A Companion to Shakespeare's Works

Volume II

Blackwell Companions to Literature and Culture

This series offers comprehensive, newly written surveys of key periods and movements and certain major authors, in English literary culture and history. Extensive volumes provide new perspectives and positions on contexts and on canonical and post-canonical texts, orientating the beginning student in new fields of study and providing the experienced undergraduate and new graduate with current and new directions, as pioneered and developed by leading scholars in the field.

A Companion to Shakespeare's Works

A COMPANION TO

SHAKESPEARE'S WORKS

VOLUME II

THE HISTORIES

EDITED BY **RICHARD DUTTON**
AND **JEAN E. HOWARD**

Blackwell
Publishing

Editorial material and organization copyright © 2003 by
Blackwell Publishing Ltd

350 Main Street, Malden, MA 02148-5018, USA
108 Cowley Road, Oxford OX4 1JF, UK
550 Swanston Street, Carlton South, Victoria 3053, Australia
Kurfürstendamm 57, 10707 Berlin, Germany

First published 2003 by Blackwell Publishing Ltd

Library of Congress Cataloging-in-Publication Data has been applied for.

ISBN 0-631-22633-8 (hardback)

ISBN 1-405-10730-8 (four-volume set)

A catalogue record for this title is available from the British Library.

Set in 11 on 13 pt Garamond 3
by SNP Best-set Typesetter Ltd, Hong Kong
Printed and bound in the United Kingdom
by MPG Books Ltd, Bodmin, Cornwall

For further information on
Blackwell Publishing, visit our website:
http://www.blackwellpublishing.com

Contents

Notes on Contributors

Rebecca Ann Bach is Associate Professor of English at the University of Alabama at Birmingham. She is the author of *Colonial Transformations: The Cultural Production of the New Atlantic World, 1580–1640* (2000) and has published articles on early modern English drama and culture in *Renaissance Drama, Textual Practice, SEL*, and other journals and collections. She is currently completing a book entitled *Early Modern England Without Heterosexuality*.

David Bevington is the Phyllis Fay Horton Distinguished Service Professor in the Humanities at the University of Chicago, where he has taught since 1967. His studies include *From "Mankind" to Marlow* (1962), *Tudor Drama and Politics* (1968), and *Action is Eloquence: Shakespeare's Language of Gesture* (1985). He is also the editor of *Medieval Drama* (1975), the Bantam Shakespeare in 29 paperback volumes (1988), and *The Complete Works of Shakespeare* (1992; updated 1997), as well as the Oxford *1 Henry IV* (1987), the Cambridge *Antony and Cleopatra* (1990), and the Arden 3 *Troilus and Cressida* (1998). He is the senior editor of the Revels Student Editions, and is a senior editor of the *Revels Plays* and of the forthcoming Cambridge edition of the works of Ben Jonson. He is also senior editor of the forthcoming *Norton Anthology of Renaissance Drama*.

Patricia A. Cahill is an Assistant Professor of English at Emory University. She is completing a book on Elizabethan drama to be entitled *Tales of Iron Wars: Martial Bodies and Manly Economies in Early Modern English Culture*.

William C. Carroll is Professor of English at Boston University. Among his recent works are *The Metamorphoses of Shakespearean Comedy* (1985), *Fat King, Lean Beggar: Representations of Poverty in the Age of Shakespeare* (1996), and *Macbeth: Texts and Contexts* (1999); he is editor of the Arden edition of *The Two Gentlemen of Verona* (forthcoming).

Thomas Cartelli is Professor of English and Chair of the Department of English at Muhlenberg College. He is the author of *Repositioning Shakespeare: National Formations, Postcolonial Appropriations* (1999) and *Marlowe, Shakespeare, and the Economy of Theatrical Experience* (1991), as well as numerous essays and reviews. His chapter in this volume forms part of a work-in-progress entitled *Producing Disorder: The Construction of Misrule in Early Modern England and New England*.

Cyndia Susan Clegg is Distinguished Professor of English at Pepperdine University. She has most recently published *Press Censorship in Jacobean England* (2001) and *Press Censorship in Elizabethan England* (1997). Her articles on Renaissance literature, censorship, and the history of the book appear in prominent journals and essay collections. She is currently working on a study of print and parliament.

Jonathan Crewe is Willard Professor of English and Comparative Literature and Director of the Leslie Center for the Humanities at Dartmouth College. He has published extensively on early modern and contemporary writing, and has recently edited five plays and the narrative poems for the new Pelican Shakespeare.

Linda Gregerson is Professor of English at the University of Michigan. She is the author of *The Reformation of the Subject: Spenser, Milton, and the English Protestant Epic* and is currently at work on *The Commonwealth of the Word: Nation and Reformation in Early Modern England*.

Andrew Hadfield is currently visiting Professor of English at Columbia University and is the author of numerous monographs and edited collections. His most recent works are *The English Renaissance* (Blackwell, 2000), *The Cambridge Companion to Spenser* (2001), and *Amazons, Savages and Machiavels: Travel and Colonial Writing in English, 1550–1630* (2001). He is the general editor of the Arden Critical Companions (with Paul Hammond) and his *Shakespeare and Renaissance Political Culture* will appear in 2003.

Richard Helgerson is Professor of English at the University of California, Santa Barbara. His most recent book is *Adulterous Alliances: Home, State, and History in Early Modern European Drama and Painting* (2000). He is also the author of *The Elizabethan Prodigals* (1976), *Self-Crowned Laureates: Spenser, Jonson, Milton and the Literary System* (1983), and *Forms of Nationhood: The Elizabethan Writing of England* (1992), which won the British Council Prize in the Humanities and the Modern Language Association's James Russell Lowell Prize.

James Holstun teaches English literature at the State University of New York, Buffalo. He is the editor of *Pamphlet Wars: Prose in the English Revolution* (1992) and the author of *A Rational Millennium: Puritan Utopias of Seventeenth-Century England and*

America (1987) and *Ehud's Dagger: Class Struggle in the English Revolution* (2000). He is at work on a study of Tudor rebellions and reactions to them.

Lisa Hopkins is a Reader in English at Sheffield Hallam University and editor of *Early Modern Literary Studies*. Her most recent publications are *The Female Hero in English Renaissance Tragedy* (2002) and *Writing Renaissance Queens: Texts By and About Elizabeth I and Mary, Queen of Scots* (2002).

Ivo Kamps is Associate Professor of English at the University of Mississippi and the author of *Historiography and Ideology in Stuart Drama* (1996). He is the series editor for the Early Modern Cultural Studies Series, 1500–1700 for Palgrave Press. With Jyotsna Singh he is co-editor of *Travel Knowledge: European "Discoveries" in the Early Modern Period* (2001), and he is one of the editors of the forthcoming Oxford edition of the complete works of Thomas Middleton. He is currently working with Karen Raber on a Texts and Contexts edition of *Measure for Measure* for Bedford Press.

Paulina Kewes is Senior Lecturer in English at the University of Wales, Aberystwyth. Her publications include *Authorship and Appropriation: Writing for the Stage in England, 1660–1710* (1998) and essays on Shakespeare, Dryden, and Renaissance, Restoration, and eighteenth-century drama. She has edited a volume of essays on *Plagiarism in Early Modern England* (2003), and is now completing a book on representations of history in Elizabethan and Stuart drama.

James Knowles teaches at the University of Stirling. He has worked extensively on the Jacobean masque and discovered Jonson's lost *Entertainment at Britain's Burse* (1609) in 1997. He edited a collection of essays on Shakespeare's late plays (with Jennifer Richards) and *The Roaring Girl and Other Plays* (2001). He is currently editing the complete entertainments and selected masques for the forthcoming Cambridge Works of Ben Jonson (2005) and writing a book on early modern masquing culture.

Ric Knowles is Professor of Drama at the University of Guelph and at the Graduate Center for the Study of Drama, University of Toronto. He is an editor of *Canadian Theatre Review* and editor in chief of *Modern Drama*, and he has published extensively on Shakespeare in performance and on contemporary Canadian drama and theatre. His book *The Theatre of Form and the Production of Meaning* won the 2001 Ann Saddlemyer Prize.

Willy Maley is Professor of Renaissance Studies at the University of Glasgow. His publications include *A Spenser Chronology* (1994) and *Salvaging Spenser: Colonialism, Culture and Identity* (1997). He has edited, with Andrew Hadfield and Brendan Bradshaw, *Representing Ireland: Literature and the Origins of Conflict, 1543–1660* (1993), with Andrew Hadfield, *A View of the Present State of Ireland: From the First Published*

Edition (Blackwell, 1997), and with David Baker, a collection of essays entitled *British Identities and English Renaissance Literature* (2002).

Lois Potter is Ned B. Allen Professor of English at the University of Delaware. She has edited *The Two Noble Kinsmen* for the Arden Shakespeare and recently published a study of *Othello* in the Shakespeare in Performance series by Manchester University Press. She has published on Shakespeare, Milton, the English Civil War, theatre history, and Robin Hood, and is also a frequent reviewer of plays. Her current project is a biography of Shakespeare.

Kathryn Schwarz is Assistant Professor of English at Vanderbilt University. She is the author of *Tough Love: Amazon Encounters in the English Renaissance* (2000) and is working on a new project tentatively entitled "Femininity and Intention in Early Modern England."

James Siemon is Professor of English at Boston University. He is the author of *Shakespearean Iconoclasm* (1985) and *Word Against Word: Shakespearean Utterance* (2002). He has edited the New Mermaid *Jew of Malta* (1994) and is currently editing the Arden 3 *Richard III*.

Peter J. Smith is Senior Lecturer at Nottingham Trent University. His interests are in the areas of Renaissance literature and drama with special reference to performance theory and history. His publications include *Social Shakespeare: Aspects of Renaissance Dramaturgy and Contemporary Society* (1995) and *Hamlet: Theory in Practice* (co-edited with Nigel Wood, 1996). He has edited Marlowe's *Jew of Malta* (1994) and *Edward II* (1998). Since 1992 he has been associate editor of the international journal of Renaissance studies, *Cahiers Elisabéthains*.

Virginia Mason Vaughan is the Andrea B. and Peter D. Klein '64 Distinguished Professor at Clark University in Worcester, Massachusetts. She is the author of *Othello: A Contextual History* and the co-editor of the Arden 3 *The Tempest*.

Introduction

The four *Companions to Shakespeare's Works* (*Tragedies*; *Histories*; *Comedies*; *Poems, Problem Comedies, Late Plays*) were compiled as a single entity designed to offer a uniquely comprehensive snapshot of current Shakespeare criticism. Complementing David Scott Kastan's *Companion to Shakespeare* (1999), which focused on Shakespeare as an author in his historical context, these volumes by contrast focus on Shakespeare's works, both the plays and major poems, and aim to showcase some of the most interesting critical research currently being conducted in Shakespeare studies.

To that end the editors commissioned scholars from many quarters of the world – Australia, Canada, France, New Zealand, the United Kingdom, and the United States – to write new essays that, collectively, address virtually the whole of Shakespeare's dramatic and poetic canon. The decision to organize the volumes along generic lines (rather than, say, thematically or chronologically) was made for a mixture of intellectual and pragmatic reasons. It is still quite common, for example, to teach or to write about Shakespeare's works as tragedies, histories, comedies, late plays, sonnets, or narrative poems. And there is much evidence to suggest that a similar language of poetic and dramatic "kinds" or genres was widely current in Elizabethan and Jacobean England. George Puttenham and Philip Sidney – to mention just two sixteenth-century English writers interested in poetics – both assume the importance of genre as a way of understanding differences among texts; and the division of Shakespeare's plays in the First Folio of 1623 into comedies, histories, and tragedies offers some warrant for thinking that these generic rubrics would have had meaning for Shakespeare's readers and certainly for those members of his acting company who helped to assemble the volume. Of course, exactly *what* those rubrics meant in Shakespeare's day is partly what requires critical investigation. For example, we do not currently think of *Cymbeline* as a tragedy, though it is listed as such in the First Folio, nor do we find the First Folio employing terms such as "problem plays," "romances," and "tragicomedies" which subsequent critics have used to designate groups of plays. Consequently, a number of essays in these volumes self-consciously examine the meanings and lineages of the terms used to separate one genre from another and to compare the way Shakespeare and his contemporaries reworked the generic templates that were their common heritage and mutually constituted creation.

Pragmatically, we as editors also needed a way to divide the material we saw as necessary for a Companion to Shakespeare's Works that aimed to provide an overview of the exciting scholarly work being done in Shakespeare studies at the beginning of the twenty-first century. Conveniently, certain categories of his works are equally substantial in terms of volume. Shakespeare wrote about as many tragedies as histories, and again about as many "festive" or "romantic" comedies, so it was possible to assign each of these groupings a volume of its own. This left a decidedly less unified fourth volume to handle not only the non-dramatic verse, but also those much-contested categories of "problem comedies" and "late plays." In the First Folio, a number of plays included in this volume were listed among the comedies: namely, *The Tempest*, *Measure for Measure*, *All's Well That Ends Well*, and *The Winter's Tale*. *Troilus and Cressida* was not listed in the prefatory catalog, though it appears between the histories and tragedies in the actual volume and is described (contrary to the earlier quarto) as a tragedy. *Cymbeline* is listed as a tragedy; *Henry VIII* appears as the last of the history plays. *Two Noble Kinsmen* and *Pericles* do not appear at all. This volume obviously offers less generic unity than the other three, but it provides special opportunities to think again about the utility and theoretical coherence of the terms by which both Shakespeare's contemporaries and generations of subsequent critics have attempted to understand the conventionalized means through which his texts can meaningfully be distinguished and grouped.

When it came to the design of each volume, the editors assigned an essay on each play (or on the narrative poems and sonnets) and about the same number of somewhat longer essays designed to take up larger critical problems relevant to the genre or to a particular grouping of plays. For example, we commissioned essays on the plays in performance (both on stage and in films), on the imagined geography of different kinds of plays, on Shakespeare's relationship to his contemporaries working in a particular genre, and on categorizations such as tragedy, history, or tragicomedy. We also invited essays on specific topics of current interest such as the influence of Ovid on Shakespeare's early narrative poems, Shakespeare's practice as a collaborative writer, his representations of popular rebellion, the homoerotic dimensions of his comedies, or the effects of censorship on his work. As a result, while there will be a free-standing essay on *Macbeth* in the tragedy volume, one will also find in the same volume a discussion of some aspect of the play in Richard McCoy's essay on "Shakespearean Tragedy and Religious Identity," in Katherine Rowe's "Minds in Company: Shakespearean Tragic Emotions," in Graham Holderness's "Text and Tragedy," and in other pieces as well. For those who engage fully with the richness and variety of the essays available within each volume, we hope that the whole will consequently amount to much more than the sum of its parts.

Within this structure we invited our contributors – specifically chosen to reflect a generational mix of established and younger critics – to write as scholars addressing fellow scholars. That is, we sought interventions in current critical debates and examples of people's ongoing research rather than overviews of or introductions to a topic. We invited contributors to write for their peers and graduate students, rather than tailoring essays primarily to undergraduates. Beyond that, we invited a diversity of approaches; our aim was to showcase the best of current work rather than to advocate for any particular critical or theoretical perspective. If these volumes are in any sense a representative trawl of contemporary critical practice, they suggest that it would be premature to assume we have reached a post-theoretical era. Many lines of theoretical practice converge in these essays: historicist, certainly, but also Derridean, Marxist, performance-oriented, feminist, queer, and textual/editorial. Race, class, gender, bodies, and emotions, now carefully historicized, have not lost their power as organizing rubrics for original critical investigations; attention to religion, especially the Catholic contexts for Shakespeare's inventions, has perhaps never been more pronounced; political theory, including investigations of republicanism, continues to yield impressive insights into the plays. At the same time, there is a marked turn to new forms of empiricist inquiry, including, in particular, attention to early readers' responses to Shakespeare's texts and a newly vigorous interest in how Shakespeare's plays relate to the work of his fellow dramatists. Each essay opens to a larger world of scholarship on the questions addressed, and through the list of references and further reading included at the end of each chapter, the contributors invite readers to pursue their own inquiries on these topics. We believe that the quite remarkable range of essays included in these volumes will be valuable to anyone involved in teaching, writing, and thinking about Shakespeare at the beginning of the new century.

1

The Writing of History in Shakespeare's England

Ivo Kamps

I

More than seventy historical dramas were written in England between the middle of the sixteenth century and the Revolution, the greater number of them seeing the light of day during the closing decade and a half of Elizabeth's reign. To appreciate this large and important body of plays it is vital not merely to identify its historical sources – that is, for instance, to ask what bits of Halle or Holinshed we can identify in Shakespeare – but understand why in his first tetralogy Shakespeare more or less follows Edward Hall's providential pro-Tudor historical vision while he resolutely undermines that very same vision in *Henry V* and *Henry VIII*. To begin to address this and other similar questions, it is necessary to investigate first the various developments in late sixteenth- and early seventeenth-century historiography in England. In particular, it is crucial to understand that the proliferation of new and innovative historiographical methods, styles, and goals that arose in the sixteenth century helped wreck whatever univocality may have existed concerning, among other things, England's Trojan heritage and the providential shape of its history. This proliferation did not produce a national identity crisis by any means, but it did generate enough variety of interpretation, contradiction, and disagreement to provide a basis from which to contest from within Elizabethan and early Stuart society the *grand récits* of medieval historiography and Tudor orthodoxy that we find articulated in the writings of critics such as E. W. M. Tillyard.[1]

What was the status of historical writing in the age of Shakespeare? When we read Louis B. Wright's *Middle-Class Culture in Elizabethan England* we come away with the impression that virtually all Englishmen and women in the sixteenth century, regardless of their socioeconomic background or their religious beliefs, were avid readers of historical texts.[2] The reason for this widespread appeal of historical texts was, Wright suggests, that people firmly believed that, next to the study of the Bible itself, the study of history was best suited to instruct human beings how to live a moral life.

Those belonging to Wright's so-called Elizabethan middle class who could afford them purchased copies of sixteenth-century chronicles and the less expensive chapbooks or the even more affordable broadside ballads. There is no doubt that events such as the conflicts with Rome in the early part of the sixteenth century encouraged an interest in religious, legal, and parliamentary history, and that the strife with Spain in the second half of the century promoted a fervent patriotism that found an expression in nationalistic historiography. History's popularity, however, does not give us insight into the public's sophistication concerning matters of method, innovation, and divergent interpretations. D. R. Woolf's new research amply demonstrates that there were some in the late sixteenth century who read historical texts with immense vigor. Woolf describes, for instance, a man named John Thomas, whose copy of Camden's *Britannia* is "interleaved and thickly annotated . . . adding his own comments, together with poetry and extracts from the other histories he had read [as well as] page references to passages elsewhere in *Britannia* itself, to other works of relevance to Camden's topics, and to manuscript in [John Thomas's] possession" (Woolf 2000: 90). Additional examples supplied by Woolf indicate beyond question that some early modern readers read historical texts not as "passive receptacles" but with something resembling scholarly intensity. Despite the breadth and depth of Woolf's research, however, it is not clear how widespread this way of reading historical texts was (especially before 1640), and it is an accepted critical commonplace that many more (especially Londoners) would have gotten their "history" from historical dramas by Shakespeare, Heywood, Jonsen, Marlowe, and others, rather than from proper historical texts.[3] With the exception of those in the scholarly communities of Oxford and Cambridge, most libraries during the Tudor period housed mostly religious texts.[4] What is more, even if we grant Louis Wright's thesis about the widespread public consumption of historical texts, we have to make two important qualifications: first, that the reading of history for moral edification and patriotic reasons tended to subordinate factual accuracy to literary and ideological concerns, and, secondly, that with one or two notable exceptions one would not turn to chronicles, chapbooks, and broadsides to learn about either historiographical rigor or historiographical innovation.[5] One has to assume, therefore, that Englishmen and women, with some exceptions, were not in a position to evaluate critically the historical knowledge they received.

This is not an insignificant point because this is the time when the medieval chronicle largely fades from existence and is succeeded by a wide array of "historical texts" such as "poems, plays, antiquarian tracts, [and] humanist 'politic histories'" (Woolf 2000: 8).[6] Notwithstanding Annabel Patterson's thesis about the multivocality of Holinshed's *Chronicle* (in which she argues that Holinshed deliberately included versions of events at variance with one another), there is a strong sense that history writing as a field became even more fragmented when its dominant genre, the chronicle, was phased out. Each of the newly emerging historiographical genres was shaped by a different set of principles, making the end of the sixteenth century a particularly important, yet difficult time for anyone wanting to evaluate the veracity of historical claims. Surprisingly, only a few of the historians themselves in the late sixteenth and

early seventeenth centuries display a keen enough awareness of the range of historiographical practices to evaluate the merits and shortcomings of each. Most historians
simply repeat the commonplaces about history's duty to represent the past in as life-
like a manner as possible, and to do so without malice or prejudice, so that readers
can receive moral instruction from the examples cited.

The Elizabethan and Jacobean playwrights, on the other hand, we know read the
historical texts available to them with considerable care, and, of course, with an eye
to how history might be transformed into a profitable commodity for the theatre. This
care, as I have argued elsewhere,[7] led the dramatists to a greater awareness of methodological contradictions and/or inconsistencies within the rapidly proliferating historiographical genres. This awareness made it possible for Renaissance dramatists to
appropriate for the stage not only the substance or content of the historical texts they
read, but also the historiographical methods employed in those texts. Our understanding of what Marlowe, Shakespeare, Heywood, Jonson, Massinger, Fletcher, Ford,
and others were up to in their history plays can be enhanced by examining the various
types of history writing available to them. In this essay I try to lay the foundation for
an enriched understanding of the Renaissance history play by discussing Renaissance
understandings of the term "history," and by considering historiography's development during roughly the period of Shakespeare's life. The remainder of the essay will
consider the three main "schools" of Renaissance historical thought: the providential,
the humanist, and the antiquarian.

II

Modern historians studying the field of Renaissance historiography have at times
attempted to discern a pattern or progress in its rich and sometimes perplexing heterogeneity. In an influential 1962 study, F. Smith Fussner proffered that history
writing underwent a major revolution in England in the late sixteenth century and
in the first half of the seventeenth century. Fussner argued that in the 1580s English
history writing underwent crucial changes "when more adequate facilities for research
became available, and the antiquaries began to question their medieval authorities"
(p. 300). The publication of William Camden's *Britannia* (1586), an antiquarian study
of England's Roman heritage, is a watershed event in this argument. Camden relied
on archival sources, allowing him strictly to limit both conjecture and reliance on
divine causes, and to use a comparativist's approach to test inherited historical
"truths."

The teleological character of Fussner's historical revolution has been criticized, most
recently by D. R. Woolf, who observes that Fussner's conception of a historical revolution as "the late Elizabethan and early Stuart working-out of proper historical
method" (Woolf 2000: 7) may be primarily a projection of modern (and Fussner's
own) historiographical practices onto an early modern context. Woolf maintains that
the historical revolution is less a catalyst *for* than an effect *of* a broad range of cultural

changes that are taking place in sixteenth- and seventeenth-century England. That said, Fussner's argument is more complex than Woolf's brief criticism of it here suggests, as Fussner is very much aware that "The historical revolution, unlike the scientific, resulted in no great Newtonian synthesis" (p. 305), and that the end of the Renaissance did not witness anything like uniformity of method or purpose in English historiography. However, the progressive trajectory of Fussner's argument – from error-perpetuating chronicles to sound antiquarian research – is manifest throughout *The Historical Revolution*.

Woolf has suggested that the truly significant historical revolution did not occur until the eighteenth century. The Renaissance historical "revolution" consisted of a wide array "of changes in the purpose, content, and style of historical writing" (Fussner 1962: 300), but the serious discussion of these changes was limited to "a very small segment of highly educated people, mainly men," compared to "the almost daily conversations, familial readings, public performances, and correspondence discussions of historical issues in the eighteenth century, among both men and women, involving nearly everything about the past, British, European, and Asian, as well as the older classical and biblical material" (Woolf 2000: 7). It is not necessary here to adjudicate between these two positions because Fussner and Woolf appear in general agreement that there did occur a number of legitimate innovations in the world of historiography in the late sixteenth century. The difference between their positions lies in the degree to which these innovations took hold and exactly when they permanently changed the course of historical research in England. Certainly, we have to consider that even if we can identify moments of genuine methodological innovations in antiquarian and humanist "politic histories," we cannot expect those innovations to have a particularly profound impact on the historical understanding of a populace whose ideas had been shaped for decades by stories from the chronicles and, beginning with Bale's *King Johan* and Marlowe's *Edward II*, by historical dramas.

In a succinct and still useful essay, Leonard F. Dean (1947) describes several emerging trends in history writing in the sixteenth and early seventeenth centuries (pp. 3–4). Dean notes that historians increasingly limited both the time-frame and the geographical region to be treated in a single work. Historians also increasingly believed that their work should teach moral, religious, or political lessons, that truthfulness should be "the first law of history" (p. 3), and that while God is the prime mover of history, the "historian should depict human motives since they are the secondary causes of worldly actions. Therefore, councils should be fully presented and interpreted, [and] probable thoughts invented and attributed to the various personages" (pp. 3–4). Along the same lines, Dean observes that historians increasingly tried to heighten the instructional value of their work by manipulating it rhetorically, that is, by inventing rhetorical set speeches to produce a more intense effect upon the reader (p. 4). Lastly, historians began to provide greater narrative coherence to the chronological sequences that characterize the annals and, to a lesser extent, the chronicles.

I said that Dean's formulation is still useful, but only if we realize that there are important exceptions to all the trends he identifies. The Reformation, the emergence of humanism and antiquarian research, as well as other continental influences in the sixteenth century certainly had an impact on both the method and the purposes of history writing, but even as important innovations were vigorously embraced by some historians, others merely paid lip service to them or rejected them outright in favor of time-honored medieval practices. Walter Ralegh's *History of the World*, for instance, is unashamedly universal in scope even though it is published in 1614 (well into the period where these trends could have taken hold), and begins with the creation of the world, even though Dean suggests that histories become narrower in scope. Likewise, Ralegh writes a vigorous defense of a historian's use of conjecture ("to rehearse probabilities as bare coniectures" (pp. 212–17),[8] even though antiquarian researchers had firmly rejected this practice as speculative and misleading. The so-called set speech, a distinctive feature of classical historiography going back to Thucydides' *History of the Peloponnesian War*, was an important part of humanist histories such as Thomas More's *History of Richard III* (1543),[9] but its validity was explicitly denied by Thomas Blundeville in his 1574 treatise on history writing, in which he maintains that historians "ought not to fayne anye Orations" (Blundeville 1940: 164). Still others – in fact most non-antiquarian producers of historical texts at this time – freely mixed providential historiography with a humanist emphasis on secondary causes and wedded verifiable facts with legendary materials from the chronicles. Finally, as we shall see when we come to the antiquarians, there was an important group of scholars doing historical research that cared little for the kind of moral, political, or religious didacticism prevalent in chronicles and humanist histories.

In fact, "history," although (or perhaps because) many Renaissance writers professed to define it, was not a stable term. "History" could in fact refer to an impressive variety of texts. Poems, plays, memorials, biographies, narratives of current events, political narratives, annals, chronicles, surveys, antiquarian accounts – all could bear the name of "history" in the late sixteenth and early seventeenth centuries.[10] The chorus in Shakespeare's *Henry V* asks the audience to "admit [him] chorus to this history," seemingly implying that a literary work that deals with historical matters constitutes a "history." Less plausibly (to our ears, at least), a character in Shakespeare's *Taming of the Shrew* describes the production to be staged before Sly as "a kind of history," suggesting that an entirely fictitious story can also carry the name of "history." In his letter to Walter Ralegh, Edmund Spenser claimed to "haue followed all the antique Poets historicall" such as Homer, Virgil, and Tasso when he composed *The Faerie Queene*, and to have "coloured" his epic with "an historicall fiction" (Spenser 1989: 787). For Degory Wheare, the first man to hold a chair in history at Oxford University, history was "nothing but moral philosophy, clothed in examples" (Haddock 1980: 80), whereas grammar school education used (classical) history primarily as a reservoir of rhetorical and literary conventions to be imitated (Levy 1967: 40–50). It has been suggested that by the seventeenth century all this ambiguity was cleared up as "history had become an autonomous discipline with its own purposes and methods, clearly distinguished from myth and literature, and accountable to different formal requirements and different truth criteria" (Rackin 1990: 19). I think that this assessment is too optimistic and definitive, although clear patterns of usage were beginning to emerge by the end of the sixteenth century as chronicle writers, humanists, and antiquarians gradually established practices that can be distinguished from those of poets, playwrights, religious writers, and polemicists.

These patterns, however, were undermined – in theory and practice – almost at the same time that they took shape. When, for instance, the prolific Renaissance writer Thomas Heywood composed his prose history entitled *Englands Elizabeth* (1631), he predictably turned to Holinshed's *Chronicles*, Foxe's *Acts and Monuments*, and Fabyan's *Newe Chronycles of Englande and of France* (1516) for information. Like so many other Renaissance historians, Heywood had neither the opportunity nor the inclination to search for original documents to verify or correct what his predecessors had written about England's queen. Although Heywood, by going about his project in this way, had little or no chance to contribute to what we might call new knowledge of Elizabeth's life and career, he also did not deviate from the common Renaissance practice of relying on other "authorities" without any great concern for their veracity. But in composing *Englands Elizabeth* Heywood also turned to a play about the life of Elizabeth in her minority which he himself had written circa 1603.[11] There may be several possible explanations for Heywood's decision to draw on a literary text to write a history, but I am here less interested in Heywood's particular motives than I am in the fact that he did it – and that others did it, while still others observed that this practice was hardly uncommon. In Ben Jonson's *The Devil is an Ass*, for instance, one character compliments another's knowledge of the chronicles, to which the second party heartily replies, "No, I confess I have it from the play-books, / And think they are *more* authentic" (emphasis added). As a ferocious reader of classical history and devout ex-student of the learned antiquarian William Camden, a sarcastic Jonson is merely lambasting the rapid proliferation of English chronicles at the time, and certainly not dismissing the veracity or generic distinctiveness of all historical writing. On the other side of the literature–history coin, we find Thomas More's *History of Richard III*, one of the great achievements of English humanist historiography, described by one modern historian as "almost as much fiction as . . . history, though it is a fiction imagined as though it had happened that way" (Levine 1999: 21). What these examples suggest is a trend toward cross-fertilizations and (apparent) interchangeability of history and literature in the early Renaissance, a trend also observed by Walter Ralegh in *The History of the World* (1614), where he writes that "it was well-noted by that worthy Gentleman Sir Philip Sidney, that Historians do borrow of Poets, not only much of their ornament, but somewhat of their substance" (Ralegh 1971: 213). And Sidney himself wrote in *The Defence* that the historian often has to "tell events whereof he can yield no cause; or, if he do it, it must be poetically" (Sidney 1989: 224).

It would be wrong to say that early modern men and women had no conception of truth and falsehood, but it is obvious that the difference between them – especially if the problem was couched in terms of "fact" and "fiction" – was not of paramount importance when it came to the production of historical texts. Or, to put it differently, just because a story was fictional did not mean it was false, nor was it enough to disqualify that story from being included in a "history." As observed by Joseph Levine, it was not uncommon for medieval historians to substitute legend or pure fabrication for history. In his *History of Britain*, twelfth-century Geoffrey of Monmouth, for instance, "seems to have invented (or borrowed) an entire fictional history of early Britain, culminating in the legendary Celtic King Arthur . . . What Geoffrey thought he was doing is now beyond retrieval, but it is clear that no medieval author was willing to declare his purpose by making a bold distinction between fiction and history. When they told a fiction they pretended it was history; when they recounted a history, they included fiction; and neither authors nor audience seemed much to care" (Levine 1999: 16, 17).

That the Italian humanist Polydore Vergil debunked the myth of England's Trojan origins in his history of England, *Anglica Historia* (1534, 1555),[12] written at the behest of Henry VII, of course constituted an advance in the procedures of history writing, but this advance went generally unheeded. Geoffrey of Monmouth and virtually all medieval historians maintained that Brutus, the great grandson of Aeneas, the legendary founder of Rome and son of Venus, founded Britain at the goddess Diana's behest. Careful not to offend or disillusion those who have embraced the concept of England's Trojan beginnings, Polydore Vergil declares that he "will nether affirme as trew, nether reproove as false, the judgement of one or other as concerning the originall of soe auncient a people," but nevertheless dismantles the Brutus myth by pointing out, among other things, that "nether Livie, nether Dionisius Halicarnaseus, who writt dilligentlie of the Romane antiquities . . . did ever once make rehersall of this Brutus, neither could that bee notified bie the cronicles of the Brittons, sithe that longe agoe thei loste all bookes of their monuments, as Gildas witnesseth" (Vergil 1846: 31, 30). Polydore then goes on to suggest politely that in "olde times" many nations "weare so bowlde as to derive their beginnings of their stocke from the Goddes" so that the people and cities might be more prosperous, although now such stories sound "more like fabels then the sincere witness of noble acts" (p. 31). From our modern vantage point, Polydore's findings appear judicious because he compares sources and vainly searches for evidence to corroborate the claims of earlier historians, but a number of Renaissance historians begged to differ. The noted antiquarian John Leland, who generally served the progress of historiography better than many of his contemporaries, was so outraged by Polydore's less than patriotic attack on the Brutus legend that in 1544 he challenged the Italian historian's findings in print and vigorously defended Monmouth's history of Britain (Gransden 1982: 472). As late as 1603, we find John Stow addressing the issue of Troynovant with considerable caution in *The Survey of London*. A self-styled yet sophisticated antiquarian and topographer, Stow had in his *Annales* (1592) already rejected another historian's fraudulent attempt to establish a genealogical link between the native British and the sons of Noah. Stow was also fully aware that the popular story of Britain's Trojan origins had been called into question, but he nonetheless includes it on the *Survey*'s opening page, justifying its place there by explaining that he is simply following his source, Geoffrey of Monmouth, who in turn is following the time-honored practice of Roman writers who, "to glorify the city of Rome, derive the original thereof from gods and demi-gods, by the Trojan progeny" (p. 3). Sensitive to the traditional beliefs of his readers, Stow, a man not given to embrace legend before fact, somewhat discredits the Trojan story but declines to displace it altogether with a more credible account, which he could have taken from Polydore.

Levine explains this somewhat confounding treatment of "fact" and "fiction" by suggesting that a distinction between the two terms did not enter medieval life until people were beginning to notice "a disjunction between the real features of English public life and the idealized versions of medieval fiction" that had been "invented as a set of fictional ideals to meet the needs of medieval feudalism" (Levine 1999: 19).[13] This sort of identification of an "originary" moment is always fraught with difficulty, but Levine's argument *vis-à-vis* feudalism can be seen as part of a broad fabric of late medieval and Renaissance forces that include economic changes, international commerce, the advent of print, geographical exploration, the Reformation, the rediscovery of classical antiquity – all of which contributed to an emerging sense of genuine difference between England and other nations and between England's present and past.[14] The idea here is that "difference" entails the articulation of alternatives (is one saved by works and faith or by faith alone? Does the power to make law reside with parliament or crown? Does the king's power derive from God or the people?), and that such articulations become invariably contested, and that competition between alternatives frequently leads to searches for origins and foundational documents, and that such investigations lead to greater scrutiny and the development of the methods of historical investigation.

However, even as the slow but significant changes in historiography that occurred between the arrival in England of the Italian humanist Polydore Vergil in 1502 and the death of England's greatest antiquarian, Camden, in 1623, gradually took hold, we have to admit that (a) the fact–fiction paradox continued well into the seventeenth century, that (b) medieval elements that were squarely at odds with more sophisticated humanist and antiquarian practices continued to be employed by historians (including those same humanists and antiquarians), and that (c) historiography, although it was becoming a field of inquiry gradually distinct from poetry and literature, experienced neither cohesiveness nor anything like a unitary development. One reason for historiography's eclecticism of course is that at this time it was not an academic subject, and that "neither its authors nor its readers ever received any formal training in it" (Levy 1967: 51). Another crux in the haphazard progress of English Renaissance historiography is the lingering presence of providentialist thought and its general incompatibility with the secondary causes analysis of historical events advocated by some humanists.

III

In part, the seemingly contradictory character of Renaissance historiography has its roots in providential medieval historical thought and practice. Medieval historians produced an impressive range of texts. They wrote ecclesiastical histories, universal histories (reaching back to the moment of creation), monastic chronicles (capturing the daily lives of monastic communities), topographical studies, *de casibus* histories (recounting the fall of princes for the moral edification of the reader), and so forth. But despite the different purposes and methodologies of these types of historical writing, they all shared a fundamental belief in a providentially organized cosmos. And while it was understood that God's divine plan might not always be apparent to the eye of the historian, it was taken as self-evident that "history demonstrated the workings of God's will on earth; as mankind proceeded towards its destiny, the last judgment and eternal life in heaven and hell, God rewarded virtue, punished vice and otherwise showed His omnipotence" (Gransden 1982: 454). The historian's labors, therefore, B. A. Haddock (1980) observes, were no more than an "anticipation of the detailed disclosure of a pattern of events which God had revealed in outline. Men could pursue what ends they might but they could not alter the framework of their lives. Innovation was the exclusive preserve of God" (pp. 1–2).

Shakespeare's Hamlet takes this view to its logical extreme when he says to Horatio, "We defy augury. There's a special providence in the fall of a sparrow" (5.2.157–8). Horatio has just suggested that if Hamlet's "'mind dislike anything'" about the upcoming duel with Laertes, he should declare himself unfit to fight. But Hamlet rejects augury – that is, the practice of divination from omens – on biblical grounds that everything is guided by God's will, even those minor and seemingly trivial events that appear to take place outside of God's "general providence" but which are part of his "special providence."[15] Hamlet's defiance of augury amounts to a rejection of historical interpretation: "If it be now, 'tis not to come. If it be not to come, it will be now. If it be not now, yet it will come. The readiness is all" (158–60).

However, built into this linear view of time – which stretches from creation to final judgment – was a paradoxical sense that history also repeated itself. The origins of the idea of repetition can be found in a number of classical writers and appear "based on cycles observable in nature" (Woolf 1990: 5), but the internal logic of medieval Christian thought, which preached that each human being's life is a kind of universal morality drama with the fate of the human soul as its focal point, is an equally compelling basis for the need of a powerful concept of repetition. The resulting shape of time was that of a spiral, endlessly repeating the drama of rise and fall, of sin, repentance, and mercy and punishment, and ever coming nearer the apocalypse (ibid). Plays such as *Everyman* and literary–historical texts such as Lydgate's *Fall of Princes* and its sixteenth-century successor *The Mirror for Magistrates* embody this type of cyclicism. One notable consequence of this view of history as spiral was that the details (or the facts) were of very little importance in and of themselves because their primary function was to illuminate the omnipresence of God's truth and will. In other words, Richard Grafton's 1570 preface to poet–historian John Hardyng's (1378–1464) *Chronicle* may vaguely sound like a modern political historian when he proclaims that "Chronicles dooe recorde and testifye" of the rise and decay of nations, and do this so faithfully that "thinges antique to vs bee apparent, / As yf at their doinges we had been present" (Hardyng and Grafton 1812: 8), but it is hardly Hardyng's (or Grafton's) intent to produce a detailed and accurate factual account of the past for its own sake.[16] Rather, he tells us, chronicles are texts of "great fruite and vtilitie" approved by God himself to teach us "What waies to refuse, and what to folowe." Endeavoring to establish his credentials as a serious historian, Grafton explains that he has abandoned Hardyng's verse form in the newly added chapter on Henry VIII so that he can report "worde for worde" "the truth without fraude or glose" (p. 12), only to have described in the previous stanza Richard III as the man who was plagued "With shamefull death, as Goddes vengeance" for murdering Edward V.

This mixing of a desire to report history as accurately as possible and an equally strong desire to interpret history providentially was not limited to the work of medieval historians or those like Grafton and Hall who wrote in the sixteenth-century chronicle tradition. Quite clearly, the link between history writing and providentialism promoted a kind of social and political conservatism that could serve those in power. As Gransden observes, a longing among Renaissance historians not to be at odds with crown and government made them treat

> The fifteenth century . . . as a prelude to the accession of Henry Tudor. Already John Hardyng had written of the doom which enshrouded the Lancastrian kings because of Henry Bolingbroke's illegal seizure of power and the murder of Richard II. Polydore Vergil expanded this theme: he saw God's vengeance manifested in the alternation of an unhappy reign with a more propitious one, and regarded Richard III as the wickedest of kings. This embryonic historiographical structure reached its full development in the chronicle of Edward Hall, completed in about 1532. (Gransden 1982: 470)

We have to look to the Italian humanist influence, particularly the influence of Machiavelli and Guicciardini (and Tacitus through them), on English historians such as William Camden, Samuel Daniel, Francis Bacon, and John Hayward before we can begin to discern a significant break with the providentialism that still creeps into the historical writings of More and Polydore.

Humanist historiography in Renaissance England sets itself apart from other forms of history writing by virtue of its interest in secondary causes and human psychology, in matters of politics, and in its careful attention to rhetorical/literary style. Modern historians have at times proclaimed that the advent of humanism also marked the birth of modernity, but Antonia Gransden observes that continental humanist influences on English historiography did not produce an "abrupt break with the medieval tradition," but that humanist historians accelerated already existing trends and helped bring about a "gradual shift" (p. 426). In fact, the single most crucial premise of humanist historiography – the assumption that history can teach us about the present because history repeats itself – closely resembles the medieval notion of time as cyclical. That is, humanists held that whatever predicament confronts us now, a search of history will yield an identical situation in the past which can be used to guide successful conduct in the present. In *The Prince* (1532) and elsewhere, Niccolò Machiavelli refines this historical cyclicism by relying less on specific examples than on a set of principles based on a wide range of historical examples. These principles remain essentially stable over time, and form the basis of an early attempt at political science.

Another Italian, Francesco Guicciardini, took issue with Machiavelli's cyclicism on the grounds that all historical moments are truly unique and therefore are unlikely to illuminate one another. Guicciardini concludes that "It is most misleading to judge by examples; for unless these be in all respects parallel, they are of no force, the least diversity in the circumstances giving rise to the widest divergence in the conclusions. To discern these minute differences requires a just and clear eye" (Guicciardini 1949: 211). In other words, Guicciardini understands that the differences are at least as important as the similarities, and the context of any given event shapes the meaning and significance often as much as the event itself.[17] As I have argued elsewhere, Thomas Heywood uses this particular insight to great advantage and effect in his drama about the difficult days of Elizabeth Tudor before she became queen. During Elizabeth's imprisonment in the Tower at the hands of Queen Mary, the men who have to guard the princess cautiously discuss what "a man may say, without offence," and conclude that what constitutes offense and what does not depends entirely on the historical/political context in which a statement is uttered (Kamps 1996: 79–82).

Where Machiavelli decisively separates himself from any medieval tradition of historiography is on the question of religion. Whereas most humanist historians allow for the presence of God and providence in their analyses of the world,[18] Machiavelli the pragmatist categorically divorces history from theology (Fussner 1962: 12; see also Trompf 1979: 283–91; and Kahn 1985: 186). In *The Prince* the ultimate objective is power – not heaven – and Machiavelli's universe changes accordingly. For all practical purposes, he substitutes for the Christian concept of the Wheel of Fortune (which almost randomly changes the fate of man so that no one will become proud or complacent about their salvation) the concept of an indifferent force named *fortuna*. Machiavelli also necessarily abandons the notion that one's godliness makes one perhaps a little less vulnerable to the spinning of the wheel (on the whole the good should receive less misfortune than do the wicked, though being good does by no means shield one from ill fortune), and argues instead that an individual's *virtú* (ability), combined with a knowledge of historical principles, better prepares them to deal with *fortuna*. Machiavelli never advocates amoral behavior for its own sake, but he does make it clear that "man must choose: he could live aside from the stream of politics and follow the dictates of Christian morality; but if man entered upon the *vita activa* of politics, he must act according to its laws" (Gilbert 1984: 197). Machiavelli's ideas, though usually condemned, found their way into English culture even before the middle of the sixteenth century (see Fussner 1962: 14), and we see them everywhere in the drama of the period.

In English historiography his perceived atheism is hardly welcomed, but Machiavelli's emphases on secondary causes, psychological insight, and historical and political conditions do find their way (often indirectly) into English historical thought. Nowhere is Renaissance historiography's almost schizophrenic character more apparent than in Thomas Blundeville's *The True Order and Methode of Wryting and Reading Hystories* (1574), a translation and adaptation of "the precepts of Francisco Patricio and Accontio Tridentino." This brief treatise on how to write and read historical texts – the first such metahistorical treatise to be printed separately in England – yokes together an abridged translation of Francesco Patrizi's distinctly humanist–political text *Della Historia Diece Dialoghi* (1560) and Giacomo Concio's much more traditional, and medieval, treatise. In the first part of the *Methode*, the portion adapted from Patrizi, Blundeville insists that historians ought "to tell things as they were done without either augmenting or diminishing them, or swaruing one iote from the truth. Whereby it appeareth that the hystoriographers ought not to fayne anye Orations nor any other thing, but truly to reporte euery such speech, and deede, euen as it was spoken, or done" (p. 164). The edict against the invention of speeches is noteworthy because it is an indirect criticism of humanist historians such as Thomas More, who, taking their cue from that Roman school of history writing that viewed history as a subcategory of rhetoric, believed that invented speeches would enhance history's exemplary powers. The first part of Blundeville's assertion, his uncompromising dedication to truth and factual accuracy without any embellishment whatsoever, however, is not remarkable and can be found in any number of histories of the period, including those of Holinshed, Bacon, Hardying, and others. What constitutes unadorned truth for Blundeville is a different matter. Blundeville emphasizes the historian's duty to describe a country or city's economic life, its political organization, as well as its military make-up. The historians must also convey what knowledge can be gathered about the city or country's origins, "what kinde of gouernement [it] had in his beginning, augmentation, state, declynation, and ende. And whither there were any chaunge of gouernement, for what cause, and howe the same was done, and what good or euill ensued thereof" (p. 156). Patrizi may have found his inspiration for this passage in Machiavelli, but more important to our understanding of the development of English historiography is that Blundeville elected to include it in his adaptation because it implies his appreciation for the significance of changing historical contexts. To understand a city or country at any moment in history, Blundeville argues, the historian must endeavor to understand that city or country's entire history and its political development because only then can its institutions, customs, and practices be properly contextualized. Blundeville then proceeds to a discussion of the role of the individual in history, and although he essentially follows the familiar "great men" model, we find here too the author shuns divine explanations in favor of a consideration of the context in which the "great man" acts, his objectives, his personal history, his reasons and "passions of . . . mynde," as well as any "outwarde" causes such as "force, or fortune" that may have played a role in the event. The historian's proper purview includes human psychology, biography, sociology, military affairs, and politics. Only if the historian investigates these areas thoroughly will the reader "receyve any good by his writing" (pp. 156–7).

The "profite" or benefit of properly written and researched historical texts is that they reveal ("much more playnlye" and with greater efficacy than philosophical texts), by virtue of their "perticular examples and experiences," how history can guide conduct in the present (p. 161). Blundeville shares this emphasis on exemplarity with his medieval predecessors, but with the crucial difference that medieval exemplarity is inevitably moral in character, whereas Blundeville's humanist exemplarity uses examples to draw political and civil lessons. Blundeville's insufficient awareness of the absolute uniqueness of each historical context does not allow him to achieve Francesco Guicciardini's level of sophistication on this question, but his very insistence on the search for secondary (as opposed to divine) causes in the understanding of history makes him anticipate a historical consciousness that does not take hold firmly in England until centuries later. Blundeville's modernity, however, vanishes abruptly when we get to the last section of the *Methode*, namely the portion translated from Concio.

This section's title promises a discussion of "the methode to be obserued in reading hystories" (p. 165). If the reader is to understand "howe hystories are to bee readde," Blundeville observes, the reader must first "knowe the endes and purposes for which they are written." At first it seems unnecessary to make the point because it is evident from the earlier sections in which the purposes and the benefits have been laid out. But in the first and second paragraphs we learn that there are three reasons to read history:

> First that we may learne thereby to acknowledge the prouidence of God, whereby all things are gouerned and directed. Secondly, that by the examples of the wise, we maye learne wisedome wysely to behaue our selues in all our actions . . .
> Thirdly, that we maye be stirred by example of the good to follow the good, and by examples of the euill to flee the euill. (p. 165)

Now, until this point in the treatise, Blundeville has mentioned God just once and only in a perfunctory manner (p. 164), let alone given any indication how the kind of history writing he advocates will yield any insight into the workings of divine providence. Likewise, exemplarity's role has taken on a distinctly medieval quality, exhorting readers to live moral lives by following historical examples of goodness and avoiding those that are evil.

What is more, if Blundeville's translation of Patrizi emphasizes the importance of secondary causes above all others, his adaptation of Concio offers a familiar medieval argument that reverses that order, even if the evidence does not support such a reversal. "As touching the prouidence of God," Blundeville writes,

> We haue to note for what causes and by what meanes hee ouerthroweth one kingdome & setteth vp an other. For though things many times doe succeede according to the discourse of mãs reason: yet mans wisedome is oftentimes greatlye deceyued. And with those accede[n]ts which mans wisdome reiecteth and little regardeth: God by his prouidence vseth, when he thinketh good, to worke marueylous effects. And though he suffreth the wicked for the most part to liue in prosperitie, and the good in

aduersitie: yet we maye see by many notable examples, declaring aswell his wrath, and reuenge towardes the wicked, as also his pittie and clemencie towardes the good, that nothing is done by chaunce, but all things by his foresight, counsell, and diuine prouidence. (p. 165)

When we see the wicked prosper, it is a sign of God's providence; when we see the good suffer, it is an indication of God's providence. If we see the wicked punished, that too is a sign of God's providence; and if the good receive pity and mercy, this is also to be taken as evidence of God's providence. In short, everything is a manifestation of God's providence. This view of course creates a contradiction within the exemplarity model, because if God sends prosperity and adversity to the good and the wicked alike, then historical examples cannot effectively guide our behavior, unless of course we have *a priori* notions about good and evil and heaven and hell that supersede any historical examples and make them irrelevant as anything other than an affirmation of what we already know to be the case. Blundeville, however, makes the precise opposite assertion when he writes that we read history so that "we may learne thereby to acknowledge the prouidence of God" (p. 165).

What is remarkable about all this is not that Blundeville appears to believe that providence illuminates history and that history illuminates providence (in a Christian context this is less contradiction than a commonplace), but that he identifies two radically different ways of conceiving of the past but fails to recognize the profound methodological and epistemological differences between *explaining* an event in social, economic, political, or psychological terms, and merely *accounting* for it by attribution to God's will. If the schizophrenic character of Blundeville's hybrid text (perhaps inadvertently) highlights the disjunction between providential and secular humanist historiography, Ralegh's *History of the World*, published exactly forty years after the *Methode*, almost entirely confounds any differences between the two by once again equating history with providence. History, Ralegh asserts, allows us to "behold how [the world] was gouerned: how it was couered with waters, and againe repeopled: How Kings and Kingdomes have florished and fallen; and for what virtue and piety GOD made prosperous; and for what vice and deformity he made wretched, both the one and the other" (Ralegh 1971: 48). In other words, a king or kingdom falls because its ruler acts immorally and incurs God's displeasure; and not because a ruler refuses "to act immorally" and therefore loses his grip on power, as Machiavelli suggests in *The Prince* (pp. 54–5). Indeed, in the second book of *The History* Ralegh goes so far as to chastise some historians for recording "information of humaine counsailes and euents, as farre forth as the knowledge and faith of the writers can affoord; but of Gods will, by which all things are ordered, they speak onely at random, and many times falsly. This we often finde in prophane writers" (p. 212). The absence of a consideration of "second causes" is not a problem as long as the historian refers "all vnto the will of God" (p. 213). This of course does not mean that Ralegh was not a keen interpreter of political events in history or that *The History* (which concludes at 168 BC) had no perceived bearing on early seventeenth-century English life. James I was upset enough with Ralegh's book to suppress it "for divers exceptions, but specially for being too sawcie in censuring princes" (p. 11). Francis Bacon's *The History of the Reign of King Henry the Seventh*, on the other hand, though it too falls short of modern historiographical standards, enthusiastically follows the emphases and precepts of Italian humanist thought, as it depicts "with detached coolness the acts that *necessity*, as opposed to justice, requires" (Weinberger 1996: 11), the all-important events surrounding the birth of the Tudor dynasty. These examples illustrate that something like "progress" toward modern historiography is discernible, but that that progress is haphazard and limited to the work of specific historians.

Antiquarian scholars set out to "investigate the laws, customs, and institutions of England" (Fussner 1962: 95). For us it is not difficult to recognize the vital contributions made by these scholars to the development of historical thought and practice. Unlike the chronicle writers and the early humanist historians, antiquarians did not easily accept and incorporate the "facts" and interpretations provided by previous generations of historians. They insisted on original, often archival, research and scrupulously compared and discredited sources, where chroniclers had commonly opted to be uncritically inclusive and accumulative. However, antiquarians were a relatively small and elite gathering of mostly well-to-do men (some of them were titled, some were lawyers, diplomats, heralds, or official record keepers, though John Stow was a tailor) that worked in a closed society known as the Elizabethan College of Antiquaries, an organization founded in 1586. The discourses produced by antiquaries, however, were not meant to compete in the public marketplace of historical ideas. Antiquarians conducted mostly group research and presented reports of their findings to the college. Some of this research had great political potential as it dealt with legal precedents and the ancient constitution, the rights of parliament, and the powers of the crown. There is little evidence that antiquarians did this research for the purpose of intervening politically, but it is clear that others, including James I, recognized the increasing importance of "precedent" in the struggle between king and parliament. In 1614, when the Society of Antiquaries planned to resume its meeting, King James expressed "a little dislike of [the] Society; not being inform'd that we had resolv'd to decline all Matters of State" (quoted in Fussner 1962: 95).

More than anything, antiquarians desired to reconstruct, through study of both textual and physical remains of the past, an "exact memory" of the objects of antiquity (Levine 1987: 73, 77). In this respect, they were on the surface not all that different from their chronicle-writing and humanist contemporaries. In fact, we find the wish to create a perfect record of the past – "As yf at their doinges we had been present" (Hardyng and Grafton 1812: 8) – expressed in virtually all chronicles and "politic" histories.[19] There are at least four factors that most clearly distinguish antiquarians from chroniclers and narrative historians. First, antiquarians had little or no interest in using the past for the purpose of moral didacticism. Secondly, antiquarians were interested in "antiquity for its own sake" (MacCaffrey 1970: xvi) and did not try to make historical events applicable to the present; nor, thirdly, did they concern themselves with providential explanations. And, fourthly, their historical interests were of a synchronic rather than a diachronic nature. Modern historians, F. Smith Fussner and J. G. A. Pocock prominent among them, have hailed antiquarians as those who introduced "modern" research principles essential to the continued development of history writing, but antiquarians were in their own time frequently the object of scorn and derision. The primary objections against antiquarian scholarship were that it was obscure, had little relevance to the present, and therefore served no pedagogical or utilitarian function. Philip Sidney, for instance, described antiquarians as obsessed with "mouse-eaten records" and "better acquainted with a thousand years ago than with the present age" (Sidney 1989: 220). And Arnaldo Momigliano observes that antiquarians were thought of as "imperfect historians who helped to salvage relics of the past too fragmentary to be the subject of proper history" (Momigliano 1966: 7). To all but a few in early modern England, "history that did not teach was utterly inconceivable" (Levy 1967: 7).

As has been pointed out time and again, the English Renaissance is marked by a renewed fascination with the texts of antiquity and their rapid proliferation beyond the walls of the old monastic libraries. In a wider European context it has been noted that the desire to determine the authenticity and exact meaning of these texts gave rise to Renaissance philology (Levine 1987: 76). Lorenzo Valla's use of general linguistic analysis combined with his ability to discern anachronistic word usage allowed him to expose the "Donation of Constantine" as a fraud. Valla argued that the vocabulary and idiom of the "Donation" did not fit the linguistic characteristics of the early fourth century, the period in which it was thought to have been written, and thereby refuted the legal footing for the Papal States. In England the antiquarian John Selden introduced essentially the same principle by coining the word "synchronism." The term "implied a strict adherence to principles of chronology in the use and interpretation of sources" (Woolf 1990: 213). If a text was claimed to have been written in a particular historical period but it revealed "some trace of debt to a later period, either in handwriting or contents," then it had to be a fake (ibid).

In addition to legal and textual scholarship, antiquarians also concerned themselves intensely with the objects of the past, such as road maps, monuments, inscriptions, road signs, building foundations, and coins. In contrast with other historians who always sought to establish a link of relevance between objects and events of the past and the present moment, antiquarians studied historical artifacts for their own sake and for what they revealed about the nature of cultures of those who produced and/or used them. Because of this desire to study the past on its own terms, antiquarians had little use for narrative and only infrequently sought to establish diachronic causality chains. Instead they wrote in a synchronic or "systematic order," so that they could "collect all the items that are connected with a certain subject, whether they help to solve a problem or not" (Momigliano 1966: 3). Antiquarian John Leland grasped "that the many new devices of Italian humanism could be employed not only to resuscitate classical antiquity but to recover the whole of the British past" (Levine 1987: 82). In his *Britannia*, for instance, fellow antiquarian William Camden organizes his labors favoring the ancient division of Britain into Roman provinces over Britain's sixteenth-century division into counties. To produce his chorography of Britain, Camden claimed to have traveled the land and to have consulted public records, old deeds, ecclesiastical registers, the archives of cities and churches as well as monuments.[20] No chronicle writer or humanist historian of the period could boast the same. There is no doubt that Camden's *Britannia* resonated with the public in part because of a revived interest during the Tudor period in England's Trojan origins. But Camden was clearly not seeking popular acclaim or trying to capitalize on the revival. First, he published the 1586 edition only in Latin,[21] severely limiting its audience, and he explicitly rejected the Trojan legend, instead emphasizing the French roots of many of England's most prominent families.

In his *Remains Concerning Britain* the antiquarian restraint of Camden's scholarship is equally clear. Discussing the rightful claim of English monarchs to the title *Defensor fidei*, Camden recalls the saga of "*Brithwald* the Monke," which is "often recorded in our Histories" (Camden 1605: 8–9). Brithwald apparently became deeply concerned with the succession of the crown because "the blood Royall was almost extinguished," but then heard a divine "voyce, which forbade him to be inquisitive of such matters resounding in his eares. *The kingdome of England is Gods owne kingdome, and for it God himselfe will provide*. But these, & such like are more fit for a graver Treatise than this." The final sentence in this quotation is not in italics in the original, but it is the one we need to emphasize because it displays Camden's blend of patriotism and religious fervor, but then exiles both from the historical investigation. The remaining chapters of the *Remains* go about the business of collecting information about Christian names, surnames, unusual names, anagrams, proverbs, epitaphs, money, and sundry other items. Most of the *Remains* reads like a barely digested and non-contextualized gathering of facts, quotations, poems, and epitaphs. In some ways it is no more than a carefully organized archive. It has been observed that sixteenth-century antiquaries "were content to explore the past, find and describe its remainders, and leave it at that" (Breisach 1983: 177). Some antiquarian texts are adequately described in this fashion, but it may be too severe a judgment of the sum of their labors. One example will illustrate the point.

In his remarkable *History of the Most Renowned and Victorious Princess Elizabeth Late Queen of England* (first published in Latin in 1615 under the title *Annales rerum Anglicarum et Hibernicarum regnante Elizabetha*), Camden may appear restrained and to let the facts speak for themselves, but he certainly relies on his readers' ability to recognize irony and on their shared feelings of patriotism and Protestantism to properly understand the meaning of the facts. Describing the year 1588, the year of the Spanish Armada, Camden relates dryly how after prolonged rumors of war, it was now a "certain Truth" that "a most invincible Armada was rigged and prepared in Spain against England, and that the famousest Captains and expertest Leader and old Souldiers were sent for out of Italy, Sicily, yea and out of America into Spain" (Camden 1970: 308). The superlatives used to describe the power of the invincible Armada go unchecked in Camden's narration, except that they are clearly modulated by the outcome of the battle, known to every English man and woman. The very invincibility of the Armada (which Camden stresses but which he ascribes to various reports, implying his own restraint) of course only heightens the greatness of England's victory.

Camden then proceeds to tell us by means of a long quotation how the pope and various prominent Catholics tried to persuade the king of Spain to undertake this venture against England:

> That seeing God had blessed him [Philip II of Spain] with such exceeding great Blessings and Benefits, Portugal with the East-Indies and many rich Islands being laid of late to his Dominions, he in like manner would perform somewhat which might be pleasing and acceptable to God the Giver of so great Good things, and beseeming the Grandeur and Majesty of the Catholick King. But nothing could there be more acceptable to God, or more beseeming to him, than to propagate and enlarge the Church of God. That the Church of God could not be more gloriously nor more meritoriously be propagated, than by the Conquest of England, and replanting the Catholick Roman Religion, and abolishing Heresie there. (Ibid: 308–9)

The zealous Protestant historian John Foxe might have taken this occasion to vent against the corrupt and cruel Rome, but Camden studiously refrains from editorializing and merely continues to describe how the Armada was put together (310ff.). However, in light of the Armada's devastating defeat, even an ardent Catholic would have to consider the possibility that the pope and other prominent Catholics interpreted God's will erroneously. That Camden does not hit his reader over the head with this appraisal hardly makes it any less obvious. Even when recounting the Armada's inglorious end Camden relies on simple irony instead of grand interpretation: "And thus this great Armada, which had three complete Years in rigging and preparing with infinite Expense, was within one Month's space many times fought with, and at last overthrown, with the Slaughter of many men, not an hundred of the English being missing, nor any Ship lost, save onely that small one of Cock's: (for all the Shot from the Tall Spanish ships flew quite over the English:)" (pp. 326–7). The interpretation lies in the stark contrast between the extraordinary preparation of the Armada and its fairly simple defeat. The standard interpretation – the English Protestant God defeats the Spanish Catholic God is offered, but not as Camden's own. Camden simply relates how the queen "commanded publick prayer," and how she herself went to Paul's Church to give "most hearty Thanks to God," and where she "heard a Sermon, wherein the Glory was given to God alone" (p. 328).[22] Camden's *Annales* is not a study of antiquity but it contains ample evidence of the author's desire and ability to synthesize and interpret the "remainders" he describes, albeit through the use of irony, juxtaposition, and a firm knowledge of what his readers know to be true.[23] It is also true, however, that Camden's history of Elizabeth is not typical of most antiquarian research in the period, which was quite austere and content to let the facts speak for themselves.

But it was the sheer commitment to rigor, the archive, and to philological competence that set the antiquarians apart from other historians of the period. Moreover, antiquarians such as Camden, Selden,[24] and Henry Spelman separated divine causes from human causes even more decisively than did the humanists Polydore Vergil and Thomas More. Of course we cannot forget D. R. Woolf's thesis that the historical revolution that was to incorporate these antiquarian skills and innovations did not occur until long after the age of Shakespeare. Until the late seventeenth century, narrative and antiquarian methods were hardly ever practiced in unison.

But that does not mean that antiquarian innovations are any less important to Elizabethan and Jacobean drama than are the providentialism and psychological and political analyses of the chronicles or the humanists' "politic" histories. This essay has concerned itself with historiography in Shakespeare's time, and not with historiography's impact on the drama. In closing, however, I do wish to say a word about that impact. In my view, the drama's borrowings from the historians greatly exceed the level identified by a number of well-known older studies by E. M. W. Tillyard, Felix E. Schelling, M. M. Reese, and Alvin Kernan. According to these critics, playwrights' interaction with historical texts is limited to a scouring of the chronicles for content fit for a play, and, at times, for historical patterns that would give a proper shape to content. Irving Ribner and, more recently, Phyllis Rackin, Graham Holderness, and Paola Pugliatta have gone beyond these matters to consider what *theories* of history writing might be appropriated (and investigated) on the public stage. My own contribution to this more recent trend is premised on the claim that playwrights such as Marlowe, Shakespeare, Thomas Heywood, Dekker, and Ford aggressively appropriated and sometimes even simulated for their own purposes the plurality of historiographical methods described in the present essay. I have argued elsewhere that the playwrights were *more* acutely aware than most historians of the apparent contradictions and inconsistencies in the various historical methods that all purported to yield a true and accurate account of the past (Kamps 1996). In *Henry VIII*, for example, Shakespeare and Fletcher dramatize four distinct historiographical methods (providential, antiquarian, early humanist, and humanist) and give us insight into the very process of historiographical production, not to elevate one approach over the others or to push a particular ideological agenda, but to show that there are legitimate alternatives to the potent providentialism of Cranmer's prophetic speech at the christening of the infant Elizabeth. Entering the historical fray in different fashion, John Ford offers a controversial presentation of Perkin Warbeck, the man who claimed to be the Yorkist heir to the throne occupied by Henry VII. Taking a stance against "the libertie of vsing coniecture in Histories," practiced by Ralegh (1971: 212–17) and many other historians, Ford simply refuses to interpret the identity of Perkin Warbeck beyond what the factual record grants, thereby castigating Hall, Holinshed, Gainsford, and Bacon, who all readily perpetuate the official Tudor line that Warbeck was an obvious fraud. In this manner, dramatists like Shakespeare, Fletcher, and Ford, who were important disseminators of historical knowledge in late Elizabethan and early Jacobean London, claimed for the stage historiographical methods and capitalized on the internal confusion in the field of history writing to achieve powerful dramatic and political effects.

Notes

1 See Patterson (1994) and Rackin (1990: 1–12, 13).

2 See also Dean (1947: 1–2); Rackin (1990: 1–3); Levy (1967: 202–36, esp. 234).

3 Discussing the importance of orality in medieval and Renaissance culture, Woolf himself admits that "prior to 1600, and perhaps even a century later, most people would have heard their history in one form or another long before they read it, if they ever read it at all" (Woolf 2000: 83).

4 See Woolf (2000: 134–6).

5 Holinshed's *Chronicle* would be such an exception, especially now that Patterson has shown it to be a far more complex and thoughtful text than was commonly assumed by critics.

6 For a detailed account of the chronicle's demise, see Woolf (2000, 11–78).

7 See Kamps (1996).

8 "For he doth not faine, that rehearseth probabilities as bare coniectures; neither doth he depraue the text, that seeketh to illustrate and make good in humane reason, those things, which authoritie alone, without further circumstance, ought to haue confirmed in euery mans beliefe" (Ralegh 1971: 217).

9 The 1543 date refers to the inclusion of More's *History* in Richard Grafton's edition of *The Chronicle of John Hardyng*.

10 See Woolf (1990: 16) and Levy (1967: 153–4).

11 See Heywood, *If You Know Not Me* (pp. 222–3).

12 The first edition of *Anglica Historia*, published in Basle in 1534, dealt with the period from Roman Britain to 1509; the third edition of 1555 went to 1537.

13 For a different view, see Kelley (1998: 103).

14 J. G. A. Pocock (1987) notes, for instance, that the humanists' wish to "return to the ancient world as it really was" placed them "on the threshold of the modern historical consciousness" (p. 4). Kelley (1998) observes, "Scholars in the Middle Ages also had an appreciation of classical historiography, including the rhetorical forms and values on which this rested. Yet this historical sense was selective and subordinated to deep religious commitments and inhibitions which frustrated both a discriminating perspective on the ancient world and a clear perception of the differences not so much as 'modern' as a world darkening or 'grown old,' with a bright future reserved for things spiritual and posthumous. In general, chronological awareness was tied to a rigorous concern for the Year of Our Lord, and geography to small circles of local experience, natural as well as human; and historical knowledge was limited to rumors of farther-off happenings and relevance to the myopic concerns of monastery, cathedral, court, and, eventually, city" (p. 130). For the impact of foreign travel on English consciousness, see Kamps and Singh (2001).

15 See Matthew 10: 29; and explanatory note in Norton Shakespeare.

16 "When the historian spoke of the 'truth' of histories, he meant their moral as much as their factual veracity; he never had in mind the kind of precise, literal truth denoted in the nineteenth century by Ranke's famous phrase 'the past as it actually happened'" (Woolf 1990: 12).

17 For comparative treatments of Machiavelli and Guicciardini, see Kelley (1998: 146–52); Gilbert (1984); Pocock (1975).

18 As Gransden observes, "The humanists, like their medieval predecessors, saw history as the manifestation of God's will on earth; the future was predicted by prodigies and portents, and the Wheel of Fortune continued to turn. But the humanists laid greater emphasis on natural causation: God remained the prime mover of events, but usually worked through secondary, natural causes. This view led to a careful analysis of motives, especially of psychological, but also of political ones" (Gransden 1982: 427).

19 See, for instance, Edward Halle (1548), who suggests that "memorie maketh menne ded many thousande yere still to live as though thei were present: Thus fame triumpheth upon death, and renoune upon Oblivion, all by reason of wryting and historie" (p. ii).

20 See "Mr. Camden's Preface to the Reader."
21 The English authorized translation (produced by Philemon Holland) did not appear until 1610.
22 Woolf makes the same point about a different part of the *Annales* (Woolf 1990: 124).
23 But see MacCaffrey (1970), who argues that Camden "seeks to accomplish [this] not by praising her merits but, more obliquely, more delicately, by laying out the record of her reign. To him that record is self-evident; its very recital will command the admiration of the world and posterity. What Camden did not quite grasp is that the record by itself, unadorned by interpretation or examination, is intellectually unassimilable by his readers. The relentless flow of historical facts informs their minds without illuminating their understanding" (p. xxxi).
24 For an excellent treatment of Selden, see Woolf (1990: 200–42).

REFERENCES AND FURTHER READING

Blundeville, T. (1940) [1574]. *The True Order and Methode of Wryting and Reading Hystories, According to the Precepts of Francisco Patricio, and Accontio*, ed. H. G. Dick. *Huntington Library Quarterly*, 2, 149–70.
Breisach, E. (1983). *Historiography: Ancient, Medieval and Modern*. Chicago: University of Chicago Press.
Camden, W. (1789). Mr. Camden's Preface to the Reader. *Britannia or Chorographical Description of the Flourishing Kingdoms of England, Scotland, and Ireland*, vol. 1, trans. R. Cough. London.
——(1970) [1615]. *The History of the Most Renowned and Victorious Princess Elizabeth Late Queen of England*, ed. W. T. MacCaffrey. Chicago: University of Chicago Press, 1970.
——(1984) [1605, 1614, 1623]. *Remains Concerning Britain*, ed. R. D. Dunn. Toronto: University of Toronto Press, 1984.
Dean, L. F. (1947). *Tudor Theories of History Writing*. Contributions in Modern Philology No. 1. Ann Arbor: University of Michigan Press.
Fussner, F. S. (1962). *The Historical Revolution in English Historical Writing and Thought, 1580–1640*. London: Routledge and Kegan Paul.
Gilbert, F. (1984). *Machiavelli and Guicciardini: Politics and History in Sixteenth Century Florence*. New York: Norton.
Gransden, A. (1982). *Historical Writing in England II: c. 1307 to the Early Sixteenth Century*. Ithaca, NY: Cornell University Press.
Guicciardini, F. (1949). *Ricordi*, trans. N. H. Thomson. New York: S. F. Vanni.
Haddock, B. A. (1980). *An Introduction to Historical Thought*. London: Edward Arnold.
Halle, E. (1548). *The Union of Two Noble and Illustre Famelies of Lancastre & Yorke*. London.
Hardyng, J. and Grafton, R. (1812) [1570]. *The Chronicles of John Hardyng*. London.
Heywood, T. (1964). *If You Know Not Me, You Know No Bodie; or, The Troubles of Queene* Elizabeth. *The Dramatic Works of Thomas Heywood*, vol. 1. ed. R. H. Shepherd. New York: Russell and Russell, 89–247.
——(1982) [1631]. *Englands Elizabeth: Her Life and Troubles, During Her Minoritie, from the Cradle to the Crowne*, ed. P. R. Rider. New York: Garland.
Holderness, G. (1982). *Shakespeare's History*. New York: St. Martin's Press.
Holderness, G., Potter, N., and Turner, J. (1988). *Shakespeare: The Play of History*. Iowa City: University of Iowa Press.
Kahn, V. (1985). *Rhetoric, Prudence, and Skepticism in the Renaissance*. Ithaca, NY: Cornell University Press.
Kamps, I. (1996). *Historiography and Ideology in Stuart Drama*. Cambridge: Cambridge University Press.
Kamps, I. and Singh, J. G. (eds.) (2001). *Travel Knowledge: European "Discoveries" in the Early Modern Period, 1500–1800*. New York: Palgrave.
Kelley, D. R. (1998). *Faces of History: Historical Inquiry from Herodotus to Herder*. New Haven, CT: Yale University Press.
Kernan, A. B. (1975). *From Ritual to History: The English History Plays*. Vol. 3 of *The Revels History of Drama in English*, 4 vols. London: Methuen, 262–99.

Levine, J. M. (1987). *Humanism and History: Origins of Modern English Historiography*. Ithaca, NY: Cornell University Press.

——(1999). *The Autonomy of History: Truth and Method from Erasmus to Gibbon*. Chicago: University of Chicago Press.

Levy, F. J. (1967). *Tudor Historical Thought*. San Marino, CA: Huntington Library.

MacCaffrey, W. T. (1970). Introduction. *William Camden's The History of the Most Renowned and Victorious Princess Elizabeth Late Queen of England*. Chicago: University of Chicago Press, xi–xxxix.

Machiavelli, N. (1987) [1532]. *The Prince*, ed. Q. Skinner and R. Price. Cambridge: Cambridge University Press.

Momigliano, A. (1966). *Ancient History and the Antiquarian*. Studies in Historiography. London: Weidenfeld and Nicolson, 1–39.

——(1981). The Rhetoric of History and the History of Rhetoric: On Hayden White's Tropes. *Comparative Criticism: A Yearbook*, ed. E. S. Shaffer. Cambridge: Cambridge University Press, 259–68.

Patterson, A. (1994). *Reading Holinshed's Chronicles*. Chicago, IL: University of Chicago Press.

Pocock, J. G. A. (1975). *The Machiavellian Moment: Florentine Political Thought and the Atlantic Republican Tradition*. Princeton, NJ: Princeton University Press.

——(1987). *The Ancient Constitution and the Feudal Law: A Study of English Historical Thought in the Seventeenth Century*. Reissue. Cambridge: Cambridge University Press.

Pugliatti, P. (1996). *Shakespeare the Historian*. New York: St. Martin's Press.

Rackin, P. (1990). *Stages of History: Shakespeare's English Chronicles*. Ithaca, NY: Cornell University Press.

Ralegh, W. (1971) [1614]. *The History of the World*, ed. C. A. Patrides. Philadelphia, PA: Temple University Press.

Reese, M. M. (1961). *The Cease of Majesty: A Study of Shakespeare's History Plays*. London: Edward Arnold.

Ribner, I. (1957). *The English History Play in the Age of Shakespeare*. Princeton, NJ: Princeton University Press.

Schelling, F. E. (1902). *The English Chronicle Play: A Study in the Popular Historical Literature Environing Shakespeare*. New York: Macmillan.

Shakespeare, W. (1997). *The Norton Shakespeare*, ed. S. Greenblatt, W. Cohen, J. Howard, and K. Maus. New York: Norton.

Sidney, P. (1989). *A Defence of Poesy*, ed. K. Duncan-Jones. New York: Oxford University Press.

Spenser, E. (1989). Letter to Walter Ralegh. Appendix 1. *The Faerie Queene*, ed. A. C. Hamilton. New York: Longman, 737–8.

Stow, J. (1987) [1603]. *The Survey of London*, ed. H. B. Wheatley. London: Everyman.

Tillyard, E. W. M. (1962) [1944]. *Shakespeare's History Plays*. New York: Collier Books.

Trompf, G. W. (1979). *The Idea of Historical Recurrence in Western Thought: From Antiquity to the Reformation*. Berkeley: University of California Press.

Vergil, P. (1846). *Polydore Vergil's English History*, ed. H. Ellis. Camden series, vol. 36. London: Camden Society.

——(1950). *The Anglica Historia of Polydore Vergil, A.D. 1485–1537*, ed. and trans. D. Hay. Camden series, vol. 74. London: Royal Historical Society.

Weinberger, J. (1996). Introduction. *Francis Bacon, The History of the Reign of King Henry the Seventh*. Ithaca, NY: Cornell University Press, 1–20.

Woolf, D. R. (1990). *The Idea of History in Early Stuart England*. Toronto: University of Toronto Press.

——(2000). *Reading History in Early Modern England*. Cambridge: Cambridge University Press.

Wright, L. B. (1953) [1935]. *Middle-Class Culture in Elizabethan England*. Ithaca, NY: Cornell University Press.

2
Shakespeare and Contemporary Dramatists of History
Richard Helgerson

As a dramatic genre fit to stand alongside the classically sanctioned genres of comedy and tragedy, the history play is both distinctly Shakespearean and distinctly retrospective. Only with the posthumous division of Shakespeare's plays in the 1623 First Folio into "comedies," "histories," and "tragedies" did the notion of such a genre receive clear articulation, and all subsequent discussion has taken the ten plays the Folio editors printed as "histories" to be the genre's defining exemplars. This Shakespearean dominance has had some good effects. Without it, history plays by writers other than Shakespeare would have received even less attention than they have. After all, the only reason this volume contains a chapter on other "dramatists of history" is because those others can be compared to Shakespeare. But it also has disadvantages. For most of us, the English history play is what Shakespeare and his Folio editors made of it. Plays by other writers have routinely been accepted as true expressions of the genre only to the degree that they resemble his. The result has been a considerable narrowing in our understanding of the variety of perspectives on the English past – and thus on the English nation – that were available to Elizabethan theatregoers.

Perhaps it would be liberating simply to set aside for the moment our usual concern for generic clarity. *George a Green*, *Arden of Faversham*, *The Shoemaker's Holiday*, *Look About You*, and *The Whore of Babylon*, to name some fairly extreme examples, may not be history plays in anything like the way we have learned to understand that genre from reading Shakespeare, but each presents, as do many other plays critics regularly dismiss as too comical, too sentimental, too domestic, or just too unhistorical, a vision of England and the English past that once competed with Shakespeare's.

In proposing this temporary disregard for generic clarity, I can claim at least some support from Elizabethan practice. Until the Folio editors took ten of Shakespeare's plays and called them "histories," early modern playwrights and publishers were no clearer in their generic labeling than I intend to be. Shakespeare's own quartos, the single-play editions that appeared over the three decades prior to the Folio, provide a telling example. Though their title pages do include a *History of Henry IV* – our *1*

Henry IV – and a *Chronicle History of Henry V*, they also identify *3 Henry VI*, *Richard III*, and *Richard II* as "tragedies," and they supply no generic label at all for *2 Henry VI* and *2 Henry IV*. So of the seven Shakespearean history plays that appeared in quarto editions, only two got described as such. Nor did the quartos limit the term to plays the Folio was later to identify that way, for among them we also find *The True Chronicle History of King Lear*, *The Tragical History of Hamlet*, *The Famous History of Troilus and Cressida*, and *The Most Excellent History of the Merchant of Venice*. Opening our attention to a broader range of plays thus violates no generic restriction the Elizabethans were at pains to maintain.

This is not to say that rights to the term "history" were not hotly contested in Elizabethan England. They were. But that contest was waged less by playwrights than by the new "politic" historians, men like Francis Bacon, William Camden, John Hayward, and John Selden. Intent on denying the claim of the massive and miscellaneously capacious chronicles of such compilers as Richard Grafton, Edward Hall, Raphael Holinshed, and John Stow, these writers did what they could to reserve the term for their own more critical and sharply focused studies of the great affairs of state. Shakespeare's sensitivity to this campaign may have had something to do with what he made of materials he borrowed from the chroniclers. The politic historians' sense that histories should be made exclusively "of deeds done by a public weal or against a public weal, and such be either deeds of war, of peace, or else sedition and conspiracy" (Blundeville 1574: sig. Aivᵛ) closely matches what we find in his work. And certainly the success the politic historians had in imposing their views has had a significant part in moving latter-day critics to accept a definition of the history play that puts a high premium on its political focus. To a large extent, our notion of history has been theirs. But that notion had not yet taken firm hold in the theatrical world of the 1590s and the first years of the seventeenth century, when most of the plays concerning England's past were written and produced. To impose it retroactively on that far more diverse historical culture as a way of deciding which plays deserve attention and which don't would be to miss much that was going on. Though the theatre saw no contest over generic nomenclature comparable to that engaged by the politic historians, it did present rival scriptings of England's past, rival accounts of who and what mattered. Ignoring generic categorizations, however helpful such categorizations may be for other purposes, may help bring the full range of those rivalries into clearer view.

One immediate fruit of such a strategy would be to increase from ten to fourteen the number of Shakespeare's own plays that would be available for consideration. To the Folio's *King John*, *Richard II*, two parts of *Henry IV*, *Henry V*, three parts of *Henry VI*, *Richard III*, and *Henry VIII*, we could add *Macbeth*, *King Lear*, *Cymbeline*, and perhaps even *The Merry Wives of Windsor*, the only comedy Shakespeare set in England and a play that proclaims its attachment to history by including among its principal characters a figure made famous by his role in the two *Henry IV* plays, Sir John Falstaff. But here expanding the canon of Shakespearean plays that engage England and its history is of less importance than is setting those plays, however many of them we suppose there to have been, against the thirty or so plays by other writers that undertake a similar engagement. As the other chapters in this volume amply attest, Shakespeare's own English history plays, even if we stick only to the Folio's ten, are hardly monolithic in their concerns. But they do nevertheless share partialities that show up with striking clarity when they are seen against the backdrop of a larger, more heterogeneous company.

In what follows I will describe five distinct, though often overlapping, interests that are strongly represented in the non-Shakespearean drama of history, but that Shakespeare himself neglects, marginalizes, or actively opposes. To provide some focus for this discussion, I will pay special attention to a series of plays dealing with a single, fairly limited period of English history and then bring in other plays as they share interests with those. There would be many such possibilities. One characteristic of the historical drama produced in the half century between the appearance of the first such play, *The Famous Victories of Henry V*, in 1586 and the last, *Perkin Warbeck*, in 1633 is its repeated rewriting of the same or closely related material.[1] Shakespeare's own "Henriad," the two parts of *Henry IV* and *Henry V*, is just such a rewriting of *The Famous Victories* itself, and it in turn provoked an angry rebuttal in the form of the two-part *Sir John Oldcastle*. These Henry plays would be one likely place to begin, and I will want to return to them. But a historically more distant series of reigns and a less familiar group of plays can perhaps give us an even fresher and more varied introduction to the early modern theatrical writing of the English past. Like his Henriad, Shakespeare's *King John* (1596) drew heavily on an earlier rendition of much the same material, the anonymous *Troublesome Reign of John, King of England* (1591).[2] And like the early Henry plays, these closely related plays on the reign of King John were followed by others that put this historical moment in a markedly different light: Anthony Munday and Henry Chettle's two-part *Downfall and Death of Robert, Earl of Huntington* (1598), the anonymous *Look About You* (1599), and Robert Davenport's *King John and Matilda* (1628). In these different plays, Shakespeare's along with the rest, we get not only five or six radically different views of King John, but also five or six different systems of theatrical value and thus five or six different Englands.

Politics and the Elect Nation

Why should King John have appealed to so many dramatists? The preface "to the gentleman readers" of the 1591 quarto edition of *The Troublesome Reign* makes its claim quite explicit:

> You that with friendly grace of smoothed brow
> Have entertained the Scythian Tamburlaine
> And given applause unto an infidel,
> Vouchsafe to welcome with like courtesy
> A warlike Christian and your countryman.

> For Christ's true faith endured he many a storm
> And set himself against the man of Rome,
> Until base treason by a damned wight
> Did all his former triumphs put to flight.
> Accept of it, sweet gentles, in good sort,
> And think it was prepared for your disport.

This preface celebrates John as an English Tamburlaine, a great warrior king comparable to Marlowe's Scythian conqueror. Given the date of the play and the extraordinary popularity of Marlowe's work, such a connection was certainly inviting. But there is a problem. John does not fit the Marlovian mold. Though he does fight the French, he is no Tamburlaine. His wars are notably unheroic and inconclusive. If there is any spark of Marlovian spirit in this play, it belongs not to John but rather to "the Bastard," the illegitimate son of John's elder brother, Richard Coeur de Lion. So why, if the dramatist wanted to present a heroic image of royal military valor, didn't he simply take King Richard as his subject? Because he had a far more pressing ideological agenda, one that Richard's glory as a crusader would not have served. What made John an irresistible subject to this dramatist was the same thing that appealed to John Bale in his virulently anti-Catholic *King Johan* more than sixty years earlier: John's conflict with the "man of Rome" and his death at the hands of a popish monk. No Tamburlaine, the King John of *The Troublesome Reign* is a tragically failed precursor of those Tudor defenders of England's religious sovereignty, Henry VIII and Elizabeth I.

The Troublesome Reign is the first of what have sometimes been called "elect nation" plays, plays that follow the lead of mid-century Protestant historiographers like John Bale and John Foxe in seeing England as a new Israel, a nation chosen by God (Spikes 1977). Though we often think of Puritans and other radical reformers as enemies of the theatre, in this regard reformed religion and the public stage made common cause. In the years shortly following her death, Elizabeth herself, who in *The Troublesome Reign* is prefigured by John, appeared in at least two such plays: as the Protestant princess suffering for her faith under the rule of her Catholic sister Mary in the first part of Thomas Heywood's *If You Know Not Me, You Know Nobody* (1604) and as the Fairy Queen, the great opposite of the popish Empress of Babylon, in Thomas Dekker's allegorical *Whore of Babylon* (1606). King John in *The Troublesome Reign* and the Elizabeth of *The Whore of Babylon* nevertheless depart from the usual pattern of such plays. Most of their Protestant protagonists are not reigning monarchs but rather subjects who suffer from the combined enmity of royal and ecclesiastical power. Princess Elizabeth in *If You Know Not Me* is herself just such a figure, and so are Sir John Oldcastle in the two *Oldcastle* plays (1599) written by Michael Drayton, Richard Hathway, Anthony Munday, and Robert Wilson, Cromwell in the anonymous *Thomas Lord Cromwell* (1600), Wyatt in Dekker and John Webster's *Sir Thomas Wyatt* (1602), Katherine Parr in Samuel Rowley's *When You See Me, You Know Me* (1604), and the duchess in Thomas Drue's *Duchess of Suffolk* (1624). Rarely in these plays are kings actively malevolent. In this regard, Queen Mary is an exception. But they are regularly misled by scheming Catholic bishops. As in Foxe's *Book of Martyrs*, the elect nation, whose history these plays present, can thus only sporadically be identified with the monarchic state.

Finding *Sir John Oldcastle* on the list of elect nation plays should alert us that, theatrically at least, Shakespeare was not of this party. As I have already remarked, *Sir John Oldcastle* was written to rebut Shakespeare's Henriad. Borrowing from *The Famous Victories of Henry V*, Shakespeare had made Oldcastle the companion of Prince Henry's lawless youth. Indeed, Shakespeare went well beyond *The Famous Victories* in giving his Oldcastle the unmistakable language of Puritan religiosity. Such a characterization could only be seen as a direct affront to the memory of a man reformers regarded as a Protestant hero and martyr. Why Shakespeare should have indulged in it can be no more than a matter of speculation. But the affront was real and could hardly have been accidental. For whatever reason, Shakespeare wanted to besmirch Oldcastle's reputation and make him look like a comic hypocrite. The reaction, whether from religious admirers of Oldcastle or, more likely, from Oldcastle's noble descendants, must have been swift, for Shakespeare immediately backed down. He changed the name to "Falstaff" and then went on to protest in the epilogue to *2 Henry IV* that "Oldcastle died a martyr, and this is not the man."[3] But for his opponents, this was not enough. The damage had been done and could only be undone with a response in kind. Thus Drayton, Hathway, Munday, and Wilson's two-part play (only the first part of which survives) celebrating Oldcastle's religious faith and loyalty to his king, a play whose prologue declares, "Let fair truth be graced, / Since forged invention" – clearly Shakespeare's "forged invention" – "former time defaced."

Shakespeare's *King John* is guilty of no comparable defacement, no similarly direct affront – not, that is, if one takes *The Troublesome Reign* as "fair truth." But, still, *King John* would not easily be mistaken for an elect nation play. Though Shakespeare generally follows his predecessor – presuming, of course, as most critics do, that *The Troublesome Reign* is the earlier play – scene by scene and often speech by speech, he cuts away almost all the most virulently anti-Catholic rhetoric. Gone, too, are scenes of monkish licentiousness and treachery and prophecies of a king – Henry VIII – who will one day free England from the Roman yoke. Though Shakespeare lets us hear by report that a monk has poisoned King John, he all but suppresses the growing animosity between what *The Troublesome Reign* calls "our popelings" and the king and eliminates altogether the planning of the king's murder by abbot and monk. And though Shakespeare's John does still denounce the pope's legate as a "meddling priest" and insists, as did his counterpart in *The Troublesome Reign*, on his own position as "supreme head" of the English state and church (3.1.163 and 155), the whole balance of the play has shifted. Instead of sectarian propaganda, Shakespeare provides, as Hershel Baker (1997: 806) has remarked, "a daring exploration into the murky depths of *Realpolitik*." In this, Shakespeare adheres more faithfully to the principles of the new politic historians than they were often willing to do themselves.

Even among Shakespeare's own history plays, *King John* stands alone, for it does less than any other to engage the emotions of its audience. Lacking the endearing, if politically disabling, piety of Henry VI, the bold evil of Richard III, the tragic pathos of Richard II, the triumphant political and military skill of Henry V, and the imposing splendor of Henry VIII, Shakespeare's King John makes us think more than he makes us feel. But for all its uniqueness, *King John* resembles Shakespeare's other history plays in focusing its attention and its dramatic energy on the getting, keeping, and losing of political power. Similar issues do, of course, arise in the work of other early modern dramatists of English history. But no other dramatist shares the singular intensity of Shakespeare's focus on the workings of power at the highest level of the monarchic state. The interest of those other dramatists most often centers elsewhere. With the elect nation plays, religious truth is that center. If a monarch like John or Elizabeth is the momentary repository of religious truth, his or her political struggles will rightly assume paramount dramatic importance. But if for a time truth resides with lesser figures, even with figures as politically insignificant as Sir John Oldcastle or the Duchess of Suffolk, that is where the drama of history will turn its attention. In Shakespeare's *King John*, papal interference poses an acute political problem, a problem of impossibly divided sovereignty. In *The Troublesome Reign*, the implications of that same interference are more nearly apocalyptic than political, less a conflict between rulers and institutions than between Christ and Antichrist. This is not to make of Shakespeare a modern secularist. He was, on the contrary, intensely concerned, particularly in the *Henry VI* plays and *Richard III*, with the providential design of history. But divine providence, as represented in his history plays, agrees with him in confining its attention to the greatest affairs of state.

A Nation of Yeomen and Good Fellows

As its title suggests, the next of the plays that feature John and his reign, Munday and Chettle's *Downfall and Death of Robert, Earl of Huntington*, departs still further than *The Troublesome Reign* from this Shakespearean axis. These new authors care less about John himself, who now figures neither as Protestant hero nor as center of political speculation, and more about the chief victims of his usurpation and lust, the Earl of Huntington and his beloved Matilda Fitzwater – otherwise known as Robin Hood and Maid Marian.

Huntington and Matilda's suffering at the hands of abusive power might be thought to link this two-part work to the elect nation plays. And, indeed, the association of sixteenth-century earls of Huntington with the Puritan cause, the play's sharp anti-clericalism, and its celebration of a virtuous fugitive band has suggested an appeal to Protestant Nonconformists (Bevington 1968: 295–6). But, if so, that appeal would have been muted by the blackening of John's character, the near omission of his conflict with Rome, and the identification of Huntington with Robin Hood, not a particular favorite of radical reformers. No, the closest affiliations of the two Huntington plays are less with sectarian evocations of an elect nation than with three separate, though sometimes related, tendencies, all three virtually absent from Shakespeare's English histories. The first invests greatest representative value in yeoman heroes; the second does the same for aristocratic intercessors between king and people; and the third most prizes virtuous female objects of lawless royal desire. In his double role of Robin Hood and Earl of Huntington, Munday and Chettle's title character gives dramatic expression to the first two of these tendencies. The third finds its ideal in Marian/Matilda.

The Robin Hood of ballad, folk play, and holiday festival on whose legend Munday and Chettle drew lacked the Earl of Huntington's noble title. He was a yeoman outlaw, not a persecuted aristocrat. So foreign to this popular hero is his new found gentility that Munday and Chettle seem occasionally unsure whether their noble Robert Hood is, in fact, the legendary outlaw or is just playing the part. "Henceforth," says Earl Robert, "I will be called Robin Hood. / Matilda shall be my Maid Marian" (p. 142). It sounds as though he needs a Maid Marian because the real Robin, the Robin of May Day games, had one. Nor would this be the only instance of such aristocratic masking. In George Peele's *Edward I*, the Welsh Prince Lluellen takes the part of Robin Hood, while in Shakespeare's *As You Like It*, the banished Duke Senior lives in the forest of Arden "like the old Robin Hood of England" (1.1.116). But whether Munday and Chettle's Earl of Huntington really is Robin Hood or is, like Lluellen and Duke Senior, only masquerading, the yeomanly associations of the role persist. Robin's greenwood fellows, Little John, Much the miller's son, Scarlet, Scathlock, and Friar Tuck, do clearly come from the lower reaches of society; they are sworn to give their master no title of "earl, lord, baron, knight, or squire" (p. 153); and repeated allusions link them with that other yeoman hero of early modern English drama, George a Green, the jolly pinner of Wakefield. In the anonymous 1590 play devoted to George a Green, George captures the rebellious Earl of Kendall, brags that "a poor man that is true, / Is better than an earl if he be false" (ll. 31–2), refuses a knighthood, and fights Robin Hood himself to a draw. Yeomanly pride and valor go together with fierce loyalty to the rightful king, the same loyalty Munday and Chettle's Robin feels toward the absent King Richard, whose throne Prince John is scheming to usurp.

Considered more broadly, what both the yeomanly side of the Robin Hood plays and the closely linked *George a Green* point to is a conception of the true England as a comradely band of "good fellows."[4] Shakespeare's Henry V draws on the rhetoric of such fellowship in his rousing speech before the Battle of Agincourt: "We few, we happy few, we band of brothers, / For he today that sheds his blood with me / Shall be my brother" (4.3.60–3), and his youthful time of tavern revelry with Falstaff, Bardolph, and Poins provides a simulacrum of the thing itself. But Henry is no good fellow. Nor does Shakespeare suppose he could be. Good fellowship, irrespective of rank, is an idle dream that cannot withstand the alienating reality of royal history as Shakespeare conceives of it. Henry's disguised meeting with some of his common soldiers on the eve of Agincourt provides a good test case. In other plays – *George a Green*, *Sir John Oldcastle*, Heywood's *1 Edward IV*, and Samuel Rowley's *When You See Me, You*

Know Me – the meeting of a disguised king and his common subjects discovers their shared humanity and enforces the bond of good fellowship. The appearance of King Richard, dressed in Robin Hood's Kendal green, at the end of the first Huntington play serves a similar function. It proves that yeomen and king belong to the same merry company. The meeting in *Henry V* does just the reverse. It reveals an unbridgeable gulf, a gulf no good fellowship could ever span, between commoner and king.

Noting differences of this sort, critics have praised the irony and complexity of Shakespeare's historical sensibility and deplored the "nostalgic but false romanticism" of his competitors (Barton 1975: 99). There is certainly some justification for this preference. Shakespeare is more politically acute than his contemporaries. But the yeomanly good-fellow plays are not without complexities of their own. For one thing, their jolly high spirits often accompany a threatening lawlessness. Compared to the Robin Hood of medieval ballads, Munday and Chettle's Earl of Huntington is a relatively tame figure, but he and his merry band are nevertheless outlaws who support themselves by thievery. Likewise, the commoner the disguised Henry V meets in the first part of *Sir John Oldcastle* is a highway robber, who reminds the king of his own thieving youth. And in *When You See Me, You Know Me*, King Henry VIII meets, fights, and bonds with the notorious thief and murderer, the self-proclaimed "good fellow," Black Will, who had made an earlier stage appearance as the hired killer of Arden of Faversham. "Let not a little wipe" – that is, their own armed encounter – "make us enemies," says the still disguised king. "Clap hands, and be friends" (ll. 1305–6). Shakespeare's Prince Hal also claps hands and at least pretends to be friends with Falstaff and his thieving crew, but for Hal, unlike his counterpart in *The Famous Victories*, this is always a pretense. He uses the appearance of good fellowship for his own politic ends. In the more comical histories, good fellowship, including its lawless, anarchic, clownish, and carnivalesque sides, seems an end in itself. Where, on becoming king, Hal banishes even the appearance of all that, many of the non-Shakespearean dramatists of history make it central to their idea of England and its history. Unlike Shakespeare, they encourage their audiences to imagine themselves as members of a potentially disruptive community of good fellows.

Such disruption did, however, bump up against firm limits. Popular rebellion is never allowed a sympathetic portrayal. Four plays include such episodes: *The Life and Death of Jack Straw* (1591), *Sir Thomas More* (1595), *1 Edward IV* (1599), and Shakespeare's *2 Henry VI*, the play its quarto edition calls *The First Part of the Contention Betwixt the Two Famous Houses of York and Lancaster* (1591).[5] Much of the clowning and carnivalesque revelry that characterizes the good-fellow plays can be found here as well. And so can the leveling ideology implicit in the notion of good fellowship. "Neighbors, neighbors," says Parson Ball in the sermon that galvanizes the Peasants' Rebellion in *Jack Straw*,

> the weakest now a days goes to the wall,
> But mark my words, and follow the counsel of John Ball.
> England is grown to such a pass of late,
> That rich men triumph to see the poor beg at their gate.

> But I am able by good scripture before you to prove,
> That God doth not this dealing allow or love.
> But when Adam delved, and Eve span,
> Who was then a gentleman?
> Brethren, brethren, it were better to have the community
> Than to have this difference in degrees. (ll. 76–85)

That such sentiments got expressed at all is a matter of some consequence. Certainly these were not views whose circulation Elizabeth's government would particularly have encouraged. No wonder then that Edmund Tilney, the man charged with censoring plays, should have intervened to block the production of *Sir Thomas More*. "Leave out the insurrection wholly and the cause thereof," he wrote in the margin of the play's manuscript (p. 17). We may guess that only the savage mockery to which each subjects the rebellion and its leaders saved the other three plays, *Jack Straw*, *1 Edward IV*, and Shakespeare's *Contention*, from similar censorship. Unlike the respectable Londoners who take arms in *Sir Thomas More*, their rebels are clearly identified as fools and knaves. Shakespeare's Jack Cade, to cite only the most conspicuous example, has one man hung for knowing how to read, beheads another for founding a grammar school, and kills a third, one of his own followers, simply for calling him "Jack Cade." Even in a theatre that sometimes celebrated lawless good fellows, Cade and his counterparts in *Jack Straw* and *1 Edward IV* were aggressively discredited.

But if rebellion was beyond the pale, the leveling trickery of disguise was very much within it. Not only do kings disguise themselves to meet with their common subjects, but characters of all sorts indulge in frequent shape-shifting. Not every change in costume is a sign of egalitarian good fellowship. Richard II's masquing in *Woodstock* and John's in *King John and Matilda* are, on the contrary, tools of oppression. But most serve both as a shield against the abuses of power and as marks of festive comradery. That is certainly true of the many disguisings in *George a Green*, *Edward I*, *The Blind Beggar of Bednal Green* (1600), and the first Huntington play, but it applies as well to the disguises persecuted Protestants assume in *Sir John Oldcastle* and *The Duchess of Suffolk*. Role playing itself is a quality these plays link with English good fellowship and invite their audiences to admire. In line with this admiration, Munday and Chettle take the metatheatrical impulse to a still further level and present the whole of the two Huntington plays as the rehearsal of performances supposedly scripted by the early Tudor poet John Skelton and intended for King Henry VIII. Thus audiences would have seen the Lord Admiral's Men, the company that put on these plays, playing Skelton and his company playing Huntington and his men playing Robin Hood and his. In such a many-layered confection, playing itself becomes the basis of England's continuity through time.

For sheer multiplicity of disguising, even the Huntington plays must, however, yield to the curious but closely related *Look About You* (1599). With at least a dozen and a half shape-shiftings, including repeated crossdressing in gender, age, and status, just keeping track of who in this play is really who must have been more than most audiences could have managed. Yet this dizzying succession of role changes, more excessive than what one finds in even the most extravagant comedy of disguises, presents itself as a drama of history, and at least one critic has written at length in defense of this claim (Lancaster 1969). Set half a generation earlier than *The Downfall of Robert, Earl of Huntington, Look About You* concerns that moment when Henry II's sovereignty was challenged by his wife, Queen Elinor, and their sons, Henry, Richard, and John. At the play's opening, the kingdom is divided. By its conclusion, order has been restored. Clearly, the credit must belong, though it would be difficult to say just how, to the seemingly endless series of disguisings that at one time or another put a great many of the play's characters into one another's clothes. Not all these characters are particularly appealing. Skink, the most agile of the play's many shape-shifters, is a serial murderer, and Prince John is a tyrant in the making. But if Skink and John are not quite the good fellows the play is most eager to celebrate, they too find a place in this strangely anarchic nation of festive excess, a nation that in variously attenuated ways is to be found as well in many Elizabethan dramas of history.

Good Lords and Suffering Commoners

As Robin Hood, the Earl of Huntington evokes a legendary England of jolly yeomen and festive merriment, of roguish good fellowship and comic disguise. As a nobleman with a special concern for the welfare of his less privileged fellow subjects, he belongs to a slightly different category, the category of "good" earls and "good" dukes who mediate between king and commons. Good Duke Humphrey in what was probably Shakespeare's first history play, *The Contention* (aka *2 Henry VI*), is the earliest of these figures. Where the other nobles in this play – Queen Margaret, Duchess Eleanor, Cardinal Beauford, and the dukes of Somerset, Suffolk, Buckingham, and York – scheme to advance themselves and their power, Duke Humphrey and his closest supporters act on behalf of the king and the common people. To serve the public good is, as these men understand it, the true purpose of government.

Given this opening to Shakespeare's career as a dramatist of history, it is remarkable that such concerns play so little part in his subsequent work. Duke Humphrey dies by the third act of *The Contention*, the victim of his wife's ambition and the envy of his less public-minded peers, and by the play's conclusion Cade's Rebellion has destroyed all sympathy for popular suffering or discontent. From then on, through the remaining eight Shakespearean history plays of the 1590s, we hear nothing more from kings or noblemen about the public good. Not until *Henry VIII*, more than twenty years later, does Henry's queen Katherine intervene in the council of her husband to draw the king's attention to the excessive taxation levied on his common subjects. "Taxation? / Wherein? and what taxation?" (1.2.37–8), responds the king. King Henry's neglect had also been Shakespeare's. Whatever English history meant to Shakespeare, it did not mean a concern for the fortunes of the common people. In his history plays, kings and nobles are valued for many qualities, but, with the exception of Duke Humphrey at the very beginning and Queen Katherine at the very end, an interest in the public good is not one of them.[6]

This neglect on Shakespeare's part is all the more conspicuous when we compare his plays to those of the other dramatists of history, for they repeatedly follow the lead he gave and then abandoned. Concern for the poor is, of course, central to the Earl of Huntington's behavior as Robin Hood. The first article of the vow each of his men must take is that "you never shall the poor man wrong" (p. 154). But it figures no less obviously in a surprisingly large number of other plays. Sir John Oldcastle, who is known as "the best man to the poor that is in all Kent" (p. 126), is first seen distributing alms, and scenes of almsgiving begin and end *The Duchess of Suffolk*. "I spend my labors to relieve the poor," says the imprisoned Princess Elizabeth in *If You Know Not Me* (p. 30), while More in *Sir Thomas More* and Cromwell in *Sir Thomas Cromwell* are both remarkable for interventions on behalf of their common fellow subjects. Perhaps the most elaborately dramatized of all the acts of mediation on behalf of suffering commoners are those undertaken by the penitent citizen's wife, Jane Shore, in the two parts of Heywood's *Edward IV*. Having been elevated to something like noble status by her liaison with the king, Mistress Shore spends all her energy visiting hospitals and prisons and carrying petitions to the otherwise neglectful king. And she, like all the others, is not only a defender of the poor commons but is also herself a victim of royal power. In the next section, I will want to return to Jane Shore and her sufferings, but here the figure who most immediately invites comparison with what we find (or don't find) in Shakespeare is still another noble defender of the people and political martyr, the title character of the anonymous *Thomas of Woodstock* (1592).

Woodstock has two obvious connections to Shakespeare's history plays. It picks up on the Duke Humphrey episodes of *The Contention*, constructing a whole play centered on a character who nearly resembles Shakespeare's "good duke." And it competes with Shakespeare's *Richard II* by supplying a strikingly different interpretation of that failed king's reign. The similarities to *The Contention* are unmistakable. Woodstock and Humphrey, both dukes of Gloucester, are also both lord protectors of the realm during the minority of their royal nephews, Richard II and Henry VI, and both are displaced and eventually murdered once their royal masters come of age. More important, they are alike in their unwavering loyalty to the crown, their equally unwavering devotion to the commonweal, and their lack of any distracting personal ambition. But there is also a significant difference. Where Shakespeare kills off his good duke midway through the play and then goes on to undermine with Cade's Rebellion the position Humphrey of Gloucester had represented, *Woodstock*'s author persists in regarding "plain" Thomas's regard for the public good as the moral center of his play. And when Shakespeare, some two or three years later, wrote a play of his own about Richard II, he all but ignored those popular grievances that had so preoccupied *Woodstock*'s lord protector.

Woodstock takes its dramatic energy and interest from the representation of royal oppression. Owing more to Marlowe's *Edward II* (1592) than to *Woodstock*, *Richard II* takes its from the representation of royal suffering. Shakespeare's play alludes so obliquely to Richard's blank charters, his farming out of the kingdom, and even his responsibility for his uncle's murder that it would be difficult for anyone who had not seen *Woodstock* to know what is meant. But in *Woodstock* itself, these abuses are not only explained in detail; they are vividly dramatized. The effects of Richard's misrule on his suffering subjects, Thomas of Woodstock most prominent among them, are what most engage our attention in *Woodstock*. How do the common people respond to the tyrannical demand that they sign blank charters giving the king and his minions the right to assess their property at whatever rate they find convenient? How do they experience the king's dividing of the land into four parcels that are then rented out to tax farmers, interested only in their own enrichment? How do they take the disappearance of their chief defender, plain Thomas of Woodstock? Questions like these have no place in *Richard II*, no more than does Queen Anne's lament in *Woodstock* that "distressèd poverty o'erspreads the kingdom" (p. 108). *Richard II*'s queen is also troubled by the effect of her husband's misrule, but the victim who most engages her sympathy is Richard himself. "But soft, but see," she says at the sight of the imprisoned king,

> or rather do not see,
> My fair rose wither; yet look up, behold,
> That you in pity may dissolve to dew
> And wash him fresh again with true-love tears. (5.1.7–10)

"Let us sit upon the ground," says her husband a little before his arrest, "and tell sad stories of the death of kings" (3.2.155–6). Both the queen and the king reserve their most impassioned rhetoric for the pitiful spectacle of the king's own, largely self-inflicted wrongs, and so does Shakespeare. If ever there was a play that solicited tears for a fallen king, *Richard II* is it. Nor is the difference between *Richard II* and *Woodstock* merely an isolated difference between plays that happen to choose different moments in the same reign as their subjects, one the death of Woodstock, the other the death of Richard. No, the difference is, on the contrary, systematic and repeated. Though the stories are not all sad, stories of kings do claim the greatest share of Shakespeare's attention. For the other early modern English dramatists of history, stories of suffering subjects, including especially those noble subjects who have devoted themselves to the welfare of the poor commons, seemed of far greater moment.

This does not, however, mean that Shakespeare's version of history propped up monarchy any more reliably than did the plays of his rivals. With regard to *Woodstock* and *Richard II*, the reverse seems, in fact, to have been the case. The first three quarto editions of *Richard II* omit the scene of Richard's deposition, presumably because such a scene was thought politically dangerous, and on the eve of the Earl of Essex's abortive rebellion against Queen Elizabeth, his supporters ordered a special production of *Richard II*. "I am Richard II," fumed the queen. "Know you not that?" (Chambers 1930, II: 326). Though after his execution, ballads appeared lamenting Essex as another Woodstock, Duke Humphrey, Oldcastle, Huntington, Cromwell, or More –

that is, as a champion of the people struck down by the malevolent workings of power
– he and his supporters clearly felt that a play that presented a king's overthrow would
do more to strengthen their cause than one showing the defeat and death of a popular
lord. Some years later, Henry Wotton, describing an early performance of Shakespeare
and Fletcher's *Henry VIII*, remarked that the play's many scenes of "pomp and majesty"
were "sufficient in truth within a while to make greatness very familiar, if not ridiculous" (Chambers 1930, II: 344). Perhaps he was right. Perhaps Shakespeare's history
plays did make greatness familiar and thus susceptible to a more critical regard (Orgel
1982 and Kastan 1986). But those plays still identified English history as the near
exclusive province of just such royal greatness. What other Elizabethan dramatists of
history, including the anonymous author of *Woodstock*, invited their audiences to consider was that history might have other concerns, that England was, in short, not
merely or even primarily the "royal throne of kings," the "sceptered isle," the "earth
of majesty," that in *Richard II* Shakespeare's John of Gaunt so memorably evokes
(2.1.40–1), but rather the home of England's common subjects.

History's Objects of Desire

Poisoned by the Prior of York and his henchman Sir Doncaster, the Earl of
Huntington dies in the first act of the second part of the two-part play that bears his
name. For the remaining four acts, attention focuses on King John's sexual pursuit of
Huntington's bereaved fiancée, Maid Marian – or, rather Matilda Fitzwater, as the
play now calls her. Already in *Part One*, John's schemes to bring Matilda under his
control had given strong evidence of his tyranny, and the play's comic ending had
been especially marked by his renunciation of those unruly desires, a renunciation he
repeats with still greater vehemence at Huntington's death in *Part Two*:

> When John solicits chaste Matilda's ears
> With lawless suits, as he hath often done,
>
> . . .
>
> He craves to see but short and sour days;
> His death be like to Robin's he desires;
> His perjured body prove a poisoned prey
> For cowled monks and barefoot begging friars. (pp. 246–7)

Knowing from Foxe's *Book of Martyrs*, *The Troublesome Reign*, and Shakespeare's *King
John* just how John was in fact to die, Elizabethan audiences would have felt the full
irony of this self-condemnation. But this play is not John's tragedy, and so it ends
with the dying Matilda, whose tragedy it is, vainly praying that John will be spared
the curse to which his treatment of her has made him subject.

   Why should Munday and Chettle have refocused their play on the sufferings of the
virtuous Matilda? What claim had she on the attention of history? Before trying to

answer, we should notice that Munday and Chettle were not alone in interesting them-selves in her. Four years earlier, both Michael Drayton and Richard Barnfield had written poems about Matilda, and she appeared once again in 1597, a year before Munday and Chettle's play, in another of Drayton's works, *England's Heroical Epistles*. Nor was Matilda the only woman to be rewarded for her suffering at the hands of a lustful English monarch by having her story told in verse. Fair Rosamond, the mis-tress of Edward II, who was poisoned by Edward's queen Elinor, was made the subject of Samuel Daniel's *Complaint of Rosamond* (1591), and both Matilda and Rosamond followed in the wake of Mistress Shore, who had been featured in the second edition of the enormously influential *Mirror for Magistrates* (1563) and who reappeared in several poems in the 1590s, before her stage apotheosis as "Jane" Shore in Heywood's *Edward IV*. In making Matilda the central figure of the second Huntington play, Munday and Chettle were thus participating in a widespread literary fashion. But why should that fashion have gained such prominence? What values were engaged by the literary depiction of these suffering women?

Whatever the answer – and I will try in a moment to point to at least a few facets of it – it is worth remarking that in his history plays Shakespeare resisted this fashion. Though he did write a long poem, his *Rape of Lucrece* (1594), on the Roman arche-type of such figures and even remarked in the preface to that poem on the political repercussions such an event could have – "the state government changed from kings to consuls" – he follows *The Troublesome Reign* in saying nothing of Matilda in his *King John* and departs from all his sources in making no more than a dirty joke of Shore's wife in *Richard III*. Nor does he anticipate *Look About You* in recalling the fate of fair Rosamond or in giving dramatic prominence to Richard Coeur de Lion's amorous pursuit of Lady Faulconbridge. Women do figure significantly in Shakespeare's earli-est history plays as demonic warriors, ambitious harridans, and dangerous adulteresses (Howard and Rackin 1997), but early and late he denied them the central role so many other dramatists of history gave them as the persecuted objects of royal desire – unless, that is, one wants to think of his merry wives of Windsor in this way, with the marauding Falstaff as a surrogate king, or to credit Shakespeare, as many critics have done, with the Countess of Salisbury episode in the anonymous *Edward III* (1590). But even these exceptions illustrate Shakespeare's difference. *The Merry Wives of Windsor* was clearly for him a play on the remotest margins of history, while the Countess of Salisbury episode is just that: an episode in a play that centrally concerns the king not the countess.

The contrast with plays featuring Matilda or Shore's wife is undeniable. In them, women take history's center stage, leaving the kings who oppress them in an affec-tively marginal position. Whatever England means in these plays is more nearly asso-ciated with these women than with their tormentors. In defending her chastity against the king's attack, the Countess of Salisbury neatly defines the values in question: "To be a king is of a younger house / Than to be married" (2.1.262–3). Private, domes-tic virtue matters more than royal desire. Nowhere is this preference more powerfully presented than in Heywood's *Edward IV*. Though Jane Shore does yield to the king's command, she takes no pride in the political power she has gained and feels nothing but regret for the home and the marriage her obedience to the king has destroyed. That home, rather than the king's dealings with his foreign and domestic foes, is what Heywood encourages his audience to value. In Heywood's play, England and English history depend more on Jane and Matthew Shore's relation to one another than on anything King Edward can hope to accomplish (Helgerson 2000: 33–56).

The public significance of this preference for the home over the state is suggested by the last of the plays on the reign of King John, Robert Davenport's *King John and Matilda*. In many ways little more than a rewriting of the final four acts of the second Huntington play, *King John and Matilda* nevertheless adds an element familiar to our own memories of King John but not so much as mentioned in the John plays of the 1590s: Magna Carta. By the late 1620s, when Davenport's play was written and produced, repeated conflicts between the Stuart kings and their parliaments had given Magna Carta a prominence it had not enjoyed thirty years earlier. It was now recognized as both the principal event of John's reign and the chief bulwark of English liberty. But what seems most remarkable is that in a time of intense Elizabethan nostalgia, when non-Shakespearean dramas of history of the sort discussed in this chapter were regularly being revived and imitated as part of a mounting discourse of subjects' rights (Butler 1984: 198–210), a playwright of this new generation would have linked Magna Carta so directly to a story of sexual oppression. For Davenport and his audience, the rights of Englishmen, the sanctity of their homes and property, were symbolically invested in the sexual bodies of their wives and daughters. In Matilda's father, Fitzwater, the leader of the barons' revolt, Davenport does also furnish a plain-speaking defender of the public good very much in the mold of Thomas of Woodstock or Humphrey of Gloucester. But the play's emotional energy remains focused on Matilda herself. Though it is undoubtedly true that John's desire for her, like Edward's desire for Jane Shore, gives Matilda a historical significance she would not otherwise have, once endowed with that significance she and the domestic values with which she is identified displace the king as the prime agent of history. The real drama of history is ultimately more hers than his.

Citizen Nationhood

Up to this point, our exploration of the non-Shakespearean drama of history has been guided by plays featuring King John. *The Troublesome Reign* directed us to a repeated interest in England's Protestant identity as an elect nation. The Robin Hood side of the two Huntington plays linked up rather to a legendary yeomanly England, whose penchant for comic shape-shifting was most extravagantly revealed in another John play, *Look About You*. Huntington's alternative role as a nobleman with a keen concern for the common people then recalled the theatre's presentation of a whole range of similar "good" aristocrats, while Matilda in *Part Two* of the Huntington plays and in *King John and Matilda* brought to our attention women who not only shared something of her fate but who were also, like her, made to represent a domestic England, an England of strongly defended subjects' rights. But there remains one further concern to which no play that includes John can lead us, for no such play centers on London or any other English town. As an introduction to this final version of Englishness – a citizen Englishness – let's go back to a play that has already come up in each of the last three sections, Heywood's *Edward IV.*

Edward IV begins with a rebellion intended ostensibly to restore the deposed Henry VI but aimed more immediately at the sack of London. In the absence of King Edward, who is generally absent whenever he is most needed, the mayor, the aldermen, the guildsmen, and their apprentices organize themselves "to vanquish this rebellious rout" and "preserve our goods, our children, and our wives" (p. 14). Their success recalls the earlier victory of Londoners over the rebellious peasants of 1381 – a victory staged in *Jack Straw* – and justifies the city's prominent inclusion in the "Chronicles of England" (p. 18). But victory proves the prelude to a grievous defeat. Though no loutish rebel makes good on his threat to make love with a city wife, the king himself, the greatest rebel of all, does just that. At the mayor's victory feast, King Edward sees Jane Shore, the wife of one of the city's most valiant defenders, falls in love with her, and ends by commanding her submission to his desires. We have already noticed Jane Shore's role as mediator between king and people and as the representative of a violated domesticity. But she is also very much a Londoner, a figure who stands for the city's liberties and its civic pride. And *Edward IV*, the two-part play she so completely dominates, is, as much as anything else, a play about London (Howard 1999).

This focus on London and its relation to England's royal history had been anticipated a few years earlier by Munday's *Sir Thomas More*, the story of another Londoner who had his own unhappy encounter with the dangerous business of kings. And within a year of its first production, *Edward IV* itself had a part in prompting Thomas Dekker's comic celebration of London, *The Shoemaker's Holiday* (1599), which was in turn followed a few years later by the second part of Heywood's *If You Know Not Me*, a play that is given over almost entirely to the London story of Sir Thomas Gresham and the building of the Royal Exchange. At about the same time, and perhaps provoked by these celebratory accounts, the newly revived boys' companies were presenting London's craftsmen and merchants in a more satiric vein in plays like *Westward Ho!* (1604), *Eastward Ho!* (1605), *Michaelmas Term* (1605), *A Trick to Catch the Old One* (1605), and *The Knight of the Burning Pestle* (1607). The struggles between gentlemen and citizens that are central to so many of these plays, both the more celebratory and the more satiric ones, had their effect as well in shaping rival repertories. Gentlemen's plays at the private theatres vied with citizens' plays at the public theatres (Harbage 1952). But only the citizens' plays made a claim to participating in the drama of history. They alone link London's present to both a civic and a monarchic past.

What particularly distinguishes these plays is their interest in the cultural topography of London, in the historical construction of civic space. In this regard, Jane Shore's body figures the walled city itself. The violation of one is the violation of the other. The difference with Shakespeare is striking. Not only does Shakespeare leave

Mistress Shore and the London perspective associated with her out of his *Richard III*, but in *The Contention*, where a rebellion similar to that in Heywood's *Edward IV* does take place in London, the city functions as little more than a neutral backdrop, a battlefield like any other across which the rival forces of Lancaster and York contend (Sullivan 1998: 197–229). Far from such neutrality, Heywood's London marks and is marked by those who live there. *Edward IV*'s lord mayor, John Crosby, was named for Cow Cross, near Islington, where "an honest citizen did chance to find [him]," and he in turn gives his name to Crosby House, a poorhouse he endows in Bishopgate Street (p. 58). Similarly, Londoners "from the love they bear" to Jane Shore "and her kind husband . . . forever after mean to call the ditch" where they died "Shore's Ditch, as in memory of them" (p. 192). Nor is Heywood's *Edward IV* alone in this topographical focus. *The Shoemaker's Holiday* commemorates Simon Eyre's building of Leadenhall; *If You Know Not Me* gives still more attention to Gresham's Royal Exchange; and *Sir Thomas More* charts More's life as a movement from the city to the court and then to the Tower and the scaffold.

The last decade of Elizabeth's reign and the first decade of James's – that is, the very years when the drama of history most flourished – was also marked by an extraordinary burst of cartographic and chorographic descriptions of England, descriptions that in foregrounding the land of England necessarily displaced the royal body as the chief sign of national identity and, at the same time, competed for attention with king-centered history. Urban chorographies, John Stow's massive *Survey of London* (1598) most prominent among them, had their place in this movement. Stow, in particular, reads London as a palimpsest on which the city's richly layered history is written. The London-oriented dramatists of history do something of the same sort and with much the same effect – an effect quite foreign to Shakespeare's occasional evocations of London in his history plays – of pushing royal concerns to the side. Only at the end of *When You See Me* does Elizabeth appear to inaugurate and name the exchange Gresham has built, and the unnamed king – probably Henry V – in *The Shoemaker's Holiday* performs a similar and similarly tardy function with regard to Simon Eyre's Leadenhall. Edward IV's presence in Heywood's play is of course far more disruptive, but he, too, is rather a troubling visitor to the city than the protagonist of its history, while Henry VIII, though ultimately responsible for More's promotion, undoing, and death, never appears in *Sir Thomas More*.

Instead of focusing in Shakespeare's manner on the political history of the monarchic state, these plays give their attention to London – and particularly to London as a place of productive labor and commerce. The disguised Edward IV approaches Jane Shore as she presides over her husband's goldsmith shop, and Simon Eyre's shoe factory is the principal setting of *The Shoemaker's Holiday*. Business affairs are vital to the plot of both plays. Eyre's timely purchase of a shipload of imported goods propels his meteoric rise from master shoemaker to sheriff and then to lord mayor, while Edward's seduction of Jane is conducted under the metaphoric guise of shopping:

> *Jane.* What would you buy, sir, that you look on here?
> *King.* Your finest jewel, be it not too dear. (p. 66)

And though the commercial dealings in *When You See Me* are spectacularly unsuccessful, they, too, are recounted in considerable detail, and Gresham's untroubled acceptance of such massive reverses testifies to the enormous scale of his former profits. A man who can lose £60,000 without a qualm must once have made a great deal of money. Futhermore, the foundations Eyre and Gresham endow, Leadenhall and the Royal Exchange, were both marketplaces central to London's commercial life. No wonder then that among the rebels' taunts in *Edward IV* is this: "At Leadenhall, we'll sell pearls by the peck, / As now the mealmen use to sell their meal" (p. 10). What the rebels propose is nothing less than the wanton subversion of London's commercial base, a base erected by the labors of men like Simon Eyre.

The confrontation in the opening scenes of *Edward IV* of carnivalesque rebels and responsible, hard-working citizens should not, however, lead us to conclude that London is only a place of work. On the contrary, the London histories share with the yeomanly plays a strong element of hearty good fellowship. All four of those London histories – *Sir Thomas More, Edward IV, The Shoemaker's Holiday*, and the second part of *If You Know Not Me* – include scenes of extravagant feasting, scenes that interestingly serve to define the city's relation to the crown. Queen Elizabeth – "Queen Bess," as they familiarly call her – attends Gresham's feast to celebrate the opening of the Royal Exchange, as the unnamed king attends Eyre's in *The Shoemaker's Holiday*, a play whose very title commemorates urban festivity. As befits the tragic turn each of the other London plays takes, its moment of festivity is broken, rather than graced, by a royal intervention. I have already mentioned that the king first sees Jane Shore at the lord mayor's feast in *Edward IV*, and in *Sir Thomas More*, More is called "in haste" (p. 158) from the banquet he gives the lord mayor and aldermen to the meeting of the king's council that begins his downfall. But whether beneficent or destructive, the king represents a political force in terms of which both the work and play of London must ultimately define themselves. Like each of the other areas of ideological commitment we have noticed shaping the early modern drama of history, civic nationhood can sometimes marginalize but can never wholly ignore the monarchic state and the imperious claims of its history, a history Shakespeare was so brilliantly bringing to the stage.

Rival Companies, Rival Englands

The differences between Shakespeare and the other dramatists of history are, as I have said, systematic and repeated. Where Shakespeare focuses his dramatic attention on what might be called the problematics of early modern kingship, his contemporaries are more interested in the problematics of subjecthood. Where, that is, Shakespeare is most concerned with the getting and keeping of power, the others ask rather how subjects are to weigh their duty to the king against other fundamental commitments, including the commitment to religious truth, to yeomanly good fellowship, to the public welfare, to home and marriage, to the city and its liberties.

Though the sharpness of his political focus was unique, Shakespeare was not alone in putting the king and kingship at the center of attention. *The Famous Victories of Henry V, Edward III*, Peele's *Edward I, The Troublesome Reign of John, King of England, The True Tragedy of Richard III*, Marlowe's *Edward II*, and John Ford's *Perkin Warbeck* all do something of the same sort. But with the exception of *Perkin Warbeck*, which did not appear until 1633, all these plays were first produced by 1592 and thus belong only to the earliest development of the English history play. Moreover, all but Peele's *Edward I* turn in a distinctly Shakespearean orbit. *The Famous Victories, The Troublesome Reign*, and *Edward II* helped shape Shakespeare's Henriad, *King John*, and *Richard II*; *The True Tragedy* may have done the same for *Richard III*; Shakespeare himself seems to have had a part in writing *Edward III*; and *Perkin Warbeck* quite consciously revives a long-abandoned Shakespearean mode. But if Shakespeare's distinctive concerns were shared, particularly in the period up to 1592, those early years also saw the appearance of plays that variously anticipate the alternative emphases that were later to become so frequent: Robert Greene's *Friar Bacon and Friar Bungay* (1589), *George a Green, Arden of Faversham* (1591), and *Jack Straw*. And from 1593 on, Shakespeare's king-oriented plays and his rivals' subject-oriented ones divided the field in a relatively clear and consistent way.

That division was not, however, merely between dramatists. It was also between acting companies, theatres, and perhaps even audiences. Beginning in 1594, all Shakespeare's histories, like all the rest of his plays, were written for the Lord Chamberlain's Men, who in 1603 became the King's Men and who played successively in the Cross Keys Inn, the Theatre, the Curtain, and the Globe, before adding a "private" theatre, the Blackfriars, in 1608. With the single exception of the anonymous *Thomas Lord Cromwell*, which also belonged to the Chamberlain's Men, all the more subject-oriented plays about England's past were produced by companies and in playhouses managed by Philip Henslowe, either by the Admiral's Men (who became Prince Henry's Men) or by Lord Worcester's Men (renamed Queen Anne's Men) at the Rose, the Fortune, or the Red Bull. Such evidence as we have would seem to suggest that Shakespeare's company aimed at and probably succeeded in attracting a somewhat more elite audience than the companies managed by Henslowe, whose clientele was reputedly more popular. Did different kinds of history plays have a part in sorting out these audiences? Did Shakespeare follow the lead of the politic historians as a way of attracting more privileged spectators? And did the Henslowe dramatists draw more heavily on Foxian history, broadside ballads, romantic tales, and urban legends in an effort to consolidate their more popular following? Too many plays from the repertories on each side are lost for us to speculate with any confidence about such intentions (Hunter 1997: 359–63). What the surviving evidence does allow us to say is that audiences going to the Theatre or the Globe to see the Chamberlain's Men put on one of Shakespeare's history plays could have anticipated having a very different experience than audiences going to the Fortune or the Red Bull to see the Admiral's Men or Queen Anne's Men stage a historical play by Chettle, Munday, Dekker, Heywood, or Drayton. Sometimes the plays at one theatre would be specifically responding to the plays at the other, as was clearly the case with the Henslowe company's *Sir John Oldcastle*. But even when they weren't, they might as well have been, so strikingly consistent were the differences between them.

For us, coming to these plays four hundred years later, it is impossible to regard the rivalry between them as in any way even. Shakespeare has so decisively outdistanced his competitors that we find it hard to believe that they ever ran in the same race. Indeed, just admitting that there may once have been viable interests that Shakespeare left out is beyond many of us. Seen alone, as he usually is, Shakespeare multiplies and diversifies like Darwin's Galapagos finches to fill all the ideological niches available. Nothing we could ever want is missing. But what a careful reading of the other Elizabethan dramatists of history can help us to see is that Shakespeare's overwhelming artistic supremacy is not quite the same as universality. His is as much a brilliance of exclusion as of inclusion. And what he excluded – often deliberately excluded – can most readily be seen by doing what many Elizabethan theatregoers must have done, by shuttling back and forth from the Henslowe theatres to the theatres where Shakespeare played, by juxtaposing Shakespeare's *King John* and Munday and Chettle's Huntington plays, Shakespeare's *Richard II* and the anonymous *Woodstock*, Shakespeare's Henriad and Drayton, Hathway, Munday, and Wilson's *Sir John Oldcastle* or Dekker's *Shoemaker's Holiday*, Shakespeare's *Richard III* and Heywood's *Edward IV*. Such comparisons will take nothing from our admiration for Shakespeare's poetic and theatrical genius. But they will make clear that his was not, even in his own time, the only way or perhaps even the most politically attractive way of imagining the English past.

NOTES

1   Except where otherwise noted, dates for plays cited in the text of this chapter are taken from the *Annals of English Drama* (1989) and are meant to indicate a best guess about the year of first production. They should in most cases be understood as no more than imperfect approximations.

2   I follow most recent editors in dating Shakespeare's *King John* 1596 rather than 1591, the date preferred by the *Annals of English Drama*.

3   Quotations from Shakespeare are from *The Riverside Shakespeare* (1997).

4   Knapp (2002), in an argument that links Shakespeare more closely to contemporary dramatists of history than I do in this chapter, makes much of good fellowship as a sign of an ecumenical supranationalism closely associated with the religious views of Erasmus.

5   On the strength of its Lollard Revolt, *1 Sir John Oldcastle* could also be added to this list. Despite the play's strong Lollard sympathies, this revolt is subjected to much the same ridicule as are the popular rebellions in the four other plays. In fact, it is Sir John Oldcastle himself who reveals the plot and is thus responsible for the uprising's failure.

6   A possible exception to this pattern of neglect is the moment when mad Lear on the heath remembers other "poor naked wretches" and exclaims, "O, I have ta'en / Too little care of this!" (3.4.28 and 32–3). But even at this point, Lear remains far more concerned with filial ingratitude – and thus with his own suffering – than with any responsibility he, as king, may have had for the welfare of his subjects.

REFERENCES AND FURTHER READING

Annals of English Drama, 975–1700, 3rd edn. (1989). Ed. A. Harbage, S. Schoenbaum, and S. S. Wagonheim. London: Routledge.

Baker H. (1997). Introduction to *King John*. *The Riverside Shakespeare*, 2nd edn., ed. G. B. Evans. Boston, MA: Houghton Mifflin.

Barton, A. (1975). The King Disguised: Shakespeare's *Henry V* and the Comical History. In *The Triple Bond: Plays, Mainly Shakespearean, in Performance*, ed. J. G. Price. University Park: Pennsylvania State University Press.

Bevington, D. (1968). *Tudor Drama and Politics: A Critical Approach to Topical Meaning*. Cambridge, MA: Harvard University Press.

Blundeville, T. (1574). *The True Order and Methode of Wryting and Reading Hystories*. London: W. Seres.

Butler, M. (1984). *Theatre and Crisis, 1632–1642*. Cambridge: Cambridge University Press.

Chambers, E. K. (1930). *William Shakespeare: A Study of Facts and Problems*, 2 vols. Oxford: Clarendon Press.

Clarke, F. W. and Greg, W. W. (eds.) (1911). *The Comedy of George a Green*. Oxford: Malone Society Reprints.

Drayton, M., Hathway, R., Munday, A., and Wilson, R. (1984). *1 Sir John Oldcastle*, ed. J. Rittenhouse. New York: Garland Publishing.

Harbage, A. (1952). *Shakespeare and the Rival Traditions*. New York: Macmillan.

Helgerson, R. (1992). *Forms of Nationhood: The Elizabethan Writing of England*. Chicago, IL: University of Chicago Press.

——(2000). *Adulterous Alliances: Home, State, and History in Early Modern European Drama and Painting*. Chicago, IL: University of Chicago Press.

Heywood, T. (1851a). *The First and Second Partes of King Edward the Fourth*. In *The Dramatic Works of Thomas Heywood*, 2 vols., ed. J. P. Collier. London: The Shakespeare Society, 1.1–202.

——(1851b). *If You Know Not Me, You Know Nobody* [parts 1 and 2]. In *Two Historical Plays on the Life and Reign of Queen Elizabeth*, ed. J. P. Collier. London: The Shakespeare Society.

Howard, J. E. (1999). Other Englands: The View from the Non-Shakespearean History Play. In *Other Voices, Other Views: Expanding the Canon in English Renaissance Studies*, ed. H. Ostovich, M. V. Silcox, and G. Roebuck. Newark: University of Delaware Press.

Howard, J. E. and Rackin, P. (1997). *Engendering a Nation: A Feminist Account of Shakespeare's English Histories*. London: Routledge.

Hunter, G. K. (1997). *English Drama, 1586–1642: The Age of Shakespeare*. Oxford: Clarendon Press.

Kastan, D. S. (1986). Proud Majesty Made a Subject: Shakespeare and the Spectacle of Rule. *Shakespeare Quarterly*, 37, 459–75.

Knapp, J. (2002). *Shakespeare's Tribe: Church, Nation, and Theater in Renaissance England*. Chicago, IL: University of Chicago Press.

Lancaster, A. (1969). *Look About You* as a History Play. *Studies in English Literature*, 9, 321–34.

Muir, K. and Wilson, F. P. (eds.) (1957). *The Life and Death of Jack Straw*. Oxford: Malone Society Reprints.

Munday, A. and Chettle, H. (1874–6). *The Downfall and Death of Robert, Earl of Huntington*. In *A Select Collection of Old English Plays*, 4th edn., 15 vols., ed. W. C. Hazlitt. London: Reeves and Turner, 8.93–327.

Munday, A. and Others (1990). *Sir Thomas More*, ed. Vittorio Gabriele and Giorgio Melchiori. Manchester: Manchester University Press.

Orgel, S. (1982). Making Greatness Familiar. *Genre*, 15, 41–8.

Ribner, I. (1957). *The History Play in the Age of Shakespeare*. Princeton, NJ: Princeton University Press.

Rossiter, A. P. (ed.) (1946). *Woodstock: A Moral History*. London: Chatto and Windus.

Rowley, S. (1952). *When You See Me, You Know Me*, ed. F. P. Wilson. Oxford: Malone Society Reprints.

Shakespeare, W. (1997). *The Riverside Shakespeare*, 2nd edn., ed. G. B. Evans. Boston, MA: Houghton Mifflin.

Snider, J. W. (ed.) (1979). *The Troublesome Raigne of John, King of England*. New York: Garland.

Spikes, J. D. (1977). The Jacobean History Play and the Myth of the Elect Nation. *Renaissance Drama*, 8, 117–49.

Sullivan, G. A., Jr. (1998). *The Drama of Landscape: Land, Property, and Social Relations on the Early Modern Stage*. Stanford, CA: Stanford University Press.

3

Censorship and the Problems with History in Shakespeare's England

Cyndia Susan Clegg

Raphael Holinshed's letter dedicating the 1577 *Chronicles of England, Scotland, and Ireland* to Lord Burghley astutely registers the conditions shaping the reception of historical writing in early modern England. After wisely "craving onlie" that his reader "make a freendlie construction" of his meaning, he reminds his reader that "Manie things being taken out as they lie in authors, may be thought to give offense in time present, which referred to the time past when the author writ." He then offers the assurance that history is "not onlie tolerable, but also allowable" (Holinshed 1577, I: v,). Holinshed here reveals important things about the reception of historical writing: first, that past accounts of past events resonated poorly with sixteenth-century readers; then, that offense was "thought" and, similarly, that meaning was conferred by the reader; and finally, that historiography met with ecclesiastical censors' favor.

Three incidents involving historical writing confirm Holinshed. In 1614 a clergyman accused of treason for writing about "his Majestie's sacred person and gouvernment" justified himself by confessing that according to "the example of preachers and chroniclers, kings' infirmities are to be laid open" (Willis-Bund 1879, I: 140). During the clergyman's imprisonment, two histories whose recent publications had been "allowed" – that is, approved for publication by the ecclesiastical reviewers – were called in. In another instance, a group of leaders in Elizabeth I's government drew up treason charges in 1600 against an influential member of the aristocracy. He was accused of conspiring with the King of Spain to overthrow Elizabeth and place the Infanta on the English throne. His intent could be proven by a history published the previous year on the times of Richard II. Finally, a continental press issued a book in 1592 on the Elizabethan succession – a topic English statute prohibited – which traced the Spanish Infanta's lineage from Henry Bolingbroke, who, the book maintained, had been the legitimate heir because parliament elected him when Richard II willingly resigned. When the first printed edition of a play on Richard II appeared a few years later, it lacked a long scene representing Richard's deposition that could be read as corroborating the illegal continental book. In each of these instances, the offending historical matter had appeared in countless prior histories that had been both tolerated and allowed. The unfriendly construction these books' meanings received were "thought" by particular readers, in whose minds written histories became associated with treasonable acts, even though the histories themselves were not inherently seditious.

Although Holinshed directs us to readers as the source for the problem of history in Shakespeare's England, scholars repeatedly look to the censorship of Sir Walter Ralegh's *The History of the World*, Sir John Hayward's *The first parte of the life and raigne of king Henrie IIII*, and William Shakespeare's *The Tragedie of Richard II* – the familiar histories whose censorship is outlined above – as evidence that historical writing was inherently dangerous. Adding to these both editions of Holinshed's *Chronicles*, Edward Ayscue's *A historie contayning the warres, treatises, marriages, betweene England and Scotland*, William Martyn's *The history and lives of twentie kings of England*, William Camden's *Annales*, Samuel Daniel's *Philotas*, and Ben Jonson's *Sejanus* seems to lend credence to those scholars who believe that historical writing attracted special attention in early modern England because its monarchs and their ministers engaged in a kind of general "public surveillance" to ensure that cultural forms followed their prescriptions. "The writing of history was specifically included in the province of official censorship" because "the history of the realm," according to Annabel Patterson (1984), "belonged to the monarch" (p. 129). This essay weighs the case for a general surveillance of historical writing against both special contexts that conditioned some histories' reception and licensing practices to discover if the "authorities" really saw history as a special problem.

Most scholars assume historical writing's vulnerability to censorship as simply a given. This may be seen, for example, when, writing about Michael Drayton's "Historical Epistles," Jean Brink remarks, "Writing about English history carried with it certain risks in the late 1590s" (Brink 1990: 42). Probably the oldest case for historical censorship – one that has influenced four generations of scholars – was made in 1908 by Phoebe Sheavyn, who maintained that for English Renaissance writers even "the most innocent allusion to current politics was liable to be tabooed" by a government living in constant fear of insurrection: "Writers of history, in verse or prose, were driven to passing lightly over any incidents and speeches which might have been made to bear an evil construction" (Sheavyn 1967: 45). The "evil" from her perspective was whatever "toucheth the deposing of a King" (p. 61). More recently, Janet Clare's *"Art Made Tongue-Tied By Authority": Elizabethan and Jacobean Dramatic Censorship* (1990) applies Sheavyn's principle that the representation of insurrection provoked censorship to Renaissance drama. Clare finds the government engaged in a "policy of keen surveillance of any potentially subversive activity," which "especially extended to restrictions on the publication of history of topical interest" (p. 42). History plays "more so than any other genre," according to Clare, were especially vulnerable to censorship (p. 55). Clare argues that *Sir Thomas More, Woodstock, Doctor Faustus, Jack Straw, 2 & 3 Henry VI*, and *Richard II* "were censored because they staged issues that were topical or referential; since it was perceived that these plays had the potential to kindle or inflame public disorder" (p. 27).

Brink, Sheavyn, and Clare, like most scholars who correlate censorship with historical writing, argue from three events: John Hayward's "prosecution" for referring to contemporary events in *The first part of the life and raigne of King Henrie IIII*; Hayward's association with Robert Devereux, the second Earl of Essex; and the 1599 so-called "bishops' ban," which, among other things, required that English histories be approved for print by "some of her Majesty's Privy Council" (Arber 1875, III: 677). Scholarly report and assessment of these "events" is often inconsistent – and sometimes inaccurate. Clare even credits to the bishops' ban Shakespeare's abandoning of English chronicles in favor of classical histories as dramatic sources (Clare 1990: 74). While scholars like Clare associate censorship with some aspect of the Hayward–Essex–1599 bishops' ban rather loosely, others, like Annabel Patterson, see an intrinsic relationship because of the status of all historical writing and its relationship to the state. "Historiography, in the sixteenth and early seventeenth century," according to Patterson, "was no academic discipline but a matter of public interest, both in the sense that the material of English history was popular material for the emergent national theater, and because (for a set of reasons which included this same popular appeal) the government regarded historical materials as subject to its own control" (Patterson 1988: 41). Patterson lists several occasions of historical censorship that testify to the government's attitude: the stay imposed on *Mirror for Magistrates* during the reign of Mary; the censorship of the 1587 edition of Holinshed's *Chronicles*; Master of the Revels Edmund Tilney's marginal instructions on the manuscript of *Sir Thomas More* to "Leave out ye insurrection wholly & ye cause thereof"; the absence of the deposition scene in the 1597 and 1598 quartos of Shakespeare's *Richard II*; "the scandal over Sir John Hayward's *History of Henry IV*" which was published in February 1599 with a dedication to the Earl of Essex; the "Bishops' Order" of June 1, 1599; Fulke Greville's inability to obtain access to documents for a proposed history of Elizabeth's reign; and the 1615 stay issued on sales of Sir Walter Ralegh's *History of the World* (Patterson 1988: 41). The explanation Patterson offers for recurring repressive measures is that "the authorities . . . at the turn of the sixteenth century were dictating what form the stories of English national experience, past and present, should take" (p. 57). Like Sheavyn and Clare, Patterson locates the authorities' problem with history in its representation of rebellion and deposition.

Richard Dutton's work on dramatic censorship effectively counters Clare's (and Sheavyn's) arguments while paradoxically invoking Patterson. Dutton dispels the notion of a generally censorious climate by clarifying the Master of the Revels' role as dramatic censor. Employing the standards of the court, the Master sought to contain topical allusion within acceptable limits rather than eliminate it altogether. What was unacceptable, according to Dutton, was direct allusion to the king or his representatives. Dramatic censors, then, fixed their attention "on immediately provocative matters rather than on *potentially* subversive matters" (Dutton 2000: 8). This directly challenges Clare's position that the government engaged in a "policy of keen surveillance of any potentially subversive activity" that "especially extended to restrictions on the publication of history of topical interest" (Clare 1990: 42) and argues against history plays' proclivity to censorship.

This presents a conundrum. Dutton's evidence on the Revels Office denies as a principal motive for censorship historical writing's "potential to kindle or inflame public disorder" at the same time that Patterson's list demonstrates the perils of historiography. One may, however, have it both ways – but only by attending to their difference in focus. By including the 1599 Bishops' Order (or "ban") in the list of witnesses, Patterson's argument becomes generic; that is, it is organized around the authorities' interest in the "publication" of history. Subversion necessarily belongs to intentionality. Provocation, however, resides in reception. Dutton's position is that dramatic censors were concerned with the drama's reception. Dutton's central contention that "early modern readers . . . read plays and other texts analogically, often 'applying' quite exotic fictions to contemporary persons and events" – grows directly out of Patterson's hermeneutic theory articulated in *Censorship and Interpretation*.

> . . . politically charged analogical reading was *normal*, the *usual* condition of writing and reading in the period, and not just something that happened when scandals such as those surrounding Chapman's *Byron* plays or *A Game at Chess* drew attention to it. Alert readers will have spotted in my phrasing an allusion to Annabel Patterson's book, which rehearses a good deal of the evidence for the practice. (Dutton 2000: xi)

Dutton, however, goes beyond Patterson in maintaining that the censors were quite aware of this analogical reading and "usually chose to ignore it unless they deemed the 'application' to be too transparent or provocative" (ibid). The problem with censorship was that "no censor could hope to regulate what an audience of such readers [those inclined to analogical reading] might infer from, or over-read upon, any given text at any given moment" (p. xv). What Patterson's list of witnesses actually testifies to is the inability of censors to regulate readers and to dictate the conditions under which these particular examples of historical writing would be read. By examining both licensing practices and also the conditions which shaped the reading of historical writing that was censored during the reigns of Elizabeth I and James I, it will become clear that the censorship of history, even English history, was far from an "ordinary" practice. Not only was most historical writing no more subject to official scrutiny than other genres, but also when historical writing did meet with censorship, local and immediate contexts dictated the acts.

One measure of government interest in controlling the publication of history can be found in Stationers' Company licensing practices. Although Company regulations required that anything printed should receive a Company license that would be entered in the Company's register books, a comparison of titles entered in the register with titles of extant printed books reveals that entrance rates for all works excluding ballads varied significantly – from a high of 79 percent in the 1560s and 1570s to a low of 37 percent in the last five years of James I's reign. (Licensing practices relating to ballads were themselves highly irregular.) During the latter half of the sixteenth century, approximately 65 percent of the books printed in England were entered in the Stationers' Registers, but between 1600 and 1625 only an average of 39 percent were entered. This apparent lack of compliance derives in part from the fact that subsequent editions of a text were rarely entered – even when they underwent substantial revisions – and in part from the number of works that were printed under royal privileges. It also reflects some laxness on the part of Company officials. Furthermore, Company officials were not especially rigorous in requiring the entry of histories; indeed, during the reign of James, they exhibited less concern about histories than other works. Before 1600, 42 percent of histories were entered, compared to an overall entry rate of 65 percent. In 1600–25, 37 percent of histories were entered, compared to 39 percent overall.

Stationers' Company regulations also required that ecclesiastical censors review and approve works before printing. Here again, compliance varied. In the late sixteenth century 25 percent of the Stationers' Register entries indicate an ecclesiastical authorizer's name, while during the reign of James 83 percent of entries name authorizers. Despite this apparent variation, the actual number of works receiving official approval ranged between one-tenth and one-third of all titles. During the reigns of both Elizabeth and James certain classes of books – religious texts and books by continental authors, for example – were far more likely to receive notice of official approval than were conduct books, books on trade and husbandry, or classical literature. The masters and wardens of the Stationers' Company exercised considerable discretion in enforcing the requirement for pre-print approval. One measure of this discretion appears in the presence of some register entries with the special condition that the title receive authorization. Although important conditional entries exist for histories, Company officials were only slightly more concerned about inadequately authorized histories than they were about other classes of writing (2.2 percent of all titles entered in the registers received conditional entries, compared with 2.5 percent of histories). In 1600–25 the authorization rates of histories and other titles were equal at 32 percent. At the end of the sixteenth century, however, historical writing appears to have been monitored more closely. Although the total number of works that received official scrutiny was fairly close (14 percent of histories compared to 20 percent overall), histories were nearly twice as likely as other works to be entered in the Company's register books with an indication of authorization.

While Stationers' Company's records in the late sixteenth century seem to suggest that officials expected all historical writing to meet state standards, this is not entirely the case. Officials were most concerned about histories by continental authors. From 1560 to 1600 nearly half the histories by continental authors – most in translation – were authorized before entry (47 percent), while the authorization rates for British and classical histories were 16 percent and 5 percent respectively. Special concern for histories by continental authors also extended into the seventeenth century. Between 1600 and 1625, 61 percent of histories by continental authors were authorized before entry, compared with 28 percent of British histories, and 33 percent of classical histories. This effectively means that during the reigns of both Elizabeth and James histories, except those by continental authors, were far *less* likely to receive official review than other books. Authorization rates for continental histories during the reign of James, while more than double those for British histories, still fell below the general rate (61 percent compared to 83 percent). During the reign of Elizabeth, however, histories by continental authors were twice as likely to be scrutinized! Furthermore, seven of the Stationers' Registers' nine conditional entries for histories were for histories by continental authors. The most telling conditional entry, on November 19, 1608 for Louis de Mayerne Turquet's *General History of Spain* (STC 17747) reads, "Provided the everye sheete is to be by Master Etkins revised and by Aucthority allowed."

While this evidence argues that most historical writing was no more subject in any significant way to regulatory control than other kinds of writing, the existence of the 1599 "Bishops' Order" (or "bishops' ban") is persistently offered as evidence to the contrary. This ban, in my opinion, represents a red herring in understanding the censorship of history. On June 1, 1599, Archbishop of Canterbury John Whitgift, and Bishop of London John Bancroft, issued an order to the Stationers calling in nine satires and everything written by Thomas Nashe and Gabriel Harvey; prohibiting further printing of satires, epigrams, or works by these authors; and requiring that English histories receive Privy Council approval and that no plays be printed "excepte they bee allowed by suche as have aucthorytie." Rather than reflecting a general anxiety about the effects of satire or the dangers of histories and plays, as has been widely believed, the order responded to a unique historical moment – the national crisis surrounding England's invasion of Ireland led by Robert Devereux, the second Earl of Essex – and sought to quell criticism of Essex and the government. Not coincidentally, the 1599 ban immediately followed Bishop Bancroft's suppression of the second edition of John Hayward's *The first parte of the life and raigne of king Henrie IIII* (sales of its first edition had been stayed until its dedication to Essex was excised) – and may not be understood properly apart from the Hayward censorship and the Irish crisis.

During the late winter and early spring of 1599, Earl Marshall Essex's departure preparations were fraught with faction and conflict – especially between Essex's party and that of Robert Cecil. Essex, the subject of malicious "bruits," recognized the dangers inherent in being absent from court. "I am not ignorant," Essex wrote Lord Willoughby, "what are the disadvantages of absence; the opportunities of practising enemies when they are neither encountered nor overlooked" (*Salisbury*, IX: 10). During this distressing time, Hayward's *Henry IIII* appeared with its dedication to Essex. To eliminate the association between this book and his name, Essex immediately wrote Archbishop Whitgift, his friend and ardent supporter, asking him to suppress the dedication, which he did. By the time that the second edition of Hayward's history appeared at the end of May, the political climate for Essex had badly deteriorated. Essex's military efforts had faltered from the moment he arrived in Ireland. Conditions had forced him to march on Munster despite the Irish Council's order to confine his operations to Leinster. The effort was going so badly the Privy Council held all Irish communications secret and prohibited speaking or writing about the war (PRO, SP 12/271, 33). Essex's earlier concerns about the perils at home were warranted: the court turned against him (*Salisbury*, IX: 125). The significance of all this was not lost on Privy Councilor Whitgift, who saw the inherent dangers in the reappearance of Hayward's book for Essex. By having Hayward's history confiscated and burned, Whitgift spared Essex any false comparisons his enemies might make between the earl and the book. A few days after suppressing *Henry IIII*, Whitgift and Bancroft issued their censorship order – an order that effectively destroyed satires directed at Essex (Clegg 1997b: 210–16).

The relationship usually understood between *Henry IIII* and Essex is one of treason and usurpation. From this perspective Essex distanced himself from the book because he feared the parallel to a traitor (the book being about Lancaster leading a rebellion in England), but such a reading strikes me as curious. When the book first appeared, Essex was, after all, the queen and Privy Council's appointee to lead English forces *against* Tyrone, a traitor *to* England. The earl's wish to dissociate himself from Hayward's text can be understood more appropriately as his response to the message the book aimed at him rather than a warning to others (to Elizabeth? to the public?) about Essex's ambitions. *Henry IIII*'s preface emphasizes the importance of learning from history, but the book focuses less on Lancaster *leading* a rebellion than on the dangers of political faction. By its account, divisiveness and bad government are destroying England during Lancaster's exile. During this time, Richard II, away in Ireland, loses support at home. Cognizant of both his own political vulnerability and the difficulties inherent in the Irish mission, Essex understandably would not want his name associated with a history representing the dangers of political faction, especially one depicting a leader's lost domestic influence while in Ireland. Such "bad press" for Essex and an Irish expedition would mitigate the advantages he sought at court against his rival, Robert Cecil.

One important piece of evidence that insists that the requisite Privy Council licensing of histories belongs to the moment of crisis over Ireland – one so serious that a gag order was in place – is the Stationers' Company's records of subsequent licensing and authorization. From this we learn that English histories continued to be published without Privy Council authorization, and plays were printed without being allowed by authority. For example, an entry on August 28, 1599 for two plays, the first and second parts of John Heywood's *Edward IV*, makes no mention of authorizers, ecclesiastical or otherwise. No entry in the Stationers' Register subsequent to the ban names a Privy Councilor as authorizer. On January 12, 1600 an entry names the cleric Abraham Hartwell as the authorizer of a history of Henry VIII. That plays were not necessarily authorized and histories were not reviewed by Privy Councilors subsequent to the 1599 order (nothing in the registers suggests otherwise) demonstrates a contemporary disregard for the "bishops' ban" that insists that beyond the immediate moment of the ban's issuance in June of 1599, it should not be taken too seriously as evidence that the state closely monitored historiography. This, of course, does not mean that histories did not present particular problems in Elizabethan and

Jacobean England. The point, I believe, is that their problems were quite *particular*. To illustrate this, I will return to those three instances of censorship I briefly sketched at the beginning of this essay: *Richard II*, *The first part of the life and raigne of king Henrie IIII*, and *The History of the World*.

Shakespeare's *Richard II* has occupied a prominent place in discourses of censorship, especially since it is presumably the play performed on the eve of the Essex rebellion, which, in turn, reportedly prompted Elizabeth to say, "I am Richard II. Know ye not that?"[1] The play's association with one rebellious act has often led to the conviction that the deposition scene was censored from the play's Elizabethan quartos because Elizabeth's government would not tolerate its representation of rebellion. The play, probably written in 1595, was first printed in 1597, most likely from Shakespeare's foul papers or a transcription of them. Two editions of substantively the same text followed in 1599. In 1608 the play was reprinted, only this time 163 lines were added in which Richard relinquished the symbols of his kingship before parliament. Even without the deposition scene, the earlier quartos depict bad government, rebellion, deposition, and "bodily harm" to the king. The "deposition" scene may have provoked suppression, however, because its representation of parliament apparently corroborated *A Conference upon the Next Succession* (1595) by Robert Doleman (Robert Parsons), a work Elizabeth's government regarded as highly offensive on many grounds. Contemporary with Shakespeare's play, Parsons's book not only subscribed to the central tenets of continental Catholic resistance theory, particularly the secular nature of political society and the monarch's subjugation under law, but it also denied the Tudor succession's legitimacy and favored the Spanish claim via John of Gaunt. Its argument for the Lancastrian line's legitimacy depends upon the premise that an act of parliament legally deposed Richard II. The 1608 Quarto's ritualized reenactment of Richard's abdication in the deposition scene conflates three parliamentary events, which in Holinshed's *Chronicles* (Shakespeare's source) represent parliament's voice (both Lords and Commons) as *consenting* to Richard's abdication and Henry's accession. While these events remained distinct in the source, when Shakespeare compressed them into one scene that inverted their order, it suggests that the Commons urged Richard's deposition (Clegg, 1997b).

The parallels between Shakespeare's *Richard II* and Parsons's *Conference upon the Next Succession* point to the difference between historical writing that becomes dangerous in its reception and dangerous historical writing. Parsons used history to make a seditious argument, that is, to teach the lesson of Tudor illegitimacy and to speak directly to the Elizabethan succession – a topic declared treasonous by statute. With or without the deposition scene, Shakespeare's play teaches neither the virtue nor necessity of rebellion. Had it done so, I suspect that far more than the deposition scene would have been eliminated! It is curious, however, that understanding writing history as a perilous occupation depends upon a book that represents the events of Richard's fall in much the same way as Shakespeare's play. John Hayward's *The first parte of the life and raigne of king Henrie IIII* appears in virtually every account of the dangers of historiography in Shakespeare's England. These accounts, however, rarely address the censorship proper of *Henry IIII* (as I did earlier), but instead persistently link the book's suppression to Essex's 1601 treason trial – a matter frequently misunderstood.

The story of Hayward and Essex has been retold so many times that I regret having to return to it here. Unfortunately, errors have been repeated and new errors introduced virtually every time the story appears. Accurately told, however, this is not the story of a hapless historian accused of treason. Nor is it one of the queen's displeasure. This is an instance where the leading member of a faction in Elizabeth's government, Robert Cecil, one of Essex's greatest rivals and enemies, turned a book censored for entirely different reasons into a brilliant piece of propaganda so effective it impressed the dangers of writing history on a generation of writers – and left as its legacy the conviction that writing history in early modern England was hazardous. In July 1600, over a month after a government inquiry at York House exonerated the Earl of Essex for alleged misconduct in Ireland, a document was drawn up stating, "The Earle of Essex is charged with high Treason, namely that he plotted and practised with the Pope and king of Spain for the deposing and settling to himself as well the Crowne of England, as of the Kingdom of Ireland" (PRO, SP 12/275, 33). The accusation depends on evidence from William Alabaster, Thomas Wright, and some "credible persons" in Ireland, as well as an alleged relationship between Essex's actions and John Hayward's "treasonable" book, *The first part of the life and raigne of king Henrie IIII*. Bundled with the treason charge are John Hayward's confession and Edward Coke's notes and interrogatories relating to *Henrie IIII*; statements from Samuel Harsnett, the ecclesiastical authorizer who approved Hayward's book's publication; and the examinations of William Alabaster and Thomas Wright. The treason charge has been regarded variously as a vestige from the York House inquiry, as something related to Essex's 1601 rebellion, or as part of a government effort to intimidate Essex that included prosecuting Hayward.[2] More often, however, interest in the charge and its related documents has been displaced from Essex to John Hayward's presumed treason in writing *The first parte of the life and raigne of king Henrie IIII*.[3] The repeated misreading of the treason charge derives from both an insistence that it must somehow be linked to an actual action brought against Essex and a recurring neglect of such seemingly unimportant figures as Alabaster and Wright. When all the named figures receive equal consideration, it appears clear that an effort was afoot to gather information that, if it were made public, would thoroughly discredit Essex and eliminate him from political life. Although some scholarship has tended to underplay faction's importance in Elizabethan politics, this untried treason case argues both that a faction opposing Essex existed and that it employed the evidence it compiled to condemn Essex in the court of public opinion.

Three months after Essex's uninvited return from Ireland in August 1599, articles of accusation were entered in Star Chamber against the earl for misusing resources, deferring his departure for two months after he received his orders, not immediately pursuing the Earl of Tyrone upon his arrival in Ireland, turning over control of the army and giving the sword into a deputy's hands without license, and leaving his charge and coming into England (PRO, SP 12/273/37). Spared a Star Chamber trial because Elizabeth intervened, Essex was summoned before a private proceeding at York House on June 5, 1600 – Chamberlain referred to it as a "hearing" (PRO, SP 12/274/5). On June 11, 1600, Sir Gelly Meyricke, Essex's steward, wrote to the Earl of Southampton that "The Lords and the rest freed his Lordship from any disloyalty . . . all had one counsel which was fitting to clear the Queen's honour, which, God be thanked, I hear she is well satisfied" (*Salisbury*, X: 178). Despite the apparent satisfaction, Essex remained a "prisoner, but at his own custody" until the end of August, when he was freed but denied the court. By mid-October Essex was "much in town, fed with hope" (SP 12/275/94). The story's end is well known: the earl, unable to regain Elizabeth's favor and, hence, his place at court, planned to obtain the queen's presence by force. The queen gained information about the earl's plans, and on February 8, 1601, the Lord Keeper and Lord Chief Justice were sent to him to summon him to court. Essex refused, took them prisoner, and "issued out into London on a sudden resolution" with some of his followers, who when they met two or three companies of "foot and 50 or 60 horse," returned to Essex House. After some resistance, they were arrested there by the queen's forces (PRO, SP 12/278/50). Before a jury of their peers, Essex and Southampton were tried for treason on February 19, 1601; the charges were "Essex's attempt to surprise the court, his coming in arms to London to raise rebellion, and defending his house against the queen's forces" (PRO, SP 12/278, 110).

Neither John Hayward nor his book appear in the numerous examinations preceding Essex's 1601 treason trial. According to Francis Bacon, Elizabeth had first brought the book to his attention, asking if he didn't find it treasonous, in late fall 1599. Although Bacon found no treason, in January or February 1599/1600 Edward Coke read the book closely. His notes containing excerpts from Hayward's book reveal he was looking for parallels between Hayward's book and contemporary events. He was particularly interested that Richard II was "without childe," that he borrowed money from Londoners, that he extracted money under the name of benevolences, that he was "repayed" by a rebellion in Ireland, that his councilors were corrupt, and that noblemen applauded Bolingbroke's efforts against him (PRO, SP 12/244, 61). Chief Justice Popham subsequently drew up interrogatories to be administered to Hayward which sought to establish that Hayward falsely introduced material into his history to strengthen contemporary parallels, that Essex was somehow connected with its conception, and that the book adhered to contemporary resistance theory by permitting a subject to depose a king and finding a king's death beneficial to the commonweal (PRO, SF 12/244/5).

The Privy Council did not require Hayward's presence until May 17, 1600, when he appeared and was enjoined "to give his attendance upon theire Lordships in theire syttings to answere that which might be objected against him," but he was apparently not detained at this time (*APC*, XXX: 328). What transpired in the meeting between Hayward and a skeleton Council consisting of Egerton, Nottingham, Buckhurst, Cecil, and Popham went unrecorded in the official minutes, even though they note the session. On July 11, 1600, Hayward made a confession, again before

Egerton, Nottingham, Buckhurst, and Cecil, which responded to Popham's interrogatories. Although he did not implicate Essex, he confessed to inserting material
into the archbishop's speech "tending to prove" that deposers of kings had some
success and to introducing benevolences into the time of Richard II, even though they
first appeared later in his sources. Two days later the Privy Council issued a letter to
Sir John Peyton, Lieutenant of the Tower, to receive Dr. John Hayward into his
custody, "and see him safely kept . . . untill you shall receave other dyreccion" (*APC*,
XXX: 499). Hayward was not tried in Star Chamber, as is widely believed, for writing
his history. Certainly Attorney General Coke entered no indictment as was customary for state-initiated actions in Star Chamber. Nor was Hayward tried for treason.
The letter to Peyton suggests that a few Privy Councilors had Hayward detained until
he might be of further use. Hayward was again interrogated in January 1601, this
time before Coke and Peyton. Once again, Coke sought to establish a connection
between Essex and Hayward's history. That this interrogation took place in January
1601 insists upon the anachronism of efforts to identify Hayward's book with Essex's
February failed *coup d'état*. Hayward's book could not have been a cause in a trial
against Essex for a rebellion he had not *yet* committed. Hayward and his history,
however, became useful because they could implicate Essex in another entirely different act of treason – one described in the July 1600 treason charges.

The 1600 document, which Dutton (2000: 171) correctly identifies as a charge of
treason that was never brought to court, begins, "The Earle of Essex is charged with
high Treason, namely that he plotted and practised with the Pope and king of Spain
for the deposing and settling to himself as well the Crowne of England, as of the
Kingdom of Ireland" (PRO, SP 12/275, 33). Dutton observes that for whoever was
considering prosecuting the Earl of Essex for treason, the earl's involvement with
Hayward's book "stood on a par with negotiating with Jesuits and Irish rebels" (p.
171). According to English treason statutes, neither Hayward's book nor consorting
with Jesuits and Irish rebels constituted high treason; plotting to overthrow the queen
with either the pope, the Spanish king, or Tyrone, however, did. The 1600 document
charging Essex with treason outlines the evidence; those accompanying it – the interrogations of Hayward, Alabaster, and Wright – support the charge.

High treason, however, was a serious matter, one that would require a special commission of *oyer* and *terminer* for trial, and the case Coke outlined in the 1600 treason
charge had some serious problems. However treasonous Hayward's book may have
been in Coke's mind, Hayward's confession did not establish treasonous intent on the
part of either himself or Essex. Furthermore, the principal witnesses to Essex's collusion with the pope, William Alabaster and Thomas Wright, were Catholics who,
although currently imprisoned, had previously enjoyed some government favors.
Their usefulness as principal witnesses in a treason trial might be limited; furthermore, their examinations did not show absolutely that treason was proposed to Essex.
The case's strength depended on a third witness, Valentine Thomas, who was expected
to testify that Alabaster said that the conference between Wright and Essex concerned
the English crown and that he (Alabaster) carried letters from the pope and King of

Spain detailing to Essex the course of action – that he would befriend Tyrone, be reconciled to the pope, and be confirmed in the English crown. No examination, however, exists for Thomas, who had a checkered career as an infomer.[4] Furthermore, notable discrepancies exist between the treason charge and other statements by Alabaster and Wright. Alabaster originally indicated that he was to have sought Essex's support for the Spanish claim *after* Elizabeth's death, and his examination before Coke and Peyton addresses Essex's support for the Infanta, not his own claim to the English throne. The treason charge says Alabaster had letters from the pope and King of Spain, while Alabaster explicitly stated he did not. Any evidence that Essex proceeded in the alleged plan was only circumstantial. Nothing confirms that Alabaster contacted the earl, and the corroborating information the "reliable" Scot, David Hetheringron (Hetherington), provided Buckhurst in January 1600 was only that in Dublin one Piers Ovington had reported to him that "the kern of the Brenny was very foul and odious touching my Lord of Essex, if their speech should be true, as, namely, that he was their friend, and should be King of Ireland" (*CSP Relating to Ireland, 1599–1600*: 376).

William Alabaster, the principal witness to Essex's collusion with the pope and the Spanish king, originally a cleric in the Church of England, served as Essex's chaplain on the 1596 voyage to Cadiz. Shortly afterwards, he converted to Catholicism. In 1595 Thomas Wright, a Catholic priest, having learned that in the interest of promoting religious toleration Essex had been protecting two English Catholics, procured the same for himself (Sutton 1997: xxiii). Alabaster and Wright were both imprisoned in September 1597, Alabaster by Archbishop Whitgift for writing *Seven Motives* – which Coke and Cecil feared sought to convert Essex to Catholicism – and Wright by Cecil for his association with Alabaster. In May 1598 Alabaster escaped from the Clink (allegedly with government assistance) but was apprehended on August 1, 1599 in Rochelle. On August 8, 1599 Peyton, the keeper of the Tower, received him into his custody. Cecil's agents brought Alabaster back to England because of a document Cecil obtained in 1599, probably in June, that was in Alabaster's hand,[5] which told of Alabaster's conference with the King of Spain and his mission to Essex. The 1599 document contains the same information as Alabaster's July 22, 1600 examination and the July treason charge. The day after Peyton received Alabaster in the Tower, he wrote to Cecil that Alabaster had "some secret matters of importance touching the State" relating to "the Northern part" that were for Cecil's ears alone (*Salisbury*, XIX: 282).

Most of the interest in Hayward and Essex results from their threat to "the authorities" – even before the 1601 Essex rebellion. The circumstances surrounding the July 1600 treason charges and their assembled evidence, however, suggest that perhaps neither "the State" nor "the authorities" unanimously perceived the threats. Instead, from as early as the summer of 1599 Essex's enemies led by Cecil were working very hard to construct a damning case against the earl. Cecil's rivalry with the earl was no secret. Considerable faction on the Privy Council had preceded Essex's appointment to the Irish Lieutenancy, and, we have seen, surrounded the whole campaign.

Furthermore, once the earl obtained the lieutenancy, indeed perhaps even in it being granted to him, Cecil was determined that Essex fail. This was so well known that on July 21, 1599 the merchant Francis Cordale wrote of it to business associates in Venice:

> Therle of Essex heare in courte, hath little or no grace at all, her majestie altogether averted from hym, and wholely directed in all busynes by mr Secretary, who now rules all as his father did, and who albeit he pretends love and friendshipp to therle of Essex yet in hart is thought his greatest enemy, envying his former greatness with the Queen: and entending his utter ouerthrow, if Irish affayres take not better effect as they are not like. (PRO, SP 12/271, 106)

The "untried" high treason case looks like the means that Cecil intended to effect Essex's "utter overthrow."

Essex's actions on February 8, 1601, of course, made Cecil's plan unnecessary, but Cecil still tried his case in the court of public opinion, first in Star Chamber, then in the churches. On February 13, 1601 the Privy Council met in Star Chamber with the justices and gentlemen. Egerton, Knolls, and Nottingham all spoke to the matter at hand: that "the arch-traitor had on Sunday last assembled his company" to depose the queen. Cecil's speech wandered from the present offense to those set forth in the July treason charges. A loose transcription of Cecil's speech noted, among other things,

> That . . . this popular traytour Earl nourished apropos these 5 or 6 years to become k. of England . . . power was putt into his hand and so he meant to slip into the place of her majestie . . . That at his being in Ireland, he conspired with the Traytor Tyrone, that after he would be come into England and had removed some of her majesties servants from about her that looked into his action with Egles eyese & had governed the Queen in ther place a few monthes, Tyrone should land 8,000 of his men in England & the Queen be put aside & all made prey to Irish kerns. That these intentions so said appeared by the booke written of Henry 4th to make this time seem like the tyme of K. Richard 2 & that are to be reformed by him like as by Henry 4th . . . That this traytor that seemed to spend that time in prayer . . . harboured more preests under the colour of drawing intelligence from them than the counsell of England, and the cheefe about him were papists to whom he committed the plotting of his treasons. (PRO, SP 12/278, 54)

Cecil here demonstrated more concern with the outlines of the July treason charges than with Essex's deeds on February 8.

Directives to the clergy on how their sermons should represent Essex's treason mirror Cecil's Star Chamber speech. After telling them to dispel rumors that the earl's "only drift was to remove certain persons from Her Majesty" by reminding them that such a strategy would have placed "both Her Majesty and the Government . . . in his hands," they told how Essex should be characterized. This reverts to the picture detailed in the July 1600 charge: he plotted with Tyrone, he protected traitorous (Catholic) priests, and from Hayward's book, he plotted "how he might become an other Henry the 4th" to redress "the same abuses being now in this realm that were in the days of Richard II., the like course might be taken for redress." The preachers were to ascribe it to God's mercy that Essex's "real treason" was not committed because it was discovered before he could proceed. "Otherwise, if he had not been prevented, was there never a rebellion in England since Richard 2s tyme more desperate or dangerous" (PRO, SP 12/27B, 63). By saying that Essex's real treason had been "prevented," this last convoluted directive displays some anxiety about charging Essex with treason for his actions on February 8. The current case required bolstering from the evidence Cecil had amassed for his other treason charge. Following these orders, the Essex treason sermons along with Cecil's Star Chamber speech, ascertained that every churchgoer in London, every country justice, and most of the gentlemen and peers of the realm heard Cecil's treason case against Essex – even though its evidence would not have withstood a trial. The government never had to try the case against Essex that alleged – but might not have proven – that he conspired with the pope and his agents, Tyrone and the King of Spain, to overthrow Elizabeth and become king. Instead, Cecil used these false accusations to denounce Essex from the Star Chamber and the pulpit and to vilify him to the people so that the February charges would be more convincing. When it came to the actual trials of Essex and his co-conspirators, attorneys for the state made no mention of this other treason. The queen charged her legal council to "say nothing in this business" about Essex having "none but Papists, Recusants, and Atheists for his adjutors and abettors in their capital Rebellion." Instead, they were instructed to "restrict their charges to those that could be proven . . . for she would go with her justice untouched" (Howell 1816, I: 1341).

Posterity has persistently linked Essex's treason to Hayward's book because Cecil's propaganda campaign against Essex proved so successful, even, possibly, prompting Elizabeth's notorious identification with Richard II. Elizabeth was not alone in her sensitivity to the kinds of associations Cecil fostered. Jean Brink links revisions in the 1600 edition of Michael Drayton's "Heroical Epistles" – those on Richard II – to the perceived dangers of writing about rebellion and history (Brink 1990: 13). In his *Life of Sir Philip Sidney*, unpublished during his lifetime, Fulke Greville told of burning his manuscript of "Antonie and Cleopatra" because he feared that their "childish wantonness" might be "construed or strained to a personating of vices in the present governors and government" – a fear invited by "the practice of the world, seeing the like instance not poetically, but really fashioned in the Earl of Essex then falling" (Greville 1986: 93). Other writers less cautious about how their historical allusions might be received soon learned that powerful Privy Councilors persisted in reading the Essex rebellion into historical representation. Samuel Daniel was called before the Privy Council for his play *Philotas*, which told the story of a general favored by Alexander the Great, who was tried and executed for treason. Although some critics have questioned the play's link with Essex, Dutton demonstrates not only that the play was read as shadowing Essex's career but also that surviving correspondence among Cecil, Mountjoy (the Earl of Devonshire), and Daniel demonstrates Cecil's and

Mountjoy's anxiety about potential associations between themselves and the counselors who in Daniels's play prosecuted Philotas (Dutton 1991: 165–71). Although
Daniel satisfied his critics, he was not the only dramatist who had to answer to the
Privy Council for a history play that could be identified with Essex. Ben Jonson met
with Henry Howard's contempt because of allusions in a history play.

Although considerable caution has been exercised in reading Ben Jonson's *Sejanus
His Fall* as political allegory – and in accepting at face value Drummond's evidence
for Jonson's summons before the Privy Council – Jonson's play registers anxieties
about both an ambitious courtier's abusive use of censorship and historiography's
implicit dangers. The only evidence that Jonson went before the Privy Council for
writing *Sejanus* comes from Drummond, who says, "Northampton was his mortall
enemie for brauling on a St Georges day one of his attenders, he was called befor ye
Councell for his *Sejanus* & accused both of poperie and treason by him" (quoted in
Herford and Simpson 1925, I: 36). While scholars have found historical parallels
between Sejanus and both Ralegh and Essex and between Northampton and the noble
Silius, arguing Jonson's intention is problematic, especially since he apparently satis-
fied his Privy Council critics. The issue here, as Richard Dutton ascertains, is not that
Jonson "intended" political allegory, but that Northampton, who initiated the
Council's summons, perceived one (Dutton 1991: 10). Parallels between Sejanus and
Essex, which are anything but direct, have been seen as prompting Northampton's
response – but so have parallels between Sejanus and Ralegh.

Without identifying Sejanus with either Essex or Ralegh, one scene in the play
does suggest a remarkable parallel to Essex and Hayward that may have disturbed
Northampton – and Cecil. As one means of obtaining *de facto* control of Tiberius' government, Sejanus seeks to destroy the aristocratic party opposing him. First he accuses
Silius of treason against Rome for his conduct in the war in Gallia. Then he unleashes
his "bloodhounds" on the historian, Cremutius Cordus, whom they accuse as "A sower
of sedition in the state," proved, they tell him, by "The annals thou hast published;
where thou bit'st" (3.380–5). Cordus protests his innocence under the law of treason
because his words do not reach "either prince, or prince's parent" (3.409); he has only
written honorably of great past Romans "whose deeds, when many more . . . have writ,
not one hath mentioned without honour" (3.412–13). Claiming his legacy from previous historians underscores the falsity of the accusations against him, as does his statement that he has not written about "the prince" (the English statutory definition of
treasonous writing). The innocent books are condemned to the fire for Cordus' real
crime – his association with Silius and his party.

Cordus' responses to allegations that he has taken matter from times past to
condemn the present and foster treason bear a striking similarity to the plight of John
Hayward. In doing so, Cordus becomes more than Jonson's manifesto on the mistaken
reception of his own writing, or on the ills of censorship, or the dangers of writing
history. *Sejanus* exposes the factional nature of court politics. By reading *Sejanus* against
Elizabethan court politics, Silius' aristocratic faction, including the historian Cordus,
looks like the Essex faction. If Northampton, who was jealous of his own distinguished

family's honor, suspected this, might he not have sought reassurances from Jonson that he intended neither parallels with Essex nor identification between Northampton and the upstart Sejanus – or the politically subtle Macro? Although we may never know how Jonson satisfied his critics, his play takes exception to the idea that writing history is an inherently seditious act and reminds us instead, that it is not historiography but its political use and abuse that proves dangerous.

Once we properly understand the local contexts of the *Richard II*–Essex–Hayward–bishops' ban nexus and appropriately relinquish its hold on our understanding of historical writing and censorship, another case still remains to which arguments for historiography's perils repeatedly return – Sir Walter Ralegh's *History of the World*. Like Hayward's book, Ralegh's history both appeared at an unfortunate moment and impressed us with a far greater sense of danger than it warranted. John Chamberlain's letter of December 22, 1614 to Dudley Carleton reporting the stay on Ralegh's book actually reports two censorsious acts, the recall of Ralegh's *History of the World* and the imprisonment of Edmund Peacham for writing a seditious though unnamed manuscript. Historical interest in Ralegh has assured retelling, embellishing, and even fabricating accounts of this act of suppression, while Chamberlain's comment about the relatively obscure clergyman has attracted only marginal notation and minimal speculation outside the annals of jurisprudence – even though, at the time, the king took far greater interest in Peacham than he did in Ralegh. No one has suggested the possibility that the two could have been linked in the king's mind, as, I believe, they were. Events in 1614 suggest why.

In 1614 James had summoned parliament to gain a subsidy. Parliament's response was especially rancorous, and the House of Commons openly criticized him for his use of extra-parliamentary levies, called "impositions." James quickly dissolved the parliament and appealed to the clergy for revenues (Sommerville 1994: xxviii). In the months before Chamberlain wrote to Carleton about Ralegh's book, several clergymen, including Peacham, had been arrested for protesting the benevolences the church was levying on the king's behalf. According to Gardiner, Peacham was called before the High Commission, and papers obtained from his study during the investigation were submitted to the Privy Council (Gardiner 1884, II: 272). On December 9, 1614 Peacham was transferred from ecclesiastical custody to the Tower, and one month later the Privy Council questioned Peacham, who was charged with treason. The Privy Council's examination followed a set of interrogatories that suggest important relationships between Ralegh's history and Peacham's offense. The sixth interrogatory asked why Peacham wrote and gathered together "such a mass of slanders against the king, his posterity, and the whole state." The seventh more explicitly asked Peacham why he had written the words "The king might be stricken with death on the sudden, or within eight days, as Ananias or Nabal." The tenth demanded if Peacham knew of any plot against the prince that would justify prophesying, "The getting of the crown land again would cost blood, and bring men to say, 'This is the heir, let us kill him'." The eighth interrogatory implicates historians like Ralegh. It stated, "You have confessed that these things were applied to the king; and that, after the example of preachers and chroniclers, kings' infirmities are to be laid open" (Willis-Bund 1879, I: 410). History does not record what histories Peacham read that "laid open" the infirmities of kings, but in the king's mind, at least, Ralegh's *History of the World* must have been one of them.

Ralegh's *History of the World*, encouraged by his patron, the late Prince Henry, appeared in print in March 1613. But it was not until December 22, 1614 (four days after Peacham's interrogation in the Tower) that Archbishop Abbot wrote to the masters and wardens of the Stationers' Company, upon the king's "express direction," requiring them to "repaire unto the printer of the said booke as also unto all other stationers, and booksellers which have any of them in their Custodie, and . . . take them in" (Jackson 1957: 355–6). While the censorship of Ralegh's book has been seen as deriving from its criticism of James, it seems unlikely that Ralegh – hardly a novice to court politics – would have expected to have "wonne his spurres and pleased the King extraordinarily" (as Chamberlain indicated) by making a veiled attack on his policies (Chamberlain 1939, I: 566). The preface does harshly judge monarchy's crimes, but as a prologue to a panegyric on James that concludes "yet may it bee better spoken of His Majesty, than of any King that ever England had; who as well in Divine, as Humane understanding, hath exceeded all that fore-went him, by many degrees" (Ralegh 1614: B2v).

Although Ralegh's historical method, especially his providentialism, has merited considerable study, his peculiar perspective on providence, which is what I believe discomfited King James, has gone unremarked. Ralegh's preface repeatedly offers exempla demonstrating one version of Old Testament justice: the sins of the fathers are visited on their sons – even those who are innocent. Since providential history enjoyed a long and familiar tradition, the chaos tyrants released would have surprised neither James nor the rest of Ralegh's audience. Ralegh's particular vehicle of dead children and sudden, unexpected deaths, however, may have resonated badly with James, who according to G. P. V. Akrigg, possessed a "neurotic" fear of death (Akrigg 1962: 35), undoubtedly heightened by a recent serious fall from his horse. Although Chamberlain leaves little doubt that Ralegh was in trouble for having "laid open" kings' infirmities, the preface to *History of the World*, which envisioned the deaths of kings and their heirs as divine retribution, unwittingly touched upon the king's particular sensitivities in 1614–15.

The association between Peacham's writings and chronicles about kings probably touched another history besides Ralegh's: William Martyn's *The history and lives of twentie kings of England*. On February 26, 1615, the day after Peacham was sent to Somerset to stand trial for his treasonous writings, the Privy Council summoned William Martyn, the Recorder of Exeter, to appear. When Martyn attended the Council on March 14, 1615, he was charged with writing a history of England, "wherein were many passages so inaptly inserted, as might justly have drawne some heavy and severe censure upon him" (*APC*, XXIV: 62). Since Martyn acknowledged his fault, the Council appealed to the king, and the charges were dismissed (*APC*, XXIV: 100).

I have sought here to establish that some of the most important instances of historical censorship – those cited as proof of state surveillance of history – represent special cases that have captured the historical imagination. The relationships among these acts of censorship effectively reduce what had appeared to be multiple separate events to only three – hardly an illustration of general practice. Some other instances of histories being censored, however, do reflect state interest in historical writing, but these are unconcerned with anxieties about rebellion or fears about the dangerous nature of history. The censorship of Holinshed's *Chronicles* (both editions) and James's interest in controlling historical accounts of his mother, Mary Queen of Scots, argue a sensitivity toward the ability of historical representation to affect public opinion.

Both editions of Raphael Holinshed's *Chronicles of England, Scotland and Ireland* met with censorship. The 1577 edition came to the Privy Council's attention in December 1577. It ordered the Bishop of London to stay the sales until the text could be reformed and to call upon the Earl of Kildare to present to the Council Richard Stanyhurst, who contributed to the "History of Ireland." On January 13, 1577/8 the Council ordered the bishop to release the stay once he received notice from the Lord Treasurer that the revisions Stanyhurst had agreed to make were completed. While the *Short Title Catalogue* notes three cancels in the 1577 *Chronicles*, only the F$_7$ gathering contains significant changes. The revised text moderates a strong bias toward Kildare and removes some disparaging remarks about Archbishop John Alen. On February 1, 1587 the Privy Council sent a letter to the Archbishop of Canterbury requesting "the staye of furder sale and uttering" of a "new booke of the Chronicles of England . . . until they shall be reviewed and reformyd" (*APC*, XIV: 311). The Council's order expressed concern not with the *Chronicles* themselves but with recent additions made "as an augmentation to Hollingsheades Chronicle" that contained "sondry thinges which we wish had bene better considered, forasmuch as the same booke doth allso conteyne reporte of matters of later yeeres that concern the State, and are not therefore meete to be published in such sorte as they are delivered." The order also appointed reviewers experienced in those state matters that warranted "reformation." Henry Killigrew, a client of the Earl of Leicester and a practiced diplomat in both Scottish and Dutch affairs, served on the Dutch Council of State. John Hammond, a civil lawyer and High Commission member, frequently served as a special commissioner in all kinds of unrelated legal matters: admiralty and trade, debt, piracy, and (probably most important here) treason. Thomas Randolph, an important member of Francis Walsingham's international diplomatic network, served twice as an English envoy in France, but his principal service was in Scotland – in 1570, 1578, 1581, and 1586 – where he had recently negotiated a league between Elizabeth and James.

Holinshed's 1587 *Chronicles* were castrated and reformed in three stages. The hands of Killigrew, Hammond, and Norton clearly dictated the earliest stage of censorship. Their work removed passages in the continuation of the Scottish history that might jeopardize English–Scottish relations, especially those that showed England intervening in Scottish factional politics. In the continuation of the "History of England" their revisions enhanced Leicester's stature; distanced England from the Duke of

Alençon, who had recently offended the Dutch; and polished accounts of English legal practice to insist that fair public officers administered trials and executions in England according to the due process of law. The censors acted with the Privy Council order's requisite speed, and the revisions were promptly printed, probably during the first week of February. The version of the text that met Killigrew's, Hammond's, and Norton's requirements received further fine tuning, probably by the Archbishop of Canterbury, since a substantial part of a long history of the archbishops of Canterbury was cut. The *Chronicles'* final reformation, dictated by political circumstances that arose after the first and second revisions were completed, reflects a careful attempt to influence international and domestic opinion in anticipation of both England's efforts to negotiate a settlement in the Low Countries and also international response to Mary Queen of Scots' execution on February 8, 1587. The account of the Babington conspirators' capture, trial, and execution received careful editing that tempered vehement anti-Catholic sentiments and now demonstrated that the trial proceeded according to due process in a legal system that, while not lenient, could exhibit compassion. Finally, in addition to the state affairs that dictated the 1587 *Chronicles'* censorship, Privy Council factional interests affected the text early and late, especially the rivalry at court between Leicester, whose sympathies rested with international Protestantism, and his more conservative opponents, William Brooke, Lord Cobham, and Thomas Sackville, Lord Buckhurst, newly appointed to the Privy Council in February 1586 (Clegg 1997b: ch. 7).

The Elizabethan state's concern about how both editions of the *Chronicles* represented its actions differs little from those that motivated King James's efforts to control historical representation. In 1590, before he came to the English throne, James sought, unsuccessfully, to have an unflattering account of Scottish religious politics excised from Holinshed's *Chronicles*, probably because he was especially sensitive about anything that Elizabeth might construe as criticism of his policies. Then in 1596 James took exception to Spenser's *Faerie Queene* because the "ninth chapter of the second part" (Book V, canto ix) "contained some dishonourable effects . . . against himself and his mother deceased" (*CSP, Scotland*, XII: 359). He expressed his desire to prevent the sale of any that might come to Scotland and to have English justice punish the author, who, James believed, wrote and published under the queen's authority. Even though the English ambassador explained to the king that the book had not been published under the royal privilege, James still desired "that Edward [*sic*] Spenser for this fault may be duly tried and punished," a wish he saw unfulfilled (*CSP, Scotland*, XII: 359). With Holinshed and Spenser, James's wishes amounted to little more in England than a diplomatic scuffle, but once he became England's king, James would seek to control historical representation for similar reasons – his sensitivity about his mother and Scotland.

The affront to personal and family honor James found most biting appeared in Edward Ayscue's *A historie containing the warres, treaties, marriages, betweene England and Scotland* (1607). The king's precise objections to Ayscue's history are part of the historical record. A copy of the offending book "marked with long scores" accompanied a letter to Salisbury that told him he would find "that whereof he [the king] is offended in the last leaf of the book" (Hatfield House, Salisbury MS 122 f. 49). The last leaf of Ayscue's history contains an account of the trial of Mary Queen of Scots and her son's response. In Ayscue's account, following Mary's death, efforts were made (it does not say by whom) to provoke James to take recourse against his mother's "lamentable end." James refused, both because he saw the justice of her death and because pursuing such a course of action held potentially negative consequences for him. James's objection to Ayscue's book is understandable: Ayscue characterizes Mary as traitorous and her son as self-serving. James, however, had no recourse against the author, who was dead by the time James saw the book.

His experiences with Spenser and Ayscue taught James a caution towards representations of his mother that dictated his most significant effort to influence historical writing. According to D. H. Woolf, having attempted to persuade the French historian Jacques-Auguste de Thou to rely on William Camden's account of Mary for his *Historiae sui temporis* and failed, James ordered Camden to publish the first part of the *Annales*, which appeared in 1615. Even after Camden died in 1624, James sought to ensure that the second part would eventually be printed in England (Woolf 1990: 117–20). The first three books of Camden's *Annales* contain an account of Mary Stuart's rule in Scotland, as well as a consideration of her impact on Elizabethan politics. Camden did not gratuitously represent Mary in ways that were favorable to his patron, but instead, according to Woolf, "steered a middle course and described a worthy, virtuous, but unfortunate princess" (p. 120).

James I's several efforts to control and censor historical writing might seem to lend credibility to the idea that history was especially subject to censorship because "the history of the realm . . . belonged to the monarch." A closer look, however, has shown that James's claims on historiography had more to do with his interest in favorably influencing accounts of himself and his mother. Admittedly Peacham created a temporary anxiety about how history might be read (an anxiety that Holinshed had registered nearly forty years before in his preface to the *Chronicles*), but, for the most part, neither James nor Elizabeth saw history as a *genre* as inherently suspicious. Indeed, the censorship of Holinshed's *Chronicles*, together with James's effort to control representations of his mother, argue that the state in early modern England understood the potential power rather than the potential danger that resided in historical writing. When histories became dangerous, they did so because contemporary political events directed their reception. Historical writing in Shakespeare's England was indeed "not onlie tolerable, but also allowable" even though "Manie things being taken out as they lie in authors" were sometimes "thought to give offense in time present, which referred to the time past."

NOTES

1 Elizabeth reportedly made this remark to William Lambarde, but Lambarde did not actually write about it. John Nichols, who tells about the queen's interview with Lambarde in his 1788 *Progresses*

and Public Processions of Queen Elizabeth, relied on a report of the story in the Lambarde family papers by an eighteenth-century gentleman, Multon Lambarde, Esq.

2   See respectively, G. B. Harrison, *The Life and death of Robert Devereux, Earl of Essex* (1937), 266–7; Mervyn James, *Society, Politics and Culture: Studies in Early Modern England* (Cambridge, 1986), 416–24; and Dutton (2000).

3   See Frederick S. Siebert, *Freedom of the Press in England, 1476–1776* (Urbana, IL, 1952), 94, and Leeds Barroll, "A New History for Shakespeare and His Time," *Shakespeare Quarterly*, 39 (1988), 441–64.

4   The queen issued a declaration on December 20, 1598 that Valentine Thomas, alias Thomas Anderson, was a "lewd Caitiff," and affirmed that she gave "no credit to such things as the said Valentine Thomas has affirmed against our good brother," namely that he conspired with the King of Scotland to kill the queen (PRO, SP 12/269/20). Thomas reappears on February 15, 1601 with evidence against Essex and Thomas Wright following Essex's rebellion (PRO, SP 12/278/64).

5   Personal letter of Dana F. Sutton, October 7, 1998. According to Sutton, "The present document is written in some haste, and so employs a more flowing and ligatured style, and yet there is small room for doubt that it is written in the same hand as the much more carefully and formally written Huntington Library ms. Ellesmere 428, a 'bread and butter' written to Lord Ellesmere, Keeper of the Privy Seal, in 1596."

REFERENCES AND FURTHER READING

Acts of the Privy Council [APC] (1890–1907). Ed. J. R. Dasent, 32 vols. London.

Akrigg, G. P. V. (1962). *Jacobean Pageant of the Court of King James.* London.

Arber, E. (1875). *A Transcript of the Registers of the Company of Stationers of London*, 5 vols. London.

Ayscue, E. (1607). *A historie containing the warres, treaties, marriages, betweene England and Scotland.* London.

Brink, J. (1990). *Michael Drayton Revisited.* Boston, MA.

Calendar of State Papers Relating to Ireland during the Reign of Elizabeth I, 1599–1600 (1903). London.

Calendar of State Papers Relating to Scotland, 1547–1603 (1969). Vol. 13. Edinburgh.

Chamberlain, J. (1939). *The Letters*, 2 vols., ed. N. E. McClure. Philadelphia.

Clare, J. (1990). *"Art Made Tongue-Tied By Authority": Elizabethan and Jacobean Dramatic Censorship.* Manchester.

Clegg, C. S. (1997a). "By the choise and invitation of al the realme": *Richard II* and Elizabethan Press Censorship. *Shakespeare Quarterly*, 48, 4, 431–47.

——(1997b). *Press Censorship in Elizabethan England.* Cambridge.

——(2001). *Press Censorship in Jacobean England.* Cambridge.

Dutton, R. (1991). *Mastering the Revels: The Regulation and Censorship of English Drama.* Iowa City.

——(2000). *Licensing, Censorship and Authorship in Early Modern England.* Houndmills.

Gardiner, S. R. (1884). *History of England from the accession of James I to the outbreak of the Civil War.* London.

Greville, F. (1986). *The Prose Works of Fulke Greville*, ed. J. Gouws. Oxford.

Herford, C. H. and Simpson, P. (eds.) (1925–52). *Ben Jonson*, 14 vols. Oxford.

Historical Manuscript Commission [*Salisbury*] (1883–1976). *Calendar of the Manuscripts of the Marquis of Salisbury*, 24 vols. London.

Holinshed, R. (1577, 1587). *Chronicles of England, Scotland, and Ireland.* London.

Hostettler, J. (1997). *Sir Edward Coke: A Force for Freedom.* Chichester.

Howell, T. B. (1816). *A Complete Collection of State Trials*, Vol. 1. London.

Jackson, W. A. (1957). *Records of the Court of the Stationers' Company, 1602–1640.* London.

Patterson, A. (1984). *Censorship and Interpretation.* Madison.

——(1988). Back by Popular Demand: The Two Versions of Henry V. *Modern Drama*, 19, 29–62.

——(1989). *Shakespeare and the Popular Voice.* London.

Ralegh, W. (1614). *History of the World.* London.

Sheavyn, P. (1967) [1908]. *The Literary Profession in the Elizabethan Age*, 2nd edn. Manchester.

Sommerville, J. P. (1994). *Political Writings: James VI and I.* Cambridge.

Sutton, D. F. (1997). *Unpublished Works by William Alabaster (1568–1640).* Salzburg.

Willis-Bund, J. W. (1879). *A Selection of Cases from the State Trials*, Vol. 1. Cambridge.

Woolf, D. R. (1990). *The Idea of History in Early Stuart England: Erudition, Ideology, and the "Light of Truth" from the Accession of James I to the Civil War*. Toronto: University of Toronto Press.

4

Nation Formation and the English History Plays

Patricia A. Cahill

Increasingly, scholarship on the English histories has focused on their figurations of the nation and considered their role in consolidating the identity of the early modern nation-state. Criticism has thus taken up such matters as the plays' representation of linguistic and regional difference; their dynamics of inclusion and exclusion; their interweaving of discourses of nationhood with discourses of gender and sexuality; their selective remembering and forgetting of the past; and their relationship to specific events of the 1590s, especially the Elizabethan attempt at reconquest of Ireland, which sparked numerous rebellions and led, in 1594, to the outbreak of the Nine Years War.[1] Such work – much of it drawing, of course, on Benedict Anderson's conception of the nation as an "imagined political community" – has amply demonstrated that the histories, for all their attention to kingship, envision a world in which traditional dynastic configurations are being challenged and new models of community are visible.

In what follows, I aim to extend this work by looking at how fantasies of nationhood are bound up with certain formulations of race and class, two interrelated discourses that have been insufficiently examined in this critical literature.[2] While none of the histories focuses exclusively on either race or class, those I discuss in the first section of this essay emphasize the connections between nation and race, while those in the second part are preoccupied with the relationship between nation and class. Accordingly, I begin by looking at plays that bring the historical memory of English military victories in France to the stage: namely, *Henry V*, a play notoriously preoccupied with nationhood and haunted by the English experience in Ireland, and *King Edward III*, an anonymous work that bears a striking resemblance to *Henry V* and that, in accordance with recent scholarship, I take to be, at least partly, by Shakespeare.[3] In these plays, I argue, questions of racial identity pervade the discourse of the nation, for their fantasies of national origins are primarily worked out through a narrative of sexual origins and racialized bodies. In both plays the English nation is conjured up not simply through the commemoration of battle but also through barely repressed narratives of race and reproduction, of generation and degeneration.

In the second half of this essay, I examine *1* and *2 Henry IV*, which are both set predominantly in England and which do not so keenly engage a dialectic of racial difference. These plays assert a vision of an *abstract* English body, a social formation in which certain physical qualities – such as male "sufficiency" – may be valorized, but individual bodies seem not to matter. The staging of nationhood in these plays, I suggest, entails the envisioning of a collectivity that is defined by the adherence of its members to disciplinary techniques and new economies of labor – to the structures that, ultimately, become legible as class differences. By examining how these histories deploy the racialized physical body and the class-inflected body politic, I hope to illuminate two of the primary registers in which early modern nationhood was calibrated. In addition, I hope to disclose a dynamic that many of the histories share. Shaped by emergent conceptions of race and class, these plays do not represent static visions of the nation; instead, their plots turn on the uneasy relations between an English national body and the Other bodies that are required to sustain that imaginary figure of the Same through a representational logic of corporeal and class difference.

It is hardly surprising that *Henry V* has emerged in recent criticism as the *locus classicus* of Elizabethan discourses of the nation, for Henry's promise on the eve of the Battle of Agincourt that "he today that sheds his blood with me / Shall be my brother" (4.3.62)[4] offers one of the period's best-known articulations of the fiction of the "deep horizontal comradeship" upon which national identity depends (Anderson 1983: 6). Through Henry's interpellation of his subjects as "We few, we happy few, we band of brothers" (4.3.60), the play would seem to consolidate national identity in simple terms around the question of a subject's willingness to die for England. But, as I hope to show here, the play's seemingly simple national language of "blood" and "brotherhood" is entangled with complex narratives of racial difference. Rather than signal a triumphalist assertion of nationhood, in fact, Henry's speech signals the paradox on which the play's discourse of the nation is founded: namely, that to gain membership in the English nation is to be willing to shed one's blood on its behalf, but to be constituted as a physical body, in the terms of this play, is to be part of a narrative of generation in which one is already constituted by – indeed contaminated by – an essence that is not English.

Act 1, scene 2 of *Henry V* offers the first hints of this paradox, as it brings up the matter of origins and offspring. In this scene, which is devoted to arguments in support of Henry's right to France, Englishness is framed as merely a matter of patrilineal inheritance as Canterbury and Ely urge Henry to identify his entitlement to France with that of his great-grandfather, Edward III, the fourteenth-century warrior king who led England into the Hundred Years War with France. In fact, as Phyllis Rackin has pointed out, the play hints at the fact that Henry's claim is bound up with inheritance through the *female* line (Rackin 1990: 167). Canterbury accompanies – perhaps even supports – his assertion of Henry's right to the French throne by forcefully repudiating the so-called Salic law, according to which, so he maintains, the French prohibit female inheritance. And the play's evocation of Salic law may obliquely acknowledge that Henry's claim to the French throne actually derives not from Edward III but from that king's mother, Isabella, the daughter of Philip IV of France. As is suggested by these textual traces of a maternal order and a non-English lineage, the play's first staging of Englishness is, in part, a staging of its confused origins. The play invokes impurity precisely by repudiating it.

Supplementing these allusions to matrilineal inheritance and this encrypted narrative of the French queen as progenitor of the English king are the racialized fantasies of male parthenogenesis that surface repeatedly throughout the play. Thus the French king's explanation for French/English difference in act 2 – which involves yet another evocation of Edward III and the suggestion that Henry has inherited a predilection for war from his forefathers – is underlain by a discourse of racial generation. It describes the Black Prince as Edward's "heroical seed" (2.4.59), a phrase that suggests that he is at once Edward's offspring – literally, an embodiment of his semen – as well as that which may be sown and thus itself produce offspring. In addition, the French king's speech suggests not only that Henry is bound to other Englishmen in a web of kinship, but also that he represents a heritable essence: "The kindred of him hath been fleshed upon us, / And he is bred out of that bloody strain / That haunted us in our familiar paths" (2.4.50–2). Here, English origins are explained in terms of the engendering or breeding of a fearsome stock or "strain," a word that is clearly inflected by the discourse of racial "kinds." And here, too, the text is charged with notions of English impurity, for to be "bred out of that bloody strain" may mean both to be a product of that strain and a symptom of its exhaustion. Indeed, later in the play when the Dauphin laments that "Our madams mock at us and plainly say / Our mettle is bred out" (3.5.28–9), he will invoke precisely this notion of a worn-out "stock" of valor.

This racialized rhetoric permeates the play's many evocations of English national identity as something produced by participation in war. In Henry's speech at the siege of Harfleur, for example, the notion of a "bloody strain" is implicit in his description of his highest-ranking soldiers as the "noblest English / Whose blood is fet [i.e., derived] from fathers of war-proof" (3.1.17–18). It is also implicit in his admonition to these men to claim and manifest their Englishness by, paradoxically, both mimicking and instructing their social inferiors on the battlefield:

> Be copy now to men of grosser blood,
> And teach them how to war. And you, good yeomen,
> Whose limbs were made in England, show us here
> The mettle of your pasture; let us swear
> That you are worth your breeding – which I doubt not
> For there is none of you so mean and base
> That hath not noble lustre in your eyes. (3.1.24–30)

Inasmuch as this speech brings together the body ("blood," "limbs," and "eyes"), a geographic region of birth or acculturation (England as the site of manufacture, "pasture," and "breeding"), and an inherited disposition or "mettle," it clearly envisions the nation within the period's evolving racial paradigms. Its fantasy image of English men who are at once copies and copying matter depends upon notions of the somatic that cannot easily be subsumed in a discourse of the familial, the dynastic, the regional, or the national. Indeed, even the language of status evoked here – "Be copy now to men of grosser blood" – insists upon such difference as written on, or rather, in, the body.

Significantly, this racialized vision of English bodies entails a narrative of reproduction – of this endless work of copying and making and breeding men – that pointedly occludes the bodies and labor of women. The breeding process is here imagined as unrelated to birth or nurturance; it is not sexual but martial. Indeed, it is not all that different from that evoked in the French king's speech cited above, in which it is the "bloody strain" of war that enables Englishmen to be "fleshed" – that is, to be at once born as distinctively English flesh and born as distinctively English soldiers, men whose appetites are like those of predators who have acquired a taste for newly killed flesh. In the play's visions of England as a warrior nation, in other words, the act of reproduction is invoked in a way that insists upon a disavowal of the womb as the site of generation and, with that, a disavowal of the Frenchness with which the play identifies the womb in act 1.

This staging of this racialized national body is complicated, however, by a recurrent rhetoric of "breeding" gone awry, of reproduction or acculturation that somehow hasn't worked. Among many examples, consider the lament that accompanies the Chorus's account of the treacherous nobles – "O England! . . . What mightst thou do . . . / Were all thy children kind and natural?" – which clearly hints at the matter of "unnatural" issue and "unkind" kin (2.0.16–19). Indeed, the notion of contamination at the site of English origins seems to underlie the play's oft-noted preoccupation with racially hybrid bodies and hybrid speech, a preoccupation that may be seen in those moments when the play brings the English into proximity with the Scots, Welsh, and Irish – for example, when Pistol, the English soldier, sings an Irish love song (4.4.4.), or when Fluellen, the Welsh Captain, insists upon Henry's Welsh blood (4.7.98). This notion of degeneration at the site of generation is especially emphatic, however, when the play envisions the illegitimacy of offspring between French and English bodies – for example, Bourbon's description of the English as "bastard Normans, Norman bastards" (3.5.10) or the Dauphin's anxious prophecy that French women "will give / Their bodies to the lust of English youth, / To new-store France with bastard warriors" (3.5.29–31).

Nowhere in *Henry V* is the specter of embodied racial degeneration developed more fully, perhaps, than in the so-called "wooing scene," in which the French queen's description of the marriage of Henry and Catherine as an "incorporate league" that will ensure "[t]hat English may as French, French Englishmen, / Receive each other" (5.2.338–40) itself enacts the blurring of the two identities into one. Crucially, this scene stages a full-blown return of the repressed narrative of generation that we have seen in act 1. This return takes the form of a materialization of the ghostly French mother who haunts the royal genealogy: she appears not only in the figure of Queen Isabel but also, and especially, in the figure of her daughter, Catherine, whom Henry envisions as the mother of a "boy, half-French half-English, that shall go to Constantinople and take the Turk by the beard?" (5.2.206–9) and whom the audience might recognize as the future mother not only of Henry VI but also of another hybrid son, Edmund Tudor.

The scene's complex interlocutions of race and reproduction have much to do with its Irish subtexts, which have, of course, been noted by a diverse array of critics.[5] As Michael Neill has pointed out, the staging of the princess's apparent submission to Henry's will may be read as a gendered metaphor about the necessity, if not the pleasures, of foreign submission to English rule, for the French king's gift of his daughter to the victorious English king is legible as a fantasy solution to the struggles over control of Ireland (Neill 1994: 23). In addition, as Jonathan Dollimore and Alan Sinfield have proposed, this scene may be read in connection with the Elizabethan *regulation* of sexuality in Ireland, with polemic against English–Irish intermarriage and with statutes that prohibited English–Irish alliances of various kinds. Indeed, as they point out, Henry's evocation of his son, Henry VI – a monarch who was derided as weak and effeminate and who lost nearly all his father's French conquests – seems bound up with Elizabethan anxieties about the consequences of English–Irish mixture (Dollimore and Sinfield 1992: 151).

Implicit in the play's engagement with this rhetoric of miscegenation, I would suggest, is the notion that the relationship between sexuality and race is a mutually constitutive one. More specifically, the oft-cited Elizabethan tales about people born in England or of English descent who have "gone native" and "fallen into" Irishness,[6] are not simply stories of conversion or decline but also stories about sexual procreation and degenerate offspring. Fynes Moryson's explanation of how Ireland's first English colonizers became Irish is exemplary:

> But as horses Cowes and sheepe transported out of England into Ireland, doe each race and breeding declyne worse and worse, till in fewe yeares they nothing differ from the races and breeds of the Irish horses and Cattle. So the posterities of the English planted in Ireland, doe each discent, growe more and more Irish, in nature manners and custumes, so as wee founde in the last Rebellion diuers of the most ancient English Familyes planted of old in Ireland, to be turned as rude and barbarous as any of the meere Irish lords. (Moryson 1907–8: 481)

In this narrative, "race" clearly signifies the reproduction or "breeding" of animals as well as the inferior types or "breeds" that purportedly ensue from such intercourse. Central to this account, moreover, is the idea that it is *through* generation, in an Irish climate, that degeneration – the "turn[ing]" of "ancient English familyes" into the rudeness and barbarism that he terms "meere" Irishness – occurs. That Englishness could not be (re)produced in Ireland was in fact a commonplace: as one anonymous treatise noted in 1599, "it is a thing observed in Ireland, and growen to a

Proverbe that English in the second generation become Irish but never English"
(Quinn 1942).

Read against this context, the play's preoccupation with questions of offspring and
issue may more clearly be seen as a sign of its interest in race, and especially, in racial
degeneration. Indeed, it is striking to note that Henry woos Catherine partly by conjuring up images of bodily decline:

> A good leg will fall, a straight back will stoop, a black beard will turn white, a curled
> pate will grow bald, a fair face will wither, a full eye will wax hollow, but a good heart,
> Kate, is the sun and the moon — or rather the sun and not the moon, for it shines bright
> and never changes, but keeps his course truly. (5.2.154–9)

Imagining himself as the sun who shines bright and never changes and as the pro-
ducer of a son who similarly keeps his course, Henry optimistically absents himself
from the possibility of deterioration he describes and, in doing so, would seem to be
disavowing the specter of Englishness as a potentially depleted or mutable "stock."
But before the scene ends the specter will return as the French king presents his
daughter to Henry:

> Take her, fair son, and from her blood raise up
> Issue to me; that the contending kingdoms
> Of France and England, whose very shores look pale
> With envy of each other's happiness,
> May cease their hatred . . . (5.2.320–4)

The king's speech, which conjures up Henry as his "son" and the offspring as a product
of this male exchange who is destined to be "raise[d] up" by Henry alone, offers yet
another fantasy of generation without women. But that is not all it offers, for the
king's identification of the child as the "[i]ssue" of "her blood" betrays the play's
investment in the notion that the matter of racial difference depends, at least in part,
on women. Through this double narrative the play encodes the racial anxieties at issue
in the royal marriage. Moreover, it is surely no accident that the play takes up the
matter of offspring most explicitly in a meeting that takes place outside of England,
outside of the locale which, as we have seen, was routinely figured as the "pasture"
where English mettle is produced and preserved. By "planting" the encounter between
Catherine and Henry precisely in the land that has just been won by war, the play
encrypts the specter of racial degeneration at the heart of their (inter)national union.

Such racial anxiety over the English body dangerously mixed up with its national
Other not only concludes *Henry V*, but, equally important, is the starting point for
Edward III. In the first scene of *Edward III* a disaffected French lord rehearses the
matrilineal genealogy at issue in *Henry V* as he explains why Edward is the legitimate
heir of the French throne. In this account, Edward's three uncles — men who died and
"left no issue of their loins" — are juxtaposed with Isabella, his fertile French mother,
whose womb is figured as the "fragrant garden" that paradoxically offers, as its finest

"flower," the English king who ought, rightly, to be king of France as well (1.1.9 and 14–15). In both plays, then, violations done to a French maternal body motivate warfare and generate the dramatic narrative. Although *Edward III* resolves its narrative of maternal violation differently from *Henry V*, it too relies upon performances of English homosociality to sustain its nationalist imaginary. Indeed, as Giorgio Melchiori has noted, it stages more scenes of English chivalric practice – knighting and investitures – than any other play of the period (Melchiori 1998: 41).

Recycling material from Holinshed and Froissart, *Edward III* begins with the promise of war – more specifically, with a scene in which Edward learns of the legitimacy of his claim to France and fervently vows to win back "all the whole dominions of the realm" (1.1.83). Opening in the English court and closing with Edward's 1347 conquest of Calais – the territory that, until 1558, remained an English colony – the play's imagining of nationhood entails the same analogy that structures *Henry V*: through the staging of the French–English wars and the struggle to claim contested land, both plays imagine a triumphant conclusion to England's ongoing crisis in Ireland.

The English crisis in Ireland comes into view in this play in act 1, when the action shifts from the English court to Roxborough (in present-day Scotland), where the castle of the Countess of Salisbury is under siege by the "treacherous [Scottish] King . . . [who has] made invasion on the bordering towns" (1.1.127). The castle, a royal residence in Scotland's "English Pale," changed hands several times between the twelfth and sixteenth centuries, as the boundaries between northern England and Scotland were fiercely contested (Ferguson 1977: 38). The play's staging of this Scottish invasion strikingly conjures up the Irish rebellions of Elizabeth's reign. Thus, the Countess's fearful description of the treatment she expects at the hands of the Scots – that she will "be wooed with broad unturned oaths / Or forced by rough insulting barbarism" (1.2.7–9) and that "they will deride us in the north, / And, in their vild, uncivil, skipping jigs / Bray forth their conquest and our overthrow" (1.2.11–13) – echoes the language used in Elizabethan accounts of Ireland. And the Scottish king's detailed description of the attire and weaponry of his cohorts resonates with the proto-ethnographic descriptions of the (Scottish Irish) galloglasses offered in Elizabethan accounts of the north of Ireland.[7] While the military struggles in Ireland were notoriously protracted and difficult, the play rewrites this history, showing the Scottish invasion put down without any warfare, as the Scottish troops, learning of the approach of the English, instantly flee.

These Roxborough scenes, which are the subject of much of the first two acts, may chronicle English victory but they also stage a threat to the now-familiar vision of the nation as constituted by its members' participation in war. This threat does not take the form of these Scottish/Irish rebels; rather it shows up in the romance plot that takes up much of the first two acts and that, like the romance plot of *Henry V*, turns on the matter of race and reproduction in Ireland. The plot centers on the force of Henry's desire for the Countess. No sooner does he meet her than he denounces his wife and renounces everything that the play sets forth as the essence of English masculinity. Sequestered in his closet and pining with desire, he enlists the Countess's father to enforce his will. Dissociating himself from his knights, he bids farewell to war, refuses to go to France, and, in a climactic moment, agrees to the murder of the Queen and the Countess's husband. For much of these two acts the Countess deftly maneuvers to deflect Edward's overtures, and Edward blushes with shame, seemingly poised on the brink of destruction and aware that the fate of his would-be empire hangs in the balance.

While the play withholds explicit explanation for the abrupt transformation of the king, Elizabethan accounts of Ireland in the period of Edward III's reign – a period that has been described as a moment when "the English colony in decline faced a Gaelic society in resurgence" (Watt 1987: 307) – clearly suggest one. Elizabethan writers declared that England had very nearly lost its hold on Ireland in this period, and they interpreted this political turmoil in clear national and racial terms: Edward's reign was said to mark the beginning of the end of Englishness in Ireland. Holinshed's *Chronicle of Ireland* thus averred that this was the moment when English identity in Ireland began to bifurcate: the "English of byrth, and the English of blood falling at words, were devided into factions" so that "the realme was even upon the point to give over all and to rebel." Edward's reign also witnessed in 1367 the enactment of the Statute of Kilkenny, which was passed by Edward's son Lionel and was intended to strengthen ties among members of Ireland's English community (Hardiman 1843: 1–43). This statute was notorious for its zealous attempt to legislate Englishness in Ireland: it prohibited all inhabitants of the English colony from adopting Irish customs, speaking the Irish language, or forming alliances with the indigenous peoples. One prominent Elizabethan, Sir William Gerard, reading history through the lens of the culture's new racial paradigms, characterized the Statute as a response not to strife among different groups of English settlers but rather to English degeneration. In a 1576 report to the Privy Council, Gerard decried the current national and racial transformations – the manner in which "rebells [who] . . . refuzinge Englishe nature growe Irishe in soche sorte as (otherwise then in name) not to be discerned from the Irishe." Referring to his research in some unnamed "recordes," he summarily declared that "this degenratinge . . . beganne about the xxxth yeare of the sayd Kinge Edwarde the third his reigne" (Gerard 1931: 120).

Edward III goes further than Gerard, locating English racial degeneracy not in Edward's Ireland, but rather in the king himself. It connects Edward's crisis with the culture's mythology about the propensity of English men to "turn" Irish in Ireland, a mythology that conventionally identified the English man's degeneration with his "de-gendering" or subordination to women (Dollimore and Sinfield 1992; Carroll 1993; Jones and Stallybrass 1992; Neill 1994; Rackin 1994). Even more strikingly, the play does this through the Countess, using her to figure the specter of an Irish woman who can wreak havoc upon the king and upon the Englishness he embodies.

This narrative follows from the ambiguity that, at certain moments, the play attaches to the Countess, which allows the audience to entertain the possibility that she might not be properly English or that, like the English inhabitants of Ireland in popular tradition, she may have declined into Irishness. Indeed, her liminal place in the play — alone on the walls of a besieged castle in a frontier zone — makes visible the unstable position she occupies in its discourse of nation and race. Living in these borderlands apart from her husband who is soldiering in France, she resembles the notoriously independent wives of wealthy Irish lords, women whose autonomy New English colonizers sought to curtail (Nicholls 1972: 17).

Perhaps the most striking way in which the play portrays the Countess as Other is through its treatment of her speech, one of the Elizabethan theatre's primary means of representing Irishness (Neill 1994: 14–22; Smith 1999: 306–11). The Roxborough scenes are largely taken up with the establishment of the Countess's intimacy with the speech of the borderlands, an intimacy that many early modern writers identified as a clear sign of English degeneration. Thus, in a scene that appears to be derived from Holinshed's account of a Scottish noblewoman, the Countess taunts the fleeing Scots by repeating their boasts and mimicking their Scottish phrases (Metz 1989: 13). It will not be long before the play recalls this mimicry as Edward, recollecting a conversation with her that has not been staged, marvels at her "broad" speech and at her facility in performing the "epithetes and accents" of "her barbarous foes" (29–30, 35). In an era when it was popularly held that the women of Ireland spoke English with what Richard Stanyhurst called "a harsh and brode kind of pronunciation" the Countess's speech signaled her affiliation with Ireland (Carroll 1993: 383).

More than anything else, the play's romance plot articulates English manhood as vulnerable to the foreignness that the Countess represents. Thus, when Edward's secretary composes a sonnet comparing the Countess's constancy to that of Judith, Edward nervously invokes Holofernes' fate: "O monstrous line! Put in the next a sword, / And I shall woo her to cut off my head" (2.1.170–1). These fears for the integrity of the king's body are not Edward's alone; his secretary also observes, "when she blush'd, even then did he look pale, / As if her cheeks, by some enchanted power, / Attracted had the cherry blood from his" (2.1.6–9). Associating the Countess with these images of castration and vampirism, the play positions her as a threat to the supposed fountainhead of Englishness. Moreover, through Edward's comparison of his desire for her to the nightingale's song of "adulterate wrong" (2.2.110) — an allusion, of course, to the Ovidian myth of Philomel — the play suggests that a union between them would be not only adulterous but also racially dangerous, "corrupted by base intermixture" (*OED*).

Unlike *Henry V*, however, this play ultimately disavows its narrative of miscegenous romance, offering instead, via Edward, a vociferous assertion of the Countess's Englishness. Indeed, even before Edward makes this assertion (to which I shall return), the play works against its depiction of the Countess as a dangerous Other. Most notably, when the Countess reacts to her father's apparent collusion on Edward's behalf, the play begins to suggest that it is the king who really endangers the racial identity on which national community is imagined to depend:

> Hath he no means to stain my honest blood,
> But to corrupt the author of my blood
> To be his scandalous and vile solicitor?
> No marvel though the branches be then infected,
> When poison hath encompassed the root
> No marvel though the leprous infant die,
> When the stern dame envenometh the dug. (2.1.415–21)

Invoking images of contamination at the sight of generation – including a poisoned root that has infected its branches and a malicious woman whose venomous breast has killed a newborn – this speech positions the transgressing king as the source of racial corruption. In his response to his daughter, the Countess's father continues to link Edward with contamination through images of "polluted" chambers, "taint[ed] carrion," poison in a golden cup, and, in an echo of Sonnet 94, festering lilies that smell far worse than weeds (2.2.433–51). As the Countess declares herself to be the embodiment of "honest blood" (2.1.416) and the possessor of a soul which is "an angel pure, divine unspotted," the play transforms her into an image of unsullied English womanhood. Drawing female chastity into the net of its national and racial discourse, the play grounds Englishness – both that of the king and that of the Countess – in female sexual purity.

In the final scene of the Roxborough episodes the play assigns to the Countess – now portrayed as an English woman – the task of arresting the king's miscegenous desire by returning it to its "proper" object: the maternal body that turns out to be a repressed point of origin of Englishness in the play. Thus, in the midst of his crisis, the king twice sees in his son's facial features the imprint of the English queen: "I see the boy. Oh how his mother's face, / Modell'd in his, corrects my stray'd desire," he exclaims in act 2, and ten lines later he is still distressed by the vision, "Still do I see in him delineate / His mother's visage: those his eyes are hers, / Who looking wistly [i.e., steadily] on me makes me blush" (2.2.76–7, 87–9). Like the English queen whose steady gaze has the capacity to disrupt the king's adulterous and adulterating desire, the Countess ultimately appears in the Roxborough scenes as a disciplinary figure. Thus she audaciously tells Edward that his desire for her is a crime against heaven, for he dares, like a counterfeiter, to "stamp [God's] image in forbidden metal" (249–58). Describing her body as this proscribed matter, she also declares that his desire breaks a "sacred law" that is more consequential than kingship: "In violating marriage' sacred law / You break a greater honor than yourself. / To be a king is of a younger house / Than to be married" (2.1.260–3). Subordinating kingship to kinship, the Countess reproaches Edward and brandishes two knives that she has hidden under her cloak. Offering one to Edward with the proposal that he kill himself, she then kneels in the posture of a petitioner and insists that she will take her own life if he does not stop pursuing her.

As the play stages this melodrama, it seems to be returning to earlier moments in the text, for the Countess's display of these weapons echoes the gestures of the rebellious Scots who shortly before had flaunted their daggers. As it summons up the body of the Countess as a vessel of "pure chaste blood" (2.1.187), however, the play pointedly distances her from the world of the borderlands, linking her instead to the knights whose "blood" is elsewhere in the play a symbol of Englishness (e.g., 2.2.83). Significantly, the Countess is shown to defend Englishness itself – not simply herself and her marriage, but the king and the kingdom as well – by means of "wedding knives," by a pair of ornate knives that were, by English custom, given to brides to hang from their waist (2.2.172) (Bailey 1927: 4). These implements – specifically female, specifically English, weapons – are in fact the obverse of the Scottish swords that threatened the king in the earlier scene. While those swords stood in for the supposed barbarity of the borderlands, these knives emblematize the social order that the play imagines as necessary to allay the threats to Englishness inherent in the king's journey out of England. In staging the Countess's display of the wedding knives, in other words, the play defines the regimes of marriage as what keeps Englishness safe from racial contamination.

In portraying the Countess as the defender of the English body and a would-be martyr for marriage, the play undoes its association of her with the borderlands, whose supposed barbarity would deny the claims of English marriage law.[8] Affirming the institution of marriage and the claims of kinship, the Countess is presented as offering the "cure" for the racial degeneration and the means of preserving Englishness. At the end of this scene, accordingly, Edward and the Countess are reborn as exemplary English subjects. Edward at once repudiates his desire for the Countess as an "idle dream" (2.2.198) and reclaims his role as a guardian of English manhood, calling for his son and his knights and appointing the Countess's father as a warden to guard against incursions from the North (2.2.199–203). But the play has suggested that the Countess, the woman who keeps the king from national and racial crossings, is the real guardian of the borderlands. She, too, performs a kind of resurrection as Edward instructs her to relinquish her position as supplicant:

> Arise, true English Lady, whom our isle
> May better boast of than ever Roman might
> Of her, whose ransack'd treasury hath task'd
> The vain endeavor of so many pens. (2.2.193–6)

Alluding to the tale of Lucrece, the Roman wife whose rape and subsequent suicide were part of the founding myth of Rome, Edward imagines the Countess as inaugurating a new era of Englishness with the "treasury" of her chastity. As this chaste English wife rises into view, the threat of English racial degeneration disappears. Moreover, as the play continues, it becomes clear that the female regulation of sexuality and reproduction in these scenes has its counterpart in the male work of genocide to follow. Moreover, Edward's sojourn with the Countess is framed as producing the martial manhood on view in the play's subsequent acts. Fittingly, then, the Countess's wedding knives not only forestall English degeneration and prevent a mixing of racial kinds, but they are also the weapons that inaugurate the warfare that was the deferred promise of the play's first scene and that is imagined as the sign *par excellence* of Englishness.

Significantly, the concerns about mixing that are apparent in the romance plot show up as well in the rest of the play in which the king travels over water to France, and successfully conquers the French. In fact, as a closer look at Edward's turn from matters in Roxborough to matters in France makes clear, the scenes of genocidal violence that immediately follow the resolution of the romance plot are represented as an extension of that plot. In Edward's first appearance after his farewell to the Countess, he rue-fully announces his intent to invade France:

> Ah, France, why shouldst thou be [thus] obstinate
> Against the kind embracement of thy friends?
> How gently had we thought to touch thy breast,
> And set our foot upon thy tender mould,
> But that in froward and disdainful pride,
> Thou, like a skittish and untamed colt,
> Dost start aside, and strike us with thy heels. (3.3.27–33)

Strikingly, this speech about France's rejection of England is nothing less than a reprise of Edward's earlier petitions to the Countess, for it turns on his imagining of the English conquest of French territory as a union or "embracement" of two of the same "kind" or type, and as a sexual union, as the "kind embracement" of lovers enfolding themselves in each other's arms. Bringing the romance and war plots together, the speech represents the French lands as a "breast" that might be lovingly "touch[ed]" and as a "tender mould," a body that might willingly receive the racial imprint of the English forces.

Figuring unconquered territory as a woman, the speech not only resonates with the discourses of English/Irish mixture that we have seen in *Henry V*; it also serves as a reminder that the matter that haunts the first part of the play remains unresolved. That is, as Edward calls attention to the French refusal of union, he simultaneously returns us to the racialized romance of the Roxborough scenes: the inordinate desire to touch the taboo female body, the breast that was imagined as an "envenomed dug," the longing for embrace between different racial "kinds," the understanding of the material of the body as "tender" and vulnerable to imprint or stamping. It is not simply that the play retains this racialized language of nationhood as it shifts the scene from the English borderlands to the fields of France. Rather, it is that the play shows English violence emerging in *response* to the prohibited sexual encounter with the racial and national Other. Warfare thus comes into view as the attempt to maintain outside of England a national and racial identity that is proper to itself and that is not vul-nerable to difference.

The repressed national and racial terms of *Edward III*'s romance plot are disclosed most pointedly in the play's last scenes. Set in Calais after the English have vanquished their Scottish enemies and reclaimed the crown of France, these scenes bring the English royal family together for the first time. In the play's penultimate speech, the prince, who has returned triumphantly from the Battle of Poitiers, stands alongside the queen, who has returned from England, and the king, where he sounds the dominant note of national triumph. Imagining his deeds as the stuff of chronicles and contemplating the future readers of such a text, he petitions that "many princes more, / Bred and brought up within that little isle, / May still be famous for like victories!" and that:

> ... hereafter ages, when they read
> The painful traffic of my tender youth,
> Might thereby be inflam'd with such resolve,
> As not the territories of France alone,
> But likewise Spain, Turkey, and what countries else
> That justly would provoke fair England's ire,
> Might at their presence, tremble and retire. (5.1.220–35)

Looking into a future age marked by dissension among competing countries whose expanding dominion many in Elizabethan England viewed with anxiety, the prince fuses England's past and future, uniting chronicle history and the martial enterprises of the 1590s. Moreover, his temporal sleight of hand is accompanied by a significant geographic move. Looking outward from England, he turns, elliptically, toward Ireland. That is, his reference to sixteenth-century enemies intent on "provok[ing] fair England's ire" contains a common Elizabethan pun on Ireland as a "Land of Ire," a pun that enables him, linguistically, to establish English possession of Ireland and to fix the country in relation to Britain, the "little isle" that he does not name but implicitly identifies as the source of English manly might.[9]

Even as the play establishes the prince as the warrior around whom the English nation will be constituted, it complicates his vision of English conquests as the labor of men by returning to the imagery of reproduction with which the play began. More precisely, the prince's prayer is not simply another instance of the fantasy of male self-replication. Rather, the prayer, with its reference to the breeding of princes, calls attention to the first appearance in the play of Edward's wife, Philippa, the English queen who was celebrated in Elizabethan chronicles for having produced seven sons and who in this scene is "big with child" (4.2.45).[10] Inviting its audience to contemplate this queen's pregnant body, the play concludes by literalizing the imagined womb of its first scene and resignifying this womb as English. Reviving the narrative of male sterility and female generative power with which the play began, the prince's speech emphasizes that the play's vision of conquest depends upon the presence of the English woman with the teeming womb. Set forth as a figure of English national and racial purity, Queen Philippa – who has, so it seems, single-handedly conceived a child while in England – appears here, in the conquered land, as the sign of a new order. Her pregnant body represents the promise of English births in the new English colony and an antidote to the reproductive dangers associated with the borderlands. Staging this royal family reunion amidst the "civil towns . . . That now are turn'd to ragged heaps of stones," the play thus assigns the English woman a key role in the colonial order that is imagined to underwrite the nation: the reproduction of the English royal family functions as a metonym for the reproduction of the Englishness in the land that has been emptied out of its non-English inhabitants (5.1.203–4).

To foreground the play's conclusion – with its vehement rejection of the mixed union that *Henry V* embraces, however ambivalently – is to note a striking difference between *Edward III* and *Henry V*. What they share, however, may be equally compelling: in both, the English nation and its colony emerge not simply through acts of warfare and bloodshed; rather, both formations require generation as well as genocide. Enlisting the womb in the cause of conquest, these plays make it clear that the production of Englishness was indissolubly tied to reproduction and that Elizabethan racial understandings were of crucial importance to the emergence of national consciousness.

The racialized bonds that undergird the nation in *Henry V* and *Edward III* are far less visible in *1 and 2 Henry IV*, the plays on which I focus in the remainder of this essay. Like many of the histories that treat dissension within England, these plays represent civil war as a *failure* of kinship and look elsewhere for models of the nation. For example, *1 Henry IV* begins with the king's narration of civil war as an assault on the substance of Englishness and with the promise of a new kind of community:

> . . . Those opposed eyes,
> Which like the meteors of a troubled heaven,
> All of one nature, of one substance bred,
> Did lately meet in the intestine shock
> And furious close of civil butchery,
> Shall now, in mutual well-beseeming ranks,
> March all one way, and be no more opposed
> Against acquaintance, kindred, and allies. (1.1.9–16)

Implicit in the king's speech is a vision of the nation in which personal ties of affiliation – the ties that once bound those who are bred of one nature and substance – are to be supplanted by impersonal structures, by the ordered ranks, which affirm national unity via disciplinary regimes. This vision, I will suggest, is key to both plays – and it is key, too, to the economic relationships that the plays represent as the nation's foundation.[11]

The discourse of discipline to which I refer emerges in the play's second act when Lady Percy reveals to Hotspur that she has surreptitiously observed him in his sleep and has been alarmed by the nocturnal behavior that she has witnessed (2.4.41–9). Lady Percy's speech presents the spectacle of a man calling for order even as he himself is out of control – asleep, breathless, and drenched with sweat; in her speech, this image of the imperious warrior is subordinated to that of a man in the throes of "strange motions" and an alien passion (2.4.47). The language Hotspur speaks in his sleep is an *au courant* jargon of military command, but, in Lady Percy's account, the phrases seem to spill from his lips incoherently; represented as a list of nouns without a controlling verb, the words appear as though they are themselves caught up in the "currents of [the] heady fight" that he describes (2.4.42).[12] Bearing witness to Hotspur, Lady Percy suggests that he is possessed by his militaristic rhetoric rather than the possessor of it. In short, her speech represents Hotspur as completely under the sway of martial impulses, as a man whose speech and movements occur independently of his will.

Through this evocation of bodily constraint – of both Hotspur's unwilled movements and Lady Percy's transfixed spectatorship – *1 Henry IV* offers an arresting image of the culture's investment in what Foucault famously termed the docile body, the body whose every gesture manifests its subjectification to discipline (Foucault 1979: esp. 135–69). I am suggesting that such bodies are crucial to both parts of *Henry IV*, in which the national body politic appears as a regulated – indeed, almost automated – and virtually anonymous collectivity.

By examining the seemingly marginal and highly farcical mustering scene of *2 Henry IV* we can get a better sense of this vision of the nation as constituted by docile bodies. In this scene (3.2), Falstaff scrutinizes a group of five men whose names hint at their physical inadequacies – Ralph Mouldy, Simon Shadow, Francis Feeble, Peter Bullcalf, and Thomas Wart. These men have been assembled by Shallow, a dim-witted justice of the peace, as potential draftees for the royal army. After speaking to each of the men, Falstaff asks Shallow to choose those whom he deems most fit to serve the king, and the justice promptly selects four men. To Shallow's consternation, Falstaff immediately dismisses two of these men. In response to Shallow's meek protests, Falstaff – who has secretly pocketed bribes from the two discharged men – imperiously responds:

> Will you tell me Master Shallow, how to choose a man? Care I for the limb, the thews [i.e., strength], the stature, bulk, and big assemblance of a man? Give me the spirit, Master Shallow . . . O, give me the spare men, and spare me the great ones. (3.2.236–47)

Falstaff's disquisition on spare men and great ones parodies the rhetoric of the new military treatises that were published in profusion in the late 1590s as military science emerged as a discipline in England. Silencing Shallow and ensuring that the bribery can pass unnoticed, Falstaff claims expertise in what the period's military treatises suggested was a real art – namely, the ability to study men's bodies and recognize their "sufficiency" or readiness for war.

The discourse of discrimination on view in this scene implicitly divided English men into two classes: on the one hand, there are those men, defined by their "sufficient" bodies, who must, as one militarist put it, be "sorted, proportioned, armed, disciplined, and orderlie conducted" (Knyvett 1906: 11–12). And, on the other hand, there are the men, distinguished by their powers of discrimination, who are entrusted to carry out such disciplinary projects. In short, with the advent of military science came a new division of labor and a discourse of manly thrift, a discourse that depended upon the notion that large numbers of men were available to be mustered, arrayed, and treated as fungible material. Here, one cannot overstate the particularities of this moment: for while lowborn men had always served in English armies and systems of social inequality long precede this era, it was only with the emergence of the military profession in the early modern period that common men became legible as a kind of proto-national capital, a kind of wealth that might wisely, or unwisely, be spent.[13]

The mustering scene focuses attention on the new science of managing men, taking apart the ideology of "natural" manly distinction that critics have rightly recognized in the plays' discourse of chivalry. Underlying the farce of this scene, in other words, are traces of the culture's anxiety about the new imperatives to produce expendable men and the men who would expend them and the new practices that legislated who would be placed on either side of this economic divide. Divulging structures of inequality within early modern England, the scene affords a glimpse of how economic changes were helping to shape notions of the national body.

Foremost among the historical factors that render the scene's narrative intelligible today, of course, is the English transition to capitalism, which, as Richard Lachmann has noted, was remarkably fast as compared with the rest of Europe (Lachmann 1987: 16). According to Lachmann, "from 1570 to 1640, the portion of English peasants who were proletarianized – that is, who lost their land rights and were forced to work for wages or for poor relief payments, rose [from 8 percent] to 40 percent" (ibid). Significantly, Elizabethan militarization contributed substantially to the increase in the numbers of individuals who sold their labor rather than their goods: as men who had been peasants or artisans were pressed into military service by entrepreneurial captains, they took up places as workers within a strict hierarchy of command, a position somewhat analogous to the wage laborer.[14] The significance of these economic changes was not lost on Elizabethans; as one militarist observed, "he that is once become a souldier is now no more his own man but he under whose government he is paid" (Garrard 1591: sig. C4v).

The *Henry IV* plays continually equate men to be pressed with goods to be bought and sold, and nowhere more so, perhaps, than in this scene, which attends in detail to the Elizabethan practices of merchandising men as the men's names are repeatedly called out and checked off. Significantly, the setting for this scene is Gloucestershire, a region largely inhabited by peasant farmers in Shakespeare's day (Tawney and Tawney 1934: 52), and a locale from which more men were levied for Elizabeth's Irish wars than were levied from London or indeed any other county save Yorkshire (Cruickshank 1966: 291).

Throughout the scene Shallow continually calls attention to his muster roll, a stage property that plays a key role in the play's discourse of the national body. Muster rolls are quintessential Elizabethan texts: they began to proliferate in the 1580s and 1590s as the Privy Council increasingly sent orders to local officials to assemble men and determine their fitness for war (Wake 1935; Boynton 1967; Cruickshank 1966;

Breight 1996: 208–38). During this period, English common men underwent inspection as never before. In the 1580s the office of county muster master – which included the task of selecting, training, and inspecting troops – was permanently established and the Privy Council sent out model muster certificates on printed forms (Rowse 1955: 357; Boynton 1967: 40). General Musters – formal assemblies for inspection of all men liable for service, which were authorized by a statute of 1557 – usually happened once every four years over the course of a few days, but they happened more frequently during the Armada years and during other times of perceived danger. In the late 1580s muster masters provided Elizabeth with information about the 130,000 or so men who were deemed to be available for the nation's defense (Nolan 1994: 390–1).

Francis Bacon likened the data contained in muster books to that contained in "Carts and Mappes," and his analogy is suggestive (Bacon 1965: 21). Like Elizabethan maps and chorographies, the muster books of the period bear witness to the process by which England's inhabitants imagined a nation. Just as Elizabethan cartographers and chorographers attempted to assert control over the lesser-known portions of the kingdom by inscribing unfamiliar localities in their texts, so, too, those who carried out the muster took possession of England by recording data on common men. Enumerating the men of the realm, these inventories responded to the national imperative to quantify and mark common men as someone else's property. In an obvious sense, such texts contributed to the consolidation of non-elite English men as an abstract population; they are a key part of the prehistory of the process that Mary Poovey (1995) has identified with the late eighteenth-century efforts at "making a social body."

In *2 Henry IV* the muster book functions as a material sign of the ideology that defined one segment of the population as expendable. The muster book may appear to resemble the map that the rebels peruse in *Part 1*: representing a world largely populated by common men rather than by gentry, it attests to the expansiveness of the *Henry IV* plays, an interest that distinguishes these plays from the earlier dynastic histories (Howard and Rackin 1997). But, unlike the map, Shallow's muster book registers the "cost," as it were, of this expansiveness: as it testifies to the interests served by the census-takers and underscores the compromised terms under which non-elite men were included in the emerging national imaginary. In these texts, as common men are written into the nation, they appear as expendable items in an inventory.

At the same time, the mustering scene might be read as offering a narrative of resistance from below to this emergent nation, for the deficient bodies of the recruits are made to signify a deficient will to serve: one man (unsuccessfully) resists; two offer bribes; and the one man who declares his willingness to serve is Francis Feeble, a woman's tailor whose "weak" name and "unmanly" occupation are made to signify his lack of resolution. In other words, even as the play equates men with their deficient names and deals in the commercial logic of the muster books, it can be seen to render the refusal of these "goods" to go to market as they should. This potentially subversive "take" on the national imperative is on view in one of the scene's most risible moments in which Wart – whom Falstaff describes as a "little, lean, old, chapped, bald" fellow (252) – tries to make do with a big weapon that has been placed in his hand. Falstaff's orchestration of Wart's movements with the caliver – a three-and-a-half feet long firearm – brings to the playhouse, however parodically, the discourse of docile bodies implicit in the new science of drill. Through the hilarious encounter between Wart and Falstaff, the play pointedly alludes to contemporary treatises that articulated the "science" of matching weapons and bodies and that held out a vision of a nation comprised of uniformly competent men. Glancing toward such Foucauldian projects of docility, the play insists upon a problem at the heart of the body politic.

As the play stages the failure of the conscripts to become disciplined, well-ordered bodies, it draws attention to a world in which the relations of production are in crisis, a world – so it suggests – in which working men might be manufactured, managed, and spent otherwise. The plays lodge this critique partly through the portrayal of Falstaff, who at the end of *Part 1* announces that he has led most of his 350 soldiers to their death (5.3.35–8). Strikingly, the plays' representation of Falstaff hints at his inability to recognize the normalizing discourses and the economies of labor that are emerging around him. More specifically, the plays suggest that Falstaff fails to see in "his" merchandise something other than a consumable good; he doesn't "get" that, under capitalism, men's bodies potentially offer something more than the money he collects by using them up. To those who would exploit them, the plays suggest, men may offer a much more valuable thing – namely, their labor power, which holds out the promise of value continually being produced for nothing.

Labor power may have little meaning on the battlefield – where captains like Falstaff can get rich by the "spending" of men – but it is key to the market economy to which the tavern scenes point. It is also key to the plays' vision of the nation as a world in which there is the possibility of the organized and systematic exploitation of labor and, with that, the possibility of accumulation. As the plays conjure up this world in which men's bodies are commodities, it positions Falstaff as fundamentally out of place: he is cast as the man who misconceives the nature of what he is working with, the man who fails, in short, to see the common man as capital. Like Hotspur – the improvident warrior who leads his men to battle with the cry, "Die all! Die merrily" (4.1.135) – Falstaff is made to speak a language of extravagance and to stand opposed to an emergent discourse of husbandry and sensible expenditure of men.

By contrast, the plays set forth Hal as a solution to the crisis on view in the mustering scene, for he speaks the language of nascent capitalism that is here envisioned as key to the national body politic. As Jonathan Goldberg has observed, the play's narrative about the redemption of a son is fundamentally an economic narrative: thus Hal's "reformation" implies his embrace of habits of thrift and industry, and his arrival on the throne coincides with his being "written into the economies of an emerging middle class" (Goldberg 1992: 160). Hal himself calls attention to these economies in *Part 1* when he uses the language of accounting to explain to the king his relationship with Hotspur. Conversant in the language of "factors" and "engrossments," "accounts" and "reckonings" (3.2.147–52), Hal is alert not only to the interests of the middling sort as Goldberg demonstrates, but he is also alert to the workings of a bureaucratic apparatus like that which will help bring the nation into being.

The disciplinary structures that are integral to this vision of the nation are visible in the tavern scenes where the play focuses on Hal's interest in the practices of manly management. Consider, for example, the scene in *Part 1* in which Hal listens to the reading out of an inventory – a tavern bill – and turns his thoughts abruptly to the mustering of soldiers (2.5.495–8). Or consider the scene in *Part 2* in which Hal converses with Ned Poins, worrying aloud about whether his appetite for small beer implies a straying from his proper place (2.2.9–17). The play does more than merely summon up his royal status. It also suggests – through a speech in which he emphasizes his skill at remembering names and faces and stockings and shirts – that his "greatness" or power may have much to do with his mastery of detail and his capacity to distinguish between men. Evoking Hal as a master of the inventory, insisting on his memory and his knowledge of the particularities of men "beneath" him, the play links him to a modern discourse of knowledge as power and to the larger projects that the musters represent, namely the amassing of data about common men and the concomitant creation of a class of men who, like the recruit named Shadow, are virtually invisible.

The play alludes to this new national body as it shows Hal's interactions in the tavern, where he rehearses his place in a proto-capitalist economy and positions himself with respect to laboring men. As one of the most explicit articulations of this rehearsal, consider the scene in *Part 1* in which Hal encounters Francis the tapster, who gives him a pennyworth of sugar. Almost as soon as he has met him, he tells Poins that he has devised a scheme to amuse himself and torment the tapster: instructing Poins to call out for Francis again and again, Hal engages Francis in conversation, questioning him about his age and his loyalty to his "indenture" (2.5.43), promising him a thousand pounds in return for the sugar, and asking him whether he will rob his master. The comedy inheres in Hal's ability to set Francis in motion, to wind him up like a mechanical toy so that he runs to and fro, unsure of which command to follow and unable to say anything but "anon, anon." When Hal tires of the game, he dismisses Francis, offering some final cautionary words about the dangers of deserting his tavern post:

> *Prince.* Why, then, your brown bastard is your only drink! For look you, Francis, your white canvas doublet will sully. In Barbary, sir, it cannot come to so much.
> *Francis.* What, sir?
> *Poins.* Francis!
> *Prince.* Away, you rogue, dost thou hear them call? (2.5.73–9)

To an early modern audience the link between Hal's talk of sugar sales and his talk of Barbary may have been more obvious than they are today, for sugar was a key commodity of the early modern slave trade and Barbary was the region from which the slaves used in (Portugal's) sugar mills were transported. Revising an Elizabethan commonplace about the impossibility of washing the Ethiope white, Hal, in his parting comment to Francis, evokes an image of the white-doubletted tapster being sullied by contact with Barbary, thus reminding the tapster of the privilege of whiteness and of his good fortune in escaping such a fate.[15]

Hal's assertion of authority over Francis – more precisely, his insinuation that the English tapster has a better life than the Barbary slave – offers an early expression of the notion of a national labor force, the notion that lowborn English men are, as it were, free to labor. Much like William Harrison's *The Description of England*, which includes in its description of the "fourth and last sort of people" the proud declaration that slaves and bondsmen are unknown in England, Hal's speech invokes the horrors of African enslavement to articulate the supposed freedom of the English man (Harrison 1587: 275). Rejecting the world of Barbary slaves, Hal seems to imply that men like the simple tapster of whom he is so contemptuous must properly carry out the labors of the elite. In short, Hal's speech summons up a class of laborers who might be read as a precursor to the English working class, a class that here emerges under the shadow of slavery and service.

Subject to an "indenture" – a word that, significantly, may denote both a military contract as well as a contract for apprenticeship – as well as to the insistent and derogatory acts of naming involved in Hal's game, Francis bears a striking resemblance to the men of the mustering scene, one of whom shares his name. Moreover, through Hal's vision of the tapster rebelling against his master, the play forges a curious link between this scene and the Coventry scene in which Falstaff identifies "revolted tapsters" as part of his band of destitute soldiers (4.2.27–31) (Whitney 1994: 420). Falstaff's comments in the Coventry scene – in particular, his description of the men whom he has pressed and whom he leads across the stage as a "commodity of warm slaves," and as "slaves as ragged as Lazarus" (4.2.16–17) – may perhaps be read as yet another effort to link the pressing needs of England in the 1590s with the contemporary trade in Africans. As such, they not only point to the play's preoccupation with a nation defined by commodified labor, they also point to a key difference between Hal and Falstaff: while Falstaff, we may recall, views lowborn men as "food for powder" (4.3.66), goods that exist only to be used up in the wars, Hal carefully distinguishes between slaves and employees, seeing in Francis and his fellow workers men who can be trained to do his bidding and predicting that when he is king, he "shall command all the good lads in Eastcheap" (2.4.12–13).

My point, then, is that the play's representation of Hal's reformation – including, of course, his rejection of the "surfeit-swelled" Falstaff in favor of that almost abstract embodiment of the law, the Lord Chief Justice – is inextricably bound up with a vision of a national economy that demands men who know how to discipline subordinates and appropriate the labor of the lowborn. At a moment when the culture produced a discourse of nationhood founded on the efficient use of men and the increasing need for exacting work discipline, the play offers Hal – the lean figure whose first soliloquy marks him off as one who monitors idleness, pays off debts, and spends time wisely – as the man who would be king.

The Henry IV plays testify to the degree to which, as national consciousness emerged, Elizabethan codes of chivalry were supplanted by codes of discipline and a reevaluation – a new valuing as *property* – of the bodies of low-born English men. Paradoxically, so these plays suggest, the emergence of this new economy of "sufficient" bodies gave rise to anxieties that individual bodies would cease to matter, that the populace would metamorphose from a priceless substance to a mere Shadow. As the culture increasingly prescribed new modes of control over the bodies of boys and men and as it laid the foundation for an economy in which men's labor increasingly came to be understood as a commodity to be used efficiently, there emerged new understandings of the nation and new forms of affiliation. As I have tried to show through my readings of *Henry V* and *Edward III*, however, the old forms of affiliation through kinship did not simply disappear. Rather, they were rearticulated in new ways – shot through with racial language – as the relations between nation and colony were forged anew.

Notes

1 Recent studies of nationhood and the histories include Helgerson (1992), Jones and Stallybrass (1992), Altman (1991), Baker (1997), Highley (1997), Levine (1998), Dollimore and Sinfield (1992), Rackin (1990), Neill (1994), Murphy (1999), and Howard and Rackin (1997). Among many historical accounts of the crisis in Ireland, see McGurk (1997), Morgan (1993), Canny (1976), and Falls (1950).

2 I invoke the potentially anachronistic language of race and class here advisedly. Following Hendricks and Parker (1994), I take "race" to have signified a range of discourses and to have comprehended much more than a concern with skin color. Following Kastan (1999), I take "class" to be a "heuristic" rather than a "properly historical" category: "classes in the most precise economic definition, perhaps can be said to come into being only within the social conditions of bourgeois production, but classes, in their abstract social sense, can be seen to have existed as long as social organization has permitted an unequal distribution of property, privilege, and power" (pp. 149–50).

3 On the play's authorship, see Metz (1989: 6–20). All references are to *King Edward III* (Melchiori 1998).

4 All references to the *Henriad* are to *The Norton Shakespeare* (1997).

5 See, for example, Altman (1991: 1–32), Baker (1997), Burnett and Wray (1997), Cairns and Richards (1988: 1–12), Dollimore and Sinfield (1992), Edwards (1979), Highley (1997), Maley (1989), Murphy (1996: 38–59), and Neill (1994).

6 See, for example, Jones and Stallybrass (1992), Neill (1994: 4–10), Carroll (1993: 382–4).

7 Compare, for example, Dymmok (1843: 7).

8 See, for example, Campion (1963: 16–19).

9 For examples of this pun, see Bradshaw, Hadfield, and Maley (1993: 18).

10 Phyllis Rackin makes this point in "Women's Roles in *Edward III*," a paper presented at the Annual Meeting of the Shakespeare Association of America, Cleveland, OH, April 1998.

11 For a related argument, see Laurie Shannon's (2002) reading of the relegation of friendship to the private sphere in the *Henriad*.

12 See the glossary of war terms appended to Barret (1598), which includes at least four words from Lady Percy's speech: "sallies," "trenches," "palisadoes," and "parapets."

13 For a discussion of the emergence of the professional soldier, see Hattaway (1994).

14 See Nolan (1994: 400). Hall (1997) compares the "de-skilling process" that accompanied the industrial revolution with the technological changes that marked early modern armies (p. 235). See also Kiernan (1965), who asserts that the "common soldier was almost the first proletarian" (p. 131).

15 On the image of the white Ethiope, see Newman (1987) and Hall (1995: esp. 62–122).

References and Further Reading

Altman, J. B. (1991). "Vile participation": The Amplification of Violence in the Theater of *Henry V. Shakespeare Quarterly*, 42, 1–32.

Anderson, B. (1983). *Imagined Communities: Reflections on the Origin and Spread of Nationalism*. London: Verso.

Bacon, F. (1965). Of the true greatness of kingdoms and estates. In J. Spedding et al. (eds.) *Francis Bacon: Selection of His Works*. New York: Garret.

Bailey, C. T. (1927). *Knives and Forks Selected and Described*. London: Medici Society.

Baker, D. J. (1997). *Between Nations: Shakespeare, Spenser, Marvell, and the Question of Britain*. Stanford, CA: Stanford University Press.

Barret, R. (1598). *The Theorike and Practike of Modern Warres*. London.

Boynton, L. (1967). *The Elizabethan Militia 1558–1638*. London: Routledge and Kegan Paul.

Bradshaw, B., Hadfield, A., and Maley, W. (eds.) (1993). *Representing Ireland: Literature and the Origins of Conflict 1534–1660*. Cambridge: Cambridge University Press.

Breight, C. C. (1996). *Surveillance, Militarism, and Drama in the Elizabethan Era*. New York: St. Martin's Press.

Burnett, M. T. and Wray, R. (eds.) (1997). *Shakespeare and Ireland: History, Politics, Culture*. New York: St. Martin's Press.

Cairns, D. and Richards, S. (1988). *Writing Ireland: Colonialism, Nationalism, and Culture*. Manchester: Manchester University Press.

Campion, E. (1963). *Two Bokes of the Histories of Ireland*, ed. A. F. Vossen. Assen: Van Gorcum.

Canny, N. (1976). *The Elizabethan Conquest of Ireland: A Pattern Established, 1565–76*. Brighton: Harvester Press.

Carroll, C. (1993). Representations of Women in Some Early Modern English Tracts on the Colonization of Ireland. *Albion*, 25, 3, 379–93.

Cruickshank, C. G. (1966). *Elizabeth's Army*, 2nd edn. Oxford: Clarendon Press.

Dollimore, J. and Sinfield, A. (1992). History and Ideology, Masculinity and Miscegenation: The Instance of *Henry V*. In A. Sinfield (ed.) *Faultlines: Cultural Materialism and the Politics of Dissident Reading*. Berkeley: University of California Press, 109–42.

Dymmok, J. (1843). A treatice of Ireland, ed. Richard Butler. In *Tracts Relating to Ireland*, vol. 2. Dublin: Irish Archaeological and Celtic Society, 1–90.

Edwards, P. (1979). *Threshold of a Nation: A Study in English and Irish Drama*. Cambridge: Cambridge University Press.

Falls, C. (1950). *Elizabeth's Irish Wars*. London: Constable.

Ferguson, W. (1977). *Scotland's Relations with England: A Survey to 1707*. Edinburgh: Donald.

Foucault, M. (1979). *Discipline and Punish: The Birth of the Prison*, trans. A. Sheridan. New York: Vintage Books.

Garrard, W. (1591). *The Arte of Warre*. London.

Gerard, W. (1931). Notes of his report on Ireland – May, 1578. *Analecta Hibernica*, 2, 93–291.

Goldberg, J. (1992). *Sodomotries: Renaissance Texts: Modern Sexualities.* Stanford, CA: Stanford University Press.

Hall, B. S. (1997). *Weapons and Warfare in Renaissance Europe: Gunpowder, Technology, and Tactics.* Baltimore, MD: Johns Hopkins University Press.

Hall, K. F. (1995). *Things of Darkness: Economies of Race and Gender in Early Modern England.* Ithaca, NY: Cornell University Press.

Hardiman, J. (ed.) (1843). Statute of the fortieth year of Edward III enacted in a Parliament held in Kilkenny, AD 1367. In *Tracts Relating to Ireland*, vol. 2. Dublin: Irish Archaeological and Celtic Society, 1–143.

Harrison, W. (1587). The Description of England in volume 1 of R. Holinshed, *The Chronicles of England, Scotland and Ireland.* London. Reprinted 1808, London: J. Johnson et al.

Hattaway, M. (1994). Blood Is Their Argument: Men of War and Soldiers in Shakespeare and Others. In A. Fletcher and P. Roberts (eds.) *Religion, Culture and Society in Early Modern Britain.* Cambridge: Cambridge University Press.

Helgerson, R. (1992). *Forms of Nationhood: The Elizabethan Writing of England.* Chicago, IL: University of Chicago Press.

Hendricks, M. and Parker, P. (eds.) (1994). Introduction. In *Women, "Race" and Writing in the Early Modern Period.* New York: Routledge.

Highley, C. (1997). *Shakespeare, Spenser, and the Crisis in Ireland.* Cambridge: Cambridge University Press.

Holinshed, R. (1808) [1587]. *Chronicles of England, Scotland and Ireland*, 2nd edn., 6 vols. London: J. Johnson et al.

Howard, J. E. and Rackin, P. (1997). *Engendering a Nation: A Feminist Account of Shakespeare's English Histories.* London: Routledge.

Jones, A. R. and Stallybrass, P. (1992). Dismantling Irena: The Sexualizing of Ireland in Early Modern England. In A. Parker et al. (eds.) *Nationalisms and Sexualities.* New York: Routledge, 157–71.

Joughin, J. J. (ed.) (1997). *Shakespeare and National Culture.* Manchester: Manchester University Press.

Kastan, D. S. (1999). *Shakespeare after Theory.* New York: Routledge.

Kiernan, V. G. (1965). Foreign Mercenaries and Absolute Monarchy. In *Crisis in Europe, 1560–1660*, ed. T. Aston. New York: Basic Books.

Knyvett, H. (1906). *The Defence of the Realme*, ed. C. Hughes. Oxford: Clarendon Press.

Lachmann, R. (1987). *From Manor to Market: Structural Change in England, 1536–1640.* Madison: University of Wisconsin Press.

Levine, N. S. (1998). *Women's Matters: Politics, Gender, and Nation in Shakespeare's Early History Plays.* Newark: University of Delaware Press.

McEachern, C. (1996). *The Poetics of English Nationhood, 1590–1612.* Cambridge: Cambridge University Press.

McGurk, J. (1997). *The Elizabethan Conquest of Ireland.* New York: Manchester University Press.

Maley, W. (1989). Review of *Writing Ireland* by Cairns and Richards. *Textual Practice*, 3, 291–8.

Melchiori, G. (ed.) (1998). *King Edward III.* New Cambridge Shakespeare. Cambridge: Cambridge University Press.

Metz, G. H. (1989). *Sources of Four Plays Ascribed to Shakespeare.* Columbia: University of Missouri Press.

Morgan, H. (1993). *Tyrone's Rebellion: The Outbreak of the Nine Years War in Tudor Ireland.* London: Royal Historical Society.

Moryson, F. (1907–8). *An Itinerary Containing His Ten Yeeres Travell through the Twelve Dominions of Germany, Bohmerland, Sweitzerland, Netherland, Denmarke, Poland, Italy, Turky, France, England, Scotland & Ireland*, vol. 4. Glasgow: J. MacLehose and Sons.

Murphy, A. (1996). Shakespeare's Irish History. *Literature and History*, 5, 1, 38–59.

——(1999). *But the Irish Sea Betwixt Us: Ireland, Colonialism, and Renaissance Literature.* Lexington: University Press of Kentucky.

Neill, M. (1994). Broken English and Broken Irish: Nation, Language and the Optic of Power in Shakespeare's Histories. *Shakespeare Quarterly*, 45, 1–32.

Newman, K. (1987). "And wash the Ethiop white": Femininity and the Monstrous in *Othello*. In J. E. Howard and M. F. O'Connor (eds.) *Shakespeare Reproduced: The Text in History and Ideology*. London: Routledge.

Nicholls, K. W. (1972). *Gaelic and Gaelicised Ireland in the Middle Ages*. Dublin: Gill and Macmillan.

Nolan, John S. (1994). The Militarization of the Elizabethan State. *Journal of Military History*, 58, 3, 391–420.

Poovey, M. (1995). *Making a Social Body: British Cultural Formation, 1830–1864*. Chicago, IL: University of Chicago Press.

Quinn, D. B. (ed.) (1942). A Discourse of Ireland (circa 1599): A Sidelight on English Colonial Policy. *Proceedings of the Royal Irish Academy*, 47, 151–66.

Rackin, P. (1990). *Stages of History: Shakespeare's English Chronicles*. Ithaca, NY: Cornell University Press.

——(1994). Foreign Country: The Place of Women and Sexuality in Shakespeare's Historical World. In R. Burt and J. M. Archer (eds.) *Enclosure Acts: Sexuality, Property, and Culture in Early Modern England*. Ithaca, NY: Cornell University Press.

Rowse, A. L. (1955). *The Expansion of Elizabethan England*. London: Macmillan.

Shakespeare, W. (1997). *The Norton Shakespeare*, gen. ed. S. Greenblatt et al. New York: W. W. Norton.

Shannon, L. (2002). *Sovereign Amity: Figures of Friendship in Shakespearean Contexts*. Chicago, IL: University of Chicago Press.

Smith, B. R. (1999). *The Acoustic World of Early Modern England*. Chicago, IL: University of Chicago Press.

Tawney, A. J. and Tawney, R. H. (1934). An Occupational Census of the Seventeenth Century. *Economic History Review*, 5, 25–64.

Wake, J. (ed.) (1935). *Montagu Musters Book, AD 1602–1623*. Peterborough: Peterborough Press.

Watt, J. A. (1987). The Anglo-Irish Colony Under Strain, 1327–1399. In A. Cosgrove (ed.) *A New History of Ireland*, vol. 2. Oxford: Clarendon Press.

Whitney, C. (1994). Festivity and Topicality in the Coventry Scene of *1 Henry IV*. *English Literary Renaissance*, 24, 2, 410–48.

5

The Irish Text and Subtext of Shakespeare's English Histories

Willy Maley

My mamma asked me the other day if I knew Shakespeare was an Irishman. I said no I didn't. She said well it's right there in the Savannah paper; and sure enough some gent from the University of Chicago had made a speech somewhere saying Shakespeare was an Irishman. I said well it's just him that says it, you better not go around saying it and she said listen SHE didn't care whether he was an Irishman or a Chinaman.

Flannery O'Connor, *The Habit of Being*

There is so little to go on when you try to decipher the life of William Shakespeare. But we can say with some certainty that he was not an Irishman. Mind you, I don't know for sure if he was an Englishman either.

Frank McGuinness, *Shakespeare and Ireland*

Much Ado About Ireland

This essay does two things: addresses the key Irish allusions in Shakespeare's histories, including textual cruces like the four captains scene and Chorus to 5.0 in *Henry V*; and cavills on the ninth part of a harp with conventional criticism on the topic.

Ireland looms large in Shakespeare's work and in the political culture which produced it, but not in obvious ways (Barton 1919; Lawrence 1906; Burnett and Wray 1997). For example, the only evidence of Shakespeare's knowledge of Gaelic is a line uttered by Pistol in *Henry V* – "*Calin o custure me!*" (4.4.4), the "corrupt refrain" of an Irish song, "maiden, my treasure" (Taylor 1982: 234). Chris Ivic finds it "disquieting" that "one of the play's English soldiers speaks in broken Irish" (Ivic 1999a: 94), but more disquieting is the gloss in the Norton, "The Irish refrain of a popular ballad, meaning 'I am a girl from beside the Suir'," as reassuring to the reader as the original Irish is to the French soldier at whom Pistol aims it. Yet more disquieting is the fact that one of modern Ireland's most theoretically sophisticated critics, Declan Kiberd, can comment: "On Shakespeare's stage only fresh-faced country colleens are permitted to lisp charmingly in the patois 'Cailín ó cois tSiúire me' (I am a girl from the banks of the Suir)" (Kiberd 1995: 13). Pistol is no "fresh-faced country colleen," but this comment (politically) incorrect on every count, producing colonial discourse by projecting it into the text, is characteristic of critical responses to Shakespearean depictions of Ireland. Most critics discover only scapegoats and stereotypes in Shakespeare's Ireland, reproducing the very imperialist assumptions their arguments are ostensibly designed to contest. Kiberd's comments are put in perspective by Irish language expert Michael Cronin, who observes: "It seems a fitting tribute to the stimulating intersections between Shakespeare's work and the Irish language that, only 25 years after the dramatist's death, Joe Harris, an Irish actor in London, should sing Irish-language songs at performances of *Henry V*" (Cronin 1997: 210). It is to the stimulating intersections between Shakespeare and Ireland, and the critics, with their leading questions and quibbles, that we now turn.

James I, inspecting the documents stored in Whitehall upon his accession, exclaimed: "We had more ado with Ireland than all the world besides" (Andrews 1983: 20; Highley 1997: 1). But this pervasive presence in the state papers is strangely absent from the London stage. As Michael Neill notes:

> Given the amount of political, military, and intellectual energy it absorbed, and the moneys it consumed, Ireland can seem to constitute . . . one of the great and unexplained lacunae in the drama of the period. (Neill 1994: 11)

Andrew Murphy discerns "a failure, or unwillingness, on the part of English dramatists to engage with one of the most urgent and important political crises of the close of the sixteenth century: the war in Ireland" (Murphy 1996: 38). Murphy, like Andrew Hadfield (1997), attributes this silence to censorship arising from ongoing conflict. Joel Altman cites one contemporary, George Fenner, writing on June 30, 1599, in the midst of Essex's unsuccessful expedition: "it is forbidden, on pain of death, to write or speak of Irish affairs; what is brought by post is known only to the Council; but it is very sure that Tyrone's party has prevailed most" (Altman 1991: 12). Altman observes that the patron of Shakespeare's company was Sir George Carey, "whose signature appeared on most of the orders commanding the lords lieutenant to levy soldiers for Ireland" (p. 15).

Alan Fletcher has drawn our attention to an "aborted performance of *Much Ado About Nothing*," set for some time before May 28, 1628 at Coleraine, co. Londonderry, which he conjectures is "probably Shakespeare's play of that name" (Fletcher 2000: 238). That a production of a popular Shakespearean comedy in the newly planted province of Ulster was barred by the authorities because one of its songs was considered objectionable is intriguing, suggestive of a conflictual site of censorship and secrecy, prompting subtle allegorical depiction as well as provocative political representation. Fletcher finds it "hard to see how any of the songs in *Much Ado* might have caused . . . offence, unless it be Balthasar's song on the faithlessness of men (*Much Ado*, Act II, scene III). But if so, the commissioners must have been touchy indeed. Perhaps more likely they had been the butt of some lampoon" (ibid: 430, n. 159). Fletcher assumes the dispute revolved around the role of the commissioners and the rights of the colonists. He guesses the play was being staged by the latter, and "it is probable that the song to which the commissioners took exception was some sort of jibe, however mild, aimed at them by persons unknown" (pp. 239–40).

Perhaps the play's the thing to catch the conscience of the commissioners. Balthasar's song could credibly offend crown agents come to police a plantation:

> Men were deceivers ever,
> One foot in sea, and one on shore
> To one thing constant never . . . (2.3.57–9)

Fletcher observes that in choosing *Much Ado* "the planters . . . showed themselves aware of what was currently popular in London theatrical circles, and thus likely to please their guests" (p. 431, n. 160). Or displease them. They may also have shown themselves aware of the political uses of drama and the possibilities of oblique critique of authority (Howard 1987).

Exploring the place of Ireland in Shakespeare's histories entails rounding up the usual suspects: *2 Henry VI*, *Richard II*, and *Henry V*. Since I do not intend to dwell on it, I should mention Christopher Highley's reading of *1 Henry IV* as a play preoccupied with Ireland, the Celtic cousin Welsh Glendower – and later the English rebel Hotspur – standing in for the absent Irish figure, Hugh O'Neill, Earl of Tyrone, a very different pairing than that of Fluellen and Macmorris (Highley 1997: 86–109). Highley is one critic who looks for dramatic complexity – "ideological faultlines and moments of dissidence" – rather than colonial stereotyping in Shakespeare's treatment of Ireland, and I find his arguments compelling (ibid: p. 8). I am convinced by his reading of *Henry V* as a play that "begins forcefully to register Shakespeare's disillusioned ambivalence about the reasons behind and the consequences of English empire-building" (p. 135). This is not to praise Shakespeare's genius or even-handedness but merely to suggest that for English dramatists and poets Ireland was a demanding and rewarding text rather than an archive of negative images. One way of approaching the representation of Ireland in Renaissance drama is by thinking in terms of stereotypes and negative images (Snyder 1920). Another is to see English attitudes to Ireland in much more equivocal terms (Highley 1997).

Subtext is a slippery concept, as defined by Fredric Jameson in *The Political Unconscious* (that title itself another term for "subtext"):

> the "subtext" is not immediately present as such, not some common-sense external reality, nor even the conventional narratives of history manuals, but rather must itself always be (re)constructed after the fact . . . The whole paradox of what we have here called the subtext may be summed up in this, that the literary work or cultural object, as though for the first time, brings into being that very situation of which it is also, at one and the same time, a reaction . . . (Jameson 1981: 81–2)

Do Shakespeare's English histories reflect, represent, or respond to a hidden Ireland, or do they conjure into being an Ireland as fraught and fragmented as the England it threatens, and make of it "the official English Unconscious"? (Kiberd 1995: 656). Or guilty conscience (Arden 1979b). Subtextually speaking, do Shakespeareans bring into being the colonialism they claim to be reacting against?

David Baker, discussing *Henry V*, comments: "Ireland is not only a place elsewhere which must be pacified *in absentia*. It is also the "scene" of this drama, a terrain on which . . . power slips within its own categories" (Baker 1993: 51). For Michael Neill, "Ireland functions as a recurrent point of reference – the crucial implied term in an unstable dialectic of national self-definition" (Neill 1994: 11). Shakespeare's Ireland, according to Bernhard Klein, "is rarely more than a shadowy and indistinct background of the dramatic scenery, always only partially coming into view" (Klein 1998: para. 5). It comes into view early in *King John*, which opens with the French ambassador setting out the "most lawful claim" of Philip of France:

> To this fair island and the territories,
> To Ireland, Poitou, Anjou, Touraine, Maine;
> Desiring thee to lay aside the sword
> Which sways usurpingly these several titles. (1.1.10–13)

Philip reiterates his claim in person in the first scene of the second act:

> England and Ireland, Anjou, Touraine, Maine,
> In right of Arthur do I claim of thee. (2.1.152–3)

John persuades his nephew, "Arthur of Brittaine," to yield to him rather than rely on "the coward hand of France" to win his right. Here, Ireland goes with the territories, then gets coupled with England, before becoming a pig-in-the-middle of "Brittaine" – "Brittany" but with echoes of "Britain," especially with its Arthurian overtones – and France. This transitional, territorial tug-of-war is played out in the ensuing histories.

2 Henry VI: Discerning Kern

2 Henry VI contains more explicit Irish allusions than any other Shakespeare play, starting with Salisbury praising York's

> acts in Ireland,
> In bringing them to civil discipline. (1.1.191–2)

But York's acts have not prevented the loss of England's prized possessions, as he reflects in a soliloquy, ending thus:

> Methinks the realms of England, France, and Ireland
> Bear that proportion to my flesh and blood
> As did the fatal brand Althaea burnt
> Unto the prince's heart of Calydon. (1.1.231–4)

The crown's failure to defend its possessions in France and Ireland is seen as a sell-out by a figure who fought to establish a foothold there.

Andrew Murphy sees the Nine Years War (1594–1603) as the crucial context for the histories, so that a play like *2 Henry VI* (ca. 1591) is less ireful than *Richard II* (ca. 1595): "The relative stability of the English position in Ireland in this period is reflected in the manner in which Ireland figures in the text of Shakespeare's play" (Murphy 1996: 42). Accordingly:

> Between the 1591 play and its 1595 successor . . . we get a shift in the way in which Ireland is presented on the Shakespearean stage. In the first instance, Ireland is a territory to be deployed as an English source of strength; in the second, it is associated with a catastrophic draining away of that strength, leading to Richard's loss of power, and ultimately to his death. (Ibid: 44)

But Ireland functions in both plays as pretext or context for rebellion – York's and Bolingbroke's. Even a critic as sophisticated as Christopher Highley succumbs to the temptation to construct a narrow context for Shakespeare's interest in Ireland, so that his subtle reading of *1 Henry IV* as an Irish play is premised on the fact that the play "coincides with a critical new phase in Elizabeth's Irish wars" (Highley 1997: 87). I find Highley's general arguments convincing, but efforts to pin the plays down to specific contemporary concerns less so. The word "crisis" is as worn-out with regard to Ireland as the word "new."

Jonathan Dollimore and Alan Sinfield pursue a similar contextualizing: "The exuberance of *Henry V* leads most commentators to link it with the early stages of the Irish expedition when the successful return could be anticipated" (Dollimore and Sinfield 1985a: 219). The play's Epilogue lacks exuberance. The pessimism of the final Chorus gets lost in the optimism around the alleged Essex allusion (Rackin 1990: 84–5). Contextualization can lead to closure and containment. To see Shakespeare's preoccupation with Ireland stemming from the outbreak of the Nine Years War in 1594 and ending either with Essex's unsuccessful campaign or O'Neill's submission to Mountjoy in 1603 is narrow. The historicism that ties the second tetralogy to the Tyrone Rebellion, rather than a much more protracted and problematic relation with Ireland, is answered effectively by Marlowe's *Edward II* (1593). In Marlowe's play, Edward asks, "Shall I still be haunted thus?" and Lancaster responds:

> Look for rebellion, look to be deposed.
> Thy garrisons are beaten out of France
> And lame and poor lie groaning at the gates;
> The wild O'Neil, with swarms of Irish kerns,

> Lives uncontrolled within the English pale;
> Unto the walls of York the Scots made road,
> And unresisted drave away rich spoils. (2.2.161–7)

An editorial note reads: "Marlowe is making no precise historic reference but uses O'Neil as a general term for an Irish leader of 'kerns' or foot-soldiers, led against the 'pale' or English settlement" (Merchant 1975: 44). The name "O'Neil" was familiar to Elizabethan audiences from the celebrated visit to court of Hugh's father, Shane, in 1567 (Hogan 1947). Highley mentions the "anachronistic reference to 'Onele' " in the 1594 Quarto edition of *2 Henry VI*, which "helps to accentuate the immediacy of the rebellion" (Highley 1997: 180–1, n. 10). This is a further instance of that historicist desire to pin the play's Irish allusions to a particular context, rather than see them as part of a larger and more enduring structure. We are back with Murphy's determination to see Shakespeare's histories as driven by the urgency of the Nine Years War rather than informed by four hundred years of Anglo-Irish history. The long view is vital to an understanding of early modern Ireland. Hugh O'Neill offered his opinion of a supposed Old English ally at the time of the Nine Years War: "for being told, That Barrett of Castlemore, though an Englishman, was a good Catholick, and had been there four hundred Years; he replied, That he hated the Clown as if he had come but yesterday" (Cox 1689, I: Ded., c). That puts things in perspective. If we look at Richard's first Irish campaign in 1394–5 we see that he treated with one "Niall Oge O'Neill . . . captain of his nation" (Curtis and McDowell 1977: 64–5; Curtis 1927). Nation here means the O'Neills, but then "nation" always implies identity and exclusion.

The problem of England's two pales, French and Irish, was perennial. Art Cosgrove maintains that: "By the opening of 1460 it had become clear that, while Henry VI ruled in England, his authority was no longer effective in the two English 'Pales'" (Cosgrove 1983: 25). The loss of Calais in 1558 ended England's ambitions there, though "France" persisted in the title of English monarchs. England's association with Ireland goes back to the twelfth century. The most famous account of this first colonial encounter, by Gerald of Wales, is reproduced in Holinshed, Shakespeare's chief historical source. As Richard McCabe notes, "Holinshed's Irish *Chronicles* came to form an integral part of 'English' history, a record not of 'conquest' but of confusion" (McCabe 2002: 66). This confusion arises from the Irish material being written from an English colonial perspective, or rather two English colonial perspectives across the two editions of 1577 and 1587. We need to curb our tendency to see early modern Ireland through the lens of recent events, or to see Shakespeare's depiction of it solely in terms of the events of the 1590s, or fifteenth century. We need to think of undercurrents as well as currency.

In *2 Henry VI*, while York plots, a post arrives:

> Great lord, from Ireland am I come amain
> To signify that rebels there are up
> And put the Englishmen unto the sword. (3.1.282–4)

York and Somerset debate who should go. The Cardinal intervenes:

> My lord of York, try what your fortune is.
> Th' uncivil kerns of Ireland are in arms
> And temper clay with blood of Englishmen.
> To Ireland will you lead a band of men
> Collected choicely, from each county some,
> And try your hap against the Irishmen? (3.1.309–14)

York accepts, and wastes no time in mustering his forces:

> within fourteen days
> At Bristol I expect my soldiers;
> For there I'll ship them all for Ireland. (3.1.327–9)

York's enemies suppose that out of sight is undermined. Highley comments: "As a permanent offstage location, a land literally outside the space of representation, Ireland confers a temporary invisibility upon York which his enemies wrongly assume to be disempowering" (Highley 1997: 43). Holding Irish office allows York to build an alternative power base, and to plot against the crown from a safe distance:

> Whiles I in Ireland nurse a mighty band,
> I will stir up in England some black storm
> Shall blow ten thousand souls to heaven or hell. (3.1.348–50)

York leaves behind Jack Cade, veteran of England's Irish wars:

> In Ireland have I seen this stubborn Cade
> Oppose himself against a troop of kerns. (3.1.360–1)

Within a few lines Cade the kern-killer becomes Cade the copycat, complimented on his affinity with those same kerns:

> Full often like a shag-haired crafty kern
> Hath he conversèd with the enemy
> And, undiscovered, come to me again
> And given me notice of their villainies. (3.1.367–70)

Cade's "tactical Gaelicization," made easier by his Irish birth, is later adopted by his master (Highley 1997: 52, 53). Cade also impersonates a claimant to the throne, in pretending to be a Mortimer, another link between himself and York. If Cade succeeds, York reflects,

> Why then from Ireland come I with my strength
> And reap the harvest which that coistrel sowed. (3.1.380–1)

The kernlike nature of Kentish Cade is compounded at the very moment his rebellion is suppressed, for York returns heading a host of Irish rebels. A messenger informs the king:

> The Duke of York is newly come from Ireland,
> And with a puissant and a mighty power
> Of galloglasses and stout Irish kerns
> Is marching hitherward in proud array. (4.8.25–8)

The stage direction "*Enter the Duke of* YORK *and his army of Irish*" mocks earlier claims that his arms were intended only to remove Somerset:

> From Ireland thus comes York to claim his right,
> And pluck the crown from feeble Henry's head. (5.1.1–2)

According to Highley, Shakespeare's inventive adaptation of Hall and Holinshed at this juncture serves "to make Ireland central to the inception and staging of rebellion within England," but Highley views this as part of "a larger centripetal movement in the first two parts of *Henry VI*, whereby the nation's geographical margins are seen as encroaching upon and contaminating the core" (Highley 1997: 49). If Shakespeare makes Ireland central does this not unsettle our notion of margins and core?

Ireland advanced York's claim in *2 Henry VI*, but foretells the end of the Yorkist reign in *Richard III*, where the king recalls a grim prediction:

> a bard of Ireland told me once
> I should not live long after I saw "Richmond". (4.2.108–9)

Shakespeare's histories show that Irish rebellion can be harnessed by royal claimants, and that the greatest threat to the crown lies in Ireland, but they also show that Ireland is a double-edged sword, as Richard II found to his cost on his second campaign.

Richard II: Banishing Woes

Richard II contains the longest leavetaking in Shakespearean drama. The king spends half the play going to Ireland and the other half coming back. Claimants, pretenders, and would-be usurpers aside, he was "the only English king to visit the country between 1210 and 1689" (Ellis 1985: 25). Commenting on Bolingbroke's banishment, Green observes:

> Well, he is gone, and with him go these thoughts.
> Now for the rebels which stand out in Ireland.
> Expedient manage must be made, my liege,
> Ere further leisure yield them further means
> For their advantage and your highness' loss. (1.4.36–40)

News of Gaunt's illness prompts the king to connect another noble lost with more resources:

> The lining of his coffers shall make coats
> To deck our soldiers for these Irish wars. (1.4.60–1)

Richard has, by his own admission, kept "too great a court," forcing hard-pressed subjects to underwrite – "subscribe" to – his Irish policy. Bolingbroke's banishment is one additional source of income, and another is promised with news of Gaunt's death, as the king remarks:

> Now for our Irish wars.
> We must supplant those rough rug-headed kerns,
> Which live like venom where no venom else
> But only they have privilege to live.
> And for these great affairs do ask some charge,
> Towards our assistance we do seize to us
> The plate, coin, revenues, and movables
> Whereof our uncle Gaunt did stand possessed. (2.1.156–63)

This infamous anti-Irish speech can be read as anti-courtly critique (Arden 1979a; 1979b; Maley 1997c; O'Brien 1979). The king exits, leaving his nobles, and Ross declares:

> He hath not money for these Irish wars,
> His burdenous taxations notwithstanding,
> But by the robbing of the banished Duke. (2.1.260–2)

Here we have all the elements of Shakespeare's Ireland, by turns a drain on resources, a convenient pretext for royal adventuring, an implicit critique of courtly excess, and a site of banishment and exile. Throughout the histories, Ireland is invoked as part of a back door theory (conduit for French or Spanish invasion); domino theory (if it goes, Wales and Scotland will follow, Kent and Cornwall too); and conspiracy theory (English rebels use it as a launch pad), and sometimes all three together.

Richard departs for Ireland, and his absence is his enemies' opportunity. Northumberland, asked to "be bold," explains that Bolingbroke's party "shortly mean to touch our northern shore":

> Perhaps they had ere this, but that they stay
> The first departing of the King for Ireland. (2.1.291–2)

Richard's blank charters have summoned a chartered fleet from Port le Blanc. Green tells the queen:

> I hope the King is not yet shipped for Ireland. (2.2.42)

York asks whether messengers have been sent to inform Richard of the threat, and raises again the question of cost:

> What, are there no posts dispatched for Ireland?
> How shall we do for money for these wars? (2.2.103–4)

Which wars? The "Irish wars" mentioned three times, or the civil wars that threaten with Bolingbroke's return from banishment?

Richard may have got wind of rebellion, but there's none to waft him back to England, as Bushy explains:

> The wind sits fair for news to go for Ireland,
> But none returns. (2.2.123–4)

Bushy and Green seek refuge from "the hateful commoners," but Bagot's loyalty takes him "to Ireland, to his majesty" (2.2.141). We don't follow Bushy, just as we never followed the king. Ireland is offstage, "the unseen realm to which Richard ventures" (Murphy 1999: 113).

In *1 Henry IV* Northumberland remarks that Richard

> did set forth
> Upon his Irish expedition,
> From whence he, intercepted, did return
> To be deposed, and shortly murderèd. (1.3.147–50)

Later, Hotspur accuses Henry IV of executing

> all the favourites that the absent King
> In deputation left behind him here
> When he was personal in the Irish war. (4.3.88–90)

Finally, Worcester petitions Henry, citing the circumstances that enabled him to usurp Richard, ending with:

> the contrarious winds that held the King
> So long in his unlucky Irish wars. (5.1.52–3)

The "unlucky Irish wars" affect how we read Shakespeare's English histories, as celebration, condemnation, or both.

Michael Neill says of *Richard II* that "the play's Irish dimension may have been one of the things that commended it to the Essex plotters in 1601":

Given Essex's conviction that his failure in Ireland was due to the parsimony of the queen's support, a play that featured the deposition of a monarch after a mistaken venture in Ireland may have seemed especially germane to their cause. (Neill 1994: 13, n. 50)

Richard II was hoist by his own parsimonious petard. He had money neither for his Irish wars nor the defence of his crown. The play transmitted a mixed message, attacking weak and wasteful monarchs, and showing what fate befalls the leader of an unsuccessful Irish expedition. Elizabeth thought she was Richard, John Hayward saw Essex as Bolingbroke, but the roles could be reversed (Hadfield 1997: 49).

Highley argues that "Shakespeare depicts Ireland as an expensive and dangerous distraction to England's rulers . . . The play offers no excuse for Richard's expedition, no sense that it is needed to secure the 'scept'red' isle itself . . . Richard never explains what he sees as Ireland's importance for England, nor does he justify risking his own person in the expedition" (Highley 1997: 65). There are several things wrong with this analysis. Firstly, although the play shows Richard appropriating resources for his Irish wars, it is made clear that it is not the wars that are costly but the court. Asked what has become of the king's "daily exactions" Northumberland answers:

> Wars hath not wasted it; for warred he hath not,
> But basely yielded upon compromise
> That which his ancestors achieved with blows.
> More hath he spent in peace than they in wars. (2.1.253–6)

This refers to Richard's earlier expedition, 1394–5, and echoes York's complaint in *2 Henry VI* that England was giving away its hard-won possessions. Secondly, to say that "the play offers no excuse for Richard's expedition, no sense that it is needed to secure the 'scept'red' isle itself" ignores the fact that the "scept'red" isle is a fiction kept in place through colonialism of the kind epitomized precisely by the Irish expedition. In any case, the play does offer an excuse for Richard's expedition. Green, remember, advises the king:

> Now for the rebels which stand out in Ireland.
> Expedient manage must be made, my liege,
> Ere further leisure yield them further means
> For their advantage and your highness' loss. (1.4.36–40)

Finally, Ireland's importance for England is taken as read by all the characters in the play. The dispute is between those who want the Irish wars prosecuted properly, but feel the crown is wasting treasure elsewhere, namely at court, and those, like Richard, who want to have it both ways, but end up yielding basely upon compromise abroad as a consequence of keeping too great a court at home. The parties in the play are not divided between those who want to go to Ireland and those who do not. Richard's opponents are not opposed to his Irish expedition but argue that it is not wars that have wasted his treasure but courtly excess. As for Richard's decision to go in person to Ireland, after York's Irish rebellion in *2 Henry VI* it is easy to see why a king might think it safer to oversee Ireland himself than entrust the task to another. Highley himself notes that "York's exploitation of his Irish commission taps into an enduring unease among England's rulers . . . that the office of lord deputy provided ambitious aristocrats with the chance to build a rival power-base to that of the monarch" (p. 44). As for Ireland being "an expensive and dangerous distraction," it needs "expedient manage." The true expense is an overblown court, not a neglected colony. That Shakespeare is less critical of Ireland than of England is something critics cannot grasp.

Henry V 3.3: British Ill Done

The play with most allusions to "England" and "Englishness," Shakespeare's most nationalist drama, contains his one Irish character, only Irish lines (the Irish English of Macmorris and the Erse of Pistol), and sole contemporary reference (to the Earl of Essex's Irish expedition of 1599). It also contains one of his most talked-about scenes. *Henry V* 3.3, a scene repeatedly reinvented in its reader's image, raises many questions, not least why it only appears in the First Folio (Albright 1928; Smith 1954). In the four captains scene, the Irish officer Macmorris is introduced favourably by the English Captain Gower:

> The Duke of Gloucester, to whom the order of the siege is given, is altogether directed by an Irishman, a very valiant gentleman, i'faith. (3.3.10–12)

The Welsh Captain Fluellen dogs Gower's observation with a question:

> It is Captain Macmorris, is it not?

The Irishman's identity confirmed, Fluellen counters Gower's good opinion:

> By Cheshu, he is an ass, as in the world. I will verify as much in his beard. He has no more directions in the true disciplines of the wars, look you – of the *Roman* disciplines – than is a puppy dog. (3.3.15–18)

Fluellen's obsession with "the *Roman* disciplines" sets up the national question that follows. Macmorris enters accompanied by Captain Jamy, the Scot, whom Fluellen compliments on his knowledge of "the disciplines of the pristine wars of the Romans." Hailed by Gower, Macmorris protests that the work is prematurely halted – "O 'tish ill done, 'tish ill done, by my hand 'tish ill done" (3.3.35) – at which point Fluellen "beseeches," or besieges, him:

> Captain Macmorris, I beseech you now, will you vouchsafe me, look you, a few disputations with you, as partly touching or concerning the disciplines of the war, the Roman wars, in the way of argument, look you, and friendly communication? Partly to satisfy my opinion and partly for the satisfaction, look you, of my mind. As touching the direction of the military discipline, that is the point. (3.3.36–42)

That is not the point. Fluellen factionally undermines Macmorris for the satisfaction of his mind. Macmorris, a lot on his mind, retorts:

> It is no time to discourse, so Chrish save me . . . The town is besieched. An the trumpet call us to the breach, and we talk and, be Chrish, do nothing, 'tis shame for us all. (3.3.46–50)

Fluellen's attempt to "beseech" Macmorris draws from the latter the protest that "the town is besieched," Jamy intervenes – "Marry, I wad full fain / heard some question 'tween you twae" (3.3.57–8) – whereat Fluellen obligingly provokes Macmorris into posing the question which remains the crux of national identity in Shakespeare's histories, a provocation framed so that an objection is envisaged "under your correction":

> *Fluellen.* Captain Macmorris, I think, look you, under your correction, there is not many of your nation –
> *Macmorris.* Of my nation? What ish my nation? Ish a villain and a bastard and a knave and a rascal? What ish my nation? Who talks of my nation? (3.3.59–63)

Fluellen, having besieged Macmorris, goes on the defensive:

> Look you, if you take the matter otherwise than is meant, Captain Macmorris, peradventure I shall think you do not use me with that affability as in discretion you ought to use me, look you, being as good a man as yourself, both in the disciplines of war and in the derivation of my birth, and in other particularities. (3.3.64–9)

Macmorris reacts violently to the suggestion that Fluellen is "as good a man" as himself (70–1). To Gower's interjection, "Gentlemen both, you will mistake each other," Jamy adds, "Ah, that's a foul fault" (72–3). They are gentlemen both, both gentlemen. According to Macmorris, "the trumpet call us to the breach." After the breach, a timely stage direction announces "*A parley*" and one is called for here, too, but this is no time to discourse of discipline.

Is Fluellen's concern with "the disciplines of the wars" on the battlefield a sign of indiscipline? He tells Gower in a subsequent scene "that there is no tiddle-taddle nor pibble-pabble in Pompey's camp," and later warns Williams to "keep out of prawls and prabbles and quarrels and dissensions" (4.1.70–1; 4.8.59–60), so perhaps he learned something from his exchange with Macmorris. Essex's *Lawes and orders of Warre, established for the good conduct of the service in Ireland* (1599) emphasize "military discipline":

> Forasmuch as no good service can be performed, or warre well managed when Military discipline is not observed; And Military discipline cannot bee kept where the Rules or chiefe partes thereof bee not certainly set downe and generally knowen: I have with the

advise of the Counsaile of Warre set downe these Lawes and Orders following, and doe now publish them under my hand, that all persons in this Armie or Kingdome within my charge, may take knowledge of the saide Lawes, and the penalties set downe for the breakers of them. (Devereux 1599, A)

There follow thirty-seven "Lawes and orders". Fluellen and Macmorris would be in breach of at least two, Items 3 – "Let no man blaspheme or pay loss, prison or Court Marshall will ensue" – and 7 – "No violent private quarrels in Campe or Garrison upon paine of death" (Devereux 1599: A2). Fluellen's breach of military etiquette – debating strategy in the field – undercuts his claim to "know the disciplines of war."

But the critical consensus on the scene is that Macmorris is at fault. Joseph Leerssen comments that Macmorris "bursts out in a wholly unreasonable non-sequitur effectively prohibiting Fluellen from coming to the point" (Leerssen 1986: 95). The *non sequitur* is Fluellen's. He trundles to the point and misses it, digressing from the pressing matter of the mines to the general principles of military discipline. It is Macmorris who is interrupted and undermined. The scene runs on twin-tracks, traveling in different directions. Macmorris's preoccupation with the siege ("The Duke of Gloucester, to whom the order of the siege is given, is altogether *directed* by an Irishman") parallels Fluellen's obsession with strategy ("touching the *direction* of the military discipline"). The link is "direction," a word Fluellen borrows from Gower: "He has no more *directions* in the true disciplines of the wars." This is a conversation at cross-purposes, two trains of thought running full tilt into a head-on collision. "Nation" is the trigger term, the point where a subordinate clause jumps the tracks.

The four captains scene is "a locus classicus in Shakespeare's representation of the colonized" (Baker 1993: 43). A target-rich environment, drawing fire away from other national questions, including Henry's identification with Fluellen – "For I am Welsh, you know, good countryman" (4.7.96) – Ireland has given rise to an outburst of criticism, directed mainly against Macmorris, in whom commentators see a stage Irishman upstaging a loyal Welshman. That they manage to reconcile his alleged unruliness with a reading of the scene as serving imperial power and "British" unity speaks volumes for their ingenuity. Patricia Parker sees it as "less a demonstration of integrity than of the argument and disunity that prevent these diverse forces from answering Henry's unifying call," but she goes on to speak of "Irish intractability," keeping the pressure on Macmorris (Parker 1996: 168, 181). I want to release some of that pressure.

David Beers Quinn sees the verbal volley Macmorris fires off as a sign "that [Fluellen's] loyalties to the English Crown do not submerge his own" (Quinn 1966: 161). This, the dominant critical position, is most trenchantly articulated in Philip Edwards's famous translation, "from the Irish," as it were:

The paraphrase should run something like this. "What is this separate race you're implying by using the phrase 'your nation'? Who are you, a Welshman, to talk of the Irish as though they were a separate nation from you? I belong in this family as much as you do". This is the essence of it – indignation that a Welshman should think of Ireland as a separate nation from the great (British) nation to which the Welshman apparently thought he belonged. (Edwards 1979: 75–6)

What ish my indignation? Ish a margin and a border and a periphery and a region? Edwards makes Macmorris a Unionist before the fact. Moreover, Fluellen claimed the king as Welsh, rather than protesting his own Britishness. There was – is – no British nation, merely a state composed of several nations. Michael Neill is unconvinced by Edwards's paraphrase: "It seems to me virtually impossible to determine exactly what [Macmorris] means, and that his inarticulacy on the topic of nationality is precisely Shakespeare's point" (Neill 1994: 19). I agree with the first part of Neill's sentence but the attribution of inarticulacy to Macmorris – rather than a whole critical tradition – is unjust. Modern readings clearly derive from twentieth-century preoccupations rather than textual or contextual evidence.

Others take Edwards at his word. Declan Kiberd, after quoting Macmorris, remarks: "In other words, the captain says that there is no Irish nation . . . some of the Irishman's first notable words in English literature are spoken as a denial of his own otherness" (Kiberd 1995: 12, 13). Other words, not Fluellen's or Macmorris's. The denial is on the part of the critics. To Dollimore and Sinfield, the scene "seems to effect an effortless incorporation, one in which, as Philip Edwards has pointed out, the Irish Macmorris is even made to protest that he does not belong to a distinct nation," yet within a few lines they remark that "Ireland was the great problem – the one Essex was supposed to resolve," which sits awkwardly alongside their endorsement of Edwards (Dollimore and Sinfield 1985a: 224). David Baker also translates Macmorris's question: "What does it mean, Macmorris seems to ask, to be "of" a nation when you have no recognized nation, when those who insist that you are "Irish" also deny the existence of something called "Ireland," except perhaps as a colonial adjunct, a debased subsidiary to England, the only true nation?" (Baker 1993: 44–5). Baker's question comes only a few pages after condoning Kiberd's controversial claim that the English invented Ireland (p. 38). Does England deny the existence of its own invention? Who is dissing Ireland and Macmorris? Who sees England as "the only true nation"? Baker takes issue with those for whom "this scene is a site triumphantly occupied by the English power, and thus empty of any voice but one":

> Here, Macmorris the Irishman, along with Fluellen the Welshman and Jamy the Scots-man, those other ethnic "types" whose accents are heard in *Henry V*, are entirely absorbed into the colonizers' racial typology and reduced to ludicrous caricatures. (Ibid: 45)

By whom? Who reduces Fluellen and Macmorris to "ludicrous caricatures"? Not Gower, who regards Macmorris as "a very valiant gentleman, i' faith" (3.3.11–12). Not King Henry, who identifies with Fluellen: "For I am Welsh, you know, good countryman" (4.7.96). Baker acutely discerns that the "disparities" of the four captains scene "find their best register . . . in the very criticism that tries to police the passage":

> In order to resolve the dispute between Fluellen and Macmorris into something like a civil "communication," critics have resorted to finishing Fluellen's sentence for him, to paraphrasing MacMorris' riposte, and then to re-paraphrasing him. (Baker 1993: 46)

Far from being univocal, in the four captains scene "the voicing of imperial power gives way to a discursive heterogeneity, interrogates itself, and finds itself unable to sustain the distinctions on which it rests" (ibid). But Baker cannot resist the temptation to paraphrase, and hazards another attempt, this time to translate Fluellen's suspended sentence, "an act of linguistic colonialism":

> In Fluellen's remark, we catch colonialist discourse in the act of producing Macmorris as an "Irish" subject. He implies that as an Irishman Macmorris can be named and categorized, that however few there might be of his kind, together they form a recognizable "nation" within the colonizer's racial scheme. He assumes, that is, that this English word *refers* to the Irish, and thus he assigns Macmorris a distinct (although certainly subordinate) place in the grammar of imperial power. The Irish, like the Welsh, Fluellen implies, are "under . . . correction," and he expects to be answered in the same terms he employs. As in the colonies themselves, the English language serves to define the colonized. (Ibid: 46–7)

Fluellen's suspended sentence had as its subject military discipline. Macmorris's "kind" or "nation" was not the subject of the sentence. Michael Cronin likewise finishes Fluellen's sentence so that the Welshman "notes that there are not many of Macmorris' 'nation' on the battlefield" (Cronin 1997: 197). Neither the grammar of Fluellen's interrupted question, nor the context, suggests that he was going to ask Macmorris about the population of Ireland, or the numbers of Irish in France. "Nation" is no more "English" than "colony." No sense of subordination surfaces in Fluellen's speech, except his own insubordination in broaching, and thus breaching, discipline in the field. Item 13 of Essex's *Lawes and orders of Warre* reads simply: "No insubordination" (Devereux 1599: A2), and while Fluellen is "as good a man as" Macmorris, in pursuing a private quarrel he is arguably guilty of insubordination. Despite Baker's suggestion, Fluellen does not denigrate Macmorris as "certainly subordinate," but assumes his Irish colleague is his equal, even in matters of military discipline:

> being as good a man as yourself, both in the disciplines of war and in the derivation of my birth, and in other particularities.

The "correction" Fluellen anticipates is keyed to the topic of strategy. Macmorris chooses to correct him on another of his terms.

No critic can resist paraphrasing, however bizarre the effort, not even me. Fluellen's finished sentence might read: "Captain Macmorris, I think, look you, under your correction, there is not many of your nation directed in the true disciplines of the wars, look you – of the *Roman* disciplines." Baker ventures a further paraphrase: "Another way to put this is that, while Fluellen's half-sentence implies all the answers that make up colonialism's 'truth,' Macmorris' outburst rephrases these answers as the questions they were designed to preclude. His queries are thus definitive for (and defined by) colonialist discourse" (Baker 1993: 50). The outburst is Fluellen's. Baker rephrases Edwards rephrasing Macmorris rephrasing Fluellen. Rephrasing is risky. After all, the only truth Fluellen has faith in is "the true disciplines of the wars."

Macmorris has certainly come to be "defined by . . . colonialist discourse." Baker asks:

> Who, after all, "ish" Macmorris? Who is this self-alienated character, a foreigner in an English army, and what does "nation" mean when he says it? Has he borrowed an English term to denote an Irish synonym (which is?), or is he speaking now as an Englishman, fracturing a language other than his native dialect? (Ibid: 48)

Synonym? A nation is a Nym with a Pistol. For Baker, Macmorris's "inability to utter the copula, to say 'is' as the English would have said it, becomes a sign of the ambiguity which invades assigned identity when Macmorris speaks their language" (ibid). Whose language? Shakespeare's English characters speak "broken" French and Irish, broken English too. They say "Tis," less "English" to our ears than when the plays were written. In a play where the only Irish line is uttered by an Englishman in France, one should not be too hasty to assign languages. David Lindley, reading Jonson's Irish masque, puts scare quotes around "standard" English, reminding readers no such thing obtained in the period (Lindley 1986: 353). As Michael Cronin remarks:

> It is an ironic feature of Shakespeare's posthumous reputation that, although he was promoted as the literary incarnation of English linguistic greatness, his plays contain within them attitudes towards language difference, particularly with respect to the Celtic rim, that are by no means triumphalist and homogeneous. (Cronin 1997: 201)

We should be wary of phrases like "Celtic rim," which play into the hands of Anglocentrism, but wary too of Celticism, like Matthew Arnold's infamous claim that Shakespeare "touches the Celtic note so exquisitely that perhaps one is inclined to be always looking for the Celtic note in him" (Arnold 1867: 126; Cronin 1997: 205).

Macmorris's questioning style is contagious. Andrew Hadfield asks: "What is Macmorris asking here? Is he denying the efficacy of his Irishness and affirming a solidarity with the other Britons with whom he is fighting? Or is he anticipating an attack on his national identity and so preparing to defend the loyalty of the Irish to the English/British crown?" (Hadfield 1997: 50). Same difference, surely? Heads you win, tails you don't lose. In a scene full of questions, must we confine ourselves to one? Macmorris fires off a battery. As Philip Edwards notes, the subject of the central question – "Ish a villain and a bastard and a knave and a rascal?" – "may be

Ireland, Macmorris, or Fluellen" (Edwards 1979: 248–9). Baker adds England to the mix, remarking that "MacMorris' assertive voice shifts within the multidirectional terms of his speech" (Baker 1993: 48). Is the villain he who talks of "my Nation" whether that nation is Macmorris's or anyone else's? According to Andrew Gurr: "MacMorris's outburst . . . might be said to fit his role in the English army, just as well as it fits his Irishness. Mercenaries were thought to be rascals and knaves and villains, and had no nation, as the French Herald's segregation of them from the French dead affirms" (Gurr 1989: 372). This turns Macmorris, Gower's "valiant gentleman," into one of those "stout Irish kerns" York went to Ireland to fight and returned leading in *2 Henry VI*.

Macmorris is introduced in complimentary terms, identified as an Irishman directing an English duke, and praised by an English captain. The stage Irishman of Shakespeare criticism is a much more sophisticated character in the play, complimented even by the colleague who thinks him an "ass" with respect to "the true disciplines of the wars." To Gloucester, he's valuable. To Gower, he's valiant. To Fluellen, as good a man as himself. To critics out to scapegoat and stereotype him, a "barbarian [who] must be absorbed and converted into the tropes of English colonial power; in this sense the threatening difference Macmorris represents is furiously repudiated" (Baker 1993: 50). Critically, it certainly is. Michael Neill sees Macmorris as a "disruptive" influence who "must be banished from the action" – hence his failure to reappear, but the banishing is critical, not dramatic (Neill 1995: 272; Berger 1985).

Gary Taylor conjectures that the four captains scene was cut from the 1600 Quarto because "The Irishman may have seemed rather less funny after Essex's return than he did in spring of 1599" (Taylor 1982: 313). I never laughed first time round, and neither did Michael Cronin: "To characterize the encounter between Macmorris, Fluellen and the others as simply a failed exercise in verbal comedy is to miss the point. In a play . . . dominated by the problematic of translation – emotional, political and linguistic – and haunted by the nightmare of non-equivalence [this scene] takes on a significance that far exceeds the tribute of easy laughter" (Cronin 1997: 199–200).

Joel Altman argues that "theatergoers attending a performance of the Lord Chamberlain's servants as they played the matter of France in a London beset by the matter of Ireland in the spring of 1599 are not likely to have experienced it in a simple way," but then alludes to the "audience's deep-seated hostility toward a notoriously barbaric neighbor" (Altman 1991: 4, 7). Who talks of my nation? Shakespeare creates an Irish captain praised by an English duke and an English colleague. The critics conjure up a barbarous stereotype.

Although he goes on to complicate Macmorris's identity in productive ways, Andrew Murphy says "we are presented with an English army that is . . . paradigmatic of the nation as a whole, as its membership is shown to include English, Welsh, Scots, and Irish representatives" (Murphy 1996: 51). But how do we get from the make-up of an army – notoriously diverse in the period – to "the nation as a whole"? And what "nation"? This is where Macmorris comes in. The "furious repudiation of difference" detected by Edwards is an apt characterization of critical reactions to this scene.

Ish it a margin? For Jonathan Dollimore and Alan Sinfield, "the Irish, Welsh and Scottish soldiers manifest not their countries' centrifugal relationship to England but an ideal subservience of margin to centre" (Dollimore and Sinfield 1985a: 217). Claire McEachern sees margins within margins:

> Caricature functions to isolate Macmorris, but in Fluellen's leek-wearing it serves to assimilate cultural chauvinism to the totality of Britain via a tolerance for a bit of quaintness. Although Fluellen is "a little out of fashion" . . . as Henry puts it, he clearly ranks as the favored subcultural exponent, with an authority both guaranteed and subordinated by an ethnic kinship to Henry himself. (McEachern 1996: 107)

Phrases like "the totality of Britain" and "tolerance for a bit of quaintness" are out of place with regard to the play, but reflect a critical conviction, that Britain is a totality even before it exists and that "quaintness" – or cultural difference – is to be tolerated at best. This discourse of totality and (in)tolerance produces the subculture it purports to uncover. McEachern cites Henry's claims to Welshness, but not in a way that explains what's "subcultural" about it, or the ethnicities of Jamy or Macmorris. Similarly, Highley speaks of a "meeting of margins and center," but the marginal figures in this scene are Scottish and English (Highley 1997: 146). The meeting of minds, and mines, is Irish and Welsh.

According to Stephen Greenblatt:

> By yoking together diverse peoples – represented in the play by the Welshman Fluellen, the Irishman Macmorris, and the Scotsman Jamy, who fight at Agincourt alongside the loyal Englishmen – Hal symbolically tames the last wild areas in the British Isles, areas that in the sixteenth century represented, far more powerfully than any New World people, the doomed outposts of a vanishing tribalism. (Greenblatt 1985: 42)

To speak of a "New World" and describe Scotland, Wales, and Ireland as "the last wild areas of the British Isles" or "the doomed outposts of a vanishing tribalism" is problematic. Any allusion to a politically charged geographical entity called "the British Isles" is questionable. British ill done! Where is the Englishman Gower in Greenblatt's summary, the captain who considered Macmorris to be "valiant" rather than "vanishing"? Michael Neill invokes "warring Irish septs," but what of those warring English septs who are the stuff of Shakespeare's histories? Whose language is this? That of the sixteenth century, or that of a critical tradition that assumes the incivility of the non-English nations of the emerging British state?

Ish it a region? Are Ireland, Wales, and Scotland nations making up a nascent (now senescent) multi-nation state, or are they regions (together with Kent and Cornwall) of a British nation that is merely England writ large? Cronin refers to "regional dialects" and McEachern speaks of "regional captains" and their "dialects," but the words "region" and "dialects" are absent from the text (Cronin 1997: 196; McEachern 1996: 127). A language is a dialect with an army and a navy. Macmorris does not ask what is his region. Citing G. L. Brook's *The Language of Shakespeare* to the effect that "native dialects had acquired the status of national languages," Michael Cronin counters, claiming that while the "Celtic languages, Welsh and Gaelic" are national, Scots and Irish English are not (Cronin 1997: 199). This goes with the grain of colonialism. All talk of "region" and "dialect" is implicitly imperialist. In the play itself, Gower upbraids Pistol for mistaking Fluellen's Welshness as a sign of weakness, and appropriately enough he does so in a language that needs glossing:

> I have seen you gleeking and galling at this gentleman twice or thrice. You thought, because he could not speak English in the native garb, he could not therefore handle an English cudgel. You find it otherwise. And henceforth let a Welsh correction teach you a good English condition. (5.1.66–70)

This is the same Gower who referred to Macmorris as "valiant," so perhaps an Irish correction is required for those critics who have been "gleeking and galling" at Shakespeare's Irish captain.

Ish it a colony? Ish it a kingdom? Within a few years of the Kildare Rebellion, the first great Old English rising of the sixteenth century, Henry VIII declared himself King of Ireland (Bradshaw 1977; Ellis 1976). He had hitherto styled himself *Dominus Hibernia*, lord of Ireland. Henry VIII's Irish parliament turned a lordship into a kingship through "An act that the king of England, his heirs and his successors be kings of Ireland" (Curtis and McDowell 1977: 77). According to Karl Bottigheimer, "the promotion of Ireland to a kingdom in 1541 was little more than an overzealous declaration of intent" (Bottigheimer 1978: 46). Brendan Bradshaw maintains that the act had the ironic effect of encouraging the Old English "to regard themselves more as subjects of the kingdom of Ireland than as subjects of the Crown of England" (Bradshaw 1973: 77). For Edmund Spenser:

> by this Act of Parliament . . . nothing was given to King Henry which he had not before from his auncestors, but only the bare name of a King . . . what needed afterwards to enter into any such idle termes with them to be called their King, when it is in the power of the conqueror to take upon himself what title he will, over his dominions conquered. For all is the conquerors, as Tully to Brutus saith. (Spenser 1997: 18)

Richard II, asking "Is not the King's name forty thousand names?" (3.2.81), got a short reply. Despite the shared skepticism of Irish historians and English colonists, some literary critics lay great emphasis on the shift from colony to kingdom. For Michael Neill:

> It is difficult to overestimate the significance of this statute for the subsequent direction of Irish affairs, for it marks the point at which wholesale incorporation of the native

Irish into the body politic defined by English settlement became, for the first time, legally enunciated policy. Under this new dispensation a systematic war of subjugation could be presented not as the aggressive conquest of an alien people but as a defensive operation designed to secure the good order of the realm against rebels. (Neill 1994: 5)

Neill maintains that the act of kingly title "made assimilation a policy," but the statutes of Kilkenny, passed in 1366 – and issued in French – constitute a more thorough platform for that policy (Curtis and McDowell 1977: 52–9). The thirty-six statutes aimed to restore a colony deemed to have declined from its original purity. This legislation set the scene for the mixture of assimilation and intolerance evident in the sixteenth century. David Baker, in a convoluted argument, concludes that Ireland, the medieval lordship converted into a kingdom in 1541, was becoming a colony in Shakespeare's time (Baker 1997). Like Spenser, I prefer to see the act of kingly title as a blip on the screen.

Baker takes the New Historicists to task for their Anglocentrism, citing insensitivity to the non-English constituents of the emerging British state, including Greenblatt's glib characterization of Fluellen, Jamy, and Macmorris as "humorous grotesques . . . puppets jerked on the strings of their own absurd accents." But Baker himself presents us with a Fluellen endowed with an "amiably accented English" and, more tellingly, offers a Macmorris who, speaking "in an often overwrought dialect, is finally reduced to outraged and stammering questions," odd given the weight Baker attaches to the process of questioning and his central thesis that Britain is itself "a question" (Baker 1997: 23, 29). Ireland is "an intractable anomaly," but Macmorris proves all too tractable in the hands of the critics, "reduced to spitting incoherence" (Neill 1995: 272). Critics can juggle complexity with obviousness. Murphy sees the non-English captains lacking "linguistic competence" while insisting that Macmorris's speech is "a profoundly ambiguous passage" (Murphy 1999: 117, 118). Is ambiguity a sign of incompetence? Murphy makes much of the variations in Macmorris's name in speech prefixes across editions, but the variation between his speeches and the critical consensus that surrounds them is more perturbing (Murphy 1997: 227).

Critics conclude that the play offers "a voicing of imperial authority and *only* of that authority" only by playing down the significance of Macmorris's question, or paraphrasing him in the manner of Edwards (Baker 1993: 43). When a critic asks "Who *is* speaking in Macmorris' absurdly broken English?" one must respond with another question, "*Who* is speaking of Macmorris' absurdly broken English?" In this case, Baker (p. 44). For Gary Taylor, "Macmorris has sometimes made a vivid if rather crude impression – partly because the problems of the British in Ireland have continued to lend his part the thrill of topical interest" (Taylor 1982: 44). But more than "the thrill of topical interest" motivates the caricaturing of Shakespeare's only Irish character, who gets a better deal from Gower, Gloucester, and Shakespeare than from modern commentators.

Chris Ivic comes closer to the mark: "Rather than reading Macmorris's 'What is my nation?' as a plea for identity, whether Irish or (Old or New) English, it is crucial to interpret this line as an interrogative that complicates the simplistic identity politics that has served to essentialize the identities of the intermingling inhabitants of the British Isles" (Ivic 1999a: 92). Again that vexed phrase "the British Isles," which puts on the map that which it seems merely to map out. Ivic still sees Fluellen disciplining Macmorris, rather than Macmorris correcting Fluellen's undisciplined broaching of discipline. Ivic says "Fluellen's 'correction' . . . of Macmorris breaks off," but the correction is Macmorris's: "Captain Macmorris, I think, look you, under your / correction, there is not many of your nation —" (3.3.59–60). Moreover, Gower's intervention refers to both gentlemen mistaking each other, and Jamy's wish is to "see some question 'tween you twae." So why is Macmorris singled out for correction, pathologized and patronized? In a later version of his essay, Baker contends that Macmorris's question "is not a throwaway query from a minor character representing a subordinate people. It is the question that confronted every English member of Shakespeare's audience and the question that both organized and disturbed *Henry V* – until its powerful interrogations were erased" (Baker 1997: 44). Let the allusion to "a subordinate people" pass. Baker's position is taken up by Murphy, who maintains that Macmorris's question "has as much force for Shakespeare the English writer as it has for Shakespeare's Irish soldier" (Murphy 1999: 119). If Macmorris is "Old English" then the Englishness of Shakespeare's audience, even Shakespeare himself, seems less secure.

Neill alludes to Macmorris's "broken English," a phrase applied to French Katherine in the play, imagining Fluellen and Macmorris "confined to the kingdom of [their] own language," borrowing a celebrated phrase of Spenser's and turning English aspiration into Celtic confinement (Neill 1994: 19–20). Neill also speaks of "the wild Macmorris" – and later of "the wild Irish" – which jars with Gower's complimentary characterization of "a very valiant gentleman." Later, Neill refers to "Elizabeth's plantation of the Irish wilderness" (p. 32). Does he mean the rich pastures snapped up by English planters? The risk here and elsewhere is that critics are complicit with colonialist propaganda. Neill remarks that "To be Welsh or Scots (or perhaps even Irish) is to be a subspecies of English; and to speak a dialect of English is to reveal an English heart," but "subspecies" and "dialect" are Neill's terms, just as "subcultural" is McEachern's, and "a debased subsidiary to England" is Baker's. The language of criticism is saturated by the very prejudice it claims to discern in the texts.

Henry V 5.0: A Chorus of Disapproval

The Chorus in *Henry V* 5.0 compares the king's return to London with the repatriation of another heroic figure, generally thought to be the second Earl of Essex. Henry's homecoming is first compared with Caesar's to Rome, then, less enthusiastically, with Essex's anticipated arrival from Ireland:

> As, by a lower but high-loving likelihood,
> Were now the General of our gracious Empress —

> As in good time he may – from Ireland coming,
> Bringing rebellion broachèd on his sword,
> How many would the peaceful city quit
> To welcome him! Much more, and much more cause,
> Did they this Harry. (5.0.29–35)

For Highley, "The Chorus's syntactically ambivalent lines about Henry convey the exact sense of uncertainty, the mixture of danger and excitement surrounding Essex in Ireland" (Highley 1997: 158). Is the ambivalence aimed at Henry V, or "the General of our gracious Empress"? Is this a dig at Elizabeth? After all, a real empress would have an empire, not an underfunded colony up in arms. The words "lower" and "much more cause" certainly cast doubt on the worthiness of the Irish expedition. The subject of rebellion is broached, but whose? And which "General"? If Essex, as commonly assumed, then is this, as Gary Taylor asserts in his introduction to the Oxford edition, a unique instance of Shakespearean topicality?:

> Reflections of contemporary history have been suspected in many of Shakespeare's plays, but the allusion to the Irish expedition in 5.0.29–34 is the only explicit, extra-dramatic, incontestable reference to a contemporary event anywhere in the canon. (Taylor 1982: 7)

There were many Irish expeditions in Shakespeare's time, and it's hard to see what's "extra-dramatic" about this, unless we take "extra" to mean extremely, or uttered by extras, who have their part to play in drama and history.

For Annabel Patterson, the Chorus in 5.0 "demands that we juggle at least two meanings of 'history' . . . the fifteenth-century history that Shakespeare took over from Holinshed and others and rewrote to his own specifications, and the events in which he and his theater were environmentally situated in the late 1590s, and to some extent embroiled" (Patterson 1989: 71). This assumes Holinshed was not already caught up in the history of the 1570s and 1580s, as Patterson has elsewhere shown (Patterson 1994). It also assumes that fifteenth-century history was not already caught up in earlier histories. Holinshed is certainly caught up in the history of the twelfth century. Critics suggest that Macmorris is an Old Englishman, whose "hybrid surname" is "a Gallicized version of Fitzmaurice", and thus a fusion of French and Irish (Neill 1994: 19).

In his note on *Henry V* 5.0 Taylor says the general in question is "Almost certainly Robert Devereux, Earl of Essex, who left England on 27 March 1599 to suppress Tyrone's rebellion in Ireland" (Taylor 1982: 260). This argues for a date of May or June for completion of Shakespeare's play. Keith Brown maintains that an Essex victory was anticipated in August, but whatever the month mooted, such dating depends on the general being the particular – Essex – and the rebellion being Tyrone's, rather than his own (Brown 1986). According to Taylor, "though the allusion to Essex is unquestionably complimentary, the sting in its tale [*sic*] ('much more, *and much more cause*, / Did they this Harry') deserves more attention than it seems to have attracted" (Taylor 1982: 7). True, but might the allusion, if to Essex, be barbed in more ways than one, the rebellion his own, like York in *2 Henry VI*, one of the plays alluded to by the Chorus in the Epilogue? Taylor goes on to argue that this "extra-dramatic" reference betrays an underlying – subtextual – preoccupation with Ireland:

> What can hardly be disputed is the playwright's preoccupation with Irish affairs: from Captain Macmorris, Shakespeare's only Irish character (3.3), to the "kern of Ireland" and "foul bogs" (3.7.51–5), through Pistol's "*Calin o custure me*" (4.4.4), to the general "from Ireland coming" (5.0.29–34), the revealing textual error in "So happy be the issue, brother Ireland" (5.2.12), and Henry's promise to Catherine that "England is thine, Ireland is thine, France is thine" (5.2.230). This preoccupation the dramatist could confidently expect his audience to share; just as confidently he could expect their enthusiastic assent to Ely's call for "exploits and mighty enterprises" (1.2.121). (Ibid: 7–8)

But what if the sting in the tail was there at the play's head? What if confident expectation was not merely misplaced but contested? What if, as in *Richard II*, Ireland entailed risk and ruin? What if the "audience" was divided in its support of English adventurers in Ireland, as Donne's epistle to Henry Wotton, and Fluellen's allusion to "Alexander the Pig" suggest? (Highley 1997: 134–63; Murphy 1994; Quint 1982; Spencer 1996). What then? A question mark hovers over the play's patriotism. Patricia Palmer complains that "When writing about early modern Ireland, postcolonialists' fixation on English literary texts – once more unto the breach with *Henry V* – quite unintentionally ends up representing colonial discourse as triumphantly omnipotent," but the critics – and the Quarto – are at fault (Palmer 2001: 5).

Taylor's "revealing textual error" reveals an intriguing approach to editing. Something not in the text – "Essex" – is put in, something in the text – "Ireland" – taken out. Those who note the absence of the reference to Essex in the Quarto forget it's not in the Folio either. Andrew Gurr judges "brother Ireland" to be a compositor's "misreading" (Gurr 1992: 214). Ivic rightly argues that to correct this supposed slip or misreading "is to purge the text of one of its most unsettling moments" (Ivic 1999a: 96). In his introduction Taylor refers to this "error" when crying foul on the Folio:

> one error in particular – the substitution of "Ireland" for the clearly required "England" in "So happy be the issue brother Ireland" (5.2.12) seems almost certain to be Shakespeare's own "Freudian slip" – a slip natural enough in 1599, a hundred lines after Shakespeare's reference to the Essex expedition in 5.0, but most unlikely to have been made by a later scribe or compositor. (Taylor 1982: 18)

The only slip here – besides punctuation – is the one that deletes "Ireland" and inserts "the Essex expedition," nowhere alluded to explicitly.

As Ivic observes, "Although many theories exist as to why the First Folio includes 'brother Ireland,' they are all based on the dubious assumption that Shakespeare intended 'brother England'" (Ivic 1999a: p. 94). In context, "brother Ireland" makes perfect sense. First, Henry salutes "our brother France and . . . our sister" (5.2.2), then Charles salutes Henry as "brother England" (5.2.10), before France's sister, Queen Isabel, utters the alleged error: "So happy be the issue, brother Ireland." Henry is "France," "England," "Ireland," titles held by conquest in two cases, usurpation in the other. Henry's subsequent speech informing Catherine that "England is thine, Ireland is thine, France is thine" (5.2.230–1) suggests that all is in order. In *3 Henry VI* Edward IV is proclaimed

> by the grace of God King of
> England and France, and Lord of Ireland. (4.8.71–2)

Note that Edward is "Lord of Ireland," not king. Neill, in his essay accompanying the Folger edition of the play, which retains "Brother Ireland," notes that the issue of it being substituted for "Brother England" may not be the "revealing textual error" which earlier editors have assumed (Neill 1995: 243). The fact that Henry VIII declared himself King of Ireland in 1541 adds weight to the suggestion that an English king could be referred to as Brother Ireland.

Neill suggests that the "general" may be Essex's successor, Lord Mountjoy, a name significant both in the play and in Shakespeare's life (Hopkins 1997: 15; Neill 1994: 20; Taylor 1982: 7). If the general is the particular, a further complication arises. The Essex expedition of 1599 was not the first. Fathers and sons are vital to *Henry V*, where Hal is haunted by his (Erickson 1988). Essex is haunted too. His father, Walter Devereux, first Earl of Essex, was in Ireland in the 1570s, served by the young Hugh O'Neill, later Earl of Tyrone (nemesis of the second earl). Walter Devereux died in Dublin in 1576 before Philip Sidney, serving under his father, Sir Henry, the Lord Deputy, could reach him. The 1587 edition of Holinshed memorialized this original Essex expedition, which expedited Essex's death:

> The first Earl of Essex's abortive plans to colonize various parts of Ulster are praised on the grounds that "he was . . . of so heroicall a mind, that if his abilitie had answered his good will, he had not bin a second, neither to Lacie, nor to Courcie, nor to anie the first conquerors of Ulster to the crowne of England". (McCabe 2002: 59–60)

Thus a failed Essex attempt at subduing the Irish, bound up with Hugh O'Neill, predates Shakespeare's play, and is prominently placed in his major historical source, admitting defeat, but acknowledging heroism.

In Shakespeare's histories Ireland stands for several things. First, for cultural confusion. Macmorris is not the only one confused about national identity. Henry V thinks he's England, France, Wales, Ireland, and he has a point, or a claim. For banishment and exile, since Bolingbroke's is bound up with Richard's Irish campaign. For breaches, including the bracketing or broaching of rebellion. Patricia Parker reminds us that "broached" in *Henry V* 5.0 is "a term that might also be interpreted in relation to the imagery of breaching in the play" (Parker 1996: 332, n. 37). For conquest, including self-conquest. For the body, particularly the nether regions or posterior. (England must protect its rear.) For barbarism, epitomized by rug-headed kerns, but also by crafty kernlike English rebels, "Irish" in their opposition. For republicanism, or at least covert criticism of the court, including Richard's own admission that royal excess has depleted resources, making heavy taxation essential to the prosecution of England's Irish wars. And finally, for warfare in the extreme, for brutality, massacre and siege, projected and performed.

The critical attitude to Macmorris betrays a larger social prejudice. Michael Neill invites us to contrast two modes of speech: "*Henry V* lurches to and fro between, at the one extreme, the Chorus's intoxicated visions of chivalric glory and the King's charismatic oratory of martial brotherhood, and, at the other, the degraded, increasingly vicious buffoonery of Eastcheap" (Neill 1995: 262–3). This is the same Henry V who stands for butchery and rape. Neill does see the two modes mirroring one another, but takes insufficient notice for my liking of his own language. The critic who finds "charismatic oratory" on one side, and "degraded, increasingly vicious buffoonery" on the other, has already taken sides.

Christopher Highley, in his efforts to distance Shakespeare from the colonial enterprise, offers a different perspective:

> In *Henry V*, Shakespeare's misgivings about Essex together with an awareness of burgeoning public alarm at the war in Ireland produce a skeptical counter-discourse about English expansionism within the British Isles. (Highley 1997: 135–6)

That "skeptical counter-discourse about English expansionism within the British Isles" should extend to the term "the British Isles." Such skepticism is arguably present as early as *2 Henry VI*, and is certainly evident in *Richard II*. But it is not necessarily a skepticism about expansionism. Rather, it is a skepticism about the colonial subtext of political authority, the economic underpinnings of the state, and the uses of exile. There is more at issue than imperialism or anti-imperialism in England's engagement with Ireland – like ideology and strategy. Opposition to Essex's Irish campaign need not mean opposition to Essex. Those most in favor of Robert Devereux being appointed Lord Lieutenant of Ireland may not have had his best interests at heart. The post of Irish viceroy was a double-edged sword, as Richard II found to his cost when he assumed the role personally. Essex, after what happened to his father, would have known the risks of assuming Irish office: "From the start, Essex knew that his leadership of the Irish campaign was a dangerous gamble that promised him either glory or disgrace" (Highley 1997: 157).

Skepticism about the motives behind sending a prominent figure to Ireland surfaces in Shakespeare's last history. The bard of England is still harping on Ireland as late as *Henry VIII* (1613), where two gentlemen discuss Buckingham's treason trial, blaming Cardinal Wolsey:

First Gentleman. . . . first, Kildare's attainder.
Then deputy of Ireland, who, removed,
Earl Surrey was sent thither – and in haste, too,
Lest he should help his father.
Second Gentleman.   That trick of state
Was a deep envious one.
First Gentleman.   At his return
No doubt he will requite it. This is noted,
And generally: whoever the king favours,
The Card'nal instantly will find employment –
And far enough from court, too. (2.1.42–9)

For King read Queen, for Cardinal read Cecil, for Surrey read Essex or York. The "trick of state" played throughout Shakespeare's histories – and English history – uses Ireland as a cover for anti-courtly criticism and a convenient posting for potential troublemakers, a source of rebellion in a double sense. The idea that Ireland was a form of exile is here related specifically to faction and court intrigue.

Surrey returns from Ireland to confront Wolsey, accusing the Cardinal of bringing down "noble Buckingham, my father-in-law":

Plague of your policy,
You sent me deputy for Ireland,
Far from his succour, from the King, from all
That might have mercy on the fault thou gav'st him. (3.2.260–2)

Plague of policy or trick of state, the use of Ireland as a last post for touchy subjects is a recurring feature of the histories, and of the criticism that they engender. John Joughin, reporting on the 1997 Dublin conference on "Shakespeare and Ireland," saw in the Essex allusion "a staple of potential dissent" and "another productive textual glitch" in Macmorris's national question (Joughin 1997: 79). I have examined both staple and glitch at length here in order to expose the colonial subtext which underpins the loaded language of criticism. Declan Kiberd, with whom I began, remarks that "Macmorris is the first known exponent on English soil of a now-familiar literary mode: the extracted confession. So he is made to say what his audiences want to hear" (Kiberd 1995: 13). For audiences, read critics.

References and Further Reading

All references to Shakespeare's plays are to *The Norton Shakespeare (based on the Oxford Edition)* (1997), ed. S. Greenblatt, W. Cohen, J. E. Howard, and K. E. Maus. London and New York: W. W. Norton.

Albright, E. M. (1928). The Folio Version of *Henry V* in Relation to Shakespeare's Times. *Publications of the Modern Languages Association*, 43, 722–56.

Altman, J. B. (1991). "Vile participation": The Amplification of Violence in the Theatre of *Henry V. Shakespeare Quarterly*, 42, 1–32.

Andrews, J. H. (1983). Appendix: The Beginnings of the Surveying Profession in Ireland – Abstract. In S. Tyacke (ed.) *English Map-Making 1500–1650: Historical Essays*. London: British Library, 20–1.

Arden, J. (1979a). Rug-headed Irish Kerns and British Poets. *New Statesman*, July 13, 56–7.

——(1979b). Shakespeare Guilty. *New Statesman*, August 10, 199.

Arnold, M. (1867). *The Study of Celtic Literature*. London: Dent.

Baker, D. J. (1993). "Wildehirissheman": Colonialist Representation in Shakespeare's *Henry V. English Literary Renaissance*, 22, 37–61.

——(1997). Imagining Britain: William Shakespeare's *Henry V*. In *Between Nations: Shakespeare, Spenser, Marvell, and the Question of Britain*. Stanford, CA: Stanford University Press, 16–65.

Bartley, J. O. (1954). *Teague, Shenkin, and Sawney: Being an Historical Study of the Earliest Irish, Welsh and Scottish Characters in English Plays*. Cork: Cork University Press.

Barton, A. (1977). He that Plays the King: Ford's *Perkin Warbeck* and the Stuart History Play. In M. Axton and R. Williams (eds.) *English Drama: Forms and Development*. Cambridge: Cambridge University Press, 69–93.

Barton, D. P. (1919). *Links between Ireland and Shakespeare*. Dublin: Maunsel.

Berger, T. L. (1985). The Disappearance of Macmorris in Shakespeare's *Henry V. Renaissance Papers*, 13–26.

Bottigheimer, K. S. (1978). Kingdom and Colony: Ireland in the Westward Enterprise, 1536–1660. In K. R. Andrews, N. P. Canny, and P. E. Hair (eds.) *The Westward Enterprise: English Activities in Ireland, the Atlantic, and America 1480–1650*. Liverpool: Liverpool University Press, 45–64.

Bradshaw, B. (1973). The Beginnings of Modern Ireland. In B. Farrell (ed.) *The Irish Parliamentary Tradition*. Dublin: Gill and Macmillan, 68–87.

——(1977). Cromwellian Reform and the Origins of the Kildare Rebellion, 1533–34. *Transactions of the Royal Historical Society*, 5th series, 27, 69–93.

Brady, C. (1994). *The Chief Governors: The Rise and Fall of Reform Government in Tudor Ireland, 1536–1588*. Cambridge: Cambridge University Press.

Brown, K. (1986). Historical Context and *Henry V. Cahiers Elisabethains*, 29, 77–81.

Burnett, M. T. and Wray, R. (eds.) (1997). *Shakespeare and Ireland: History, Politics, Culture*. London: Macmillan.

Cairns, D. and Richards, S. (1988). *Writing Ireland: Colonialism, Nationalism, and Culture*. Manchester: Manchester University Press.

Canny, N. P. (1975). *The Formation of the Old English Elite in Ireland*. Dublin: National University of Ireland.

Cosgrove, A. (1983). Parliament and the Anglo-Irish Community: The Declaration of 1460. In A. Cosgrove and J. I. McGuire (eds.) *Parliament and Community, Historical Studies*, 14, 25–41.

Cox, R. (1689). *Hibernia Anglicana*. London.

Cronin, M. (1997). Rug-headed Kerns Speaking Tongues: Shakespeare, Translation and the Irish Language. In M. T. Burnett and R. Wray (eds.) *Shakespeare and Ireland*. London: Macmillan, 193–212.

Curtis, E. (1927). *Richard II in Ireland, 1394–5, and Submissions of the Irish Chiefs*. Oxford.

Curtis, E. and McDowell, R. B. (eds.) (1977). *Irish Historical Documents, 1172–1922*. London: Methuen.

De Breffney, B. (1984). An Elizabethan Political Painting. *Irish Arts Review*, 1, 1, 39–41.

Devereux, R. (Second Earl of Essex) (1599). *Lawes and orders of Warre, established for the good conduct of the service in Ireland*. London.

Dollimore, J. and Sinfield, A. (1985a). History and Ideology: The Instance of *Henry V*. In J. Drakakis (ed.) *Alternative Shakespeares*. London: Methuen, 206–27.

——(eds.) (1985b). *Political Shakespeare: Essays in Cultural Materialism*. Manchester: Manchester University Press.

Edwards, P. (1979). *Threshold of a Nation: A Study in English and Irish Drama*. Cambridge: Cambridge University Press.

Ellis, S. G. (1976). The Kildare Rebellion and the Early Henrician Reformation. *The Historical Journal*, 9, 4, 807–30.

——(1985). *Tudor Ireland: Crown, Community and the Conflict of Cultures, 1470–1603*. London: Longman.

Erickson, P. (1988). Fathers, Sons, and Brothers in *Henry V*. In H. Bloom (ed.) *William Shakespeare's "Henry V"*. New York: Chelsea.

Fletcher, A. J. (2000). *Drama, Performance, and Polity in Pre-Cromwellian Ireland*. Cork: Cork University Press.

Franssen, P. (2001). The Bard and Ireland: Shakespeare's Protestantism as Politics in Disguise. *Shakespeare Survey*, 54, ed. P. Holland. The Shakespeare Institute, University of Birmingham, 71–9.

Greenblatt, S. (1985). Invisible Bullets: Renaissance Authority and its Subversion, *Henry IV* and *Henry V*. In J. Dollimore and A. Sinfield (eds.) *Political Shakespeare*. Manchester: Manchester University Press, 18–47.

Gurr, A. (1989). Why Captain Jamy in *Henry V*? *Archiv fur das Studium der Neuren Sprachen uns Literaturen*, 226, 2, 365–73.

——(1992). *King Henry V*. Cambridge: Cambridge University Press.

Hadfield, A. (1997). "Hitherto she ne're could fancy him": Shakespeare's "British" Plays and the Exclusion of Ireland. In M. T. Burnett and R. Wray (eds.) *Shakespeare and Ireland*. London: Macmillan, 47–67.

Henry, L. W. (1958). Contemporary Sources for Essex's Lieutenancy in Ireland, 1599. *Irish Historical Studies*, 11, 8–17.

——(1959). The Earl of Essex and Ireland, 1599. *Bulletin of the Institute of Historical Research*, 32, 1–23.

Highley, C. (1990). Wales, Ireland, and *1 Henry IV*. *Renaissance Drama*, 21, 91–114.

——(1997). *Shakespeare, Spenser, and the Crisis in Ireland*. Cambridge: Cambridge University Press.

Hogan, J. (1947). Shane O'Neill Comes to the Court of Elizabeth. In S. Pender (ed.) *Feil-scribhinn Torna: Essays and Studies Presented to Professor Tadhgua Donnchadha on the Occasion of His Seventieth Birthday*. Cork: Cork University Press, 154–70.

Holderness, G. (1991). "What ish my nation?": Shakespeare and National Identities. *Textual Practice*, 5, 74–93.

Holinshed, R. (1976) [1807–8] *Chronicles of England, Scotland, and Ireland*, 6 vols. Reprinted with an introduction by V. Snow, ed. H. Ellis. New York: AMS Press.

Hopkins, L. (1997). Neighbourhood in *Henry V*. In M. T. Burnett and R. Wray (eds.) *Shakespeare and Ireland*. London: Macmillan, 9–26.

Howard, J. E. (1987). Renaissance Antitheatricality and the Politics of Gender and Rank in *Much Ado About Nothing*. In J. E. Howard and M. F. O'Connor (eds.) *Shakespeare Reproduced: The Text in History and Ideology*. London: Methuen, 163–87.

Ivic, C. (1999a). "Our Inland": Shakespeare's *Henry V* and the Celtic Fringe. *Ariel: A Review of International Literature*, 30, 1, 85–103.

——(1999b). Incorporating Ireland: Cultural Conflict in Holinshed's Irish Chronicles. *Journal of Medieval and Early Modern Studies*, 29, 437–98.

Jameson, F. (1981). *The Political Unconscious: Narrative as a Socially Symbolic Act*. London: Methuen.

Jones, A. R. (1987). Italians and Others: Venice and the Irish in *Coryat's Crudities* and *The White Devil*. *Renaissance Drama*, 18, 101–20.

Joughin, J. J. (1997). Shakespeare and Ireland (report on an international conference held at Trinity College, Dublin, 20–23 March). *The European English Messenger*, 6, 2, 78–80.

Kiberd, D. (1995). *Inventing Ireland: The Literature of the Modern Nation*. London: Jonathan Cape.

Klein, B. (1998). Partial Views: Shakespeare and the Map of Ireland. *Early Modern Literary Studies*, 4, 2. 5.1.1–20. online journal. URL: http:purl.oclc.org/emls/04-2/kleipart.htm.

Lawrence, W. J. (1906). Was Shakespeare ever in Ireland? *Shakespeare Jahrbuch*, 42, 65–75.

Leerssen, J. T. (1986). *Mere Irish & Fior-Ghael: Studies in the Idea of Irish Nationality, its Development and Literary Expression Prior to the Nineteenth Century*. Amsterdam: John Benjamins.

Lindley, D. (1986). Embarrassing Ben: The Masques for Frances Howard. *English Literary Renaissance*, 16, 2, 343–59.

McCabe, R. (2002). Making History: Holinshed's Irish *Chronicles*, 1577 and 1587. In D. J. Baker and W. Maley (eds.) *British Identities and English Renaissance Literature*. Cambridge: Cambridge University Press, 51–67.

McEachern, C. (1996). Speaking in Common: *Henry V* and the Paradox of the Body Politic. In *The Poetics of English Nationhood, 1590–1612*. Cambridge: Cambridge University Press, 83–137.

McGuinness, F. (1997). *Mutabilitie*. London: Faber and Faber.

Maley, W. (1997a). Fording the Nation: The Abridgement of the British Problem in *Perkin Warbeck* (1633). In A. Murphy (ed.) special early modern issue of *Critical Survey*, 9, 3, 11–31.

——(1997b). "This sceptred isle": Shakespeare and the British Problem. In J. Joughin (ed.) *Shakespeare and National Culture*. Manchester: Manchester University Press, 83–108.

——(1997c). Shakespeare, Holinshed and Ireland: Resources and Contexts. In M. T. Burnett and R. Wray (eds.) *Shakespeare and Ireland*. London: Macmillan, 27–46.

Merchant, W. M. (ed.) (1975). *Christopher Marlowe: Edward the Second*. London: Ernest Benn.

Murphy, A. (1994). Gold Lace and a Frozen Snake: Donne, Wotton, and the Nine Years War. *Irish Studies Review*, 8, 9–11.

——(1996). Shakespeare's Irish History. *Literature and History*, 5, 38–59.

——(1997). "Tish ill done": *Henry the Fifth* and the Politics of Editing. In M. T. Burnett and R. Wray (eds.) *Shakespeare and Ireland*. London: Macmillan, 213–34.

——(1999). "The remarkablest story of Ireland": Shakespeare and the Irish War. In *But the Irish Sea Betwixt Us: Ireland, Colonialism, and Renaissance Literature*. Lexington: University Press of Kentucky, 97–123.

Neill, M. (1994). Broken English and Broken Irish: Nation, Language, and the Optic of Power in Shakespeare's Histories. *Shakespeare Quarterly*, 45, 1–32.

——(1995). *Henry V*: A Modern Perspective. In B. A. Mowat and P. Werstine (eds.) *Henry V: The New Folger Library Shakespeare*. New York: Washington Square Press, 253–78.

O'Brien, C. C. (1979). Shakespeare: Not Guilty. *New Statesman*, July 27, 130.

O'Connor, F. (1979). *The Habit of Being*. Letters edited and with an introduction by S. Fitzgerald. New York: Farrar, Strauss, Giroux.

Orgel, S. (ed.) (1969). *Ben Jonson: The Complete Masques*. New Haven, CT: Yale University Press.

Palmer, P. (2001). *Language and Conquest in Early Modern Ireland: English Renaissance Literature and Elizabethan Imperial Expansion*. Cambridge: Cambridge University Press.

Parker, P. (1996). *Shakespeare from the Margins: Language, Culture, Context*. Chicago, IL: University of Chicago Press.

Patterson, A. M. (1989). Back by Popular Demand: The Two Versions of *Henry V*. In *Shakespeare and the Popular Voice*. Oxford: Blackwell, 71–92.

——(1994). *Reading Holinshed's Chronicles*. Chicago, IL: University of Chicago Press.

Piveronus, P. J. (1975). The Desmond Imperial Alliance of 1529: Its Effect on Henry VIII's Policy toward Ireland. *Éire-Ireland*, 10, 2, 19–31.

Potter, D. (1983). French Intrigue in Ireland During the Reign of Henri II, 1547–1559. *International History Review*, 5, 159–80.

Quinn, D. B. (1966). *The Elizabethans and the Irish*. Ithaca, NY: published for the Folger Shakespeare Library by Cornell University Press.

Quint, D. (1982). "Alexander the Pig": Shakespeare on History and Poetry. *Boundary 2*, 10, 49–67.

Rabl, K. (1987). Taming the "Wild Irish" in English Renaissance Drama. In W. Zach and H. Kosock (eds.) *National Images and Stereotypes*, vol. 3. of *Literary Interrelations: Ireland, England and the World*. Tubingen: G. Narr, 47–59.

Rackin, P. (1990). *Stages of History: Shakespeare's English Chronicles*. London: Routledge.

Smith, W. D. (1954). The *Henry V* Choruses in the First Folio. *Journal of English and Germanic Philology*, 33, 38–57.

Snyder, E. D. (1920). The Wild Irish: A Study of Some English Satires against the Irish, Scots, and Welsh. *Modern Philology*, 17, 147–85.

Spencer, J. M. (1996). Princes, Pirates, and Pigs: Criminalizing Wars of Conquest in *Henry V*. *Shakespeare Quarterly*, 47, 160–77.

Spenser, E. (1997). *Edmund Spenser, A View of the State of Ireland (1633): from the first printed edition*, ed. A. Hadfield and W. Maley. Oxford: Blackwell.

Taylor, G. (ed.) (1982). *Henry V*. Oxford: Clarendon Press.

Welch, R. (1994). *The Kilcolman Notebook*. Dingle, Co. Kerry: Brandon Press.

Werstine, P. (1998). "Is it upon record?": The Reduction of the History Play to History. In W. S. Hill (ed.) *New Ways of Looking at Old Texts: Papers of the Renaissance English Text Society, 1992–1996*. Tempe, AZ: Medieval & Renaissance Texts & Studies in conjunction with Renaissance English Text Society, 71–82.

White, D. G. (1957–8). Henry VIII's Irish Kerne in France and Scotland. *The Irish Sword*, 3, 213–25.

6
Theories of Kingship in Shakespeare's England
William C. Carroll

Kings are justly called gods, for that they exercise a manner or resemblance of divine power upon earth. For if you will consider the attributes to God, you shall see how they agree in the person of a king.

King James, 1610

To see our monarchical power and regal prerogative strained so high and made so transcendent every way, that if the practise should follow the positions, we are not like to leave to our successors that freedom we received from our forefathers, nor make account of any thing we have longer than they list that govern. Many bold passages have since been [spoken] in the lower house [of parliament], and among the rest a wish that this speech [of James's] might never come in print: but what issue this business now in hand will come unto, God knows.

Chamberlain 1939, II: 301

Commonwealths and realms may live, when the head is cut off, and may put on a new head, that is, make them a new governor, when they see their old head seek too much his own will and not the wealth of the whole body, for the which he was only ordained.

Ponet 1556: D7

The first epigraph above is by King James I, in his speech to parliament, March 21, 1610, the second is by John Chamberlain, writing to Sir Ralph Winwood on May 24, 1610, regarding James's speech, and the third is by John Ponet, in his *A Short Treatise of Politic Power* of 1556. Taken together, these three comments might well serve as exemplary markers of contemporary positions on the subject of kingship and its powers in early modern England. An exile from the rule of the Catholic Queen Mary, Ponet knew firsthand what the excesses of monarchical power might bring, and his *Treatise* fashions a justification for overthrowing a legitimate monarch by attacking not her faith, but the philosophical assumptions of unchecked rule; resistance to tyranny was therefore based on constitutional and contractual principles. Ponet's position was hardly triumphant in his lifetime, however, and would find its most articulate exposition in the writings of Scottish (after the deposition of Mary Queen of Scots in 1567) and French (after the Huguenot massacre in 1572) authors. This discourse, which might be termed "contractual" or "resistance" theory, was certainly a minority discourse in Shakespeare's time, yet looming over all discussions of kingship theory in this period are the events of 1649, when a legitimate, ruling king was brought to execution.

At the opposite extreme from Ponet's position was the elaborate, complex discursive system developed by Tudor and Stuart monarchs for generations, boldly expressed in James's claim – before parliament, no less – that kings were chosen by God, were like God, and were subject to no man's rule; thus, there could be no justification whereby any citizen or group of citizens could dare to overthrow a legitimate monarch. This "providentialist" theory enjoyed the full support of the state propaganda apparatus for over a century and as "official" discourse was systematically disseminated throughout the kingdom; opposition to these principles, rhetorical or actual, received swift rebuke.

A third position, as reflected in Chamberlain's letter, can also be discerned, however. Chamberlain was clearly a supporter of the monarchy, and close to the court and its expanding circles of influence. Yet Chamberlain, like others at the time, was disturbed by what he took to be the excessive claims linking the institution of kingship to divine power ("strained so high and made so transcendent"), with the attendant possibilities of abuse, and spoke for the ancient freedoms which "we received from our forefathers," but which "we are not like to leave to our successors" if things continue as they have. This ingrained traditional sense of "freedom" – of rights and obligations taken for granted – was just what James, a Scot whose country had no such common law traditions, had not understood about England. James's boldness – or his insensitivity – in making such a claim before parliament led not to its acceptance as a theoretical position, but in a familiar irony, to a resistance to it: "Many bold passages have since been [spoken] in the lower house" against it, some perhaps too inflammatory to be quoted directly. Chamberlain's own uneasiness, and his account of parliament's resistance to James's claims, anticipates the events of 1642 and parliament's eventual role in the deposition and execution of James's son, Charles I.

I do not mean to suggest that these three philosophical positions, amplified below, can possibly account for the variety of writings on the nature of kingship in this period, but they do offer a way to begin. One must also resist the continual temptation to frame a teleological argument, with the events of 1642–9 acting as a magnet, or black hole, toward which each historical moment inevitably moves. Still, one cannot escape the fact that a political movement so opposed to the absolutist claims (if not the local reality) of monarchy eventually did move from rhetoric to action – the killing of a king.

Providential Theory

At the heart of the "providential" theory of kingship is the concept of the monarch ruling as the chosen vice-regent of God, independent of the consent of the commons, unfettered by ecclesiastical authority, outside of and prior to the laws of the kingdom – all summed up in the term, "divine right." The consolidation of this theoretical position occurred over many decades of the sixteenth century, particularly from the time of Henry VIII's break with Rome. Successive monarchs invariably claimed that God was on their side, but as practical politics met various forms of resistance, theories of sovereignty were developed to explain and justify the righteousness, justice, and undeniability of monarchical decisions in terms not just of divine approval, but of divine direction *through* the monarch. Resistance to a king's earthly authority was thereby reinterpreted not just as a form of treason, but also as rebellion against God himself. The centralization of state power in terms of bureaucratic and political machinery – a process which continued throughout the Tudor period, reaching a high point in the reign of the Cecils – was accompanied by a centralization and intensification of various forms of discursive powers as well. Indeed, the rhetoric of monarchical authority generally outstripped the reality of monarchical power, and in one of those paradoxes Foucault has taught us to see, the greater the claims of divine monarchical authority, the more certain we can be that such claims were resisted or disputed. Perhaps the most extreme claims about the divinely ordained authority of a king occurred in the writings of Sir Robert Filmer, in his *Patriarcha: Or the Natural Power of Kings* (ca. 1630), *The Anarchy of a Limited or Mixed Monarchy*, and *The Necessity of the Absolute Power of All Kings*; the latter two works, published in 1648, made these claims even as Charles I languished in prison, just one year before his execution.[1] Clearly, the *assertion* of the divine right of kings was one thing, its application in the material world of politics something else.

One of the most influential formulations justifying monarchical power and infallibility was the doctrine of the King's Two Bodies. This concept derived from medieval political and religious thought, as Ernst Kantorowicz has shown, but was codified and disseminated in a highly polemical form during Queen Elizabeth's reign. In a court case of 1562, Elizabeth's lawyers (as quoted in Edmund Plowden's *Reports*) argued that a lease granted by Edward VI, Elizabeth's predecessor, was valid even though he was not of legal age; the lawyers agreed

> that by the Common Law no Act which the King does as King, shall be defeated by his Nonage. For the King has in him two Bodies, *viz.*, a Body natural, and a Body politic. His Body natural (if it be considered in itself) is a Body mortal, subject to all Infirmities that come by Nature or Accident, to the Imbecility of Infancy or old Age, and to the like Defects that happen to the natural Bodies of other People. But his Body politic is a Body that cannot be seen or handled, consisting of Policy and Government, and constituted for the Direction of the People, and the Management of the public weal,

and this Body is utterly void of Infancy, and old Age, and other natural Defects and Imbecilities, which the Body natural is subject to, and for this Cause, what the King does in his Body politic, cannot be invalidated or frustrated by any Disability in his natural Body. (Quoted in Kantorowicz 1957: 7)

This distinction between the mortal and the political body has a certain plausibility, but also led to unexpected consequences, as we shall see; one can easily see the advantages to the monarchical position in such a theory, since no *personal* action of the monarch could be invalidated, and no matter how incompetent or diseased the monarch was, as king he was nevertheless perfect.

Given the distinction between these two bodies, how were they unified? The answer is that the Body politic was the greater and more inclusive of the two:

the Body politic includes the Body natural, but the Body natural is the lesser, and with this the Body politic is consolidated. So that he has a Body natural, adorned and invested with the Estate and Dignity royal; and he has not a Body natural distinct and divided by itself from the Office and Dignity royal, but a Body natural and a Body politic together indivisible; and these two Bodies are incorporated in One Person, and make one Body and not divers. (Ibid: 9)

The result, then, is something like the mystery of the Holy Trinity, two bodies in one, though not the same. Among the immediate practical implications of this concept is that the king (as opposed to the individual body natural who is king) is infallible; the Body natural may have craven desires or petty motivations, but these mortal flaws cannot be used to invalidate a monarchical decree.

In the doctrine of the King's Two Bodies, too, there seemed to be a solution to some of the troubling questions of monarchical succession, for the Body politic (as the queen's lawyers argued in another case) was not subject to death, as the Body natural was:

for as to this Body [politic] the King never dies, and his natural Death is not called in our Law . . . the Death of the King, but the Demise of the King, not signifying by the word (*Demise*) that the Body politic of the King is dead, but that there is a Separation of the two Bodies, and that the Body politic is transferred and conveyed over from the Body natural now dead, or now removed from the Dignity royal, to another Body natural. So that it signifies a Removal of the Body politic of the King of this Realm from one Body natural to another. (Ibid: 13)

Hence the saying, "The king is dead, long live the King." Moreover, since there was never a gap in time between one monarch and the next, there was therefore no time or necessity for any other agent – such as parliament or any other agent of the people – to interfere with royal succession; as we will see below, this doctrine was in effect a refutation of any possibility of construing royal investiture as a matter of election rather than inheritance. What this doctrine could not do, however, was identify to whom the kingship would go if the monarch, as in Queen Elizabeth's case, had no heir.

The doctrine of the King's Two Bodies continued as a viable argument throughout the Stuart reign, though King James, as we will see, would stress other concepts justifying monarchical power. Still, the idea that the two Bodies could be distinguished eventually rebounded against the Stuarts, for in 1642 parliament would employ it for its own purposes, summoning "in the name and by the authority of Charles I, King body politic, the armies which were to fight the same Charles I, king body natural" (Kantorowicz 1957: 21). The parliament at the same time asserted its superiority to the monarch:

> The High Court of Parliament is not only a Court of Judicature . . . but it is likewise a Council . . . to preserve the publick Peace and Safety of the Kingdom, and to declare the King's pleasure in those things that are requisite thereunto, and what they do herein hath the stamp of Royal Authority, although His Majesty . . . do in his own Person oppose or interrupt the same. (Ibid)

Using the doctrine of the King's Two Bodies *against* the king could hardly have been conceived by Queen Elizabeth's lawyers in 1562, yet perhaps more significant than this irony is the fact that the weapon was wielded not by a disgruntled individual, but by parliament, which asserted once again the supremacy, not of the king, but of the king-in-parliament.

While Queen Elizabeth made many pronouncements regarding her role as monarch, and clearly had various strategic positions to defend, she herself wrote relatively little about the philosophy or theory of kingship, seeming to want to keep her beliefs ambiguous. King James, on the other hand, was unusual in that he wrote and spoke so directly about the nature of kingship. In two major works published in Scotland before he succeeded Elizabeth as king of England – *The True Law of Free Monarchies* (1598) and *Basilikon Doron* ("The King's Testament," 1598) – James delineated key theoretical positions. In *True Law* he defined the grounds of kingly authority and royal prerogative (that is, the powers belonging to the king alone, rather than to parliament or some other institution), while in *Basilikon Doron* he spoke as the father-king giving practical advice to his son Prince Henry toward the day when he would become king.[2] When James became King of England as well as Scotland in 1603, both works were reprinted in London, in multiple editions; the English were eager to find out as much as possible about their new, foreign, and relatively unknown king. *Basilikon Doron* was especially popular, running through as many as nine versions printed in London in 1603 alone, with more than twelve thousand copies in print (Wormald 1991: 150). Yet *True Law* and *Basilikon Doron* had been directed toward a specifically Scottish audience, and their arguments were based in a context of Scottish, not English, political history and political institutions; the Scottish parliament, to take one example, was vastly weaker than the English parliament, a fact which James would soon discover. Yet many English readers took James's writings as signs of what James would do as king of England.

In these two works, and in his various speeches to the English parliament between 1604 and 1610, James articulated three essential points – each of which would be contested by his opponents; James's positions were distinct from, though complementary to, the doctrine of the King's Two Bodies that had been promoted by the Elizabethan regime. First, the king is God's lieutenant on earth. Only God has the power to exalt or depose a king; if a people chafes under their king, they must suffer his misrule until God removes the king. The king's *right* to the throne does not derive from man, but from God; thus the kingship cannot be elected, but can only be inherited, in a chain of monarchs that goes back to the Bible. Second, the king is not bound by the law, for the king came before the law; thus parliament cannot "make any kind of law or statute, without [the king's] scepter be to it, for giving it the force of a law" (James 1598: 202). The kingship possesses many powerful "prerogatives" (a term that soon became controversial) that cannot be abridged; what they are, and how far they extended, were sources of contention throughout James's reign. Third, it follows that the king cannot be lawfully deposed, or his power restricted, by any act of parliament, or by any uprising of the people. Even a tyrannical king must be obeyed by his people. Shakespeare places a version of this traditional belief in the mouth of John of Gaunt, in *Richard II*, when Gaunt resists the Duchess of Gloucester's call for him to revenge his brother Woodstock's death by order of Richard:

> God's is the quarrel; for God's substitute [i.e., Richard],
> His deputy anointed in His sight,
> Hath caused his [i.e., Woodstock's] death; the which if wrongfully
> Let heaven revenge, for I may never lift
> An angry arm against His minister. (1.2.37–41)

The king's right to the throne, it was claimed, is absolute, and his powers also absolute. This term, which was initially a wholly positive concept – *absolute* meaning perfect, complete, unrestricted, or unimprovable – eventually also became a term of negative judgment, suggesting "too much," and finally virtually a synonym for "tyranny."[3] Hence the term "absolutism," (negatively) indicating a form of rule that was without limits, arbitrary, unchecked. Sir Thomas Smith, in *De Republica Anglorum* (1583), asserted that the king "hath absolutely in his power the authority of war and peace, to defy what Prince it shall please him, and to bid him war, and again to reconcile himself and enter into league or truce with him at his pleasure or the advice only of his privy council" (Smith 1972: 58–9), but he also noted that "in time of peace, the same [absolute power] is very dangerous, as well to him that doth use it, and much more to the people upon whom it is used" (ibid: 16–17) because man's imperfect nature is soon corrupted by such power, which turns into tyranny.

In his speech of 1610, after several years of struggle with parliament, James tried to have it both ways, asserting his divine right and monarchical power, but allowing that every king who is not a tyrant will willingly submit himself to the laws of the land – even though he is above those laws.[4] In the end, James would permit others to discuss *why* he did something, but, he maintains, "I will not be content that my power be disputed upon" (James 1610: 531).[5] This speech was in response to a petition protesting James's attempt to exclude parliament from discussing "impositions" (i.e., a particular tax) because they were his prerogative; for parliament, it was a matter of free speech. James eventually conceded the point, but his 1610 speech only exacerbated the controversy, as is evident in Chamberlain's letter, quoted above. And as yet another observer, John More, wrote to Sir Ralph Winwood of this speech, "the most strictly religious [members of James's audience] could have wished that his Highness would have been more sparing in using the Name of God, and comparing the Deity with Princes' sovereignty" (Winwood 1725, III: 141–2). But linking sovereignty to divinity was the heart of the providentialist claim.

The arguments on behalf of the divine right of kings by James and his followers proceeded from a foundational assertion about God's will, but they were also conducted through an elaborate system of analogies derived from the natural world. The order of God's law and the law of nature were said to be in perfect agreement with the (status quo) order of the political world. In *True Law* James developed one ancient trope which was invoked throughout the Tudor–Stuart period:

> The King towards his people is rightly compared to a father of children, and to a head of a body composed of divers members: for as fathers, the good princes and magistrates of the people of God acknowledged themselves to their subjects . . . And the proper office of a king towards his subjects agrees very well with the office of the head towards the body, and all members thereof: for from the head, being the seat of judgment, proceedeth the care and foresight of guiding, and preventing all evil that may come to the body or any part thereof. The head cares for the body, so doth the king for his people. As the discourse and direction flows from the head, and the execution according thereunto belongs to the rest of the members, every one according to their office, so it is betwixt a wise prince, and his people. (James 1598: 204)

Tracing his argument back to the Bible's commandment to "Honor thy father," Sir Robert Filmer, in *Patriarcha*, extended James's assertion to a universal application:

> In all kingdoms or commonwealths in the world, whether the prince be the supreme father of the people or but the true heir of such a father, or whether he come to the crown by usurpation, or by election of the nobles or of the people, of by any other way whatsoever, or whether some few or a multitude govern the commonwealth, yet still the authority that is in any one, or in many, or in all these, is the only right and natural authority of a supreme father. There is, and always shall be continued to the end of the world, a natural right of a supreme father over every multitude . . . If we compare the natural rights of a father with those of a king, we find them all one, without any difference at all but only in the latitude or extent of them. (Filmer 1680: 22–3)

In his speech to parliament in March 1604, James developed several related analogies, many of which also derived from ancient texts: "I am the husband, and all the whole Isle is my lawful wife; I am the head, and it is my body; I am the shepherd, and it is my flock" (James 1604: 488). Thus, as the father is to the child, the husband to the wife, the head to the body, and the shepherd to the flock, so is the king to his people, whose only response can be one of submissive, unthinking, feminized obedience. The theory of divine right constructed an order of the natural world which exactly duplicated that of God's relationship to man. To put it in more modern terms: the discourse of power worked to naturalize itself, seeking to freeze into place the hierarchical relations of the status quo. The resort to "natural" analogy was a powerful discursive weapon, but eventually such analogies were recognized and resisted as oppressive ideological constructions.[6]

Given this patriarchal theory of a king's divine right, the chief duty of a subject was obedience to monarchical authority, and the Tudor–Stuart monarchs employed a wide range of political and religious mechanisms to make certain that such a message was circulated widely. One such means was through the Elizabethan homilies: two authorized texts of collections of moral and political sermons – one published in 1547, the other in 1563 – were placed in every Anglican church in the kingdom, along with the Bible and the Book of Common Prayer. In many churches the sermons preached were simply these homilies. Following the Northern Rebellion of 1569 an additional sermon, "An Homily Against Disobedience and Willful Rebellion," was published in 1570 and added to the collection in 1571, replacing a 1547 sermon, "An Exhortation, concerning Good Order and Obedience to Rulers and Magistrates."[7] The new homily was considerably stronger than the earlier one, and reinforced the concept of the divine origin of kingly power. The new homily reads the rebellion of Lucifer and the Fall of Adam and Eve as a political allegory in which God as king suffers treason and rebellion from his subjects until he strikes them down:

> it is most evident that kings, queens, and other princes . . . are ordained of God, are to be obeyed and honored of their subjects; that such subjects as are disobedient or rebellious against their princes disobey God and procure their own damnation, that the government of princes is a great blessing of God given for the commonwealth, specially of the good and godly; for the comfort and cherishing of whom God giveth and setteth up princes; and on the contrary part, to the fear and for the punishment of the evil and wicked . . . all kings, queens, and other governors are specially appointed by the ordinance of God. And as God Himself, being of an infinite majesty, power and wisdom, ruleth and governeth all things in heaven and in earth, as the universal monarch and only king and emperor over all . . . so hath He constituted, ordained, and set earthly princes over particular kingdoms and dominions in earth, both for the avoiding of all confusion, which else would be in the world if it should be without such governors, and for the great quiet and benefit of earthly men their subjects. (*Homily* 1570: A3ᵛ–A4)

Even if the monarch is an evil tyrant, there is only one divinely authorized course of action: "Nay, let us either deserve to have a good prince, or let us patiently suffer and obey such as we deserve" (ibid: B3). The homily's argument is wide-ranging – from an account of the creation of heaven and earth and scriptural examples of obedience to civil authorities, to a depiction of rebellion as the most dangerous violation of all God's commandments and the destruction of rebels; worshippers are invited to recall rebellions in England's past history, and the erasure of whole noble families which had supported rebellion. The homily, with many other similar documents throughout the period, made rebellion virtually unthinkable – except that, of course, some continued to think such thoughts.

Contractual Theory

A survey of contemporary published documents on kingship theories suggests an overwhelming consensus in Shakespeare's time concerning divine right and royal authority; such claims became ever more strident and absolute as the Stuart monarchy lost more and more of its power and influence in the 1630s. Yet long before the Stuarts succeeded to the English throne, a European-wide discourse argued the limited nature of kingship and promoted the right of resistance to tyranny, even justifying the overthrow of rightfully enthroned kings if necessary. Such arguments were rightly understood to be an enormous political threat; the alleged right of the people to set aside a lawful king, either directly or through their representatives, struck at the very heart of royal ideology.

This counter-discourse challenged the most fundamental assumptions of the providentialist theory, that the king's authority derived directly and only from God. Against the royalist position that kingship preceded law and society, they argued that kingship derived from the wishes and needs of the commons in nature, and that laws were socially formed and were therefore prior to kings. Finally, responding to the notion that the king was "head" of the political body, which could not live without him, John Ponet (like others) argued that "Kings, Princes and other governors, albeit they are the heads of a politic body, yet they are not the whole body. And though they be the chief members, yet they are but members: neither are the people ordained for them, but they are ordained for the people" (Ponet 1556: G6^v). While all arguments, on either side of these questions, were ultimately based on interpretations of scriptural passages and episodes, Ponet and other English writers also based their opposition to royalist ideology on a native English tradition of the duties and limitations of a monarch, and the right of individual judgment.

Two key facts distinguished England from Scotland and continental European states in terms of limitations upon monarchical power. The first was the existence of common law, as opposed to juridical systems based on Roman precedents, or civil law; thus, Ralph Winwood, the recipient of Chamberlain's letter quoted above, would instinctively know what was meant by "that freedom we received from our forefathers," while such a concept was neither theoretically nor practically extant in Scotland. James's attempts to consolidate power would be resisted in various ways, but Sir Edward Coke – once one of James's early allies but later a forceful critic of royal policy – asserted the supremacy of common law over ecclesiastical cases and denied the power of the king to change common law by proclamation.[8] Removed from his office as Chief Justice of the King's Bench, Coke took his revenge upon James in the form of publication: his eleven volumes of *Reports* (1600–15) and his *Institutes* (1628–44; three volumes published posthumously), in which he recast, explained, and defended the common law, thus illuminating the foundation of English legal liberties.

The second fact which distinguished England from its rivals was the strength (and very existence) of its parliament. The traditional powers invested in parliament were not as great as the monarch's, in the sense of waging war, for example, but they were considerable and could not be abrogated. Queen Elizabeth discovered, as James would after her, that the power of taxation in particular gave parliament an important political position; parliament could certainly be ignored for long stretches of time, not even called into session, but eventually the royal purse would be empty, and new revenues had to be generated, and so parliament would be called back into session. Tudor and Stuart parliaments enacted many other important statutes, of course, and refused to enact notable royal initiatives (James's 1604 bill for the legal and political union of England and Scotland, for example), but perhaps the most important thing about parliament was simply its legal–political status in English thought. In *De Republica Anglorum* Sir Thomas Smith encapsulates this traditional view: "The most high and absolute power of the realm of England, consisteth in the Parliament" (Smith 1972: 48). While "in war where the king himself in person, the nobility, the rest of the gentility, and the yeomanry are, is the force and power of England: so in peace and consultation" the parliament represents the whole order of the kingdom:

> For every Englishman is intended to be there present, either in person or by procuration and attornies, of what preeminence, state, dignity, or quality soever he be, from the Prince (be he King or Queen) to the lowest person of England. And the consent of the Parliament is taken to be every man's consent.

And it is the parliament that "abrogateth olde laws, maketh new, giveth orders for things past, and for things hereafter to be followed" (p. 49). In England, Smith asserted, "the most high and absolute power of the realm of England consisteth in the Parliament," not in the king. The "king-in-parliament" was, in the English tradition that James inherited, the ultimate power.[9]

Expressing a reverence for the traditions of English common law, ancient privileges, or the representative authority of parliament was permissible, depending on the circumstances of the moment, but the more radical concepts of royal limitation associated with Ponet were rarely if ever heard during Queen Elizabeth's reign; articulating the logic of deposing a lawful king was one thing during Queen Mary's reign, but not at all relevant or permissible thereafter. Opposition to Queen Elizabeth's rule or individual policies would generally be expressed in conservative terms which preserved the sanctity of the monarch herself and cast blame on her ministers, courtiers, or other subjects. The philosophical discourse opposing divine right theory and unchecked monarchical rule flourished instead in two foreign countries closely linked during Elizabeth's rule: Scotland and France.[10]

Just as John Ponet's *Short Treatise* was in effect a justification for the deposition of the Catholic monarch Queen Mary of England, so George Buchanan's *De Jure Regni apud Scotos* (1579) provided a theoretical justification for the deposition of Mary, Queen of Scots (King James's mother) in 1567. One of the major scholars in sixteenth-century Europe, Buchanan (though a Protestant and a leader in the reformed Church of Scotland) had found favor with Mary, and became her tutor, and eventually James's tutor. When Mary was forced to abdicate her crown, following the murder of her husband Lord Darnley and her remarriage, three months later, to the suspected murderer, the Earl of Bothwell, Buchanan was appointed one of the commissioners to investigate her actions. His *De Jure Regni* argued that the Scots had indeed been justified, by the laws of nature and of God; no person, not even the monarch, was above the law authorized by the people: "Our kings received from our ancestors an authority which was not absolute, but which was limited within definite bounds. Confirmation, moreover, is supplied by immemorial usage and by the people's assumption, without objection being made, of certain rights . . . bad princes . . . should no more be immune to punishment than are the robbers for whom we are commanded to pray. Nor does it follow from the fact that good rulers ought to be obeyed that the bad ones ought not to be resisted" (Buchanan 1949: 107, 113). Near the end of his life, Buchanan began writing the history of Scotland, the *Rerum Scoticarum historia*, which in effect provided the historical illustration of the political theories expounded in the *De Jure Regni*. Rejecting Buchanan's political stance (and perhaps recalling Buchanan's notorious rigor as a tutor, about which he had nightmares), James as king of Scotland worked to discredit and destroy Buchanan's major political work. In 1584 the Scottish parliament passed an act to punish authors of slanderous works against the monarchy, specifying by name only two works: "the books of the *Chronicle* and *De jure regni apud Scotos* made by umquhile [i.e., now deceased] Mr. George Buchanan" (Gatherer 1958: 6). In the *Basilikon Doron* James himself urged his son to be well versed in history, but went on, "I mean not of such infamous invectives, as Buchanan's or Knox's Chronicles" (James 1603: 176).[11]

While Scottish Protestants like Buchanan supplied justification for the deposition of Mary, Queen of Scots and English Protestants like Ponet did the same for resisting Queen Mary of England, the most insistent and powerful resistance texts, founded on a theory of kingship at odds with the providentialist divine-right concept, were written in the immediate aftermath of the St. Bartholomew Day's massacre of Protestants throughout France in 1572.[12] Several Huguenot resistance treatises appeared soon afterward: François Hotman's *Francogallia* (1573), Theodore de Beza's *Du droit des magistrats* (1574), and the anonymous *Le Reveille-Matin* (1574), *Le Politique* (1574), and *Le Tocsain* (1577), among others. Perhaps the most important of these polemics, at least in English politics, was the *Vindiciae contra Tyrannos*, by (a pseudonym) Stephano Junio Bruto Celta ("Stephanus Junius Brutus, the Celt"), first published in 1579.[13] The authorship of the *Vindiciae* remains unclear, but there is no doubt about its popularity, as gauged by its publishing history, with nine additional Latin editions by 1622, as well as translations into French and Dutch in the 1580s. The "Fourth Question" of the *Vindiciae* was translated into English and published in 1588 as *A Short Apology for Christian Soldiers*. The entire work was translated into English and printed twice in the next hundred years, both times in years linked to revolutionary political events: 1648 and 1689.

Virtually all of these Huguenot "monarchomachs" ("king-killers," according to one of their opponents – Skinner 1978: 301) argued that the cynical political principles of Niccolò Machiavelli were the guiding principles of royal government; resistance to such tyranny was justified on both political and religious grounds. The *Vindiciae* took up four related questions, the very asking of which could have been considered treasonous in England:

1   "Whether subjects are bound and ought, to obey princes, if they command that which is against the law of God."
2   "Whether it be lawful to resist a prince which doth infringe the law of God, or ruin His church, by whom, how, and how far it is lawful."
3   "Whether it be lawful to resist a prince which doth oppress or ruin a public State, and how far such resistance may be extended, by whom, how, and by what right, or law, it is permitted."
4   "Whether neighbor princes may by right, or are bound by law, to aid the subjects of other princes, persecuted for true religion, or oppressed by manifest tyranny."

The *Vindiciae*'s arguments are based on the central concept rejected by all Tudor–Stuart monarchs and their supporters, that the relation between king and people is one of a contract – in short, the belief that kings are *elected*, not divinely given:

> We have shewed before that it is God that doth appoint kings, who chooseth them, who gives the kingdom to them: now we say that the people establish kings, putteth the sceptre into their hands, and who with their suffrages, approveth the election. God would have it done in this manner, to the end that the kings should acknowledge, that after God they hold their power and sovereignty from the people. (*Vindiciae* 1648: 46)

If the monarch fails to live up to his or her responsibilities, or commits crimes against the church or state, then the people are justified in replacing them: "If the prince fail in his promise, the people are exempt from obedience, the contract is made void, the right of obligation of no force" (p. 120). Nor was the author of the *Vindiciae* impressed by the argument of inheritance:

for so much as none were ever born with crowns on their heads, and sceptres in their hands, and that no man can be a king by himself; nor reign without people, whereas on the contrary, the people may subsist of themselves, and were, long before they had any kings, it must of necessity follow, that kings were at the first constituted by the people; and although the sons and dependants of such kings, inheriting their father's virtues, may in a sort seem to have rendered their kingdoms hereditary to their off-springs, and that in some kingdoms and countries, the right of free election seems in a sort buried; yet, notwithstanding, in all well-ordered kingdoms, this custom is yet remaining. The sons do not succeed the fathers, before the people first have as it were anew established them by their new approbation; neither were they acknowledged in quality, as inheriting it from the dead; but approved and accounted kings then only, when they were invested with the kingdom, by receiving the sceptre and diadem from the hands of those who represent the majesty of the people . . . To conclude in a word, all kings at the first were altogether elected, and those who at this day seem to have their crowns and royal authority by inheritance, have or should have, first and princi-pally their confirmation from the people . . . Now, seeing that the people choose and establish their kings, it follows that the whole body of the people is above the king. (Ibid: 49–51)

Later in the seventeenth century radical supporters of the English revolution, includ-ing Milton, would cite Buchanan and the author of the *Vindiciae* as laying the ground for limiting monarchy.

Divine-right theorists opposed all such "resistance" claims strenuously. Sir Robert Filmer, in *Patriarcha*, posed the supposed assumption of "papists" and the "divines also of the Reformed churches," which "the common people everywhere tenderly embrace . . . as being most plausible to flesh and blood" in this way:

Mankind is naturally endowed and born with freedom from all subjection, and at liberty to choose what form of government it please, and that the power which any one man hath over others was at first bestowed according to the direction of the multitude. (Filmer 1680: 3)

"This desperate assertion," Filmer argued, "whereby kings are made subject to the censures and deprivations of their subjects," follows from the notion that mankind is at "liberty to choose what form of government it please" (p. 4). The entire argument, which rests on a belief in "the *natural liberty and equality of mankind*," will collapse if this belief is rebutted.[14] Much of the argument over the nature of kingship, as is evident here, reached back to conflicting interpretations of natural law, and what were the earliest conditions of society – with or without kings, whether laws or kings were prior. Their positions were irreconcilable, given the absoluteness of the claims of divine right – a monarch could not have "partial" divine authorization, and an "absolute" (in the sense of perfect or irresistible) claim to the throne could not exist if the monarchy was a matter of election.

Points of Conflict

Much of the early modern debate about the nature of kingship revolved around two issues, both of which had enormous consequences in the practice of politics: first, whether tyrannicide was ever justified; second, whether the kingship was inherited or elected and hence, what were the principles of succession. We will briefly focus on these problem areas in more detail.

According to divine-right theorists, tyrannicide could *never* be justified, no matter how evil or incompetent the monarch. It is certainly understandable why Tudor and Stuart monarchs made such arguments, however, since the historical records of England and Scotland are marked repeatedly by just such actions. The English tended to view the Scots as savage and inferior on just this point; as one Christopher Piggott said in a famous outburst during a 1607 parliamentary debate over the proposed union with Scotland, the Scots "have not suffered above two kings to die in their beds, these two hundred years. Our king [James] hath hardly escaped them; they have attempted [to murder] him [both in the Gowry conspiracy and the Gunpowder Plot]" (Galloway 1986: 104). For speaking such unpleasant truths, Piggott was expelled from the House of Commons and confined in the Tower. Yet anyone who read the Scottish (John Major, George Buchanan) or English (Holinshed) historians would have found just what Piggott had remarked: while it was true that the Scottish kings could trace their ancestors back over a hundred generations, an embarrassingly large number of them had been deposed and/or murdered.

The English, however, were in little better position to brag. The Tudor dynasty had after all been founded on the corpse of Richard III, and the War of the Roses which led up to Richard III's defeat by Henry Tudor had been sparked by the deposition and murder of Richard II; Shakespeare wrote eight history plays on this sequence.[15] The little discourse on the subject of tyrannicide that existed in Tudor–Stuart England was almost entirely an argument against the possibility of justification; Buchanan found no sanction in official discourse, and plays which seemed to support (or at least not condemn) rebellions of any sort were few, and among those few, some were censored (e.g., *The Book of Sir Thomas More*). Queen Elizabeth herself survived rebellions, from the Northern Rebellion of 1569 to the more restricted Oxfordshire Rising of 1596, and direct attempts on her life, the most famous being the attempted coup by Robert Devereux, the Earl of Essex, in 1601. Essex's followers, in a frequently cited incident, had commissioned Shakespeare's company to put on a performance of an old play, *Richard II*, the night before their attempt, presumably so that it would inspire them and/or the audience to deposing a monarch.[16] The Elizabethan regime was indeed sensitive to the associations between Richard II and Elizabeth, and took direct action, such as the imprisonment of Sir John Hayward, who had unwisely dedicated his book, *The First Part of the Life and Reign of Henry the IIII* (1599), to Essex, and was imprisoned for having more or less vindicated Henry IV's deposition of Richard II (although several writers of the time, including Francis

Bacon, could find no trace of treason in the book).[17] Elizabeth herself, in a famous anecdote a few months after Essex's conspiracy, was reported to have exclaimed to William Lambarde, the Deputy Keeper of the Rolls, who had shown her a catalog of documents surviving from Richard II's reign, "I am Richard II, know ye not that?" If the subjects of tyrannicide and deposition were strongly suppressed during Elizabeth's reign, the need to control such ideas was felt even more strongly during James's reign, given the attempt on his life in the Gunpowder Plot, and the growing infiltration of radical writings from clandestine presses in Europe; by the reign of Charles I, English radical thought was in full bloom.

The second major issue dominating the discourse of kingship was that of the principles of succession. In the case of Henry VIII his own actions clouded the supposedly clear principle of hereditary patrilineal succession – the eldest son of the eldest son, and so forth. Henry attempted, more than once, to set forth the guidelines of who would succeed him, and how. Unhappy with both Nature and God, at least as far as his successors went, Henry wrote the English succession into his will, emending it several times, and sought (and received) an act of parliament approving his plan. The problems had begun with Henry's divorce from Catherine of Aragon (they had had a daughter, Mary), on the grounds that their marriage was illegitimate because she was the widow of his elder brother, Arthur (who had died after, but before consummating, his marriage to Catherine). Henry's marriage to Anne Boleyn, according to Catholics, was "incestuous" (as Henry had argued his marriage to Catherine was) and therefore produced a "bastard," the future Queen Elizabeth; some Catholic writers even claimed that Anne was really Henry's daughter, her mother having been his mistress before he took up with Anne. At last, with Jane Seymour, Henry eventually produced a son, Edward, but he was not the first-born. Following Henry's death, first Edward, then Mary (both died after short reigns of about five years each), then finally Elizabeth took the throne; for many European Catholics, disappointed that Queen Mary's efforts to return England to a Catholic state had failed, Elizabeth was never a "legitimate" child, hence not a legitimate monarch. And for some in England, the descendants of Henry VIII's daughters had substantial, perhaps even better, claims to the throne. Margaret Tudor, however, had married James IV of Scotland, and her descendants had been denied succession rights by Henry's will; the Stuarts' claims to the English throne were also contested on the grounds that, as Scots, they were foreigners, and non-citizens could not inherit English land. The line deriving from Henry's sister Mary, who had married Louis XII of France, then, upon Louis's death, the Duke of Suffolk, had a better but not perfect claim, according to some.

Queen Elizabeth's claim to the throne was eventually settled, by her longevity if nothing else; she had been on the throne for six years when Shakespeare was born in 1564, and for the vast majority of English adults in 1600, she was the *only* monarch they had ever known. Paradoxically, however, her very longevity eventually led to new insecurities about succession. Elizabeth's refusal to wed and consequent failure to produce an heir to the throne generated increasing anxieties as she visibly aged. Already by 1571, with the passage of the Second Treasons Act (the so-called Statute of Silence), *any* debate on the topic of the queen's successor had been legally prohibited. Nevertheless, such discussions increased dramatically in the 1590s. Robert Parsons, a Jesuit priest living in France, published his *A Conference upon the Next Succession to the Crown of England* in 1595, a bombshell which inaugurated a series of polemical books and pamphlets on the topic. Parsons's questioning of the principle of strict blood inheritance, and his advancement of a crew of pretenders (among whom James VI of Scotland, Parsons argued, had an invalid claim), aroused a furious official reaction, but many others were saying the same thing. In one of the responses to Parsons in 1602, in fact, Elizabeth's own godson, Sir John Harington, reported that even before James had been born, "it was thought as fit that for a counterpoise to the Queen of Scots' pretense [to the English throne] some other titles should underhand[edly] be set on foot at home" (Harington 1880: 41). Harington goes on to describe "the policy of the State" in secretly promoting several other candidates, more recently the Infanta, daughter of Philip II of Spain, as a counterpoise to James. Thomas Wilson observed in 1601 that "there are 12 competitors that gape for the death of that good old Princess the now Queen" (Wilson 1601: 2). Whether Elizabeth brought it upon herself or not, there was a substantial debate over succession caused by her failure to produce an heir; even if she had produced an heir, he or she would surely also have been challenged, judging by the polemics and religious conflicts of the time.

In constructing their arguments about succession, writers tended to rely on three main kinds of evidence and argument, in addition to the continuing appeal to "natural law," as we have seen above. First, there was often an appeal to religious authority: Sir Thomas Craig, for example, a strong supporter of James, argued in 1603 that "It is clear that in instituting kings God ever preferred hereditary to elective succession. He gave it his countenance in the case of David and his posterity," and in several other biblical examples Craig summons, leading to his conclusion that "kings were first instituted by God; that monarchy was introduced from the beginning, and that it was settled on an hereditary basis in order that the ambition and strife of men might be stayed; for kingship is the fairest thing in heaven as on earth" (Craig 1909: 228–9). This was certainly James's position, as he expressed it in *True Law* (with another echo of the doctrine of the King's Two Bodies):

> Monarchy is the true pattern of divinity . . . the lineal succession of crowns being begun among the people of God, and happily continued in divers Christian commonwealths: So as no objection either of heresy, or whatsoever private statute or law, may free the people from their oath-giving to their king, and his succession, established by the old fundamental laws of the kingdom. For, as he is their heritable over-lord, and so by birth, not by any right in the coronation, cometh to his crown; it is alike unlawful (the crown ever standing full) to displace him that succeedeth thereto, as to eject the former: for at the very moment of the expiring of the king reigning, the nearest and lawful heir entereth into his place. (James 1598: 194, 209)

A second ground of argument derived from secular rather than religious history. Writers on both sides of the divine right/election issue took the supposed tradition of the English or Scottish monarchies with the greatest seriousness, but drew very different lessons from those traditions. To take two Scots, for example, who consider exactly the same material: the royalist Sir Thomas Craig, in the passage quoted above, finds succession by heredity to be God's plan, while George Buchanan – in telling the story of Malcolm II in his *Rerum Scoticarum historia* – reaches just the opposite conclusion. Buchanan argues that the new law of patrilineal succession established by King Kenneth II, leading to Malcolm II's coronation, had unexpected consequences:

> An universal good to all was pretended [by those who argued for succession by heredity], in thus settling the succession, that seditions, murders, and treacheries might be prevented amongst those of the blood; and also, that ambition, with the other mischiefs accompanying it, might be rooted out from amongst the nobles. But on the contrary, when I enquire into the causes of public grievances, and compare the old [law of election] with the modern [law of heredity], it seems to me, that all those mischiefs, which we would have avoided by this new law, are so far from being extinguished by the antiquating of the old, that they rather receive a great increase therefrom. For, not to speak of the plots of their kindred against those who are actually in the throne; nor of a present king's evil suspicions of those, whom Nature and the law would have accounted as most dear to him; I say, omitting these things . . . all the miseries of former ages may seem light and tolerable, if compared with those calamaties which followed.

In arguing for this new law of heredity, kings aim to "perpetuate their name and stock," Buchanan concludes, but "how vain and fallacious that pretense is, the examples of the ancients, yea, even Nature itself, might inform them" (Buchanan 1690, Book 7: 205).

A third ground of argument might be termed that of the mystique of blood – the belief that a blood relation was inherently superior to any other connection or qualification for the kingship. In his *Treatise* on the succession (1598, written in 1595) – another of the responses to Parsons's *Conference* – Peter Wentworth reviewed the shaky grounds upon which Richard III had taken the kingship:

> Rather than he would have been without some show of succession, how bare and weak soever, [Richard] did choose to cause proclaimed at Paul's Cross, his mother an harlot, and his brethren bastards. And thus he sought the kingdom no otherwise, than by right of succession [i.e., by heredity] . . . By which you see, that even in the conceit of the usurpers themselves, the most lying, infamous and falsely forged pretense of next and most lawful blood, is to be preferred before any Parliament, as being the ground and warrant for justifying and clearing the acts and doings of the same. And if the crown might be lawfully given at the pleasure of a Parliament, what reason is there to call Rich[ard] III or any such others, usurpers[?] (Wentworth 1598: 54–5)

This primal belief in the efficacy of blood relation – even usurpers feel the need to claim it – could lead to tortured historical arguments, perhaps the greatest of which was the founding mythology of the Stuart dynasty.

Stuart kings, from James V on, traced their lineage back from the undoubted founder of the line, Walter Steward (later Stewart, now Stuart), to the mythical figure Banquo (the character from Shakespeare's *Macbeth*). According to these histories, Banquo's son Fleance flees to Wales and impregnates the Welsh princess with a son, Walter. This myth of lineal continuity appears in no history prior to that of Hector Boece in 1526, in the reign of James V.[18] The significance of the supposed link between Banquo and Walter Steward was clear – by it, the Scottish king also had a claim on the Welsh crown, and ultimately the English crown; hence, *both* sides of the Steward line were therefore of royal blood, and the Stuarts could therefore trace their line all the way back to Fergus. The Banquo-to-Fleance-to-Walter Steward myth quickly hardened into accepted historical fact.[19] When James became king in 1603 – the succession from Elizabeth having been peaceful, contrary to general expectations of violence or disturbance – he and his supporters mounted a substantial campaign of publications designed to support and reinforce James's rights by inheritance. The title of George Owen Harry's 1604 genealogy says it all:

> *The Genealogy of the High and Mighty Monarch, James, by the grace of God, King of great Brittayne, &c. with his lineall descent from Noah, by divers direct lynes to Brutus, first Inhabiter of this Ile of Brittayne; and from him to Cadwalader, the last King of the Brittish bloud; and from thence, sundry wayes to his Maiesty.*

From Noah to Brutus to Cadwalader to Fleance to James: such was the supposed unbroken line. This triumph of inheritance theory was codified in the official Succession Act of 1604, in which parliament – rather ironically, in retrospect – publicly and completely accepted all of James's claims: he is, the Act said, "lineally, rightfully, and lawfully descended" from Henry the Seventh's eldest daughter; and *immediately*, without a gap of time, upon Queen Elizabeth's death, James "did by inherent birthright and lawful and undoubted succession" become king, as "lineally, justly, and lawfully next and sole heir of the blood royal" (*Statutes*: 4.1017). This authorizing language concealed and suppressed an enormous amount of political controversy and backstage machinations regarding James's achievement of the throne.

With James's ascent in 1603 the great questions of kingship in England must have seemed at last answered: his claim to the throne, contested by some in the 1590s, triumphed in the end. His experience as a king in Scotland augured well for his immediate competence; those tiring of Elizabeth's at times capricious rule, and certainly those who could not find sufficient favor in her court, looked forward to James. More, James was a man, and while Elizabeth had used her gender shrewdly as an aspect of her statecraft, most English citizens were reluctant to countenance another female ruler. Finally, James came to the throne with not one but two sons, and so the worrisome issues of succession created by Elizabeth's childlessness seemed unlikely to afflict the kingdom again. The new king, moreover, clearly and openly stated his theory of kingship, and in a maturing nation-state, his assertion of powerful kingly prerogatives must have seemed plausible to many.

Within just a few years, however, the great optimism greeting James's ascent had waned, and voices of dissent were soon heard again. Attempts had been made on James's life, rebellion in the countryside had occurred, and the Jacobean discourse of kingship was being challenged by parliament itself. The story of Charles's reign takes us well beyond Shakespeare's lifetime, but clearly the seeds of his destruction had been planted in the contested theories of kingship deriving from John Ponet and others. These theoretical conflicts led to real, drastic political consequences.

NOTES

1   Filmer's political position in the 1630s was surely a minority one, though after the Restoration he must have seemed an exemplar of absolutist ideology.

2   Henry died in 1612, before becoming king; his brother Charles became King Charles I upon James's death in 1625.

3   Daly (1978) and Burgess (1996) both trace the history of this term into the Restoration. Even in a writer as early as Ponet, the term could be strongly negative: "Kings and princes have not an absolute power over their subjects" (Ponet 1556: G5^v).

4   The divine right of kings and the theory of monarchical absolutism were not the same thing, of course. While most accounts of royal absolutism included an element of divine-right theory, the reverse was not necessarily the case. Most Englishmen would probably have granted the theory of divine right (if it had been more discreetly stated than James seemed to do), and most would probably have rejected absolutism at the same time. Still, the discursive (if not actual) combination of the two provided a solid rhetorical argument for James's opponents.

5   James in effect adopted a "King's Two Bodies" position: no one could dispute or resist his power as king, but the motives of the Body natural could be discussed – not that such a discussion could have any impact.

6   Some later writers rejected such arguments by analogy. In his *Two Treatises of Government* John Locke took on Filmer directly: "thus we are born free, as we are born rational . . . The freedom of a man at years of discretion, and the subjection of a child to his parents, whilst yet short of that age, are so consistent, and so distinguishable, that the most blinded contenders for monarchy, by right of fatherhood, cannot miss this difference, the most obstinate cannot but allow their consistency" (quoted in Schochet 1975: 251).

7   In an ironic counterpoint, Pope Pius V issued a papal bull in 1572 that proclaimed Elizabeth's excommunication and deposition from the throne of England; it released her subjects from their oaths of allegiance to her, thereby in effect legitimating the deposition and murder of a monarch.

8   The common law itself was the inheritance of all Englishmen, and therefore it could not be taken away without consent; it was also, according to Coke, superior to royal prerogative in many cases; in particular, the king's prerogatives could not be used to violate any principle of common law.

9   For common law theorists like Coke, parliamentary or statute law was supplementary to the common law, speaking where the common law was silent, but statute law could not override common law.

10 To take one example, many Scottish intellectuals, such as George Buchanan, studied and lived in France. Mary, Queen of Scots' first marriage had been to Francis II of France, and Scotland and France often found common purpose in foreign policy opposition to England.

11 John Knox, the Calvinist Scottish minister, had justified resistance to monarchy in his *Appellation from the Sentence Pronounced by the Bishops and Clergy* (1558), among other works.

12 Many of the chief authors of so-called resistance texts were Calvinists, or at least Protestant (see Skinner (1978) for more on the religious context), but Elizabeth and James were also Protestant.

13 The title page pseudonym recalls, in part, the legendary Brutus, great-grandson of Aeneas and founder of the British race. This Brutus is often conflated with Lucius Junius Brutus, the legendary first consul of Rome, who led the Romans to overthrow the tyranny of Tarquinius Superbus, and establish a republic; Shakespeare tells part of this story in his poem of 1593, "The Rape of Lucrece." The *Vindiciae* was attributed by contemporaries to both Hubert Languet and Philippe du Plessis Mornay; the work's most recent editor concludes that "we can only say that the most likely scenario is some form of close collaboration" between the two (Garnett 1994: lxxvi). See also Garnett's textual history (pp. lxxxiv–lxxxviii).

14 Filmer reserved a special scorn (given James's own feelings about Buchanan) for the "book *De Jure Regni apud Scotos* [which] maintains a liberty of the people to depose their prince" (Filmer 1680: 4).

15 Citing Cardinal Poole, John Ponet noted that "England lacketh not the practice and experience of the same [deposing of kings and killing of tyrants]. For they deposed King Edward the Second, because without law he killed his subjects, spoiled them of their goods, and wasted the treasure of the realm. And upon what just causes Richard the Second was thrust out, and Henry the Fourth put in his place, I refer it to their own judgement" (Ponet 1556: G3).

16 Whether this play was Shakespeare's *Richard II* cannot be determined; Simon Forman reported seeing a non-Shakespearean *Richard II* (judging by Forman's plot summary) at the Globe on April 30, 1611.

17 Hayward was soon rehabilitated, however, and his *An Answer to the First Part of a Certain Conference* of 1603, a page by page refutation of Robert Parsons's *Conference*, was a substantial intervention in the succession controversy on the side of King James.

18 Boece's history, written in Latin, was the basis for Raphael Holinshed's history of Scotland, published in 1557 in English; Holinshed's history was of course used extensively by Shakespeare as source material for his plays.

19 With a few skeptics, such as Sir George Buc, the deputy Master of the Revels and a supporter of James, who said of the Fleance story, "this being not acknowledged by the best Scottish historiographers, and the thing not honorable, I may well pretermit it" from his own history (Buc 1605: A4ᵛ).

References and Further Reading

Axton, M. (1977). *The Queen's Two Bodies: Drama and the Elizabethan Succession.* London: Royal Historical Society.

Buc, Sir George (1605) *Daphis Polystephanos. An Eclog treating of Crowns, and of Garlands.* London.

Buchanan, G. (1690). *Rerum Scoticarum historia*, trans. T. Page. London.

——(1949). *Powers of the Crown in Scotland*, trans. C. F. Arrowood. Austin: University of Texas Press. Translation of *De Jure Regni apud Scotos*. Edinburgh, 1579.

Burgess, G. (1996). *Absolute Monarchy and the Stuart Constitution.* New Haven, CT: Yale University Press.

Bushnell, R. W. (1990). *Tragedies of Tyrants: Political Thought and Theater in the English Renaissance.* Ithaca, NY: Cornell University Press.

Chamberlain, J. (1939). *The Letters of John Chamberlain*, ed. N. E. McClure. Philadelphia, PA: American Philosophical Society.

Craig, Sir Thomas (1909). *A Treatise on the Union of the British Realms*, trans. C. Sanford Terry. Edinburgh: Edinburgh University Press. Translation of *De unione regnorum Britanniae tractatus*, ca. 1603–8.

Daly, J. (1978). The Idea of Absolute Monarchy in Seventeenth-Century England. *Historical Journal*, 21, 227–50.

Filmer, Sir Robert (1680). *Patriarcha: Or The Natural Power of Kings.* London. Written ca. 1630.

Galloway, B. (1986). *The Union of England and Scotland 1603–1608.* Edinburgh: Donald.

Garnett, G. (ed.) (1994). *Vindiciae, Contra Tyrannos.* Cambridge: Cambridge University Press.

Gatherer, W. A. (ed.) (1958). *The Tyrannous Reign of Mary Stewart.* Edinburgh: Edinburgh University Press.

Harington, Sir John (1880). *A Tract on the Succession to the Crown (AD 1602).* London: Roxburghe Club.

Hayward, J. (1603). *An Answer to the First Part of a Certain Conference, Concerning Succession, Published not long since under the name of R. Dolman.* London.

Homily against disobedience and willful rebellion, An (1570). London.

Kantorowicz, E. H. (1957). *The King's Two Bodies: A Study in Medieval Political Theology.* Princeton, NJ: Princeton University Press.

King James I (1598). *The True Law of Free Monarchies: Or the Reciprock and Mutual Duty Betwixt a Free King, and His Natural Subjects.* Edinburgh. Quoted from *The Works of the Most High and Mighty Prince, James.* London, 1616.

——(1603). *Basilikon Doron. Or His Majesty's Instructions To His Dearest Son, Henry the Prince.* Edinburgh. Quoted from *The Works of the Most High and Mighty Prince, James.* London, 1616.

——(1604). A Speech, As It Was Delivered in the Upper House of Parliament . . . on Monday the XIX Day of March 1603 [i.e., 1604]. Quoted from *The Works of the Most High and Mighty Prince, James.* London, 1616.

——(1610). "A Speech to the Lords and Commons of the Parliament at Whitehall, On Wednesday the XXI of March. Anno 1609 [i.e., 1610]. Quoted from *The Works of the Most High and Mighty Prince, James.* London, 1616.

Levine, M. (1973). *Tudor Dynastic Problems 1460–1571.* London: Allen.

Nenner, H. (1995). *The Right To Be King: The Succession to the Crown of England 1603–1714.* Chapel Hill: University of North Carolina Press.

[Parsons, Robert] Doleman, R. (1594). *A Conference about the Next Succession to the Crown of England, Divided into Two Parts.* N. Antwerp; actually appeared in 1595.

Ponet, J. (1556). *A Short Treatise of Politic Power, and of the true Obedience which subjects owe to kings and other civil Governors, with an Exhortation to all true natural Englishmen.* London.

Schochet, G. J. (1975). *Patriarchalism in Political Thought.* Oxford: Blackwell.

Shakespeare, W. (1992). *The Complete Works of Shakespeare,* 4th edn., ed. D. Bevington. New York: HarperCollins.

Skinner, Q. (1978). *The Foundations of Modern Political Thoughts,* 2 vols. Cambridge: Cambridge University Press.

Smith, Sir Thomas (1972). *De Republica Anglorum: A Discourse on the Commonwealth of England,* ed. L. Alston. Shannon: Irish University Press.

Sommerville, J. P. (1986). *Politics and Ideology in England, 1603–1640.* London: Longman.

Vindiciae contra Tyrannos: A Defence of Liberty against Tyrants. Or, Of the lawful power of the Prince over the people, and of the people over the prince. Being a Treatise written in Latin and French by Junius Brutus, and translated out of both into English (1648). London.

Wentworth, P. (1598). *A Treatise containing M. Wentworth's Judgment Concerning the Person of the true and lawful successor to these Realms of England and Ireland.* London.

Wilson, T. [1601]. *The State of England AD 1600,* ed. F. J. Fisher. Camden Miscellany, 3rd series, lii.

Winwood, Sir Ralph (1725). *Memorials of Affairs of State in the Reigns of Queen Elizabeth and King James I.* London.

Wormald, J. (1991). James VI and I, *Basilikon Doron* and *The Trew Law of Free Monarchies:* The Scottish Context and the English Translation. In L. L. Peck (ed.) *The Mental World of the Jacobean Court.* Cambridge: Cambridge University Press.

7

"To beguile the time, look like the time": Contemporary Film Versions of Shakespeare's Histories[1]

Peter J. Smith

In order to be marketed to film audiences and those responsible for teaching Shakespeare, reverence for the text and the author are prerequisites. This may provide us with the vital clue as to why Shakespeare on screen has made it into the canon.

Cartmell (1999: 37)

I don't like Shakespeare.

Richard Loncraine cited in Crowdus (1998: 46)

Richard Loncraine's *Richard III* (1996)

As Sir Ian McKellen's grinning Richard of Gloucester weaves his way through the formal ball in celebration of his brother's succession to the throne, ducking the gliding couples who spin past him, a graceful thirties *chanteuse*, complete with kiss-curl and under the direction of a conductor who looks more than a little like Glenn Miller, croons a musical version of Christopher Marlowe's lyric, "Come live with me and be my love."[2] The lyric was first published in the anthology *The Passionate Pilgrim* in 1599, and included in *Englands Helicon* the following year. Its popularity gave rise to a series of imitations, responses, and parodies. Marlowe's own murderous Ithamore tempts the whore, Bellamira, in *The Jew of Malta* (ca. 1589), with a catalog of earthly delights, concluding his seduction with "Thou in those groves, by Dis above, / Shalt live with me and be my love" (4.2.101–2). John Donne's weird piscatory rewriting, "The Bait," was published in 1612 and Izaak Walton included a version of the lyric in the second edition of *The Compleat Angler* (1655) over half a century after its first appearance. The poem most commonly paired with Marlowe's, however, both in print and manuscript, was written by Sir Walter Ralegh.

In what became known as "The Nymph's Reply to the Shepherd" the inventory of sensual enchantments offered by the speaker of Marlowe's lyric is refuted one by one: "Thy gowns, thy shoes, thy beds of roses, / Thy cap, thy kirtle, and thy poesies, / Soon break, soon wither, soon forgotten, / In folly ripe, in reason rotten" (ll. 13–16). Despite ending with a wistful longing, Ralegh's poem sees through the fallacious permanence of the spring which Marlowe's speaker has offered – "The shepherd swains shall dance and sing / For thy delight *each May morning*" (ll. 21–2; my emphasis). Reluctantly the Nymph rejects the prospect of eternal verdancy and effortless plenitude because, like Juliet's Nurse, she knows the bitter truth about men: "There's no trust, no faith, no honesty in men; / All perjured, all forsworn, all naught, dissemblers all" (3.2.87–8). As if to demonstrate the "female intuition" of Nymph and Nurse, it is at the exact point when the smiling Richard watches Brackenbury arrest his brother Clarence, who nervously, but without fuss, puts down his champagne and gathers his things, that the *chanteuse* changes her song seamlessly, but with trenchant significance, from the lyrics of Marlowe's utopian pastoral to those of Ralegh's bracing realism, "If all the world and love were young, / And truth in every shepherd's tongue . . ." Above all else, *Richard III* is a play about lying, and the achievement of Richard Loncraine's film version is that it never loses sight of the centrality of political mendacity.

Just as Marlowe's widespread lyric circulated and attracted the responses of his contemporaries, so the early versions of Richard's reign prompted a number of commentaries and rewritings. The general tendency of these, unsurprisingly, given that Richard's nemesis, Richmond (later Henry VII) was founder of the Tudor dynasty, father to Henry VIII and grandfather to Elizabeth I, was ideologically driven and profoundly denigratory. Richard became the victim of an orchestrated smear campaign – monstrously sinister in shape and egregiously wicked in his machinations. Polydore Vergil, Sir Thomas More, Edward Hall, and Raphael Holinshed (all of whose works were among Shakespeare's sources) transformed the last Plantagenet into a mirror for anti-magistrates – this was how *not* to do it. Of these vituperative texts, the most influential subsequently has been Shakespeare's dramatized version of the monarch's short reign. Yet, paradoxically, while Shakespeare's *Richard III* is the most feigning, it is also the most true. As Greg Walker insists in a penetrating analysis:

> Of all Shakespeare's histories it is (with *Henry VIII*) perhaps the most faithful to its sources, the most copious in the detailed borrowings from the received story. The recorded facts are there in bewildering quantity, even when they do not seem strictly necessary for the movement of the play or are incorporated into the action without clear explanation or function. (Walker 2000: 32)

Of the three best-known film versions of *Richard III* (Olivier's 1955 version, Loncraine's, and, also 1996, Al Pacino's *Looking for Richard*), Loncraine's seems to me to be the most "true" – another offshoot of Shakespeare it inevitably is, but just as Shakespeare is true to the falsity of his sources, so Loncraine is true to the falsity of his subject. Unlike, on the one hand, Pacino's Richard, who functions as a vessel into which Pacino can pour himself, a vehicle through which the actor explores notions of psychological verisimilitude with questions about motivation or plausibility (as though the character were a "real" person), or Olivier's performative Richard, on the other, in which part of the pleasure derives from watching Olivier act Richard's acting, as player and character simultaneously self-fashion, Loncraine's version is both authentic and untrue. Its wealth of detail, accuracy of costume, décor, vehicles, properties, its studied attention to London landmarks – what we might think of as its accumulation of particularities – places it in a long line of British costume dramas such as Merchant–Ivory films and popular TV and cinema adaptations of "classic works" by Charles Dickens, George Eliot, E. M. Forster or, perhaps most widespread, Jane Austen.[3] For Samuel Crowl, this plethoric detail confines the performances:

> What happens in Loncraine's film is that his period details swallow Shakespeare's tale and swamp McKellen's performance so that the audience is deprived of the pleasure of watching a great actor create a character virtually by embodying a political landscape; instead, the landscape in effect paralyzes the character. (Crowl 1997: 56)

But this is only partially to view Loncraine's achievement, for against the period details are set a series of exaggerated artificialities. The film's use of special effects such as the uncanny spider running down Lady Anne's waxen face, its computer-generated settings (the Grand Midland Hotel, St Pancras, is relocated to the South Bank, for instance), or its camply excessive final conflagration, make it conspicuously and self-consciously mannered. It is a film which relishes the real thing alongside the synthetic and Loncraine draws attention to the film's oxymoronic spirit: "I want the acting to be very real and the imagery to be very unreal" (Freedman 2000: 66).

This tension can be read in two ways – first, as McKellen notes, it results from the metamorphosis of one medium into another via an intermediate state: "We were not making a film of the play, we were making a film of a screenplay from a play" (Crowdus 1998: 46). Commenting on Baz Lurhmann's spirited annexing of Shakespeare's love story in *William Shakespeare's Romeo + Juliet* (1997), McKellen attributes its success to its wholesale transcodification: "Again, like *Richard III* in a different way, of course, it was a film. It was not photographing the play, because there is nothing more boring than that" (Crowdus 1998: 47). The second source of the film's artistic fascination is to do with the way in which it is fully conscious of the slipperiness of the history with which it is engaging and which it continues, inevitably, to promulgate. Just as Shakespeare himself was writing a play true to untrue sources, so Loncraine's film updates its story to a London that is transparently real and yet has never existed. Its locations are genuine – Bankside Power Station, Battersea Power Station, the Grand Midland Hotel, the Pearl Assurance Building in Holborn, Senate House (University of London), Shell-Mex House, Big Ben, County Hall, etc. – yet historically, it is a city of fantasy. These places have never played court to a fascistic English leader; Bankside Power Station looks nothing like the Tower of London, and so on. As McKellen remarked, "I always like to do Shakespeare in a modernish period. It's what he himself did, after all. He's never writing history – he's just using history" (ibid: 46).

In the light of this fusion of the implausible and the plausible, Marlowe and Ralegh's diptych neatly poses a series of questions about truth and temporality which

Richard III, its sources, its context(s), its remakes, and finally its content will worry at, though never resolve. How fitting then that the opening song of this adaptation of Shakespeare's play should be based on the words of two of his contemporaries and not his at all. Yet, as if to forestall our objections, the film wittily stamps the very identity of the playwright on the opening scene, superimposing a signature (or at least a set of initials) onto its signature tune. The Glenn Miller *doppelgänger* shares presumably his initials with those of the play's author; visible on the back of each music-stand is the monogram "W. S." (McKellen 1996: 58). Like the mysterious "Mr W. H." of the *Sonnets* (playfully decoded in the nineteenth-century as "Mr William Himself"; see Rollins 1944: 214–16) the playwright hovers in the background, his displaced identity articulating itself through the identities of others.

This ventriloquism – speaking on behalf of others, articulating a position through the words of others – is something with which *Richard III* is obsessed. In the council scene, the Bishop of Ely suggests that Buckingham can speak on behalf of Richard (3.4.9), while Buckingham lands Hastings in trouble by calling attention to the manner in which he would have spoken for Richard (without prior permission): "Had you not come upon your cue, my lord, / William Lord Hastings had pronounced your part – / I mean, your voice" (ll. 26–8). Like Coriolanus, Richard requires the *vox populi* to confirm his authority and, when it is not forthcoming, he is urged by Buckingham to "Play the maid's part: still answer 'nay' – and take it" (3.7.51). Between them they extort the public voice they need. Towards the end of the play Richard attempts to woo Princess Elizabeth by proxy, urging her mother to "Be eloquent in my behalf to her" (4.4.288). Stanley asks a priest to tell Richmond the fate of his son, "Sir Christopher, tell Richmond this from me . . ." (4.5.1). Richard orders Catesby to "Rumour it abroad / That Anne, my wife, is very grievous sick . . . and like to die" (4.2.52–9), while earlier in the same scene he has asked Buckingham to articulate his own thoughts: "Think now what I would speak" (l. 11). At the beginning of the play Lady Anne even attributes the power of sanguinary speech to the corpse in front of her, remarking how its "wounds / Ope their congealèd mouths and bleed afresh" (1.2.55–6).

Though not all of these instances survive in Loncraine and McKellen's screenplay, the film is acutely aware of the importance of speaking in and out of turn. Its opening image is a tickertape message delivered to King Henry's operations room which reads, "Richard Gloucester is at hand. He holds his course toward Tewkesbury." The line is an adaptation of King Edward's "We are advertised by our loving friends / That they do hold their course toward Tewkesbury" (*III Henry VI*, 5.3.18–19) ventriloquized, in the film, as a friendly tip-off, though of course it comes too late. Subsequently Richard's congratulatory speech, delivered in a pause between dance numbers at the Yorks' party, the speech we have all been waiting for, the most immediate dramatic opening in the theatre, "*Now* is the winter of our discontent . . ." (1.1.1; my emphasis), is spoken as the camera, beginning at "Grim-visaged war" (l. 9), gradually closes in on his mouth with pencil-line moustache, oddly coloured left eye and crooked, yellowing teeth. This close-up maps Richard's deformity onto that of history itself, as facial ugliness is shared by him and the recent civil strife. According to Hall's *Union of Famelies of Lancastre and Yorke* (1548), Richard was "harde favoured of visage, such as in estates is called a warlike visage, and emonge commen persones a crabbed face" (Bullough 1960: 253). It is this half-grin/half-grimace that reappears at the film's closure as "the whirligig of time brings in his revenges" (*Twelfth Night*, 5.1.373) and Richard takes us with him, laughing, to the flames of hell.

Of course, it is in the plotting against his brother, Clarence, that Richard relies most upon the efficacy of gossip. In the play Richard circulates a rumor that the king's children will be murdered by one whose name begins with the letter G (1.1.39–40) and the king is incited to suspect his own brother, George, Duke of Clarence. However, the film's naturalism calls for the cutting of the play's supernatural elements (its prophecies and curses – and so, incidentally, Queen Margaret is omitted). Thus the mysterious fiction of the letter G (which stands not only for *George*, Duke of Clarence, but with unintentional foresight on Richard's part, for Richard, Duke of Gloucester, who really will murder the king's sons) is cut.[4] However, the downfall of Clarence still has Richard as its origin. As he waves us to follow him from the gents', he cheerily informs us "Plots have I laid . . . [*Cut to jetty on the Thames*] To set my brother Clarence and King Edward / In deadly hate the one against the other" (ll. 32–5). Only then do we retrospectively remember Tim McInnerny's Catesby whispering in the king's ear while Clarence was being arrested at the dance. It is clear, with hindsight, whose side Catesby is on.

One of the most significant achievements of this adaptation is the clarity with which it renders a complicated story. Paradoxically, nowhere is this lucidity more obvious than in the opening nine minutes of the film, which contain hardly any dialogue. The title sequence of the killing of King Henry VI and his son, Prince Edward, serves to condense the events of the *Henry VI* plays and explain how King Edward IV has ended up on the throne, but it also exemplifies Loncraine's capacity to inaugurate several ideas and motifs which will reappear and resonate as the film goes on. One of these is the notion of Englishness. The only exchange between Henry and Edward upon receiving the news of Gloucester's imminent arrival is stereotypically clipped and formal:

> *Edward.* Goodnight, your majesty.
> *Henry.* Goodnight son.
> *Edward.* Father.

Edward enters his chamber throwing a bone to the black labrador in front of the fire – a gesture to the English adoration of domestic animals, the dog being the Englishman's best friend. He begins a meal of meat and two veg and pours himself a glass of red wine. Above him hangs a pastoral scene of the English countryside. As the faintest tremor of Richard's approaching army is registered by the barking dog, the photo on the table of Edward's wife, Lady Anne (Kristin Scott-Thomas), vibrates and falls over in an adumbration of the way she will submit to Richard's seduction.

A tank gun bursts through the wall, scattering books and furniture in front of it. Shooting infantry flow through the breach firing tommy-guns. Edward makes a dive for his revolver in its holster on his desk, but a masked gunman shoots him in the chest and then in the head; the river scene and green fields in the picture behind him are spattered with blood, symbolizing the bleeding of England. Subsequently a soldier, rasping loudly in his gas mask, enters the king's chamber. Henry kneels by the side of his bed, praying, and is shot at point blank range in the back of the head. There is something quintessentially English about his stiff upper lip, his fatalistic resigna- tion in the face of certain death which recalls both the bravery and the pathos of "The Charge of the Light Brigade." The soldier removes his mask with the same hand as that with which he holds his gun. Clearly his other arm is paralyzed; by now we know this is Richard. Although the king and his son have not figured long enough in the film for us to feel personally sympathetic for them, their urbanity and vulnerability contrast positively with the brutality and abruptness of their attackers – a hand-held firearm has no chance against a tank (as Richard will himself find out when Richmond bears down on him in the film's concluding moments). Moreover, the royals' clearly English martial uniforms with medals and brown leather Sam Brownes (named of course after an English military commander) differentiate them from the science-fiction-like hordes who are masked and shrouded in gas and smoke.

The film brilliantly uses this Englishness as a way of marginalizing the Woodville family by casting them as Americans – at the same time drawing a neat historical parallel. In 1936 King Edward VIII chose to abdicate in order that he could be free to marry Mrs. Wallis Simpson, an American divorcee. This constitutional crisis, as well as the king's unpalatable sympathies towards continental fascism, alienated the royal family from the establishment. Both the sense of dislocation as well as the finely honed and (still?) deeply ingrained attitude of British superiority over everything American, is seen throughout in the treatment of Queen Elizabeth (Annette Bening) and her brother, Earl Rivers (Robert Downey, Jr.). In the opening sequence we see Rivers disembarking from a plane, his arms clutching a bundle of presents and escorted by an air hostess who is obviously taken with his dashing good looks. Clearly the worse for wear, he heads off in entirely the wrong direction before being grabbed and steered back to the waiting limousine where he insouciantly shakes hands with the tailed and starched Catesby. Rivers just has time, vulgarly, to stuff a tip (the con- vention is that the English royal family never carry cash) into the hostess's top pocket before being whisked away. We next see him, from a vertiginous camera shot (remi- niscent of Alfred Hitchcock's fearful angles), entering the dance. Once inside, his cig- arette still hanging rakishly from his lips, he shakes hands with Hastings but mockingly makes the sign of the cross to the Bishop of Ely, who looks shocked. Then, with inappropriate temerity, he kisses the Duchess of York on the cheek before auda- ciously dumping all his parcels in the lap of the surprised monarch; the unctuous Catesby hurriedly relieves the king of them. Rivers then dances with his sister and nephew while the surrounding courtiers frown and look disapproving. Richmond, by contrast, formally seeks permission to dance with Princess Elizabeth and we see the two of them together in a foreshadowing of their eventual harmonious union. Within this short sequence Rivers has managed to offend the punctilious English court within which he now has to take his place.

He and his sister, accompanied by other members of the court, dine in the opulence of the Brighton Pavilion (1.3). Queen Margaret being cut, her insults are given to Elizabeth, whose screeched outbursts ("poisonous hunch-backed toad," l. 244; "bottled spider," l. 240) are clearly supposed to signal a truculent if slightly unbalanced Americanness. Lady Anne, by contrast, holds Richard's hand across the table and smiles into her napkin at the brashness of these foreigners, while Princess Elizabeth looks at the floor in shame; an English lady would never behave thus at the dinner table! Ely and Buckingham share this sense of shock and the latter attempts to calm the situation: "Have done, have done" (l. 277). But both Rivers and Elizabeth are marked out by their failure to observe decorum and it is this stereotypically transatlantic lack of social propriety on which the machiavellian Richard deliberately plays.[5] James N. Loehlin ingeniously suggests that the Americanness of the actress has a secondary or symbolic role:

> Within the film's historical framework, Bening could be read as America growing from an indifference to fascism to come to Britain's rescue in the Second World War. Ironically, Bening's prominence in the film, as imported star-power, simultaneously suggests the destructive extent to which American mass media came to dominate British culture in the years after the war. (Loehlin 1997a: 71)

While the allegorical reading is an intriguing one, the petulance of Queen Elizabeth in this banqueting scene compromises the integrity of the American war effort and, moreover, Rivers's assassination again picks up the negative connotations of this Americanness. We see him willingly tied to the bed-head of a hotel room, slurping whiskey and dragging on a cigarette while the air hostess (still in her uniform hat) begins to fellate him: Rivers is clearly over sexed and over here. As she moves down his body, out of shot, a narrow blade abruptly appears from his stomach and his scream merges into the whistle of a steam train entering a tunnel – both a smuttily English reference to the sexual act (in the nudging style of a seaside postcard) as well as another allusion to Hitchcock (*The 39 Steps*, 1935). This hotel–hostess sex is contrasted both with the demure Lady Anne at the bottom of the staircase, wordlessly inviting Richard upstairs (though instead of following her, he leans towards her only to hit the light switch and she, meekly, turns away), and the unembarrassed nakedness of Richmond and Princess Elizabeth on the morning after their (interpolated) marriage which is reminiscent of the untainted and nescient nudity in Franco Zeffirelli's *Romeo and Juliet* (1968).

Perhaps the idea of Englishness is most to the fore during the stately scene of Richard's coronation. Richard is shown, amid the trappings of monarchy, solemnly receiving the crown. As it is placed on his head so a serried gathering of Lords of the Realm put their crowns on too. The focus blurs as though we are seeing the scene through the wavering eyes of Lady (now Queen) Anne who, by this time, is a drug addict. The scene begins again, this time in black and white, and the gorgeous trappings and colors of ceremony are defamiliarized as though from her perspective, until we realize that the coronation is being watched in a darkened room on a movie projector by Richard and his entourage (which includes Buckingham, played by Jim Broadbent, and his all but unconscious queen). The sequence wittily highlights the symbiosis between royal paraphernalia and media exposure which continues to this day to be an essential, albeit generally crass, part of English culture.

The film's attitude to the English aristocracy is – much like that of Shakespeare's hazardous play – witheringly critical. King Edward IV is not merely physically sickly but pampered and politically flaccid. We see him, childlike, putting his tongue out for his nurse to give him his medication at the same time as his batman is buttoning on his collar. As he attempts to dry the wax seal on Clarence's pardon by blowing on it, he becomes quickly short of breath and begins to wheeze so horribly that the nurse is summoned to administer oxygen. Subsequently, as he presides, smug and complacent in his authority, over an uneasy *rapprochement* between the different factions of his court (2.1), we see him on the Esplanade of the De la Warr Pavilion at Bexhill-on-Sea in a wheelchair, wrapped in a blanket like Shelley's decrepit sovereign, "An old, mad, blind, despised, and dying King."[6] While John Wood's Edward represents a monarch jaded by political responsibility and finally unable to support the weight of office, Nigel Hawthorne's Clarence is a delightfully optimistic and hopelessly guileless aristocrat – what is popularly known in English as a "chinless wonder"! In the very first scene of the play Richard refers to his brother as "Simple plain Clarence" (l. 119) and Hawthorne's Duke is a bumbling bachelor (his son and daughter who appear in the play are cut), an amateur photographer whose heart, though clearly not his head, is in the right place. As Brackenbury whisks him in a motor launch over the Thames to the Tower of London (the windowless and therefore magnificently imposing Bankside Power Station), he raises his handcuffed hands to wave at Richard, who responds by fluttering his handkerchief, mockingly affectionate.

Although, as we have seen, the supernatural and prophetic aspects of the play have been cut, Clarence's foreboding dream is left in (a good decision, since it is one of the most intensely alarming speeches in Shakespeare). Clarence, in the remains of his tattered tails, tells his gaoler of falling into the sea and drowning as he is led up a tiled corridor to emerge into a featureless, concrete, circular exercise yard ringed by a moat which looks like a zoo enclosure (in fact it is the interior of a disused gasometer; McKellen 1996: 98). As he tells of "the tumbling billows of the main [and] the slimy bottom of the deep" (1.4.20–32), the heavens open and he is quickly soaked to the skin. We next see him in a bath house relaxing with his glasses on, reading the paper. Tyrrell and the Second Murderer enter to him and (the scene is heavily cut) push him under the water, slitting his throat. This avoids the awkwardness of drowning him in the malmsey butt (a scene that is unfortunately clumsily comic in the Olivier version and which, perhaps for that reason, is also omitted from Pacino's film) and, as the bath-water turns a livid red, reinforces the horror of Richard's killing machine: the utterly amoral Tyrrell (chillingly rendered by Adrian Dunbar). Cut to

Richard who is having his disabled arm massaged. A small parcel is delivered, wrapped in brown paper, and Richard opens it dextrously with his good hand: Clarence's spectacles. Richard takes off his own and regards them thoughtfully.

The relationship between Richard and Tyrrell is animated by a fearful malevolence. To begin with, Tyrrell is introduced much earlier in the film than in the play, where his main function is to report the death of the two princes in a speech of the most harrowing and extraordinary beauty. The children are described as "girdling one another / Within their alabaster innocent arms" (4.3.10–11) – unfortunately this speech is cut from the screenplay. In the film, as Richard sits at breakfast, smoking (a bronze boar stands on the table in front of him), he receives the document of Clarence's pardon and sets light to it. Requiring a murderer, Richard is introduced to Tyrrell in a stable where he is lobbing apples to a boar in a sty.

> *Richard.* Is thy name Tyrrell?
> *Tyrrell.*   James Tyrrell, and your most obedient subject.
> *Richard.* Art thou indeed?
> *Tyrrell.*   Prove me, my gracious lord. (4.2.68–70)

During this conversation Tyrrell continues to toss apples to the snorting boar. He passes one to Richard who, with a look of nasty gratification, throws the apple sharply *at* the boar, causing it to squeal in pain.

Tyrrell becomes instrumental in Richard's rise to power – the brawn to Buckingham's brain. He, Richard, and the Second Murderer (Michael Elphick) take tea on a rooftop to discuss the assassination of Clarence amid the Second Murderer's homing pigeons. Having dispensed with Richard's brother, we next see him tutting at the housemaid who is about to take fresh towels into Rivers's hotel room (though she is prevented by overhearing the sexual squeals of the air hostess), so we realize that he is involved in that murder too. Shortly after Elizabeth receives the news of Rivers's death, we see Tyrrell place his foot across the model railway track of the children, George Stanley and Richard, Duke of York, derailing their toy engine and smiling spitefully down at them. Cut to the reception of Prince Edward arriving by steam train at St. Pancras Station, with Tyrrell hovering dangerously in the background. He is next responsible for the summary execution of Hastings. Sitting opposite him at the council table after the others have left, he says matter of factly, "the Duke would be at dinner" (3.4.94); cut to a shot looking up at a trap door through which Hastings's body falls towards us before halting abruptly and dangling by the neck. As Richard instructs Tyrrell to murder "those bastards in the tower" (4.2.76) he offers him a chocolate. "Say it is done, / And I will love thee," says Richard. "It . . . is . . . done," replies Tyrrell, deliberating exaggeratedly over which chocolate to take. As he reports the death of the children we see him smother the young, gasping Duke of York with a scarlet cloth.

While Tyrrell is Richard's henchman he is also someone Richard wants to impress. Richard looks genuinely hurt by his mother's curses (the imperious Maggie Smith plays the Duchess of York) and, as she descends the stairs in front of him, we see Richard pause thoughtfully, before turning back, catching sight of Tyrrell and laughing off the insults. Having witnessed Tyrrell's capacity for infanticide it is chilling to see him dangle the bespectacled and tiny George Stanley aloft from the door of a railway carriage as Richard warns his father that his son's life is pawned against Stanley's loyalty. Tyrrell's final assassination is the garrotting of Buckingham (who has obviously been beaten up) in the back of an army truck while Richard sits in the front seat, smoking. During the final battle sequence Ratcliff drives an army jeep with Richard in the passenger seat and Tyrrell standing behind them with a mounted machine gun. As the jeep reverses away from an oncoming tank, the wheels are raised uselessly in the air by a hump in the ground. Ratcliff is shot and slumps forward. Richard, immediately, shoves him out of the jeep to die on the ground and takes his place in the driver's seat, but to no avail; the wheels spin hopelessly and Richard shouts, "A horse! A horse! My kingdom for a horse!" (5.7.7). Tyrrell calls to him "I'll help you to a horse" (in the play the line is Catesby's). Without a moment's hesitation, Richard spins round and shoots Tyrrell in the head. The bullet pierces his tin helmet and he is thrown out of the jeep. Even for Richard, this is a shocking act of betrayal and seems to be the only awful thing of which he is now capable.

Much has been written about the film's closing sequence. As Richard is chased up flights of metal stairs in the ruins of Battersea Power Station, flames surrounding him, he takes pot shots at his pursuer, Richmond. This sequence owes more than a little to the classic cop chase of the 1970s movie which usually ends with the villain falling from a flat roof or through a skylight. Here, Richard pushes open the last door and finds himself faced by a lattice of girders. There are no floors and he is several storeys up. Gingerly he makes his way out onto one of the beams, the camera (in another allusion to Hitchcock) skewed at a bizarre angle. Richmond emerges on a parallel girder. In a gesture of ostensible appeasement, Richard offers his hand, "Let's to't pell mell – / If not to heaven, then hand in hand to hell" (5.6.42–3). Because we look at him apparently from Richmond's position, it is as though he is offering *us* his hand. As he finishes the line, he smiles and falls gently, suicidally, backwards into the abyss. Richmond fires two shots (too late) and we see his face break into the same crafty grin; there seems to be nothing to choose between them. Cut back to Richard smiling up at us as he falls down into the blaze. Al Jolson's buoyant *I'm Sitting on Top of the World* begins to play and we are reminded of the classical pattern, the rise and fall of tragedy – mythically, Lucifer; historically (and iconographically in the case of Loncraine's film), Hitler; dramatically, Richard III.

Al Pacino's *Looking for Richard* (1996)

In what was considered to be one of the most iconoclastic moments of Loncraine's version, McKellen's Richard continued his opening speech in the gents' while urinating. With the kind of compelling impudence that characterizes the film in general, and McKellen's performance in particular, it is as Richard takes hold of his penis that he remarks that he is "not shaped for sportive tricks / Nor made to court an amorous looking-glass" (1.1.14–15). The implication is, as Stephen M. Buhler has pointed out, that Richard feels "alienated from his family because of his incapacity to continue the York line in any form. He is separated from the physical processes of patriarchy and cannot fully share in its triumphs" (Buhler 2000: 45). Pulling the chain of the urinal, Richard turns and washes his hands beneath a mirror while he speaks of his capacity to

> smile and murder whiles I smile,
> . . .
> And wet my cheeks with artificial tears,
> And frame my face to all occasions. (*III Henry VI*, 3.2.182–5)

It is on the last word that he suddenly catches sight of us over his shoulder, reflected in the mirror, as though we have been spying on him. Grimly, he informs us that he "is determinèd to prove a villain / And hate the idle pleasures of these days" (1.1.30–1) before jauntily heading off with "Plots have I laid . . ." The effect of this sequence is to bind us to him. By positioning us as spectators, overlooking him in the priv(ac)y of this most intimate of places, during the most intimate of bodily functions, the film strips us of any moral authority as we become petty voyeurs, caught in the act of peeping over the toilet door. McKellen rightly notes the manner in which audience discomfort would give rise to a kind of moral bankruptcy as the viewer becomes companion in Richard's thoughts and conspirator in his deeds:

> All of Shakespeare's troubled heroes reveal their inner selves in their confidential solil-oquies. These are not thoughts-out-loud, rather true confessions to the audience. Richard may lie to all the other characters but within his solo speeches he always tells the truth. I never doubted that in the film he would have to break through the fourth wall of the screen and talk directly to the camera, as to a confidant. If this unsettled the audience, so much the better. They should not be comfortable hearing his vile secrets and being treated as accomplices. (McKellen 1996: 23)

Al Pacino's *Looking for Richard*, made in the same year as Loncraine's adaptation, takes this rupturing of the fourth wall one stage further. Pacino's "socio-drama type thing" is a mixture of rehearsal, costumed playing, discussion, talking heads, *vox populi*, and interview with a "spontaneous structure driven by association and digression rather than a linear narrative" (Lanier 1998: 41). Pacino's stated intention is to "communi-cate a Shakespeare that is about how we feel and how we think today." In this way the fourth wall is not simply breached but totally done away with as Pacino con-templates not merely Shakespeare's *Richard III* but the place of Shakespeare at the end of the twentieth century, as well as cultural questions about the tension between English stage and American film traditions; different acting styles (the English actor-manager versus the Hollywood film star); the antipathy between theatrical and academic investigation; and so on. In addition, technical problems are also confronted such as soliloquy, setting, voice projection, or iambic pentameter. The film is, throughout, fully self-conscious, reflexive, as actors drop in and out of role, address the camera, wrangle between themselves over differing interpretations, seek the advice of thespians (Peter Brook, Kenneth Branagh, Sir John Gielgud, and so on) or academics (Emrys Jones or Barbara Everett). In this sense, Peter Holland has rightly identified *Looking for Richard* as "the first Shakespeare metafilm" (Holland 2000: xiv).

Looking for Richard opens with a shot of a gothic cathedral and a voice-over (with an English accent) of Prospero's "Our revels now are ended . . ." (*The Tempest*, 4.2.148–58). Pacino's laudable design seems to be to make Shakespeare, above all, readily comprehensible – "We're peddling [Shakespeare]", he tells a couple of kids he meets on the street. For example, in this opening speech (and again when it is repeated as the film's epilogue) "Leave not a rack behind" becomes "Leave not a wisp behind" – presumably because the description of a cloud as a *rack* is outmoded (*OED* lists its most recent use in this sense as 1886). Pacino is seen playing basket-ball with a youngster in front of a forbidding American tower block. The juxtaposition of English gothic architecture and massive American cityscape prompts a series of questions about intercultural negotiation and exchange; as an anonymous French girl incredulously asks, "You want to do it wiz yor American accent?" The basket-ball also suggests that Pacino is on a mission to share Shakespeare with the young, to wrench the play from the traditional authorities of tweedy professors and stiff British accents and pass it to a new generation of streetwise American adolescents. We see him mockingly blaspheme when he calls *The Annotated Shakespeare* "The Anointed Shakespeare," as though it constituted a holy book, and near the beginning he recites the opening speech of *Richard III* to an audience of teenagers only to find, upon asking them to paraphrase, that not one of them has the slightest notion what he is saying – indeed, a couple are seen "making out" in the back row in clear defiance of his cultural imperative! His voice rises with exasperation as he complains about the difficulty of the play: "In Shakespeare you have an entire company on the stage, good actors, not knowing where they're going, where they ARE!" On the other hand, Pacino is anxious to maintain some sort of Elizabethan authenticity and has (only half-jokingly) William Shakespeare sitting in the auditorium shaking his head with disappointment. "Fuck," exclaims Pacino, at this double bind.

Shakespeare, here, is a kind of cultural and spiritual savior. Early on, as the film canvasses the opinions of passers-by on a busy New York street, one ostensibly dispossessed speaker declaims passionately that Shakespearean language is the language of "feeling":

When we speak with no feeling we get nothing outta our society. We should speak like Shakespeare. We should introduce Shakespeare into the academic; know why? Because then the kids would have feelings. That's why it's easy for us to get a gun and shoot each other. We don't feel for each other. But if we were taught to *feel* we wouldn't be so violent.

This messianic Shakespeare is, paradoxically, deeply old fashioned and traditional, stretching back at least as far as Matthew Arnold and the Romantic poets; Shakespeare is unquestionably valuable, he is a civilizing influence, he is mysteriously *good* for us – here, he'll stop us shooting each other (ironic, given the amount of slaughter in *Richard III*, to name but one play)! Paradoxically, it is this mystified Shakespeare which the film endorses even as it protests that it seeks for a way to democratize and elucidate him. At one point, Vanessa Redgrave cringingly suggests that

> Shakespeare's poetry and his iambics floated and descended through the pentameter of the soul and it's the soul, if we like, the spirit of real concrete people going through hell and sometimes moments of great achievement and joy – *that* is the pentameter you have to concentrate on, and should you find that reality, all the iambics will fall into place.

Yet, elsewhere, Pacino rightly shows himself to be impatient with this kind of enigmatic twaddle; when his collaborator, Frederic Kimball, describes the iambic as "an anteater – he's very high in the back and very short, er, little front legs: ta TA" – Pacino looks directly into the camera and raises his eyebrows heavenwards, shaking his head in disbelief.

The film, then, is inconsistent in its approach to *Richard III* as well as the larger questions that surround the performance of Shakespeare in contemporary urban America. At one point Pacino finds himself at a party in conversation with a woman – half-hippie throw-back and half-New York socialite – who insists that Shakespeare is Talmudic while, at the same time, he is best interpreted via the Chinese concepts of Yin and Yang. Elsewhere a radical director talks about how she wants to stage *Macbeth* with "Lady Macbeth in a rock and roll context . . . singing the blues, doing the beat, doing her thing." In despair, Pacino confides to Kimball, "You must get me out of this. This idea is a bad idea. It's gone too far." Nonetheless, Pacino's faith in Shakespeare is unshakeable perhaps all the more because the Bard is resilient to such ridiculous appropriations. The play can be trusted magically to cast its own company: "Hopefully, somehow the role and the actor will merge . . . the actor will find the role . . . and the casting will get done." Of course this providential coincidence of actor and role is precisely that of the Method, based on the work of Konstantin Stanislavsky and promulgated especially in America through the Actors' Studio under the directorship (1951–82) of Lee Strasberg, whose pupils included Marlon Brando, Anne Bancroft, Paul Newman, and Shelley Winters. Robert de Niro, Dustin Hoffman, and Pacino himself are among its contemporary practitioners with performances marked by naturalistic, psychologically rounded characterizations.

This empathic quality verges on the obsessive as Pacino and Kimball seek (note the film's title) the essential Richard/Shakespeare beneath the script in front of them (one section is subtitled "the quest"). Pacino makes his way to the Bankside Globe which (although only half-finished) seems to inspire him. Elsewhere, in an unfortunate incident, the two of them visit the Birthplace in Stratford-upon-Avon. As Kimball waits for "an epiphany" they manage to set off a fire alarm and their visit is cut short by the appearance of a nonplused fireman. "That's a real bummer," complains Kimball. As they rehearse the ghost scene in London's West End they seek the phantoms of previous performances and Pacino emphasizes that this is "method acting type stuff." On the one hand, then, there is an awakening of faith in the wonder of Shakespeare – something understood. On the other, there is an aggressive, hard-bitten New Yorker's contempt for the intangible, a stubborn American materialism.

At the same time as the performance is underlined by this empirical or experiential approach, it continually attempts to valorize itself with reference to specialists both academic and theatrical. Kimball challenges Winona Ryder to explain why Lady Anne mourns Henry VI so publicly, suggesting that the character deliberately set out to encounter Richard of Gloucester: "Did she not have any idea that if she went out with a corpse making frequent stops [she would meet him]?" This perverse reading is rejected as Pacino asks the rest of the company for a better suggestion. His proposal that an academic's advice be sought, in an attempt to untangle the characters' motivations, infuriates Kimball:

> You know more about *Richard III* than any fucking scholar at Columbia or Harvard. This is ridiculous because you are making this entire documentary in order to show that actors truly are the possessors of a tradition – the proud inheritors of the understanding of Shakespeare, for Christ's sakes, and then you turn around and say, "I'm gonna go get a scholar to explain it to you." THIS IS RIDICULOUS!

Unsurprisingly, since it is above all an *English* authority which the film seeks to displace, it is neither to Columbia nor Harvard but to Oxford that Pacino and Kimball direct their quest. Emrys Jones is pictured in a Larkinesque bewilderment, sitting in front of a small manual typewriter (American academics all have laptops, of course), surrounded by books. He blinks awkwardly at his interlocutors, folds his arms, crosses and uncrosses his legs. "I don't really *know* why he needed to marry her historically . . . erm, it's . . ." – cut to Pacino hanging on his every word and Kimball's expression of frustration and fury in equal measure. Pacino's voice-over then goes on to give his own perfectly feasible explanation: Richard needs a queen, Anne is a Lancastrian and, were she to marry Richard, their wedlock would unite the warring factions and publicly "exonerat[e] him from his crime [of murdering her husband and father-in-law]." As so often, the sequence implies, actors are the only ones in a position to answer theatrical difficulties – academics are too far removed. As the film goes on it is notable that the academic interpolations become less frequent. Ostensibly there to provide expert help, the professorial input is ironized, even sent up.

The opinions of actors are more widely sought, though in this case, less to do with interpretative matters, than the insecurities felt by American performers, overwhelmed by the long shadow of English stage traditions. "As Americans, what is that thing," Pacino asks, "that gets between us and Shakespeare?" Derek Jacobi's paternalism verges on the patronizing:

I think Americans have been made to feel inhibited because they've been told so long by their critics, by their scholars, by all the commentators on Shakespeare that they cannot do Shakespeare; therefore they've got it into their heads that they can't and you become totally self-conscious, and I think the great thing about American actors is that they're not self-conscious, but they are when it comes to Shakespeare because they've been told they can't do it and, very foolishly, they've believed that.

Jacobi comforts himself with the thought that the foolishness is the Americans'. Gielgud's patrician pronouncement is unconscionably offensive, at the same time as it is charmingly rendered in his elegant English accent: "Perhaps they [American actors or Americans in general?] don't go to picture galleries and read books as much as we do, because I think it's the fact of how everybody looked and behaved – that one's got a sort of Elizabethan feeling of period." Even Peter Brook, a director who has spent many years working outside England pioneering internationally constituted companies, is happy to pronounce on what he perceives to be a transatlantic misapprehension:

> If you get obsessed with the text – this is a great barrier to American actors who get obsessed with the British way of regarding a text. That isn't what matters; what matters is that you have to, one way or the other, penetrate into what, at every moment, it's about.

While the arrogance of these commentators, their assured sense of cultural superiority, is attributable, in part at least, to an element of self-protection – enfranchise American Equity and that way unemployment lies – it is, in fact, a widespread prejudice. Loncraine's film, as we have seen, used the Woodvilles' foreignness, creatively, in order to stigmatize them in the eyes of the English court (to say nothing of the film's English audience). But this sense of American inferiority or lack of confidence can also be seen in critical writings on the Shakespeare film industry. In a seminal essay about cinematic Shakespeare, Lynda E. Boose and Richard Burt (1997a) point out that "offshoots" rather than "straight" versions of Shakespeare are more suitable to the American market which is, implicitly, better equipped to handle watered-down Shakespeare:

> Perhaps because Shakespeare is such a signifier for British cultural superiority, America's relationship to the Bard has frequently been marked by all the signs of a colonized consciousness. All in all the preferred American approach to Shakespeare has been decidedly oblique; up until the sudden, Branagh-inspired boom in straight Shakespeare of the mid-nineties, Hollywood has distinctly felt more comfortable reworking Shakespeare into new, specifically American narratives such as Woody Allen's *A Midsummer Night's Sex Comedy* (1982) or Paul Mazursky's *Tempest* (1982), for example. America's best made for film Shakespeare productions may, in fact, be the musicals *Kiss Me, Kate* (dir. George Sidney, 1953) and *West Side Story* (dirs. Robert Wise and Jerome Robbins, 1961), where the Bard is recreated within a particular theatrical idiom that is thoroughly home-grown. (Boose and Burt 1997a: 13)

Barbara Freedman equates Americanness and immaturity as she attributes the success of Loncraine's *Richard III* to the "film's popular appeal to a depoliticized American and Americanized international youth market" (Freedman 2000: 65). Given the crushing weight of the reputed authority of English Shakespearean know-how, as well as the degree to which transatlantic Shakespeare is taken to be inferior, underdeveloped, or downright ignorant, it is refreshing to hear the achievement of *Looking for Richard* justifiably (if a little jingoistically) described as that of "hardy, ambitious Americans who take on a powerful Old World and come out winners" (cited in Coursen 2000: 114).

In fact, the film's *mise-en-scène* – a perfectly credible medieval setting and costume – works well and the performances are generally successful:

> Only Aidan Quinn's Richmond jars: the ponderous delivery sounds uncomfortably like John Wayne. Pacino, Kevin Spacey as Buckingham, Alec Baldwin as Clarence, Kevin Conway as Hastings, Harris Yulin as the King, and Penelope Allen as the Queen deliver the poetry with vigour and an alertness to its rhythm and sense. (Sinyard 2000: 63)

The film also creatively alludes to Olivier's version in its highlighting of Richard's shadow (which Richard taps playfully with his riding crop) and its battle sequence. Perhaps the most conspicuous allusion to Olivier's film is in the physical likeness of Winona Ryder to Claire Bloom, both of whom play Lady Anne. Both actresses are small, dark, feminine, extremely beautiful, and both portray Anne as innocent and modest (in contrast to the forward portraits of Jane Shore interpolated into both versions). In these wooing scenes both Annes genuinely fall for Richard's protestations and both move to kiss him. Kristin Scott-Thomas, on the other hand, in Loncraine's version, remains wary of Richard and is still confused rather than submissive, crushed by the death of her husband (Loncraine's film, as well as Olivier's, substitutes Edward's body for the play's Henry VI which serves to intensify Anne's grief). In an acute reading, Marliss C. Desens has suggested that we are, in any case, bound to be less sympathetic to Thomas's Lady Anne than to Bloom's: "While in Olivier's film, Anne becomes the icon for the weak but innocent female victim – very much a 1950s stereotype – in Loncraine's she becomes an icon for the neurotic one – a stereotype of the 1990s" (Desens 2000: 265). But the wooing of Lady Anne also serves to illustrate a contrast in the playing of Richard.

As the two characters joust verbally, Richard, with magnificent effrontery, proposes a sexual congress:

> *Lady Anne.* And thou [art] unfit for any place but hell.
> *Richard.* Yes, one place else, if you will hear me name it.
> *Lady Anne.* Some dungeon.
> *Richard.* Your bedchamber. (1.2.109–11)

In both Olivier's and Pacino's versions, Richard's extraordinary suggestion is spoken directly to Lady Anne. In Loncraine's, however, as Richard and Anne circle the corpse on the post-mortem slab between them, he utters the line *sotto voce* directly to the camera, and she fails to hear it. This has the effect of undermining Richard's achievement, as his gross impertinence is tempered by discretion, but it also marks a clear contrast between Pacino's and McKellen's protagonists. Pacino, despite being culturally dislocated by the Americanness which so alarms him, is the real inheritor of Olivier's performance. His is a Richard of charm, confidence, wit, adroit enough "To take her in her heart's extremest hate" (1.2.219). On the other hand, McKellen's Richard conscripts rather than seduces Anne, and so this is a Richard that fails to connect as closely with the audience as the other two performances. Finally, then, McKellen's Richard is "no charming Vice-figure but a haggard, sleepless killer" (Loehlin 1997a: 75).

Kenneth Branagh's *Henry V* (1989)

Near the beginning of *Looking for Richard*, in an interview with Pacino, Kenneth Branagh recalls his first lack-lustre exposure to the playwright who would, subsequently, make him a household name:

> Now I was brought up in a school where Shakespeare was taught, in the first instance, very, kind of, straightforwardly and dully, to be perfectly honest, and we read it aloud and of course, it made no sense to us 'cause there was no, kind of, connection made.

Any account of contemporary Shakespearean film would be incomplete without some attention to Branagh. Symptomatic of his importance is his appearance on the covers of many current studies of Shakespeare on screen, for instance, Burnett and Wray (2000) (*Hamlet*); Jackson (2000b) (*Love's Labour's Lost*); Cartmell (2000) (*Henry V*); Skovmand (1994) (*Henry V*); Loehlin (1997b) (*Henry V*). Images of him on stage also appear on the covers of Shaughnessy (1994) and Jackson and Smallwood (1988) (both *Henry V*). It is because of his centrality and the volume of work written on him that I have left him till last and have dedicated the bulk of this essay to two less thoroughly documented films. Nonetheless, Branagh's significance cannot be overstated. The rash of Shakespearean films which appeared in the 1990s is due mainly to the impact of his work and especially to the success of his *Henry V*: "I was convinced that I could make a truly popular film" (Branagh 1989: 10).

Branagh, at the age of 23, was the youngest Henry V to appear at the Royal Shakespeare Company, in Adrian Noble's production of 1984. In his account of the role on stage, he notes the formative influence of Olivier's 1944 film: "My first experience of Henry V, inevitably, was Olivier's remarkable film treatment. It would come to haunt me as I attempted the role myself" (Branagh 1988: 93). While critical orthodoxy has it that films often set out to record stage versions (Loncraine's *Richard III* is based on Richard Eyre's 1990 National Theatre production), it is interesting to note here that cinema and theatre are symbiotic. Yet while Branagh's performance based itself on Olivier's film, tonally it was much darker.[7]

The circumstances surrounding the making and role of Olivier's version are well known. The film was made between June 1943 and July 1944 and premiered in London on November 22 that year. Sponsored by the Ministry of Information, it is prefaced with the caption: "To the Commandos and Airborne Troops of Great Britain, the spirit of whose ancestors it has been humbly attempted to recapture in some ensuing scenes – this film is dedicated." Made at a time of national crisis, Olivier's film was an attempt to galvanize a nation at war whose forces, on June 6 that year in the D-Day landings, attempted the kind of assault that Harry's invading armies conduct in the play. Though Olivier had returned from Hollywood in 1941 in order to enlist in the Royal Navy Volunteer Reserve, it was through film that he chose to contribute to the war effort, being fully conscious of the way Shakespeare could be mobilized as part of Britain's martial struggle: "I had a mission . . . My country was at war; I felt Shakespeare within me, I felt the cinema within him, I knew what I wanted to do, what he would have done" (cited in Donaldson 1990: 2–3). Shakespeare's poetry would have resonated with that of Britain's wartime leader: "Clearly, Henry's speeches would remind a contemporary audience of Churchill (compare Henry's 'We few, we happy few, we band of brothers', 4.3.60, to Churchill's 'Never in the field of human conflict was so much owed by so many to so few')" (Cartmell 2000: 97).

In order to heroize his Henry, Olivier strategically cut elements in Shakespeare's script which compromise the king's authority or discredit his reputation. For instance, the Southampton conspiracy which threatens domestic betrayal; the Harfleur speech in which Henry intimidates its Governor with graphic descriptions of rape and slaughter; the misgivings on the eve of Agincourt about Henry IV's guilt in the murder of Richard II; the order to slay the French prisoners (in defiance of the Geneva Convention); and, perhaps most significantly, the execution of Bardolph. The closing Chorus which recounts the ephemeral nature of Henry's triumph is also cut. Olivier's film portrays an idealized Commander-in-Chief presiding over a united army which conducts its heroic campaign with almost no internal dissension. The unity of Henry's troops is anticipated by the harmony between the various social ranks that appear in the opening sequence in the Globe Theatre: "There is a vigorous if rough-hewn camaraderie about the totality of the theatrical experience which mirrors that required of troops and generals in a war" (Davies 2000: 168). In shiny silver armor and astride a rearing white steed, Olivier's Henry is a model of chivalric heroism and an inspirational example of courage, truly worthy of the sobriquet, "This star of England" (Epilogue 5).

Branagh's film version is both a tribute to Olivier's and a departure from it. To begin with, the very decision to direct and play the title-role on film identifies Branagh as a successor to Olivier and the film echoes and converses both diegetically and extradiegetically with the 1944 version, as Peter S. Donaldson explains:

The variously nuanced rivalry is part of the film's meaning: the young filmmaker's ambition is paralleled in the French Campaign of the youthful Henry V, and, though Olivier
himself does not appear in the film, Paul Scofield, in a magisterial performance as the
French King, stands in for him, registering metaphorically the sorrow of an older generation of Shakespearean actors faced with the imperious claims of youth. (Donaldson
1991: 61)

The major distinction is one of tone and the contrast is obvious from the outset, as the
conversation between Canterbury and Ely (1.1) is conspiratorial, machiavellian, and
shady as opposed to the comic buffoonery, the dropping of papers, the audience heckles
in Olivier's version. As Branagh himself recognized: "Although Olivier's film had been
welcomed and celebrated as part of the war effort, its seeming nationalistic and militaristic emphasis had created a great deal of suspicion and doubt about the value of
Henry V for a late twentieth-century audience" (Branagh 1989: 9). In the wake of the
privations and moral collapse of the 1980s under Margaret Thatcher, which in academic circles aroused the oppositional criticism of the cultural materialists (especially
Dollimore and Sinfield 1985; Drakakis 1985; Holderness 1988; 1992), as well as the
epic and revolutionary *Wars of the Roses*, staged by the English Shakespeare Company
between 1986 and 1989, itself animated by the bleak, if short-lived destructiveness of
the Falklands war (Bogdanov and Pennington 1990: 48), *Henry V* could no longer be
viewed as an unambiguous paean to Henry's martial virtuosity. From the early days of
its RSC incarnation, Branagh was aware of this complication: "I know many people
who questioned the wisdom of putting the play on so soon after the Falklands conflict" (Branagh 1988: 98). Accordingly, Branagh's film reinstated some of the less
wholesome elements, such as the Southampton conspiracy as well as the belligerent
horror of the Harfleur speech. Even so it avoided Henry's command to slaughter the
French prisoners – an omission which Branagh was later to regret:

> I think I rather flunked and avoided [the killing of the prisoners], and although I make
> dramatic sense in the context of our picture, I could have possibly been braver about
> the way we presented it and not, as I feared we would, lose the sympathy of the audi-
> ence for the central character. (Branagh 2000: 172)

Perhaps the most notable example of Branagh's revision of Olivier's film was the
inclusion of a scene which had been staged as an interpolation in Noble's RSC version.
In the play we hear that Bardolph (one of the prince's old friends from the Eastcheap
tavern scenes of *Henry IV*) is to be executed for robbing a pax. Noble actually staged
the execution which took place in front of the king:

> Bardolph kneels, hands tied, with the armored Exeter looming at his back, before the
> silent Harry some feet away – with a long, transfixing wordless gaze. When, at Henry's
> nod, he is abruptly garroted, he offers no struggle. Gently, submissively, his head and
> shoulders sag forward onto his chest as he bows in death to become a kneeling corpse.
> (Fitter 1991: 262)

In the film version Bardolph (played by Richard Briers) is lynched over the bough of a tree by the brutal and fully armored Exeter (Brian Blessed). The pathos of the episode (and the rigor of Henry's military order) is intensified by a flashback (one of several in the film) to the riotous days of the Boar's Head Tavern in which Bardolph and Falstaff compete in a drinking game. Bardolph cheats by digging his opponent in the ribs, causing him to spill his beer. Hal is seen to be joining in with the sport and Bardolph (assigned one of Falstaff's lines from *1 Henry IV*) appeals to him, "Do not . . . when thou art king, hang a thief" (1.2.61). Hal's smile fades and he responds with melancholy foresight. "No, thou shalt." We register the shock on Bardolph's face before we cut to the present to see him, his nose slit and bloody, his head in a noose imploring Henry, silently, for mercy. With tears in his eyes, Henry nods at Exeter and Bardolph is kicked off the back of the cart as it is pulled out from under him. Lynched high in the air, his feet kick grotesquely as Henry looks on, a single tear chasing down his face. In one sense, the scene reinforces the loneliness of Hal who has lost his bed-fellow in the Southampton conspiracy and now loses an old chum from his youth, but it also serves to problematize the Olivian idea of Henry as a benevolent ruler. Though clearly upset by the episode, Branagh's Henry is steely in his determination that nothing, not even the sparing of an old friend, should jeopardize the success of his invasion. As if to underline this, Montjoy (Christopher Ravenscroft) enters on horse-back and glances up disapprovingly at Bardolph's dangling feet; so too does Derek Jacobi's Chorus, who pulls his coat and scarf around him more tightly as though to indicate that the warmth of the Eastcheap tavern is consigned firmly to the past.

In another important revision of Olivier's film version, Branagh's Henry is vulnerable and racked by doubt. As the Governor of Harfleur surrenders, Henry is hugely relieved. Clearly his muddied, wrangling, and exhausted troops could never have conducted the violent assault which Henry threatened, and the surrender of Harfleur is shown to have resulted from Henry's bluff. Moreover, the strain has taken its toll – shortly after the capitulation, Henry is shown to collapse onto the shoulder of Exeter, who catches him and helps him stumble towards the city. This moment anticipates the mixture of exhaustion and elation that follows Montjoy's admission of defeat after the Battle of Agincourt: "The day is yours" (4.7.84). In the Olivier film there is no room for this kind of doubt, but in Branagh's, even in victory, Henry is tarnished. As the slaughtered luggage boys are piled in a wagon, Henry's expression undermines the conquest:

> He gently lays the BOY down, kisses him gently on the head, and then stands up as the rest of the army gather round him as best they can. We cut close on his blood-stained and exhausted face, the dreadful price they have all had to pay for this so-called victory clearly etched into his whole being. His head drops as if in shame. (Branagh 1989: 114)

As Samuel Crowl has demonstrated, the shot is a quotation of the moment when Olivier's Henry rallies his troops from the back of a cart (Crowl 1992: plates 19, 20), but whereas Olivier's burnished monarch addresses his soldiers before Agincourt, Branagh's muddied and bloodied Henry regards his (for he has nothing to say) from the cart *after* the battle; if this is a victory at all, it is surely a Pyrrhic one. War is thus deglamorized both here and in the preceding battle sequences in which the mud and chaos derive from the Battle of Shrewsbury as it appears in Orson Welles's *Chimes at Midnight* (1966).

As has been often noted, Olivier's film incorporates, in its early Choruses at least, a self-consciousness that is truly Shakespearean and the achievements of Henry's campaign are subtly undercut by the consistent reminders that they are being staged for us "On this unworthy scaffold" (Prologue 10). Although Branagh's initial Chorus transcodifies drama to film by changing the setting from Olivier's Globe to a film studio, subsequent Choruses are absorbed by and placed *within* the fictive world of the Henry story. Thus, Jacobi is set on the white cliffs as he talks of the scene shifting to Southampton and he is actually present at the siege of Harfleur: "The CHORUS continues, his speech is urgent, breathless as if he too were caught up in the battle . . . Now we cut close on the CHORUS, he is caught up wildly in the excitement of the gunfire, smoke and explosions" (Branagh 1989: 53). At Agincourt the Chorus "emerges and begins to walk towards us as soldiers run past him towards the battlefield" (p. 101). Jacobi's Chorus, albeit that he is wearing modern dress, is part of the action, and those devices which Olivier used to defamiliarize the myth of Henry – the opening sequence at the Globe, the cardboard cut-out sets in which French castles resemble nothing so much as Santa's Grotto, the return to the Globe at the ending with Henry married to a princess played by a boy – all these devices are smoothed over and rendered inconspicuous in the Branagh version. The effect is to remove or neutralize those elements which call attention to the play's artificiality; Branagh's film attempts to expose the viewer to the horrors of war at first hand, unmediated by the framing devices of Olivier's film (or Shakespeare's play).[8]

A number of critics have found in this naturalization a reactionary politic. Chris Fitter, for instance, suggests that the film

> slides away at every point from a Shakespearean interrogation of the action and liberation of the imagination, into the political and financial security of transparent and singular meaning . . . Furthermore, the very familiarity of the film's screen conventions works to naturalize ideology rather than interrogate and defamiliarize the action. (Fitter 1991: 273)

But Branagh *has* included moments of ideological awkwardness, even (in the execution of Bardolph) inserting new ones, while, as we have seen, he regrets having cut the killing of the French prisoners. Albeit that the film is frequently accused of varnishing over the horrors of aggressive imperialism, of fobbing us off with a romanticized story of a young king's struggle to win against the odds, might it not be that this predisposition passively to accept the veracity of film derives more from the naturalistic conventions of the medium? As Fitter himself acknowledges, modern film productions "encourage a relation of docile, passive empathy from an audience distanced from the plane of action in far-reaching tiers" (Fitter 1991: 272). In the light of this suggestion, perhaps we should take heed of Graham Greene's early misgivings when he expressed himself "less than ever confident that there is an aesthetic justification for filming Shakespeare at all" (cited in Jackson 2000a: 21).

NOTES

1   The quotation in my title comes from *Macbeth*, 1.5.62–3 (all Shakespeare quotations are from Shakespeare 1988). I am grateful to Mary Brewer, Paul Edmondson, Roy Pierce-Jones, Karen Roberts, Jim Shaw, and Nik Smith who helped me locate video and other material.
2   The *chanteuse* is played by Stacey Kent. McKellen notes, "I liked Colin Good's resemblance to a young Jack Payne or Glen [*sic*] Miller" (McKellen 1996: 58).
3   McKellen (1996: 124) remembers how the props department sought out an antique Rolex worth £5,000 which appears in the film only incidentally. Throughout, Richard smokes Abdulla cigarettes.
4   In *Looking for Richard* this prophecy causes Frederic Kimball and Al Pacino all sorts of difficulties. Without noticing Shakespeare's ironic use of *G*, they propose substituting the letter *C* (for Clarence). In the final take, though, this suggestion is thankfully forgotten.
5   *Martin Chuzzlewit* by Charles Dickens contains wonderfully comical descriptions of oafish American table manners, for instance.
6   "England in 1819." The poem was written about George III, who was certified insane in 1811 and died nine years later. Coincidentally, it was for the son of this monarch, the Prince Regent, that Brighton Pavilion, shown later in the same scene, was originally constructed.
7   This essay excludes discussion of the film of Deborah Warner's National Theatre *Richard II*, with Fiona Shaw in the title role (1995). Those analyzed here are fully realized film versions, albeit based on previous stage performances. Warner's film, although excellent and interesting in its own right, is really a film recording of a theatre version and, in the interests of consistency, has been left out.
8   A more recent example of this ostensibly unmediated exposure of the audience to the horror of battle would be the opening sequence of Steven Spielberg's *Saving Private Ryan* (1998).

REFERENCES AND FURTHER READING

Bogdanov, M. and Pennington, M. (1990). *The English Shakespeare Company.* London: Nick Hern Books.
Boose, L. E. and Burt, R. (1997a). Totally Clueless? Shakespeare goes to Hollywood in the 1990s. In L. E. Boose and R. Burt (eds.) *Shakespeare, the Movie: Popularising the Plays on Film, TV and Video.* London: Routledge, 8–22.
——(eds.) (1997b). *Shakespeare, the Movie: Popularising the Plays on Film, TV and Video.* London: Routledge.
Branagh, K. (1988). Henry V. In R. Jackson and R. Smallwood (eds.) *Players of Shakespeare 2.* Cambridge: Cambridge University Press, 93–105.
——(1989). *Henry V by William Shakespeare: A Screen Adaptation by Kenneth Branagh.* London: Chatto and Windus.
——(2000). From the Horse's Mouth: Branagh on the Bard. In M. T. Burnett and R. Wray (eds.) *Shakespeare, Film, Fin de Siècle.* London: Macmillan, 165–78.
Buhler, S. M. (2000). Camp *Richard III* and the Burdens of (Stage/Film) History. In M. T. Burnett and R. Wray (eds.) *Shakespeare, Film, Fin de Siècle.* London: Macmillan, 40–57.

Bullough, G. (1960). *Narrative and Dramatic Sources of Shakespeare*, Vol. 3. London: Routledge.

Burnett, M. T. and Wray, R. (eds.) (2000). *Shakespeare, Film, Fin de Siècle.* London: Macmillan.

Cartmell, D. (1999). The Shakespeare on Screen Industry. In D. Cartmell and I. Whelehan (eds.) *Adaptations: From Text to Screen, Screen to Text.* London: Routledge, 29–37.

——(2000). *Interpreting Shakespeare on Screen.* London: Macmillan.

Coursen, H. R. (2000). Filming Shakespeare's History: Three Films of *Richard III.* In R. Jackson (ed.) *The Cambridge Companion to Shakespeare on Film.* Cambridge: Cambridge University Press, 99–116.

Crowdus, G. (1998). Shakespeare is up to date: An interview with Sir Ian McKellen. *Cineaste,* 24, 46–7.

Crowl, S. (1992). *Shakespeare Observed: Studies in Performance on Stage and Screen.* Athens, OH: Ohio University Press.

——(1997). Changing Colors like the Chameleon: Ian McKellen's *Richard III* from Stage to Film. *Post Script: Essays in Film and the Humanities,* 17, 53–63.

——(2000). Flamboyant Realist: Kenneth Branagh. In R. Jackson (ed.) *The Cambridge Companion to Shakespeare on Film.* Cambridge: Cambridge University Press, 222–38.

Davies, A. (1988). *Filming Shakespeare's Plays.* Cambridge: Cambridge University Press.

——(2000). The Shakespeare Films of Laurence Olivier. In R. Jackson (ed.) *The Cambridge Companion to Shakespeare on Film.* Cambridge: Cambridge University Press, 163–82.

Desens, M. C. (2000). Cutting Women Down to Size in the Olivier and Loncraine Films of *Richard III.* In G. Ioppolo (ed.) *Shakespeare Performed: Essays in Honour of R. A. Foakes.* London: Associated University Presses, 260–72.

Dollimore, J. and Sinfield, A. (eds.) (1985). *Political Shakespeare: New Essays in Cultural Materialism.* Manchester: Manchester University Press.

Donaldson, P. S. (1990). *Shakespearean Films/Shakespearean Directors.* Boston, MA: Unwin Hyman.

——(1991). Taking on Shakespeare: Kenneth Branagh's *Henry V. Shakespeare Quarterly,* 42, 60–71.

Drakakis, J. (ed.) (1985). *Alternative Shakespeares.* London: Methuen.

Fitter, C. (1991). A Tale of Two Branaghs: *Henry V,* Ideology, and the Mekong Agincourt. In I. Kamps (ed.) *Shakespeare Left and Right.* New York: Routledge, 259–75.

Freedman, B. (2000). Critical Junctures in Shakespeare Screen History. In R. Jackson (ed.) *The Cambridge Companion to Shakespeare on Film.* Cambridge: Cambridge University Press, 47–71.

Hedrick, D. K. (1997). War is Mud: Branagh's Dirty Harry V and the Types of Political Ambiguity. In L. E. Boose and R. Burt (eds.) *Shakespeare, the Movie: Popularising the Plays on Film, TV and Video.* London: Routledge, 45–66.

Holderness, G. (ed.) (1988). *The Shakespeare Myth.* Manchester: Manchester University Press.

——(1992). *Shakespeare Recycled: The Making of Historical Drama.* New York: Harvester Wheatsheaf.

Holland, P. (2000). Foreword. In M. T. Burnett and R. Wray (eds.) *Shakespeare, Film, Fin de Siècle.* London: Macmillan, xii–xiv.

Jackson, R. (2000a). From Play-script to Screenplay. In R. Jackson (ed.) *The Cambridge Companion to Shakespeare on Film.* Cambridge: Cambridge University Press, 15–34.

——(ed.) (2000b). *The Cambridge Companion to Shakespeare on Film.* Cambridge: Cambridge University Press.

Jackson, R. and Smallwood, R. (eds.) (1988). *Players of Shakespeare 2.* Cambridge: Cambridge University Press.

Jorgens, J. J. (1991). *Shakespeare on Film.* New York: University Press of America.

Lanier, D. (1998). Now: The Presence of History in *Looking for Richard. Post Script: Essays in Film and the Humanities,* 17, 39–55.

Loehlin, J. N. (1997a). "Top of the World, Ma": *Richard III* and Cinematic Convention. In L. E. Boose and R. Burt (eds.) *Shakespeare, the Movie: Popularising the Plays on Film, TV and Video.* London: Routledge, 67–79.

——(1997b). *Henry V: Shakespeare in Performance.* Manchester: Manchester University Press.

McKellen, I. (1996). *William Shakespeare's Richard III.* London: Doubleday.

Manvell, R. (1971). *Shakespeare and the Film*. London: J. M. Dent.

Mitchell, D. (1997). *Richard III*: Tonypandy in the Twentieth Century. *Literature Film Quarterly*, 25, 133–45.

Rollins, H. E. (ed.) (1944). *A New Variorum Edition of Shakespeare, The Sonnets*. Philadelphia, PA: J. B. Lippincott.

Rosenthal, D. (2000). *Shakespeare on Screen*. London: Hamlyn.

Salamon, L. B. (2000). *Looking for Richard* in History: Postmodern Villainy in *Richard III* and *Scarface*. *Journal of Popular Film and Television*, 28, 54–63.

Shakespeare, W. (1988). *The Complete Works*, ed. S. Wells and G. Taylor. Oxford: Oxford University Press.

Shaughnessy, R. (1994). *Representing Shakespeare: England, History and the RSC*. New York: Harvester Wheatsheaf.

Sinyard, N. (2000). Shakespeare meets *The Godfather*: The Postmodern Populism of Al Pacino's *Looking for Richard*. In M. T. Burnett and R. Wray (eds.) *Shakespeare, Film, Fin de Siècle*. London: Macmillan, 58–72.

Skovmand, M. (ed.) (1994). *Screen Shakespeare*. Aarhus, Denmark: Aarhus University Press.

Walker, G. (2000). *Richard III*: The Shape of History. In F. Guinle and J. Ramel (eds.) *William Shakespeare Richard III: nouvelles perspectives critiques*. Montpellier: Université Paul-Valéry, 31–48.

8

The Elizabethan History Play:
A True Genre?

Paulina Kewes

> The players, who in their edition divided our authour's works into comedies, histories, and tragedies, seem not to have distinguished the three kinds, by any very exact or definitive ideas . . . There is not much nearer approach to unity of action in the tragedy of *Antony and Cleopatra*, than in the history of *Richard the Second*. But a history might be continued through many plays; as it had no plan, it had no limits.
>
> Samuel Johnson, Preface to *The Plays of William Shakespeare* (1765)

"The plaies that they plaie in England . . . are neither right comedies, nor right tragedies." So speaks a participant in a dialogue printed in John Florio's *Gardine of Recreation* (1591). He is evidently disconcerted by the generic impurity of current stage fare. When asked by his companion, "How would you name them then?", he replies: "Representations of histories, without any decorum" (Florio 1591: 23). In the Induction to the anonymous domestic tragedy *A Warning for Faire Women* (ca. 1590) personified figures of History ("with Drum and Ensigne"), Tragedy ("in her one hand a whip, in the other hand a knife"), and Comedy (playing a fiddle) struggle for possession of the stage. Tragedy overcomes her rivals but her victory is short-lived; as she herself tells the spectators in the Epilogue, "What now hath faild, to morrow you shall see, / Perform'd by Hystorie or Comedie" (Cannon 1975: ll. 1–2, 2733–4). This scenario seems to challenge Florio's, for history appears not as a contamination of tragedy and comedy but as a genre alongside them. Yet the *Warning*'s distinction between history and tragedy is left vague. History promises battle-scenes and noise, but there is no suggestion that it is more factual than tragedy. John Stow's slightly later *Svrvay of London* lists among the offerings of the London theatres "Comedies, Tragedies, interludes, and histories, both true and fayned" (Stow 1598: 69). Here we find a hint of a distinction between fact and fiction, but theatrical representations of both are named histories. Title-pages of printed playbooks,[1] entries for plays in the Stationers' Register, records of payments for scripts disbursed by the theatre entrepreneur Philip Henslowe, and licenses issued by successive Masters of the Revels, reveal a multitude of references to "story" and "history" in the titles and subtitles of Elizabethan and early Stuart plays: "The Honorable Historie," "The True Chronicle Historie," "a . . . Noble Roman Historye," "The Famous Chronicle historie," "The Famous History," "A historicall comedy," "French History," "The Scottish Historie," "The Comicall Historie," "The Pleasant Historie," "The True Chronicle Historie of the whole life and death of," "The Cronicle History," "the true and honorable historie," "An Antient Storie," "The most excellent Historie," "The Tragicall Historie," "the true Relation of the whole Historie," "an Honourable History," "An Historicall Tragedy," "An English Tragical History." In *An Apology For Actors*, published in 1612 but written several years earlier, Thomas Heywood seems to imply that the history play is one of the oldest dramatic forms, its origins dating back to the legendary golden age:

> I will begin with the antiquity of Acting Comedies, Tragedies, and Hystories. And first in the golden world. In the first of the *Olimpiads*, amongst many of the active exercises in which *Hercules* ever triumph'd as victor, there was in his nonage presented unto him by his Tutor in the fashion of a History, acted by the choyse of the nobility of Greece, the worthy and memorable acts of his father *Iupiter*.

Heywood then runs through a gamut of such mythological plays written "in the fashion of a History," only to turn to what he calls "our domesticke hystories" (among which he lists plays about Edward III and Henry V) and plays about "forreigne History" (Heywood 1612: sigs. B3^r, B4^r, F3^v). In Heywood's *Apology* the conception of history as a mode of shaping the drama gives way to the idea of history as a dramatic representation of the past, whether native or foreign. Last not least, the catalog prefaced to Shakespeare's First Folio of 1623 lists the contents of the volume under the three generic categories identified in the title: *Comedies, Histories, & Tragedies*.

Are these contemporary comments and classifications a sign that the Elizabethans and the Jacobeans perceived history (or, in modern critical parlance, the history play) as a dramatic genre in its own right, separate from tragedy and comedy? If so, how did they define it? The word history, we must remember, could mean many different things in the period, and its association with faithful recording of the past was by no means obvious or straightforward. Does the evidence of the plays themselves support the existence of a distinct genre of the history play? Generations of critics have thought so, and have striven to describe this elusive generic entity, proposing a range of formal and thematic criteria for differentiating histories from tragedies and comedies. Among the most frequently cited features of the Elizabethan history play are its Englishness, its open-endedness, and its didacticism. As titles of both old and new studies of the subject indicate – Schelling's *The English Chronicle Play: A Study in the Popular Historical Literature Environing Shakespeare* (1902); *Shakespeare's English Histories: A Quest for Form and Genre* (1996) edited by Velz – Shakespeare is routinely at the center of such inquiries. How sound are these critical classifications and, more important, how useful are they as a means of understanding the place of history in early modern theatrical culture?

Content

Definitions of the history play emphasize the distinctiveness of its subject matter, its form, or its ideology. The thematic approach to the genre characteristically designates as histories the plays about the "English" past, notably the post-Conquest past. A century ago Felix E. Schelling declared that "the Chronicle Play . . . retained from first to last a character essentially national and English" (Schelling 1902: v). Many later critics have concurred (Campbell 1947; Linderberger 1975; Barton 1977; Holderness, Potter, and Turner 1987; Rackin 1990; Hunter 1997; Velz 1996; Snyder 2001). Writing in the late 1990s, Jean Howard and Phyllis Rackin reiterate Schelling's claim: "what distinguishes [English 'history plays'] from other types of drama is above all their subject matter. They deal with *English* history, and they typically focus on the reign of a particular monarch" (Howard and Rackin 1997: 11). Though not everyone aiming to identify the genre of the history play draws a sharp distinction between foreign and native subject matter – Irving Ribner, for one, acknowledges that "it is ridiculous to make generic distinctions on the basis of the national origin of subject matter" (Ribner 1965: 5) – in practice terminological slippage is ubiquitous, "the history play" becoming mere shorthand for "the *English* history play." If the genre is defined by its preoccupation with the native past, then dramatizations of foreign pasts, whether ancient or modern, do not qualify as history plays and must find a generic niche elsewhere. Commentators such as Ribner acknowledged the essentially arbitrary nature of thematic classifications, and surveyed a wide range of candidates to the status of the history play before rendering generic judgments. Recent studies of the subject are as a rule more limited in scope, confining their investigation to a small number of plays featuring the native past, or to those by Shakespeare alone.[2] Indeed, since the publication of Ribner's survey there has been only one comprehensive study of Elizabethan dramatizations of the native past – Benjamin Griffin's thoughtful and thought-provoking *Playing the Past: Approaches to English Historical Drama 1385–1600* (2001) – and none of Elizabethan historical drama more broadly.

Such an insularity of approach is problematic on several grounds. First, the preoccupation with the so-called "English" histories elides important distinctions among the various kinds of native past, for critics treat England as coterminous with Britain. Secondly, it evinces a lack of sensitivity to questions of national identity which were fundamental to representations of the past in early modern historiography, historical poetry, and historical drama. Thirdly, the thematic focus on the native past means that national history plays are artificially isolated from contemporary plays portraying foreign history.

Let us take these points in turn. Benjamin Griffin's recent, stimulating attempt to codify the genre of the history play is marked by Anglocentrism. His "Appendix A:

Plays on English History: To 1642" includes such questionably "English" histories as *Macbeth*, *The Tragedy of the King of Scots*, *Robert II, King of Scots*, *The Scottish Historie of James IV*, *Malcolm King of Scots*, *The Valiant Scot*, and *The Valiant Welshman* (Griffin 2001: 150–6). Griffin is aware that "there could be lively arguments about whether Scottish, Cornish, and Welsh subjects [he omits Irish ones] are on 'native' history in the sense intended" (p. 148), yet he chooses not to engage with those arguments. Similar assimilation of Scottish, Welsh, Cornish, and Irish pasts under the rubric of "English" history characterizes earlier accounts by Ribner (1957), Hunter (1997), and others.

As Michael Neill, Christopher Highley, and Andrew Murphy have taught us, to cite "Englishness" as the defining feature of even such ostensibly "English" histories as *2 Henry VI*, *1 Henry IV*, or *Henry V* is misleading, for these plays bring to the fore the process of national self-definition (Neill 2000; Murphy 1996; Highley 1997). They broach the ongoing crisis in Ireland by imaginatively displacing it on to an earlier, successful, colonial enterprise – the conquest and pacification of Wales, and less frequently, by suggesting analogies between the subjugation of Ireland and the failed attempt to bring Scotland under English dominion. Indeed, it is likely that many lost plays which critics such as Griffin would classify, on the basis of their titles alone, as "English" histories likewise contained strong Irish subtexts. One such play that is no longer extant, Henry Chettle's *The Life of Cardinal Wolsey* (1601), manifestly did, as is evidenced by Richard Hadson's letter to Sir Robert Cecil dated July 25, 1602: "The Earl (of Kildare)," Hadson writes,

has served the Queen as captain of the horse in Lord Gray's government in Ireland. The Queen has been pleased to call him Earl of Kildare . . . If the title should be denied him, there are other men of his family that would pretend title, not only to the honour, but also to the lands of great value which fell to the Crown in England and Ireland upon the attainder of his grandfather by the policy of Cardinal Wolsey as it is set forth and played now upon the stage in London.[3]

Hadson cites the theatrical portrayal of Kildare's attainder for treason as if it were a factual report; his letter, moreover, underlines the continued intermeshing of English and Irish pasts and its impact on successive generations. Chettle almost certainly based *The Life of Cardinal Wolsey* on Richard Stanyhurst's *The Processe of Irish Affaires (Beginning where Giraldus did End) vntill this Present Age, Being a Witnesse of Sundrie Things as Yet Fresh in Memorie.* Written for Raphael Holinshed's and others' *Chronicles of England, Scotlande, and Irelande* (1577), it was available to Chettle in the second, expanded edition of Holinshed which appeared in 1587. Stanyhurst's account is itself very theatrical, reproducing as it does Wolsey's charges against Kildare, the earl's spirited defense, and "his exhortation to his sonne the lord Thomas." "There was neuer anie erle of that house read or heard of," Stanyhurst points out, "that bare armour in the field against his prince. Which I write not as a barrister hired to plead their case, but as a chronicler moued to declare the truth" (Holinshed 1807, VI: 281ff., 286–7,

304). Stanyhurst's anti-Wolsey and pro-Kildare bias was probably imported whole-sale by Chettle into his dramatic version. That bias would not have been lost on Hadson and his addressee, Cecil.

Theatrical representations of Scottish history, or what purported to be Scottish history, too, were readily applied to the contemporary situation. The metadramatic frame of Robert Greene's *James IV* (1590) – a play based on Giraldi Cinthio, *not* on a chronicle source – invited the audience to do so: "In the year 1520 was in Scotland a king, overruled with parasites, misled by lust, and many circumstances too long to trattle on now, much like our court of Scotland this day" (Greene 1970: 11). Unlike Ireland, Scotland was an independent kingdom and Elizabethan officials were anxious lest the opprobrious portrayal of the Scots and *ad hominem* attacks on their King James VI by English playwrights impair the already fraught relations between the two countries. "It is regretted," George Nicolson wrote to Lord Burghley on April 15, 1598, "that the comedians of London should scorn the king and the people of this land [Scotland] in their play; and it is wished that the matter should be speedily amended lest the king and the country be stirred to anger" (Chambers 1945, I: 322). Nicolson's concern is understandable given that James VI was likely to succeed to the English throne on Elizabeth's death, as indeed he did only four years later.

The focus on the vexed questions of national identity and cultural stereotyping in such plays as *2 Henry VI, 1 Henry IV, Henry V, Edward I, Cardinal Wolsey, James IV,* and many others – which feature English and/or Welsh and/or Irish and/or Scottish characters and which are set both at home and in those other contested territories – seems justification enough not to dub them "English" histories. Yet there are other reasons too. Some of the so-called "English" histories are set abroad: the action of *Henry V* largely takes place in France; the anonymous *Captain Thomas Stukeley* (1596) is a veritable travelogue, its scenes shifting from England to Ireland, to Spain, to Portugal, and eventually to North Africa. Conversely, there are many plays ostensibly concerned with foreign pasts which feature English characters center-stage, or which through topical allusions, parallels, and the use of anachronism, signal the relevance of the nominally foreign past to the situation at home. A case in point is the lost play about the taking of Turnhout from the Spanish by Count Maurice of Nassau with the assistance of English troops. In a letter of October 26, 1599, Rowland White informed Sir Robert Sidney, a participant in the siege, that Sidney's and his fellow-soldiers' recent exploits – Turnhout had been captured on January 24, 1598 – were now the subject of a stage-play. Though set on the Continent, this was very much a native history play in the sense that the spectators were invited to admire the heroism of England's living military commanders with whose carriage and appearance many of them would have been familiar. To make their impersonations of the English worthies more compelling, the actors went so far as to acquire characteristic items of clothing and a suitable set of props:

> Two daies agoe, the ouerthrow of *Turnholt*, was acted vpon a Stage, and all your Names vsed that were at yt; especially *Sir Fra. Veres*, and he that plaid that Part gott a Beard

resembling his, and a Watchet Sattin Doublett, with Hose trimd with Siluer Lace. You
was also introduced, Killing, Slaying and Overthrowing the *Spaniards*, and honorable
Mention made of your Service, in seconding *Sir Francis Vere*, being engaged. (*Sydney
Papers* II: 136; cited in Chambers 1945, I: 322 n. 2)

How "foreign", then, is "the ouerthrow of *Turnholt*"? Or George Peele's *The Battell of
Alcazar* (1594) – a story of a North African civil war and its Iberian reverberations –
which shadows, under the character of the swashbuckling Englishman, Captain
Thomas Stukeley, the swashbuckling nobleman and royal favorite the Earl of Essex?
Or the anonymous *The Tragedy of Alphonsus Emperour of Germany* (1594–8), which deals,
like *Turnholt*, with English involvement in continental politics, and which portrays
Richard, Duke of Cornwall (Henry III's younger brother) accompanied by Henry's
heir Edward, Prince of Wales, contending for the crown of the Holy Roman empire
against Alphonso X of Castile? (In *Alphonsus* the words "England" and "English" occur
no fewer than sixty-one times.) And yet these plays rarely make it into accounts of
native historical drama.

The close affinity between the native and the foreign is sometimes made explicit.
For instance, the very title of the anonymous *A Larum for London, or The Siedge of
Antwerpe* (ca. 1594–1600) forces the spectator to bear in mind the connection between
home and abroad as the action unfolds. The play issues a forceful warning about the
military threat of Spain; it urges the need for watchfulness and military preparedness.
Unless the lessons of the past be learned, England will suffer as dreadful a fate as
Antwerp, which the Spaniards had captured by means of treachery and open violation of diplomatic treaties. This point is driven home through the vivid portrayal of
Spanish atrocities against Antwerp's citizens, as well as their butchery of an English
trader and mistreatment of the Governor of the English House.

Theatrical representations of continental Europe frequently blur the boundaries
between the native and the foreign. This is particularly true of plays set in the Nether-
lands, a country where confessional differences mark the lines of conflict between
Catholic Spain and its Protestant rivals. Some of these plays – for example, *Turnholt*
– chronicle England's political, diplomatic, military, or commercial involvement on
the Continent, featuring Englishmen in starring roles. Others – for example, *A Larum
for London* – may have a smaller and less conspicuous cast of Englishmen, but they
signal their topicality by drawing transparent parallels between the "foreign" past and
the "native" present. If such plays were to be treated as a special subset of "native"
histories, then it might still be possible to draw a dividing line of sorts between
"native" and "foreign" history plays. But to what end? It would be a mistake to deny
the special status of plays which dramatize the past of the British Isles. It is nonetheless counter-intuitive and ultimately misleading to separate "native" histories from
dramatizations of the more genuinely "foreign" pasts. For the history of even so
geographically remote a land as Turkey could serve to express anxieties about civil
war and disputed succession that figure so prominently in plays set in feudal England.
To illustrate: Robert Greene's *Selimus* (ca. 1591–4) uses a range of devices to evoke

correspondences between Turkey and England. Not only is the succession to the aging Emperor Bajazet uncertain and the Turkish empire riven by civil strife. There are more specific parallels too. Bajazet is poisoned by Abraham the Jew, an episode reminiscent of the supposed attempt on Elizabeth's life by her "Jewish" physician, Dr. Lopez.[4] The extensive use of anachronism, including the setting of several scenes in what is recognizably the English countryside (a native clown tending his sheep prattles about the local parson, justices of the peace, and Tyburn!), further enhances the identification of the Turkish "then" with the English "now." To paraphrase Gonzalo's lines from *The Tempest*: "This Turkey, sir, is England." The adaptability not simply of Turkish history but Greene's dramatization of it to topical ends was to find a bizarre confirmation. In 1603, eleven years after the play's première and nine years after its publication, an iconoclastic speech by the villain of the piece, Selimus, was put in manuscript circulation with a mischievous attribution to Sir Walter Ralegh under the title "Certaine hellish verses devysed by that Atheist and traitor Ralegh" (Jacquot 1953).

In the Elizabethan era history was the most common source of the subject matter of plays other than comedies. Inevitably, the particular resonances of theatrical representations of medieval England, ancient Rome, biblical Israel, or sixteenth-century Turkey would have varied. But "Englishness" of subject matter is not a convincing generic criterion. So we must ask whether the formal shape of native history plays warrants setting them apart from the mass of dramatic renditions of foreign pasts, and, more generally, whether dramatizations of the past are formally different from other kinds of drama.

Form

In contrast to those who insist on the "Englishness" of the history play's subject matter as its defining feature, others maintain that it is its dramatic form (or lack thereof) that distinguishes the genre from both tragedy and comedy. The opposition between histories and either comedies or tragedies is not as absolute, they concede, as that between comedies and tragedies, but it is there.

We know that there are history plays which are tragic, and comic, and tragicomic, and romantic, and farcical. Marlowe's *Edward II* and Shakespeare's *Richard II* are manifestly tragic in scope and effect; so is *Richard III*, though we sense that the tragic shaping of this play is very different from the other two. A powerful vein of comedy runs through both parts of *Henry IV*, but it would be perverse to describe them as comical histories. Is *Henry V* a comical history? It shows the king's military and diplomatic victories and, like most comedies, it ends in marriage but that nominally happy outcome is qualified by the Epilogue's allusion to Henry's death and the territorial losses sustained during the reign of his son, Henry VI. Multi-part plays such as *1–2 Tamburlaine, 1–3 Henry VI, 1–3 Civil Warres of France* – which may not have been originally conceived as parts of a sequence – present a special problem, for in them the "comic" or "tragic" shaping will be "spread" over two or more "instalments." Individual parts may – but often do not – share the slant of the whole. Envisaged as the first of a would-be two-part drama about a Turkish tyrant, Greene's *Selimus* advertises itself as a tragical history: "No fained toy nor forged Tragedie, / Gentles we here present unto your view, / But a most lamentable historie / Which this last age acknowledgeth for true" (Greene 1908: sig. A2ᵛ). The ending sees Selimus victorious: the play is a tragedy for others, not for him. Since part two, which presumably would have concluded with the tyrant's death, did not materialize, Selimus never got his comeuppance on the London stage.

History plays, both foreign and native, come in a variety of shapes and sizes: think, for example, of the three-part fifteen-act neo-Latin historical extravaganza, Thomas Legge's Senecan *Richardus Tertius*! Yet it is difficult to see how these various formal attributes could serve as a basis of a meaningful generic categorization. What we can say for certain is that irrespective of the provenance of their subject matter, theatrical representations of history share a range of thematic concerns and a corresponding set of dramatic techniques. Whether set in medieval England, ancient Rome, or continental Europe, a large proportion of them display a preoccupation with internecine strife and disputed succession which mirrors the anxieties of late Elizabethan politics. The portrayal of civil wars – between Pompey and Caesar, between Catholics and Huguenots, between rival North African princes, between the Lancastrians and the Yorkists – in turn relies on extensive use of drum and trumpet, battle-scenes, and crowd-scenes. In many Roman, and Turkish, and Moorish histories armies march, swords clash, mobs gather. Short scenes and swift changes of locale make these plays seem episodic, formless, unstructured. We are all familiar with such assessments of the so-called "English histories" or "English chronicle plays," but contemporaries recognized similar features elsewhere. "So was *the history of Caesar and Pompey*, and the Playe of the Fabii at the Theatre, both amplified there," reports Gosson, "where the Drummes might walke, or the pen ruffle" (*Plays Confuted in Five Actions* (1582), cited in Sibley 1931: 21).

The incidence of shared theatrical grammar and vocabulary is a strong argument against separating native from foreign histories: dramatizations of all manner of history ca. 1590–1603 have more in common in terms of themes and theatrical conventions than, say, the "English" histories of the 1590s and the "English" histories written after the accession of James I in 1603. Native and foreign history plays are best categorized as thematic groupings, *not* distinct dramatic genres. This will become apparent as we consider another influential attempt to define the history play, one undertaken by those who limit the genre to "English" histories on the basis of content but seek further justification for their categorization in the realm of dramatic form. They argue that contrary to tragedies and comedies which require formal closure, history plays (read: "English" history plays) are "open-ended," for when the play ends, history continues (Kastan 1982; Danson 2000; Snyder 2001). Not only the endings, but the beginnings of history plays are said to be "open," for scenes of genealogy which rehearse events preceding the start of action proper direct the audience to locate what they see along a historical continuum (Griffin 2001: 85ff.). This argument rests on two assumptions: first, that history plays use a range of strategies which prompt the audience to look beyond the confines of the play and contemplate the broader historical significance of the plot; and, second, that even if no overt invitation to reflect on a future that will have already become a past is issued, the audience will do so anyway. Why should these assumptions hold true for representations of the native past, which thus earn the label "history plays," and not for those dealing with foreign matter, which, perforce, must be labeled tragedies?

To consider the impact of historical drama in terms of the spectators' familiarity and engagement with the "before" and "after" is a productive way of conceptualizing the distinction between plays with historical plots and plays with fictional plots. But will it help us distinguish the *genre* of the native history play from other kinds of historical drama? In order to answer in the affirmative, one would have to prove (1) that native histories resist formal closure (and that their beginnings, too, are provisional); *and* (2) that the endings of plays dramatizing foreign pasts are more genuinely final than those of native histories (and their beginnings more sharply defined).

How do history plays begin and end? Griffin points to tropes of genealogy – such as the backward-looking Induction to the anonymous *The True Tragedy of Richard III* or the forward-looking conclusion of the anonymous *The Famous Victories of Henry V* – which in his view are characteristic of what he calls the normative plays on English history (Griffin 2001: 86–91). Such tropes, he claims, remind the audience of the prehistory or the aftermath of the plot unraveling before their eyes. More broadly, they enable, even encourage, the viewers to engage at once with the spectacle and its larger implications for England's national destiny. Yet the relevance of these points is not limited to native-subject drama, for we find similar devices designed to manipulate audience response in foreign histories such as Peele's *The Battle of Alcazar* and Greene's *Selimus*. The former opens with a lengthy introduction by the Presenter who stages two dumbshows. The Presenter's speech sets the scene for what is to follow, explaining to the spectators the intricate political situation: Sebastian, King of Portugal is committed to assisting the Moorish pretender to the throne of Morocco, Muly Mahamet, against his uncle and rightful ruler, Abdelmelec, who is in turn backed by Emperor Amurath. To clarify these rather complex dynastic and political relationships, the Presenter restages some recent events in the dumbshows, offering running commentary throughout. He then invites his audience to "see this true and tragicke warre, / A modern matter full of bloud and ruth, / Where three bolde kings confounded in their height, / Fell to the earth contending for a crowne, / And call this warre *The battell of Alcazar*" (Peele 1594: sig. A3^r). At the start of Greene's *Selimus* Emperor Bajazet orders his attendants to retire and launches into a troubled soliloquy. Bajazet meditates on the nature of kingship and his own position as an aging ruler of a vast empire and father to three sons who, he fears, will rise against him and wage war against each other in pursuit of the crown. In the process he summarizes the major events of his reign and elucidates Turkish dynastic politics (Greene 1908: sigs. A3^r–A4^v). Like rehearsals of genealogy or opening dumbshows,

Bajazet's soliloquy is a means of situating the present conflict in the context of what has come before.

As for dramatic endings, it is true that the conclusion of a play dramatizing Turkish history – which was obviously less familiar to contemporaries than native lore – would hardly provoke consideration of "what happened next" in the same way as a play about Richard II or Richard III. Yet the knowledge of even Turkish history may well have been more substantial, and may have been perceived as more relevant to contemporary concerns, than we might expect. Apart from various book-length Turkish chronicles which would have been accessible only to the literate and the better-off, Elizabethans could look up a succinct account of the rise of the Turkish empire in one of the many editions of that great historical bestseller of Elizabeth's reign, John Foxe's *Actes and Monuments*. Foxe's mini-history of the Turks discussed their religion – Islam, government, customs, and rulers – Selimus (or "Zelymus" as Foxe calls him) among them. Foxe lamented the harsh lot of Christians in Turkish captivity of which, he felt, his compatriots ought to be made aware "because we Englishmen being farre off from these countries, and little knowing what misery is abroad, are the lesse moued with zeale and compassion to tender their grieuances, and to pray for them whose troubles we know not" (Foxe 1632, I: 993). Copies of *Actes and Monuments* were to be found in most parish churches, and its contents were widely disseminated through readings to both the congregation and the less formal gatherings of interested parishioners. But the dramatist could communicate the extra-textual significance of the historical figures and events he portrayed without depending on his audience's knowledge of Turkish goings-on. He could frame his representation of the Turkish past in such a way as to invite the spectators to contemplate developments postdating the nominal closure of his play. In *Selimus* Greene effects this in several ways. First, in his dying moments Corcut (Selimus's unfortunate brother and victim, and recent convert to Christianity) prophesies the fall of the tyrant. Secondly, in the final scene of the play Selimus himself outlines his plans for future conquests. Thirdly, the Epilogue forecasts a sequel and offers a preview of its contents: "Next shall you see him with triumphant sword, / Dividing kingdomes into equall shares, / And give them to their warlike followers. / If this first part Gentles, do like you well, / The second part, shall greater murthers tell" (Greene 1908: sig. K3^r). (Note the similarity between this Epilogue and the concluding lines of the Chettle–Munday Robin Hood play, *The Downfall of Robert, Earle of Huntington* (1598), spoken by the Presenter Skelton: "Well iudging hearers, for a while suspence / Your censures of this Plaies unfinisht end: / And *Skelton* promises for this offence, / The second part shall presently be pend . . .": Meagher 1980: 282.) Finally, the continuity of the Turkish past represented in Greene's play and present-day Turkish affairs is made manifest by the prosy title of the first edition: *The first part of the Tragicall raigne of Selimus, sometime Emperour of the Turkes, and grandfather to him that now raigneth. Wherein is showne how hee most unnaturally raised warres against his owne father Bajazet, and prevailing therein, in the end caused him to be poysoned: Also with the murthering of his two brethren, Corcut, and Acomat* (1594). Anyone so much as glancing at the quarto playbook would realize that, despite having perpetrated parricide, fratricide, and usurpation, the historical Selimus managed to secure succession for his line.

Given the remoteness and exoticism of Turkey, to cite *Selimus* as an example of an open-ended foreign history play may seem perverse. Theatrical representations of ancient Rome and late sixteenth-century France yield more obvious illustrations of structural open-endedness of foreign historical drama. For very different reasons, both these pasts were familiar to a large proportion of the audience. The playwrights who set out to dramatize them relied on that familiarity and frequently invoked it in ways which mirror the use of genealogical tropes in native history plays and of prophecy and anticipation in *Selimus*.

First, the Roman past. Though history was not part of the formal syllabus either in grammar schools or at universities, young Englishmen absorbed the history of ancient Rome through their study of Latin and rhetoric. They read Cicero, Livy, Tacitus, Florus, Suetonius, Caesar, and many others. When the first Oxford and Cambridge chairs of history were founded in the early seventeenth century the incumbents were required to teach not the history of England (or Great Britain) but that of ancient Rome. Acquaintance with the period in Roman history which impinged on the emergence of Christianity would have been reinforced by Foxe's ecclesiastical history and the Sunday sermon. Theatre audiences may therefore have had some superficial familiarity with such figures as Lucrece, Julius Caesar, Brutus, Cassius, Augustus, Nero, and Caligula. Addressing the question of adaptation of historical materials for the stage, Gosson ranked among "histories that are known . . . the life of Pompeie; the martial affaires of Caesar, and other worthies" (*A Third Blaste of Retraite* (1580), cited in Sibley 1931: 124). Six years later, in an oration celebrating Elizabeth's birthday on September 7, 1586, Edward Hake, Mayor of Windsor and member of Gray's Inn, concluded his review of pagan (read: Roman) examples of relations between the rulers and the ruled with an emphatic endorsement of their universal familiarity: "What shoulde I stande longer to sette forth unto you the performance of these or the like of the premisses in the worneoute ages, the stories thereof being so rife, as that no man almoste of any quality can bee ignorant therein?" (Nichols 1823, II: 463).

So whether prompted by suggestive allusions in the plays themselves or not, Elizabethan audiences – always allowing for differences in sex, social standing, and education – were inevitably drawn to reflect on developments outside the fictive frame of the Roman play they were watching. Thomas Lodge's *The Wounds of Civill War. Lively set forth in the true Tragedies of Marius and Scilla* (1588) closes with Scilla's resignation of the dictatorship followed almost immediately by his death. So by the end of the play both eponymous heroes are dead, but their personal tragedies are set within the greater tragedy of Rome. That the civil broils the spectators have witnessed are merely a prelude to further bloodshed is signaled by Pompey's presence on the scene. It is prefigured, too, by Scilla's response to the plebeians who dare taunt him now that he is no longer in a position of power: "My friends, these scorns of yours perhaps will move / The next dictator shun to yield his state" (Lodge 1969: 5.5.249–50). Not long after the real Sulla's death, Julius Caesar's unwillingness to "yield his state" and his adoption of the title of perpetual dictator would in fact lead to another civil war, the eventual fall of the Roman republic, and the institution of rule by one man. Those watching Shakespeare's *Julius Caesar* (1599) would have been aware that the alliance of Octavian Caesar and Mark Antony that culminated in their victory over Brutus and Cassius at Philippi would be merely temporary, and that the erstwhile allies would soon turn against each other. Hints of their forthcoming breach are scattered throughout the latter part of the play and the ascendancy of the new Caesar foreshadowed by – for instance – Octavian's imperious insistence on leading the right wing at Philippi against Antony's express wishes. Possibly the most compelling example of a Roman play that both evokes the past and also maps out the future of Rome is Jonson's *Sejanus* (1603). Not only do the Germanicans continually dwell on old Roman virtue that they feel has vanished with the suppression of the republic. Cremutius Cordus, a chronicler of the recent civil wars, is condemned to death and his book to the fire. The pivotal scene of his trial makes manifest the monarchical state's concern about the impact of Cordus's account in which Brutus and Cassius, champions of the republic and Caesar's killers, are held up as heroes. Neither the characters on stage nor the audience are allowed to forget what Rome once was and how far it has departed from that ideal by the time Tiberius came to power. That the process of moral degradation will continue is implied by the rise of the new, yet more evil and corrupt favorite in place of the old one: Sejanus's fall ensures Macro's rise. It is further suggested by the foreshadowing of Caligula's tyranny that, we know, will prove worse than Tiberius'. Jonson's tragedy is fashioned as a snapshot in the continuum of Rome's history, its recurrent allusions to the before and after urging the viewers to interpret the fall of Sejanus in the context of the fall of Rome, tragedy of the individual framed by tragedy of state. The so-called Roman plays, then, demand that the spectators reflect on the significance of the events represented within the larger frame of Rome's rise and fall.

For the Elizabethans, the history of ancient Rome was over and done with. It could be reconsidered and retold but its continuity with the present was broken (even if the papacy was occasionally figured as the new incarnation of the corrupt Roman empire). By contrast, the recent continental past merged seamlessly with the present. Consider, for example, dramatic representations of the French wars of religion such as Thomas Dekker and Michael Drayton's lost *1–3 Civil Warres of France*, written in quick succession between September and December 1598. These plays directed the thoughts of the audience to well-known recent happenings across the Channel, the final installment quite possibly glancing at Henry IV's reconversion to Catholicism in 1596. The Dekker–Drayton trilogy is no longer extant, but the formal and historical openendedness of representations of recent French history is apparent in Christopher Marlowe's *The Massacre at Paris* (1593). Centering on the Catholic slaughter of the Huguenots on St. Bartholomew's Day in 1572, *The Massacre* concludes with the assassination of Henry III in 1589. That is, the final scene is set a mere four years prior to the date of the play's first performance in January 1593. Henry III's dying words urging his erstwhile followers to support the claim of Henry Bourbon direct the audience outside the fictive frame: "My lords, / Fight in the quarrel of this valiant prince, / For he's your lawful king, and my next heir: / Valoyses line ends in my tragedy. / Now let the house of Bourbon wear the crowne; / And may it never end in blood, as mine hath done" (Marlowe 1986: 5.5.91–6). By highlighting dynastic change embodied in the figure of Henry Bourbon – now France's reigning monarch – the ending of *The Massacre at Paris* compels the audience to ponder the impact of French domestic politics upon the balance of power in Europe, and, in particular, to reflect on what the transition from the Catholic Valoises to the Huguenot Bourbons has meant for England.

Any dramatization of the past evokes memories of what had come before and foreshadows what was to come later. It therefore establishes a broad frame of reference, encouraging the audience to situate the events represented in the context of what they know (or are told) actually happened. And it is anyone's guess which would have seemed more topical of dynastic claims of Richard, Duke of York, in Shakespeare's *2 Henry VI* or the depiction of European confessional politics and England's role in them in Marlowe's *The Massacre at Paris*.

Ideology

If neither subject matter ("Englishness") nor form (open-endedness) clearly distances the "Elizabethan history play" from comedy and tragedy, what other kind of evidence could be cited in support of its generic identity? According to Irving Ribner (whose approach is itself indebted to earlier critics, notably Felix E. Schelling and Lily B. Campbell), history plays share a deeper affinity with prose historiography than they do with other plays. Ribner identifies didacticism as the principal purpose of Elizabethan historical writings, whether dramatic or non-dramatic, and on that basis argues that the history play is "a separate dramatic genre." A history play, he contends, "was one which fulfilled what Elizabethans considered the purposes of history" (Ribner 1965: 11, 12). The trouble with this definition is that it assumes (1) a consensual understanding of the aims of history and (2) an ideological uniformity among Elizabethan history plays. Put forward almost half a century ago when E. M. W. Tillyard's "Elizabethan world picture" – which it endorses and applies – reigned supreme, Ribner's definition constructs historical writings as an embodiment of state ideology. In his view no play without a clearly articulated, coherent message qualified as a history play, no matter how extensive its reliance on the historical record. And that message could be one and one only: to inculcate obedience and uphold the authority of the chief magistrate – the queen. Paradoxically, given its authoritarian slant, Ribner's approach to historical drama has of late gained fresh currency among adherents of Marxism, New Historicism, and Cultural Materialism. Ribner's description of what Elizabethans took to be the purposes of history may have been reassessed and reinterpreted in light of modern scholarship of Renaissance historiography, but his followers retain the underlying assumption that history plays and chronicles essentially attempted to do the same thing. "The drama appropriated not only the substance of history-writing," writes Ivo Kamps, "but also its methods and aims" (Kamps 1996: xiii). Where for Ribner, however, those aims and methods remained static throughout the Elizabethan era, his recent followers such as Rackin, Kamps, Pugliatti, and others invoke a more dynamic conception of historiography which, they claim, was reflected in the drama.

Tillyard's "Elizabethan world picture" has long been discredited. We all know that sixteenth-century chronicles, such as those by Hall or Holinshed, did not embody a uniform ideological stance, and that the late sixteenth and early seventeenth centuries witnessed important developments in thinking about and writing history. Some were products of continental influences, notably Machiavelli and Guicciardini; others, such as the antiquarian projects of Camden and Selden, were more home-grown (Woolf 1990; 2000). Yet this knowledge is put at the service of somewhat schematic readings of history plays in general and of Shakespeare's "English" histories in particular. If Tillyard was able to claim every play in the canon as an illustration of the providential view of history, recent commentators – those publishing in the last decade or so – see particular plays (and even characters) as embodiments of rival historiographies. In *Stages of History* Phyllis Rackin argues that "The order of . . . composition [of Shakespeare's histories] follows the progress of Renaissance historiography, as history becomes increasingly problematic and truth more and more difficult to determine." In the *Henry VI* plays, she contends, events "are explained in the Machiavellian terms of politic history . . . in *Richard III*, by contrast . . . the principle of historical causation is clearly providential" (Rackin 1990: 29, 27–8). Ivo Kamps has gone further and identified the interplay between three types of Renaissance historiography – providentialist, humanist, and antiquarian – in one play, the Shakespeare–Fletcher *Henry VIII* (Kamps 1996: ch. 4).

This approach to historical drama places high value on early modern historiography, especially its "politic" and antiquarian varieties. Yet at the same time it is predicated on unfavorable comparisons of prose historiography to theatrical representations of the past. For whenever modern scholars cite the sources of history plays, they are routinely critical of them. Rackin condemns Renaissance history writing for being "univocal" and "monologic" (Rackin 1990: 23, 25, 27), a view effectively refuted by Annabel Patterson in her *Reading Holinshed's Chronicles* (1994). Graham Holderness, Nick Potter, and John Turner contrast the eclecticism of historical drama with what they call "the stolid factual preoccupations of the Tudor historiographical narratives" (Holderness, Potter, and Turner 1987: 20). Paola Pugliatti is no less scathing: "nothing better than compliance with the official political theories," she says, "could be expected from the chroniclers." By contrast, Shakespeare is praised for having practised "a problem-oriented, multivocal kind of historiography." It is this "kind of historiographical perspective that his practice might have contributed to creating if contemporary English historians had been ready to capture its novelty" (Pugliatti 1996: 23, 25). The superiority of Renaissance playwrights as reporters of the past is succinctly stated by Kamps. "One central conclusion that emerges from this study," he writes in the introduction to his *Historiography and Ideology in Stuart Drama*, "is that the dramatists often show themselves to be better expositors of history than the historians; they show themselves to possess a clearer understanding of historiography's literary origins and its limitations as a knowledge-producing practice" (Kamps 1996: 13).

The study of theatrical representations of history in the context of Elizabethan historiography can be illuminating. Unlike traditional source study, this kind of inquiry enables us to address broader questions about political and ideological uses of history in plays and about the drama's contribution to political thought. Reading historical drama alongside other forms of history writing in both prose and verse has the added advantage of avoiding the spurious association of the history play with "English" subject matter. It is thus salutary that in his account of Stuart history plays Kamps devotes a chapter to a foreign history play, John Fletcher and Philip Massinger's *The Tragedy of Sir John Van Olden Barnavelt* (1619), which depicts a recent political crisis in the Dutch Republic. The danger is, however, that plays come to be judged according to how historiographially sophisticated and ideologically progressive they are. Let me illustrate. Taking for granted that the drama must keep in step with developments in historiography, Kamps repeatedly flattens the historiographical outlook of Elizabethan drama in order to emphasize the corresponding complexity of early Stuart plays. He asserts, for example, that "the typical Elizabethan history play plot follows the rebellion–chaos–restoration trajectory" (an assertion that will not withstand close scrutiny), and proceeds to argue that this "generic form" is aborted in the Stuart *Perkin Warbeck* (Kamps 1996: 180). Elizabethan plays emerge from Kamps's account as inferior on several grounds: they toe a reactionary line, their treatment of history lacks refinement, and their plots are schematic, since "it took until well into the Stuart dynasty before residual Tudor ideology lost its grip and before a playwright could . . . abandon Tudor forms of historical representation" (p. 181). Whereas for Ribner the more ideologically sound a history play the better, for Kamps the more subversive of ideology the better. And as such judgments are meted out, it is easy to forget that we are discussing scripts written for performance, not tracts in dialogue-form designed for silent reading.

The "historiographical" approach to history plays is a promising one. It has the potential to enhance our understanding of early modern historical culture and of the drama's contribution to it. History plays are rightly interpreted as a form of history writing, alongside prose historiography, historical poems, historical ballads, and historical pamphlets. Yet so far practitioners of this approach have not come up with a convincing way of differentiating history plays from other kinds of drama. Or, rather, the criterion they have proposed – the history play's conformity to what Elizabethans took to be "the purposes of history" – is virtually impossible to apply since those purposes themselves continue to be debated and contested.

Shakespeare

Whether they adopt subject matter, form, or ideological/historiographical content as a generic criterion, most scholarly accounts of the history play concentrate on Shakespeare. The title-page of the First Folio of 1623 listed histories alongside tragedies and comedies, and the catalog prefaced to it assigned ten plays to this category: *King John, Richard II, 1–2 Henry IV, Henry V, 1–3 Henry VI, Richard III,* and *Henry VIII.* Undeterred by the fact that several of them had been published previously with other generic labels – for instance, on its first appearance in print, in the Quarto of 1595, *3 Henry VI* had called itself *The true Tragedie of Richard Duke of York, and the death of good King Henrie the Sixt, with the whole contention betweene the two Houses Lancaster and Yorke* – many scholars have seized on the Folio classification as definitive and proceeded to construct a generic theory around it (Hunter 1997: 155ff.; Griffin 2001: 15–17). Does the Folio classification reflect a perception that the ten plays labeled "histories" form a coherent generic grouping or was it merely dictated by convenience? What are we to make of the fact that when some of those plays were published in Shakespeare's lifetime, though apparently without his consent or involvement, their title-pages exhibited nothing like the uniformity of the posthumously printed, dignified Folio? Even if the grouping tells us something about Shakespeare's own generic practice, how useful is it in dealing with the writings of his contemporaries?

The Folio's designation as histories of a sequence of plays with names of English kings in their titles has provided fuel for arguments that "Englishness" of subject matter is the essential feature of the history play. This assumption, as we have seen, has had an unfortunate effect on the study of historical drama. Shakespeare's Roman plays (not so distinguished in the Folio) have long been treated as a distinct grouping (and have received massive critical treatment); recently, the historical dimension of the Scottish *Macbeth* and of the "British" *Lear* and *Cymbeline* has been much debated (Norbrook 1987; Marshall 2000; Wortham 2000). But since Shakespeare did not dramatize the recent past of continental Europe, of Asia, or of Africa, history plays dealing with French, Turkish, or Moorish themes have received scant critical attention.

Once the Folio "histories" are construed as a valid and coherent generic class (rather than an *ex post facto* grouping), the question arises about Shakespeare's contribution to the genre of the "English history play." It is well known that there are both amateur and professional dramatizations of native history which predate Shakespeare's: Bale's *King Johan,* 1538; Thomas Norton and Thomas Sackville's *Gorboduc,* 1562; Thomas Legge's *1–3 Richardus Tertius,* 1579; the anonymous *Famous Victories of Henry V,* 1586, and others. It is equally well known that Shakespeare drew on some of these plays for his own versions (*1–2 Henry IV* and *Henry V* are indebted to *The Famous Victories; Richard III* seems to echo *Richardus Tertius;* and *Richard II* is Shakespeare's response to Marlowe's *Edward II*). He has been nonetheless repeatedly described as the inventor of the history play (Ribner 1965: 91; Wikander 1986: 49; Pugliatti 1996: 22–3). Even recent commentators such as Lawrence Danson and Susan Snyder have not resisted the temptation to cast the Bard in this "originary" role (Danson 2000: 87; Snyder 2001: 84). From crediting Shakespeare with the invention of the genre, there is only a short step to treating his "English histories" as normative. His predecessors can be safely disposed of as inept precursors; those who came after him can be dismissed as epigones and contaminators of the "true genre" which he has bequeathed to them, a point to which I shall return.

Even if united in their focus on the post-Conquest past, the plays classed as histories by the Folio are hardly alike in form. It is well nigh impossible to devise a formal scheme that would accommodate all of them, let alone devise a scheme that would account for them and for history plays by others. What is, one might ask, the common formal principle of *Richard III* and *Henry V*?

One way of dealing with the formal diversity of Shakespeare's histories has been to think in terms of cycles and structural patterns. Scholars have identified two "tetralogies," the first comprising *1–3 Henry VI* and *Richard III*, and the second comprising *Richard II*, *1–2 Henry IV*, and *Henry V*. That leaves out the early *King John* and the late *Henry VIII* which was written in collaboration with John Fletcher, as well as the collaborative *Sir Thomas More* to which Shakespeare is known to have contributed. There is nothing wrong with such descriptive labels. They serve as useful critical shorthand. Unfortunately, those who speak about the first or second tetralogy, or of Shakespeare's York–Lancaster cycle, often appear to treat these labels as if they possessed some sort of immanent validity.[5] Yet Shakespeare neither composed the individual plays in the chronological order of history nor did he conceive of them as a grand historical sequence. Critical discussion of such notional entities as the first or second tetralogy may be an exciting intellectual exercise. However, no such sense of wholeness and pattern would have been accessible to Elizabethan audiences: although there is some evidence that acting companies mounted two-part plays on successive days, what most spectators experienced was a single play as an afternoon's entertainment.

The corollary of casting Shakespeare as the creator of the history play and its most distinguished and prolific practitioner is a kind of generic Darwinism. The history play is assumed to have evolved towards Shakespeare and to have declined when he has abandoned it.

The Rise and Fall of the History Play?

What are the origins of the Elizabethan history play? Irving Ribner singles out the debt of early Tudor histories such as Bale's *King Johan* (1538) to the morality play tradition (Ribner 1965: 34ff.). Following Ribner, Ivo Kamps credits Bale with the transformation of the morality play into an "embryonic" history play (Kamps 1996: 63). David Kastan and Benjamin Griffin associate the development of historical drama with medieval saint plays (Kastan 1982: 42; Griffin 2001: 29–45); Griffin, moreover, points to the links between provincial festive drama such as the Coventry "storial" show of the conquest of the Danes and the early public-stage histories such as the anonymous *Famous Victories of Henry V* (Griffin 1999; 2001: 46–63). G. K. Hunter identifies the history play's Senecan vein in Thomas Legge's neo-Latin *Richardus Tertius* (Hunter 1997: 167–71). Like most modern attempts to define the history play, these genealogical researches focus on representations of the native past. And yet similar motifs and conventions occur in dramatic versions of foreign pasts. The influence of the moralities can be discerned not only in Bale but also in early Elizabethan foreign histories such as Thomas Preston's *Cambises* (before 1569) and R. B.'s *Appius and Virginia* (ca. 1564). Equally, Coventry's festive shows were not limited to the patriotic rendition of the victory over the Danes, but included, as Griffin himself notes, a play about the fall of Jerusalem. Legge's Senecan *Richardus Tertius* was matched by his neo-Latin trilogy about Jewish history, *Solymitana Clades,* or *The Destruction of Jerusalem.* There is no reason to suppose that Elizabethan playwrights who dramatized Hall or Holinshed learnt nothing from earlier figurations of Roman or Jewish history, or that those who turned for their source materials to Josephus or Plutarch ignored earlier dramatic versions of native history. In other words, the genetics of the Elizabethan history play need to be readjusted so as to take note of the extensive affinities among dramatizations of a variety of pasts produced in a variety of cultural and geographical contexts: the provinces, the universities, the Inns of Court, Whitehall, and London's public stages.

Studies such as Ribner's, Hunter's, and most recently Griffin's, embody the paradigm of the rise, flowering, decline, and fall of the history play – even if Ribner starts his account with *King Johan* and *Gorboduc,* Hunter with *Famous Victories* and *Richardus Tertius,* and Griffin with saints' lives and festive celebrations. They perpetuate the myth that there is a definable dramatic genre called the history play, which is distinct from both comedy and tragedy, which features the "English" past, and which reaches its artistic maturity with Shakespeare, swiftly declining thereafter. Moreover, the drop in the number of plays dealing with the post-Conquest past in the second decade of the seventeenth century is taken as a sign of the death of the history play (Schelling 1902: 1; Ribner 1965: 266ff.; Barton 1977: 69, 78; Pugliatti 1996: 4; Holderness, Potter, and Turner 1987: 16; Griffin 2001: 127–47). Among the causes of the history play's alleged demise modern commentators variously cite: the encroachments of romance; the exhaustion of usable subjects and themes and the emergence of the notion of definitive dramatic treatment; the lack of talent among the new generation of playwrights; and the virtual impossibility heroically to dramatize native kingship with the very unheroic James on the throne. With the notable exception of Ford's *Perkin Warbeck,* which is cast as the last great history play, the few later specimens of the genre are routinely disparaged.

There are several problems with this kind of literary history. The exclusive association of the history play with "English" subject matter, and the claim that the genre becomes extinct with Ford's *Perkin Warbeck* (ca. 1625–33), foster the impression that no later plays take up the native past, or, if they do, that they must be qualitatively inferior to the normative "English" histories. Yet if we turn over the pages of the *Annals of English Drama* beyond the year 1642 which marks the closure of the theatres, we find several full-length dramatic pieces and pamphlets in dramatic form which represent very recent occurrences in the British Isles: *The Irish Rebellion, Cola's Fury, or Lirenda's Misery, Crafty Cromwell*, and *The Famous Tragedy of Charles I*. New native histories appear after the Restoration in 1660 when theatres reopen. (As for *Perkin Warbeck*, its transmission from stage to page neatly illustrates the instability of generic categories: though styled "The Chronicle History of Perkin Warbeck" on the title-page of the first edition, it had been entered in the Stationers' Register as "a Tragedy called Perkin Warbecke.") *Perkin Warbeck*'s claim to be the last "English" history play of the Renaissance is challenged by plays of whose existence previous commentators had not been aware. In 1639, several years after the conjectural date of *Perkin*, Sir Henry Herbert licensed the Red Bull company to produce Philip Massinger's "History of Will: *Longesword*, son to Rosamund" (Bawcut 1996: 205). Given Massinger's record of artistically accomplished and politically engaged drama, we may surmise that had it survived, this lost play might well have rivaled *Perkin*.

The Circulation of History in Elizabethan England

The Elizabethan history play is not a "true" genre if by that is meant a dramatic form clearly distinguishable from the Elizabethan tragedy and the Elizabethan comedy. As we have seen, some scholars, such as Felix Schelling, Irving Ribner, and most recently G. K. Hunter and Benjamin Griffin, have treated plays on native history in isolation from plays set in foreign lands, and on that misleading basis have left the impression that the history play died in the 1630s. Others, from E. M. W. Tillyard and Lily B. Campbell, to Phyllis Rackin and Ivo Kamps, have tended to concentrate on a narrow range of plays, principally Shakespeare's, and have been too ready to regard plays merely as projections of contemporary ideologies. Others still, for example Matthew Wikander and Herbert Linderberger, have adopted a sweeping transhistorical approach which crosses the centuries from the England of Shakespeare to the Germany of Brecht, but which uproots dramatic treatments of history from the contexts which produced them. Such attempts to define and limit the genre of the history play often lead to the imposition of rigid categories and distinctions. What is to be gained by drawing a line between dramatic works which should be described as history plays and those which should not? If we want to understand the place and uses of history in early modern drama, we should be willing to consider any play, irrespective of its formal shape or fictional element, which represents, or purports to represent, a historical past, native or foreign, distant or recent (sometimes very recent). It makes sense, in other words, to treat *Richard II*, *The Massacre at Paris*, *Julius Caesar*, and *James IV* as Elizabethan history plays, since all four portray, or – in the case of *James IV* – affect to portray, figures and events drawn from history: of medieval England (and Wales and Ireland), late sixteenth-century France, late republican Rome, and early sixteenth-century Scotland (and England) respectively.

This may seem a strange assertion to make in an essay written specially for a companion to Shakespeare's histories which through its contents implicitly categorizes as such only the two tetralogies and *King John*. By urging a rethinking and defamiliarization of the received critical vocabulary, I am not suggesting that we abandon altogether such long-standing terms as "the histories" or "the Roman plays" though I believe that to speak of the "English histories" is fraught with problems. In any event, dispensing with those labels would hardly be feasible. Generations of critics, historians of literature, editors, directors, and students have long referred to Shakespeare's plays named after England's kings as "histories"; *Julius Caesar*, *Antony and Cleopatra*, and *Coriolanus* have been customarily (and *Titus Andronicus* and even *Cymbeline* occasionally) labeled Roman plays. The pragmatic value of such classifications should not be mistaken for a theory of dramatic genres.

There are two ways of approaching historical drama. One is to think about its literary and dramatic properties. The other is to regard historical drama as one among a number of ways in which a society saturated in history, and turning to it instinctively to interpret the present, looked to the theatre for both instruction and entertainment. If we choose that second perspective we understand, as otherwise we would not, how easily dramatists moved from drama and poetry to the writing of history. Ribner and Kamps, and Schelling and Campbell before them, sensed that point. Rather than comparing one history play with another, might we not do better to set historical drama alongside other forms in which the past was represented and with which it so often overlapped?

Historical drama differs from other modes of figuring the past, for it partakes of two worlds: the world of performance and the world of reading. History plays were written to be staged. But they also circulated in manuscript and printed form. As scripts for performance they can be placed alongside other modes of staging history such as coronation pageants, mayoral pageants, Accession Day tilts and other martial games, installations in the Order of the Garter. Or there are royal progresses and entertainments mounted by local authorities – for example, during her visit to Norwich on August 16, 1578 the queen was greeted by "one which represented king Gurgunt, sometime king of England" (Holinshed 1807, IV: 376). As reading matter, history plays share an affinity with historical poems, pamphlets, almanacs, and prose historiography, whether chronicles, politic histories, chorographies, or antiquarian researches.

Those frontiers were easily crossed. Richard Grafton was a printer–publisher who issued both John Hardyng's *Chronicle* (1543) and Edward Hall's *The Vnion of the two noble and illustre famelies of Lancastre & Yorke* (1548), each with a continuation compiled out of Polydore Vergil, Thomas More, and others. Grafton was also a historian in his own right. His successful *Chronicle at large* (1568) appeared with a commendatory preface by Thomas Norton, co-author of *Gorboduc*, author of *Orations of Arsanes*, and possible contributor to Foxe's *Book of Martyrs*, who became the first City Remembrancer in 1571. Grafton was to draw on his knowledge of historical lore when codevising the coronation pageants for Elizabeth in 1559, the first of which, staged at Gracechurch Street, was suggestively entitled "The Uniting of the Two Houses of Lancaster and York." The iconographic model of the pageant was the frontispiece of the 1550 edition of Hall's *Vnion* that had issued from Grafton's press:

> Vpon the lowest stage was made one seate roiall, wherein were placed two personages representing king Henrie the seuenth, and Elizabeth his wife, daughter of king Edward the fourth; either of these two princes sitting vnder one cloth of estate in their seates, none otherwise diuyded, but that the one of them which was king Henrie the seuenth, procéeding out of the house of Lancaster, was inclosed in a red rose, and the other which was quéene Elizabeth, being heire to the house of Yorke, inclosed with a white rose . . . (Holinshed 1807, IV: 161)

The second level of the pageant featured children representing Henry VIII and Ann Boleyn, the third – top-most level – a child representing Elizabeth herself. The verses declaring the meaning of this historical tableau had been penned by Richard Mulcaster, who was rewarded by the crown "for makyng of the boke conteynynge and declarying the historyes set furth by the Cyties pageantes at the tyme of the Quenes Highnes comyng thorough the Cytye to her coronacion, xlˢ which boke was geuyn vnto the Quenes Grace" (Corporation of London Records Office, Repertories, xiv, fol. 143ʳ; cited in Anglo 1997: 346, n. 4). The explanatory verses were delivered to the queen by another child:

> . . . as ciuill warre,
> and shead of bloud did cease,
> When these two houses were
> vnited into one;
> So now that iarre shall stint,
> and quietnesse increase,
> We trust, ô noble queene,
> thou wilt be the cause alone. (p. 162)

Elizabeth faced a second mirror image of herself at the next pageant, "The seat of worthie gouernance," in Cornhill Street, "wherein was placed a child representing the quéenes highnesse" (p. 163). At yet another pageant, of Time and Truth, she graciously received a copy of the English Bible presented to her by a child representing Truth – the Protestant religion. Elizabeth is known to have been involved in the planning of the pageants, and there is evidence that costumes for them were lent by the crown. So the new queen was herself a spectator, actor, and – alongside Grafton and others – co-author of her coronation pageantry (Anglo 1997: 346; Bergeron 1978; Wilson 1980: introduction; Hackett 1996: 41–8).

In due course Grafton published an account of Elizabeth's coronation entry in his *Abridgement of the Chronicles of Englande* (1562) and expanded it for the 1572 edition (Anglo 1997: 347, n. 2). A competing account, originally issued in pamphlet form, was incorporated into Holinshed's chronicle (1577, 1587). Elizabethan and Jacobean playwrights, in their turn, appropriated elements of the spectacle and substance of the coronation pageantry for their scripts. We find scenes indebted to individual pageants in the anonymous *True Tragedy of Richard III* (1586), in Thomas Heywood's *If You Know Not Me, You Know Nobody* (1604–5), in Thomas Dekker's *The Whore of Babylon* (1606–7), even in the synopsis of Richard Venner's historical con-show *Englands Joy* (1602). From these and other interactions we can see the gains of crossing the frontier from historical drama to the wider world of historical understanding in the society that produced it.

ACKNOWLEDGMENTS

The research for this essay was carried out during my tenure of a Visiting Fellowship at the Harry Ransom Humanities Research Center at the University of Texas, Austin, in July 2001. I am grateful to the HRHRC for its generous support and to the library staff for their unfailing efficiency, courtesy, and helpfulness.

NOTES

1   See "Appendix B: Printed Plays with 'History' in Title-Page, 1557–1642," in Griffin (2001: 158–61).
2   Shakespeare's Roman plays are not usually classified as histories; for exceptions to this rule see Siegel (1978) and Wilders (1978).
3   *Hatfield MSS. Calendar of the Manuscripts of the Marquis of Salisbury at Hatfield House, Hertfordshire*, 1883–1915, xii.248, cited in Sibley (1931: 22–3).
4   Since Lopez was apprehended in 1594, this would suggest the later date for the play's composition. Alternatively, Greene's casting a Jew in the role of poisoner might have acquired "fortuitous" topicality in the wake of Lopez's apprehension.
5   Sherman Hawkins, for one, makes an elaborate case, complete with graphs and diagrams, for an overarching "structural pattern in Shakespeare's histories" (Hawkins 1991). Paul Yachnin aims to solve what he terms "the structural problem" in the *Henry IV* plays by treating *2 Henry IV* as a sequel to, rather than the second part of, *1 Henry IV* (Yachnin 1991). Though Yachnin's approach is less dogmatic than Hawkins's, both these scholars emphasize the connections between the plays at the expense of their individual unity.

REFERENCES AND FURTHER READING

Anglo, S. (1997). *Spectacle, Pageantry, and Early Tudor Policy*. Oxford: Clarendon Press.
Barish, J. (1970). *Perkin Warbeck* as Anti-History. *Essays in Criticism*, 20, 151–71.
Barton, A. (1975). The King Disguised: Shakespeare's *Henry V* and the Comical History. In J. G. Price (ed.) *The Triple Bond: Plays, Mainly Shakespearean, in Performance*. University Park: Pennsylvania State University Press, 92–117.
——(1977). He That Plays the King: Ford's *Perkin Warbeck* and the Stuart History Play. In M. Axton and R. Williams (eds.) *English Drama: Forms and Development*. Cambridge: Cambridge University Press, 69–93.

Bawcut, N. W. (ed.) (1996). *The Control and Censorship of Caroline Drama: The Records of Sir Henry Herbert, Master of the Revels 1623–73*. Oxford: Clarendon Press.

Bergeron, D. (1978). Elizabeth's Coronation Entry (1559): New Manuscript Evidence. *English Literary Renaissance*, 8.

Campbell, L. B. (1947). *Shakespeare's "Histories": Mirrors of Elizabethan Policy*. San Marino, CA: The Huntington Library.

Cannon, C. D. (ed.) (1975). *A Warning for Fair Women*. The Hague: Mouton.

Chambers, E. K. (1945). *The Elizabethan Stage*, 4 vols. Oxford: Oxford University Press.

Danson, L. (2000). *Shakespeare's Dramatic Genres*. Oxford: Oxford University Press.

Florio, J. (1591). *Gardine of Recreation*, in *Florios Second Frutes*. London.

Foxe, J. (1632). *Acts and Monvments of Matters Most most speciall and memorable, hapening in the Church, with an vniuersall Historie of the same*, 7th edn., 3 vols. London.

Greene, R. (1908). *The Tragical Reign of Selimus*. Oxford: Malone Society Reprints.

——(1970). *The Scottish History of James the Fourth*, ed. N. Sanders. London: Methuen.

Griffin, B. (1999). The Breaking of the Giants: Historical Drama in Coventry and London. *English Literary Renaissance*, 29, 3–21.

——(2001). *Playing the Past: Approaches to English Historical Drama 1385–1600*. Woodbridge: D. S. Brewer.

Hackett, H. (1996). *Virgin Mother, Maiden Queen: Elizabeth I and the Cult of the Virgin Mary*. Basingstoke: Macmillan.

Hawkins, S. (1991). Structural Pattern in Shakespeare's Histories. *Studies in Philology*, 88, 16–45.

Heywood, T. (1612). *An Apology For Actors*. London.

Highley, C. (1997). *Shakespeare, Spenser, and the Crisis in Ireland*. Cambridge: Cambridge University Press.

Holderness, G., Potter, N., and Turner, J. (1987). *Shakespeare: The Play of History*. Iowa City: University of Iowa Press.

Holinshed, R. et al. (1807). *Holinshed's Chronicles of England, Scotland, and Ireland*, 6 vols. London.

Howard, J. E. and Rackin, P. (1997). *Engendering a Nation: A Feminist Account of Shakespeare's English Histories*. London: Routledge.

Hunter, G. K. (1989) Truth and Art in History Plays. *Shakespeare Survey*, 42, 15–24.

——(1997). *English Drama, 1586–1642: The Age of Shakespeare*. The Oxford History of English Literature, vol. 6. Oxford: Clarendon Press.

Jacquot, J. (1953). Ralegh's "Hellish verses" and the "Tragicall raigne of Selimus." *Modern Language Review*, 48, 1–9.

Kamps, I. (1996). *Historiography and Ideology in Stuart Drama*. Cambridge: Cambridge University Press.

Kastan, D. S. (1982). *Shakespeare and the Shapes of Time*. London: Macmillan.

——(2001). Shakespeare and English History. In M. de Grazia and S. Wells (eds.) *The Cambridge Companion to Shakespeare*. Cambridge: Cambridge University Press, 167–82.

Larum for London, A. (1913). Oxford: Malone Society Reprints.

Linderberger, H. (1975). *Historical Drama: The Relation of Literature and Reality*. Chicago, IL: University of Chicago Press.

Lodge, T. (1969). *The Wounds of Civil War*, ed. J. W. Houppert. London: Edward Arnold.

Marlowe, C. (1986). *The Complete Plays*, ed. J. B. Steane. London: Penguin Books.

Marshall, T. (2000). *Theatre and Empire: Great Britain on the London Stages under James VI and I*. Manchester: Manchester University Press.

Meagher, J. C. (ed.) (1980). *The Huntingdon Plays: A Critical Edition of The Downfall and the Death of Robert, Earl of Huntingdon*. New York: Garland.

Murphy, A. (1996). Shakespeare's Irish History. *Literature and History*, 3rd series, 5, 38–59.

Neill, M. (2000). *Putting History to the Question: Power, Politics, and Society in English Renaissance Drama*. New York: Columbia University Press.

Nichols, J. (ed.) (1823). *The Progresses and Public Processions of Queen Elizabeth, Among which are Interspersed*

Other Solemnities, Public Expenditures, and Remarkable Events, During the Reign of that Illustrious Princess, 3 vols. London.

Norbrook, D. (1987). *Macbeth* and the Politics of Historiography. In K. Sharpe and S. N. Zwicker (eds.) *Politics of Discourse: The Literature and History of Seventeenth-Century England.* Berkeley: University of California Press, 78–116.

Patterson, A. (1994). *Reading Holinshed's Chronicles.* Chicago, IL: University of Chicago Press.

Peele, G. (1594). *The Battell Of Alcazar, Fought in Barbarie, betweene Sebastian king of Portugall, and Abdelmelec king of Marocco. With the death of Captaine Stukeley.* London.

Pugliatti, P. (1996). *Shakespeare the Historian.* Basingstoke: Macmillan.

Rackin, P. (1990). *Stages of History: Shakespeare's English Chronicles.* Ithaca, NY: Cornell University Press.

Ribner, I. (1965). *The English History Play in the Age of Shakespeare*, 2nd edn. Princeton, NJ: Princeton University Press.

Schelling, F. E. (1902). *The English Chronicle Play: A Study in the Popular Historical Literature Environing Shakespeare.* New York: Macmillan.

Sibley, G. M. (1931). *The Lost Plays and Masques 1500–1642.* Ithaca, NY: Cornell University Press.

Siegel, P. (1978). *Shakespeare's English and Roman History Plays: A Marxist Approach.* Rutherford: Fairleigh Dickinson University Press.

Snyder, S. (2001). The Genres of Shakespeare's Plays. In M. de Grazia and S. Wells (eds.) *The Cambridge Companion to Shakespeare.* Cambridge: Cambridge University Press, 83–97.

Spikes, J. D. (1977). The Jacobean History Play and the Myth of the Elect Nation. *Renaissance Drama*, n.s., 8, 117–49.

Stow, J. (1598). *A Svrvay of London.* London.

Velz, J. W. (ed.) (1996). *Shakespeare's English Histories: A Quest for Form and Genre.* Binghamton, NY: Medieval & Renaissance Texts & Studies.

Wikander, M. H. (1986). *The Play of Truth and State: Historical Drama from Shakespeare to Brecht.* Baltimore, MD: Johns Hopkins University Press.

Wilders, J. (1978). *The Lost Garden: A View of Shakespeare's English and Roman History Plays.* London: Macmillan.

Wilson, J. (1980). *Entertainments for Elizabeth I.* Woodbridge: D. S. Brewer.

Woolf, D. R. (1990). *The Idea of History in Early Stuart England.* Toronto: University of Toronto Press.

——(2000). *Reading History in Early Modern England.* Cambridge: Cambridge University Press.

Wortham, C. (2000). *Shakespeare and the Matter of Britain: Five Shakespeare Plays in their Jacobean Context.* Aldershot: Ashgate.

Yachnin, P. (1991). History, Theatricality, and the "Structural Problem" in the *Henry IV* Plays. *Philological Quarterly*, 70, 163–79.

9

Damned Commotion: Riot and Rebellion in Shakespeare's Histories

James Holstun

Introduction

Contemporary Shakespeare criticism sometimes suggests that, prior to the explosion of feminist, cultural materialist, and new historicist theory twenty years ago, critics always began by assuming a hierarchical worldview governing all cultural production. But as Robin Headlam Wells (1985) suggests, Tillyardism was a mid-century phenomenon: earlier historical criticism did not hesitate to note Tudor challenges to Tudor absolutism. However, this assumption of order has not by any means disappeared, for the vision springs eternal of Shakespeare as Elizabethan world picturer, acolyte of "the" Tudor theory of history, king's dramatist, and creature of a hierarchical premodern episteme or discursive regime. Frequently, this old/new view assumes that Shakespeare wrote prior to class as such, so that we should continue to contrast the micropolitical and negotiated, but holistic world of his pre- or early modern drama with that of a fractious and class-riven modernity.

To suggest some problems with this rough-hewn, two-phase historicism, I will compare two small libraries of works focusing on riot, rebellion, and revolution. The first is modernist and sadly non-existent:

> *The Psychopathology of Capitalist Everyday Life* (1920): Freud analyzes the verbal slips arising from malnutrition and exhaustion among public health patients in postwar Vienna, then their search for "the organizing cure" through the Austrian Social Democratic Party.
>
> *Le Temps transformé* (1921): Proust cancels and preserves the Commune in a seven-volume account of proletarian Parisian daily life and working-class militancy.
>
> *Mrs. Holloway* (1922): Woolf's stream-of-consciousness narrative about an imprisoned, fasting, and force-fed English suffragist.

Maccabee (1923): Joyce's joco-messianic epic about a fiftyish Jewish salesman who joins James Connolly's Citizen Army and dies in the 1916 defense of the Dublin General Post Office.

The Factory (1924): Kafka's jagged parable about the baffling extraction of surplus value among workers in a Prague glassworks.

Deborah's Song (1936): Faulkner's account of Nat Turner's great-great-granddaughter, who works for the biracial Southern Tenant Farmers' Union and organizes the Delta plantation owned by Barrick Turner, her white third cousin twice-removed.

The East Is Enlightened (1949): Horkheimer and Adorno on the immanent, practical, critique of Kantian emancipation conducted by the Chinese Red Army and the Viet Minh, including the influential excursus, "Spartacus, or Manifesto and Enlightenment."

Now it's no hanging crime that so many modernists tended to ignore the collective political activity of communists, fascists, and working men and women going on all around them. Indeed, some modernists didn't (witness Yeats, Marinelli, Eisenstein, Rivera, Bloch, Brecht, MacDiarmid, Dos Passos, Hikmet), and neither did many other writers who were modern if not modernist (Zola, Trotsky, Dreiser, Smedley, Wright, Greene, Olsen, Sembene). Even these high modernists, when subject to allegorical reading procedures, yield crucial perspectives on the social struggles of their era. But before reading them against the grain, we should perhaps read them with it, and concede that their active and passive ignorance of popular political praxis forms a crucial, determining aspect of high modernism. And we should also perhaps avoid extrapolating from these works a modern ideology of order that made riot, rebellion, and revolution utterly unthinkable for the twentieth-century mind.

The second library – early modernist and gloriously actual – is Shakespeare's drama, which constitutes a virtual encyclopedia of the various forms of riot and rebellion in early modern England:

2 Henry VI: baronial revolt, urban riot, and peasant rebellion, with sources in the Great Rebellion of 1381, Cade's Rebellion, Kett's Rebellion, the London riots of the 1590s, and O'Neill's Rising (Caldwell 1995; Cartelli 1994; Patterson 1989; Wilson 1986).

Romeo and Juliet: urban feud, with sources in intra-gentry and inter-class rioting in 1590s London (Fitter 2000).

Richard II: aristocratic coup, with sources in opposition to Elizabeth in the 1590s (Barroll 1988; Norbrook 1996).

1 Henry IV, 2 Henry IV: baronial and popular revolt, with sources in the Pilgrimage of Grace, Kett's Rebellion, and the Northern Rebellion (McAlindon 1995; Scoufos 1979; Cartelli 1994).

The Tempest: slave rebellion, sea and land mutiny, with sources in New World exploration and settlement narratives (Greenblatt 1988: 129–64; Linebaugh and Rediker 2000: 8–35).

As You Like It: anti-enclosure riot, forest riot, with sources in the Oxfordshire Rising and other disturbances of the 1590s (Wilson 1993: 63–82).

Coriolanus: urban food riot, plebeian republican coup, with sources in the Midlands Insurrection of 1607 (Patterson 1989: 121–52).

King Lear: petty treason, with a servant violently resisting a noble master (Strier 1995: 165–202).

The Book of Sir Thomas More: urban riot, with sources in the Evil May Day riots and continuing struggles against "strangers" protected by Tudor absolutism.

The list could be longer. Shakespeare dramatized all four of the successful Tudor rebellions: two of them directly (Henry Tudor's baronial coup in *Richard III*, the people's rejection of the "Amicable Grant" in *Henry VIII*), and two of them indirectly, as I will argue, in *2 Henry VI* (Northumberland's 1549 coup against Lord Protector Somerset, and Mary's 1553 coup against him).[1] We simply cannot plot onto the reductive axis of premodernity–modernity a propensity for or against representing urban riot, aristocratic revolt, and peasant rebellion. Nor can we neatly distinguish between these premodern forms of collective action and more modern movements as between unselfconscious classes "in themselves" and revolutionary classes "for themselves."[2] There's too much "for themselves" back then; there's too much mere "in themselves" today.

The rebellions of mid-Tudor England had a seismic effect on the great cultural renaissance of late-Tudor England. They formed a varied body of practical efforts, prompting a response in the form of military assaults, reform legislation, and a remarkable corpus of social theory by contemporary "Commonwealthsmen," including fiction, poetry, drama, economics, polemic, and sermons. The two most significant rebellions were the Pilgrimage of Grace (1536–7) and the Rebellions of 1549. The Pilgrimage of Grace formed an enormous, cross-class, multi-phase revolt against the Henrician Reformation in Lincolnshire, Yorkshire, Lancashire, Westmoreland, and Cumberland. Its most recent historian calls it a commons revolt that aristocrats struggled to tame and shape from within and without (Hoyle 2001). It combined conservative efforts to restore the old religion with radical economic initiatives, particularly in the "Captain Poverty" risings in Richmondshire, and the strange, reforming aftermath of the revolt in the rising of godly Sir Francis Bigod. It presented so great a threat that the Duke of Norfolk, Henry's general, finding himself outnumbered by Pilgrim forces, made what both he and Henry called a bad-faith promise of pardon and redress of grievances. When redress never appeared, Henry used the new rising that resulted as an excuse to arrest and execute 178 Pilgrimage leaders.

The rebellions of 1549 brought England closer to a genuine popular social revolution than it has come between 1381 and the present day. These included the largely Catholic Prayer Book Rebellion in the West, the largely Protestant rebellions of East Anglia, and a number of significant associated risings, both Protestant and Catholic, in many other counties. Kett's Rebellion in Norfolk was particularly significant, since it declared itself a manifestly Protestant movement in solidarity with Protector Somerset's reformist regime. It aimed to preserve the social wealth accumulated by the Roman Catholic church for a newly reformed nation, not for a new agrarian aristocracy. Like so many early modern rebellions, it had deep roots in its community, and it was considerably more orderly than the gentlemen's riot that eventually crushed it. Fletcher and MacCulloch (1997) compare the camps of 1549 (and those of the 1590s that recalled them) to the open-air meetings of the assizes (pp. 119–20). MacCulloch calls them "fiestas of justice" and compares "the camp meetings of the Primitive Methodists two and a half centuries later, when humble folk once more asserted their dignity and identity in a troubled and threatening world" (MacCulloch 1986: 303).

Robert Kett, a prosperous local landowner and tanner of Wymondham, was first the victim of anti-enclosure rioters, then, remarkably, their leader. A massive commune of 16,000 campmen gathered on Mousehold Heath, outside Norwich. They established ties to allies in the city, then commenced military drill and regular church services using Cranmer's brand-new prayer book. They instituted a formal judiciary, a governing assembly representing the local hundreds, and regularized provision through requisition. They sent formal petitions for political, religious, and economic redress to the king and protector. Like many agrarian rebels of the period, they called for a return to the level of rents and fines under Henry VII, and the removal of enclosures instituted since his time. This program may sound like simple-minded agrarian nostalgia, but given the intervening inflation, and their calls for a radical limitation of customary rights for gentlemen and lords of manors, it sounds more like a canny plan for a smallholders' revolution. Had they succeeded, says S. T. Bindoff, they would have "clipped the wings of rural capitalism" (Bindoff 1949: 9).

These earlier conflicts were of pressing interest in the 1590s, when England was racked by dearth, when London saw a series of gentry feuds and plebeian riots of various descriptions, many of which find echoes and substantial reflections in Shakespeare's plays. Particularly when considering his histories, we need to compare not two but three historical moments: the Lancastrian, Yorkist, and early Tudor moment of his chronicle sources; the revolutionary upheavals of mid-Tudor England, when large-scale peasant rebellions rose up in class struggle against the absolutist class-state and the capitalist mode of production; and the late Tudor and early Stuart crises contemporary with Shakespeare himself, which prompted his examination of these earlier crises.

But all this is not to say that Shakespeare's plays pulse with confident celebrations of plebeian revolutionary energy, partly, no doubt, because of his sensibility and class: his interest in maintaining a tempered class hierarchy and increasing his stake in it through labor as a playwright and canny investment in theatre and other commercial enterprises, coupled with his intermittent philo-monarchism and disgust at the cheesy breath of the mutable many – invoked frequently enough to suggest genuine obsession, if also a lack of intimate familiarity with the meaty breath of the fixéd few. But his temperance also suggests a realistic awareness that late-Tudor turbulence was far from mid-Tudor crisis. The key point of transition was the defeat of Kett's Rebellion.

After the campmen defeated the first army sent to disperse them, the government sent another, including a large force of German mercenaries unlikely to be softened by any sympathy with English commoners, and commanded by John Dudley, Earl of Warwick, who would become Duke of Northumberland in 1551. The results were catastrophic for the campmen (perhaps 3,000 slaughtered immediately, and many tortured and hanged thereafter), for Somerset (denounced as a class traitor, deposed as protector, and eventually executed by Northumberland), and for any large-scale popular revolt by English small producers. The unsuccessful late-Tudor rebellions pale in comparison to the successful Tudor Rebellions, all of which were over by 1553. They even suffer by contrast with earlier failures, as we can see when we compare the Pilgrimage of Grace to the abortive recusant Northern Rebellion of 1569 and Essex's madcap rising of 1601, or the risings of 1549 to Hacket's Revolt of 1591 and the Oxfordshire revolt of 1596 (Manning 1988: 207, 220–9).[3]

These late-Tudor rebellions failed partly because of strategic errors, partly because of a stronger nationalist and religious ideology born of conflict with Catholic Spain and the "moderate" Elizabethan Anglican settlement, and partly because the capitalist transformation of English agriculture had further separated yeomen community leaders like Kett from the rural poor. Fletcher and MacCulloch argue that these later rebellions typically lacked a key structural precondition for the earlier ones: an alliance of "high" and "low" politics in a cross-class coalition. Despite its undoubted turbulence, late-Tudor England remained, in important ways, a post-revolutionary era lacking that sense of revolutionary possibility that fired the nation in the years of the First and Second Tudor Reformations, and that would reappear in 1641: "The efforts of the pathetic Oxfordshire conspirators and the Earl of Essex proved to be a far cry from Bosworth Field, or indeed from Naseby" (Fletcher and MacCulloch 1997: 115–28, 127).

So we should refrain from viewing Shakespeare's failure to adopt a uniformly sanguine view of plebeian revolt as a sign of gentry affinity or an embrace of Tudor estates theory, much less as a canny recognition that any struggle for popular liberation is doomed from the start.[4] Rather, it suggests a rational and pragmatic response to the straitened circumstances of class conflict in the 1590s, when a sympathetic observer might advise peasants and artisans against rebelling, not out of a metaphysic of order, but out of empirical evidence that rebellion could lead only to the gibbet and further expropriation. Given the significantly mixed textures of Shakespeare's histories, we should resolve them neither toward a resolute populism, nor toward a resolute anti-populism, nor toward some Olympian stance of "wonderful philosophic impartiality," to recall Coleridge's view of Shakespeare's stance in *Coriolanus* (Coleridge 1967, II: 135–6).[5] Rather, we should address them within the concrete writing situation of a despairing, late-Tudor Commonwealthsman who found himself torn between a profound sympathy for exploited English commoners and an upwardly mobile anxiety about what their revolutionary liberation might entail for him, between historical memory of revolutionary mass action in mid-Tudor England and political awareness of the slim chances for reviving it in late-Tudor England.

Shakespeare's mixed and muted populism may come into sharper focus when we contrast it with the blithe, armigerous bloody-mindedness of the Northumberland–Leicester literary faction, from Sir John Cheke's railing attack on Kett's campmen in *The Hurt of Sedition*, to Sackville and Norton's representation of a peasant rebellion crushed in *Gorboduc*, to Sidney's portraits of merrily hewn and hanged peasants in both versions of *Arcadia*, to Spenser's flailing attacks on English and Irish peasant rebels throughout *The Faerie Queene*. For these and other ruling-class writers, the mid-Tudor rebellions joined the continental and medieval English risings in a horrified mono-syllabic litany: from Ball and Wat and Jack Straw, from Cade and Kett and John-a-Leyden, good Lord deliver us. They could be invoked in order to premasticate and precognize the various isolated manifestations of social revolt for easier ruling-class control and consumption (Hill 1975).

But Shakespeare never portrays plebeian revolt without considerable sympathy, though his sympathies tend to be oblique, interspersed with antipathies, fragmented, lying athwart the main plot lines. In this essay I will examine three moments in Shakespeare's presentation of revolt and its aftermath: *The Second Part of King Henry VI*, his first history, which reworks chronicle accounts of Kett's Rebellion in a populist direction; the second tetralogy, with its scathing critique of Tudor order rhetoric and ruling-class massacre; and *Henry VIII*, his final history, which focuses directly on Tudor England, producing a joyful celebration of one, perhaps two, successful rebellions. I'll conclude with a brief word on the compatibility of Shakespeare's Catholic origins and his populist sympathies as a late-Tudor Commonwealthsman.

2 Henry VI: Commotion Dispersed

Shakespeare's sympathy with the tragedy of Somerset and the campmen appears in *2 Henry VI* not so much in his representation of Cade's Rebellion as in his dramatization of petitioning by commoners, and of four diverse killings: Peter Thump's heroic slaying of his drunken master, the noble conspirators' villainous assassination of the betrayed Duke of Gloucester, Walter Whitmore's retributive execution of the overbearing Duke of Suffolk, and Alexander Iden's cowardly slaying of the famished Jack Cade.

Petitions formed a crucial discursive genre of populist revolt in Tudor England.[6] Historians continue to debate the extent of Somerset's social radicalism and his sympathy with the campmen in Norwich and elsewhere during the summer of 1549. What is no longer controversial is the remarkable extent of their communication through petitions. Ethan Shagan has analyzed Somerset's responses to petitions arriving from camps in Norfolk, Suffolk, Oxfordshire, St. Albans, Hampshire, Somerset, and Essex. Somerset offered pardons, an early parliament, a general resolve to initiate far-reaching social reforms, and a surprisingly friendly tone. To the petitions of the Suffolk campmen, those "loyal subjects," he wrote, "your articles be well considered and perused by us and indeed we will not dissemble with you, we see them for the most part founded upon great and just causes and assure you there be few articles there but before your motion have been known thought upon considered and fully proposed by us to be redressed." Far from a traditional, paternalist ritual, this exchange shows Somerset constructing "popularity" through "a conscious effort to appeal downward for support from those outside the political establishment, creating a power-base independent of either the court or local affinities" (Shagan 1999: 59, 37 n. 1).

In act 1, scene 3 of 2 *Henry VI*, a passage with no source in the chronicles of Lancastrian England, Shakespeare presents several petitioners approaching Gloucester, but intercepted by the Duke of Suffolk and his paramour, Queen Margaret. The first two bring petitions with a Tudor feel. The first objects to ecclesiastical abuse, protesting "against John Goodman, my lord Cardinal's man, for keeping my house and lands and wife and all from me" (1.3.18–20). The second protests against agrarian enclosures, the flashpoint of the mid-Tudor Crisis, sparked in part by Somerset's decrees ordering the restoration of enclosed commons, which earned him the wrath of Northumberland and the disapproval of Holinshed (1965, III: 916–17). Shakespeare's Suffolk finds himself personally implicated:

> *Suffolk*. . . . What's yours? [*He takes the supplication*] What's here? [*Reads*] "Against the Duke of Suffolk for enclosing the commons of Melford"! [*To the* SECOND PETITIONER] How now, Sir Knave?
> *Second Petitioner*. Alas, sir, I am but a poor petitioner of our whole township. (1.3.21–5)

It's not clear why Shakespeare specifies Melford, Suffolk, or "Long Melford," as the First Quarto calls it (Knowles 1999: 382). But it featured prominently during the mass popular resistance to Cardinal Wolsey's extortionate Amicable Grant, which Shakespeare would later dramatize in *Henry VIII*, as we will see. And during the camping time of 1549, Suffolk hosted several camps to rival Kett's in Norfolk, and a steady flow of petitions and responses to the protector. In the Folio, disgusted at the English custom of petitioning, Queen Margaret calls the petitioners "base cullions" and sends them packing (1.3.44). In the First Quarto Suffolk tears up the Suffolk man's petition and rejects the whole concept of petitioning:

> [*He tears the papers.*]
> So now show your petitions to Duke Humphrey
> Villains get you gone and come not near the court,
> Dare these peasants write against me thus. (Knowles 1999: 382)

In both versions Suffolk allows the third petition to get through, since it works against his rival Machiavel, the Duke of York. Peter Thump, apprentice to the armorer Thomas Horner, charges his master with treasonous assertions that "York was rightful heir to the crown" (1.3.29–30). Gloucester orders their trial by combat (1.3.205–11), and in a contest before the king, the queen, and his fellow apprentices,

Peter miraculously slays his master, who has drunk too many premature celebratory toasts (2.3).

Where Holinshed's servant falsely charges his master with a generalized treason (Holinshed 1965, III: 210), Shakespeare's truly charges his with specifically Yorkist sedition. Where Holinshed presents a plain trial-by-combat at Smithfield, Shakespeare presents a sort of moderated apprentice riot at court, with four "neighbours" and four "prentices" cheering on their favorites: "drink, and fear not your man"; "Fight for credit of the prentices" (2.3.65, 72–3). And where Holinshed's "false servant . . . lived not long unpunished" and was hanged at Tyburn, Shakespeare's Henry proclaims Peter's "truth and innocence," and leads him off to a reward (2.3.104–7).[7] This is loyalist traditionalism of a sort. But in dramatizing an alliance of Lancastrian low and high against middling and high Yorkist usurpers and rebels, Shakespeare reproduces the logic of many sixteenth-century rebellions, including the populist royalism of Robert Kett and his campmen, who declared their alliance with King Edward and Protector Somerset against enclosing lords and gentry.

Patterson shows that a populist reading of *2 Henry VI* (whose subtitle in both Quartos and Folio is "with the death of the Good Duke Humphrey") ought to begin with the populist sympathy that Shakespeare's commoners direct toward martyred Humphrey Plantagenet, Good Duke of Gloucester, uncle and Protector to Henry VI (Patterson 1989: 47–8). This argument gains additional force when we hear its resonance with the populist Tudor sympathy directed toward the martyred Edward Seymour, Good Duke of Somerset, uncle and Protector to Edward VI. Cardinal Pole implied the connection between the two Protectorships in a 1549 letter to Somerset, as did Somerset in his response. Diarmaid MacCulloch notes that "the story of Henry's childhood prominently featured Humphrey Duke of Gloucester, who provided a useful precedent for a good duke chosen as Protector" (MacCulloch 1999: 63). John Bale thought Rome murdered Humphrey (Norbrook 1984: 41). John Foxe compared the two protectors at length on the grounds of their struggles with truculent bishops of Winchester (Gloucester with Henry Beaufort, Somerset with Stephen Gardiner), their persecution and execution by noble enemies, and their common "zeal" in religion. Foxe instances Gloucester's "discerning and trying out the false lying miracle and popish hypocrisy" of "the blind beggar at St. Alban's" (Foxe 1965, VI: 296, 713), and we know that Shakespeare drew on Foxe's account to depict Gloucester's demystifying "cure" of Simpcox in act 2, scenes 1–2.[8]

If Shakespeare's Gloucester figures Good Duke Somerset, then his Suffolk figures Bad Duke Northumberland, notorious encloser, opponent of Somerset's efforts at "popularity," and slayer of campmen and Somerset alike.[9] Shakespeare's Suffolk joins with Queen Margaret, Cardinal Beaufort, and the Duke of York against Gloucester, charging that his "sumptuous buildings" have "cost a mass of public treasury" (1.3.131–2). As they plan Gloucester's murder, Suffolk worries that "The commons" will "haply rise to save his life" (3.1.240). They proceed to have him strangled – onstage in the Quartos (Knowles 1999: 393) – a base form of death, graphically described by Warwick, that plebeianizes him (3.2.160–78). The commons respond furiously, assaulting the palace and calling for Suffolk's death (3.2.122–9, 236, 243). As Patterson (1989: 48) notes, a new high/low alliance emerges immediately to replace the old one, and Salisbury becomes the new popular spokesman (3.2.245–71).

Similarly, Northumberland's faction on the Privy Council began to organize against Somerset in 1549, charging that he ambitiously sought his own glory through his "sumptuous and costly houses."[10] In October 1549 they denounced the recently deposed and imprisoned Somerset for his efforts to enlist the people in an alliance with him and the king against them, saying that he had circulated the following petition among them:

> Good people, in the name of God and King Edward, let us rise with all our power to defend him and the Lord Protector against certain lords and gentlemen and chief masters, which would depose the Lord Protector, and so endanger the King's royal person, because we, the poor commons, being injured by the extortious gentlemen had our pardon this year by the mercy of the King, and the goodness of the Lord Protector for whom let us fight, for he leaveth all just and true gentlemen, which do no extortion and also us the poor communalty of England. God save the King and my Lord Protector and all the true Lords and gentlemen and us the poor communalty. (Dasent 1890–1907: 331)

In 1551 Northumberland and the Privy Council had Somerset arrested, tried, and condemned to death, using a statute originally aimed at Kett's rebels. In January 1552 a great crowd disobeyed the City Council's curfew and attended his execution, raising a seditious tumult until Somerset himself ordered them to maintain order.[11]

Shakespeareans considering Kett's Rebellion often stop at the fact that the rebellion itself began with a group of disgruntled commoners assembling in Wymondham, Norfolk (Kett's home), for a pageant honoring Thomas Becket (Fletcher and MacCulloch 1997: 64–5). But Shakespeare's interest in the rebellion extended considerably further. He could easily have known more details, if not through Alexander Neville's *De furoribus Norfolciensium Ketto Duce*, an ornate, neo-Tacitean narrative of 1575, then through its translation, condensation, and development in both the 1577 and 1586 editions of Holinshed, the first substantial account of Kett's Rebellion published in English (Holinshed 1965, III: 963–87). He might also have known it from *The Hurt of Sedition*, Sir John Cheke's frothing attack on the campmen, written between the first and second royalist assaults. Both editions of Holinshed reprinted it whole, directly after their accounts of Kett's Rebellion, "as a necessary discourse for every good English subject" (Holinshed 1965, III: 987–1011; 987).

During their six-week sojourn on Mousehold Heath, Kett's campmen repeatedly attacked the sumptuary signs of class: plucking off the clothing of Norwich's deputy mayor, mocking the coat of Northumberland's herald as "but some pieces of popish copes sewed together," forcing the gentlemen of Norwich to disguise themselves by doffing their apparel and hiding in the woods, and stripping a captured Italian mercenary of his "gorgeous apparel" ("very costly and cunningly wrought," Neville laments), then hanging him naked from an oak at Mount Surrey House. Neville is astonished at their failure to seek ransom, "although there would have been given £100 for his life" (Neville 1615: G4^v–G5^r, I1^v, D2^r, F4^{r-v}). Holinshed comments that their violence

> shewed what courtesy might be looked for at such cruel traitors' hands, that would thus unmercifully put such a gentleman and worthy soldier to death: for whose ransom, if they would have demanded it, they might have had no small portion of money to have satisfied their greedy minds. But it seemed that their beastly cruelty had bereft them the remembrance of all honest consideration and dutiful humanity. (Holinshed 1965, III: 972, 974)

In the first assault, the campmen also captured Lord Sheffield, who

> declared what he was, and offered largely to the villains, if they would have saved his life. But the more noble he shewed himself to be, the more were they kindled in outrageous fury against him. And as he pulled off his headpiece, that it might appear what he was, a butcherly knave named Fulkes, who by occupation was both a carpenter and a butcher, slat him in the head with a club, and so most wretchedly killed him. (Ibid: 974)

The idea never occurs to Neville or Holinshed that the campmen might have slain Sheffield and the Italian mercenary as a bit of leveling peasant potlatch – a theatrical squandering of potential ransom in symbolic recognition of the fact that no campman in a similar situation could have expected any response but *sursum cordum, alis dictus hangum meum*, to quote the sardonic law/pig Latin of *Iacke Strawe*'s apprehensive peasant rebel, Tom Miller (1593: D4^r).

But the idea occurs to Shakespeare, as he adapts this episode in *2 Henry VI*, just before he turns to Cade's Rebellion, in his account of the execution of the Duke of Suffolk. Drawing on Halle (1970: lxxvi^v), Holinshed quickly narrates Suffolk's capture and beheading by unnamed sailors employed by the Duke of Exeter, constable of the Tower of London (Holinshed 1965, III: 220). Shakespeare uses Holinshed's account of Kett's Rebellion to turn this encounter into a complex episode of class struggle. First, he turns these servants of Exeter into an independent crew of pirates (4.1.108, 140). Their Captain, who has captured Suffolk's ship, distributes the captive gentlemen as booty: one to the Master, one to the Mate, and the third, a disguised and unrecognized Duke of Suffolk, to one Walter Whitmore. Whitmore, who has lost comrades and one of his eyes in the capture, swears that he will slay his captive in revenge. Suffolk emphasizes his membership in the Order of the Garter by displaying a badge: "Look on my George – I am a gentleman, / Rate me at what thou wilt, thou shalt be paid." Whitmore responds, "And so am I; my name is Walter Whitmore" (4.1.30–2).

Suffolk startles because of a previous prophecy that he would die by wa(l)ter (1.4.72–3). This prophecy may allude to a story, recorded in some of the chronicles and hinted at in Halle and Holinshed, that Suffolk's astrologer told him he would be safe if he got out of the Tower of London, only to be captured by Exeter's ship, the *Nicholas of the Tower* (Virgoe 1965: 493). But where that delphic irony runs a noble circuit, from Exeter's Tower to his *Tower*, Shakespeare's runs a plebeian one, from water to Wa(l)ter, with a passing hint, perhaps, of Wat(Tyl)er. Whitmore spurns the gentlemanly economy of capture and ransom, saying that he hopes to be proclaimed a coward if ever "merchant-like I sell revenge." With the debonair flourish of a courtly masquer, Suffolk throws off his ragged cloak and reveals himself as

> a prince,
> The Duke of Suffolk, William de la Pole . . .
> [T]hese rags are no part of the Duke.
> Jove sometime went disguised, and why not I?

But Suffolk's gentle sumptuary gesture misfires. The Captain responds, "But Jove was never slain as thou shalt be." And he and Whitmore produce a series of sardonic puns on Pole, poll (decapitate), and pool (sewer): "pool? Sir Pool! Lord! / Aye kennel, puddle, sink, whose filth and dirt / Troubles the silver spring where England drinks" (4.1.45–6, 48–50, 73–5). Here, the Lieutenant redirects the excremental anti-Kett rhetoric of Holinshed and Cheke.[12]

Suffolk suddenly recognizes the Captain as his former servant, an "Obscure and lousy swain," "jady groom," and "base slave" who "kissed thy hand and held my stirrup," and "Bare-headed plodded by my foot-cloth mule." Thus he drives the play faster towards its second instance of a servant slaying his master. The Captain imagines Suffolk's head mounted on a pole, "And thou that smiledst at good Duke Humphrey's death / Against the senseless winds shall grin in vain" (4.1.51, 53, 54, 68, 76–7). He produces a long, eloquent denunciation (4.1.71–103). But like Lord Sheffield, with his helmet off and his gentle mien shining out to no avail, Suffolk remains incredulous:

> *Suffolk.* I go of message from the Queen to France;
> I charge thee waft me safely 'cross the Channel.
> *Captain.* Walter –
> *Whitmore.* Come, Suffolk, I must waft thee to thy death. (4.1.114–17)

After Whitmore strikes off Suffolk's head, the Captain magnanimously remits one gentleman's ransom, and sends him back to the queen with Suffolk's head and body (4.1.141). Thus a base groom becomes a pirate captain, then the avenger of a murdered duke. By transforming this execution from an action by the Duke of Exeter's servants to a pirate crew's freely chosen act of solidarity with the martyred Duke of Gloucester, Shakespeare recalls not only Kett's Rebellion, but its aftermath in 1553. After Edward died and Northumberland attempted to install his daughter-in-law, Lady Jane Grey, on the throne, Mary established her rule largely through the support of East Anglican Protestant commoners and former campmen who remembered that

Northumberland had slaughtered them in 1549, and declared their sympathy with Mary, remarkably enough, as godly solidarity.[13]

Shakespeare's account of these loyalist/revolutionary pirates suggests either that his knowledge of mid-Tudor revolts produced an intuitive sympathy with late medieval populism, or else (or also) that he knew the relatively obscure chronicle sources suggesting that Suffolk was intercepted not by regular navy but by a pirate fleet, that his executioners may have been acting in concert with York and Cade's rebellion, and that they held to a radical commonwealth ideology. When Suffolk insisted on his safe-conduct pass from the king, they responded, "they did not know the said king, but they well knew the crown of England, saying that the aforesaid crown was the community of the said realm and that the community of the realm was the crown of that realm" (Virgoe 1965: 501). Shakespeare's commoners approach this stridency when they insist they would save Henry from a serpent (Suffolk), even "if your highness should intend to sleep / And charge that no man should disturb your rest, / In pain of your dislike, or pain of death" (3.2.255–7).

These thoroughly populist scenes mitigate ahead of time Shakespeare's frequently unsympathetic portrayal of Jack Cade, and they inflect the more sympathetic scene of Cade's death.[14] After the failure of his rebellion, Cade flees, and several days later finds himself famished and driven to a stand, like the campmen, after Northumberland cut off their food supply to Mousehold Heath. On his hands and knees, Cade forages for greens in the enclosed garden of Alexander Iden, a prosperous Kentish homeowner, who is out for a stroll in the company of five servants, musing with ostentatious Horatian moderation that he seeks "not to wax great by others' waning" (4.9.18). After Cade sees and defies him, Iden first denies that he would combat a "poor famished man," then, after horrifying mockery of Cade's famished weakness, draws on him without warning and says "Let this my sword report what speech forbears" (4.1.41, 51). Cade rises from his knees, draws, fights, loses, names himself, blames his weakness, reasonably enough, on "the ten meals I have lost," and dies (4.9.59–60). In death as never quite in life, Jack Cade becomes an authentic peasant rebel, starved nearly to death and treacherously butchered.

Looking less like a doughty hero than like the mercenary Falstaff of Shrewsbury Field, Iden stabs Cade's corpse – a gesture difficult to picture in performance without a response of, at best, cynical disgust. He then begins to calculate that a grateful king will knight him and award him a coat of arms bearing the image of a bloody sword (4.9.63–8). This recalls London's coat of arms, which still bears an image of the sword of Lord Mayor William Walworth, who slew a mounted peasant rebel charging young King Richard (Knowles 1999: 4.10.70n.).[15] But given the unequal nature of the contest, Shakespeare may be imagining that less heroic William Walworth of *The Life and Death of Iacke Straw*, who moves with unseemly haste from arresting Jack Straw to stabbing him:

> Villain I do arrest thee in my prince's name,
> Proud rebel as thou art take that withal;   *Here he*

Learn thou and all posterity after thee,   *stabs him.*
What 'tis a servile slave, to brave a king. (1593: E2^r)

In Shakespeare's next scene we find that Iden does indeed wax by Cade's waning: he enters Henry's presence with Cade's head, kneels down an esquire, and rises up a knight with a thousand marks (5.1.64–80).

The Second Tetralogy: Commotion Crushed

Shakespeare's second tetralogy might seem at first an unpromising site for a sympathetic meditation on Tudor rebellion, particularly if we find a current of mystified sacred absolutism at work in the play. For Ernst Kantorowicz, Bolingbroke/Henry IV generates the turmoil of Lancastrian England when he slays Richard and sacrilegiously separates the king's two bodies (Kantorowicz 1957: 24–41). But rather than reading medieval hierarchalism forward into Tudor England, perhaps we should see Shakespeare reading Renaissance resistance theory backward. In *The Tenure of Kings and Magistrates* Milton assimilates pre-absolutist baronial counsel with kings to post-absolutist republican magistracy: dukes, earls, marquises, and barons "were at first not hereditary, not empty and vain titles, but names of trust and office," who "drew up a charge against Richard II, and the Commons requested to have judgement decreed against him, that the realm might not be endangered."[16]

As David Norbrook suggests, the neo-medieval Elizabethans viewing (or writing) *Richard II* might have been hankering, not for Ricardian absolutism, but for baronial resistance to it: the play might have offered them a precedent for a rebellious amalgam of neo-medieval aristocratic constitutionalism and early modern republicanism. Famously, eleven of Essex's rebels saw a special performance of the play by the Lord Chamberlain's Men on February 7, 1601, the night before they rose against Elizabeth. Norbrook also argues that Shakespeare's view of the barons as magistrates acquires an enhanced popular dimension in the rest of the second tetralogy (Norbrook 1996: 46). In these plays Shakespeare balances the machiavellian policy associated with Henry IV and King Harry, not through a full-fledged celebration of peasant revolt, but through a baronial/popular moral economy that delivers an elegy for murdered plebeians and a critique of the ideology of order typically invoked against them.

First, he creates a sort of "cannon fodder track" through the three plays, one that sympathetically memorializes the English commoners chewed up in the wars waged by English absolutists on their aristocratic enemies in England and in France. This track stretches from Falstaff's description of his impressed regiment in *1 Henry IV*, almost all of them massacred in battle (4.2.11–68, 5.3.30–7); to his survey in *2 Henry IV* of his emaciated, fatalistic, and generally unpatriotic draftees (3.2.1–254); to the remarkable debate in *Henry V*, on the night before Agincourt, between the disguised King Harry and the common soldier Michael Williams, who focuses on the difference in defeat between ransomed kings and soldiers with their throats cut

(4.1.83–211). After the miracle of Agincourt, this debate remains unresolved, despite (or because of) Henry's glove trick and lordly benison – a haughty sumptuary revelation of kingly identity and post-bellum munificence that leaves Williams unpersuaded and unimpressed, like a disarmed Walter Whitmore: "I will none of your money" (4.8.62).

Second, Shakespeare traces what we might call – after E. P. Thompson's "Moral Economy of the English Crowd" – the immoral economy of the English absolutist: the cynically amused ability of Henry and his sons to greet rational, traditional petitioning with calumny, lies, and murderous betrayal. In *1 Henry IV*, after the Earl of Worcester delivers a long, articulate, and detailed indictment of Henry's broken oaths to his fellow nobles, Henry ignores him completely. Like the Duke of Suffolk with the petitioners, he focuses on the medium, not the content of Worcester's speech, and engages in pure class abuse:

> These things indeed you have articulate,
> Proclaimed at market crosses, read in churches,
> To face the garment of rebellion
> With some fine colour that may please the eye
> Of fickle changelings and poor discontents,
> Which gape and rub the elbow at the news
> Of hurly-burly innovation;
> And never yet did insurrection want
> Such water-colours to impaint his cause,
> Nor moody beggars starving for a time
> Of pell-mell havoc and confusion. (5.1.72–82)

Here, Shakespeare partly adapts Holinshed, who says the Percies and others represented themselves as "procurers and protectors of the commonwealth" showing their charges against the king "to diverse noblemen, and other states of the realm." But Shakespeare eliminates Holinshed's sneering asides about these "contrived forgeries" (Holinshed 1965, III: 23, 25) – or rather, he attributes them to the sneering king. Henry's horror at moody starvelings jostling each other for news at the market cross suggests not a baronial but an ideological conflict: the Edwardian Privy Council's horror at Somerset's popularizing effort to establish friendly relations with the campmen and recruit the people to his cause. Baronial solidarity begins to resemble the godly, cross-class mid-Tudor public sphere, or even a gathering of armed commoners.

The next such moment occurs in *2 Henry IV*, when Henry's forces encounter the rebels in the Forest of Gaultres, and Westmorland denounces the Archbishop of York and the other rebels in the same post-feudal tones of railing attack on class traitors:

> If that rebellion
> Came like itself, in base and abject routs,

> Led on by bloody youth, guarded with rags,
> And countenanced by boys and beggary;
> I say, if damned commotion so appeared
> In his true native and most proper shape,
> You, reverend father, and these noble lords
> Had not been here to dress the ugly form
> Of base and bloody insurrection
> With your fair honours. (4.1.32–41)

Taking on Worcester's role in the previous play, the Archbishop delivers a long, principled petition in various "articles" asking the king for redress, previously denied (4.1.74). When Westmorland simply contradicts him, and attempts to trace out a conspiracy theory, York sounds an authentically mid-Tudor note:

> *Westmorland.* What peer hath been suborned to grate on you,
> That you should seal this lawless bloody book
> Of forged rebellion with a seal divine?
> *Archbishop of York.* My brother general, the commonwealth
> I make my quarrel in particular. (4.1.90–4)

York turns to the classic populist trope of Tudor rebellion by boldly personifying a plebeian collective and mocking the idea of a rancorous baronial mastermind. Here, he recalls the Long Melford weaver, John Green, during the successful resistance to Henry VIII's "Amicable Grant." When the Duke of Suffolk asked the Suffolk rioters who led them, Green responded "that Poverty was their captain, the which with his cousin Necessity, had brought them to that doing" (Holinshed 1965, III: 709).[17] York also recalls the Pilgrims of Grace speaking as yet another "Captain Poverty" (Hoyle 2001: 8, 22, 217–18), or perhaps Latimer, "the Commonwealth of Kent," that shadowy leader of the 1549 Kentish commotions (Fletcher and MacCulloch 1997: 66).

Regrouping and apparently backing down, Westmorland grants the justice of the rebels' lawless bloody book, and insists that Henry has granted Prince John full commission to grant their demands. Mowbray is suspicious, but the Archbishop relents. When John arrives, he swears "by the honour of my blood" that "these griefs shall be with speed redressed" (4.1.281, 285). The rebels take him at his word and disperse their superior forces, and Lord Hastings reports them returning peacefully to their rural homes "Like youthful steers unyoked." At this point, Westmorland and Prince John arrest the chief rebels and send them off to execution, quibbling that they promised reform of the grievances, not pardon for the grievants. Meanwhile, John picks up Hastings's metaphor with a murderous euphemism, as he orders his troops to "pursue the scattered stray" (4.1.328, 346) – a pastoral epithet Jack Cade had ironically applied to himself (4.9.23). The rebel Sir John Coleville surrenders to Falstaff, and his defiant final words heighten the contrast with John's treachery. John denounces him as a "famous rebel," and Coleville begins with what sounds like hierarchical grov-eling in an effort to mitigate his rebellious action: "I am, my lord, but as my betters are / That led me hither." But he abruptly reverses this impression, concluding with heroically suicidal defiance: "Had they been ruled by me, / You should have won them dearer than you have" (4.2.58–60). The "ruled by me" idiom – a favorite of peasant rebels struggling to create solidarity[18] – points toward his own ignored advice to his "betters," who were (prudentially, at least) his inferiors.

John continues with his mopping up operation, and makes plain the offstage carnage:

> *Prince John.* Have you left pursuit?
> *Westmorland.* Retreat is made, and execution stayed.
> *Prince John.* Send Coleville with his confederates
> To York, to present execution. (4.2.63–6)

Holinshed offers conflicting accounts of this encounter: the first emphasizes Westmorland's (not John's) deceit, without hinting at the murder of the dispersed common soldiers, while the second says the rebel leaders surrendered unconditionally, leaving their still-mustered troops lawfully subject to attack, with no deceptive promise of pardon (Holinshed 1965, III: 37–8). Shakespeare combines the two accounts for maximum vilification of his absolutists, who slay nobles and common-ers one by one, after implied pardon and redress. Scoufos first compared this scene to Henry VIII's treacherous response to the Pilgrimage of Grace (Scoufos 1979: 125–6), and McAlindon (1995) has followed her suggestion up. The connection may gain some added resonance from the fact that Doncaster was the site both of Bolingbroke's false promise to his fellow nobles that he had no regal ambitions, recalled by Worcester in *1 Henry IV* (5.1.42, 58), and of Norfolk's 1536 false promise of pardon and redress to the Pilgrims. But Prince John's instantaneous betrayal evokes rather the conclusion of Kett's Rebellion, when an enclave of diehard campmen accepted Northumberland's promise of pardon. Immediately after they surrendered, he proceeded to hang "nine of the chiefest procurers of all the mischief," while "Some others of them were drawn, hanged, and quartered, and their heads and quarters set up in public places for a terror to others."[19] Indeed, Northumberland presided over trials and the executions in Norwich for almost two weeks (Russell 1859: 151). If Shakespeare is indeed allud-ing critically to this account, he is the only writer, from Neville and Holinshed to present-day historians, who has sensed any conflict at all between the pardon and the gibbet.

Finally, *Henry V*. In *The Hurt of Sedition* Sir John Cheke views the orderly campmen of Mousehold Heath through bloodshot gentry eyes and vents the standard ruling-class calumny: "no doubt thereof, ye would have fallen to slaughter of men, ravish-ing of wives, deflowering of maidens, chopping of children, firing of houses, beating down of streets, overthrowing of all together" (Holinshed 1965, III: 997). As he began his first tetralogy, Shakespeare may have followed Cheke's vision when he dramatized (particularly in the Quarto versions) Cade's wanton, extra-judicial murders, his encouragement of rape. However, as he concludes his second, he shows Cheke's fantasy in the flesh, but in a surprising person. Camped before "half-achievèd" Harfleur, King Harry takes on the godlike tones of Marlowe's Tamburlaine before Damascus, for he threatens that his soldiers will begin

> With conscience wide as hell, mowing like grass
> Your fresh fair virgins and your flow'ring infants . . .
> What is't to me, when you yourselves are cause,
> If your pure maidens fall into the hand
> Of hot and forcing violation? . . .
>   why, in a moment look to see
> The blind and bloody soldier with foul hand
> Defile the locks of your shrill-shrieking daughters;
> Your fathers taken by the silver beards,
> And their most reverend heads dashed to the walls;
> Your naked infants spitted upon pikes,
> Whiles the mad mothers with their howls confused
> Do break the clouds, as did the wives of Jewry
> At Herod's bloody-hunting slaughtermen. (3.3.85, 90–1, 96–8, 110–18)

Holinshed's Harry sacks Harfleur after its surrender and expels its citizenry, offering the deserted city up for English colonization – which tends to undercut his claim that it was already English (Holinshed 1965, III: 73–4). At first, it seems that Shakespeare's does not, for after this speech, Harfleur capitulates, Harry tells Exeter "use mercy to them all" (3.3.131), and the scene ends. But within two scenes, King Charles is warning that "Harry England . . . sweeps through our land / With pennons painted in the blood of Harfleur" (3.5.48–9). This image either exaggerates the bloodshed from the initial assault on Harfleur, or hints at a bloodbath after its surrender. If the latter, then King Harry, strangely absent from the military action of *2 Henry IV*, has found within himself some of his brother John's power to say and unsay. Mark Thornton Burnett (1987) sees Marlowe's Tamburlaine embodying the early modern ruling-class fear of vagrants on a rampage. Shakespeare returns us to early modern reality, in which the nobility and gentry responded to relatively orderly and non-violent forms of plebeian "rebellion" with hysterical charges of an impending anarchy, and preemptive cavalry charges and hangings. He shows Tamburlaine's power placed utterly at the disposal of an absolutist project, but divided between Harry and his *lumpen* soldiery. When Harry hears of a French counter-attack, he orders, "Then every soldier kill his prisoners," to which Pistol, his swaggering tinhorn Tamburlaine, responds, "*Coup' le gorge*" (4.6.37–9).[20] In Shakespeare, this murder precedes and provokes the French murder of the luggage train boys, though a convenient story reverses the order of the atrocities (4.7.1–9). In keeping with Shakespeare's general despair at the prospects for popular self-liberation in the late 1590s, *Henry V* is a long way from celebrating a rebellious moral economy, but it does preserve a critical perspective on the way in which a ruling-class rhetoric of order displaces its own practice of murder and rapine.

Henry VIII: Commotion Unreproved

Shakespeare's decision to base his tetralogies in pre-Reformation England, with only traces of a Lollard subplot, suggests not so much a hankering for medieval Catholicism as an inclination temporarily to bracket theological dispute in order to view more clearly the social and socio-religious struggles of early modern England. For exceptions that pointedly prove the rule, we need simply consider the two plays about Tudor England that he wrote or helped to write: *The Book of Sir Thomas More* and *Henry VIII*. Both plays struggle to sidestep the theological issues that ripped the century apart. In return, they gain a clear and sympathetic focus on class struggle: on the Londoners in the Ill May Day riots of *Sir Thomas More*, who strain against the abusive "strangers" protected by Henrician absolutism; on the rioters against the Amicable Grant in *Henry VIII*, who strain against the corrupt counselor Wolsey, and his king.

Henry VIII (or *All Is True*) dramatizes the popular sympathy toward both the cast-off Catholic Queen Katherine of Aragon and nearly martyred Protestant Archbishop Thomas Cranmer, effacing the religious chasm that would have (indeed, did) set them violently against each other. This strange sort of combination, along with an impulse to save Shakespeare from responsibility for what they see as an inferior play, has led many editors and critics into wantonly ungrounded speculation about his joint authorship with the relatively godly and clumsy John Fletcher.[21] But Bullough argues for Shakespeare's sole authorship by noting that both *2 Henry VI* and *Henry VIII* offer relatively fragmented *de casibus* plots in which characters come into contact with the king, one after another, then rise or fall or both (Bullough 1966: 449–50). We might compare the odd couple of Katherine and Cranmer to Henry VI (the saintly martyr revered by Tudor Catholics) and Gloucester (the proto-Protestant martyr revered by Tudor gospellers).

Henry VIII also returns to *2 Henry VI* by building in two Gloucester/Somerset figures. First, the good Duke of Buckingham is brought low by a conspiracy among rivals who fear his ties to the people. The fatal, perjured testimony against him comes from his estate surveyor, whom he has fired for oppressing his tenants (1.2.174). At his execution Buckingham entreats the crowds threatening to rescue him to submit to authority (2.1), suggesting Foxe's narrative of Somerset's death (Foxe 1965, VI: 292–5) much more than Holinshed's of Buckingham's (Holinshed 1965, III: 662). Second, Queen Katherine herself appears on stage looking like a combination of Gloucester and the anonymous petitioner of Long Melford, for she presents to Henry as "my petition" the popular grievances against Wolsey's Amicable Grant. She reports that the desperate assembled people, threatened with economic catastrophe and hunger, have begun to "vent reproaches / Most bitterly" against Wolsey, and the king himself,

> Whose honour heaven shield from soil – even he escapes not
> Language unmannerly, yea, such which breaks
> The sides of loyalty, and almost appears in loud rebellion. (1.2.18, 27–9)

The remarkable thing in Shakespeare's play, as in the royal response to the Amicable Grant itself, is the absence of the condign punishment that we expect for such grumblings. Katherine intercedes effectively with the king, who immediately chastises Wolsey and orders the sending of "our letters with / Free pardon to each man that has denied / The force of this commission" (1.2.100–2). To find a similar utopian treatment of popular revolt in Shakespeare, with commotioning commoners managing to alter the *polis* without being massacred, we would have to look to the first scene of *Coriolanus*, where an equally desperate riot of hungry plebeians forces the patricians to modify the Roman constitution by adding the tribunate. In both plays we should probably hear coded echoes of popular discontent as well as Jacobean parliamentary controversies over supply.

Later in the play, Stephen Gardiner, Archbishop of Winchester, tries out a little Tudor order rhetoric against Thomas Cranmer. The people are wild horses who must be tamed "with stubborn bits." If the king doesn't do so, then

> Farewell all physic – and what follows then?
> Commotions, uproars – with a general taint
> Of the whole state, as of late days our neighbours,
> The upper Germany, can dearly witness,
> Yet freshly pitied in our memories. (5.2.57, 61–5)

Gardiner's hysterical homily derives from Foxe (1965, VIII: 24, 25), but also from Halle's chronicle for 1525, the year of the Amicable Grant: "In this troublous season the uplandishmen of Germany, called the bowres, rose in a great number, almost an hundred thousand, and rebelled against the princes of Germany, of which a great number were slain and destroyed" (Halle 1970: cxlii^v). Here, Shakespeare's Catholic machiavel combines Ulysses' "untune that string" speech in *Troilus* (1.3.74–137) with the *reductio ad Münsterum*, the favorite trope of the Tudor theorist of order: each new hint of popular resistance, no matter how small, threatens a domestic outbreak of murderous Anabaptistry. But Henry frees Cranmer from suspicion, ratifying the opinion of his probity held by "the common voice" (5.3.208). We move immediately in the play to an account of Elizabeth's christening, Cranmer's prophetic sermon about her, and the attendant celebrations.

Holinshed describes these celebrations rather quickly as "solemn ceremonies" at court (Holinshed 1965, III: 786–7). In Shakespeare, the common people's celebrations produce something like an unpunished mid-Tudor commotion. Their riotous festivity suggests Tudor drama could be not simply a mirror of rebellion, but rebellion itself: a porter worries about the cudgel work of "the youths that thunder at a playhouse" (5.3.55). The Lord Chamberlain warns against the violent behavior of the "multitude," the "lazy knaves," the "trim rabble . . . Your faithful friends o' th' suburbs" (5.3.61, 64, 65) – the site of most theatres and of most London insurrections after 1595 (Manning 1988: 211). The Porter tells the Lord Chamberlain,

> An't please your honour,
> We are but men, and what so many may do,
> Not being torn a-pieces, we have done.
> An army cannot rule 'em. (5.3.68–71).

This strangely excessive response seems to point in a utopian direction, beyond the immediate occasion. It finds a rhetorical corollary in Cranmer's excessive oration at the christening, which is completely Shakespeare's invention. For he praises the baby girl as "the maiden phoenix" who will "create another heir / As great in admiration as herself" (5.4.41–2). This is partly an effort to make a mystical plus of Elizabeth's childlessness and James's irregular succession. But in celebrating Elizabeth so strongly and so strangely, Shakespeare, Cranmer, and the crowd suggest that Henry is either an absolutist knave or an absolutist fool: his errors or lapses throughout the play include the isolation of Katherine, the oppression of the commons, the execution of Buckingham, the abuses by Wolsey and Gardiner. Henry Wotton, who attended a 1613 performance of the play, noted that its "many extraordinary circumstances of pomp and majesty" were "sufficient in truth within a while to make greatness very familiar, if not ridiculous" (Shakespeare 1997: 3117). The play's final *de casibus* tragedy, then, is Henry's own, as Cranmer's prophetic sermon and London's riotous antimasque crowd him offstage.

And just as Shakespeare's hopeful Henricians saw the newborn Elizabeth as the alternative, populist monarch that she never quite became, so nostalgic Jacobeans saw her as the beloved populist queen that she never really was. Strangely enough, they could also see her on the verge of a glorious Second Coming. As Cranmer's prophecy makes Henry the foil for his Protestant daughter, Elizabeth Tudor, so Shakespeare's play makes James the foil for his godly daughter, Elizabeth Stuart, frequently depicted as an Elizabethan phoenix reborn. *Henry VIII* probably celebrated her 1613 wedding to Frederick, Elector Palatine. Because of the Thirty Years War, Elizabeth would become the exiled Winter Queen, whose literary and religious cult would be a locus of godly opposition to her Arminian and absolutist father James, and her brother Charles after him.

When first performed, then, *Henry VIII* engaged this emergent opposition with a jubilant baptismal/nuptial riot.[22] And in a Caroline revival twelve years after Shakespeare's death, it joined in a new oppositional alliance of low and high politics that England had not seen since the mid-Tudor crisis. In the 1620s John Eliot and other parliamentarians joined anonymous verse libelers and men and women in the streets against George Villiers, Duke of Buckingham, favorite to both James and Charles: the most powerful and most hated man in the nation. The epidemic of anti-Buckingham riots frequently took the form of mutiny by unpaid soldiers and sailors.

It began on May 16, 1626, at the Fortune Playhouse, when "a crowd, consisting mostly of sailors, assaulted a constable and attempted to rescue some of their mates who had been arrested" (Manning 1988: 215). In June 1628 a crowd of apprentices, the trim rabble that thundered at the playhouses, happened upon John Lambe, Buckingham's astrologer ("the Duke's Devil"), as he left the Fortune. They beat him to death, inspiring the most popular English poem of 1628: "Let Charles and George do what they can / The Duke shall die like Dr. Lambe." On July 29, 1628, Buckingham imprudently commissioned a Globe revival of Shakespeare's *Henry VIII* – a choice that suggests unfamiliarity with the play and perhaps some mischievous advice. He left in a huff just after the scene depicting the execution of his namesake. A short while later, in a manuscript newsletter, Robert Gell observed that "Some say, he should rather have seen the fall of Cardinal Wolsey, who was a more lively type of himself, having governed this kingdom eighteen years, as he hath done fourteen." Four weeks later, Lieutenant John Felton stabbed Buckingham to death (Holstun 2000: 143–91).

Commotion, Catholicism, and the Commonwealth

I began this essay by criticizing the sort of binary historicism that contrasts "the pre-modern" and "the modern." One influential version of this historicism contrasts Catholic premodernity to Protestant modernity – a contrast frequently accepted not only by the proponents of the idea of Protestantism-as-progress, but also by its critics. As the former group wanes, the latter waxes, partly because its critique of Protestant iconoclasm resonates in a comforting way with the postmodern critique of the Enlightenment. For this group, Shakespeare's long-suspected and increasingly documented connection to the underground culture of Elizabethan Catholicism makes him look more and more like a critic of Protestant modernity: if not an orthodox believer in Catholic visions of possession, purgatory, spectacular ritual, and transubstantiation, then surely a sympathetic believer in their theatrical power and presence. Stephen Greenblatt has powerfully articulated this view in *Hamlet in Purgatory*: Hamlet's obsession with the ghost of his father, who seems to hail from a purgatory denied by Elizabethan Protestantism, figures Shakespeare's fascination with the Catholic institution, and his ties to his son Hamnet and his recusant father, John, both recently dead. Greenblatt observes, brilliantly, that "the power of Shakespeare's theater is frequently linked to its appropriation of weakened or damaged institutional structures." Fifty years after the Edwardian reformation, he turned to the controversy over purgatory, and found "a crucial body of imaginative materials" about specters and remembrance, which were now "available for theatrical appropriation." Shakespearean theatre became in part a sort of retrospective and imaginative "cult of the dead" (Greenblatt 2001: 253–4, 249, 258).

But for Shakespeare, those weakened or damaged institutional structures extended beyond formal theology to the social gospel – the radical social theory and collective projects of early- and mid-Tudor social radicals, Catholic and Protestant, courtly intellectuals and laboring commoners.[23] As a Catholic or ex-Catholic or non-Protestant or para-recusant late-Tudor Commonwealthsman, Shakespeare occupies an unusual position, but not an unprecedented one. *Utopia* gives us the most famous example of Tudor Catholic Commonwealth ideology – shadowed but not erased by More's distinctly anti-communist writings. We might also turn to that large body of mid-Tudor Protestant Commonwealthsmen who remember with critical complexity their earlier lives as Catholics, even Catholic clerics: Henry Brinkelow, Thomas Becon, Hugh Latimer, William Forrest, Thomas Lever, and John Hales. The full name of the largely Catholic rising of 1536–7 was "The Pilgrimage of Grace for the Commonwealth." Robert Kett himself had close ties to the former abbot of Wyndonham Abbey and served in its chapel Gild of Saint Thomas of Canterbury. Robert Crowley, the greatest literary artist among the Commonwealthsmen, wrote a dangerously sympathetic work on Kett's campmen in *The Way to Wealth* (1975: 1–353, 130–50), and an extended allegorical poem, *Philargyrie of greate Britayne*, in which a tyrannical Henrician giant exchanges a thievishly Wolseyan Catholic counselor named "Hypocrisie," for a thievishly Cromwellian Protestant counselor named "Philaute" (Crowley 1980).

The most sympathetic mid-Tudor response to Kett's Rebellion was *The Spider and the Flie* (1556) by John Heywood: friend to More and husband to his niece, maternal grandfather to John Donne, court poet and musician to Mary Tudor, and lifelong Catholic. Like the late-medieval setting of Shakespeare's tetralogies, Heywood's insect allegory insulates him from immediately theological issues, enabling him to conduct an exercise in Commonwealth critique of agrarian capitalism. Heywood combines Kett's 1549 rebellion and Mary's 1553 coup against Northumberland to create a classic Tudor alliance of high and low politics. The Maid of the House (Mary) comes to the aid of the flies (commoners) in their efforts to resist spiders (gentlemen landlords) covering all the holes in window lattices with their webs (enclosing common fields). After crushing the leader of the spiders (Northumberland), she becomes something like Good Duke Somerset or even Robert Kett, for she establishes a relatively tolerant regime and removes most of the webs, thus restoring the half-remembered, half-imagined smallholders' utopia from the reign of Henry VII. The resonance with the uncrushed Catholic/Protestant populism of *Henry VIII* is considerable.

Shakespeare's distance from the Elizabethan settlement, and even his sympathy with Catholicism, do not necessarily imply a backward-tending anti-rationalist sensibility for which we should damn him or (more likely, these days) laud him. His rational sympathy with the dead extends beyond Catholic purgatory to the gibbets of London, the starving streets and fields of England, and the slaughterhouse of Robert Kett's Norwich.

NOTES

Thanks to Joanna Tinker, Richard Dutton, Chris Fitter, Jean Howard, and Chris Kendrick for their comments, to Chris Fitter for sharing his work in progress on Shakespeare the Commonwealthsman and for some help with Peter Thump, and to Christa Pijacki for showing me the connections between the death scenes of Suffolk and Jack Cade in *2 Henry VI*. I will generally quote from *The Norton Shakespeare*, which largely follows the Folio. I will indicate readings drawn from the Quartos; Knowles's edition of *2 Henry VI* includes a complete facsimile version of the first Quarto (Knowles 1999: 376–407).

1   In *Tudor Rebellions* Fletcher and MacCulloch (1997) suggest that these rebellions are frequently over-looked as such because none dared call them treason (p. 115). This superb, brief study, with primary documents and a full bibliography, is the best place to begin a study of the subject.

2   In *Ehud's Dagger* I discuss some of the debates surrounding the use of class analysis to understand early modern literature and social history (Holstun 2000: 85–112). See also Andy Wood's excellent essay on the frequently binary language of social conflict in Tudor and early Stuart England (Wood 2001).

3   However, see Manning on the London riots of 1595, "the most dangerous and prolonged urban uprising in England between the accession of the Tudor dynasty and the beginnings of the Long Parliament" (Manning 1988: 208).

4   "Almost every central feature of postmodern theory can be deduced, read off as it were, from the assumption of a major political defeat" (Eagleton 1997: 23). Eagleton's comment explains both the plausibility of "postmodern Shakespeare" (so far as the term suggests a determinate parallel between two defeated and defeatist moments) and its limitations (so far as the term suggests that Shakespeare also subscribes to a metaphysical view of the end of history).

5   For powerful readings in these three modes, see Patterson (1989: 32–51), Helgerson (1992: 193–246), and Greenblatt (1988: 21–65), who suggests that Shakespeare wrote at a time "when none of the alternatives for a resounding political commitment seemed satisfactory; when the pressure to declare himself unequivocally an adherent of one or another faction seemed narrow, ethically coarse, politically stupid; when the most attractive political solution seemed to be to keep options open and the situation fluid" (p. 175 n. 65). I think Shakespeare responded to the calcified political situation of the 1590s, not with optimistic withdrawal, but with critical despair of anything like a solution.

6   Patterson (1993) begins an essay on early modern petitioning with a discussion of the petition to Duke Humphrey (pp. 57–79).

7   Halle (1970) is ambiguous as to whether it was the living servant or the dead armorer who was hanged and beheaded at Tyburn (*King Henry VI* lxviii^r).

8   See also Francis Thin's survey of protectors, including Gloucester and Somerset, in the second edition of Holinshed, just after the account of Somerset's execution (Holinshed 1965, III: 1036–59). Gloucester's ambitious wife Eleanor may have suggested to late-Tudor audiences Seymour's wife Anne Stanhope, who was "widely regarded as the cause of the duke's downfall through her aggressive personal style" (MacCulloch 1999: 204). Foxe blames Somerset's downfall on his execution of his brother Thomas, and their conflict on the antipathy of their wives (Foxe 1965, VI: 297, 283). John Ponet referred to Somerset as the "good duke" and to Warwick as "thambicious and subtil Alcibiades of england" (13r).

9   For the epithet "good duke" applied to Gloucester, see Shakespeare (1997: title page; 1.1.156, 159, 190; 1.3.4; 2.2.74; 3.2.123; 4.1.76) and Foxe (1965, III: vii, 709, 711, 713, 714; VI: 296); applied to Somerset, see Foxe (1965, VI: 292, 293, 296). This mid-Tudor conflict continues in the play's parting contrast between two fortuitously named lords: the Yorkist Richard Nevill, Earl of Warwick and "Kingmaker," and the loyalist martyr Edmund Beaufort, Duke of Somerset, eventually slain by Warwick's son Richard (5.2). Holinshed's Warwick is "full fraught . . . with good qualities right excellent and many" (Holinshed 1965, III: 238), while Shakespeare's is a treacherous machiavel strongly associated with the heraldic bear and ragged staff (5.1.140–214; 5.3.2) – a favorite of the Dudleys, and prominently displayed in Norwich after the massacre.

10   Foxe (1965, VI: 286; see also VI: 288) and Holinshed (1965, III: 1017).

11   Holinshed (1965, III: 1032, 1034–5); Foxe (1965, VI: 292–5).

12 See Knowles (1999: 136–9) on this passage. Holinshed says Kett's rebels "inkennelled themselves there on the same hill," the first use of the word in English (Holinshed 1965, III: 965), but derived from Neville, who refers to the rebels as "lurking those thick woods, as dogs in their kennels" [*et in sylvosis illis latibulis canum instar delitescentes*] (Neville 1615: C1ᵛ). Cheke compares Kett's Camp to "a sink in a town" and complains of "So many grievous faults meeting together in one sink" (Holinshed 1965, III: 992, 996).

13 Holinshed (1965, III: 1069); MacCulloch (1986: 309–10; 1999: 123).

14 For some readings of Shakespeare's mixed sympathies with Cade in these earlier scenes, see Patterson (1989: 48–51), Greenblatt (1990), Caldwell (1995), Wilson (1986), and Cartelli (1994).

15 Holinshed depicts Wat Tyler, not Jack Straw, menacing Sir John Newton with a dagger before Walworth kills him (Holinshed 1965, II: 740–1). Wat and Jack – those valiant roofers – frequently blur identities in accounts of the Great Revolt.

16 Milton (1962, III: 220; see also 220 n. 112, 343–4).

17 Shakespeare likely enough read this paragraph in Holinshed (or Halle, his source), since he quotes directly from the previous one in *Henry VIII:* Queen Katherine presents the petition against the Amicable Grant, which forced clothiers to "put off / The spinsters, carders, fullers, weavers" (1.2.33–4), quoting directly from Holinshed (1965, III: 709) and Halle (1970: cxliʳ). For Green's coming from Long Melford, see MacCulloch (1986: 293–4).

18 *Iacke Strawe* (1993: 1.58, 1.63; 3.765, 3.773, 3.853).

19 Holinshed (1965, III: 983).

20 This line is only in the Quarto. Sinfield and Dollimore (1992) find a conflict between populist critique and absolutist elements in *Henry V*; Fitter (1991) finds the former dominant.

21 See McMullan (2000: 180–200) on the authorship controversy. Joint or collective authorship is quite possible, but the reasons for assuming it here don't seem much more pressing than for many other plays frequently attributed to Shakespeare alone.

22 Walter Cohen discusses the play's metadramatic dimension, and its implied criticisms of both Henry and James (Shakespeare 1997: 3117).

23 Whitney R. D. Jones (1970: 24–9) helpfully differentiates four groups of Commonwealthsmen: the Catholic More group (More, John Rastell, Heywood, Starkey, Pole, Lupset, and Elyot), early Protestants (Frith and Tyndale), the Cromwell group (Starkey, John Rastell, Bale, Marshall, Armstrong, and Morrison), and the "Commonwealth party" (Somerset, Hales, Latimer).

References and Further Reading

Archer, I. (1991). *The Pursuit of Stability: Social Relations in Elizabethan London.* Cambridge: Cambridge University Press,

Barroll, L. (1988). A New History for Shakespeare and His Time. *Shakespeare Quarterly*, 39, 441–64.

Beer, B. L. (1982). *Rebellion and Riot: Popular Disorder in England During the Reign of Edward VI.* N.p.: Kent State University Press.

Bindoff, S. T. (1949). *Kett's Rebellion, 1549.* N.p.: Historical Association Pamphlet.

Bullough, G. (1966). *Narrative and Dramatic Sources of Shakespeare, Volume 4.* London: Routledge.

Burnett, M. T. (1987). Tamburlaine: An Elizabethan Vagabond. *Studies in Philology*, 84, 308–23.

Caldwell, E. C. (1995). Jack Cade and Shakespeare's *Henry VI, Part 2. Studies in Philology*, 92, 18–79.

Cartelli, T. (1994). Jack Cade in the Garden: Class Consciousness and Class Conflict in *2 Henry VI.* In R. Burt and J. M. Archer (eds.) *Enclosure Acts: Sexuality, Property, and Culture in Early Modern England.* Ithaca, NY: Cornell University Press.

Cheke, J. (1549). *The Hurt of Sedition.* In Holinshed (1965, III: 987–1011).

Coleridge, S. T. (1967). *The Literary Remains of Samuel Taylor Coleridge.* New York: AMS Press.

Crowley, R. (1975). *The Select Works of Robert Crowley*, ed. J. M. Cowper. New York: Kraus Reprint.

——(1980). *Philargyrie of greate Britayne*, ed. J. N. King. *English Literary Renaissance*, 10, 47–75.

Dasent, J. R. (ed.) (1890–1907). *Acts of the Privy Council*. London.

Eagleton, T. (1997). Where do Postmodernists Come From? In E. M. Wood and J. B. Foster (eds.) *In Defense of History*. New York: Monthly Review Press, 17–25.

Fitter, C. (1991). A Tale of Two Branaghs: *Henry V*, Ideology, and the Mekong Agincourt. In Ivo Kamps (ed.) *Shakespeare Left and Right*. New York: Routledge, 259–76.

——(2000). "The quarrel is between our masters and us their men": *Romeo and Juliet*, Dearth, and the London Riots. *English Literary Renaissance*, 30, 154–83.

Fletcher, A. and MacCulloch, D. (1997). *Tudor Rebellions*, 4th edn. London: Longman.

Fletcher, A. and Stevenson, J. (eds.) (1985). *Order and Disorder in Early Modern England*. Cambridge: Cambridge University Press.

Foxe, J. (1965). *The Acts and Monuments of John Foxe*, 8 vols, revd. and ed. G. Townsend. New York: AMS Press.

Greenblatt, S. (1988). *Shakespearean Negotiations: The Circulation of Social Energy in Renaissance England*. Berkeley: University of California Press.

——(1990). Murdering Peasants. In *Learning to Curse: Essays in Early Modern Culture*. New York: Routledge, 99–130.

——(2001). *Hamlet in Purgatory*. Princeton, NJ: Princeton University Press.

Halle, E. (1970). *The Union of the Two Noble Families of Lancaster and York (1550)*. Menston: Scolar Press.

Helgerson, R. (1992). *Forms of Nationhood: The Elizabethan Writing of England*. Chicago, IL: University of Chicago Press.

Heywood, J. (1967). *The Spider and the Flie*. New York: Burt Franklin.

Hill, C. (1975). The Many-headed Monster. In *Change and Continuity in Seventeenth-Century England*. Cambridge, MA: Harvard University Press.

Hobday, C. (1979). Clouted Shoon and Leather Aprons: Shakespeare and the Egalitarian Tradition. *Renaissance and Early Modern Studies*, 23, 63–78.

Holinshed, R. (1965). *Holinshed's Chronicles of England, Scotland, and Ireland*, 6 vols., ed. H. Ellis. New York: AMS Press.

Holstun, J. (2000). *Ehud's Dagger: Class Struggle in the English Revolution*. London: Verso.

Howard, J. E. (1994). *The Stage and Social Struggle in Early Modern England*. London: Routledge.

Hoyle, R. W. (2001). *The Pilgrimage of Grace and the Politics of the 1530s*. Oxford: Oxford University Press.

Jones, W. R. D. (1970). *The Tudor Commonwealth 1529–1559*. London: University of London and Athlone Press.

Kantorowicz, E. (1957). *The King's Two Bodies: A Study in Mediaeval Political Theology*. Princeton, NJ: Princeton University Press.

Knowles, R. (ed.) (1999). *William Shakespeare: King Henry VI, Part II*. Walton-on-Thames: Thomas Nelson.

Life and Death of Iacke Straw (1593). London.

Linebaugh, P. and Rediker, M. (2000). *The Many-Headed Hydra: Sailors, Slaves, Commoners, and the Hidden History of the Revolutionary Atlantic*. Boston, MA: Beacon Press.

McAlindon, T. (1995). Pilgrims of Grace: *Henry IV* Historicized. *Shakespeare Survey*, 48. Cambridge: Cambridge University Press, 69–84.

MacCulloch, D. (1984). Kett's Rebellion in Context. In P. Slack (ed.) *Rebellion, Popular Protest and the Social Order in Early Modern England*. Cambridge: Cambridge University Press, 39–62.

——(1986). *Suffolk and the Tudors: Politics and Religion in an English County 1500–1600*. Oxford: Clarendon Press.

——(1999). *Tudor Church Militant: Edward VI and the Protestant Reformation*. London: Penguin Books.

McMullan, G. (ed.) (2000). *William Shakespeare and John Fletcher: King Henry VIII*. Croatia: Arden Shakespeare.

Manning, R. B. (1988). *Village Revolts: Social Protest and Popular Disturbances in England, 1509–1640*. Oxford: Clarendon Press; New York: Oxford University Press.

Marx, K. (1973). The So-called Primitive Accumulation. In *Capital, Volume 1*. New York: International, 713–74.

Milton, J. (1962). *Complete Prose Works of John Milton*, ed. D. M. Wolfe. New Haven, CT: Yale University Press.

Neville, A. (1615) [1575]. *Norfolkes Furies, or a View of Kett's Campe*, trans. R. Woods. London.

Norbrook, D. (1984). The Reformation and Prophetic Poetry. In *Poetry and Politics in the English Renaissance*. London: Routledge, 32–58.

——(1996). "A Liberal Tongue": Language and Rebellion in *Richard II*. In J. M. Mucciolo (ed.) *Shakespeare's Universe: Renaissance Ideas and Conventions*. Menston: Scolar Press, 37–51.

Patterson, A. (1989). *Shakespeare and the Popular Voice*. Oxford: Blackwell.

——(1993). *Reading Between the Lines*. Madison: University of Wisconsin Press.

Ponet, J. [attrib. D.I.P.B.R.W.] (1556). *A Shorte Treatise of Politke Power*. N.p.

Russell, F. (1859). *Kett's Rebellion in Norfolk*. London: Longman Brown.

Scoufos, A.-L. (1979). *Shakespeare's Typological Satire: A Study of the Falstaff–Oldcastle Problem*. Athens, OH: Ohio University Press.

Shagan, E. H. (1999). Protector Somerset and the 1549 Rebellions: New Sources and New Perspectives. *English Historical Review*, 114, 34–63.

Shakespeare, W. (1997). *The Norton Shakespeare, Based on the Oxford Edition*, ed. S. Greenblatt, W. Cohen, J. E. Howard, and K. E. Maus. New York: Norton.

Sinfield, A. and Dollimore, J. (1992). History and Ideology, Masculinity and Miscegenation: The Instance of *Henry V*. In A. Sinfield (ed.) *Faultlines: Cultural Materialism and the Politics of Dissident Reading*. Berkeley: University of California Press, 109–42.

Slack, P. (ed.) (1984). *Rebellion, Popular Protest and the Social Order in Early Modern England*. Cambridge: Cambridge University Press.

Stirling, B. (1949). *The Populace in Shakespeare*. New York: Columbia University Press.

Strier, R. (1995). *Resistant Structures: Particularity, Radicalism, and Renaissance Texts*. Berkeley: University of California Press.

Tawney, R. H. (1967). *The Agrarian Problem in the Sixteenth Century*. New York: Harper.

Thompson, E. P. (1991). The Moral Economy of the English Crowd in the Eighteenth Century. In *Customs in Common*. New York: New Press, 185–258.

Virgoe, R. (1965). The Death of William de la Pole, Duke of Suffolk. *Bulletin of the John Rylands Library*, 47, 489–502.

Wells, R. H. (1985). The Fortunes of Tillyard: Twentieth-century Critical Debate on Shakespeare's History Plays. *English Studies*, 66, 391–403.

White, H. C. (1944). *Social Criticism in Popular Religious Literature of the Sixteenth Century*. New York: Macmillan.

Wilson, R. (1986). "A Mingled Yarn": Shakespeare and the Cloth Workers. *Literature and History*, 12, 164–80.

——(1993). *Will Power*. Hemel Hempstead: Harvester Wheatsheaf.

Wood, A. (2001). "Poore men woll speke one daye": Plebeian Languages of Deference and Defiance in England, *c*. 1520–1640. In T. Harris (ed.) *The Politics of The Excluded, c. 1500–1850*. Basingstoke: Palgrave, 67–98.

Wood, E. M. (1991). *The Origin of Capitalism*. New York: Monthly Review Press.

Wood, N. (1994). *The Foundations of Political Economy: Some Early Tudor Views on State and Society*. Berkeley: University of California Press.

10

Manliness Before Individualism: Masculinity, Effeminacy, and Homoerotics in Shakespeare's History Plays

Rebecca Ann Bach

Shakespeare's history plays, all of which depict England in disorder, are profoundly interested in how manliness is constructed and maintained.[1] Because gender roles and the social order were deeply intertwined in Renaissance England, masculinity surfaces constantly as a point of tension in *King John* and the plays of Shakespeare's first and second tetralogies (the three parts of *Henry VI*, *Richard III*, *Richard II*, the two parts of *Henry IV*, and *Henry V*) (Amussen 1993). Today we live in a world in which men and women are, by definition, separate kinds of people; our culture expends enormous energy from the birth of a child creating and maintaining the distinctions between men and women (Rackin 1994; Fausto-Sterling 2000). In contrast, in Renaissance England there was no firm biological distinction between men and women (Laqueur 1990). Manhood was measured in terms of its relation to femininity, but it was also measured in terms of rank, service relations (duty), bravery, adherence to religious codes, age, and nationality and race (for lack of better terms).[2] Manhood had to be achieved in Shakespeare's England, and the qualifications for manhood in his history plays differ strikingly from the qualifications for manhood in the twenty-first century (Breitenberg 1996; Orgel 1996; Spear 1993; Smith 2000).[3]

As Shakespeare's history plays contemplate who should be king and how kings should rule, they ask what kind of a man a king should be; they ask how kings and nobles should be related to women and womanliness, and how kings and nobles should conduct male–male relations; they also ask whether common men and boys can act like men. In texts of the English Renaissance many people whom we would see as men – including boys, men who violate their duty, cowards, Catholics (and atheists and Puritans), Frenchmen (and Italians, black men, Jews, and other non-English people), and men of low status – are depicted as more like women than they are like men.[4] Shakespeare's history plays are especially concerned with demonstrating the womanliness (or monstrosity) of men who violate their duty to God, their king, and their country. Such men are often described in the history plays as "effeminate."

They are effeminate because they act like women – i.e., they are frail, unable or unwilling to fight, or subordinate – and also because they desire women. In the character sketches appended to Thomas Overbury's wildly popular 1614 poem *His Wife*, "An Amourist" is described as someone who is "translated out of a man into folly; his imagination is the glasses of lust, and himself the traitor of his own discretion" (Overbury 1632: F). In today's dominant culture men are defined as masculine partially because they have heterosexual desire. "Real men" may not eat quiche, but they do love women and especially their own sexual pleasure with women. In contrast, in English Renaissance texts, men who love their own sexual pleasure with women are just like women, hotbeds of sexual desire, "translated out of [men] into folly." Or they may be boys, who by definition are not men (Fisher 2001).

If the history plays disapprove of desire between men and women, they condone loving and desiring behavior between men, behavior and language that we can term "homoerotic." The usages that the *Oxford English Dictionary* cites for "homoerotic" suggest that the twenty-first-century term is generally used in relation to homosexuality, either as synonymous with homosexuality or as distinguished from it. In the twenty-first century the homoerotic is in an inverted but similar relationship with masculinity. Behavior described as homoerotic either signifies that one is homosexual and therefore only problematically masculine or (often in the realm of sports) that one is not a homosexual and is therefore masculine. This relationship between masculinity and loving and desiring behavior between men was quite different in English Renaissance texts because Shakespeare's culture lacked both the ideology of homosexuality and the ideology of heterosexuality (Goldberg 1992: 162). Men were supposed to serve one another, to love each other deeply, and to express their love openly. In fact this behavior was more masculine than expressions of love and desire for women, which endangered a man's masculinity. In Shakespeare's service culture, service relations between men were expressed in loving and desiring terms. Expressing love and desire for a woman, however, put a man in the position of serving a woman. Since women belong below men in this culture, such service debased a man. Throughout the history plays the most manly of men directly express their love and desire for one another.

A related difference between Shakespearean masculinities and modern masculinities has to do with how Shakespeare and other English Renaissance writers treated what they called the "self." In a service culture, links between men are crucial. Homoerotic behavior and masculinity as categories did some of the work of maintaining and preserving those links. Masculinity was oriented toward collective rather than personal identity. In contrast, "effeminate" men in the history plays focus on their personal advancement at the expense of service ties, ties to God, and kinship links between men (including father–son, brother–brother, and in-law relations between men). Michael McKeon suggests that a "schematic distinction" between the " 'traditional' and 'modern' ways of organizing experience" can be "expressed as the difference between a 'vertical' hierarchy of interlocking rungs and a 'horizontal' differentiation of discrete interests" (McKeon 1995: 300). A modern social system prioritizes and validates individual achievement and self-assertion, crucial aspects of men's "discrete interests."[5] Shakespeare's history plays, which display the virtues of, and challenges to, a "traditional" system, prioritize collective achievement and degrade self-actualizing goals and the pursuit of individual pleasure. In *2 Henry VI* Young Clifford exhorts his troops to stay and fight:

> Let no Souldier flye.
> He that is truly dedicate to Warre,
> Hath no selfe-loue: nor he that loues himselfe,
> Hath not essentially, but by circumstance
> The name of Valour. (TLN 3258–62; 5.3.36–40)

Masculinity, which often goes by "the name of Valour" in the history plays, is diametrically opposed to "selfe-loue," a kind of love displayed by effeminate cowards such as the second tetralogy's wonderful Falstaff. Shakespeare's history plays display masculinity, effeminacy, and homoerotic behavior in order to reinforce what I call "collective masculinity," an ideology that constituted, and helped to maintain, Shakespeare's service culture.

Homoeroticism and Collective Masculinity

Loving language and behavior between men is part of the glue that ideally serves to hold the English polity together in the history plays. The specter of homosexuality haunts modern horizontal relations between men, so modern texts reserve the language of love and desire and the bodily expression of love for relations between men and women. This specter was absent in Shakespeare's history plays, which continually display what Mario DiGangi calls "orderly" rather than disorderly homoeroticism. Acknowledged love between men maintained the vertical hierarchy. True love in both modern and Renaissance texts reinforces and produces true masculinity. In modern texts that true love is generally heterosexual and that masculinity is produced partly to reinforce heterosexuality. In Shakespeare's history plays, however, as in other drama from the late sixteenth century, true love is homosocial, born between and reinforcing essential male bonds (Stanivukovic 1999; Bach 1998). When Bolingbroke in *Richard II* welcomes Harry Percy into his service he promises this love: "I count my selfe in nothing else so happy, / As in a Soule remembring my good Friends: / And as my Fortune ripens with thy Loue, / It shall be still thy true Loues recompense" (TLN 1155–8; 2.3.46–9). Since Bolingbroke breaks his oath of service to his king, deposing Richard in his quest to become Henry IV, he cannot keep his promise of loving friendship to Percy; however, in the history plays, when promises of love between men are kept, they confirm both men as masculine. This type of loving discourse between men, which saturates the history plays, is deeply unfamiliar to twenty-first-century eyes; and it is generally ignored in readings of Shakespeare's plays because the specter of homosexuality haunts late modern discussion of love between men.

In the last part of act 3, scene 2 of *2 Henry VI*, Queen Margaret and her lover Suffolk are left on stage after King Henry has banished Suffolk. Entreating Suffolk to leave quickly so she can experience her grief, Margaret abruptly pulls him back, crying, "Oh go not yet. Euen thus, two Friends condemn'd, / Embrace, and kisse, and take ten thousand leaues, / Loather a hundred times to part than dye" (TLN 2068–70; 3.2.355–7). When Margaret reaches for a metaphor to describe the couple's tragic separation, she does not find a paradigmatic story of tragic male–female love. Instead she compares their leave-taking to the separation of two friends, hugging and kissing, preferring death to parting. In the world Shakespeare's audiences would find familiar, love between male friends was frequently elevated above male–female love as the pinnacle of loving connection (Montaigne 1603; Bray 1994; Mills 1937; Masten 1997; Smith 1994, 2000).[6] The history plays confirm this elevation of friendship over male–female love. "Suffolk's passion for Margaret deprives him of his manhood, reducing him to the condition of a gentle, genderless infant," and Henry quite clearly would have been better off loving his friend Gloucester and rejecting his wife (Rackin 1994: 71).

The traitorous Henry, Lord Scrope of Masham, has been Henry's "bedfellow" in *Henry V*, and his treasonous plans disturb Henry all the more for that fact. Henry finds it almost beyond belief that such a man "that didst beare the key of all [his] counsailes, / That knew'st the very bottome of [his] soule" could betray him (TLN 725–6; 2.2.93–4). Henry laments that Scrope has "with jealousie infected / The sweetnesse of affiance" (TLN 755–6; 2.2.123–4). It is this "sweetnesse of affiance," this homoerotic expression, that should tie noble men to one another and especially to their liege lord. Some critics have suggested that the fear of sodomy haunts Henry's display of his love toward Scrope (Corum). I would argue, however, that this is a reading that imports our own specter of homosexuality into homoerotic representations in Shakespeare's plays. There is no evidence that sodomy haunts these love relations; indeed their ubiquity argues otherwise. The history plays do not worry about love between men; they approve it completely and see no need to distinguish it from physical expressions of love. A modern squeamishness about male–male love may tempt us to cordon off this love and proximity from sexual expression, but, as Valerie Traub (1991) suggests, we have no better proof that love between men and women leads or does not lead to sexual expression.

There *is* a specter haunting love between men in Shakespeare's history plays but it has a radically different form than the modern specter of homosexuality. It is the specter of severed bonds between men, a specter that included what we would now call heterosexuality. Loving bonds between men are depicted in these plays as much less threatening than men's bonds with women, but the history plays sometimes despair of the possibility that men might stay true to one another and, therefore, to God and England. In *2 Henry VI* Shakespeare suggests that had Henry loved Gloucester properly during his lifetime he could have saved his kingdom. Margaret berates Henry for loving Gloucester more than he ever loved her; but the play argues strongly that Henry *should* have loved Gloucester more than he loved his wife. His tie to an unfaithful woman is part of his downfall; his tie to his loving adviser might have saved him from unfaithful men. In *Richard III* the weak and sickly King Edward attempts to use loving bonds between men to unite his kingdom. In front of his king, Lord Hastings vows, "So prosper I, as I sweare perfect loue"; and his rival Rivers replies, "And I, as I loue *Hastings* with my heart" (TLN 1139–40; 2.1.16–17). But Rivers and Hastings will never love one another as they profess, and Edward is too effeminate, too tied to women and to his own personal pleasure, to broker true love between men. *Richard II*'s Northumberland flatters Bolingbroke – the future Henry IV – with loving words: "our fair discourse hath beene as sugar. / Making the hard way sweet and delectable" (TLN 1111–12; 2.3.6–7). A comedy like *Measure for Measure* worries about what happens when a man, Angelo, regrets and withdraws his sweet words toward a woman, Mariana, leaving her without a social space – "neither Maid, Widow, nor Wife" (TLN 2550–1; 5.1.176). Shakespeare's history plays worry about what happens when men regret and withdraw their sweet words toward other men. Northumberland may be being depicted as an unctuous flatterer in this dialogue; but that is only because we in the audience know that in the two parts of *Henry IV* he will withdraw those loving words and rebel against his anointed ruler. In themselves his words of love are the currency of collective masculinity. The potentially counterfeit quality of Northumberland's sweet words does not devalue that currency.

Just as Shakespeare depicts the negative consequences of love between men and women, he does not hesitate to display homoeroticism used for evil purposes. In *King John* the illegitimate king woos his faithful follower Hubert into vowing to kill Arthur, the legitimate heir to the crown. The scene is full of erotic energy. John draws Hubert near to him, perhaps whispering,

> O my gentle *Hubert*,
> We owe thee much; within this wall of flesh
> There is a soule counts thee her Creditor,
> And with advantage meanes to pay thy loue:
> And my good friend, thy voluntary oath
> Liues in this bosome, deerely cherished.
> Giue me thy hand. (TLN 1318–24; 3.3.19–25)

Hand in hand, John and Hubert conspire to kill Arthur, their souls in such communion that John never has to state his purpose openly. Like Edward wooing Lady Gray in *2 Henry VI*, John woos by indirection; and because he and Hubert share a plighted love, Hubert is much less resistant, much more in tune with his lover, than Lady Gray is to Edward. It is true that Edward woos Lady Gray for sexual purposes, while John woos Hubert for his political ends. But the history plays always enmesh sex and politics. John's seduction scene is no less eroticized than Margaret and Suffolk's love scenes in *1* and *2 Henry VI*, and it serves a very similar political end. Shakespeare's history plays depict a world in which homoerotic bonds between men should ideally make and remake a stable social order. Those bonds and expressions can be perverted to evil ends, but in themselves they are ideal; they do not threaten a man's male identity.

In sexual terms, *2 Henry VI*'s brutal rebel leader, Jack Cade, promotes horizontal relations between men and crticizes homoeroticism. Cade entices his men with visions of a land without hierarchy (except, of course, subjection to himself) – "henceforward," he claims, "all things shall be in Common" (TLN 2651–2; 4.7.16). He harps continually on the (hetero)sexual bonanza that will be reaped by him and his men. In the Quarto text of the play he promises his followers, "He that will lustily stand to it" – meaning both stand up to the enemy and have an erection –"shall go with me and take up these commodities following – item, a gown, a kirtle, a petticoat, and a smock" (4.7.136–8). The economic gain promised in Cade's rebellion is figured as (female sexual) booty. In contrast to this new order, Cade publicly displays the old order: Lord Saye's and Sir James Cromer's heads on poles. Cade orders his followers to have the two men's heads "kisse one another: For they lou'd well / When they were aliue" (TLN 2765–6; 4.7.138–9). "For with these borne before vs, insteed of Maces," he commands, "Will we ride through the streets, & at euery Corner / Haue them kisse" (TLN 2770–1; 4.7.142–3). Shakespeare characterizes Cade as an acute observer of aristocratic mores (Cartelli 1994). In the history plays men kiss each other on the hands and on the lips to seal their love for one another. Cade proposes to set up a sexual order in which male–female sexual expression replaces male–male homoerotic behavior. In psychoanalytic schemas such a replacement may seem the true story of male sexual maturation; in *2 Henry VI* Cade's plan is far from idealized.

As many critics have argued, *2 Henry VI* does not simply condemn Cade and his rebellion. That rebellion, manipulated as it is by a nobleman (York) for use in his own treasonous schemes, can certainly be read as a parody of aristocratic violence and brutality. But the play presents Cade and his men so critically that it is hard to read their sexual scheme as idealized in any way. If his rebels have real grievances against the nobles, they also plan to make leather out of their enemies' skins. Cade invokes a social order in which "common" (hetero)sexual pleasure replaces homoerotic aristocratic rule in the same scene in which he sentences Lord Saye to death. Shakespeare characterizes Saye as a good Christian man, a man who rejects greed, lying, and murder in favor of God's justice and especially justice for the poor; Saye pleads for his life on the basis of his Christian character. In his condemnation of Saye, Cade condemns himself, as Shakespeare is wont to have his evil characters do. Cade's invocation of the new sexual order is also, and not coincidentally, accompanied by his tolerance and even encouragement of rape. In the Quarto version of the play a sergeant enters the scene pleading for justice because the butcher who follows Cade has raped the sergeant's wife. The butcher represents the rape as his own lay justice against the sergeant who would have arrested him, and Cade encourages him to rape her again: "Dick, follow thy suit in her common place" (4.7.125). A viewer or reader can hardly miss the comparison of Cade's "justice" with Lord Saye's, the man whose homoerotic

bonding Cade is displaying on a pole. And the comparison strongly favors homoeroticism. A world in which Saye and Cromer kiss looks much better than a new
sexual order in which Cade and his men take their pleasure with women.[7]

Christian Male Identity in Shakespeare's History Plays

As the example of Saye's plea for mercy suggests, and as the history plays continually
reiterate, English Renaissance masculinity was deeply bound up with Christian identity. Since the history plays necessarily tell stories of war, military prowess, and
murder, they frequently return to the conflicts between Christian male identity and
male warrior identity. The soon-to-be triumphantly heroic Henry V might seem to
settle the issue of Christian versus warrior manhood when he swears to his father that
he will cleanse himself from his youthful sins: "I will weare a Garment all of Blood,
/ And staine my fauours in a bloody Maske: / . . . This, in the Name of Heauen, I
promise here" (*1 Henry IV* TLN 1955–6, 1973; 3.2.135–6, 153). However, before the
final battle in *Henry V*, Henry worries about his relationship to God. Like every
monarch depicted in the history plays, the man who we will see maturing from Prince
Hal to the good King Harry must negotiate his role as a man and king in relation to
God. *Henry V* makes this negotiation less fraught than it is in the plays of the first
tetralogy, but it is never easily accomplished in the history plays.

Shakespeare's history plays make it clear that while men of the church, men devoted
to God, ideally should not fight, a king must be a warrior as well as a churchman to
be a fully masculine ruler. At the same time, the history plays require that a manly
warrior must fight in God's name and be devoted to God. These linked requirements
for masculinity can form a fatal Renaissance catch-22, especially for rulers, because
the plays acknowledge that a major strain of Christian identity requires peace, humility, and mercy for one's enemies, while warrior identity requires bloody killing. The
pious Henry VI's masculinity, in particular, is continually challenged in the first tetralogy. In *2 Henry VI* York claims the kingship because of Henry's unsuitability for the
job: "That Head of thine doth not become a Crowne / Thy Hand is made to graspe
a Palmers staffe / And not to grace an awefull Princely Scepter" (TLN 3091–2;
5.1.96–8). York's son, who will become a moral monster in *Richard III*, echoes his
father's logic when he claims in the next scene that "Priests pray for enemies, but
Princes kill" (TLN 3294; 5.2.6). Although Shakespeare could expect his audience to
recognize this Richard as monstrous and to distrust his statements throughout the
plays, Richard's logic is in part the logic of the first tetralogy. These plays are conflicted about whether a king should be a man who fights or a man who prays and
whether a man can fight and pray simultaneously. Thus Henry's sincere devotion to
God makes him unable to fight when his kingdom is at stake. He cannot even
condemn his enemies. When the evil Cardinal Beaufort dies a tormented hell-bound
man, Henry cautions, "Forbeare to iudge, for we are sinners all" (*2 Henry VI* TLN
2165; 3.3.31). This is an absolutely proper Christian response, but it is also a sign of

Henry's inability to take charge and exercise the judgment that belongs to the anointed representative of God on earth.

Depicting Henry's tortured fall from power and the horrible civil wars that result from his indecisiveness and ineffectuality, the first tetralogy questions his manhood. Henry's devotion to God can be, and often is, read by the characters surrounding him as cowardice, the one quality which automatically demotes a Shakespearean man from full masculine status. The most manly of men, like Talbot, are brave beyond belief, but they are also devoted to God in their words if not in their actions. Talbot continually invokes God's name (see *1 Henry VI* TLN 1996–2007; 4.2.45–56 for one example). Henry VI, nominally Talbot's commander, falls far short of masculinity if measured by Talbot's manly example, and the Henry VI plays imply that, therefore, he falls short of manliness while he lives. In retrospect, however, the history plays elevate Henry VI as a good man and an example of godliness. He is called "gentle, milde, and vertuous," a "deare Saint," and "holy *Harry*" (*Richard III* TLN 287, 2549, 2796; 1.2.106, 4.1.69, 4.4.25). These posthumous revisions, however, cannot erase the first tetralogy's anxiety about Henry's masculinity. He will not fight; his presence disheartens his soldiers; and he refuses to assert his patriarchal prerogative to make his son a king after his death. Henry can accede to saintly masculinity after his death, but he fails basic tests for earthly masculinity when he is still the king.

As Henry V says before Harfleur, "In Peace, there's nothing so becomes a man, / As modest stillnesse, and humilitie: / But when the blast of Warre blowes in our eares, / Then imitate the action of the Tyger" (*Henry V* TLN 1086–9; 3.1.3–6). In the first tetralogy the problem for Henry V's son (Henry VI) is that England is never at peace, and he is such a pious man that he cannot be a tiger. But when we look at all the history plays together, we can see that man's tigerish nature is as dangerous as is any potentially fatal "modest stillnesse" in wartime. War is dangerously close to murder, and bloody conduct can endanger a man's soul, which is essential to masculine identity. *Richard III* treats us to the spectacle of Richard, a very tigerish man posing as a pious man of God in order to win the people's acclaim and, thereby, the crown. Throughout the history plays men claim to fight for God, but all of the plays worry about the inherent contradiction within verbal constructions like King John's when he calls himself "Gods wrathfull agent" (*King John* TLN 384; 2.1.87). Wrath is, of course, a mortal sin, and even *Henry V*, the play about England's most successful warrior king, worries about men dying well "when Blood is their argument" (TLN 1991; 4.1.136). From the advent of Christianity, service to God has always coexisted uneasily with warrior ideals.[8] The history plays put Christian masculinity next to male warrior identity, and they demonstrate the necessity of both as well as their potential incompatibility.

The plays of the first and second tetralogies and *King John* treat English history well before the Reformation. They are, however, post-Reformation plays, and, as well as dwelling on the potential incompatibility of Christian and warrior masculinities, they display the fissures in Christian male identity that accompanied the Reformation. Some of the history plays, especially the anti-Catholic *King John* and *1 Henry VI*, are not sure whether, by definition, a man who represents the Catholic church can be a true man. In the first two *Henry VI* plays the Bishop of Winchester, who becomes Cardinal Beaufort in *2 Henry VI*, compromises his Christian masculinity because he violates his role as a churchman, behaving "More like a Souldier then a man o' th' Church" (Salisbury *2 Henry VI* TLN 195; 1.1.184). He is also depicted as less than masculine in his service to the pope rather than to some mythical essential Christianity. During a bitter quarrel with Winchester, Gloucester, *1 Henry VI*'s avatar of mature manhood, suggests that Winchester is the pope's servile child. Gloucester offers to use Winchester's purple bishop's robes "as a Childs bearing Cloth" to remove him physically from the Tower's grounds (TLN 408; 1.4.41). Of course, Gloucester's men defeat Winchester's because Gloucester is comparatively liberated and manly. *King John* goes further than *1 Henry VI*, proleptically depicting England's independence from the pope which is displayed partially as an ascension to manhood. In *King John* both the English and the French king refuse to be "Rome's slaves," and whatever their other failings as kings and men, the audience is meant to cheer their manly stance against the pope.[9] Collectively, the history plays depict Christian identity as fraught, but they never dispute its necessity for true manhood.

Masculinity and Subjection in the History Plays

The king's service to God is the limit case in a service culture that requires that all proper men serve other men. If *King John* depicts liberation from service to the pope as manly, Shakespeare by no means suggests in that play that a king should be liberated from service to God. In Shakespeare's history plays proper masculinity is constituted in subjection. The equation of masculinity and subjection is deeply foreign to modern codes of masculinity, but it is essential to a vertical hierarchy. The history plays continually represent the masculinity of subjected men and the effeminacy or beastliness of men who reject subjection. The language of subjection – words like "duty," "liege," "servant," and "subject" – rings throughout the history plays, demarcating men's relationships to one another and their relationships to their own place as subjects.

In *Richard II* the Bishop of Carlisle eloquently defends Richard's rule against Bolingbroke's challenge on the grounds that all men are fundamentally their king's subjects. When Bolingbroke offers to take the crown in God's name, Carlisle replies,

> Mary, Heauen forbid.
>
> . . .
>
> What Subiect can giue Sentence on his King?
> And who sits here that is not *Richards* Subject?
>
> . . .
>
> I speake to Subjects, and a Subject speakes
> Stirr'd vp by Heauen, thus boldly for his King.
> (TLN 2034, 2041–2, 2052–3; 4.1.105, 112–13, 123–4)

Carlisle speaks for subjection as the master code for men. To be unequivocally affirmed as men in the history plays, male characters must speak and behave as subjects of their superiors, and kings must subject themselves to God.

The codes of masculine subjection are clearly understood in the history plays by all men – both those who confirm their masculinity as they follow those codes and those who violate those codes. Those codes require that men deny their personal desires in favor of their king and country, and therefore, those codes work for collective masculinity and against self-actualization. The most masculine men, in fact, desire nothing so much as being subjected to their male superiors. For example, Gloucester's subjection to Henry means that he must deny his bond to Eleanor – he has no desire to put his wife above his king and country. Gloucester's servingmen, who owe their duty and subjection to him, offer to rescue her, but Gloucester abides by his king's decisions even when the king will not protect him from his enemies. The play shows the price of that loyalty – Gloucester is killed by nobles who pretend to be the king's loyal subjects but instead reach for personal power. The play, nonetheless, asks us to applaud Gloucester's loyalty till death rather than Suffolk's and Winchester's self-serving refusal to subject themselves to their king. Gloucester's loyal subjection makes him "a man / Iust, and vpright," a man for whom his servingmen would willingly have their "bodyes slaughtred" (*1 Henry VI* TLN 1308–9, 1316; 3.1.97–8, 104). Subjection is a game in which a man wins his masculinity, a game played to the death by Gloucester and potentially by his servingmen.

The situation surrounding Henry IV's pardon of the Duke of York's son Aumerle in *Richard II* also points to the price men must pay within this system if they are to obey the codes of subjection which make them truly masculine men. York explains to his wife, the Duchess, that he and his family and all of England's nobles are now Bolingbroke's (Henry IV's) "sworne Subjects" (TLN 2406; 5.2.39), and that he has pledged himself in parliament for his son Aumerle's loyalty to Henry. Subsequently, York discovers a treasonous letter on Aumerle's body. The Duchess cannot believe that York will sacrifice his own son's life for his loyalty to the new king. But York is unbending, counseling Henry to kill his son Aumerle rather than to forgive his treasonous intentions. York is a loyal subject, and his total subjection to even his newly anointed kind ends up saving Aumerle's life. The conversations between York, his son, the Duchess, and the king expose what Pierre Bourdieu might call "the fundamental *illusio*" of masculine subjection, "the investment in the game itself, the conviction that the game is worth playing all the same, right to the end, and according to the rules" (Bourdieu 2001: 74). In the history plays the "game" of subjection is fundamental to masculinity. York is a subject before he is anything else, before he is a husband certainly, and even before he is a father; therefore he is willing and even eager to play the game to its fatal end, regardless of its price for his family. But Shakespeare shows us what Bourdieu terms "the double-edged privilege of indulging in the games of domination" (p. 75). If York is to be a loyal subject and retain his power in England, he must deny his love for his son and throw his wife from him as an "vnruly Woman" (TLN 2487; 5.2.110). This loyal subjection is quite costly in personal terms.

But Shakespeare also shows his audience the costs of not playing the game when York vows, "Now by mine Honor, my life, my troth, / I will appeach the Villaine" (TLN 2449–50; 5.2.78-9).[10] If York were to put his son and wife before his king he would lose his "Honor"; he could not be a man in this system were he to divide his loyalty between his family and his king.

Shakespeare works very carefully in these scenes to demonstrate that the price York is eager to pay is not negligible and that Henry (Bolingbroke), the man to whom York has subjected himself, is not untainted. York and the Duchess have only one son and they will never have another, and that son is York's and not the product of his wife's infidelity (always the central question for fathers in Shakespeare's plays (Rackin 1991: 324)). In addition, Henry stole the crown from the man who had been York's lord. Telling his wife the story of Henry and Richard entering London, York weeps as he describes the dust "throwne vpon [Richard's] Sacred head" (TLN 2397; 5.2.30). York is potentially sacrificing his only son for a man who ignominiously stole the crown from an anointed king whom York had loved and protected. To modern eyes, York's words and actions in these scenes make little sense. Indeed, when this play was rewritten in 1681, Aumerle, not York, weeps over Richard (Crowne). But while Shakespeare carefully outlines the case against York's actions, he affirms the codes York lives by. His audience should understand that a man's honor in relation to his lord is sacrosanct, as is even this newly appointed king's life. To defend Aumerle, as his mother the Duchess does, is to defend treason and murder. York should be first and foremost his king's subject, and subjection's personal cost is part of its value.

Subjection is the name of the game, the way to power, in the power structure Shakespeare depicts in the history plays. Thus Henry IV, when he is seeking the crown as Bolingbroke, continually swears his duty, loyalty, and subjection to Richard. If he did not play that game he would never have been able to usurp the crown because no men would have followed a man who violated those rules. Just as Shakespeare's effeminate men and moral monsters speak homoerotic love and display themselves as good Christians even while they illicitly desire women, hate and murder men, and serve the devil or the pope, villainous characters in the history plays speak the language of subjection as they serve their own ends. All men who seek power must display their own subjection.

One of the most perennially fascinating characters in Shakespeare's history plays, Sir John Falstaff, sends up the "fundamental *illusio*" of subjection, but he does so at the price of his own power. Falstaff is a character who intimately understands all the rules of the games of masculinity, including the game of subjection, but chooses to flout those rules just the same. In *1 Henry IV* Shakespeare allows Falstaff to expose the deadly price of the pursuit of male honor without exacting any real penalty, but in the darker *2 Henry IV* Shakespeare makes Falstaff pay the price of his refusal to subject himself to his prince. In an Eastcheap tavern Falstaff unknowingly abuses the prince's character in front of his (disguised) face. Caught out by the prince, Falstaff says that by abusing the prince to the tavern inhabitants he was playing the "part of a carefull Friend, and a true Subject" by ensuring that the lowly "Wicked" people of the tavern would not love Hal (TLN 1347; 2.4.294). Later in the play, when Hal's brother Prince John encounters Falstaff and the rebel Coleville who has surrendered to Falstaff, Falstaff informs John that "a famous true Subject [i.e., Falstaff] tooke him" (TLN 2299; 4.2.57). In both instances Falstaff openly parades his abuse of the codes of subjection. He knows that Hal understands that his verbal abuse of Hal stems from his refusal to subject himself. Falstaff also knows that the game of subjection requires a show of subjection from every man to the prince. Therefore he claims a position as subject that he never intends to occupy; but unlike a villain like Richard III, Falstaff makes that claim knowing that his audience within the play understands its inaccuracy. Hal is fully aware that Falstaff is not his subject and will never be contained within the codes of subjection. Likewise, Prince John never believes that Falstaff is either a "famous true Subject" or that he took Coleville. In front of both princes Falstaff plays with the codes of subjection, thereby ensuring his own disempowerment. Because he will never be a subject, Falstaff will also never advise a king; he cannot even truly be a man in this system, because a real man subjects himself in the history plays.

Effeminacy in the History Plays

As Bruce Smith suggests, Falstaff's "metamorphosis into a woman" in *The Merry Wives of Windsor* "is altogether appropriate" (Smith 17).[11] Falstaff is effeminate, like a woman, in the history plays because he is a coward, because he is self-indulgent and unruly, and also because all of his appetites are out of control. Falstaff, unlike manly men in Shakespeare's history plays, loves life (even when it means cowardice) and loves sex with women. The history plays mark men who share these traits with Falstaff as effeminate. Falstaff shares his cowardice with other effeminate characters in the history plays: the prissy courtier who demands Hotspur's prisoners but dislikes the smell of the battlefield (*1 Henry IV* TLN 355–86); Mortimer, who lies in his Welsh wife's lap and misses the battle (*1 Henry IV* TLN 1742–9; Rackin 1990: 172); Justice Shallow, who sits out the war talking about his early sexual exploits (*2 Henry IV* TLN 1534–59); and Falstaff's cohort Pistol, who, as I argue elsewhere, loves to be a "honey sweet Husband" but will never fight a battle (*Henry V* TLN 824; Bach 2001). The link between cowardice and effeminacy is still current in the twenty-first century, as is its obverse, the link between bravery in combat and masculinity. However, the other trait shared by all of these effeminate characters is their sexual interest in women. This link between effeminacy and a man's sexual desire for women has disappeared in modern sexual ideology.

Falstaff, characteristically, displays his interest in women and simultaneously manifests his knowledge of the rules that require that a truly masculine man will disdain involvement, especially sexual involvement, with women. Playing Henry IV in a scene with Prince Henry, Falstaff tells his "son" that he has heard that he has a "vertuous" companion: "And now I remember mee, his Name is *Falstaffe*: if that man should be lewdly giuen, hee deceiues mee" (*1 Henry IV* TLN 1383–5; 2.5.387–8). When the two characters switch roles in the scene, Falstaff, playing the prince, "vtterly den[ies]" that Falstaff is "a Whore-master" (TLN 1427–8; 2.5.428). Continually showing his prince his sexual proclivities, Falstaff then repudiates those proclivities to his face. He understands the rules which deny proper manhood to a man invested in sex with women. He does not intend to play by those rules, but he does intend to be taken as if he did. Unfortunately for him, as the plays indicate, this is a game he cannot win. Masculinity and this type of effeminacy are as antithetical as masculinity and cowardice.

Like the plays of the second tetralogy, the plays of the first tetralogy warn against emasculating male involvement with women. If the inability to live up to the codes of warrior masculinity costs Henry VI the kingdom and his status as a real man while he is alive, Edward IV loses his kingdom and his life because of his effeminacy. Edward's sexual interests mean that he neglects his essential ties to men, ties that could have cemented his power. Instead of linking his kingdom firmly with King Louis's France by marrying Louis's sister-in-law, Edward chooses to marry for pleasure. This marriage to Lady Gray humiliates his ambassador, Warwick, the kingmaker, throughout most of the first tetralogy. To his brothers Clarence and Richard, Edward declares, "They are but *Lewis* and *Warwicke*, I am *Edward*, / Your King and *Warwickes*, and must have my will" (3 *Henry VI* TLN 2039–40; 4.1.15–16). Shakespeare uses the word "will" here in at least two of its early senses: "power of choice in regard to action" and "carnal desire and appetite" (*OED* "will" 6a, 2). Both usages indicate that Edward is unfit to rule.

The history of the usage of the word "will" is one small piece of the history of the transition from collective masculinity to individual masculinity. One of the word's more negative connotations, "undue assertion of one's own will; wilfulness, self-will," becomes obsolete over the seventeenth century (*OED* "will" 9a). The first definition the *OED* offers, "desire, wish, longing . . ." becomes "coloured by or merged" with sense 5, "the action of willing or choosing to do something" over the eighteenth and nineteenth centuries (*OED* I.1a, II.5). In 1861 John Stuart Mill wrote, "Will, the active phenomenon, is a different thing from desire, the state of passive sensibility" (*OED* II.5a). In Shakespeare's time "will" often signified "desire" and both will and desire could have very negative connotations, especially when a man indulged his "will" in the sense of his carnal appetite. "*Will*" in that sense did not denote a positively valued "active phenomenon." In Shakespeare's time "will" could also have very positive connotations, especially when it meant God's will. A man's individual will, however, becomes valuable only when masculinity is organized around a "'horizontal' differentiation of discrete interests" (McKeon 1995). In Shakespeare's texts a man's "will" could easily signify as a "willfulness" that would disrupt vertical relations between men and lead a man to lose himself in his sexual desire.

Regarding his marriage to Lady Gray, Edward states, "And for this once, my Will shall stand for Law" (TLN 2076; 4.1.49). To a modern ear this statement could sound like masterly self-assertion, part of Edward's kingly prerogative. In 3 *Henry VI* Edward's statement shows that he is mastered by his sexual desire; he is no master;

instead he is a woman's servant. Edward not only sacrifices state interests by offending Louis and the Lady Bona, he also marries Lord Scales's daughter and heir to Lady Gray's brother, Rivers, and Lord Bonville's daughter and heir to Lady Gray's son. Thus his wife's interests supplant the interests of his brothers. The dispute between the brothers is not a dispute about personal marital pleasure (at least not for Clarence and Richard). It is a dispute about alliances among men, Richard and Clarence's prospective alliances with Lord Scales and Lord Bonville. These are the alliances that Edward as king should sponsor. Edward makes his "will" the law at the cost of those alliances, rejecting the homosocial ties that might have served him and his kingdom for a tie to a woman that will lead him to undermine collective masculinity. Edward's distorted priorities (in the play's terms) are signaled by his hesitancy to claim the kingdom in the fourth act of *3 Henry VI*. His "will" is unquestionable when it comes to women, but he must be goaded into strongly claiming the crown.

To harp on Edward's lust, as I have done in this section, is to risk sounding like the monster Shakespeare makes out of the historical Richard III. In *Richard III* Richard uses Edward's interest in women against him constantly (see, for example, 3.7.177, 74,72). Richard can use Edward's lust against him, however, because everyone in the play understands lust as effeminating and as endangering both a man's judgment and the process of patriarchal inheritance. Just as part of Falstaff's appeal as a character lies in his ability to expose and parody the ruling codes of masculinity, audiences find Richard III fascinating because they can watch him manipulate men and women. His ability to manipulate Clarence, the Lord Mayor, and the citizens in these scenes comes from his understanding that they subscribe to a code of masculinity that equates a man's sexual interest in women with his weakness and instability.

Unlike the other history plays, *Richard III* is ambivalent about male effeminacy. The play contains the only positive usage of the word "effeminate" in the history plays, indeed in the entire Shakespeare canon. In the famous scene in which Buckingham directs the crowd to acclaim Richard as England's king, Buckingham presents Richard as a model of Christian masculinity, a man who attends to his soul rather than to his body. He commends Richard's "tendernesse of heart, / And gentle, kinde, effeminate remorse" (TLN 2431–2; 3.7.199–201). Perhaps Shakespeare has Buckingham praise Richard for being like a woman because he is really more like a monster. Earlier in the play, Richard's brother Clarence, who has been framed by Richard, asks his murderers to "Relent, and save [their] soules." The first murderer replies, "Relent? no: 'Tis cowardly and womanish," to which Clarence says, "Not to relent, is beastly, sauage, diuellish" (TLN 1096–7; 1.4.243–5). In Buckingham's false praise of Richard to the crowd and in this murder scene we see a standard of behavior that, instead of opposing manliness to cowardice and effeminacy, opposes womanliness to savagery. *Richard III* has a "beastly, savage, diuellish" man at its center, a man who takes violence so far that what could look like womanly cowardice becomes far preferable to manly aggression. Of course, the play does not argue that men should be women, just that savage murderers should possess some of the qualities that women should ideally possess. The qualities that Buckingham ascribes to women – "tenderness of heart / And gentle, kinde . . . remorse" — are, of course, qualities of Christian manhood, the very qualities that excluded Henry VI, while he lived, from full manliness. Thus *Richard III*'s depiction of effeminacy exposes a fundamental contradiction in English Renaissance masculinity.

The play, however, is not ambiguous about its condemnation of male sexual interest in women. Edward is a weak king throughout his short reign, and he dies from what the prophetic Margaret calls "Surfet" (FN 666; 1.3.194). It is not accidental that Edward's death from surfeit associates him with Falstaff, who also appears to die of his overindulgence. The history plays link sexual appetite to effeminacy and to death in bed for men. In a seeming contradiction, effeminacy in the history plays is also linked to youth. But the association of youth, male–female sex, and death in bed is perhaps not contradictory in a culture in which youth, male–female sex, and death (off the battlefield) are all associated with male weakness. *1 Henry VI* opens with England's nobles quarreling at Henry V's funeral. Winchester praises the church for Henry's success in life, but Gloucester counters, "None doe you like, but an effeminate Prince, / Whom like a Schoole-boy you may ouer-awe" (TLN 44–5; 1.1.35–6). Henry VI's youth will make him weak and susceptible; and while a man like Gloucester will play a good father to the young king, Henry is easy prey for the vicious men around him. Wooing Margaret in the play's fifth act, Suffolk says in an aside, "*Henry* is youthfull, and will quickly yeeld" (TLN 2536; 5.5.55). Suffolk understands that young men are weak in a specifically sexual sense, that they "quickly yeeld" to women's beauty. This understanding lies behind Henry IV's fears about his son, whom in *Richard II* he calls a "yong wanton, and effeminate Boy" (TLN 2506; 5.3.10).

York also worries about Richard's youth in these same terms, when he tells the dying John of Gaunt that Richard's ear is "stopped" with "Lasciuious Meeters to whose venom sound / The open eare of youth doth alwayes listen" (TLN 660–1; 2.1.19–20). In the same speech York regrets that Richard's "will doth mutiny with wits regard" (TLN 669; 2.1.28). Richard II attends to his "will," to fashion, his flatterers, and his own desires, rather than to his country's interests and his elder's "counsell." Once again, personal desire and a lack of attention to collective masculinity endanger a man's masculine reputation. Holinshed claims that Richard's followers procured women for the king (*Norton Shakespeare* 980 n. 2). Shakespeare has Bolingbroke imply that Richard has spent "sinful hours" with Bushy and Green. I would suggest that those "sinful hours" do not preclude Richard's sexual involvement with women; and his sexual involvement with men would also not preclude sexual exploits with his male followers. That is, Shakespeare does not reject Holinshed's characterization of Richard as a promiscuous heterosexual king and, therefore, recharacterize him as a promiscuous homosexual. Writing before those categories came into existence, Shakespeare characterizes him as a man with promiscuous desire, a man out of control and womanly. In *Richard II* we see a king whose youth leads him to be ruled by desire.

Richard's effeminacy is overdetermined. Shakespeare even renders Richard's attachment to England as an effeminate bond. When he returns from his Irish wars, he embraces his native country "As a long parted Mother" would (TLN 1368; 3.2.8).

Additionally, Richard's penchant for long-winded speeches helps to characterize him as effeminate, especially as it is contrasted with Bolingbroke's warrior masculinity. In the play's first scene Mowbray asks that he be allowed to fight with Bolingbroke: "Let not my cold words heere accuse my zeale: / 'Tis not the triall of a Womans warre, / The bitter clamour of two eager tongues, / Can arbitrate this cause betwixt vs twaine" (TLN 53–5; 1.1.47–50). Richard, who finally cancels the battle between Mowbray and Bolingbroke, would certainly win "a Womans warre" himself. Shakespeare's Richard loves to talk, and he speaks some of Shakespeare's most compelling poetry. But if this poetry adds to Richard's fascination as a character, it also helps to characterize him as effeminate.

The link between talking and effeminacy is strongly indicated within Shakespeare's second tetralogy. Hotspur characterizes the bombastic Glendower as like "a rayling Wife" (*1 Henry IV* TLN 1691; 3.1.156). And Hotspur himself momentarily endangers his own masculine reputation by breaking into a talking jag, which his father calls "this Womans mood" (TLN 565; 1.3.235). Like Richard, Hotspur is one of Shakespeare's most compelling characters, and his charm, which stems as much from his flowery speeches as it does from his manly actions, is a good indication of the paradoxical relationship between Shakespeare's drama and effeminacy (Rackin 1990: 173; Levine 1986). Shakespeare's drama is an oral art form, and in Shakespeare's history plays many men with varying relations to ideals of masculinity talk long-windedly. This does not make them all like women. In fact, their speeches characterize men as men as well as making them like women. In their strictures on language Shakespeare's history plays display and reproduce dominant masculinities; and Shakespeare himself is clearly well aware that this reproduction sits uneasily with the theatre's inherent effeminacy.

Can Boys and Common Men Be Men?

Shakespeare's drama was staged by men and boys. As Will Fisher's recent work suggests about English Renaissance culture generally, boys are distinctly not men in Shakespeare's history plays. The Hostess in *1 Henry IV* searches her house for Falstaff's missing goods "Man by Man, Boy by Boy, Seruant by Seruant" (TLN 2058–9; 3.3.48–9). Likewise, *Henry V*'s Chorus describes the people of England waiting on shore for Henry's triumphant return to England as "Men, Wiues, and Boyes" (TLN 2860; 5.0.10). Boys constitute a separate category, a category not subsumed under the label "Man." Scrope tells the dejected Richard II that all of England is in arms against him, including the boys: "Boyes with Womens Voyces, / Striue to speake bigge, and clap their female ioints / In stiffe vnwieldie Armes: against thy Crowne" (*Richard II* TLN 1471–3; 3.2.109–11). This usage of "female" is the first the *OED* cites for the obsolete definition "Womanish; effeminate; weakly" (*OED* "female" 6). In the history plays boys have effeminate body parts because they are like women, not like men. When King John's Bastard is looking for a set of insults with which to cow

Louis the Dauphin, he calls Louis's soldiers "boyish Troopes" (TLN 2387; 5.2.133). With this gendered insult the Bastard shores up English masculinity by contrasting it to French boyishness.

However, the history plays, obsessed as they are with the problems of masculinity, are also deeply interested in boys who do behave like men, rejecting their effeminacy in the pursuit of manliness. Such boys set examples for men that are designed to teach men to reject effeminate behavior. Thus in *1 Henry IV* Prince John's mature behavior on the battlefield shows his brother how to act like a man: "O this Boy, lends mettall to vs all" (TLN 2982; 5.4.23).[12] What makes John special is that he is an exception to the rule that boys are essentially cowardly, essentially like women. Boys in the twenty-first century are taught to be like little men from birth. In the history plays, however, boys are expected to be like women; therefore, when they behave like brave men, their behavior is exceptional, and it is also an example for men, who in these plays can always slip toward effeminacy should they let desire rule.

Once again, Falstaff's discourse offers a wonderful take on the ruling codes of masculinity. In *2 Henry IV* Falstaff meets the courageous Prince John on the battlefield. After John has failed to believe in Falstaff's pretended valorous "capture" of Coleville, Falstaff has a lengthy soliloquy on the virtues of sack that includes this passage:

> Good faith, this same young sober-blooded Boy doth not loue me, nor a man cannot make him laugh: But that's no maruaile, hee drinkes no Wine. There's neuer any of these demure Boyes come to any proofe: for thinne Drinke doth so ouer-coole their blood, and making many Fish-Meales, that they fall into a kinde of Male Greene-sicknesse: and then, when they marry, they get Wenches. They are generally Fooles, and Cowards; which some of vs should be too, but for inflammation. (TLN 2324–33; 4.2.79–86)

It would be clear to Shakespeare's audiences, as it is to modern readers and audiences, that the basic premise of Falstaff's arguments in favor of drunkenness is false. Those audiences may well have witnessed the scene in *1 Henry IV* in which Prince Henry, in need of a weapon during the play's final battle, tries to borrow Falstaff's pistol and comes up instead with a bottle of sack. Not only does sack not increase Falstaff's courage, it is his substitute for valor. By association, Falstaff's unwillingness to fight (his addiction to sack) is clearly responsible for his neglect of his troops in that play, most of whom are killed, and all of whom he dismisses as "foode for Powder, foode for Powder" (TLN 2440–1; 4.2.58). Rather than reinforcing collective male ideals and homosociality, as alcohol does in modern beer commercials, sack in the history plays is a medium through which a man escapes his male obligations and lets his womanly desires master him.

In this speech about Prince John and sack we see Falstaff's characteristic trick of using the codes of masculinity against themselves. He calls John a "demure boy" who will not be able to father sons and may even be a coward. We, of course, see a Prince John who is acting like the consummate man despite the fact that he is a boy. In the logic of what I have elsewhere termed testicular masculinity, male bravery is a signal that a man will father sons (Bach 1998). Prince John has proven in both *1 Henry IV* and *2 Henry IV* that he is as far from having "Male Greene-sicknesse" as can be. Falstaff on the other hand, in his love of sack, indicts himself as a fool and coward. Falstaff's soliloquy reinforces masculine codes at the same time that it parodies their use. He attempts to use those codes against the boy/man who personifies them. However, his behavior on this and other battlefields indicates the truth of the system. A man addicted to sack can hardly be a man, but a noble boy who masters his desires and will always fight rather than drink is on his way to dominant masculinity.

Falstaff complains to Bardolph in *1 Henry IV* that he has been ruined by the "villainous Company" he keeps:

> I was as vertuously giuen, as a Gentleman need to be; vertuous enough, swore little, dic'd not aboue seuen times a weeke, went to a Bawdy-house not aboue once in a quarter of an houre, payd Money that I borrowed, three or foure times; liued well, and in good compasse: And now I liue out of all order, out of compasse. (TLN 2017–23; 3.3.12–17)

In this speech Falstaff outlines the requirements for gentlemanly behavior: a gentleman should not swear, gamble, patronize whores, or renege on debts. Falstaff does all of these things as often as he can, and he is well aware that his behavior does not suit his station. At the end of the play he vows that if he is made a lord for his actions on the battlefield (for the fights in which he has pretended to engage) he will reform his appetites: "If I do grow great again, Ile grow lesse? For Ile purge, and leaue Sacke, and liue cleanly, as a Nobleman should do" (TLN 3129–31; 5.4.156–7). It is unclear how we are to take this vow, and indeed an actor might perform it with a wink, but in *2 Henry IV*, of course, Falstaff is back in the tavern, consorting with men below his station, and quite evidently living "as a Nobleman should [not] do." Falstaff's requirements for noble and gentlemen's behavior are the history plays' requirements as well. And the history plays not only hold noble and gentle men to high standards for manly behavior, they also suggest that men below the status of gentlemen, as well as men who violate those standards, are not really men.

. The standards that Falstaff outlines for noble and gentlemanly behavior are the standards for masculinity in the history plays. In a tautological and hierarchical understanding of human behavior, the history plays assert that base men are naturally base, less than men. They are lesser because they live in a lesser relationship to the dominant men whom they serve. The history plays clearly show that Shakespeare was not living in a world, or writing fictional worlds, in which "all men are created equal." When Henry V reads the roll of the English dead after the battle of Agincourt, he names three noblemen and a gentleman and adds "None else of name: and of all other men, / But fiue and twentie" (*Henry V* TLN 2824–5; 4.8.99–100). Noble men have names; common men are numbers. In the *Henry IV* plays the common men in the tavern resemble boys and women, creatures who have difficulty controlling their appetites and who cannot reason like noblemen and gentlemen. There are common men in Shakespeare's history plays who are not represented as effeminate: men like

Gloucester's servants in *2 Henry VI*, the soldiers at Agincourt in *Henry V* and other soldiers, assorted gamekeepers, messengers, sheriffs, watchmen, and mayors. However, those common men are never offered as masculine role models. Instead, when Henry V rouses his troops to fight against the odds at Agincourt, he promises that their valor will "gentle" their "Condition[s]" (TLN 2306; 4.3.63). If valor is a condition for manhood in the history plays, noble and gentle men are supposed to be naturally valorous, and common men who display valor are naturally gentlemen.

Noble men in Shakespeare's history plays often behave very badly in relation to their duty and their king, but unless they prove themselves murderous monsters or render themselves effeminate by cowardly or sexually desirous behavior, they are still men. Their desire for power does not detract from their masculinity although it may make them evil. Although the history plays show many rebellions led by nobles, when we do see a rebellion of common men with a common leader in Jack Cade's uprising in *2 Henry VI*, we see bloody base men who are sexually desirous and who rape and pillage without conscience. To the noble Westmorland, the natural leaders of rebellion are "bloodie Youth," and those who naturally sanction rebellion are "Boyes and Beggarie" (*2 Henry IV* TLN 1900–9; 4.1.32–41). Westmorland's associations between "Boyes" and poor men and poor men and cowardly rebellion are the associations made by the history plays generally. When the apprentice, Peter, accuses his master, Horner, of treasonous words against Henry VI, and the two men are ordered to fight to a death, both men drink heavily, encouraged by their common peers, and both display their cowardice (*2 Henry VI* 2.3.59–100). Poor men, like boys, are emasculated and out of control.

Unlike poor men, noble and gentle men are the definition of true men throughout the history plays. After Lady Anne has softened toward him, Richard III wonders that she could forget her dead husband Edward when "The spacious World cannot againe affoord" "A sweeter, and a louelier Gentleman" (*Richard III* TLN 432, 429; 1.2.232, 229). Likewise, Bolingbroke accuses Bushy and Green of misleading Richard II, whom he calls "a Prince, a Royall King, / A happie Gentleman in Blood, and Lineaments" (TLN 1320–1; 3.1.8–9). Although Richard's masculinity is questioned throughout the first three acts of *Richard II*, Richard is reinvested with masculinity at the end of his life when Exton, who has killed him for his new "friend" Henry IV, praises Richard for being "As full of Valor, as of Royall blood" (TLN 2785; 5.5.113). In *1 Henry IV* the rebel leader Sir Michael reassures the Archbishop of York about the strength of their forces which include "a Head / Of gallant Warriors, / Noble Gentlemen" (TLN 2614–15; 4.4.25). Henry IV's general, Westmorland, offers the rebels the king's mercy, for they are sure to lose a battle when the king's forces are "more full of Names than" theirs (*2 Henry IV* TLN 2020; 4.1.152). Both sides are sure, as are the history plays generally, that English nobility is synonymous with military strength and valor which can be, of course, synonymous with masculinity.

Base men, in contrast, are hardly the definition of manliness and, unlike noble and gentle men, they go by a number of degrading epithets in the history plays. In *1 Henry IV* the thief Gadshill offers a Chamberlain a share in his loot with the oath "as I am a true man," to which the Chamberlain retorts that he will take it instead as Gadshill is "a false Theefe." Gadshill, speaking as a proleptic democrat, argues, "Goe too: *Homo* is a common name to all men" (TLN 731; 2.1.87). The history plays disagree. Noble men and gentlemen are "true" men; but common men may well be "Hindes and Pezants, rude and mercilesse" (Messenger, *2 Henry VI* TLN 2569; 4.4.32). Stafford calls Cade's followers "the filth and scum of Kent" and he calls Cade himself a "base Drudge" (TLN 2442, 2471; 4.2.109, 136). Richard III asks his troops to fight against people he calls "A sort of Vagabonds, Rascals, and Run-awayes, / A scum of Brittaines, and base Lackey Pezants." He implores, "If we be conquered, let men conquer us" rather than French peasants (TLN 3802; 5.6.46–7, 62).[13] When Richard II's queen overhears a gardener discussing Richard's fall from power, she upbraids him: "Dar'st thou, thou little better thing then earth, / Diuine his downfall?" (*Richard II* TLN 1890–1; 3.4.79–80).

Pejorative labels are applied to common men by admirable and by despicable characters in Shakespeare's history plays. These labels pass without comment and, with the exception of thoroughly disreputable men like Gadshill, the men in question do not quarrel with their designations. In the conversation between Richard II's queen and the gardener, the gardener knows more than the queen does about Richard's fate, but he does not object to being called "thou little better thing than earth." The gardener is a better judge of men than Richard is, and he has ordered his garden better than the king has ordered the garden of England, but the gardener (who does not have a name) is not the man the king is. "Vile" and "base" in Shakespeare's history plays signify simultaneously in their pejorative senses, senses that we can still use, and in the sense of low-born (*OED* "vile," "base"). The gardener, a figure for the common man, does not assert his rights as a man, rights that have only come to be seen as natural after the philosophical and political revolutions of the seventeenth and eighteenth centuries (and even then often only for privileged white men). Reading or watching Shakespeare in the twenty-first century we may forget that he wrote for a world in which not all men were, by definition, men. This is, however, one of the truths about men and masculinity in the history plays.

"Selfe-love" versus Collective Masculinity

If common men can only rarely reach for masculinity, French men in Shakespeare's histories have little or no chance of behaving like true men. The Dauphin in *Henry V* is just one of the French men whose masculinity is impugned in the history plays (Bach 2001). In an attempt to persuade his father to take up arms against the English, the Dauphin in *Henry V* claims, "Selfe-loue, my Liege, is not so vile a sinne, / As selfe-neglecting" (TLN 966–7; 2.4.73–4). The history plays believe the opposite; in fact, they promote self-neglect for men. The Dauphin's approval of self-love, which might sound like modern common sense, is additional evidence of his effeminacy. Modern audiences have been trained by novels and films to admire individuality and self-actualization. Counter-intuitively for those audiences, Shakespeare's history plays praise self-neglect for men, even for kings. In this praise, the history plays contribute to Shakespeare's culture's interest in masculine self-abnegation. Self-abnegation is an essential aspect of warrior masculinity, which requires men to sacrifice their lives, and it is also an essential aspect of Christian masculinity, which requires men to deny personal desire.

"Selfe-loue" is the negative counterpart to collective masculinity. Historically, its positive redefinition accompanied the rise of the individual and individuality, the rise of horizontal relations between men. By the middle of the nineteenth century Ralph Waldo Emerson could claim that "Society everywhere is in conspiracy against the manhood of every one of its members . . . Whoso would be a man, must be a non-conformist" (Emerson 1951: 35). In his essay "Self-Reliance" Emerson touted the virtue of rebellion against society's strictures and the opinions and actions of other men.[14] But individualism became one of the truths of masculinity slowly and unevenly, as the history of the compound words created from the word "self" indi-cate. With the rise of the "ordinary individualist self" came many new words like "self-reliance" (coined in the nineteenth century). The *OED* offers the following def-inition for "self-reliance": "Reliance upon oneself, one's own powers, etc. (*rarely* with unfavorable implication)." The first usage the dictionary cites is from 1833; and the only usage "with unfavorable implication" is from Edward Meyrick Goulburn's 1862 text, *Thoughts on Personal Religion*. Goulburn worries about people who fail to resist temptation because they still have "some particle of self-reliance lurking at the bottom of [their] hearts." Goulburn's worry indicates that in the mid-nineteenth century reliance upon the self could still be unfavorably compared to reliance upon God. By the end of the nineteenth century Matthew Arnold, no friend to the masses, could argue that the English people, "A very strong, self-reliant people . . . keeps its eye on the grand prizes . . . won only by distancing competitors, by getting before one's com-rades, by succeeding all by one's self" (Arnold 1962: 13). This praise of self competed throughout its elevation to the status of a good with a Christian masculinity that praised self-neglect, but in Shakespeare's history plays the praise of self-neglect has no competition.

Shakespeare's history plays are as invested in self-neglect as Emerson and Arnold are in self-reliance. Rather than praising self, self-actualization, and personal devel-opment, Shakespeare's history plays offer instead praise of collective masculinity, the homosocial bonds that self-loving men, by definition, do not work to promote and that they may even actively destroy. This collective masculinity is the province of true leaders of men, men such as Talbot. Invested in honor, Talbot cares nothing for his self; he fights with his men for his king and for God. Collective masculinity is another name for men's duty to other men and to God, duty that is meant to supersede per-sonal concerns. So the Chorus in *Henry V* praises Bolingbroke's son Henry V for "Being free from vain-nesse, and selfe-glorious pride; / Giving full Trophee, Signall, and Ostent / Quite from himselfe, to God" (TLN 2869–71; 5.0.20–2). Although the two parts of *Henry IV* and *Henry V* depict Henry's maturation from wild prince to successful military ruler, they care not a whit for Henry's "self"; rather, they show Henry rejecting what we would now call personal desire in order to embrace collective masculinity.

In contrast to real men like Talbot and Henry V, the history plays offer self-loving male characters, like Falstaff, King Edward, and Richard III, who violate collective masculinity at every turn. These characters are great fun to watch, but they are also counter-examples for men's behavior, men who behave like women or monsters rather than men. Their investments in their own selves compromise their masculinity and bring them together against the collective masculinity that the history plays promote. Within the history plays the man most dedicated to self-actualization is Richard III, the king whom Shakespeare ahistorically portrays as more monstrous than human. The history plays deny human status to people whom we would now term, and who would term themselves, disabled. Lady Anne calls Richard a "lumpe of fowle Deformitie" whose "inhumane" slaying of Henry VI causes his dead body to bleed (*Richard III* TLN 234, 237; 1.2.57, 60). And that dead body does indeed bleed on stage, offering material proof to audiences of Richard's association with the devil. Shakespeare gives Richard the theatrical power to persuade Anne to marry him, but that persuasive ability is offered as yet more proof of Richard's moral deformity (as it is also proof of women's weakness). Richard's mother's rejection of him is depicted as natural, a rejection of the inhuman. While in a modern understanding of character the Duchess's rejection of her son would cause his inhumanity, Shakespeare depicts Richard as morally deformed because he is physically deformed, and this deformity justifies his mother's denial of her son.

In the history plays outward appearance reflects a man's constitution, a constitution embedded in his social relations. These plays display and promote what Ann Rosalind Jones and Peter Stallybrass call the "long regime of livery" in which clothes, symbols of "debts of love, of solidarity, of servitude, [and] of obedience," make the man (275, 273). Michel Foucault, in his history of sexuality, calls another aspect of this regime "a symbolics of blood," a system in which blood rather than personal development defines a man (Foucault 1980: 148). Shakespeare's Richard III rejects the "symbolics of blood" and "the long regime of livery," asserting himself *qua* self for the space of five acts. His self-assertion, like his body, is a sign of his moral monstrosity. Created in a culture that predicated masculinity on "debts of love, of solidarity, of servitude, [and] of obedience," Richard reveals his inhumanity when he acknowledges no ties to his family or friends. In *1 Henry IV* Hotspur complains to Blunt, the king's representative, that Henry (when he was Bolingbroke) abused the ties between men that Northumberland's support brought to him. Hotspur claims that the peers of the realm "Layd Gifts before [Bolingbroke], proffer'd him their Oaths, / Gaue him their Heires as Pages" (TLN 2540–1; 4.3.73–4). Richard cannot tie the peers of the realm to him; in a nasty perversion of the ties that should bind, he, instead, takes Lord Stanley's heir George as surety for Stanley's loyalty, threatening to chop George's head off should Stanley revolt to Richmond. Richard briefly claims to be completely self-reliant at the end of the play: "*Richard* loues *Richard*, that is, I am I" (TLN 3645; 5.5.137). This assertion of an "I," so crucial to modern identity, is damning in the system that begot this character, and even Richard himself acknowledges to the audience that he finds in himself "no pittie" to himself (TLN 3665; 5.5.157). In the end, even this character, whose monstrosity consists as much in his self-reliance as it does in his physical appearance, bows to the power of collective masculinity and God's word, the force of which that masculinity is designed to support. Within the "regime of livery" self-assertion is no match for the power of collectivity.

In the process of making their cases against the "I" the history plays rehearse challenges to the dominant models of masculinity that they approve. From the perspective of the twenty-first century the behavior and interests of men like Suffolk, Falstaff, Edward, and Jack Cade may look compelling; they can even look like drafts for future masculinities. Indeed, in the Restoration and the eighteenth century most of Shakespeare's history plays were rewritten, and the effeminate men within them made into masculine role models.[15] Athough we may be tempted to believe that Shakespeare had these transformations in mind when he wrote these characters, I suggest that we resist that temptation. As Margreta De Grazia suggests, it is perhaps a mistake "to make the nascent dominant before history does" (De Grazia 1996: 21). Shakespeare's history plays offer us a look at masculinities, effeminacies, and homoerotics in a world before the glorification of self-love, a world that was different from our own: not necessarily better, not necessarily worse, but necessarily different. Reading for those differences can help us to think about our own gendered, individualistic, and sexualized world.

NOTES

1   Due to space constraints, I am treating the history plays without real attention to their different texts. On the significance of attention to original texts see Marcus (1996). In addition, my use of the name Shakespeare in relation to *1 Henry VI* is a shorthand for the men who wrote the play together. See the textual note in *The Norton Shakespeare*, and see Masten (1997) on collaboration. Unless otherwise noted, quotations are taken from a facsimile of Shakespeare's First Folio, cited by through line numbers (TLN). Following the TLNs are citations from *The Norton Shakespeare*.

2   There is a growing literature on the meaning of nations and nationality in the English Renaissance (too big to cite here). On race, see especially Kim Hall's *Things of Darkness* (1995) and my *Colonial Transformations* (2000).

3   Psychoanalytically oriented feminist critics produced important studies of masculinity in Shakespeare in the 1980s and early 1990s (Kahn 1981; Adelman 1992; Erickson 1985). For the most part, those studies conceive of masculinity in relationship to a post-Freudian, relatively transhistorical understanding of sexuality and gender. Often these critics use the history plays to illustrate a point about immature masculine bonds and desires. As should become clear, I do not believe that the history plays subscribe to Freudian or post-Freudian understandings of sex and gender.

4   On Jews and gender in Shakespeare's England see Shapiro (1996) and Metzger (1998). In *1 Henry IV* Falstaff swears that he tied up the men he robbed with the oath "I am a Jew else, an Hebrew Jew" (2.5.164–5).

5   The change McKeon is describing is a change in male–male relations. Carole Pateman's *The Sexual Contract* (1988) goes into detail about the implications of this shift for women and male–female relations.

6   The friends in Margaret's metaphor are ungendered. It is Margaret's masculinist sympathies that
     make me see them as male friends. The text leaves open the possibility that these are two female
     friends. See Traub (1991).

7   See Howard and Rackin (1997: 215) on the place of rape in modern sexual ideology.

8   See Allen Frantzen's forthcoming work for some of the history of this problematic. By the late
     twentieth century, ideals of masculinity could include military cowardice in the face of nearly in-
     explicable and ridiculous military goals – see *Catch 22* and *M*A*S*H*, for example.

9   In her remarkable book *Whores of Babylon* (1999) Frances Dolan suggests that many people in
     Shakespeare's audience would have been uncomfortable with the anti-Catholicism that these plays
     promote.

10   See also Mowbray's argument (also about his subjection to his king) to Richard II: "Men are but
     gilded loame, or painted clay / . . . Mine Honor is my life" (*Richard II* TLN 187, 190; 1.1.179,
     182).

11   For other important work on Falstaff's effeminacy, see Parker (1987) and Traub (1989).

12   On the word "mettall" and masculinity see Bach (2001).

13   On the pejorative connotations of the word "peasant" see Patterson (1989: 32).

14   See Newfield (1996) on the limits of Emerson's praise of individualism.

15   See my forthcoming book, *Early Modern England Without Heterosexuality.* One example that I discuss
     at length in the book is Richard II's transformation in Nahum Tate's *The History of King Richard the
     Second.*

References and Further Reading

Adelman, J. (1992). *Suffocating Mothers: Fantasies of Maternal Origin in Shakespeare's Plays, Hamlet to The
     Tempest.* New York: Routledge.

Amussen, S. D. (1993). *An Ordered Society: Gender and Class in Early Modern England.* New York:
     Columbia University Press.

Arnold, M. (1962). "Democracy." *Democratic Education.* In *The Complete Prose Works of Matthew Arnold,*
     vol. 2, ed. R. H. Super. Ann Arbor: University of Michigan Press.

Bach, R. A. (1998). The Homosocial Imaginary of *A Woman Killed With Kindness. Textual Practice,* 12, 3,
     503–24.

——(2000). *Colonial Transformations: The Cultural Production of the New Atlantic World 1580–1640.* New
     York: Palgrave.

——(2001). Tennis Balls: *Henry V* and Testicular Masculinity or According to the *OED,* Shakespeare
     Doesn't Have Any Balls. *Renaissance Drama.*

Bourdieu, P. (2001). *Masculine Domination,* trans. R. Nice. Stanford, CA: Stanford University Press.

Bray, A. (1994). Homosexuality and the Signs of Male Friendship in Elizabethan England. In *Queering
     the Renaissance,* ed. J. Goldberg. Durham, NC: Duke University Press, 40–61.

Breitenberg, M. (1996). *Anxious Masculinity in Early Modern England.* Cambridge: Cambridge Univer-
     sity Press.

Burnett, M. T. (1997). *Masters and Servants in English Drama and Culture: Authority and Obedience.* New
     York: St. Martins Press.

Cartelli, T. (1994). Jack Cade in the Garden: Class Consiousness and Class Conflict in *2 Henry VI.* In
     Enclosure Acts: Sexuality, Property, and Culture in Early Modern England, ed. R. Burt and J. M. Archer.
     Ithaca, NY: Cornell University Press, 48–67.

De Grazia, M. (1996). The Ideology of Superfluous Things: *King Lear* as Period Piece. In *Subject and
     Object in Renaissance England,* ed. M. De Grazia, M. Quilligan, and P. Stallybrass. Cambridge:
     Cambridge University Press, 17–42.

DiGangi, M. (1997). *The Homoerotics of Early Modern Drama.* Cambridge: Cambridge University Press.

Dolan, F. E. (1999). *Whores of Babylon: Catholicism, Gender and Seventeenth-Century Print Culture*. Ithaca, NY: Cornell University Press.

Emerson, R. W. (1951). Self-Reliance. In *Emerson's Essays*. New York: Harper and Row.

Erickson, P. (1985). *Patriarchal Structures in Shakespeare's Drama*. Berkeley: University of California Press.

Fausto-Sterling, A. (2000). *Sexing the Body: Gender Politics and the Construction of Sexuality*. New York: Basic Books.

Fisher, W. (2001). The Renaissance Beard: Masculinity in Early Modern England. *Renaissance Quarterly*, 54, 155–87.

Foucault, M. (1980). *The History of Sexuality, Volume 1: An Introduction*, trans. R. Hurley. New York: Vintage Books.

Goldberg, J. (1992). *Sodometries: Renaissance Texts, Modern Sexualities*. Stanford, CA: Stanford University Press.

Hall, K. F. (1995). *Things of Darkness: Economies of Race and Gender in Early Modern England*. Ithaca, NY: Cornell University Press.

Howard, J. E. (1997). Introduction. *Richard Duke of York. The Norton Shakespeare*, ed. S. Greenblatt, W. Cohen, J. E. Howard, and K. E. Maus. New York: W. W. Norton, 291–7.

Howard, J. E. and Rackin, P. (1997). *Engendering a Nation: A Feminist Account of Shakespeare's English Histories*. New York: Routledge.

Kahn, C. (1981). *Man's Estate: Masculine Identity in Shakespeare*. Berkeley: University of California Press.

Laqueur, T. (1990). *Making Sex: Body and Gender From the Greeks to Freud*. Cambridge, MA: Harvard University Press.

Levine, L. (1986). Men in Women's Clothing: Antitheatricality and Effeminization from 1579 to 1642. *Criticism*, 28, 121–43.

McKeon, M. (1995). Historicizing Patriarchy: The Emergence of Gender Difference in England, 1660–1760. *Eighteenth-Century Studies*, 28, 3, 295–322.

Marcus, L. S. (1996). *Unediting the Renaissance: Shakespeare, Marlowe, Milton*. London: Routledge.

Masten, J. (1997). *Textual Intercourse: Collaboration, Authorship, and Sexualities in Renaissance Drama*. Cambridge: Cambridge University Press.

Metzger, M. J. (1998). Now by My Hood, a Gentle and No Jew: Jessica, *The Merchant of Venice*, and the Discourse of Early Modern English Identity. *Publications of the Modern Languages Association*, 113, 1, 52–63.

Mills, L. J. (1937). *One Soul in Bodies Twain: Friendship in Tudor Literature and Stuart Drama*. Bloomington, IN: Principia Press.

Montaigne, M. de (1603). Of Friendship. In *The Essayes of Lord Michaell de Montaigne*, trans. J. Florio. London.

Newfield, C. (1996). *The Emerson Effect: Individualism and Submission in America*. Chicago, IL: University of Chicago Press.

Orgel, S. (1996). *Impersonation: The Performance of Gender in Shakespeare's England*. Cambridge: Cambridge University Press.

Overbury, Sir Thomas (1632). *His Wife. With Additions of New Characters*. The fifteenth impression. London.

Parker, P. (1987). *Literary Fat Ladies*. London: Methuen.

Paster, G. K. (1993). *The Body Embarrassed: Drama and the Disciplines of Shame in Early Modern England*. Ithaca, NY: Cornell University Press.

Pateman, C. (1988). *The Sexual Contract*. Stanford, CA: Stanford University Press.

Patterson, A. (1989). *Shakespeare and the Popular Voice*. Oxford: Blackwell.

Rackin, P. (1990). *Stages of History: Shakespeare's English Chronicles*. Ithaca, NY: Cornell University Press.

——(1991). Genealogical Anxiety and Female Authority: The Return of the Repressed in Shakespeare's Histories. In *Contending Kingdoms: Historical, Psychological, and Feminist Approaches to the Literature of Sixteenth-Century England and France*, ed. M.-R. Logan and P. L. Rudnytsky. Detroit, MI: Wayne State University Press, 323–44.

——(1994). Foreign Country: The Place of Women and Sexuality in Shakespeare's Historical World. In *Enclosure Acts: Sexuality, Property, and Culture in Early Modern England*, ed. R. Burt and J. M. Archer. Ithaca, NY: Cornell University Press, 68–95.

Shakespeare, W. (1968). *The First Folio of Shakespeare. The Norton Facsimile*, ed. C. Hinman. New York: W. W. Norton.

——(1997). *The Norton Shakespeare*, ed. S. Greenblatt, W. Cohen, J. E. Howard, and K. E. Maus. New York: W. W. Norton.

Shapiro, J. (1996). *Shakespeare and the Jews*. New York: Columbia University Press.

Smith, B. R. (1994). *Homosexual Desire in Shakespeare's England: A Cultural Poetics*. Chicago, IL: University of Chicago Press.

——(2000). *Shakespeare and Masculinity*. Oxford: Oxford University Press.

Spear, G. (1993). Shakespeare's "Manly" Parts: Masculinity and Effeminacy in *Troilus and Cressida*. *Shakespeare Quarterly*, 44, 409–22.

Stanivukovic, G. (1999). "The blushing shame of souldiers": The Eroticism of Heroic Masculinity in John Fletcher's *Bonduca*. In *The Image of Manhood in Early Modern Literature: Viewing the Male*, ed. A. P. Williams. Westport, CT: Greenwood Press.

Tate, N. (1681). *The History of King Richard the Second. Acted at the Theatre Royal Under the Name of the Sicilian Usurper*. London.

Traub, V. (1989). Prince Hal's Falstaff: Positioning Psychoanalysis and the Female Reproductive Body. *Shakespeare Quarterly*, 40, 456–74.

——(1991). Desire and the Difference it Makes. In *The Matter of Difference: Materialist Feminist Criticism of Shakespeare*, ed. V. Wayne. Ithaca, NY: Cornell University Press, 81–114.

11

French Marriages and the Protestant Nation in Shakespeare's History Plays

Linda Gregerson

The true and natural old English nation never esteemed nor loved the French: they have it sunk so deep and deeply laid up in their heart as the savor wherewith their young shells were seasoned to the sun from grandfather to father, who in teaching them to shoot would have them imagine a Frenchman for their butt, that so in shooting they might learn to hate kindly, and in hating learn to shoot nearly.

John Stubbs, *A Gaping Gulf*

"Brave Death by speaking, / Imagine him a Frenchman, and thy foe"

1 Henry VI 4.7.25–6

I

The apex of national consolidation in Shakespeare's earliest history plays is an event those plays can only look back to: Henry V's conquest of France in the early fifteenth century. That conquest would serve many generations as a touchstone for English patriotism, but its memory is chiefly an embittering one in the three plays of *Henry VI* and in *Richard III*. As the Duke of Buckingham will observe in another of Shakespeare's history plays, "this French going-out" has had "a most poor issue" (*Henry VIII* 1.1.73, 87). "Poor issue" describes all too accurately the dynastic, fiscal, and geopolitical disasters whose relentless unfolding constitutes the action of Shakespeare's first tetralogy. In its biological connotation, "poor issue" also suggests the flaw that lies in marriage; in the history plays, as in the double play of history – Lancastrian and Tudor – against which these plays resonate, the marriages most shattering to English fortunes and English self-regard are French.

Prior to the historical events recounted in the first tetralogy, the present Henry's father, Henry V, had taken a French wife in order to consolidate his triumphs on the battlefield; the treaty sealed by that marriage confirmed his title as "King of England and Heir of France." But the princely "issue" of that marriage has achieved mere infancy at the beginning of the plays that bear his name; his reign has been launched prematurely by his father's early death; he is destined for a long and vulnerable minority. The military "issue" of the father's triumphant treaty is the series of spectacular losses hastily recited before "dead Henry's corse" in the first scene of *Henry VI Part 1*: "Guienne, Champaigne, Rheims, Orleance, / Paris, Guysors, Poictiers . . . all quite lost" (*1 Henry VI* 1.1.60–1). The messengers come fast on one another's heels with their dire news: "If Henry were call'd to life again, / These news would cause him once more yield the ghost" (*1 Henry VI* 1.1.66–7). Foreboding saturates the scene, the first scene in the first play in the sequence of ten that will arguably constitute Shakespeare's most significant contribution to generic innovation on the English stage. The single genre quite unthinkable without the Shakespearean contribution – the English history play – is a genre in which the English nation is recurrently invited to contemplate its own contingency.

The foreboding has not lessened in the opening scenes of *Henry VI Part 2*; indeed, it has been compounded with a dire fulfillment. The news this time is the marriage of Henry VI to Margaret of Anjou, who is delivered to the king by his proxy Suffolk in the first lines of the play. Preparations for this marriage had already cast a pall over the final scenes of *1 Henry VI*: Suffolk's surrogacy was shown to be sinister and self-interested; the king's capitulation to Suffolk's marriage brokering entailed the breaking of an earlier betrothal to the daughter of the Earl of Arminack, and thus the peace treaty of which that betrothal had been a part. The king has shown himself to be an unreliable ally as well as an incapable guardian of his own and his country's interest. Not all dramatic scenes may be said to be governed by point of view, unless that point is understood as multiple, but the first scene of *2 Henry VI* is forcefully governed by the reactions of the Duke of Gloucester who, since the death of Talbot, has had to assume the mantle of constancy: in a maelstrom of chaotic statecraft and personal duplicity, he is the only figure the play can at present put forth to serve its audience as a center for moral consciousness and affective identification. And in Gloucester's devastated response as he reads the articles of marriage ("Some sudden qualm hath struck me at the heart, / And dimm'd mine eyes": 1.1.54–5), Shakespeare's English audience is made to understand just how far the unmanning of English monarch and English nation has progressed. Margaret has brought neither money nor land to the English, but costs the nation both: England cedes to Margaret's father both Anjou and Maine, "the keys of Normandy" (1.1.114) lately won with English blood; and England is exorbitantly taxed to pay for fetching the new queen out of France, which is to say, the English are made by this marriage to finance their own disinheritance. The rebel Jack Cade nicely captures the upshot of the marriage, even as he mistakes the identity of the key marriage broker: "Lord Say," Cade cries, "hath gelded the commonwealth, and made it an eunuch; and more than that, he can speak French, and therefore is a traitor" (4.2.164–7).

Crude as it is, Cade's construction of commonwealth by means of opposition to things French is echoed throughout this earliest cycle of Shakespearean history plays. Talbot, the chief exemplar of martial English manhood, speaks in a tragic mode what

Jack Cade speaks in the comic: beholding his dead son on the battlefield outside Bordeaux, Talbot tries to will the boy back to life: "Brave Death by speaking," he says to the corpse, "Imagine him a Frenchman, and thy foe" (*1 Henry VI* 4.7.25–6). In her extended study of the Jack Cade rebellion of 1450 and its representation in *2 Henry VI*, Ellen Caldwell (1995) has examined in detail the significant documentary remains of that rebellion: fifteenth-century accounts of the uprising, popular songs and poems, lists of pardons issued in the aftermath of rebellion, and, most remarkable of all, several versions of the rebels' list of grievances. These grievances were delivered in the form of a petition to King Henry VI, were circulated among contemporaries, and were preserved in later chronicles of the fifteenth-century turmoil. The Cade rebellion, of course, is only one of many historical referents at the heart of Shakespeare's play, and a highly mediated referent it is, liberally conflated with aspects of the earlier (1381) and very different Peasant's Revolt, distilled for theatrical embodiment, adapted to the colors and politics of comic relief. It is a resonant precursor all the same, worth consulting as we try to understand the logic of playhouse adaptation, the informing ground of theatrical elision and innovation.

Of repeated concern to the historical persons associated with Cade's rebellion was the rise of a predatory class of "new men," members of the king's household faction who have alienated the traditional aristocracy, diverted to their own use the king's revenue, and forced the impoverished monarchy to burden the commons with excessive taxation and other extortionate practices. One version of the rebels' petition provides a striking contribution to political theory, insisting throughout "that the king, who had sworn at his coronation to keep the law, is responsible to his subjects" (Caldwell 1995: 28, 31). But shadowing all other grievances, dwelt upon in every version of the petition and, to the point of obsession, in the fifteenth-century chronicles that narrate the rebellion and its sequelae, is "loss of France." The social and economic costs of the Hundred Years' War – soldiers dead and maimed, trade disrupted, coastal counties pillaged by demobilized troops, the alms rolls swollen by families displaced from Norman estates, the country burdened by taxation and extraction of provisions – these costs were born by magnate and smallholder, yeoman and artisan, tradesman and clergyman alike. "Loss of France" was not only a prolonged material blow; it was also a blow to the nation's understanding of itself, as Shakespeare's first tetralogy makes clear: "Of England's coat one half is cut away" (*1 Henry VI* 1.1.81). And for Shakespeare's audience, this loss was not merely the stuff of ancient history. The reign of Shakespeare's queen, their present queen, had begun with the final humiliating expulsion from Calais, the last English foothold in France.

Sixteenth-century hostilities between English and French – the native air to Shakespeare's native audience – mimicked and painfully reprised an earlier hundred-year span of overt warfare (the so-called Hundred Years' War) and a full five hundred years of violently asserted and patently imperfect "union" (the cultural, material, and political aftermath of eleventh-century conquest). French and English had been, at least on the level of their landholding elites, problematically construed to be two parts of a single realm for over half a millennium: the foreign and the familial were inextricably entwined. But sixteenth-century relations between the English and the French differed from their antecedents in one momentous respect. For added to the struggle over sovereignty, birthright, identity, and land was now the struggle over religion. The church of Western Christendom had split in two.

That split is the reverberant story of sixteenth-century England, unfolding not only in the ordinary course of time but also, and perhaps more notably, with retroactive force. For "the recognition of anachronism," writes Phyllis Rackin (1990), "was a basic premise of Reformation thought" (p. 10). In other words, as Rackin explains, the church and the understanding it embodied in material practice were no longer perceived to be transhistorical and incapable of change. The church was seen – at least by an increasingly vocal and influential minority – to have altered, to have fallen away from its primitive foundations; it needed to be reformed. This discovery of historical difference, as Rackin reminds us, had revolutionary implications. Acknowledging the possibility of change and thus of rupture, deliberate or inadvertent, better or worse, the epistemological insights of the Reformation helped prepare the way for correlative changes in sixteenth-century English historiography. Chronicles from the latter part of the century begin to acknowledge a distinction between first causes (the will of the Creator) and second causes (the vicissitudes of human affairs, political struggle, conflicting motives and aptitudes) (ibid: 5–6). The narrative of history in these chronicles becomes much messier than it had been before: disorderly, non-linear, filled with contradiction and contingency. And the drama of history? This is where Rackin's insight is even more radical than her own explications would allow. The nature of theatrical performance, especially in a theatre like Shakespeare's – market-driven, rapidly evolving, opportunistic and experimental, catering to a fickle and heterogeneous audience – makes anachronism an investigative instrument for embodied dissonance. In the theatre we are contemplating not merely the discovery of sudden or progressive change over time, not merely the branching structure of cause and effect *per se*, but the simultaneous triggering – in a single place at a single time and among a single group of people or even a single mind – of contradictory understandings.

The Shakespearean history play was a profoundly innovative form, a veritable laboratory for the discovery of the specifically theatrical anachronism described above. An example from the earliest of the history plays will serve as a case in point: in the fifth act of *1 Henry VI* the young King Henry is offered a treaty of peace. This treaty has been brokered by the pope and the Holy Roman Emperor; it is fated to be ephemeral; it is shadowed by the corrupt machinations of the new-made Cardinal, formerly Bishop of Winchester, who is willing to "sack this country" in service of his own ambition (5.1.62). Against this mordant background, the young King Henry VI is eager to embrace an illusory tranquility: "I always thought," he says, "It was both impious and unnatural / That such immanity and bloody strife / Should reign among professors of one faith" (5.1.11–14). "Unnatural," "one faith": these lines, I would argue, were meant to register as ominous with Shakespeare's audience, were meant to induce a primitive revulsion and to constitute a moral touchstone, as when in the later play *1 Henry IV* Hotspur, Mortimer, and Glendower propose to carve up the body of

England among them. It is, for the audience of *1 Henry VI*, the fourth decade of Elizabeth's reign. England and France are *not* of one faith. To hear an English king declare that they are, even though that king has been dead for a century, is as much as to hear that England shall be betrayed. The logic is something like the retroactive logic of "premature anti-fascism": in the words of Shakespeare's Henry VI, Shakespeare's audience would have discerned the outlines of dangerous Catholic sympathies. "All his mind is bent to holiness," says Margaret with contempt in the play that is the sequel to this; "To number Ave-Maries on his beads" (*2 Henry VI* 1.3.55–6). Rosary beads are not the transhistorical trappings of piety, not in the anti-papist England of the latter sixteenth century; they are synecdoche, and a phobically inflected synecdoche, for Roman Catholic observance. Shakespeare's England was an England imagined over against a Catholic Europe.

II

The Reformation gained a foothold in England on the heels of a succession crisis. Henry VIII put aside one wife in favor of another, presumably more fertile, one. Four wives later, he died, and England under his three surviving heirs went through a dizzying succession of official religions, from the zealous Protestantism of young Edward VI, to the "bloody" counter-insurgency of Roman Catholicism under Mary, and thence to the ambiguous Anglicanism of Elizabeth. Elizabeth's was the longest of the Tudor reigns and looks to us like a period of remarkable stability, but from a contemporary perspective her 45 years on the throne unfolded as one long succession crisis, for Elizabeth never produced an heir. As long as it seemed as though she *might* produce an heir – and she let it seem so for a very long time – her possible marriage was a subject of intense political interest. For over a decade, and much to the alarm of her Protestant subjects, the queen's nuptial negotiations centered on Francis, Duke of Alençon and brother to the French King Henry III. As cruxes for nationalist feeling and parables of national endangerment, French marriages appear with considerable regularity not only in the history plays that dominate the early Shakespearean stage but in a number of literary and quasi-literary publications that circulated in the 1570s. Elizabeth's Protestant subjects were deeply alarmed by the proposed marriage to a French duke; their letters, petitions, allegorical poems, and political pamphlets have much to reveal about the story the Tudor nation told itself in its later decades about its own constituent character.

Witness this passage from a pamphlet of 1579:

> The true and natural old English nation never esteemed nor loved the French: they have
> it sunk so deep and deeply laid up in their heart as the savor wherewith their young
> shells were seasoned to the sun from grandfather to father, who in teaching them to
> shoot would have them imagine a Frenchman for their butt, that so in shooting they
> might learn to hate kindly, and in hating learn to shoot nearly.

This pamphlet was published when Elizabeth's marriage negotiations with Alençon were at their height. Its printer, Hugh Singleton, was affiliated with a number of prominent Protestant activists, including Edmund Spenser. Its author, John Stubbs, was a barrister at Lincoln's Inn, brother-in-law to Sir Edward Coke, the Lord Chief Justice of England, and also to Thomas Cartwright, the famous Puritan divine. Stubbs was himself a devout Puritan, much alarmed at the prospect of a Catholic resurgence in England. His pamphlet, *The Discovery of a Gaping Gulf Whereinto England Is Like to Be Swallowed by another French mariage, if the Lord forbid not the banes . . .* , expostulates against the queen's French suitor and goes much further: in the passage above and in many passages of a similar tenor, it casts enmity to France as a constitutive feature of English national identity. From grandfather to father to son, writes Stubbs, the patriarchal transmission of "true and natural" Englishness requires the recurrent imaginative conjuring of the enemy French. The English learn to hate "by kind"; the English grow into kindness, or national likeness, by means of hate. Stubbs tacitly admits – and how could he not, given the Norman invasion and its sequelae? – that the French are also "kind," or proximate kin. And as the "nearness" of this enemy testifies, the process by which any nation distinguishes its own kind from the Other is a precarious one. Unstable and dissolving boundaries give nationalist hatred its edge of panic.

And where Stubbs writes "nation," a modern reader will frequently detect the logic of "race." The French, Stubbs argues again and again, are so foreign to the English, so culturally and linguistically and somatically outlandish as to be outside the bounds of healthy mingling. But how could this be? The French and the English had been systematically mingling since the eleventh century – at least the propertied classes and their culture had – and this was precisely the ground of dispute: who should rule the France and England that were properly one? "No king of England," says Shakespeare's Henry V, "if not king of France" (*Henry V* 2.2.193). Conflicting claims pitted father against son, brother against brother, nephew against uncle – this was a *domestic* dispute if ever there was one, as a play like Shakespeare's *King John* makes evident. But shaping Stubbs's invective is not merely the timeworn fact that hatreds close to home are frequently the most violent; there is also the historically specific fact that this particular domestic quarrel – this quarrel over French and English *domus* – had been newly inflected by division within the Christian church. The French so radically "othered" by Stubbs are French *Catholics* – the excrescence of Rome.

The specter raised most obsessively in Stubbs's polemic – the gaping gulf itself in all its phobic corporeality – is the specter of radical exogamy or miscegenation. Marriage between the English queen and the French Duke of Alençon, the author insists, would be just such a "contrary coupling" as St. Paul excoriates in scripture:[1] "an uneven yoking of the clean ox to the unclean ass, a thing forbidden in the law" (p. 9). In Stubbs's descriptions of "such wicked willing matches" (p. 14) as the proposed marriage between Elizabeth and her French suitor, one may hear the note of hysteria that has so frequently and in diverse historical settings attended condemnations of interracial sexuality. This strange marriage would be "more foul and more gross" than any of those that have heretofore corrupted the children of God and brought his wrath upon them (p. 19). The French will "weaken the very knees and hams of our realm" (p. 47). "We should be pressed down with the heavy loins of a worse people and beaten as with scorpions by a more vile nation" (p. 36). Alternately invoking the images of bodily corruption and sexual violence, Stubbs obsessively represents the proposed French marriage as a site of carnality and contagion. Ironically, given the sex of England's current monarch, he also portrays the French alliance as a site of dangerous effeminization: insinuating its way into England through the (female) body of the English monarch, French degeneracy threatens to impair English manhood.

Permeating Stubbs's argument against the French is his insistence that their corruption is congenital. The queen's present suitor, he reports, descends from a race notorious for its unsoundness of body. To Alençon's father and brothers he ascribes – and with considerable satisfaction – the somatic porousness and deficiency normally associated in this period with the female. Death entered Henry II through the eye (where he was wounded in a joust) and Francis I through the ear, writes Stubbs, "which rotted him while he was yet alive." Charles IX was afflicted "in every vent of his body." Henry III "wants one of his loins to sit upon his seat," a plague that is "common" to the House of France (pp. 22–3). Stubbs's inventory of the bodily afflictions of the House of France make chilling reading for us now: it was as a direct result of this pamphlet that Stubbs himself was to lose his right hand on the scaffold. But as he wrote (and to all appearances for the rest of his life) John Stubbs of the unfortunate surname measured his own wholeness not in hands or feet but in alien corruptions, which is to say, by taking it upon himself to alienate corruption. An obvious instance is the venereal disease known in England at this time as the "French disease" (and known to us since as syphilis). This disease has brought to Europe a dangerous corruption from the East, writes Stubbs, and the French religion, with its "Turkish and Italian" contaminants (p. 3), has brought a parallel "sickness of mind." In French licentiousness and effeminacy, so the logic goes, we may read an inherent sympathy to the oriental splendors of the Roman church.

At the threshold of the contagious body and the contagious mind, orality poses a particular danger for Stubbs's construction of Englishness. The French language, he writes, is itself a sign of the serpent: Elizabeth "may know [her suitor] by his hissing and lisping" (p. 4). And in their churches the French revert to an even more objectionable language – to popish Latin. Bred upon the body of the English queen and in the mouths of English children, these mixed and outlandish noises would produce a mongrel tongue. If Nehemiah thought it "an ill-favored noise to hear [the] children gibber in the streets half Hebrew, half Ashdod," "how much more ill-favored it were for us that in our churches speak the language of Canaan to join with them that in their Mass mumble the strange tongue of Rome" (pp. 10–11). Now in Nehemiah 13, whence this business about gibberish derives, it is Jewish *men* who have consorted with the "wives of Ashdod." Not least among the remarkable ironies of Stubbs's citation here is that the language he condemns as "strange mumble" of the female line is none other than the Roman father tongue, the language in which English schoolboys of the sixteenth century were still being trained to think on a civic scale, trained in public eloquence and the logic of state. In the chronicle history of Geoffrey of Monmouth, Rome – the line of Aeneas and his grandson Brute, or Brutus – had been father to the British nation; but the Rome of the popes has switched gender and sunk to iniquity, has become a Whore of Babylon. Annexing to his own cause the oppositional logic of nation-building that pervades the Hebrew Bible and fervidly ignoring the complex – and contested – series of cultural appropriations that have produced his own religious perspective, Stubbs invokes the wrath of God upon the wicked intermarriage of "Christian true Jews and Popish bastard Israelites" (p. 14). "Christian true Jews": that's "us," the Protestant English. And "Popish bastard Israelites": that's them, the Catholic French. And this from a man who excoriates a mongrel progeny.

When, in the second of Shakespeare's history plays, the treacherous Suffolk faces death, he shows his true colors in bilingual equivocation. Recalling a prophecy that condemned him to die "by water," Suffolk is alarmed to learn that his captor's name is Walter – "Water" – Whitmore. "Yet," he ventures, "thy name is Gualtier, being rightly sounded" (*2 Henry VI* 4.1.33). One of Suffolk's captors strikes "water" even closer to home. Suffolk's given name, an imperfectly anglicized French name, is William de la Pole: "Poole! Sir Poole! . . . Ay, kennel, puddle, sink, whose filth and dirt / Troubles the silver spring where England drinks. / Now will I dam up this thy yawning mouth / For swallowing the treasure of the realm . . . By thee Anjou and Maine were sold to France . . . reproach and beggary / Is crept into the palace of our king, / And all by thee" (4.1.70–4, 86, 101–3). The metaphoric logic of this invective appears to be overdetermined (Suffolk is the stagnant water that at once contaminates and consumes, or diverts for private use, England's nurturing "silver spring"), but the lieutenant who contemptuously puns on Suffolk's surname clearly attributes the duke's downfall to his own inherent corruptions. The traitor who dies "by water" dies from a surfeit of self. Having betrayed his king and his country into a demeaning French marriage, having wracked his nation and advanced himself as paramour to the king's French wife, Suffolk tries to escape his English ruin by appealing to French pronunciation – Gaultier for Walter. French is the last resort of a scoundrel.

In 1579 Elizabeth Tudor was 46 years old. Although her physicians formally testified to the queen's continuing ability to bear children (she presumably continued to menstruate), their depositions were received with widespread skepticism. "How unlike it is for her to have any [children]," writes Stubbs, "how dangerous for her to have but one, and how her years do necessarily deny her many" (p. 85). This line of argument may appear to be a little at odds with the mongrel offspring that so occupy the author elsewhere in his polemic. And, indeed, Stubbs finds it difficult to decide whether to be more dismayed at the assured prospect of barrenness in this ungodly marriage, or at the prospect of fecundity. Given her age, he writes, "the very point of most danger to Her Majesty for childbearing" (p. 51), to bring Elizabeth to childbed were as much as to bring her to her deathbed. For all his overheated rhetoric, Stubbs is not simply being hysterical here. The infant and maternal mortality rates of early modern England are blessedly foreign to most readers now,[2] but this should not obscure the fact that the intimate association of birth and death in this period was far more than a mere poetic figure. And the continuity of the English royal line, of *any* royal line, upon which the national well-being so vividly depended, was at best a precarious business. How much more vivid that precariousness must have been when the royal line had come to its present terminus in the body of an aging female monarch. A king might lose any number of wives and infants in childbed and still maintain a viable hope of producing heirs and sparing his nation civil war. A 46-year-old queen facing pregnancy and parturition for the first time would have brought her nation to a nearly intolerable prospect of danger. And so, in the cause of the Protestant commonwealth, which is the sovereign's body politic, John Stubbs takes considerable speculative liberties with the sovereign's "very self self . . . which is her natural body" (p. 68). He tactlessly invokes her age, her dubious fertility, and, worst of all, her implausibility as an object of honest desire, and all the time steadfastly professes himself a loyal subject to her person and her law. Elizabeth and her most intimate alliances were for Stubbs, as for his compatriots, Puritan and Catholic alike, the problematic vehicles of national and religious aspiration.

III

Henry VIII was the last of Shakespeare's history plays; indeed, we now believe, the last of his plays for the English stage. It was first performed in 1613, some ten years after the death of Elizabeth, and concerns itself with the events that led up to Elizabeth's birth in 1533, including the complex drama of her father's break with Rome. The Act of Appeals in 1533 declared that the king, not the pope, had jurisdiction over ecclesiastical as well as secular cases in England; the Act of Supremacy (1534) fulfilled the logic of the earlier Act by declaring that the king, not the pope, was the supreme head of the Church of England. The complex anachronisms of *Henry VIII*, its retroactive prolepsis and its revisionist historiography, resonate with two competing patterns of national disillusionment: the widespread disillusionment with the religious prevarications of the Elizabethan Settlement in the later sixteenth century and the more precipitous disillusionment with the Stuart monarchy in the early seventeenth century, often expressed in nostalgic celebrations of Elizabeth's reign.

Like the plays of the first tetralogy, *Henry VIII* begins with reports of another "French going-out," this time the lavish meeting of French and English kings at the Field of the Cloth of Gold in 1520. Unlike the late Lancastrian wars this meeting was ostensibly triumphant, but that triumph is illusory. Many an English peer, we learn in act 1, has been ruined by the expense of this lavish, competitive display of amity; what England has gained for its pains is a league no sooner made than broken, and an infestation of French manners at home. These customs are of course unmanly and corrupt: the courtiers "have all new legs [i.e., new manners of deportment], and lame ones . . . the spavin / And springhalt reign among 'em" (1.2.10–12); that is, their affectations are indistinguishable from (sexual) disease. The very words in their mouths suggest obscenity: they "oui away / the lag end of their lewdness" (1.3.34–5).[3]

The effeminizing function of the new French manners and the new French mouthings is evidenced precisely by their efficacy in seducing the ladies, according to the logic that too much "service" to women impairs virility.

So what are we to make of it in Shakespeare's play when Henry Tudor courts Anne Boleyn in the guise of a masquer who "speak[s] no English" but only French (1.4.56)? And what about the fact (quite thoroughly suppressed in Shakespeare's play) that Anne Boleyn had spent eight years of her young life as maid of honor in the French and Burgundian courts: "no one," writes a contemporary, Lancelot de Carles, "would ever have taken her to be English by her manners, but a native-born Frenchwoman" (Ives 1986: 58)? Anne's ascendance makes Katherine of Aragon "a stranger now again" (2.3.17) in her adopted country. Hence, though her key political allies are the Holy Roman Emperor and the pope, Katherine refuses to be addressed in the language of international diplomacy: "O, good my lord, no Latin; / I am not such a truant since my coming, / As not to know the language I have liv'd in. / A strange tongue makes my cause more strange . . . Pray speak in English" (3.1.42–6). The irony of Katherine's cause, of course, is that Henry has put her aside on the grounds of Levitical incest, on the grounds that this stranger out of Spain, the widow of his older brother Arthur, is too much of kin to be his wife. "Ye turn me into nothing," says Katherine, "I am old" (114, 120), though at the age of 43 she is fully three years younger than Elizabeth will be when she entertains the French suitor who so alarms John Stubbs. And Elizabeth, despite the triumphalism of her christening in act 5 of this play, enters *Henry VIII* as something of a stranger too: she is not the hoped-for male child, and she hasn't yet learned the language (she will thank you, says the king, "when she has so much English": 5.4.14).

The simplest answer to the questions raised a moment ago about Anne Boleyn is that Shakespeare perforce reads history backwards. Anne's retroactive association with English Protestantism makes her a figure of national consolidation, no matter where she acquired her courtly charms; Cranmer the Protestant Reformer stands godparent to her daughter. But the prophecy Shakespeare assigns to Cranmer at the end of his play is history *written* backwards, a proleptic eulogy to the virgin Queen Elizabeth, mostly remarkable for its strategic amnesia. Less than three years after the triumphal christening that closes Shakespeare's play, for example, Anne Boleyn had been condemned for treason, adultery, and incest, and her young daughter, later Shakespeare's queen, had been retroactively bastardized. Anachronism is too blunt a concept to account for the displaced sedimentations of historical consciousness at work in Cranmer's "prophecy," whose nominal futurity is in fact an uncanny rescripting of the (authorizing) past. This displacement actively maintains a double resonance, testifying at once to the present's *interest* in and resistance to the past. In the play's historical elisions and revisions we may hear the distinct chords of narrative and ideological dissonance.

And it is ideological dissonance, troubling overlay to the poetics of praise, that characterizes the only two scenes in *Henry VIII* that allow the English populace to make so much as a reported appearance. This is a play, recall, like Shakespeare's others:

written for and performed upon the popular stage, where people of every class and condition – apprentices and shopkeepers, artisans and city wives – mingled in a single audience, where the common people of London, all but the truly poor, might gain admission for a penny. And yet, within the play, the massed public is a figure for satire and disapprobation. At Anne's coronation in *Henry VIII*, "Great-bellied women / That had not half a week to go, like rams / In the old time of war, would shake the press . . . No man living / Could say 'This is my wife' there, all were woven / So strangely in one piece" (4.1.73–81). Anne herself, we may remember, was six months pregnant at the time of her coronation in 1533. And at the christening which follows closely upon this coronation, the crowds are comparably oppressive: "have we some strange Indian with the great tool come to court, the women so besiege us? Bless me, what a fry of fornication is at door! On my Christian conscience, this one christening will beget a thousand, here will be father, godfather, and all together" (5.3.33–8). In the charges of bawdy incitement we may hear the sort of criticism that was routinely leveled at the Elizabethan public stage. In the monstrous mingling, in the proprietary and procreative confusion, we may hear something more: a radical undermining of legitimate and orderly succession (the ostensible subject of celebration in Shakespeare's play) by unseemly and prolific miscegenation. But note how *The Gaping Gulf* has been transmogrified: what was for Stubbs a figure for contamination by the Catholic French is in Shakespeare a figure for the English mob, the mob, that is, of commoners. For during Anne's coronation, our stage informant reports, the lords and ladies decorously "fell off" some distance from the queen (4.1.62–5). It is the "people" who make a monster of confusion.

But am I not guilty myself of confusing the playwright with one of his dramatic characters, and a minor one at that? Is the "gentleman" who reports this scene an objective observer? Of course not. He has not so much as a name to distinguish his point of view from that of the social class with which he is identified. On the other hand, does the powerful (and complexly gendered) phobic imagery ("great bellied women . . . like rams / In the old time of war") serve exclusively to characterize the perspective of the (anonymous) dramatic persona who gives it voice? Is its resonance effectively restricted, in other words and *in this case*, by speaker attribution? Again I would answer, of course not. The England celebrated in Cranmer's prophecy at the end of the play, the England in which "every man shall eat in safety / Under his own vine what he plants" (5.4.33–4), is an England made both of and in spite of its own people. It is still in this sense the England that bred and killed Jack Cade.

Shakespeare's histories are inflected at every turning by the perspectives of landed and courtly elites. This recurrent inflection, the profound ambivalence with which the life of the commons is rendered, as in the second tetralogy, and frankly ludic or sinister representations of the mob, as in *Henry VIII* and *1 Henry VI*, have frequently discomfitted Shakespeare's modern readers. Criticism in our own era has as frequently construed its task as the comprehensive identification of the ideological propositions with which Shakespeare is "really" aligned. Do the plays unfold a pattern of skepticism and subversion from below? Or do they, albeit with complexly distributed awareness and compassion, ultimately endorse a monarchical and feudal, i.e., conservative, regime? This binary imperative, this will-to-crack-the-political-code, has arguably more to say about our own self-representations than about late Tudor and early Stuart England and has in any case obscured for us what is truly remarkable in Shakespeare's treatment of the relationship between kingship and nation, which is to say, its radical provisionality. Monarchy was *always* precarious in its ability to "stand for" the English people. The story was never that of a consolidated feudal elite progressively displaced by absolutist innovation, nor that of uncontested monarchy thrown into disarray by the grasping classes of early modernity, nor any tale so linear by half. The monarch was always a precarious vehicle for national stability and national aspiration. The tenuousness of this representational contract is the story of history plays. It is a story, I would argue, much illuminated by the life and career of the Puritan John Stubbs.

Stubbs was a radical in religion, Stubbs was excessively earnest, Stubbs was reckless in the cause of truth as he perceived it – these strike us as highly un-Shakespearean traits, if not the transhistorical signs of conceptual obtuseness. But the drama of the sixteenth-century public stage takes its life blood from the disorderly jostling of just such noisy, irreconciled imperatives. For Stubbs, the imagined communities of faith and nation – communities continually *made*, mutually implicated, and precariously maintained – were indissolubly linked to the vicissitudes of factional politics and dynastic consolidation. Beginning with the domestic upheavals that immediately preceded, and legitimized, the birth of Elizabeth, the fate of England willy-nilly had become the fate of Reformed religion. Sixteenth-century England had much to fear when it contemplated the tumultuous period that had gone before: a Hundred Years' War fought on a foreign terrain construed as domestic; the civil, familial Wars of the Roses; both prolonged engagements driven by a single logic, by dynastic contention over a disputed royal succession. Sixteenth-century England might well fear the consequences of a splintered royal line. What distinguished sixteenth-century England from the tumult that had gone before was an additional splintering, this time within the Christian church. England's break with Rome, inscribed as it was with erotic and political intrigue, personal expedience, mere accident, added one more pole of difference to the process by which the nation had recurrently to think itself into being. The break with Rome prompted an anxious reinvestment in monarchy, an anxious contemplation of its flaws and plausibility. In the formative, Reforming England of John Stubbs and William Shakespeare, kingship had to be reimagined and French marriages became expedient vehicles for the troubled contest over self and nation.

IV

How then shall we think about one of the sturdiest theatrical triumphs in the Shakespearean canon, the ever-delightful, all-but-indestructible wooing scene in *Henry V*, act 5? Age cannot wither nor mediocre acting dim the magic of this scene. War gives way to erotic play, the naked realities of conquest and negotiated truce give way to the stylizations of romantic comedy. How is it that Shakespeare's audience agrees to conspire in its own diversion from known circumstance? Henry V's French marriage is frank policy; it is not love. And yet it is staged in the rhythms of love. Henry's performance is perfect; his very ineptitude at French is part of his charm, and is also reassurance that this king will not be subsumed by French manners and French power. In its conspicuous theatricality the scene is at once a continuation of the meditation on kingship found in *Henry IV, Parts 1* and *2*, and antidote to all that is anxiously discovered in those earlier plays. The dubiousness of Bolingbroke's title to the throne is underscored throughout the second Shakespearean tetralogy by an emphasis on kingly role-playing. Anointed Richard fails to be a public king. Usurping Bolingbroke assumes the throne on a wave of popularity, by playing majesty more effectively than majesty plays itself. Bolingbroke the king makes himself rare, so as to seem more kingly. Bolingbroke coins false kings on the battlefield so as to protect his person. Hal rehearses kingship as a species of urban ethnography.

At the beginning of *Henry V* dynastic claim to France is a matter for pedantic clerics, lost to common memory, and lost to the king's own knowledge. In performance, the obscurities of Salique law must be either tedious or comic; in either case, the confessed point is that Henry's "cause" is more a pretext than a principle. It is also a diversionary tactic staged by churchmen whose real motive is the preservation of their own wealth and prerogative (1.1). How is it that these manipulated fictions and the disturbing vistas they open up are "solved" or "repaired" by a fiction more transparent yet? By the wooing scene between Henry and Kate? The unstable and conspicuously performative nature of kingship, which had been the source of political and moral anxiety in *Richard II* and *Henry IV, Parts 1* and *2* – the surrogate kings behind which the "real" king hides, a prince's precarious apprenticeship under the shadow of a dubious succession – all these instabilities are here stripped of anxiety and transposed to a celebratory key. Henry's incompetence with the French language is a positive credential; it might almost have reassured Jack Cade. The domestic and affective premise of the wooing scene is neither discrediting to the larger military and diplomatic purview nor discredited by its palpable expedience. In a remarkable piece of theatricality the playwright invites his audience to savor its own layered understanding while collaborating on the ceremonial performance of personal and political tautology.

The ability of monarch to "stand for" a nation has been at issue throughout the English histories. It has, from a thousand directions, been cast in doubt. But now the theatrical is made to perform its own cure. The contract extends its courtesy in both directions. Katherine and Henry have jobs to do; their domestic and reproductive lives are pawns to dynastic considerations, issues of sovereignty and property. And yet they are willing to play it as love, and Shakespeare's audience is willing to endorse them. It is crucial that the audience should have been introduced to Katherine in earlier parts of the play. The charm of those earlier scenes is premised on a series of cultural slurs: the French can't talk right, they expose themselves with inadvertent obscenities, they pursue trivialities while armies go to war. Amused by the agreeable embodiment of cultural prejudice and, quite possibly, by a complementary manifestation, recognizing a witty sendup of their own inclination toward patriotic boosterism, Shakespeare's audience has the opportunity to find Katherine charming despite the disadvantage of her nationality and her tongue. The audience is made to be "in love" with her, in love with her on Henry's behalf; the audience is proxy for the king, a party of advance men. So, contrary to reason or to extra-theatrical reality, when King Henry professes his "love" for Katherine, this profession has some plausibility. Wooing the princess, he becomes "our" surrogate; he woos on our behalf. He stands for England, which wins with force and wins again with charm. This marriage is not a capitulation, as Henry's son's will be, as Henry's son's *has been* in the earlier tetralogy; it is rather the capstone of conquest. Henry is in no danger of becoming infected with Frenchness; he is rather the means by which all the world, or all the world gathered inside the Globe, becomes English.

V

When John Stubbs published his pamphlet attacking on personal, biblical, and what we would now call geopolitical grounds the proposed French marriage of his queen, the author, the bookseller William Page, and the printer Hugh Singleton were brought before the law as "authors and sowers of seditious writing" and were condemned to have their right hands cut off. The Act under which they were condemned was of disputed applicability: devised for the protection of King Philip during Mary Tudor's lifetime, it was held by some legal authorities to have "died with Queen Mary."[4] The Lord Chief Justice of England ultimately ruled that the Act was still in force, since properly speaking "the king of England never dieth": the state thus authorized the violent inscription of its power upon the natural body of its subjects by appealing to the mystical body of the king. There is some aptness in the fact that Stubbs should have suffered under an Act of Philip and Mary, since, according to his own argument, the abomination of the proposed French marriage very much consisted in its likeness to the abomination of that earlier Spanish marriage. Elizabeth's chief and earliest benefit to England, according to Stubbs, was "that she redeemed it, and yet not she but the Lord by her, from a foreign king" (p. 36), that is, from Philip of Spain. Stubbs's insistence on Elizabeth's instrumentality ("and yet not she but the Lord by her") is not merely another sign of his tactless indifference to his monarch's personal vanity. Nor is it the sign of sheer, unworldly religious fanaticism. That Stubbs took his *own* instrumental status seriously indeed, that he conceived it to be part of a complex and pragmatic intersection of both sacred and secular power, is amply witnessed by his subsequent career, in the aftermath of his notorious publication.

John Stubbs's hand required three blows of the ax when it was severed on the public scaffold. And before he was taken bleeding back to prison, Stubbs removed his hat with his left hand, now his only hand, and said "God save the Queen." But the speech I find even more remarkable is the less-frequently cited speech he uttered some moments *before* his mutilation: "I am sorry for the loss of my hand," he said, "and more sorry to lose it by judgment . . . Before I was condemned, I might speak for mine innocency; but now my mouth is stopped by judgment . . . If there be any among you that do love me, if your love be not in God and Her Majesty, I utterly deny your love" (Berry 1968: xxxv). Confronted by the corporal inscription of state power, Stubbs professed loyalty to the queen and her legal executors even above his loyalty to his own good motives. He granted, in other words, the power of the queen's law to come between himself and his own innocence, granted and scrupulously observed power's power to produce reality. And, far from ending with this famous scaffold scene, John Stubbs's story continued through a further eleven years of public life. He served, after his release from prison, as Steward of Yarmouth and judge in the borough court, as secretary to Her Majesty's military commander in the Lowlands and in France, as an elected member of parliament, and as sometime propagandist for Elizabeth's chief counselor and treasurer – her right hand – Lord Burghley. Defending Burghley's *Execution of Justice in England* in 1587, Stubbs loyally endorsed, and in writing, the state's authority to cut off what it deemed to be sedition.

In 1589–90 Stubbs served with the English army in defense of the Huguenots and Henry of Navarre. Since the loss of Calais at the beginning of her reign, Elizabeth had avoided the quagmire of continental warfare that had compromised so many of her predecessors. But under pressure from the activist Protestant faction at court she had in the 1580s reluctantly committed troops to the Lowlands and to France. Lord Willoughby de Eresby (having earlier succeeded Philip Sidney as governor of Bergen-op-Zoom and Earl of Leicester as commander of English forces in the Low Countries) was appointed in September 1589 to command an army of 4,000 in aid of Henry of Navarre. In four months of active service Willoughby's army in France played an important role in the capture of Vendome, of Mons, of Alençon, and of Falaise, but received no money or supplies from either England or from Protestant France: "more died from hunger and cold than in battle." Among those who served with Willoughby was his cousin by marriage, John Stubbs.

As was common under Elizabeth, as under her forebears, the English army received no regular pay or victualing during all its months – they were winter months – on the Continent; its soldiers died *en masse* of exposure and disease. Among John Stubbs's last writings is an extant letter to Burghley, which describes with remarkable temperance the hardships endured by the English troops and petitions for desperately needed supplies and reinforcements. In this letter Stubbs thanks his Lord and his queen for the privilege of serving in so good a cause and signs himself, "Mr. John Stubbe written with his left hand. Being with my Lord Willoughby in France in aid of the King of Navarre." Stubbs died in the course of Willoughby's retreat, died in France, ironically enough, and was buried "on the seashore." Henry of Navarre survived both military and political vicissitudes to assume the throne of France, but not before he dismayed his Protestant supporters by converting to Roman Catholicism.

Benedict Anderson has pointed out that in a political order organized dynastically, miscegenation is perforce the norm for hereditary rulers. (Its one alternative – systematic royal incest – is not unheard of but is considerably rarer.) For centuries the royal families of Europe intermarried as a matter of principle and policy: mixed lineage was a necessary adjunct of consolidated rule and was itself a sign of "superordinate status" (Anderson 1991: 21). So a faithful subject's horror at the prospect of his queen's French marriage was a far more peculiar reaction than we are likely at first to apprehend. An English Puritan like John Stubbs could accommodate a great deal of what we perceive to be ideological dissonance: he saw no contradiction between service to his country in its parliamentary body of elected representatives and service to his country in the person of his queen; he insisted, even upon the loss of his hand and amidst the dying soldiers shamefully abandoned by the leaders who had sent them as a token force to France, that loyalty to his faith and to the English state was one. But Stubbs offered clamorous resistance when his queen proposed to marry a duke from Catholic France, and his voice was merely one in a general outcry. Sir Philip Sidney wrote to the queen directly and at length with his protest. French marriages became a common target of opprobrium on the English public stage. The Spanish ambassador advised his monarch that England might well dissolve into civil war if plans for the marriage to Alençon were to go forward. This was not just age-old xenophobia; it was a sign that something of consequence had altered in the popular imagination of Reformation England. The monarch was still a crux of collective identity and was to remain so well into the seventeenth century; but the logic that governed the English collectivity, that articulated its boundaries, shaped its self-representations, and grounded its sovereignty, was no longer the logic of dynasty *per se*. It was the logic of a Protestant nation.

NOTES

1   The source of Stubbs's Pauline attribution remains unclear, but the Old Testament version of the prohibition appears in Deuteronomy 22: 10.

2   Their exact proportions have been the subject of much scholarly debate, but as evidence that the mortal dangers of childbirth were felt to be significant in early modern England, they were sufficient to have spawned an entire literary subgenre. For examples of the mother's last will and testament to her unborn child, see Jocelin (1624) and Leigh (1627).

3   Compare, in *Titus Andronicus*, Aaron's rendering of the sounds made by the nurse as he kills her: "Weeke, weeke! so cries a pig prepared to the spit" (4.2.146). The murderer makes his victim alien and obscene, translates her outside the realm of the human altogether.

4   For an account of Stubbs's trial, see Berry (1968). Of the lawyers who spoke up against the Act of Philip and Mary, William Camden reports that one was committed to the Tower, another forced to give up his position. See his *Annals of Queen Elizabeth*, cited in Berry (1968: xxxiv).

REFERENCES AND FURTHER READING

Anderson, B. (1991). *Imagined Communities: Reflections on the Origin and Spread of Nationalism*, revd. edn. London: Verso.

Berry, L. E. (ed.) (1968). *John Stubbs's Gaping Gulf with Letters and Other Relevant Documents*. Charlottesville: University Press of Virginia.

Caldwell, E. C. (1995). Jack Cade and Shakespeare's *Henry VI, Part 2*. *Studies in Philology*, 92, 1, 18–79.

Doran, S. (2000). *Elizabeth I and Foreign Policy, 1558–1603*. London: Routledge.

Holt, M. P. (1986). *The Duke of Anjou and the Politique Struggle during the Wars of Religion*. Cambridge: Cambridge University Press.

Ives, E. W. (1986). *Anne Boleyn*. Oxford: Blackwell.

Jocelin, E. (1624). *The Mothers Legacie, To her unborne Childe*. London.

Leigh, D. (1627). *The Mothers Blessing: Or, The Godly Counsaile of a Gentle-woman, not long since deceased, left behind her for her children*. London.

Rackin, P. (1990). *Stages of History: Shakespeare's English Chronicles*. Ithaca, NY: Cornell University Press.

Stubbs, J. (1968) [1579]. *The Discovery of a Gaping Gulf whereinto England Is Like To Be Swallowed by an other French mariage . . .* In L. E. Berry (ed.) *John Stubbs's Gaping Gulf with Letters and Other Relevant Documents*. Charlottesville: University Press of Virginia.

12
The First Tetralogy
in Performance
Ric Knowles

The performance history of Shakespeare's first tetralogy troubles traditional wisdoms of Shakespearean theatre history, performance criticism, history itself, and even "Shakespeare," in a variety of ways.[1] The theatrical record is one of adaptation, serial performance, ensemble playing, and theatrical doubling which ghost the textual, authorial, and thematic doublings that haunt these plays, disrupting their unities and rendering insecure the use of Shakespeare in the construction of authorized English history and English subjects. Indeed, the infrequency with which the plays have been performed, and the degrees to which they have been adapted, may have to do with their potential to destabilize: (a) Shakespearean theatre history as the record of the performances of great (male) actors in star roles; (b) the dominant discourses of theatrical training and tradition, which focus on the creation of unified psychological character; (c) the neo-Aristotelian discourses of unified dramatic action; (d) the discourses of individual authorship and authority; and (e) the cultural role of "Shakespeare" as it relates to the construction of England as an imagined community through the policing of official history.

Controversy has surrounded the dating and order of composition of these plays, and the degree to which they constitute a tetralogy. Each play excepting *1 Henry VI* exists in significantly different Quarto and Folio versions with different titles or generic designations. Their classification as "chronicle histories" is more hybrid and open than are tragedy or comedy, and has been subject to a wider range of interpretation. Even the authorship of *1 Henry VI* is in question.[2] These controversies, of course, reflect different agendas. Conservative critics who find providential or hierarchical social visions in the plays tend to conflate the Quarto and Folio texts and assume Shakespearean authorship, a chronological ordering of composition, a coherent generic classification, and the operation of each play as the self-contained part of a larger unity. Cultural materialist, feminist, and other "radical" scholars have tended to find fissures in these unities, to find the cultural work performed by the plays to be more or less socially destabilizing, and to evince more interest in the plays in performance as products of, and productive of, their own times and cultures than as interpretations of Shakespeare.

Theatrical productions of Shakespeare have long struggled against criticism from literary scholars on the basis of their capacity to pervert the authoritative, written texts and to function as autonomous cultural productions rather than reproductions of a stable Shakespearean original. The controversies that surround the dating, authorship, text, and genre of the plays of the first tetralogy have made them more open than most to intervention by producers who wish to speak to their contemporaries in the performative present. The scripts' instabilities, then, have made of these plays of English history as war and insurrection themselves a battleground in the (re)production of the imagined community of England: at one end of the continuum, anxieties about indeterminacy in the Shakespearean representation of history have led producers to impose throughlines and closures that hold in check the plays' centrifugal tendencies in the interests of cultural affirmation; at the other, more radical practitioners have seen their discontinuities as opportunities for social critique. The battle is over the ownership and use of history in the constitution of English subjectivities.

Although my focus is on performances of the tetralogy as such, it is worth pausing briefly to consider the plays performed in isolation in order to understand their structural and performative difference when played together. The *Henry VI* plays have only a brief theatre history since they premiered at the Rose Theatre in the 1590s, and the stagings that constitute it have tended toward the affirmation of official history and its traditional exclusions of othered groups and memories.[3] John Crowne's and Ambrose Philips's adaptations of *2 Henry VI*, in 1681 and 1723 respectively, appropriated the story of Cardinal Beaufort in the interests of stirring up anti-Catholic sentiment, the first in the face of the "Popish plot" to assassinate Charles II, the second in the context of the Jacobite conspiracy against George I. Crowne's version of *3 Henry VI* (also 1681) warned against the dangers of Whiggism. In the nineteenth century James Anderson's *2 Henry VI* at the Surrey Theatre in 1864 and Osmond Tearle's *1 Henry VI* in Stratford in 1889 celebrated the nation on the birthday of its bard, shoring up empire and patriarchy in an unequivocal modeling of England for the Englishman. The only significant exception to this history of conservative appropriation is the 1994 *3 Henry VI* staged by Katie Mitchell for the Royal Shakespeare Company (RSC) at Stratford's "Other Place," which shared many features with performances of the tetralogy. Mitchell presented an "unremitting exploration of the viciousness of human behaviour" (Holland 1994), but that behavior was explicitly aristocratic and male, and was effectively framed by ritual comforts enacted by veiled women who escorted the dead from the stage, and by program excerpts from the 1448–71 domestic correspondence of Margaret Paston while her sons fought in the wars. Sensitive to the exclusions enacted by the play, Mitchell's *mise-en-scène* introduced voices that are otherwise silenced, and disrupted the Shakespearean text through interpolated prophetic passages "spoken most often by characters marginal to the action" (Holland 1994) which were legible at once as peripheral to the plot, omitted by the author, and yet (extra-dramatically) authoritative. The production ended, after the exit of Edward IV with his son and brothers, with Queen Elizabeth alone on the stage. Removing her crown she began a quiet Kyrie, the female celebrant incorporating the audience in a commemorative ritual for the victims of men's wars. The final effect may have been cathartic, but it rendered catharsis as much the object as the effect of the representation, making it visible as a coping tactic of those othered by wars, plays, and official history.

In addition to their life as independent plays, the *Henries* have on four occasions been staged in Britain as a trilogy: Frank Benson directed them at Stratford in 1906; Robert Atkins produced edited versions at the Old Vic in 1923; Douglas Seale directed all three in 1951–3 at the Birmingham Rep, taking a conflated, two-part version to the Old Vic in 1956–7; and Terry Hands directed the three plays virtually uncut for the RSC in 1977–8.[4] Again, these productions tended to reproduce a dominant national narrative, containing divergent memories within received history. Benson, who saw the plays as "laying the foundation of the English empire" (quoted in Knowles 1999: 6), staged them as a celebration of Shakespeare "as the national genius who spoke for the English and memorialized their history at a crucial stage in the integration of what is now 'Great Britain'" (Burns 2000: 68). Although Margaret – "the Queen whose ambition disturbed England" – was considered sufficiently prominent to be played by Mrs. Benson, "the female parts were hardly at their highest level" ("S" 1906: 587), and "there was little sympathy for Cade and his rebels" (Hattaway 1991: 48). Women and the lower classes, for Benson, were threats to rather than constitutive of the English nation.

Seale and Hands invoked the discourses of textual authority, claiming to present the plays in their original form, a strategy that exposed productive tension among conservative reviewers honoring "faithfulness" to an authoritative text but expressing anxiety about a lack of "order" within it (see Hattaway 1991: 48; Anon 1952; Nightingale 1977). Seale cut more than Hands, however, at the Old Vic at least, where excising the Talbot–Joan sequences had the curious effect of "anticipating feminist critics of today" by making Margaret the trilogy's central character (Knowles 1999: 9). Reviewers, however, were divided along gender lines. While male critics noted Rosalind Boxall's strength in the role, they typically described her, in the language of 1950s misogyny, as "vituperative" (Kemp 1954: 125), "a man-eating wife" (Keown 1952), and contrasted her to a "delectable" Lady Grey, Bianca to a Margaret who "wander[ed] in from 'The Taming of the Shrew'" (Hobson 1952). Audrey Williamson, however, described sympathetically a character "developed with sureness from a black-haired girl eager for a great match and poignantly disappointed in it, to the woman rallying to the fierce protective pride of motherhood and queenhood" (Williamson 1957: 130).

Hands presented "the pure Shakespeare text," according to B. A. Young (1977), "in a style that Burbage himself would have recognized." Homer Swander found the production "legitimately Shakespearean," "authorized by the scripts," "in plan and execution a single work," and "Shakespeare's considered final version . . . with which he was well pleased" (Swander 1978: 162), but others who approved of the project were less enthusiastic about the result. G. K. Hunter reluctantly found it "diffuse and dull" (Hunter 1978: 105); Roger Warren judged that "to tell a story simply is insufficient. Shape, development, and finally meaning were absent" (Warren 1978: 148). Irving Wardle (1977) phrased the problem succinctly: "It is one thing to theorize about the play's inexorable logic but, in performance, the grand design breaks up into one damned thing after another."

In a decade informed at the RSC by Peter Brook's *The Empty Space* (1968), Hands seems to have forgotten Brook's lesson that if you simply let the play speak, "it may not make a sound" (p. 43). Worse, it will reinforce audience preconceptions or operate as a conceptual vacuum to be filled by the taken-for-granteds of dominant ideology. If Hands "imposed no directorial thesis at all" (Daniell 1979: 247), some critics nevertheless found "the message ever present and ever vivid" (Barber 1977), even if no two agreed on what it was. The representation of gender and class was also open: male critics felt free to project their fantasies onto Helen Mirren's under-interpreted Margaret, who, like the plays' other women, was consistently described in sexualized language.[5] Steve Grant, critiquing the production's lack of political edge, described her as "nothing more than a pouting cock-tease." Critics similarly projected their political desires onto the production's representation of class. Some felt that Hands's depiction of the Cade rebellion took "Shakespeare's own clear view . . . that the worst horror that can be visited upon mankind is anarchy" (Anon 1978), while others saw the scenes more sympathetically: "Cade is played with such understanding . . . that it is hard not to fall in on his side" (Young 1977). David Isaacs (1977) puts his finger most precisely on the problem: "Jack Cade may be a charlatan, but he is leading a band of men who are genuinely expressing a grievance. [Hands], having failed to emphasise the groundswell of grassroots feeling, he has left the play in a lofty political vacuum."

Among the things that rushed in to fill that vacuum was the company's training and technique. Hunter argued that, left to their own devices, "the actors . . . act their hearts out in giving Stanislavski-esque 'depth' to the characters" (Hunter 1978: 105), and for Daniell this was welcome. He saw in the production the tragedy of "a human group . . . eaten by destruction or ambition, swayed by fantasy or insight . . . like the Shakespeare we have always known" (Daniell 1979: 275). What he didn't find was any analysis of the social or historical forces that have constituted "the Shakespeare we have always known," or the "we" who do that knowing. What the "Hands off" approach produced was a formalist Shakespeare that privileged the ideologies of actor training and directorial constructions of unity and focus, "author"-ized official history, naturalized dominant constructions of gender, class, dramatic character, and human subjectivity (not to mention race, sexuality, and other forms of difference), and led to cultural affirmation by way of "an archeology of mystification" (Hodgdon 1991: 87).

Understood as a tragedy recounting "The Life and Death," as the Folio running title has it, of a central character, *Richard III* has been one of the most frequently performed plays in the repertoire, and has served as a star vehicle contributing to the commodity value of every major actor since Burbage.[6] As tragedy – or as the tragic melodrama of Colley Cibber's adaptation, which held the stage from 1699 to the end of the nineteenth century – *Richard III* has been comfortable within traditional stage history. But in order to achieve that comfort, performances of the play have required dramatic revisioning, usually in the form of excising the play's multiple voices of memory – the voices, that is, of women – and increasing the central focus on the individualist, tragic role of Richard as agent of history. Cibber's adaptation set the pattern for subsequent versions, including those claiming to have restored the "original Shakespearean text." Using only 800 lines of Shakespeare and shortening the script by almost half, Cibber rewrote Richard to be more "resolute" and "muscular," and rewrote the action to pit him "against a smaller range of innocent victims whose pasts have been wiped clean" – and therefore to erase their memories from the historical record (Jowett 2000: 85). He cut Margaret completely, together with the lamentation of the women in 4.4. Cibber's adaptation rendered the play cleaner, more masculinist, more tragic, and more culturally affirmative, and it (or its ghosted traces) has functioned as the play's (ideological) unconscious ever since. When performed as chronicle history, however – which most often means when linked with the *Henry VI* plays – *Richard III* can become a play with a memory, full of characters, many of them women, whose stories we know, and full of points of independent interest that rupture the play's self-containment and pressure expectations established by four hundred years of solo performance. Within the tetralogy, moreover, "Margaret emerges as a gigantic character, and her appearance to curse again in *Richard III* is made a hundredfold more comprehensible with the knowledge of her place in the forerunning plays" (Jackson 1953: 50).

Although the plays of the tetralogy were presumably not performed together in Shakespeare's lifetime, and may not have been written as a series, there is enough internal evidence to suggest that they functioned for audiences as a kind of serial. But the original performances are unrecoverable, and the performance history of the tetralogy as a linked group is limited to four professional productions in Britain in the past four decades, by Peter Hall and John Barton at the RSC in 1963–4, Michael Bogdanov and the English Shakespeare Company (ESC) in 1987–9, Adrian Noble at the RSC in 1988–9, and Michael Boyd at the RSC in 2000–1.[7]

Hunter notes that to perform the plays of the tetralogy "in sequence, with the same actors playing the major roles" (Hunter 1978: 91), is an interpretative decision, but the impact of that decision is unclear. For Hunter, who is inclined to celebrate "the individual plays' centrifugal tendencies" (p. 93), to do so is questionable, because it involves "giving depth and continuity to the depiction of the same characters in play after play . . . creat[ing] a forward trajectory and momentum which the plays do not necessarily require" (pp. 92–3). But it also creates a retrospective sense of memory, gendered female, that contests the more exclusionary history that *Richard III* seems to produce before our eyes. And while the creation of continuities can create individual "star" parts and privilege "character" over role, it can also produce the monumentally resistant female role of Margaret, the only character to appear in all four plays, and the best role for women in Shakespeare. The same practice can also produce, through extended rehearsal periods and extensive doubling, a disjunction between actor and role and a democratic "company feel" that works against heroic individualism and the privileging of stars.

For many who wish to celebrate these plays as nation-forging epics, performing them in sequence emphasizes their vast scope and grand design, and invites comparisons with Aeschylus and Wagner. Others, suspicious of master narratives, view the plays' design as serial, like populist television "soaps" (gendered female), where characters central to one action disappear for an extended time before returning to perform secondary roles in different episodes. For them the imposition of grand designs is artificial, and militates against the productively disruptive quality of the plays' narrative fissures, intertexts, and voices from the margins. Theatrical productions of the tetralogy tend to be more complicated, then, in terms of their representational politics, than those of the individual plays. They can work towards containment, subsuming the discontinuities of the individual plays within a larger closure, but they can also work serially to "substitute indeterminacy and continuity for closure" (Hodgdon 1991: 10), and with their modes of production (of theatre and of history) on display they can resist effacing the inconsistencies of historical change and cultural memory-making within the confines of metaphor, self-contained action, or official history. Inventing new forms and structures of rehearsal and presentation, the plays performed as a series can be disruptive at the level of political unconscious, where their interventionist potential can play itself out in disarticulations of various kinds of authorial, textual, imperial, and patriarchal authority.

In 1963–4 Peter Hall and John Barton produced *The Wars of the Roses* for the RSC, the first tetralogy condensed, rewritten, and presented as a trilogy. Barton cut over 6,000 lines and wrote or borrowed some 1,400. The revisions clarified the action, reduced digressions, increased continuity, and imposed "greater reflectiveness on the characters" (Burns 2000: 311). The result was transhistorical epic – "symphonic," according to Ronald Knowles, where the Shakespeare scripts are "polyphonic" (Knowles 1999: 16). Lines were moved from play to play and character to character, the action was restructured, rearranged, and telescoped, linking passages were added, and the resulting three plays were renamed after their three kings: *Henry VI*, *Edward IV*, and *Richard III*. The first built towards the deaths of Gloucester, Suffolk, and Beaufort, ending with Henry's vow to govern better; the second focused on the Yorkists and ended with Edward's call for music; and the third maintained its overall shape but heavily cut the women's roles. All three were acted in a bleak medieval world of chain-mail, iron, and armor.

The production was self-consciously the product of its time, reflecting "what we found meaningful in the 1960s in Shakespeare's view of history" (Barton and Hall 1970: ix), "respond[ing] to the way the youth of the 1960s questioned authority" (Knowles 1999: 16), and participating in a 1960s search for "relevance." What it responded to most directly, however, was a curious conflation of E. M. W. Tillyard's "Elizabethan World Picture," Jan Kott's "Grand Mechanism" of history, and Peter Brook's "Theatre of Cruelty" experiments with the work of Antonin Artaud.[8] The

Brook/Artaud influence of "radical" experimental theatre led to a ritualistic style of performance designed to confront suffering directly by staging the immediacy of the theatrical event itself rather than the mimetic (re)presentation of life. Under this influence the *Wars* shocked audiences out of any complacency they may have had about Shakespeare at Stratford. The Artaud influence also sorted well with Kott's bleak articulation of history in *Shakespeare Our Contemporary*, which Hall had read in proof *en route* to rehearsals. In Kott's view, twentieth-century Europe had prepared audiences to understand an Elizabethan conception of history as unending bloody struggle, in which men exercise their will to dominate, successively climbing "the staircase of power" while "the implacable roller of history crushes everybody and everything" (Kott 1967: 39). Kott's "staircase of power" must have resonated for Hall with Tillyard's "great chain of being," which he had encountered when he and Barton were students together at postwar Cambridge. Hall unquestioningly accepted Tillyard's wartime views about the absolute need for hierarchical order: "All Shakespeare's thinking," he argues, "religious, political, or moral, is based on a complete acceptance of this concept of order. There is a just proportion in all things: man is above beast, king is above man, and God above the king . . . Revolution, whether in the individual's temperament, in the family, or in the state or the heavens, destroys the order and leads to destructive anarchy" (Barton and Hall 1970: x). These influences shaped a theatrically thrilling but politically troubling production whose effects still linger in "radical" Shakespearean stagings where "Brechtian" is recast as an aesthetic, Shakespeare becomes "our contemporary," and the conservative comforts of catharsis are replaced by existential despair. Alan Sinfield has argued that what may be political critique in Kott is legible in the Hall–Barton *Wars* only as politically disabling commentary on the universal "human condition" (Sinfield 1985: 161).

The 1963–4 production may have failed to answer Sinfield's (1985) plea for "treating Shakespeare as a historical phenomenon, implicated in values which are not ours but which can in production . . . become contestable" (p. 179), but it did represent *itself* as historical and provisional, and it may have moved some distance towards Sinfield's other stated goal: to "take aspects of the plays and reconstitute them explicitly so that they become the vehicle of other values" (ibid). It did present a radical break from the performance tradition represented only six years earlier by Seale at the Old Vic, introducing a commitment to political commentary, a "dry, cool, and intellectual" style of verse speaking that "depended on a rational appraisal of the material" (Beauman 1982: 268), and, through the designs of John Bury, who had recently come to the RSC from Joan Littlewood's radical Stratford East, a "Brechtian style of Shakespeare production" (p. 238). The *Wars* also managed, in Hall's terms, to "disturb its audiences" at Stratford (Addenbrooke 1974: 66), accustomed until then to a natural alliance between Shakespeare and bourgeois conservatism, and contributed to a theatrical and social paradigm shift that culminated in the events of 1968. Finally, it modeled – by reviving eighteenth-century practices of radically rewriting Shakespeare – a productive method of disarticulation and rearticulation: after this, "faithfulness" to the text and "legitimacy" of interpretation might no longer be the taken-for-granted measures of cultural value. Perhaps it did, after all, make English history, Shakespeare's values, and our own "contestable."

The response of critics and audiences certainly suggests contestation, and nowhere more so than over its representation of gender. On the one hand, the production has been celebrated for creating "the fully-fledged tetralogical character of Margaret" (Potter 1988: 12). Peggy Ashcroft's Margaret was played with a French accent and was legibly "other" to this English male enterprise – the war and *The Wars* – and critics unanimously praised her "quite marvellous, fearsome performance" (Hope-Wallace 1964). Her first entrance was bolstered by an interpolated offstage line, "I'll not go with thee. Know'st thou not who I am?," and her father was cut from the subsequent wooing scene with Suffolk, leaving her "stronger and more autonomous" from the outset (Potter 1988: 107). She took her place, too, at the council table and assumed the role of protagonist in *Edward IV*, sitting to Henry's right and appropriating his "Lords, take your places." Her strongest moments were at the murder of York, where "her portrayal of weakness in cruelty, helplessness in victory" (Brown 1965: 152) prepared audiences for a Margaret in *Richard III* who "drew strength from her continuing role in the sequence" (Lull 1999: 34) and who established herself firmly as the voice of memories the erasure of which the rest of the play enacted and inscribed as the most brutal necessity of the Grand Mechanism – of history and history writing. The power of Ashcroft's Margaret as the voice of othered memory, however, rested very much in the performative work of the actor, which the gender politics of the rest of the production tended to contain within the shaping of patriarchal historical narrative. In spite of their respect for the actor, reviewers' descriptions of Margaret were replete with othering characterizations and misogynist references to "female cunning, vituperation, and violence" (Shulman 1963). One traced her growth from "sub-deb, sub-bitch" to "bedraggled crone with glittering eye," "battle axe" and "gorgon" (Hope-Wallace 1964). And of course the women's parts in *Richard III* were severely cut, "thereby emphasizing untempered male aggression and nihilism" (Lull 1999: 34) and leaving Margaret's a solo voice.[9]

What little sympathy there was for the commoners within the production's great chain of being derived from the fact that "the great ones, almost to a man, are arrogant, savage, and fickle: and so, aping them, are the common people" (Tynan 1963). As this suggests, the rebellion was presented for its parallels with "the main plot," and its placement between a council scene pieced together from *3 Henry VI* 4.4 and an invented exchange about Margaret and the Cliffords framed it within the voices of the rulers (Hodgdon 1991: 94). The rupture effected by the rebellion was effectively contained as thematic analogy rather than history-from-below: the voices of the people, like those of the women, remained unheard.

The three parts of Adrian Noble's *Plantagenets* in 1988–9, adapted by Noble with playwright Charles Wood, consisted of *Henry VI* (compressing material from *1 Henry VI* into the first act and ending with Beaufort's death); *The Rise of Edward IV* (opening with the Cade rebellion and proceeding to the end of *3 Henry VI*); and *Richard III: His Death*, trimmed to reflect the eschatological focus suggested by the title. Noble and Wood did not engage in major rewriting, but like Barton's their revisions clarified the action, reduced its digressions, and strengthened its continuities. The result, however, was less epic than pageant, a pictorially splendid medieval costume parade across the late 1980s stage.

Noble's production was oddly introduced by a "marvellous essay about power and the manipulation of history" by Alan Sinfield that the reviewer from *City Limits* wished the director had read (Gardner 1988). For the production itself was under-theorized, "comparatively apolitical" in conception (Burns 2000: 317), but irretrievably conservative in impact. In their introduction to the published script, Noble and Wood articulate no conceptual position, but argue the "clear narrative convenience of reducing the number of protagonists . . . the dramatic advantages of shape and focus . . . [and] the need to simplify the actuality of politics . . . to enhance and illuminate the dramatic stature of an individual" (Noble 1989: viii). They express no awareness that such clarity, simplicity, unified shape and narrative focus are themselves ideologically coded. In most respects Noble's production was otherwise diametrically opposed to that of Hall and Barton, perhaps most obviously in its ornate style and its eschewing of contemporary relevance. It was easily the most theatrically, aesthetically, and politically conservative staging of the tetralogy to date. As Charles Osborne (1988) wrote, approvingly,

> Shakespeare's concern for social order based on submission to a just, or even an unjust, authority is allowed to make its uncomfortable points without impeding the narrative flow of the plays. His chauvinistic view of Joan of Arc is not softened, nor is any attempt made to disguise his scornful attitude to the lower classes.

In fact, Noble betrays (and attributes to Shakespeare) neo-conservative sentiments when he characterizes the Cade sequences of *2 Henry VI* as "a Peronist rebellion": what the rebels really want is "strong government and a revival of national pride" (Noble 1989: 9). Perhaps as a consequence of this view Noble cut the petitioner who complains about Suffolk's enclosure of common lands and the appropriation of his own house, wife, and land by the Cardinal's man. He also cut the Cade scenes "so severely . . . that there was no time for the rebels' claims to be understood by the audience" (Hattaway 1991: 59).

The production was more sensitive to gender than class. Penny Downie's Margaret was reviewed as "the lynchpin of this saga" (Robertson 1988), and Julia Ford's Joan was equally well received. The roles were linked by a rearrangement that placed Margaret's first entrance after Joan's death, showing "Margaret in a sense taking over where Joan left off, a new Frenchwoman to scourge the English" (Downie 1993: 20). But these performances seem less the result of analysis by the director than character work by actors left to their own devices. Downie attributes to Noble an intention "to present the sense of English xenophobia," and a consequent awareness on her own part of Margaret's "foreignness . . . her not-quite belonging" (p. 115), but she seems to have been as isolated in rehearsals as Margaret is in the plays: "as our preparation time went on I found myself increasingly alone with the part, discovering many things between me and the page," and creating a fundamentally naturalistic character out of her own Stanislavskian devices (p. 115). The result included some powerful moments featuring strong women, but these came within a context that was only fitfully productive in shifting the gendered economies of the scripts. Joan, for example, was cut from the scene between Lucy and the French following the death of Talbot, allowing it to focus exclusively on male honor. But the capture and death that followed allowed her a dignity that the Shakespeare script denies. Joan "makes a dignified assertion of her chastity," according to Dominique Goy-Blanquet (1988), one of the production's few women reviewers,

> after and not before her vain attempt to save herself by pretending she is pregnant. Her denial of her humble father is tactfully omitted, and she dies under a halo of light which gives the lie to the British soldiers' coarse insults.

Those insults included sexual abuse and black religious parody, and her burning flesh served as a visual and olfactory backdrop to the diplomatic negotiations for peace (and Henry's marriage). As Barbara Hodgdon notes, Joan and Margaret were marked here as pawns of English empire, and when at the end of the act "a huge Cross of St. George descend[ed] to obscure Joan's figure . . . still on the scaffold,"

> English might and myth erase all signs of the dangerous female presence, first by demonizing her as a spectacle that shapes the war's conclusion, then by masking that sight with a seal of Christian approval. (Hodgdon 1991: 92)

The production took advantage of the opportunity offered by doing the plays in sequence to allow lived memory, gendered female, to speak in the face of the male English History that *Richard III* is (re)writing before its audiences' eyes. Downie describes how, "when [Margaret] walks on in the third scene . . . it is as if she brings with her all the memories of everybody's blackest deeds in the battles of the past" (Downie 1993: 134), and many reviewers praised the power of the chorus-of-women scenes, which suffered from significant cuts but were allowed to establish a strong community of grieving women. Within the context of the production's style of presentation, however, the scenes read simply as acknowledgments of the necessary cost of closure, reifying the female and the foreign as the tragic price of peace. For from the outset, when troops of English soldiers emerged from the grave of Henry V as "the survival of his spirit" (Burns 2000: 318), *The Plantagenets*, "staying in a sumptuously realized mediaeval period" (Taylor 1988), framed itself as a pageantic celebration of The English Nation. As Michael Ratcliffe (1988) argued of a production in which "rich heraldry returns to the Histories on the main Stratford stage of the RSC, the tone . . . surprisingly, is not political but aesthetic. The disturbing resonances of history are not sounded." Reviewers approvingly described the revival of high-culture verse-speaking in set speeches that were both delivered (Downie 1993:

135) and received (with applause) "as if they were great arias in an opera" (Tinker 1988). "The overall effect is operatic in the best way," gushed Russell Jackson, "tableaux, ensembles, arias, spectacle. *The Plantagenets* seems designed to satisfy the British theatre-goer's appetite for Wagner" (Jackson 1990: 83). The show ended "on a heartening major chord" (Taylor 1988): "Bloody civil war and political opportunism ravage the land. But God's guiding hand is leading England to a haven of Tudor calm and prosperity, and at the close of *Richard III* the cycle ends with a great affirmative Amen" (Edwards 1988).

But not everyone was celebrating. Partly because of its high ticket prices and conspicuous expenditure Lois Potter (1990: 180) notes the impact of its "expensive decor," and Russell Jackson (1990: 83) that refitting the Barbican stage for its transfer to London cost £50,000, the production, implicitly situated "within the protective provinces of high culture," reinforced

> the assumption that this theatrical commodity was aimed at a particular audience for whom economic considerations (and the class distinctions they reassert) disappear, subsumed within visions of "Shakespeare's" larger cultural authority. Such a move not only eliminates critique from a sphere of potential socio-political engagement but enables the critical community to locate "Shakespeare speaking" within an aesthetic realm, a strategy that assumes that "pure" or "classic" theatre does not constitute a political arena. (Hodgdon 1991: 98)

This high-culture positioning was coupled with xenophobic Englishness ("England itself singing the clear tunes of its history" (Edmonds 1988)); a reverence for "Shakespeare" ("he's the ruler against which we measure ourselves," said Noble (Berry 1989: 174)); and a conservative nostalgia for the colorful and uncontestable history of the land. What Noble's *Plantagenets* achieved was a cathartic release from responsibility for political action, produced through "a blood purge of pestilent elements ending in . . . optimism" (Ratcliffe 1988). "No wonder," wrote Lyn Gardner (1988), "that after nine hours the audience gave Henry VII such a welcome – you could tell by his haircut that this was the sort of chap to make the trains run on time." The critical consensus on this "vast dramatic national anthem of blood and death and restoration" (Morley 1988) seems to have been that, "much to the audience's enjoyment, the production was unashamedly patriotic and heroic" (Hattaway 1990: 54). Received history was affirmed and reproduced for its subjects as (passive) consumers.

The plays of the first tetralogy, again condensed to three, comprised the second part of a touring, seven-play cycle of Shakespeare's histories, *The Wars of the Roses*, directed by Michael Bogdanov for the ESC in 1987–9. Bogdanov newly reshaped and retitled the plays, added some three hundred lines of bridging sequences, and repositioned scenes, in order both to place the plays within the larger context of the ESC *Wars* and draw parallels between the represented action and the contemporary world of Margaret Thatcher – the "home" period for what amounted to an eclectic historical précis of England from the Edwardian opening of the *Henries* through both world wars to the present. The minimalist design accommodated costumes that ranged from frock coats to pin-stripes, medieval armor to camouflage fatigues. Music drew from Mozart and Monteverdi as well as Philip Glass and Louis Armstrong, and all the battle scenes were backed by Byrd's *Mass for Four Voices*. The first play, *Henry VI: The House of Lancaster*, telescoped *1 Henry VI* into one act ending with Joan's death, while the second act ended with Beaufort's death and the Suffolk lynching. *Henry VI: The House of York* opened with York's return from Ireland and the Cade rebellion, moving efficiently to the "son who killed his father, father who killed his son" before the interval, with the second act focusing on the rise of Richard. *Richard III* added only an interpolated cocktail-party prologue reviewing "the story so far,"[10] and was lightly trimmed. Like Hall and Barton's, Bogdanov's structure was epic, but in a more accurately Brechtian sense, though his dynastic retitlings, focusing on noble houses, evoked national myth-making in echoing the house of Atreus.

Located at the opposite end of the political spectrum from *The Plantagenets*, Bogdanov's *Wars* derived from a socialist, anti-centrist perspective and what might loosely be called a postmodernist aesthetic of stylistic collage. It is a sign of its manifest intent, if also one of its areas of compromise, that the same reviewers who hadn't mentioned ticket prices for *The Plantagenets* voiced regret that those who would most enjoy these *Wars* might not be able to afford them (see Hodgdon 1991: 98). Neither Bogdanov nor his work evinces any interest in faithfulness to Shakespeare, nor is his primary goal the interpretation of the classical text. His main focus is on reaching audiences, notably those outside of London, who have neither access to nor interest in the Shakespeare of high culture. His express purpose is to tour clear, comprehensible, and demystified productions that embed language, action, and character within the larger social texts of their own times (Berry 1989: 217–18). He uses modern dress to signal character, clarify class distinctions (p. 218), and point up parallels between fifteenth- and twentieth-century politics (p. 221); he uses accents to indicate regional allegiances and highlight "continuing regional problems" (p. 221); and he tries to ensure that the company and the audience know "how every single character and every single line fits into social and political structures" (p. 224). His *Wars* was less about *presenting* England's History than engaging in the ongoing (re)*making* of history (and "the nation") as part of the larger social project of negotiating cultural memory and value in the present.

Not surprisingly, these interests manifested themselves most clearly in the production's representation of class, which generally demonstrated the producers' "willingness to take the non-noble characters seriously" (Potter 1990: 175): the demeaning contest between Peter the apprentice and his drunken master in *2 Henry VI* was cut, and the three citizens in 2.3 *Richard III*, usually cut, were individually and sympathetically characterized. The Cade rebellion is difficult to stage sympathetically as class struggle, but Bogdanov came to it within an unusual context. The ESC *Wars* started in 1986 with *1* and *2 Henry IV* and *Henry V*, inspired by Bogdanov's noting a parallel between Margaret Thatcher's crusade to the Falklands and Henry IV's advice to "busy giddy minds with foreign quarrels" (see Berry 1989: 221). When the first tetralogy (and *Richard II*) were added, Michael Pennington, who played Henry V in the first round, was cast to play Jack Cade. Outfitted in a sleeveless Union-Jack t-shirt echoing the flag that had earlier draped Henry V's coffin, Pennington's Cade was accompanied by flag-waving followers chanting football-hooligan cheers, as Pistol and company had when they accompanied Pennington's Henry V to Agincourt. This staging did not present analogues to left-wing political activism, but parallels, in the "patriotic" hooliganism of English football fans and the violence of the National Front, with officially sanctioned English thuggery both at Agincourt and in the Falklands. Lois Potter notes the dangers in such representations of working-class violence, quoting Isobel Armstrong's observation that "the brutalization which is the result of oppression can actually appear to justify the ruthless power exercised to control it" (Potter 1990: 80). But Armstrong herself, questioning "how far it is ever possible to control the way you are interpreted" (and accepting a conundrum that always faces dialogical representation), found in Bogdanov's processually "work[ing] out of [his] politics through theatre" evidence "that it is possible to make a coherent critique through Shakesperean production" (Armstrong 1989: 12).[11] The production succeeded, she argues, by "push[ing] the plays toward radical critique" through "foregrounding their deconstructive moments" – and, I would add, engaging in radical disarticulations of the Shakespearean script. This is perhaps nowhere more true than in the representation of the intersection of class, gender, and the "other" in and around the role of La Pucelle.

This Joan was a sturdy peasant girl with a rural accent who first entered in a class-coded workman's cap and breeches. Her later comment on the "silly stately style" of the tribute to Talbot not only marked her as alien to English "honour," it also marked a class divide. She did not condemn her country, and she was spared the denial of her father and betrayal of her class. But the sequences surrounding Joan involved more than the sympathetic representation of a frequently demonized role. As Hodgdon (1991) argues, Bogdanov's *House of Lancaster* "foreground[ed] the way in which males – subjects as well as rulers – contain the threats of female power by expressing their own power through women" (p. 90). In the wake of Joan's undercutting the "silly" heraldic style, a peasant woman ran across the stage, terrified, with a group of leering soldiers in pursuit. They forced her roughly off as one undid his trousers. "It is this female figure," says Hodgdon, "rather than Joan, whom Margaret replaces, and her ensuing encounter with Suffolk reprises just such a rape" (p. 90). It also enacted, with Suffolk's sword held to Margaret's throat as he bargained with her father, a deal between two men over the body of a woman.

Just after Suffolk announces, 'But I will rule both her, the King, and realm,' the raped woman, her clothes half torn away, stumbles onto the stage; exiting, Suffolk passes her without a second glance.

    Strafing continues as Joan enters . . . she kneels, spotlit, on the white-carpeted stage, asking her spirits for signs. Earlier . . . Andean flute music suggested the spoken sign of that spiritual link; here the only sound is an occasional burst of gunfire punctuating the silence. As Joan crawls slowly forward, York appears with two bereted commandos: one carries a red gasoline can, the other an automobile tire. Although her father is absent, she speaks her genealogy as though insisting on her own history, curses York, and is finally captured . . . (ibid: 91)

The negotiated peace that follows was backed – and upstaged – by Joan's hideous "necklacing" and the return of the Andean music. Joan's voice and spoken history, and by extension all voices oppressed, silenced, othered, or appropriated by power, imperialism, and official history, then as now, were oddly privileged, and this first act's final image haunted the production throughout.

But gender analysis flagged after Joan's death, and the representation of Margaret was the production's weakest point, as Bogdanov fell into the trap of historical analogy, unable to resist casting and coiffing Shakespeare's iron lady to resemble the contemporary Margaret, effacing her foreignness and leaving no room for feminism. Where Penny Downie's Margaret had functioned as the counter-voice of memory to implacable history, June Watson's, her "old khaki uniform absurdly covered with medals, showed her unwillingness to forget the past and her inability to learn from it" (Potter 1990: 173). Hers was not the strong central character performed by Ashcroft, and her presence troubled the plays' gender economies no more than the later Margaret troubled those of British parliament. In *Richard III* the interpolated prologue set the tone. Elizabeth was present only with Edward, as "HIS QUEEN" (Bogdanov and Pennington 1990: 297); the rest of the women appeared under the heading, "THE LADIES IN MOURNING":

MARGARET, mourning her son and her late husband, King Henry VI.
LADY ANNE, mourning her late husband and her father-in-law, the late king.
THE DUCHESS OF YORK, mourning everybody. (ibid: 298–9)

The cultural work performed by the ESC *Wars*, however, was most effective at the level of structure and style, where its major features were (1) an interrogative dramatic form that resisted closure and reflected a dialectical sense of history as the ongoing project of the present rather than stable record of the past; (2) a dialogical representation of human, political, and dramatic subjectivity as socially constructed "role" rather than psychologically constituted "character"; and (3) a populist and pluralist aesthetic and intellectual sensibility that resisted the seamless presentation of historical period as either coherent "style" or coherent "worldview." Reviewers stressed the production's soap-opera structure and pop-culture intertexts. The same reviewers often found the characters shallow, as though the actors were demonstrating rather than inhabiting their roles, as indeed they were – playing social *gests* rather than psychological studies. What these reviewers seem to be marking is the *Wars'* shifting of Shakespearean production into the realm of postmodernity, where everything is contestable, the icons of "our culture" are dislodged, and the originary authority of "the work of art" is undermined by the proliferation of simulacra. Lois Potter struggles with issues of form, performance style, and politics in the production, but finally gives up on any new-critical "search for patterning" or for a monologic political "message." She determines that what was most significant was "the production's . . . power to shock . . . Shakespeare's words are normally the object of so much reverence that any obvious alteration of them – or any comic juxtaposition of Elizabethan English and modern situations – can seem like an attack on god" (Potter 1990: 180–1). But while Bogdanov's *Wars* may have been irreverent in its disarticulations of "the Bard," its eclecticism eschewed postmodernism's lack of historicity, embracing its rejection of master narratives while insisting on legible historical and social difference (see Hodgdon 1991: 89), and on historicizing the present moment of production.[12]

Finally, many found the trilogy structure itself dissatisfying, expressing disappointment at the lack of formal closure when *Richard III* turned unexpectedly comic, more "the reverse of the trend that we see in 'Henry VI'" than its cathartic conclusion (Johnson 1989). For the show staged two endings. After a ghostly reprise of Richard's murders on the eve of Bosworth Field, Bogdanov cleared the space of everything but smoke, searchlights, and gunfire. When the lights came up the scene had reverted from camouflage fatigues to medieval armor, black for Richard, gold for Richmond, and they battled with broadswords. Nasty and brutish rather than heroically pictorial, the fight ended when Richmond thrust his sword into Richard's neck to the final, heraldic strains of Samuel Barber's "Adagio for Strings," and the stage went black. But only for a moment. When the lights came up it was on a contemporary television studio. Richmond entered in a business suit, greeted his family (carefully arranged as a backdrop), and after a make-up adjustment and a round of palm-pressing delivered his state of the nation address – "England hath long been mad, and scarred herself" – to a theatre audience watching on monitors. At the end, the national anthem swelled as the lights faded and the three screens flickered with Richmond's frozen image. As Hodgdon argues,

> If the first ending simultaneously celebrates and deflates the precise moment of power's transfer through contradictory tensions between image and sound . . . the second reverses that process so that the commodified image of the ruler comments on the play's last words. Replicated three times, that multiple representation constitutes the new order's uninterrupted, unitary discourse about itself . . . What Bogdanov's transformations make possible is less a deformation of Shakespeare's play than a contemporary authentication of its cultural function that foregrounds its own production processes. His *Richard III* translates the Elizabethan text of power to celebrate not just this particular theatrical event but those occurring elsewhere in the social text – on every occasion where the representation of power becomes an image produced and re-produced for an audience of (subjected) spectators. (Hodgdon 1991: 125–6)

In 2000–1 Michael Boyd staged the full tetralogy, lightly cut and framed as part of another RSC project, *This England*, which mounted all of Shakespeare's history plays in different venues with different directors and casts for each play or group of plays.

Boyd resisted the temptation to restructure, rewrite, or impose a monological concept, but like the Hall–Barton *Wars* his production was played out on a bleak and bloody metallic set and outfitted in spare medieval costumes. Although in interviews Boyd located the plays within the contemporary contexts of Israel, Palestine, Yugoslavia, and Northern Ireland (Remen-Wait and Johnson 2001: 20), the production worked less through contemporary reference than a non-iconic representational economy of open signs (loosely emblematic feathers, rocks, and ladders), an interdisciplinary performance style, and a fluid use of space. On and around the long thrust of the Swan Theatre, the RSC's 500-seat "Elizabethan-style" venue in Stratford, these productions structured a dialogic space that engaged audiences more actively in the process of meaning-making than had previous productions confined within modernist spaces or framed by proscenium-arch pictorialism.[13] The stage floor became "an irregular oblong" (Billington 2000), grounded at one end by an enormous set of brazen gates, with seven entrances at ground level, six of which were shared with the audience. The contact was still closer at balcony level, where actors appeared to interrupt or observe the action from almost anywhere. The heavens provided still more entrances, as actors flew in on ropes and ladders, were hoisted out on hooks, or descended by trapeze. Actors' bodies, including bodies in motion, were very much a part of the non-iconic, open design of the representational economy. In fact, in lieu of a unitary conceptual frame we were offered a presentational company style and a mode of engagement – a sense of complicity rather than consumerist reception – that seemed indebted to Boyd's work on small-scale political theatre at Glasgow's Tron Theatre and the influence of politicized, movement-based companies such as London's Cheek by Jowl and Théâtre de Complicité. Over a 17-week rehearsal period for the *Henries* that included rope classes and workshops on ritual, the creative team collaborated to develop a design context, visual and aural, that drew eclectically on different performance disciplines and resisted a logocentric focus on text. Movement director Liz Rankin worked to develop "an expressionistic style" for the battle scenes using ropes and ladders, creating "a sense of disintegration of order that's physical, literal, hierarchical" (Remen-Wait and Johnson 2001: 26). Working with an aerial artist in the cast she drew on circus imagery and skills, including rope climbing and trapeze, and in combination with *carnaval*-inspired rhythms by composer Jimmy Jones produced an underlying sense of the inverted populist world of Bakhtinian carnivalesque.

This style shaped the production from the outset. Battle scenes, underscored by ominous *samba reggae* rhythms, included "a three-man cartwheeling ladder show at Rouen" (Maddox 2000), and the percussive aerial attack of the Gunner's Boy as human cannonball in *1 Henry VI* 1.4, which left its victim hanging by one leg, realistically bloodied by make-up sleight-of-hand, while a clutch of emblematic red feathers fell. Even severed heads performed variety routines, ventriloquized acts of nodding, kissing, or, in the case of Suffolk's head in Margaret's lap, singing a lament. Nowhere was the style more effective than in the representation of class. The Cade rebellion was a party. The scenes were accompanied by Mexican folk music, and Cade himself descended from the heavens by trapeze. The stage was crowded with seething, tumbling bodies; the atmosphere was infectious. The scenes' brutalities were not softened, but theatricalized, and the eviscerations – a human liver was magically sliced out before our eyes – were brutal, dangerous, and exhilarating: the audience shared in the unruly pleasures of inversion and release.

In addition to the commoners and the audience, the third collective represented was the company. Like most stagings of the tetralogy, this one drew praise for its ensemble work, but seldom has such work seemed so democratic, energetic, or committed – "the commitment generated," according to associate director Sarah Esdaile, "through creative contribution." Here, the extensive use of doubling involved actors who played star roles one moment turning within seconds to swell a progress or join a mob. Nor was the doubling unrelated to the action. Esdaile talks about "a continuing theme of persona" through the plays, a "theme" enhanced by carefully plotted doubling, not hidden, but revealed. Lois Potter has said that these plays in performance not only employ but are essentially *about* doubling (Potter 1990: 181), and this has never been more true: not only the actors but the characters they played returned as memories to haunt the performance. Indeed, it was often unclear whether an actor was reincarnated in a new role or as the ghost of a previous one, for ghosts and doublings haunted the shows throughout.

The most prominent of these were ghosts of the cycle's most prominent victims: Humphrey, Duke of Gloucester, for example, returned in *2 Henry VI* with echoing footsteps around the periphery of the audience to preside over the death of Beaufort, latching a meat hook to his back and hoisting him to the flies. Gloucester showed up thereafter to ghost the demise of each of the conspirators who had helped him to his grave, and also as Lewis of France to whom Margaret, ironically, appealed for aid. The ghosting was legible, perhaps, as retribution, but above all it signaled the persistence of (dis)embodied memory in the face of "the tyranny of individualism" – a concern that Boyd insists is central to the plays (Remen-Wait and Johnson 2001: 21). Perhaps the most prominent of the revenant doublings, which elaborated on this pattern, was that of the Talbots, father and son, whose hauntings, in full battle gear and sporting their wounds, continued throughout the tetralogy, insisting on the role of memory, but also appropriating for heroic men what in Shakespeare's *Richard III*, at least, is women's memory work. They showed up in *Part 1* as silent witnesses to Joan's capture and death. In *Part 2* they first performed the spirits conjured by Margery Jourdain and then enacted Suffolk's death by Wa(l)ter, fulfilling their own prophecy and revenging the betrayal that led to their deaths. In *Part 3* this dead father and son played the son who had killed his father and the father who had killed his son. Finally, in *Richard III*, old Talbot played the role of Stanley while his son (Sam Troughton, whose father had played Henry V earlier in the season) inherited the role of Richmond.

But the most clearly marked of the doublings was Fiona Bell's. A splendid Joan with a striding gait and Scottish lilt that marked her otherness, she was shadowed throughout by attendant spirits, women dressed in red velvet who echoed all her actions. Her capture and death, conflated, were brutal, though she rose to her defense with some dignity. York bound her to a ladder under the supervision of the Talbot ghosts and her own attendant spirits before slipping his knife beneath her skirt, "proving" her a virgin by the blood on his hand, and committing her to the fire in the pit. Slamming the trap shut as her screams reverberated, he licked his bloody fingers. But seconds later, across the length of the stage, Bell re-entered magically as Margaret, dressed in the same red velvet as Joan's spirits: La Pucelle had lost her accent, but she had gained her revenge, witching her way into the English court. The doubling made thematic sense, of course, but it also made of Bell's a commanding role in the tetralogy, and lent her overwhelming authority in the final play, where she lurked in the peripheries carrying as totemic memory the skeletal remains of Edward, and watched the fulfilment of her curses from the balcony.

But the plays' gender analysis, like that of Bogdanov's *Wars*, was clearest early on. Like much of the production's most effective cultural work, this was effected structurally and stylistically within the given context of history as the story of men's wars. In *Part 1* the stage design, color scheme, and blocking pictured war as a series of brutal penetrations. The dominant structure, the set's hulking metal gates, protruded outward in a semi-circle from upstage like a late medieval chastity belt. It was presided over by a gatekeeper with a ring of keys whose blood-red costume linked him to the women, and who manned the gates throughout, emerging thence to drag or escort corpses from the stage. The cities under siege were mostly French, of course, and the French were unsubtly effeminate; but whatever side attacked whatever city, the inevitable forced entry gendered war and its histories masculine and configured women's bodies as endlessly permeable, the property of men and price of war.

Much was made of the fact that David Oyelowo, playing Henry, was the first person of color to portray an English king at the RSC. With renewed racial tension in England and the National Front winning voter support, it was time a national theatre company portraying English history recast and reconstituted "Englishness." Nor was Henry the only person of color in the company: both king and king-maker were black men, the former bringing "moral strength" to the production (Billington 2000), while the latter, a tall, regal Warwick, brought power and authority. There may have been some anxiety about disrupting in this way the surface of the representation, in that, alone among the cast and eschewing the otherwise-observed principle of doubling, these actors could be identified exclusively with a single character. Neither Henry nor Warwick doubled roles, and Rashan Stone, the production's only other actor of color, playing Clarence, doubled only in small parts. For the most part, however, the production observed comfortably the central tenet of color-blind casting, the optimistic liberal notion that race should and therefore can disappear, and the audience would forget the fact that Clarence alone among the York family is non-white. (They would also, presumably, take as incidental the fact that until *Richard III* Clarence alone among the brothers, like Warwick among their allies, betrays the family.) But for one brief moment the company's three men of color found themselves on stage alone together, when Henry chose Warwick and Clarence as his joint protectorate in *3 Henry VI*. The image was startlingly disruptive to the veneer of the representation and the pretenses of color-blind casting, as three "brothers" were seen to establish allegiances beyond familial brotherhood, and audiences were perhaps confronted with their own attitudes to race and the English nation, onstage and off.

The performative work of the production was effected in part through its process of production and its structures of closure. The danger of "tetralogy thinking" (Hodgdon 1991: 76) – reading the end, and therefore the predetermined shape of the cycle backwards through the action – was tempered by rehearsing *Richard III* in isolation after the other plays had opened. This *Richard* did complete one arc, a sense of flagging carnival that had begun to set in after the Cade rebellion, and it did present a kind of fulfillment, as the ghosts of Richard's victims peopled not only his dreams on the eve of Bosworth Field, but also his earlier coronation and later death. But the production also brought to a head in less comfortable ways the earlier plays' practice of implicating the audience, making them complicit in the action, and insisting on their judgment. *Richard III* opened with Adrian McArdle's campy, "panto" Richard, and a risky new optics. After their involvement in moments of carnival and their imaginative completion of the plays' non-iconic representational economy, the audience found themselves laughing broadly at a McArdle/Richard playing stand-up comic downstage center. Even before speaking he surveyed the audience and stretched his arms – "ta da!" – at which the house went wild. This carried forward into the wooing scene, where laughter spilled over into moments of sexual aggression as Richard shoved Anne violently against the metal gates as part of his "wooing" practice – an act implicitly condoned by an audience who laughed broadly at "was ever woman in this humour wooed?" The laughter carried over, too, into the encounter with Clarence as we watched, on one level of representation, Richard ridding the world, not only of meddling women, but of traitorous people of color – readings made available by Margaret's lurking presence and the revenant wanderings of Henry. The action proceeded to the end-of-act wooing of the "troops of citizens" – here the audience. The scene, again, was very broadly played as the house lights were brought up and the audience watched the theatrical technologies of its manipulation played out. On "Refuse not, mighty lord, this proffered love," Buckingham physically raised the hand of an audience member in approval, and, functioning as cheerleader, urged "us" in one voice to shout "God save Richard, England's worthy king." Richard waved, acknowledging a round of applause (for Richard or McArdle? Buckingham or Boyd?), before the lights faded to the interval.

When the show drew to its customary close, then, it may have been with some uncomfortable understanding of the mechanisms by which the land and stage had been purged – of what, exactly? women? people of color? the French? on whose behalf? – before the happy return of a young and squeaky-clean white male order in the person of Richmond/John Talbot. But after Richmond had crowned himself and the stage was cleared, Richard's body remained. The last of the revenants, he rose to face Oyelowo's Henry as the lights went down.

I began this essay by suggesting that to consider the first tetralogy in performance is to enter contested and contestable terrain; to write against a kind of critical and theatrical history that privileges unities, stabilities, certainties, and star roles; and to address Shakespeare in production, not as a history of the theatrical interpretation of stable, authoritative literary "texts" – as "illustrated official histories" of nation – but as a complex and conflicted record of the contestatory representational terrain of variously constituted performance texts. Whether an individual production suggests repressed anxieties in its attempts to contain the centrifugal tendencies of the plays, as did *The Plantagenets*; treats their instabilities as an opportunity for radical critique, as did the ESC *Wars*, or more monologic intervention, as did those of Hall and Barton; or constructs more complex, self-reflexive processes and representational economies, as did Boyd's production, the first tetralogy in the theatre would seem to render Shakespeare, English history, and the gendered, raced, and classed constitution of English subjectivities the objects of critique, appropriation, and struggle in the ongoing negotiation of national cultural memories.

NOTES

1   I am deeply indebted to Barbara Hodgdon for her extraordinary scholarly generosity in sharing her extensive research and notes with me; to the staff of the Shakespeare Centre Library for their time and help; to Christine Bold, Barbara Hodgdon, Skip Shand, and Carol Rutter for company at and conversation about Michael Boyd's 2001 production; to Carol Rutter for her hospitality; and to Christine Bold for her generous help and always acute insight in reading and commenting on drafts of this chapter.

2   For recent accounts of the controversies around dating, text, and authorship see the *New Cambridge Shakespeare* editions (Hattaway 1990, 1991, 1993; Lull 1999) to which all citations to the plays refer. For a full consideration of "The Shakespearean Tetralogy" see Crane (1985); for a discussion of Quarto versus Folio versions of *2* and *3 Henry VI* see Urkowitz (1988, 1989), and of *Richard III* see Urkowitz (1986). *1 Henry VI* exists only in the 1623 Folio, where it was published (as *The first Part of Henry the Sixt*), with parts two (*The second Part of Henry the Sixt, with the death of the Good Duke Humphrey*) and three (*The third Part of Henry the Sixt, with the death of the Duke of Yorke*) in the section entitled "Histories." The 1594 Quarto of *2 Henry VI* was entitled *The First part of the contention betwixt the two famous Houses of Yorke and Lancaster*; the 1595 Quarto of *3 Henry VI* was called *The true Tragedy of Richard Duke of Yorke, and the death of good Kind Henrie the Sixt, with the whole contention betweene the two Houses Lancaster and Yorke*. *Richard III* was first published in Quarto in 1597 as *The Tragedy of King Richard the third. Containing, His treacherous Plots against his brother Clarence; the pitiefull murther of his innocent nephewes; his tyrannical usurpation: with the whole course of his detested life, and most deserued death*. In Folio it is called *The Tragedy of Richard III* on its title page, but is grouped with the other "Histories," and its running title is *The Life and Death of Richard III*.

3   In addition to those I mention here, *1 Henry VI* was produced in 1994 at the Outdoor Theatre in New York by the American Theatre of Actors; Edmund Kean appeared in Thomas Merivale's adaptation of (mostly) *2 Henry VI* in 1817; Frank Benson produced *2 Henry VI* in Stratford in 1899, and Jerry Turner in Oregon in 1977, with interpolations from the other plays; and Theophilis Cibber and Richard Valpy produced thoroughgoing adaptations of (mostly) *3 Henry VI* in 1723 and 1795, respectively. Charles Kemble's 1795 abridgement of the final play in the tetralogy was not performed.

4   There have also been a number of productions in the US and Canada, including an edited version at the Pasadena Community Playhouse in 1936, a serial production over three years at the

Oregon Shakespearean Festival in 1953–5, single-play conflations at the Great Lakes Shakespeare Festival in 1964 and at Stratford, Ontario in 1980, and a two-play abridgement at Oregon in 1991–2.

5 David Daniell (1979), for example, somewhat obsessively focused on the conjunction of adolescence and sensuousness in "a very young, seductive, and pliant" Margaret (p. 258) in *1 Henry VI*, and seemed unable to consider any of the women's roles in any but erotic terms. He describes "a humanly desirable Margaret, her sensuous adolescent body offer[ing] the third level of eroticism in the production. First Joan, assertive and roughly available; then the Countess, trying to act out the Lady of the Castle, to be won by the Hero. Here in Margaret is slim grace, youth, and knowing, tender sexual promise" (pp. 257–8). The later Margaret prompted sympathy among male reviewers for Henry as "the most spectacularly henpecked husband in English drama" (Cushman 1977).

6 The history of *Richard III* in production is too long and too well documented to rehearse, but see Hankey (1988) and Colley (1992). The best short introduction is in Jowett (2000: 72– 110).

7 The adapted tetralogy was also performed as *The "War" of the Roses* at the New Jersey Shakespeare Festival in 1983. What follows, however, limits itself to analyses of production and reception within a manageable time frame in a single (if divided) nation, excluding performances of the Bogdanov production in Australia, Hong Kong, Japan, Canada, and the US and the Boyd tetralogy in Michigan. Similarly, although the Hall–Barton and Bogdanov productions were taped, and two other television versions of the tetralogy exist (an adaptation directed by Michael Hays in 1960 for Peter Dews's *The Age of Kings*, and Jane Howell's 1982 version for the BBC's complete Shakespeare series), I will limit myself to specifically theatrical technologies of production and reception. The scripts of the Hall–Barton and Adrian Noble versions are both published (see Barton and Hall 1970; Noble 1989). For comparative analysis of the productions' cuts and rearrangements offering more detail than I can provide here see Hunter (1978), Dessen (1993), and Potter (1990). The best theorized analyses of Hall–Barton, Noble, and Bogdanov, as well as the trilogy as produced by Hands, are in Hodgdon (1991).

8 For accounts of the *Wars* in the context of the history of the RSC see Addenbrooke (1974), Beauman (1982), and Sinfield (1985).

9 At various other points, too, Barton's rearrangements had negative effects on the production's gender economy, as in the conflation of the two scenes concerning Henry's marriage at the end of *Henry VI*, where "Margaret's relation to Suffolk as well as to Henry becomes subsumed within a formal – and ideological – coherence that privileges male experience" (Hodgdon 1991: 78). Even Potter's celebration of the production's elevation of Margaret to star status is qualified by his lament at Barton's having curtailed her defiance at her son's death, having "follow[ed] Shakespeare in abandoning her to an offstage exile [in *Edward IV*], her disposition labelled a 'trifle'," and having "allowed [her] to slip away [in *Richard III*] to permit Richmond to step unassisted into his proforma hero's spotlight for the finale" (Potter 1988: 109).

10 The text for this is published in Bogdanov and Pennington (1990: 297–9) and in Jowett (2000: 397–8).

11 Armstrong is discussing the ESC *Henrys* rather than the *Wars*, but the point holds true of both.

12 I am addressing the politics of the production in the UK, but it should be said that the ESC funded its English dates and very English shows with money from Ireland (the Irish Allied Bank) and the colonies (Toronto's then-owners of the Old Vic, Ed and David Mirvish and the revenue from international touring), and took very little into account on their international tour the politics of meaning-making at the point of reception. In fact the project *on tour* can be read as neocolonialist, funding essentially English *Wars* by draining wealth from the colonies.

13 My assessment of the production is based on viewing the three *Henry VI* plays at the Swan in January–February 2001, and the full tetralogy in Ann Arbor, Michigan, in mid-March. I am discussing the Swan performances here because, in addition to the different political and cultural

context in the US generally, the material conditions (including monetary) were quite different at the much larger Power Center auditorium in Ann Arbor (capacity 1,390), with its vast, if somewhat modified, proscenium-style stage. The staging, too, was rearranged there to privilege as pictorial backdrop what at the Swan was shared and contestable space, and the audience contact used throughout seemed considerably more forced and intrusive. The subtitles given to the individual *Henry VI* plays, too, were rendered more mythical and apocalyptic in America: "The War Against France," "England's Fall and the Chaos" became "The War," "The Fall," and "The Chaos," *tout court*.

REFERENCES AND FURTHER READING

Addenbrooke, D. (1974). *The Royal Shakespeare Company: The Peter Hall Years*. London: Kimber.

Anon. (1952). King Henry VI – Part III. *The Times*, July 22.

Anon. (1978). *Sunday Times*, April 24.

Armstrong, I. (1989). Thatcher's Shakespeare? *Textual Practice*, 3, 1–14.

Barber, J. (1977). Stratford Looks at England Divided. *Daily Telegraph*, July 14.

Barton, J. with Hall, P. (1970). *The Wars of the Roses*. London: BBC.

Beauman, S. (1982). *The Royal Shakespeare Company: A History of Ten Decades*. Oxford: Oxford University Press.

Berry, R. (1989). *On Directing Shakespeare*. London: Hamish Hamilton.

Billington, M. (2000). When Three Become One. *Guardian*, December 16.

Bogdanov, M. and Pennington, M. (1990). *The English Shakespeare Company: The Story of "The Wars of the Roses" 1986–1989*. London: Nick Hern.

Brook, P. (1968). *The Empty Space*. Harmondsworth: Penguin Books.

Brown, J. R. (1965). Three Kinds of Shakespeare: 1964 Productions at London, Stratford-upon-Avon and Edinburgh. *Shakespeare Survey*, 18, 147–55.

Burns, E. (ed.) (2000). *King Henry VI Part 1*. New Arden Shakespeare, 3rd series. London: Tomson.

Colley, S. (1992). *Richard's Himself Again*. New York: Greenwood.

Crane, M. T. (1985). The Shakespearean Tetralogy. *Shakespeare Quarterly*, 36, 282–99.

Cushman, R. (1977). Thrones, Coffins and Roses. *Observer Review*, July 17.

Daniell, D. (1979). Opening Up the Text: Shakespeare's *Henry VI* Plays in Performance. In J. Redmond (ed.) *Themes in Drama 1: Drama and Society*. Cambridge: Cambridge University Press, 247–77.

Dessen, A. C. (1993). Stagecraft and Imagery in Shakespeare's *Henry VI*. *Yearbook of English Studies*, 65–79.

Downie, P. (1993). Queen Margaret in *Henry VI* and *Richard III*. In R. Jackson and R. Smallwood (eds.) *Players of Shakespeare 3: Further Essays in Shakespearian Performance by Players with the Royal Shakespeare Company*. Cambridge: Cambridge University Press.

Edmonds, R. (1988). A Haunting, Horrifying Marathon. *Birmingham Evening Mail*, October 24.

Edwards, C. (1988). Review of *The Plantagenets*, dir. Adrian Noble. *Spectator*, November 5.

Esdaile, S. (2001). Panel discussion. Rackham Auditorium, Ann Arbor, Michigan, March 18.

Gardner, L. (1988). Review of *The Plantagenets*, dir. Adrian Noble. *City Limits*, November 10.

Goy-Blanquet, D. (1988). Strange, Eventful Histories. *Times Literary Supplement*, November 4–10, 1229.

Hall, P. and Barton, J. (1970). *The Wars of the Roses*. London: BBC.

Hankey, J. (1988). *Plays in Performance: Richard III*, 2nd edn. Bristol: Bristol Classical Press.

Hattaway, M. (ed.) (1990). *The First Part of King Henry VI*. New Cambridge Shakespeare. Cambridge: Cambridge University Press.

——(ed.) (1991). *The Second Part of King Henry VI*. New Cambridge Shakespeare. Cambridge: Cambridge University Press.

——(ed.) (1993). *The Third Part of King Henry VI*. New Cambridge Shakespeare. Cambridge: Cambridge University Press.

Hobson, H. (1952). Salute to Genius. *Sunday Times*, July 27.

Hodgdon, B. (1991). *The End Crowns All: Closure and Contradiction in Shakespeare's History*. Princeton, NJ: Princeton University Press.

Holland, P. (1994). In a World With No Use for Goodness. *Times Literary Supplement*, August 26–30, 3.

Hope-Wallace, P. (1964). Wars of the Roses. *Guardian*, January 13.

Hunter, G. K. (1978). The Royal Shakespeare Company plays "Henry VI." *Renaissance Drama*, n.s. 9, 91–108.

Isaacs, D. (1977). Lofty Politics . . . *Coventry Evening Telegraph*, July 14.

Jackson, B. (1953). On Producing *Henry VI*. *Shakespeare Survey*, 5, 49–52.

Jackson, R. (1990). Shakespeare Production in the British Theatre: Too Much of a Good Thing? In *Shakespeare et La Guerre*. Paris: Les Belles Lettres, 79–88.

Johnson, B. (1989). Review of *The Wars of the Roses*, dir. Michael Bogdanov. *Daily Telegraph*, February 18.

Jowett, J. (ed.) (2000). *The Tragedy of King Richard III*. The Oxford Shakespeare. Oxford: Oxford University Press.

Kemp, T. C. (1954). Acting Shakespeare: Modern Tendencies in Playing and Production with Special Reference to Some Recent Productions. *Shakespeare Survey*, 7, 121–7.

Keown, E. (1952). *King Henry the Sixth, Part Three*. *Punch*, August 6.

Knowles, R. (ed.) (1999). *King Henry VI, Part 2*. The Arden Shakespeare, 3rd series. Walton-on-Thames: Thomas Nelson.

Kott, J. (1967). *Shakespeare Our Contemporary*. London: Methuen.

Lull, J. (ed.) (1999). *King Richard III*. New Cambridge Shakespeare. Cambridge: Cambridge University Press.

Maddox, D. (2000). A Truimphant, Turbulent Trilogy. *Stratford-upon-Avon Herald*, December 21.

Martin, R. (2000). "A Woman's generall: what should we feare?": Queen Margaret Thatcherized in Recent Productions of *2 Henry VI*. In E. J. Esche (ed.) *Shakespeare and his Contemporaries in Performance*. Aldershot: Ashgate, 321–38.

Morley, S. (1988). Review of *The Plantagenets*, dir. Adrian Noble. *Punch*, November 4.

Nightingale, B. (1977). A King in Mind. *New Statesman*, July 22.

Noble, A. (1989). *The Plantagenets*. London: BBC.

Osborne, C. (1988). Review of *The Plantagenets*, dir. Adrian Noble. *Daily Telegraph*, October 24.

Potter, L. (1990). Recycling the Early Histories: "The Wars of the Roses" and "The Plantagenets". *Shakespeare Survey*, 43, 171–81.

Potter, R. (1988). The Rediscovery of Queen Margaret: "The Wars of the Roses", 1963. *New Theatre Quarterly*, 4, 105–19.

Ratcliffe, M. (1988). Review of *The Plantagenets*, dir. Adrian Noble. *Observer*, October 20.

Remen-Wait, K. and Johnson, B. (ed.) (2001). *Shakespeare's Histories*. Ann Arbor: University of Michigan Press.

Robertson, A. (1988). Review of *The Plantagenets*, dir. Adrian Noble. *Time Out*, October 26.

"S" (1906). Shakespeare Memorial Performances at Stratford. *The Athenaeum*, 4098, May 12, 587–8.

Shulman, M. (1963). A Shakespeare Marathon Brimful with Excitement. *Evening Standard*, July 18.

Sinfield, A. (1985). Royal Shakespeare: Theatre and the Making of Ideology. In J. Dollimore and A. Sinfield (eds.) *Political Shakespeare: New Essays in Cultural Materialism*. Ithaca, NY: Cornell University Press, 158–81.

Swander, H. (1978). The Rediscovery of *Henry VI*. *Shakespeare Quarterly*, 29, 146–63.

Taylor, P. (1988). Review of *The Plantagenets*, dir. Adrian Noble. *Independent*, October 24.

Tinker, J. (1988). Review of *The Plantagenets*, dir. Adrian Noble. *Daily Mail*, October 24.

Tynan, K. (1963). Gang War in Armour. *Observer Weekend Review*, July 21.

Urkowitz, S. (1986). Reconsidering the Relationship of Quarto to Folio Texts of *Richard III*. *English Literary Renaissance*, 16, 442–6.

——(1988). "If I mistake in these foundations Which I build upon": Peter Alexander's Textual Analysis of *Henry VI*, Parts 2 and 3. *English Literary Renaissance*, 18, 246–9.

——(1989). Rewriting Shakespeare?/Shakespeare Rewriting? Unpublished paper, Shakespeare Association of America.

Wardle, I. (1977). Henry VI, Part II. *The Times*, July 14.

Warren, R. (1978). Comedies and Histories at Two Stratfords, 1977. *Shakespeare Survey*, 31, 141–53.

Williamson, A. (1957). *Old Vic Drama 2: 1947–1957*. London: Rockliff.

Young, B. A. (1977). Henry VI part III. *Financial Times*, July 15.

13

The Second Tetralogy: Performance as Interpretation

Lois Potter

Before the History Cycles

Non-performance, like performance, is a form of interpretation. While the group of plays dealing with Richard II, Henry IV, and Henry V never dropped out of the repertory so completely as the Henry VI plays, they suffered for much of the eighteenth and nineteenth centuries from the theatre's focus on leading roles and star actors. The absence of good roles for women, especially when Mistress Quickly and Doll Tearsheet were expurgated into insignificance, also worked against them. The one genuinely successful history play, *Richard III* – in Colley Cibber's adaptation (1700), which held the stage for the next two centuries – was as destructive to the other plays as its hero had been to other characters. Cibber had improved the title role not only by inserting material from *3 Henry VI* but also by borrowing lines traditionally cut from other plays: for instance, Richard acquired the Chorus's eve-of-Agincourt description from *Henry V*, here transferred to Bosworth Field, and a death speech based on Northumberland's curse in *2 Henry IV* 1.1.153–60, a scene which also furnished most of the dialogue for the opening of Cibber's play.[1] Thus, most revivals of *2 Henry IV* omitted 1.1, beginning instead with the entrance of Falstaff and his page. But Falstaff, in any case, had already taken on a life of his own. Arguably, he achieved transcendental status as early as *The Merry Wives of Windsor*, but it was confirmed in the short "droll" (*The Bouncing Knight*) excerpted from *1 Henry IV* and performed during the mid-seventeenth century period when the playhouses were officially closed. The later plays, essays, stories, and operas in which Falstaff figures have little if anything to do with his original historical context. Hotspur in Part 1 and Henry IV in Part 2 became leading tragic roles, contending for interest with Falstaff; in the adapted version of *2 Henry IV*, the king's soliloquy on sleep opened the last act of the play, thus making it a self-contained tragedy which could be performed on its own.

What brought about a revival of the history plays as a whole in the nineteenth century was a new interest in recreating the visual appearance of the past through picturesque, beautiful – and supposedly accurate – sets and costumes. *Henry V*, like *King John*, had been a consistent favorite on patriotic occasions in the eighteenth century, though its choruses, perceived as archaic, had often been cut. Macready's *Henry V* (1839), which revived and "illustrated" them with stage tableaux, started a tradition of spectacular production. Even *Richard II*, despite its lack of a heroic central figure, became a popular play when Charles Kean (1857) introduced vividly imagined tableaux like the entry of Richard and Bolingbroke into London. Two years later his revival of *Henry V* interpolated the king's triumphal entry into London, a deliberate intertextual parallel.

Historical research into the periods depicted in the plays eventually led to similar research on the theatre for which they had been written. This scholarship in turn refocused interest away from the plays as mirrors of a historical period and toward their intended effect in the age when they were performed. German scholars, the first to take a serious interest in the Elizabethan stage, were the first to describe the history plays as a national epic. Franz Dingelstedt's tercentenary production at Weimar in 1864 gave all but one play of the two tetralogies, though his translations, heavily cut and given strong curtain lines, might better be described as adaptations. Dingelstedt's rationale for omitting *1 Henry VI* was not, as one might expect, that he found the treatment of Joan of Arc offensive, but that audiences were already familiar with her story from Schiller's *Maid of Orleans* (Dingelstedt 1867, II: 10). In other words, he took the value of the plays to derive from their participation in a narrative rather than from their individual character.

There is no evidence that Shakespeare's own public ever saw the English history plays in sequence; surviving records suggest that even the two parts of *Henry IV* were rarely performed together (Crane 1985: 291–5). Nevertheless, the most important influence on twentieth-century interpretation of those plays – critical and theatrical – has been the belief that these plays are a continuous and coherent whole. Productions of complete cycles have usually reinforced this view by choosing a homogeneous performance style, often with a single set for all the plays. In the last years of the twentieth century the taste for disjunction and contradiction associated with postmodern aesthetics led to a reaction against this approach. The process as a whole lasted only fifty years.

It had one precursor. In 1901 Frank Benson produced, at what was then the Memorial Theatre in Stratford-upon-Avon, his "Grand Cycle of Shakespeare's Plays, *King John* to *Richard III*" – or, to use the phrase of the local newspaper, "The Feast of Kings" and "the first of the new century" (*Stratford-upon-Avon Herald*, April 16, 1901). It was not quite complete (it included only Part 2 of both *Henry IV* and *Henry VI*) and it was only in 1906 that the company performed the complete group, apart from *Richard III*, in chronological order. Most of the plays had been rehearsed and performed individually rather than conceived as part of a cycle; they had also been drastically cut and rearranged (there was, for instance, no Chorus in *Henry V*). Still, the conditions of performance had their effect on interpretation: the role of Henry IV, traditionally given to an older actor, was now played by a younger man who could also be the Bolingbroke of *Richard II*. One critic also complained that Benson's Hal, perhaps with Agincourt in mind, was "so impressed with the hollowness of the life he was leading that a genuine laugh never escaped his lips" (*Birmingham Gazette*, April 28, 1894). However, it was the closest anyone in England had ever come to making connections between the plays.

It would take almost fifty years to create another opportunity. The performance of even one history play is an expensive operation. Unlike Germany, the English-speaking world lacked subsidized theatres. Productions of the plays in cycle form had to wait for the emergence of the director, designer, and large subsidized theatre companies (Shewring 1996: 93). Even now, theatres outside the UK can mount productions of the history cycles only at the rate of one play a year (thereby, perhaps, replicating the conditions in which audiences first saw them). This purely material consideration explains why so much of this essay will be focused on British productions. But it is worth mentioning a few others. A number of directors have conflated the two parts of *Henry IV*, usually by cutting scenes in Part 2 that largely repeat those of Part 1 and by removing passages in which characters either prophesy the future or recall the past. Samuel Leitner's invaluable *Shakespeare Around the Globe* discusses many other conflated and adapted versions. Orson Welles was the first and most important adapter. His initial project was intended for the stage, a condensed, two-part version of the two tetralogies under the title *Five Kings*. He completed only the first part, which failed on the American stage in 1939; it failed again when he tried to revive it in Dublin in 1960, but another version finally became the film *Chimes at Midnight* (1966) – which, as will become clear below, has influenced a number of later stage productions.

The Histories as the History of the RSC

The most persuasive arguments for the unity of the history plays were published during World War II. In 1944 J. Dover Wilson's *The Fortunes of Falstaff*, a close reading of the Henry IV plays, argued that they could be more easily understood when read as a single play (Wilson 1944: 89–91). E. M. W. Tillyard's classic *Shakespeare's History Plays* also appeared in 1944. Tillyard is often associated with, even blamed for, the "jingoistic" *Henry V* film of Laurence Olivier (also 1944), which became a sort of straw man for later versions. In fact, he did not even care much for the play, which he described as showing "a great falling off in quality" compared to the *Henry IV* plays (Tillyard 1944: 306). Nor was his view of Hal uncritical: he felt, for instance, that the prince's treatment of Francis was "brutal," and, though he duly explained it according to the concept of "degree," he did not condone it (pp. 276–7). However, his belief that "Shakespeare conceived his second tetralogy as one great unit" (p. 234) was indispensable to the directors of the 1951 Stratford production of the second tetralogy. The production coincided with the Festival of Britain, a deliberate exercise in morale-boosting in a country where rationing had only just ended. (The Old Vic's

Henry V, which opened before the Stratford one, got its biggest laugh on the line, "these English are shrewdly out of beef" (Williamson 1957: 58).)

In the interest of thematic unity the Stratford production used a single permanent set (by Tanya Moiseiwitsch) for all four plays, and retained the same casting for nearly all the roles – though, as Michael Redgrave played both Richard II and Hotspur, the Harry Percy of the earlier play was a different actor, made up and wigged to look as much as possible like Redgrave's Hotspur. The Aumerle of *Richard II* even played York in *Henry V*, though, as the Aumerle plot in the earlier play was completely cut, the significance of the relationship was lost (David 1973: 131). (In fact, the identity of these two characters goes unnoticed in most productions, since Aumerle/York does not appear in the intervening Henry IV plays.) More important was the rethinking of characterization that accompanied the enterprise. In the book-length account of the history cycle by J. Dover Wilson and T. C. Worsley, it is interesting to notice how often the word "must" appears, usually to explain a directorial choice based on something that is going to happen in a later play. Although Richard II is obviously the central figure of his own play, he appears only there, whereas Bolingbroke figures in three plays; therefore Richard "must not engage too predominating a share of our sympathy" while Bolingbroke "must win us by his dignity, nobility and virility" (Wilson and Worsley 1952: 28). Just as Bolingbroke/Henry IV had been revealed as a vitally important role, so Hal/Henry V turned out, when all three plays were taken into account, to have the longest role in Shakespeare (McMillin 1991: 4). So Hotspur "must not outshine Hal"; Falstaff "must" be "an old ruffian" who deserves to be rejected; Hal's destiny as the hero of Agincourt "must be evident in its kernel from the very beginning" (Wilson and Worsley 1952: 28–9). Shakespeare has been accused of writing "winners' history": this was a "winners' production." T. C. Worsley claimed, "One will never again think of these plays as single entities, and when they are played as such we shall feel them to have been lopped" (*New Statesman & Nation*, November 3, 1951: 489).

But the tetralogy made special, perhaps excessive, demands on its audiences. As J. Dover Wilson put it, "when a trilogy is in question one must sit and watch the whole series before one has any right to frame final conclusions about its characters" (Wilson and Worsley 1952: 4). Yet relatively few spectators were able to do what Wilson recommended. Because of the technical difficulties of rehearsing and mounting a new production, the plays were introduced into the repertory at one-month intervals, and those who could not get to Stratford until late in the season missed the opportunity to see them all together. Even among those who did manage to see the entire sequence, there was disagreement. Worsley, who initially felt that *Richard II* was stylistically different from the rest of the cycle, was eventually converted: knowledge of *Richard II*, he claimed, "gives a double edge to almost everything that is said in the subsequent play, either by the King's party or the rebels" (*New Statesman & Nation*, November 3, 1951: 489). Richard David argued that, on the contrary, the play did this only because it had been made to do so. As an example of how the plays lost as much as they gained by their juxtaposition, he pointed to the fact that the

Stratford production had been less successful than the Old Vic *Henry V* with Alec Clunes; the play "has a size and an immediacy that as the peroration to a political treatise it must forgo, a sparkle and verve that are lost when it is trimmed to fit a tetralogy" (David 1973: 138).

David added that the series as a whole had falsified the plays by seeing *Henry V* only as the culmination of a triumphant progress and not as the prelude to the Wars of the Roses. Whether or not they were influenced by this comment, the next RSC directors to approach the histories, Peter Hall and John Barton, did so via the first tetralogy – rewritten, reduced to three plays, and called *The Wars of the Roses*. They returned to the second tetralogy in 1964, the year of the Shakespeare quatercentenary. Theatrical technology and rehearsal conditions had improved so much since 1951 that it was possible in 1964 for the plays to rehearse together, to open in quick succession, and to use a simple permanent set (by John Bury) that was capable of more extensive transformation than Moiseiwitsch's. It was thus possible for audiences to see and appreciate the sequence as a whole, in all-day and all-weekend performances.

Brecht (whose Berliner Ensemble had paid a famous visit to London in 1956) was immediately identified as an obvious influence on the 1964 cycle. "Again and again," wrote Ronald Bryden, "as unshaven, carefully muddied soldiery pulled their little canteen-wagons into stark, straw-strewn farmyards, I looked for Mother Courage to follow with her children" (*The New Statesman*, April 24, 1964: 652). In fact, the resemblance to Brecht was mainly physical (and the 1951 Old Vic *Henry V* had also used wagons). A far more Brechtian production had been given in Villeurbanne, France, in 1957; director Roger Planchon made characters undercut their idealistic language by, for instance, eating while they spoke (Leiter 1986: 186–7). Some reviewers, noting the RSC's emphasis on physical pain, relatively new in British theatre, also noted that the company had recently made a study of Artaud's theatre of cruelty (see Brown 1965: 149). But Artaud's indifference to text, and Brecht's willingness to adapt it freely, were both at the opposite extreme from what the company, with its careful training in verse speaking, was trying to achieve. In fact, the RSC was influenced by Chekhov as much as by Brecht – which is why *2 Henry IV*, generally described as an inferior play in 1951, was the most highly praised play in the 1964 cycle. Robert Speaight, who wrote a particularly sympathetic account of the production, describes what was to be the RSC house style for about a decade: "every moment of every play is squeezed for the last ounce of meaning it contains . . . We remember Hal burning Falstaff's unsettled invoices in the last flickering candle at the Boar's Head; Fluellen's pocket Xenaphon; and Bolingbroke's toy soldiers. The pace is leisurely; one never feels that the actors have been told to get a move on" (Speaight 1964: 388). Chekhovian atmosphere and pauses allowing for subtextual reading dominated the scenes which Speaight, in common with other reviewers, mentioned most often: Falstaff's melancholy attempts at love with Doll Tearsheet; the deathbed reconciliation of Henry IV with his son; the conversations among the old men in Shallow's orchard; Hal's simple, "Falstaff, goodnight," at the end of the tavern scene, after which one knew that "nothing would ever be the same" (Speaight 1964: 385). Even the usually triumphant

1 Henry IV had as its final image the hanging of Worcester and Vernon. This emphasis on the dark side of the plays was to characterize many subsequent Stratford productions.

As in 1951, the best reviews went to Henry IV (Eric Porter) and Falstaff (Hugh Griffith), the characters who develop most radically and who benefit most from being given time to do so. Sometimes, also as in 1951, the characters were accused of "mortgaging" the present role for the one in the next play (Speaight 1964: 381, 386). Ian Holm's Hal, like Richard Burton's in 1951, was visibly thinking ahead to his kingship, though, unlike Burton, he was able to maintain the lightness of the tavern scenes. Although some reviewers found this actor's Henry V disappointing (as they had, previously, found his Richard III), the production sometimes gained from the knowledge that the *Henry VI* plays would follow it. Holm, like the Chorus's description of England, was a "little body with a mighty heart." Montjoy, initially unimpressed by him, had already changed his mind by the end of his first scene with the English troops, a fact that was evident when he said, with a new respect, "Thanks to *your Majesty*." (Hall and Barton seem to have started an RSC tradition of making Montjoy a sympathetic representative of France, in place of the Constable, the token "good Frenchman" of the Olivier film.) This king was not only small himself, he was destined to live "small time, but in that small most greatly." A number of Henries, including Branagh and even the otherwise unsympathetic Pennington, have indicated some kind of physical vulnerability, usually in the aftermath of Harfleur. Holm did the same; he also made clear, from this point on, his increasing sense of mortality. Thus, in the wooing scene, his suggestion to Katherine that they beget a son who will be an even greater warrior than himself, began as a joke but quickly turned serious. When Katherine said, "I do not know dat," Holm replied, with an almost frightening urgency, "No, 'tis hereafter to know." This king wanted an heir, and he knew that he must have one as quickly as possible. The presence of the Dauphin in this scene, though it contradicts both the Quarto and the Folio playtexts (and history, since he was dead by the time the treaty of Troyes was signed), was also used to throw the audience's minds forward to the events of *1 Henry VI*, where another Dauphin is crowned king by Joan of Arc (Hodgdon 1991: 203). The 1964 cycle emphasized the political significance after the wooing as the Dauphin and Katherine pleaded on opposite sides of their father in dumbshow; when the king granted Henry's final request, thus effectively disinheriting the Dauphin, the latter rushed off stage in fury. Then the Chorus spoke the Epilogue, with its reference to the loss of France, usually cut in non-cycle productions. This ending was less depressing than it might have been, because, whereas the rest of the cast wore plain costumes which were timeless as much as medieval, the Chorus was played as a flashily dressed Elizabethan who belonged very much to his own era. For this patriotic and rather unreflective actor, the loss of France, however sad, was definitely in the past; he ended on an upbeat note, reminding us of the opportunity to see the theatre's Henry VI plays.

Looking at English productions of the Henry IV plays up to the mid-1970s, Scott McMillin notes that:

The Stratford cycle of 1951 was part of the transformation that was brought about at the Shakespeare Memorial Theatre after the war. The 1963–64 cycle brought a new Royal Shakespeare Company out of the Stratford organisation and helped it become the most influential English company of the 1960s. The 1975 cycle served to resolve a financial crisis in the same company. (McMillin 1991: 11)

One might add that in 1982 Trevor Nunn opened the company's new London theatre, the Barbican, with the two parts of *Henry IV*. And the theatre marked the arrival of the millennium, almost inevitably, by returning to the history plays. Aware of the history plays as part of its own history, the Royal Shakespeare Company has given one production of a cycle each decade, each time with a sense that it was embodying something about its sense of itself as a theatre at least as much as about Shakespeare studies or the current state of Britain.

Each new production of the plays as a cycle had to come to terms with the problems revealed by the previous one. It had become apparent in 1951 and 1964 that *Henry V* (like *Richard III*) sometimes suffered by coming at the end of a four-play sequence: the hero's "journey" is already over at the end of *2 Henry IV* and he risks becoming one-dimensional thereafter (Loehlin 1997: 108). Alan Howard had already played Henry VI in Terry Hands's production of all three *Henry VI* plays. In the cycle of 1975–6, also directed by Hands, the company chose to open with *Henry V* and rehearsed it in conjunction with *1 Henry IV* and *The Merry Wives of Windsor*; *2 Henry IV* was later added; *Richard II* and *Richard III* followed. Allowing a single actor, under a single director, to play all the kings apart from Henry IV might seem like a return to the age of Henry Irving, except that Irving would have directed the plays as well as starring in them. But the sequence justified itself through the notion of role-playing as a means of growing up. Alan Howard played what was probably the most psychologically complex Hal of the late twentieth century, caught in an impossible relationship with an embarrassing father, Emrys James, whose Henry IV was described by Richard David as "a crabbed, pawkey, devious, self-pitying politician" (David 1978: 199). The difficulty with making England's royal family so neurotic was, as McMillin (1991: 80) points out, that Brewster Mason's dignified Falstaff could hardly be a threat of any kind to a political world already thoroughly sick. The sickness, moreover, was psychological rather than political. Hal's main need was not to inherit the crown but to win his almost impossible struggle toward self-realization, while in *Henry V* (a very popular production, which toured widely) his struggle took the form of the need to weld the members of his disparate army into a band of brothers. Henry's three "real" brothers were given unusual prominence and made to look as much as possible like the tall, red-haired Alan Howard. Particular emphasis was laid on Thomas of Clarence, since he had been described in *2 Henry IV* as Henry's favorite brother, but Hands cut the Duke of Bedford out of the cast because he would be remembered as John of Lancaster from *2 Henry IV*, a figure whose *realpolitik* would be out of keeping with the mood of Agincourt (Beauman 1976: 116). Other links among the three Henry plays were carefully brought out. The most famous example was the hanging of Bardolph, an episode only reported in the playtext but depicted more and more explicitly in productions of the 1980s and 1990s in order to underline the tensions in Henry's situation.

The notion of a difficult group enterprise was carried into the production. To the surprise of spectators who had already seen the visually spectacular end of *2 Henry IV*, with the new king in gold armor against a snowy landscape, the actors began in rehearsal clothes (then an unusual device). But the production did not sustain this level of austerity, or this appeal to the audience's imagination, for long. Appropriately, the first costumed character to appear was the French ambassador of 1.1, dressed as a bishop: Hands had found historical justification, since two churchmen had been part of the embassy; he also wanted to balance Canterbury and Ely with the French "spirituality" (Beauman 1976: 116). Moreover, the interpretation made the English, who looked almost like twentieth-century soldiers, more "real" than the French, who were beautiful anachronisms, a little like those of the Olivier film, wearing gold armor to emphasize their distance from their own soldiers. But the "liberal" attitude of the production embraced the French too. Because the cast size had been reduced, for reasons of economy, the characters who remained could be more richly characterized by inheriting some of the lines of others; Montjoy, in particular, benefited from these transpositions. Hal's search for a father, a theme of the *Henry IV* plays, continued into their sequel because Emrys James, his father in the previous plays, returned as the Chorus and also spoke Burgundy's lines in the final scene. Henry himself spoke Queen Isabel's lines ending the play.

Pope wrote that every speech of Shakespeare was uniquely appropriate to its speaker (Smith 1962: 48); Johnson, though he would not go so far, agreed that "it will be difficult to find any that can be properly transferred from the present possessor to another claimant" (ibid: 116). In a cycle that had been particularly concerned with ideas of acting and identity, Hands's moving of dialogue from speaker to speaker can be seen either as an attempt to make characters more "consistent" or, on the contrary, as an indication of the postmodern preference for disintegration rather than organic unity. Postmodernism certainly seems to explain some theatrical devices that worked to destabilize rather than homogenize the plays: characters from one scene shared props and theatrical space with those supposedly far away, as if to remind the audience that the miles that separated them existed only in its imagination. Adrian Noble's production of the *Henry IV* plays in 1992 also brought characters into each others' space and used the heights and depths of the acting area for surreal effects: Hal and Falstaff made their first entrance from under the stage, with red light and smoke, suggesting to one spectator that they were rising from hell (Hattaway 1994: 366). The tavern was also red. Some reviewers thought of Bosch, but the effect was also of a womb. Hal (Michael Maloney) went there in search of warmth and comfort, which, with Robert Stephens as Falstaff, was the main quality of this production. Perhaps the best gloss on it was what Welles told Keith Baxter, the Hal of *Chimes at Midnight*: "The film is a love story. Never, ever, forget that. Everything else – the politics, the comedy, the battles – they all drop into their place. What the film is *about* is Love, and love betrayed" (Baxter 1998: 79). The focus at the RSC, too, was on interiority rather than history, and Noble might have been influenced not only by *Chimes at Midnight* but also by *My Own Private Idaho* (1991), which modernizes the Falstaff–Hal relationship and, as Baxter points out, draws on Welles for some of its images (Baxter 1998: 97).

In keeping with the postmodern ethos, then, the RSC directors, having chosen to celebrate the millennium with another history cycle, under the title "This England," decided to entrust the plays to several different directors and to stage them in three different venues, thus removing any possibility of a unifying permanent set. Actors carried over from play to play, though not from tetralogy to tetralogy. In Pimlott's spare, modern *Richard II*, Adam Levy played Harry Percy as a caricature of a fanatical member of a commando brigade, but as Hotspur in Michael Attenborough's more traditional *1 Henry IV* he became a psychologically credible character. William Houston's Hal commanded authority even when he became Henry V in Edward Hall's controversially modern production. The stylistic dissonances did not prevent the sequence from being very well reviewed and indeed perceived as a unity. But this time the unity was not based on a sense of nationhood, or the concept of the king as a symbol of every human being's need to play a role. It derived from the image of earth itself (a small symbolic mound in *Richard II*, it covered the whole stage in the *Henry IV* plays), in its double meaning of country and grave. At a public debate at the Barbican (April 2001) as to whether the history plays still had anything to say about England and Englishness, a reporter found that participants were reluctant to ascribe any single view to Shakespeare, but "Everyone was comfortable with him as the universal Questioner" (Patrick Carnegy, *Spectator*, May 5, 2001).

Politics and Gender (The English Shakespeare Company and Feminist Histories)

The apparent turning away from political approaches to Shakespeare on the part of the RSC helped to provoke the formation of the one cycle production that did not start at Stratford. The English Shakespeare Company, formed in 1986 by director Michael Bogdanov and actor Michael Pennington, began by taking the two *Henry IV* plays and *Henry V* on tour, then expanded the cycle to include *Richard II* and the first tetralogy (reduced to a trilogy). Bogdanov's attraction to the histories was twofold: he thought they could offer a genuinely popular and populist kind of theatre experience, and he saw in them a clear parallel to contemporary Britain, particularly in the division between conservative England, which had re-elected Margaret Thatcher in 1986, and Scotland, Ireland, and Wales, which had voted against her. Beginning with the "Henrys" (IV and V, that is), the company eventually added *Richard II* and the Henry VI–Richard III group (see chapter 12, this volume), thus creating the "Wars of the Roses" series that toured internationally with great success. The productions were constantly changing in the course of the run, not only because new cast members sometimes took on new doubles, but because the addition of new plays shifted the balance of the old ones. This brief account is necessarily incomplete, but the importance of the sequence lay less in what actually happened than in its reception.

The productions were intended to *look* political, which meant that they drew attention whenever possible to contemporary parallels. Bogdanov knew the collection *Political Shakespeare* edited by Jonathan Dollimore and Alan Sinfield (1985), to which he refers in the book that he and Pennington wrote in the aftermath of the venture. For him, the main value of the essays was that they revealed "the underlying political subversion" of Shakespeare's plays (Bogdanov and Pennington 1990: 27). Some of them, however, also raise questions relevant to the entire project of political theatre. For instance, the Marxist critic Margot Heinemann (1985) contended that "the visual representation of historical context and class contrast" is an essential part of a production (p. 224). Bogdanov had always brought out class contrasts, but he invariably preferred modern dress, and used it for the three "Henrys." Once the other plays had been added, however, the cycle's 100-year sweep required the ESC to convey some sense of a changing world. With an eclectic mixture of costumes that prevented the historical settings from being taken too literally, the company gave a general sense of the period from 1800 (Richard II was dressed as the Prince Regent) to the present (Richard III had a computer instead of a throne). Bolingbroke and his supporters represented the next generation's "Victorian values." The phrase, first used by Margaret Thatcher to denote what the Conservative government of the 1980s hoped to restore, was defined by Bogdanov as "greed, avarice, exploitation and self" (Bogdanov and Pennington 1990: 24). But the Boar's Head was a modern dive, where Hal took part in contemporary youth culture, or counter-culture.

Both Michaels agreed that Prince Hal (also played by Pennington) was a "dirty rat" (p. 49) and Henry IV a cold bureaucrat. The result was "the bleakest father–son relationship in modern productions" (McMilin 1991: 114). There was no reconciliation at the end of Part 1. Instead, Bogdanov, as he admits (Bogdanov and Pennington 1990: 54–5), borrowed an idea from Orson Welles's *Chimes at Midnight*. Welles might in turn have taken it from *The Fortunes of Falstaff*, where it is part of J. Dover Wilson's answer to Maurice Morgann's famous defense of Falstaff (1777). Morgann argued that Falstaff must have been genuinely courageous at Shrewsbury because he is treated with more respect in Part 2 than in Part 1. Wilson suggested that this respect was the result of Hal's generous willingness to let his old friend claim credit for the killing of Hotspur – which, he noted, Henry IV never specifically ascribes to his son (Wilson 1944: 89–91). Welles's film makes some characteristic transpositions to create a scene in which the king, after initially congratulating Hal, meets Falstaff with the body of Hotspur and rejects his son as a liar. The device is useful as an explanation for the estrangement between father and son that continues into Part 2 in spite of their apparent reconciliation at the end of Part 1, and has been used in other productions that give the two plays in quick succession.

Henry V was the most notorious production of the sequence, drawing as it did on the recent Falklands War and the jingoistic reactions that it had inspired. The soldiers from Eastcheap, like the English football hooligans who were currently invading Europe, set off to war half drunk, carrying signs saying "Fuck the Frogs"; as in the Terry Hands production, there was a big laugh when the exit of this rowdy crowd was followed by the entrance of the French king dourly commenting, "Thus comes the English with full power upon us." As in 1964, the Dauphin's furious exit in the final scene made it clear that Henry's victory was already under threat.

Like Terry Hands, Bogdanov expressed his view of the plays both inside and outside the production. Thus, as with the 1975 cycle, it is easy to see the gap between intention and reception. The ESC gave a good deal of pleasure to a general audience, and to many young theatregoers, but often failed to satisfy the critics most sympathetic to the directors' political views: Michael Hattaway, for instance, accused the company of relying too much on "cultural gesturing" (Hattaway 1994: 365). It is arguable that the most genuinely subversive aspect of the productions was not their obvious paralleling of medieval and contemporary figures but their willingness to take liberties with the text. In an important essay in *Political Shakespeare*, Alan Sinfield comes close to saying that genuinely radical Shakespeare is an impossibility: the RSC's 1960s productions demonstrated only that all politicians are corrupt and one political system no better than another. He goes on to claim that Shakespeare's position as cultural authority prevents even radical productions from having any effect, since "the idea of the real Shakespeare from whom it all emanates nevertheless registers cultural authority, and implies that every innovation has been anticipated. The underlying pressure is towards deference and inertia" (Sinfield 1985: 178). The only solution he offered was that directors should rewrite Shakespeare or appropriate him for their own purposes (p. 179). The ESC's use of audible extra-textual ad-libs, its Ballad of Harry le Roy (originally written to explain events before *1 Henry IV* but retained even after *Richard II* had joined the cycle), its commentator who cynically summed up the web of family intrigue at the beginning of *Richard III*, registered as subversive because they could be recognized as intrusions into – almost attacks on – the Shakespearean text. Even so, the kind of audience that felt culturally empowered by the production style was not necessarily the kind that the company wanted. One reviewer claims that some school groups at *Henry V* "identified with the jingoist punks and roared their approval" (Julia Pascal, *Jewish Chronicle*, May 1, 1987).

Class politics are more obvious in the plays than gender politics. But the histories in general, and Falstaff in particular, have always had a reputation for being unpopular with women: the eighteenth-century writer Elizabeth Inchbald called *1 Henry IV* a play "which all men admire, and which most women dislike" (quoted in Sprague 1964: 50). She could have been thinking either of its male-oriented subject matter or of the limited opportunities it offered for female performers. Bogdanov, who had strong feminist credentials (he directed a famous *Taming of the Shrew* in 1978), foregrounded female roles whenever possible, treated characters like Mrs. Quickly and Doll Tearsheet seriously, and, unlike most directors, made Queen Isabel an important part of the final scene of *Henry V* (Henderson 2000: 340). The company's extensive doubling (Queen Isabel had also been Mrs. Quickly) limited the number of women actors who could be employed but, on the other hand, improved their acting opportunities. Jean Howard and Phyllis Rackin have pointed out the contrast between the second tetralogy and the first, where Margaret, though a demonized figure, has the strongest and largest role. In *1 Henry IV* women speak only 4 percent of the dialogue and it is mostly non-standard, marginalized speech: Lady Percy is the exception, but even she is criticized by her husband for her choice of oaths (Howard and Rackin 1997: 24). To show that characters who have close relationships with women are thereby diminished in authority, they point to the so-called "Welsh scene" (*1 Henry IV* 3.1) in which both Hotspur and Mortimer are seen with their wives. In a historical context, Rackin argues, Mortimer is both a victim of female seduction and a "frightening figure" because of his association with the foreign, especially in a play where Welsh women are first mentioned as the perpetrators of unspeakable brutalities on the dead bodies of English men (p. 137). Bogdanov sees the Welsh scene very differently. For him, it shows "the meeting of two cultures, a love born of an internal communication transcending all verbal barriers; a plea for communal harmony and understanding, for the banishing of bigotry and prejudice." He believed that this plea was Shakespeare's own, and found that audiences were always moved by the Welsh dialogue and song, even without understanding the words (Bogdanov and Pennington 1990: 54). If theory and performance seem particularly far apart at this point, it is partly because (1) much feminist interest in the plays has to do with female absences, which by their nature do not lend themselves to dramatization and (2) the effect of the Welsh song is largely non-verbal and cannot be deduced from a reading of the lines that surround it. To put it in the terms that Kate McLuskie uses in *Political Shakespeare*, the female spectator (or critic) can adopt this particular feminist reading only by "refusing the pleasure of the drama and the text" (McLuskie 1985: 97).

The most obvious way of making the histories more attractive to female performers is to create a stronger female presence – for instance, by crossdressing the major roles. This is not a new idea: a Mrs. Webb played Falstaff in the 1786 London season: "It produced a large audience," according to a theatre historian, "but did not add to her fame" (quoted in Sprague 1964: 50). Pat Carroll played a successful Falstaff in *The Merry Wives of Windsor* at the Shakespeare Theatre, Washington, DC in 1990, but said that she would not have felt equally able to play the Falstaff of the history plays. Charles Kean's *Henry V* (1859) gave the role of Chorus to his wife and leading lady, costumed as Clio, the Muse of History; many other nineteenth-century productions also made this character female, to soften the play's virtually all-male emphasis. The creation of all-female companies has opened up possibilities for playing major non-romantic roles. But when the Company of Women performed an all-female *Henry V* in 1994–5, James Loehlin found it not noticeably different from other anti-war productions, except insofar as it made Henry's treatment of Katherine and Alice in the final scene more openly brutal (Loehlin 1997: 164–7; cf. Henderson 2000: 340–1).

Gender politics have been implicit in *Richard II* at least since Frank Benson's revival in 1896, which made it, along with *King John*, the most popular history play in the Stratford festival for several seasons. It is generally assumed that the enthusiasm for these plays was patriotic, a result of the excitement over Queen Victoria's diamond jubilee of 1897 and Britain's recent victories in the Boer War. But it was not simply Gaunt's great patriotic speech that kept audiences coming back to see *Richard II*. The athletic Benson, whose company played sports every day, seems an incongruous defender of the aesthete-as-king, but it is hard to overlook the fact that his revival came only a year after the trial of Oscar Wilde. Accounts of his performance suggest that he made Richard a *modern* hero, charming, ineffectual, and artistic. A reviewer describes him in the deposition scene: looking in the mirror for which he had called, he absent-mindedly mounted the steps to the throne; then, just as he was about to sit, came to himself "with a short laugh and an apologetic gesture" (*The Sketch*, March 17, 1897). At the end of the scene, as the new king's procession passed out, Richard remained behind, "feebly marking time with an upraised hand to the sounds of the receding martial music, often previously played for his pleasure" (*Leamington Spa Courier*, April 26, 1901). C. E. Montague's famous and often-quoted review, which defined Benson's Richard as a "capable and faithful artist" in an "incapable and faithless king," largely established the acting tradition for the role in the first half of the twentieth century (see Sprague 1964: 47–8). In Beerbohm Tree's production of 1903, a version which, as Barbara Hodgdon notes, is seen entirely from Richard's point of view (Hodgdon 1991: 132), the elaborate framing of Tree's farewell to the queen, accompanied by emotional music, suggests another agenda, the reclaiming of the upper-class "dandy" figure for heterosexuality. By 1948, Harold Hobson thought, the play had become "almost the favorite of Shakespeare's plays"; his remark seems tinged with disapproval (Sprague 1964: 37). Barbara Hodgdon attributes the disappointment with Redgrave's Richard in the 1951 cycle to "its initial homophobic interpretative communities" (Hodgdon 1991: 143); the problem may have been, rather, the demystification of a role that had become a conflation of unexamined and idealized contradictions: an artist whose creations are never available for criticism; a man accused of effeminacy who dies fighting and who seems to love his wife, in a distant, poetical way, as much as she loves him. When Ian McKellen played the role in repertory with Marlowe's *Edward II* for the Prospect Company on tour (directed by Richard Cottrell) in 1968, the doubling led to the assumption that Richard was likewise meant to be seen as a homosexual (Shewring 1996: 89). Though this was supposedly not the production's intention – McKellen took on the role of Marlowe's king only after another actor had refused it (Gibson 1986: 59) – the date is significant, coming as it does immediately before the abolition of the office of Lord Chamberlain. Post-1968 productions of the play did not need to code sexuality as a form of art. In Bogdanov's production Richard was an irresponsible artistic dabbler. While York offered him well-meaning advice, the king drew a caricature of his uncle, finally handing it to him by way of an answer.

The strand of feminism associated with Judith Butler argues that femininity is a performance. Howard and Rankin note the paradox involved in the association of theatricality with the feminine: characters like Richard II and Richard III, even when condemned in the text, are also "empowered by their theatricality, because of its inevitable attraction for a theatre audience" (Howard and Rackin 1997: 152). Casting a woman in the role of Richard, as in Deborah Warner's National Theatre production of 1995 with Fiona Shaw, problematizes the whole question of Richard's "manliness." The production was obviously not meant to be gender-blind, nor was it a *tour de force* of impersonation, like, say, Bernhardt's Hamlet. But director and actor did not choose the attractive option of playing Richard as someone for whom baronial bickering was simply a lot of macho nonsense. As Benedict Nightingale objected, the character seemed more like a child refusing to take adult quarrels seriously. The reviewer, though he admits that he was gripped by the production, was puzzled as to what Shaw was trying to convey about Richard's sexuality: "He seems momentarily attracted to David Threlfall's Bolingbroke, whom he pats, strokes and, not long before pronouncing his banishment, gives a smacking kiss on the lips. And Graham Crowden's Gaunt contemptuously manhandles Shaw in the same way, as if to accuse Richard of effeminacy" (*The Times* [London], June 5, 1995). There seemed to be too many variables: a woman playing a man, a man playing a king, a king losing his identity, a woman losing hers. If the standard way of treating a man with contempt is to feminize him, what happens when he is already female? However interesting these questions might be in the abstract, they did not problematize the play itself so much as the entire theatrical experience. In this respect, the production was characteristic of the 1990s.

Metatheatricality and the Undercutting of Authority

The theatrical self-consciousness of the late twentieth century can be traced to critical, especially feminist, interest in the process of acting and viewing and to an increased interest in performance studies. Terry Hands's *Henry V* crystallized a number of these issues when it was commemorated in a book, *Henry V for the Centenary Season* (1976), written and compiled by Sally Beauman. Along with the text used in the production, it contains extensive notes by Terry Hands and the actors explaining their interpretations and their reasons for cuts and transpositions. Gary Taylor's *Moment by Moment by Shakespeare* (1985) contains a chapter on the same production, which Taylor saw nineteen times. He lays particular emphasis on audience reactions (of varying degrees of sophistication) and on the discrepancy between audience response and actors' intention. This discrepancy in turn gave rise to the complex anti-theatrical arguments of Harry Berger, Jr. Against what was becoming a received view – that performance was the ultimate test of the viability of any critical interpretation – Berger maintained in *Imaginary Audition* (1989) and in many of the essays collected as *Making Trifles of Terrors* (1997) that performance-centered criticism reduces the text to the impoverished single meaning that can be conveyed in a single performance (Berger 1989: 40). W. B. Worthen's response to Beauman's book, and to other accounts of Shakespeare in production, also led him, though for different reasons, to reject what he calls "*the Authority of Performance*," since the theatre is only "one site among many where 'Shakespearean' meanings are produced in contemporary culture" (Worthen 1997: 38). Berger's and Worthen's objections to a performance-centered approach are based on a distrust of the effects of its hegemony: for the one, the theatre oversimplifies character psychology; for the other, the subordination of performers to author means the marginalizing of many kinds of theatricality. In the last part of this chapter I shall look at some of the ways in which productions of the histories have played with questions of authority and theatricality.

The difficulty of working outside the tradition of psychological realism is evident from one of the earliest attempts to do something different with the histories. Barton's *Richard II* in 1973 questioned the very notion of personal identity by suggesting that Richard and Bolingbroke are virtually identical in their roles and their ultimate mortality. (For a full description of this landmark production, see Wells 1976; for an attack on it, see Coursen 1992: 141–2.) Richard Pasco and Ian Richardson alternated the roles of Richard and Bolingbroke. The play began with the two actors holding the crown between them; then an actor dressed as Shakespeare chose the one whose turn it was to play the king and he was formally robed. Originally, Barton had intended that the actors themselves would not know from one night to another which of them was to play which role, but the idea had to be abandoned because spectators who wanted to see both actors in each part needed to know the casting schedule (Shewring 1996: 122–3). Barton had also thought originally of directing them separately as far as possible, so that neither would know how the other was going to play his role, but this ultimately proved to be unnecessary, as the two performances developed in different directions (Speaight 1973: 402). The production externalized the play's imagery, sometimes rather obviously: a snowman melted, followed by a brief glimpse of spring, to echo both Richard's image of himself as a mockery king of snow and the Duchess of York's lines on the new-come spring; Richard's "Down, down, I come" at Flint Castle was (at least, early in the run) the cue for the descent of the platform on which he was standing; he was even killed with a crossbow, possibly a non-verbalized pun, or possibly a way of saying that Bolingbroke had become the Ancient Mariner, forever forced to wander and retell his story because of his killing of a sacred creature. The most striking and consistent image was that of the mirror: Richard looked in it and smashed it, as prescribed, but also wore its frame around his neck. Bolingbroke, disguised as the Groom, visited him in prison and the two men looked through the frame at each other, as if recognizing their essential likeness. This production style was evidently not realistic: though the mirror was visible to both Richard and Bolingbroke, most of what the audience saw could have existed only as part of the mental world inhabited by these two characters. Yet, within a production that seemed to externalize their feelings, the two fine actors gave subtle, internalized performances in the best Chekhovian tradition. By contrast, Ariane Mnouchkine's production from La Cartoucherie, taken on a world tour in 1984, started from the view that "Richard has no psychology" (Shewring 1996: 167). Adopting an eclectic mixture of devices from Asian theatre and Italian commedia, she externalized Richard's divine/royal status in his white face and the stylized gestures of a Kabuki actor; his

"Now mark me, how I will undo myself" became a ritualized disrobing like the ritual robing in Barton's production.

But such theatricality is possible outside the Anglo-Saxon world precisely because the text is already at one remove from the audience. Late twentieth-century Shakespeare acting in Britain combined immense respect for the verbatim delivery of the text with a willingness to subvert it through subtextual acting. However, since the subtext was always assumed to be more "real" than the text, the ultimate effect was to make Shakespeare's characters seem still richer because of what lay beneath their words. Anne Righter and James Winny, among others, have shown that the history plays are inherently metatheatrical: characters are compared to actors and perform for each other's benefit. But, when given a choice, the theatre has generally chosen to imply an essential nature in these characters, separate from the multiple roles that they play. Thus, at the end of *2 Henry IV*, Hal rejects Falstaff and the knight, despite his hopeful words, is left in the tragic isolation that can easily be read into the subtext of his lines. No wonder Part 1 has almost always been the more popular play: "So long as *Part One* is staged by itself, Falstaff ends at the peak of his renown, full of resiliency" (McMillin 1991: 2). But the actual end of Part 2 is an Epilogue in which the speaker dances and refers to Falstaff's probable reappearance in a play about Henry V and France. David Wiles suggests that the speaker was Will Kemp himself, the original Falstaff and a famous dancer, commenting on his own role and under-cutting his apparent defeat (Wiles 1987: 128). Some sense of what might originally have happened could be seen in the ESC cycle, when the actor of Falstaff reappeared as the Chorus in *Henry V* and was enthusiastically applauded on his entrance. But even the ESC production did not allow this effect in Part 2 itself, preferring to focus on Falstaff's banishment as a real event, raising real issues.

Doubling, a necessity in the large casts of the history plays, has traditionally worked to draw attention to the actor rather than the character, as when Laurence Olivier (Old Vic, 1945) and Roy Dotrice (Stratford, 1964) followed a brilliant performance of Hotspur in Part 1 with an equally brilliant one of Justice Shallow in Part 2. On the other hand, the doubling of Hotspur and Pistol (by John Neville at the Old Vic in 1955 and by John Price in the ESC production) was less an actorly *tour de force* than a point about the parodic relation between the two characters. But attempts at doubling within a single play often founder on the audience's determination to treat the production realistically. The reviewer of a *Richard II* at the Old Globe in San Diego, California, complained that the doubling of Gaunt with the Gardener – presumably intended to draw a parallel between their concerns for the land and their ineffectual attempts at counseling – looked like an attempt to save money (Dan Sullivan, " 'Richard II' at Old Globe in San Diego", *Los Angeles Times*, June 13, 1986). The atmosphere of the ESC cycle, where the audience came to feel that it knew the individual actors, made it easy to accept multiple doubles as part of the experience, but it seems essential for the production to make it clear that no one is attempting to conceal the practice.

A similar movement from role to character has occurred in productions of *Henry V*. The Chorus, a theatrical device, is a blank page on which director and actor can write what they choose. In the eighteenth century the speaker was treated as an actor, speaking multiple prologues and an epilogue; then he or she became a personification (Time for Macready, Clio for Charles Kean). In the late twentieth century the Chorus (sometimes called simply Chorus, as if that were a proper name) began to develop a personality (usually male), which allowed him to lose something of his authoritative, or authorial function. It was understandable that some reviewers thought that the Chorus of the 1964 *Henry V*, in his Elizabethan costume, was meant to be Shakespeare himself. He occupied a peculiar relationship to the other actors, all of whom wore medieval costume and never indicated that they knew they were in a play. The dissociation between the two may have been intended simply to indicate that they occupied two different imaginative planes, but John Russell Brown thought that the Chorus was being deliberately undermined, "as if the directors thought that all he said had to be ironically wrong" (Brown 1965: 151). One possible interpretation was that the audience, thanks to its participation in the act of imagination, understood the play better than the Chorus. Another – especially if the Chorus was intended for Shakespeare – was that the actors understood their play better than its author.

At first sight, it might seem that the ultimate symbol of Shakespeare's status as the ultimate authority is the fact that, after years of adapting the plays to fit them for contemporary theatre, scholars and architectural historians joined forces to adapt the theatre to fit it for Shakespeare's plays. "Shakespeare's Globe" was reconstructed as near as possible the original sites where the history plays were first performed, and, after early experiments with the space, it officially opened in 1997 with Mark Rylance, its artistic director, as Henry V. Though the publicity around this event made the new theatre sound both archaic and conservative, it quickly became apparent that its most remarkable feature was the role that it gave the audience. Richard Olivier's production, like most others, tried not to be simplistic or chauvinistic in its treatment of the French. Each of the Chorus's speeches was given to a different actor, and it was the French king who spoke the Epilogue that revealed how quickly the English "lost France" again. But some members of the audience, apparently assuming that they were expected to play patriotic Elizabethans, booed the French and cheered the English on every entry, as well as giving wolf-whistles to the boy-actor who played Katherine (Kiernan 1999: 111). Actors in turn responded to the audience. When the French lords directed their contempt for the English directly at the rowdy spectators, the effect was merely to stir them on to more antagonism. On the other hand, when a few of the audience cheered the statistics about the French killed at Agincourt, Rylance turned his back on them and read the rest of the note only to those on stage; at the end, "he turned back to the audience, to find his disrespectful 'soldiers' now suitably chastened" (Kiernan 1999: 20). Much discussion of the theatre has focused on the supposed inauthenticity of the spectators' behavior, and Rylance himself agreed that this is sometimes "false" – people are "shy and unused to expressing themselves in a public place and so they fall into received patterns of response" (Kiernan 1999: 132). When the Globe performs a history play, the relation of king to subject, actor to spectator, can be made visible. The theatre has shown itself surprisingly capable of playing interiority (in fact, Rylance's Henry had an inner life from the start), but it has also created an audience for presentational acting and a willingness to accept productions that move between the two kinds of acting.

Steven Pimlott's *Richard II*, which inaugurated the RSC's "This England" series in 2000, makes a fit ending to this study, since it experimented with what might be called the subject position of the spectator. Before each half of the play, the soundtrack played a cacophony of barely audible words (they seemed to be from the play; one phrase was "Our scene is altered from a serious thing"). Richard spoke the beginning of his prison monologue at the start, and the same lines were also spoken by other characters during the play. The words, since they had once been written, existed apart from their speakers. At the beginning, the lights were dim; it was with hesitation, as if he already knew what would follow, that Richard told Gaunt to call the appellants to his presence. As he set his foot on the steps to his throne, the lights came up and the entire acting space was brightly illuminated, as it would remain (sometimes with non-naturalistic, theatrical changes of color) for the rest of the play. Richard apparently knew that he was about to set off a chain of events, or a ritual, that he had experienced before. So, while some characters appeared to think that they were speaking their own words, others were equally aware that they were not. As in the Loncraine film of *Richard III*, Shakespeare lines that made no sense in a modern context became "quotations from Shakespeare." When Richard read off the formulaic language for the duel, he had to suppress a flicker of amusement at its reference to the adversaries "plated in habiliments of war."

Whether or not he had read Harry Berger's work on the history plays, Pimlott's production hinted at possibilities that Berger himself takes to be beyond realization in performance. Berger's argument – which displaces intention from author to characters in the interest of psychological complexity – is that Richard's "project" is "to get himself deposed, pick out a likely 'heir' to perform that service, reward him with the title of usurper, and leave him with a discredited crown and the guilt of conscience for his labor" (Berger 1997: 169). Since what Richard "wants" is what the play does, this means that characters are complicit in their own fates, although this complicity is unstated and probably unrecognized. Samuel West's highly theatrical performance suggested that he was doing what the audience wanted him to do (he arrived at the deposition scene draped in the flag of St. George, with its red cross underscoring his religious claims as well as his patriotic ones). Perfectly at ease in his role, he was the only character who never addressed the audience directly.

A similar complicity was evident in the Aumerle plot of act 5. This young man's stupidity in walking around with an incriminating document in plain view must often have struck readers and spectators; it parallels Edmund's treatment of the forged letter incriminating Edgar, which of course he intends his father to see. In this production Aumerle's character was ambiguous from the start. In 1.3, for example, he described himself as giving a *hypocritical* tearful farewell to his cousin, but we were left with the possibility that it might have been a *sincere* tearful farewell. The treasonous document was so visible that it looked as if he intended York to discover it, but some sort of death wish might also have motivated him; his mother had difficulty persuading him to ride to the court; just as she pushed him offstage, the new king entered, saying, "Can no man tell me of *my* unruly son?" In other words – as in the productions by Hands and Noble already described – Henry IV knew something which, for the purposes of the next scene, he could not possibly know.

In keeping with this non-naturalistic awareness was the characters' sense of their audience. Doubling was underlined for comic effect, as when Carlisle, almost daring us to laugh, announced that Norfolk (a part which he himself had played) had died, "As surely as I live" (4.1.93). Ross, Willoughby, and Northumberland addressed to us their lines condemning Richard's failure to rule effectively; Bolingbroke motioned to us to rise in tribute to the dead Duke of Norfolk, and his henchmen looked threateningly at those who failed to do so; Carlisle emerged from our midst to make his appeal against the usurpation, which he urged us to "resist" and "prevent"; and Bolingbroke, again looking at us, declared sourly that he had "little looked for at *your* helping hands" (4.1.152). Our role as audience – supposedly part of the play but unsure how to "act" without spoiling it – was constantly called in question. But it soon became apparent that Bolingbroke was equally unsure of the kind of play in which he had been asked to perform. During the short exchange that begins with Richard's "I'll beg one boon" (4.1.292), Bolingbroke thought that he had finally recognized the play's genre, and he completed his line, "Go, some of you, convey him to the Tower" as if it were the punchline of a stand-up comedian. To his disgust, no one thought it was funny. In his final scene the other characters walked offstage while he spoke couplet after couplet – as if he had simply disappeared or as if they had ceased to exist once they ran out of lines (the supply, after all, was not infinite; it was confined to the contents of that soundtrack).

Pimlott's complex interpretation was curiously involving in spite of its elaborate games with the audience, precisely because it demanded to be interpreted. The other productions in the tetralogy demanded less from their audience, because the plays were less inherently difficult. Michael Attenborough's *Henry IV* offered admirably balanced performances of the major characters, with the psychological depth that one expects in these more realistic plays. Edward Hall's expressionistic *Henry V*, instead of trying to avoid the play's clichés, took them to extremes: the French wore berets, smoked Gauloises, and sang "La Vie en Rose" (Ian Johns, *The Times*, March 26, 2001). What was particularly interesting about this tetralogy, apart from the fact that it was not really a tetralogy, was that it seemed unlikely to become the kind of influence on other productions that previous histories had sometimes been. Another unifying factor, which received a good deal of publicity at the time, was extra-dramatic. Observant spectators could note that the opening lines of *Richard II*, the first play in the sequence, were spoken by Samuel West, son of two famous actors; that his usurper (David Troughton) was from another theatrical family; and that Richmond, whose lines in *Richard III* bring the cycle to an end, was played by David Troughton's son (also named Sam). Given that these various successions involved neither usurpation nor murder, and appeared to be the result of merit, they might have been a comment on political history, an argument for hereditary monarchy, or simple whimsy. The determination to treat each segment of the histories for itself, instead of looking to the past or the future, had made interpretation part of the experience of performance.

NOTE

1   Act, scene, and line references to Shakespeare's plays are taken from *The Norton Shakespeare*, ed. Stephen Greenblatt et al. (New York: W. W. Norton, 1997).

REFERENCES AND FURTHER READING

Baxter, K. (1998). *My Sentiments Exactly*. London: Oberon Books.

Beauman, S. (ed.) (1976). *Henry V for the Centenary Season at the Royal Shakespeare Theatre*. Oxford: Pergamon Press.

Berger, H., Jr. (1989). *Imaginary Audition: Shakespeare on Stage and Page*. Berkeley: University of California Press.

——(1997). *Making Trifles of Terrors: Redistributing Complicities in Shakespeare*. Stanford, CA: Stanford University Press.

Berry, R. (1989). *On Directing Shakespeare: Interviews with Contemporary Directors*. London: Hamish Hamilton.

Bogdanov, M. and Pennington, M. (1990). *The English Shakespeare Company: The Story of "The Wars of the Roses"*. London: Nick Ahern Books.

Brown, J. R. (1965). Three Kinds of Shakespeare. *Shakespeare Survey*, 18, 147–55.

Coursen, H. R. (1992). *Shakespearean Performance as Interpretation*. Newark: University of Delaware Press; London: Associated University Presses.

——(1996). *Shakespeare in Production: Whose History?* Athens, OH: Ohio University Press.

Craik, T. W. (ed.) (1995). Shakespeare, *Henry V*. Arden 3, Nelson. London: Routledge.

Crane, M. T. (1985). The Shakespearean Tetralogy. *Shakespeare Quarterly*, 36, 282–99.

David, R. (1973). Shakespeare's History Plays: Epic or Drama? *Shakespeare Survey*, 6, 129–39.

——(1978). *Shakespeare in the Theatre*. Cambridge: Cambridge University Press.

Dingelstedt, F. (1867), Introduction to *Shakespeare's Historien: Deutsche Bühnen-Ausgabe von Franz Dingelstedt*, 3 vols. Berlin.

Gibson, J. L. (1986). *Ian McKellen: A Biography*. London: George Weidenfeld and Nicolson.

Hattaway, M. (1994). Shakespeare's Histories: The Politics of Recent British Productions. In M. Hattaway, B. Sokolova, and D. Roper (eds.) *Shakespeare in the New Europe*. Sheffield: Sheffield Academic Press.

Heinemann, M. (1985). How Brecht Read Shakespeare. In J. Dollimore and A. Sinfield (eds.) *Political Shakespeare*. Manchester: Manchester University Press.

Henderson, D. (2000). The Disappearing Queen: Looking for Isabel in *Henry V*. In E. J. Esche (ed.) *Shakespeare and His Contemporaries in Performance*. Aldershot: Ashgate, 339–55.

Hodgdon, B. (1991). *The End Crowns All: Closure and Contradiction in Shakespeare's History*. Princeton, NJ: Princeton University Press.

——(1993). *Henry IV, Part Two*. Manchester: Manchester University Press.

Howard, J. E. and Rackin, P. (1997). *Engendering a Nation: A Feminist Account of Shakespeare's English Histories*. London: Routledge.

Kiernan, P. (1999). *Staging Shakespeare at the New Globe*. London: Macmillan.

Leggatt, A. (1988). *Shakespeare's Political Drama: The History Plays and the Roman Plays*. London: Routledge.

Leiter, S. L. (ed.) (1986). *Shakespeare Around the Globe: A Guide to Notable Postwar Revivals*. New York: Greenwood Press.

Loehlin, J. N. (1997). *Henry V*. Manchester: Manchester University Press.

McLuskie, K. (1985). The Patriarchal Bard: Feminist Critics and Shakespeare: *King Lear* and *Measure for Measure*. In J. Dollimore and A. Sinfield (eds.) *Political Shakespeare*. Manchester: Manchester University Press.

McMillin, S. (1991). *Henry IV, Part One*. Manchester: Manchester University Press.

Righter, A. (Barton) (1977). *Shakespeare and the Idea of the Play*. New York: Greenwood Press.

Shewring, M. (1996). *King Richard II*. Manchester: Manchester University Press.

Sinfield, A. (1985). Royal Shakespeare: Theatre and the Making of Ideology. In J. Dollimore and A. Sinfield (eds.) *Political Shakespeare*. Manchester: Manchester University Press.

Smith, D. N. (ed.) (1962) [1903]. *Eighteenth-Century Essays on Shakespeare*. New York: Russell and Russell.

Speaight, R. (1964). Shakespeare in Britain. *Shakespeare Quarterly*, 15, 377–89.

——(1973). The Stratford-upon-Avon Season. *Shakespeare Quarterly*, 24, 400–4.

Sprague, A. C. (1964). *Shakespeare's Histories: Plays for the Stage*. London: Society for Theatre Research.

Taylor, G. (ed.) (1984). Shakespeare, *Henry V*. Oxford: Oxford University Press.

Taylor, G. (1985). *Moment by Moment by Shakespeare [US title: To Analyze Delight: A Hedonist Criticism of Shakespeare]*. London: Macmillan.

Tillyard, E. W. M. (1944). *Shakespeare's History Plays*. London: Chatto and Windus.

Trewin, J. C. (1978). *Going to Shakespeare*. London: George Allen and Unwin.

Wells, S. (1976). *Furman Studies: Royal Shakespeare*. Greenville, SC: Furman University.

Wiles, D. (1987). *Shakespeare's Clown: Actor and Text in the Elizabethan Playhouse*. Cambridge: Cambridge University Press.

Williamson, A. (1957). *Old Vic Drama 2: 1947–1957*. London: Rockliff.

Wilson, J. D. (1944). *The Fortunes of Falstaff*. Cambridge: Cambridge University Press.

Wilson, J. D. and Worsley, T. C. (1952). *Shakespeare's Histories at Stratford, 1951*. London: Max Reinhardt.

Winny, J. (1968). *The Player King: A Theme of Shakespeare's Histories*. London: Chatto and Windus.

Worthen, W. B. (1997). *Shakespeare and the Authority of Performance*. Cambridge: Cambridge University Press.

14

1 Henry VI

David Bevington

The vexed questions of authorship and chronology remain as vexed as ever, in all three *Henry VI* plays but especially in Part 1. A swing of the pendulum is plainly discernible. Theories of disintegration, prevalent in the nineteenth century, were cast into disrepute in most of the twentieth century. Today the pendulum appears to be swinging back toward theories of multiple authorship and a comparatively late date for *1 Henry VI* (after Parts 2 and 3), assisted no doubt by a postmodern inclination toward authorial indeterminacy but also backed by improved rigor in scholarly method. An indication of the uncertainty today about issues of date and chronology appears in this interesting circumstance: since the appearance of Gary Taylor's substantial essay arguing the case for multiple authorship in 1995, two critical editions of the play have appeared, one of which, the Arden 3 edition by Edward Burns, accepts Taylor's argument, while the other, the New Cambridge edition by Michael Hattaway, emphatically does not. (Hattaway's edition appeared before Taylor's article made it into print, but took into account an earlier version of it, along with earlier work by Taylor as editor of the play for the Oxford Shakespeare; see Wells and Taylor (1987: 217ff.).) As Fredson Bowers used to say, you pays your money and you takes your choice.

Broadly speaking, those critics who admire *1 Henry VI* and find thematic and theatrical integrity in it favor a single authorship and a date preceding Parts 2 and 3, while its critics are eager to lay its presumed defects at the door of other dramatists like Nashe, Greene, and Peele. Edmund Malone is struck by unevenness of diction, figures, allusions, and versification, prompting him to look for parallels in the writings of Kyd, Marlowe, Peele, and Greene. Frederic Fleay assigns parts of the play to Thomas Lodge. E. K. Chambers, while performing yeoman service in discrediting the methods of the disintegrators – most of all their reliance on subjective criteria of taste and on too-easy verbal comparisons to other dramatists – is openly skeptical of any unitary claim to Shakespeare's authorship; he puts forward some cogent textual arguments (such as the fact that the Folio's elaborate stage directions often begin with

"Here," unusual elsewhere in Shakespeare) along with observations that betray a dislike
for the verse, such as the heroic couplet passages in the scenes of Talbot's death, featuring "the duplication of a tasteless comparison of Talbot and his son to Dedalus and
Icarus" (Chambers 1930, I: 289). John Dover Wilson argues at length that Shakespeare
revised "basic texts" of the *Henry VI* plays that had been plotted by Greene, and then
composed by Greene and Nashe with some assistance from Peele. Wilson bolsters his
case with parallel citations aplenty, but at bottom his criteria are whether the quality
of the verse is up to his expectations for Shakespeare (Wilson: 1952). Marco Mincoff
insists that the Countess of Auvergne episode is "a pointless excrescence," only one
among many pieces of evidence that "the play is not stylistically of one piece" and is
chiefly "in a style unlike anything of Shakespeare's that we know" (Mincoff 1965).

Conversely, David Riggs acknowledges a fragmentation of structure and style in
the play, but asks if it is unusual for "a major poet at an early age to be relatively
expert in one form and the merest apprentice in another" (Riggs 1971: 94). Robert
Ornstein, admitting the possibility of multiple authorship, argues that "It is better
to accept the poetry of the *Henry VI* plays as Shakespeare's earliest (and rapidly maturing) efforts than to save his reputation as a poet by suggesting that he was an opportunistic botcher of other men's plays" (Ornstein 1988: 35). M. M. Reese sees little to
be gained from debating the issue, since "in matters of this kind there are dogmatists
who will never yield and discussion is inevitably inclusive. To accept Shakespeare's
responsibility for the three parts is convenient and not necessarily wrong" (Reese
1961: 165). Carol McGinnis Kay, wishing to argue a unity of effect through recurrent images of animals and traps, accepts the view that all three *Henry VI* plays are
Shakespeare's and written in chronological order (Kay 1972). So does Barbara
Hodgdon, who wants to find a consistent "directorial eye" in the early history plays
(Hodgdon 1980). Leo Kirschbaum believes that we should trust the conscientious-
ness of Heminges and Condell as Shakespeare's friends and colleagues (Kirschbaum
1952).

In terms of chronology, the polarization is much the same. Proponents of a consistent authorial presence in *1 Henry VI* tend to favor an early date, before the writing
of Parts 2 and 3 (as indicated above in the analyses of Kay and Hodgdon). F. P. Wilson,
quoting from Nashe's eloquent praise of Lord Talbot as a model of heroism, proposes
that "for all we know there were no popular plays on English history before the
Armada and that Shakespeare may have been the first to write one" (Wilson 1953:
108). Andrew Cairncross presents an extensive argument for authorial integrity
and for an early date for *1 Henry VI*, before Parts 2 and 3, but mars his case by much
hypothetical emendation and regularization of the verse to make it sound more
"Shakespearean" (Cairncross 1962). Hattaway opts for a date of 1589–91 (Hattaway
1990: 34–41). Ernst Honigmann favors a date around 1589 (Honigmann 1985: 59ff.)
Conversely, E. K. Chambers is insistent on a later date (Chambers 1923: 129–31),
as is John Dover Wilson. Edward Burns views the play as a "prequel," that is, "a
dramatic piece that returns for ironic and challenging effect to the narrative roots of
an already familiar story" (Burns 2000: 4–5).

The most comprehensive analysis of the questions of authorship and date is that of Gary Taylor (1995). Extending arguments proposed earlier by Chambers, he deals carefully with judgmental and aesthetic criteria as notoriously subjective (albeit still potentially useful in context), and focuses primarily on textual evidence. The fact of inclusion in the First Folio need not argue for Shakespeare's unassisted authorship, since arguably he collaborated on plays in that collection, including *Timon of Athens*, *Macbeth*, and *Henry VIII* – though all of these instances can be contested, whereas plays like *The Two Noble Kinsmen*, *Pericles*, *Cardenio*, *Edward III*, and *Sir Thomas More* that are often thought to be collaborations were excluded by Heminges and Condell from the 1623 edition. The ordering of the *Henry VI* plays in the First Folio can be accounted for by an understandable desire to present the plays in their historical sequence. Setting out to write a trilogy in the late 1580s or early 1590s would have been unusual, if not unprecedented. As John Dover Wilson observed in 1952, the early printed versions of Parts 2 and 3, *The Contention* and *The True Tragedy*, make no mention of Talbot in Part 1. *The Contention* makes no use of Holinshed, whereas Part 1 and *The True Tragedy* do – a circumstance more easily explained if Part 1 were written last, or at least after *The Contention*. *The Contention* and *The True Tragedy* were performed by mid-1592, as Greene's parody of a line from the latter play (see Carroll 1985) would seem to indicate. If the "Harey the vi" recorded in Henslowe's diary as performed by Strange's Men at the Rose in the spring of 1592 and marked as "ne" was indeed new at that time, and if it was indeed Shakespeare's play (for evidence see Born 1974), *The Contention* and *The True Tragedy* would have had to be written and performed in a remarkably short period of time.

Textually, in Taylor's analysis, spelling and compositorial habits point, in his view, to two and possibly more hands at work, with the distribution of these hands suggesting different authors rather than scribes. The word "Here" in stage directions in Part 1, as noted by Chambers, is rare elsewhere in the canon. The use of feminine endings in blank verse lines confirms distinctions already established in this analysis; so too with compound adjectives and the relative frequency of alternative forms like *between/betwixt*, *O/Oh*, and *amongst/among* (see also Taylor and Jowett 1993: 248–51). Taylor therefore proposes that much of act 1 was by Thomas Nashe, and that substantial portions of the play were by other authors not so certainly identifiable. Shakespeare is left with little more than 2.4 (the scene in the Temple Garden) and much of act 4 involving the death of Lord Talbot.

Taylor's is a serious and impressive study. Yet Michael Hattaway, for one, is prompted to offer a rebuttal. As Taylor allows, not all of the items marked as "ne" in Henslowe's diary were newly written and performed; the indication could mean "newly adapted." Peter Alexander (1929) has argued that the entry probably refers to another play, although that view is now largely discounted. Part 1 must have been written by mid-1592, in time for Thomas Nashe's encomium of Talbot in *Pierce Penilesse his Supplication to the Divell* (Stationers' Register, 8 August), and that tribute might seem to point to a current play, but it could have been written earlier. The use of Holinshed might have seemed appealing to Shakespeare soon after the publication of that work's second edition in 1587, and, since Holinshed is used in it mainly for the scenes involving Joan Pucelle and the Dauphin (Bullough 1966: 3.75–7), whereas a major portion of the play is based on Hall's *Union of the Two Noble and Illustre Families of Lancaster and York*, the pattern of using sources in the three *Henry VI* plays is easy enough to understand whether Part 1 was written first or last. The failure of Parts 2 and 3 to recall Lord Talbot may simply mean that in the onrush of events a great deal of action turns out to be sequential and episodic. Interruptions owing to the plague, and shifting alliances among the acting companies of the late 1580s and early 1590s, all conspire to provide enough uncertainty that a sequence of dating still remains murky (Hattaway 1990: 34–41; see also Hammond 1981: 54–61).

On the authorship question as well, matters remain unsettled. The main contention of those who resist Taylor's arguments is that, at an early stage of his career, Shakespeare may have been "moving freely between the various verse registers that were being deployed in the plays in which he was probably acting" (Hattaway 1990: 42–3). Other critics substantially endorse this view that the varying texture of *1 Henry VI* can be explained as the product of an experimenting and absorptive mind. The debate continues, but Taylor's work certainly is receiving serious attention, and deserves to do so.

These questions of authorship and chronology might seem technical, and are sometimes dismissed as unimportant, but they do in fact bear significantly on the central issue of the play's unity and integrity as a piece of dramatic writing. Is *1 Henry VI* a jumble of fragmented pieces, written in a distracting medley of styles, or is it informed by coherent ideas and image patterns? Increasingly, the critical impulse has been to find coherence.

Take, for example, the episode in which the Countess of Auvergne attempts to entrap Lord Talbot by her enticing hospitality and thereby rid France of her chief enemy (2.3). The episode is not to be found in the chronicles. Marco Mincoff finds it "a pointless excrescence" (Mincoff 1965: 279). More representatively, Sigurd Burckhardt addresses what he calls "the disintegrationist heresy" by analyzing the Countess episode as an instance of interrupted ceremony. To Burckhardt, a characteristic of Shakespeare's so-called "immature" style is authorial self-awareness of this apparently disjointed kind of writing. Greene's admonition about the "upstart crow, beautified with our feathers" should be read as evidence of "a young poet's inevitable and natural tendency to imitate his elders." The Countess episode deftly illustrates a style resulting from these circumstances: it approaches a prevailing image of static order and harmony, based on an analogy of the kingdom to the family, and critiques it. This is the way it fits into a play that begins and ends with the interruption of the ceremonial mode. What appears to be episodic in Shakespeare's early style is, in retrospect, calculated and revealing. Savage spectacles move toward ordered conclusions (Burckhardt 1968).

James Riddell endorses Burckhardt's reading of the Countess episode as well integrated into the play as a whole, going one step further by insisting that the Talbot we encounter in this scene is the same Talbot as in the later scenes in Bordeaux

(Riddell 1977). David Bevington (the present author), joined by several critics, finds coherence in the Countess episode by noting ways in which this daunting lady is a counterpart to Joan Pucelle and Margaret of Anjou – dominating females to whose temptations weak men succumb while strong men (notably, Talbot) successfully resist (Bevington 1966; Richmond 1967; Berry 1975; Kastan 1982: 116; Bassnett 1988; Howard and Rackin 1997: 59; Holderness 2000). As William Hawley observes, the Countess episode clearly demonstrates the way in which "the superior masculine force of pure self-representation over misplaced feminine desire must be acknowledged by her [the Countess's] utter submission" (Hawley 1992: 20). The fact of this episode's having no direct chronicle source might seem to point to the author's particular interest in this sequence, rather than suggesting irrelevance.

The figure of Talbot is an appealing one to critics looking for unity in *1 Henry VI*. Talbot is, after all, the focus of Nashe's warm praise of the play, and was evidently the object of veneration in the play's early success. To Robert Jones, who, in a way characteristic of integrationists sees *1 Henry VI* as "the first play of the first tetralogy," Talbot embodies the ideal of an heroic historical heritage that can live anew in the present if the English people will but heed the lesson (Jones 1991). Talbot keeps alive the spirit of Henry V when that heritage proves to be squandered in the royal successor; Talbot's own son, and the noble father–son relationship we witness at the time of their deaths, is to be seen in juxtaposition with the failures of young Henry VI, who has not understood how renewal of the heroic spirit is to be attained through generational succession and historic fame. For James Bulman, the binding force in *1 Henry VI* is the epic vein of an heroic drama, using language that Shakespeare inherited from epic tradition and from conqueror plays like *Tamburlaine*. Talbot's death takes the form of traditional *de casibus* tragedy, showing us in this case a mighty representative of chivalric virtue "victimized by vicious historical necessity" (Bulman 1985a: 26–37). Ronald Berman points out the thematic force in the *Henry VI* plays of the configuration of fathers and sons, stressing the instructive contrast between the Talbots and the Plantagenet family constellation (Berman 1962). Wayne Billings similarly observes that the peace-loving King Henry VI lacks *virtù* and love of glory, while his adversary, the Duke of York, is valiant in war but conniving in times of peace; only Talbot manages to combine true valor with personal integrity. No dramatist but Shakespeare, in Billings's view, was capable of the overview of English history that informs meaningful juxtapositions such as these (Billings 1972). Michael Manheim's study of the "weak king dilemma" in this and other history plays is in substantial agreement; and so is Harold Goddard, who finds Henry VI "the most critically neglected of Shakespeare's kings" (Manheim 1973; Goddard 1951).

Joan Pucelle fascinates most critics who come to this play, partly because of the character assassination and more importantly because of the deep anxieties about gender that her presence generates. Richard Hardin traces the mythmaking that took place in the time of the Reformation and the resulting animosity, in England, toward a French heroine. Edward Hall was the first to develop the assault fully, as contrasted with the French account of Enguerand de Monstrelet. Shakespeare takes much of his material from Hall, but then highlights the caricature of Joan by drawing on

Holinshed's rendition of the meeting of Joan and the Dauphin, her pregnancy, and still more. Indeed, Shakespeare goes well beyond his sources in satiric defamation by inventing many details of the first conversation and love scene between Joan and her besotted royal admirer (Hardin 1990). As David Riggs and Edward Berry observe, Joan is an "extended parody" of the chivalric ideal embodied in Lord Talbot (Riggs 1971: 104; Berry 1975: 20).

A key to Joan's centrality in providing a unity for this play lies in gender and family relations. Coppélia Kahn, interested in masculine self-definition, contrasts the pattern of emulating the father seen in the Talbot family with the chaotic rivalries seen elsewhere in the *Henry VI* plays. In Kahn's view, the play implies an idealized relationship whereby the son should not try to excel the father in striving to be worthy of him, and in these terms young John Talbot is a dutiful son. Yet there is an opposite danger, into which he does fall: that of failing to achieve his own separate identity. As Kahn puts it, the son is too strongly "identified with his father in death." Family relationships, and especially those between males, are thus problematic in the early histories, beset by huge risks of undifferentiated merger or, conversely, of anarchic self-assertion. Given these weaknesses in men, liaisons with women "are invariably disastrous because they subvert or destroy more valued alliances between men." Joan, above all, is "a composite portrait of the ways women are dangerous to men": she emasculates them both by usurping the male role of warrior and by using her sexual appeal to dominate men. Joan is thus at the center of *1 Henry VI*'s absorbing study of the deep connection between gender and political history (Kahn 1981).

Graham Holderness further elaborates ways in which women, especially Joan, are figures of transgression, deeply problematic in a world "sustained by the explicitly masculine values of physical heroism and military achievement." Even Talbot "has serious problems with women who refuse their allotted role in traditional society"; he is unable to explain the "unnatural strength" with which Joan overcomes him in combat, other than to ascribe that power to witchcraft (Holderness 2000; see also Von Rosador 1990). Shakespeare, by going beyond his sources in his caricature of Joan, gives support to Talbot's view, to such an extent that Marilyn French sees in the dramatist himself a hatred of sexuality and of women with which he wrestles; woman is, for him, both a destroyer and a restorer of harmonious wholeness (French 1981: 325–6). Catherine Belsey, too, sees in the women of *1 Henry VI* the paradox that "Woman to man / Is either a god or a wolf" (Belsey 1985: 183).

Joan's daunting role in *1 Henry VI* invites topical elucidation. One of the more controversial readings is that of Leah Marcus, who pursues extensively an analogy between Joan and Queen Elizabeth. Both act "like a man." Elizabeth donned male military attire for her appearance before the army at Tilbury in the year of the Armada, referred to herself as a "prince," and ambivalently adopted roles for herself both as husband of her nation and as virgin mother to her people. Shakespeare's Joan, in a play written four years or so after the Armada victory, "has a similar uncanny, befuddling effect on English warriors and their accustomed roles." The "woman on top" arouses male anxieties about female dominance in both cases (Marcus 1988: 51–96). The argument is intriguing but tenuous because it relies on analogous parallels (Joan's naming of her lovers "is both a displacement and a display of rumors like those which dogged the English queen": p. 71) that can be accounted for by the omnipresence in English culture of the period of anxieties about female transgression; John Knox was exercised about the "monstrous regiment" of Mary Tudor before Elizabeth came to the throne, and the controversy about female rulers was generally widespread. One wonders what Elizabeth's subjects, and she herself, would have thought of the comparison if it appeared evident to them.

More substantially, Gabriele Bernhard Jackson proposes a topical link between Talbot and the Earl of Essex in 1591–2, "when English troops under Essex had been sent to France for the particular purpose of besieging Rouen; the play unhistorically dramatizes that city's recapture from the French." This parallel not only illuminates a striking feature of the play's departure from its sources; it also has the considerable advantage of proposing a compliment to Elizabeth, rather than an insult. As Sir William Lucy sadly escorts offstage the dead bodies of Talbot and his son, he defiantly proclaims, "from their ashes shall be reared / A phoenix that shall make all France afeard" (4.7.92–3). Here is a topical resonance that can hardly be doubted. The phoenix was one of Elizabeth's emblems. At the same time, the play can be seen to deal with what was controversial about Essex's campaign: the reluctance of Elizabeth to put Essex in charge, and the perennial conflict between the queen's own policy of negotiation and minimal expenditure on the one hand and Essex's wasteful bravado on the other. Essex is in this sense no Talbot: he was hotheaded, rash, and extravagant, as in his knighting of many of his followers in defiance of the queen's known wishes for restraint. The analogy is thus not perfect, but it does allow audiences to speculate on issues that were in the forefront of war policy when the play was written and performed (Jackson 1988). One might add that even at an earlier date, say 1589, the same problem of caution at court undercutting military effort on the Continent was endemic; it had been a constant factor in Elizabeth's troubled relations with Leicester in the Lowlands shortly before his death in 1588. Jackson also asks whether the satirical portrait of Joan might not remind Elizabethan viewers of their own queen at Tilbury, but does so in a way that leaves the topic open: audiences are invited to ponder the prospect of an Amazonian, domineering woman in time of war, but in such an ambiguous way that one cannot be sure if any topical criticism is intended.

Jean Howard and Phyllis Rackin reinforce Jackson's point that "Joan may have been the first female character to appear on stage in armor and that she was one of the first to appear there in masculine attire of any sort" (Howard and Rackin 1997: 45–6). In part we are invited to be fascinated by Joan's bravura, even attracted by it; at the same time, Joan's transvestite costume "prepares for her final association with the demonic" (Rackin 1990: 199). Donald Watson, following up on Jackson's work, usefully explores the possible resonances in *1 Henry VI* of Essex's siege of Rouen in 1591 (Watson 1990: 40).

Nina Levine cogently asks if the play's ambivalent exploration of issues of gender and power may not be illuminated by a consideration of the annual Accession Day tournaments that were such an important political spectacle in the 1580s and 1590s.

Levine's wish is not to "unlock" the play's meaning this way, or to claim a direct source, but rather to see the Accession Day spectacle as (in Richard McCoy's terms) a "formal ritual by which the queen and the nobility came together to negotiate long-standing conflicts of power and privilege." Essex figures prominently here, as in Jackson's topical analysis. The 1590 tilt is full of suggestive symbolisms demonstrating what Eric Mallin calls "a forum for the visibility of masculine courtier power" (Levine 1998; McCoy 1989: 2–3; Mallin 1990: 157). One might add that the situation in 1588–9 was as rife with topical possibilities, so soon after the death of Leicester.

Another topical approach to Joan Pucelle is to look at contemporary attitudes toward witchcraft. Deborah Willis shows how, in Shakespeare's first tetralogy, "witches, wives, and mothers are endowed with similar nightmare powers; by both magical and nonmagical means they manipulate males and make them feel as if they have been turned back into dependent children." When the English burn Joan at the stake, "they are punishing not only a rebel and a class upstart but also a betraying mother, in this case a phallic mother, a mother who at first seemed to have it all – breast, womb, and phallus – now reduced to futile stratagems [*sic*] that display only the relative powerlessness of the maternal body in the male public world." Hence the usefulness of studying Joan's fate in the broader context of English witch-hunts (Willis 1994: 100–1). John Cox similarly explores a "highly charged atmosphere" in the years immediately after the Armada victory that lent energy to the scapegoating of a "demonically inspired character" who is both foreign and a witch (Cox 2000: 141). Cox proposes still another way to read the play topically, as an "extraordinarily bleak" response to anxieties in the post-Armada years and to the larger pattern of an old aristocracy in decay – the departure of Talbot, as it were, and the baleful arrival on the scene of a new, educated, privileged class typified by Suffolk (Cox 1989: 83, 87).

Although Margaret of Anjou's appearance as the intended bride of King Henry and the paramour of Suffolk is a belated one in *1 Henry VI*, she too is seen as a unifying figure dramaturgically because of her final place in the iterated parade of domineering women. As a "masculine" mother in a world of civil and familial conflict, Margaret "comes to possess a witchlike power" (Willis 1994: 102). Thomas Heywood, in his *Exemplary Lives* (1640), saw fit to enthrone Margaret in his list of Amazonian female Worthies, along with Deborah, Judith, Esther, Penthesilea, Artemisia, Boadicea, Ethelfleda, and Queen Elizabeth (Wright 1946). As Gwyn Williams shows, the illicit affair between Margaret and Suffolk is unhistorical; Shakespeare's invention here points toward a thematic continuity, both in *1 Henry VI* as a self-contained play and as a link forward (possibly a "prequel") to Part 2. Recent stage productions that have sometimes cut the Margaret–Suffolk love affair, along with the Countess episode, have robbed the play "of passages of high and complex human interest and made such productions heavy with history, shorn of those parts of these plays which perhaps most interested their author, partly because he invented them" (Williams 1974: 310, 319).

The question as to whether *1 Henry VI* embodies the "Tudor myth" of providential history has been sharply debated in the past forty years or so, and remains at the center of the larger critical discourse over the play's unity or lack of unity. E. M. W. Tillyard's espousal of the Tudor myth has become a favorite whipping boy. He sees the hand of God in England's destiny. Joan is, as she declares, "Assigned . . . to be the English scourge" (1.2.129). What then, asks Tillyard, were the sins that God sought to punish by inflicting England with this scourge? Preeminent was "the murder of Richard II, the shedding of blood of God's deputy on earth." The theme of *1 Henry VI* is "the testing of England, already guilty and under a sort of curse, by French witchcraft." Lord Talbot, "a great and pious soldier," is the "Morality hero" of this drama, "and the witchcraft is directed principally at him." This providential view serves the Tudor cause because it looks forward to Henry Tudor, Henry VII, as the eventual restorer of order once the English have suffered sufficiently for that original crime and its aftermath in civil slaughter. Such was the perspective on history provided by the chroniclers whom Henry commissioned to argue in this way, and the interpretation made its way into the chronicles of Hall and Holinshed. This view of Shakespeare's history plays demands an overview of them as a tetralogy, a cycle, and indeed only part of a massive epic survey of fifteenth-century history that includes the second so-called tetralogy as well. Not surprisingly, Tillyard is fully persuaded of the single authorship of Shakespeare for all these plays and for the composition of the first cycle in chronological order, with *1 Henry VI* written first (Tillyard 1964: 161–73). Lily B. Campbell offers a supporting view, showing how widespread was the Tudor myth in Elizabethan historiography in Polydore Vergil, Hall, Sir Walter Ralegh, and others, and arguing that Shakespeare's intent was to "use history to teach politics to the present" (Campbell 1968: 82–4, 123–5). Robert Pierce sympathetically applies Tillyard's conclusions to a discussion of the family and the state as reflecting a "doctrine of correspondences." "What infects the kingdom infects everything in it" (Pierce 1971: 35–52). Irving Ribner accepts uncritically a providential reading (Ribner 1965: 104–6).

The corrective to Tillyard began with A. L. French, who, in 1968, pointed out that the word "scourge," in the sense of an "instrument of divine chastisement," is used once by Joan herself, whereas it is used of Talbot no less than three times (French 1968). The argument was expanded by French in 1974: the death of Richard II is referred to only five times in the entire first tetralogy, and then only in a perfunctory and legalistic way as a matter of genealogical debate. More substantially, the first tetralogy undercuts notions of order, justice, and moral equity. Some deaths are seen as divinely retributive; others appear to be more wanton, or the bad luck of war or even old age (such as the deaths of Salisbury and Bedford in *1 Henry VI*). Talbot is defeated because he has been let down by factional rivalries among the English. History in this play is "subversive" (French 1974). More or less at the same time, Henry Ansgar Kelly came to a similar view. Talbot's death is in no way ascribed to Joan Pucelle; Exeter's pessimistic soliloquies predicting disaster for England merely point out that child-rule breeds the occasion when envious rivalry can do its work; the end of *1 Henry VI* arrives with promise of carnage to come and "without implicating to any discernible extent the operation of divine providence." The English chroniclers provided their own spin to bolster a state-sponsored Tudor myth, but Shakespeare as a dramatist had other aims (Kelly 1970: 218–53). David Frey, writing in 1976, challenged, "on the widest level possible, the notion that God's hand may be seen in the affairs of England"; piety and goodness are not divinely protected but instead are incessantly rebuffed (Frey 1976: 10ff.).

David Scott Kastan provides some much-needed balance in the debate. The early history plays do indeed feature a reiterated providentialism, he points out, as in Mortimer's dying remembrance of how Henry IV "Deposed his nephew Richard, Edward's son, / The first-begotten and the lawful heir / Of Edward king, the third of that descent" (*1 Henry VI*, 2.5.63–6), with predictable and morally serious consequences. Yet "this is not to say that Shakespeare uncritically accepts the providential assertions of his characters." Providentialism is there, but "as a model of historical causation to be probed and challenged." King Henry's own providential belief is best understood not as objective evidence of divine control of human history "but of his unfitness to rule." Shakespeare's own historiography owes at least as much to a humanistic model in which history is "the record of an endless recurrence of events under more or less identical circumstances." If history is repetitive, "time has value as it can provide models for future action." This humanistic model too, in Kastan's view, is held up for critical scrutiny in *1 Henry VI*. Time can be relentless, bringing men to their deaths without any necessary increase in knowledge of themselves. This is the profound sense in which *1 Henry VI*, like the plays that follow it, is open-ended historically and theatrically (Kastan 1982: 13–25; see also Siegel 1986: 71–2).

In a subsequent article, Kastan argues convincingly that the very fact of putting monarchs on the stage was subversive "because representation became itself subversive." The process of "counterfeiting" in the theatre demystified ideologies of order and degree by showing the monarchy continually involved in a "dispiriting drama of human motives," using pageantry as a fictitious prop. Representation "is powerful and dangerous," argues Kastan, and not as easily contained or coopted as Stephen Greenblatt and other New Historicists are inclined to argue. Kastan thus agrees with Stephen Orgel that "To mime the monarch was a potentially revolutionary act" (Kastan 1986; Greenblatt 1988: 21–65; Orgel, "Making Greatness Familiar," 45).

The issue of providentialism has inevitable consequences for one's view of the interplay between predestined fate and free will. M. M. Reese's balanced view is that Shakespeare is attempting to reconcile the orthodox providential view of history with a view that "man, while not the total author of his fate, does by his own actions cooperate in his destiny, however slightly or obscurely." The dramatist's attitude is thus "not wholly fatalistic." Talbot is the tragic hero caught in an impossible situation where his death is determined by chaotic forces beyond his control, and yet he has it within his choice to die nobly and to gain immortal fame for his greatness of courage (Reese 1961: 165–80).

In the wake of the rebellion against Tillyard's worldview critics have generally sought unity in *1 Henry VI* and other early history plays in what Philip Brockbank calls "the frame of disorder" (Brockbank 1961). Whatever might appear chaotic or episodic is by design. Shakespeare's dramatic design in the early history plays, argues Roger Warren, is "that of setting one extreme against another, and especially of leading the audience to expect a particular consequence, and then reversing that expectation by presenting quite a different result, often the complete opposite of the one expected." The siege of Orleans is full of such ironic reversals. The play opens with an interrupted funeral procession for the dead Henry V. Anti-climax is a recurrent feature of dialogue and action. Such contrasts "help to provide the structure for the entire central action" of Part 2, and Part 1 as well (Warren 1984). The argument here follows that of Hereward T. Price, who insists that Part 1 is so brilliantly constructed that no one other than Shakespeare could have undertaken the task (Price 1951: 24–37). John Blanpied's metatheatrical approach to *1 Henry VI* finds an intentional design in the play's "counterconsciousness" and incessantly ironic perspective in the face of a "collapse of order and ceremony." Shakespeare "subtly undermines the authority of the monumental past" by "asserting those theatrical techniques that seem designed to dignify it." "A pattern has emerged," and it is one of theatrical subversion, of presenting human action as a kind of play (Blanpied 1975). The metatheatrical essence of the play is an "experimental quality of confusion" in which "everything straightforward and sturdy turns doubtful and inconclusive" (Blanpied 1983: 26–41).

Larry Champion explores the early history plays as expressive of Shakespeare's "search for dramatic form." In *1 Henry VI* coherence is strengthened by the choric utterances of Exeter, Bedford, and Lucy, thereby establishing "the fundamental theme" of political discord which "lends coherence to the welter of activities which make up the plot" (Champion 1980: 12–24). Surely it is not accidental that these plays "comprise a virtual discourse on authority" (Champion 1990: 71–81). Edna Zwick Boris finds artistic coherence in the attention Shakespeare gives "to the sanctions of lawful rule, general consent, and dedication to the common good"; parliament scenes, such as 3.1 of *1 Henry VI* and the rose-plucking scene in the Temple garden that precedes it (2.4), astutely dramatize the political struggle in such a way as to reveal the thoughtfulness and complexity of Shakespeare's understanding of constitutional issues (Boris 1978: 25, 30–2). At the same time, argues Richard Helgerson, the play shows little regard for commoners; it is as though Shakespeare wished to "efface, alienate, even demonize all signs of commoner participation in the political nation" (Helgerson 1992: 214). For Moody Prior, intent on studying "the drama of power," the central unifying question is, "Who has the right to be the king of England?" (Prior 1973: 103). Paul Dean finds a "powerful and richly textured" coherence in the play's use of its sources, especially the "romance" histories of Greene, Lyly, and others (Dean 1982). For S. C. Sen Gupta, unity is best found in the way in which Shakespeare responsibly condenses his chronicle sources, not as a "mere fantasia" as some have supposed but as a coherent representation "that is not unhistorical in substance" (Sen Gupta 1964: 59; see also Saccio 1977: 91–100; Norwich 1999: 221–8).

Studies of language and imagery in *1 Henry VI* tend to find a unifying principle in the play's imagistic presentation of violence. Again, the principle of artistic order is to be found in disorder. For David Frey, the early history plays are unified by a pattern of images grouped around the hunters and the hunted, the butchers and the slaughtered: on the one hand lions, wolves, foxes, ravens, serpents, and kites; on the other hand doves, whelps, sheep, oxen, lambs, wrens, heifers, deer, and chickens (Frey 1976: 12–19). Carol McGinnis Kay similarly defends the unity of these plays in terms of major image patterns involving animals, "specifically dragons, bears, wolves, deer, lions, sheep, horses, worms, mules, mice, dogs, rabbits, oxen, bees, and fish." The list continues particularly in *1 Henry VI* with owls, the phoenix, doves, eagles, leopards, sheep, and wolves, presented in ways that involve the weaker animals in "the endless harassment of traps, snares, chains, cages, and hunts," as when Lucy describes Talbot at Bordeaux as "girdled with a waist of iron, / And hemmed about with grim destruction" (4.3.20–1). Images of birds in flight connect with the picture of Talbot and his son as Daedalus and Icarus (4.6.54–6). Patterns of enclosure dominate the first play and differentiate it from Part 2, in which imagery of slaughter is predominant (Kay 1972).

Robert Ornstein celebrates the Temple garden scene especially (2.4) as a "triumph of the dramatic imagination over the inartistic formlessness of Tudor historiography." His case is bolstered by the fact that the scene is highly original, without a model in the chronicles, and that it is generally credited to Shakespeare even by those who argue for multiple authorship. The scene is noteworthy for its emblematic imagery of plucking of the white and red roses (Ornstein 1988: 36–42). The scene is an instance of what John Wilders calls "the lost garden" in the history plays, using the garden as an emblem of "the temporary nature of human achievement"; Shakespeare portrays history, in Wilders's view, "as a series of attempts by individuals to satisfy their need for permanence, and their necessary failure to create it" (Wilders 1978: 22, 27–8). James Bulman, too, sees the Temple garden scene as central to the play's emblematic integrity: drawing on Virgil's *Georgics*, Shakespeare looks at England as a garden whose decay (as Caroline Spurgeon puts it) is "brought about by ignorance and carelessness on the part of the gardener." In the Temple garden scene and elsewhere, Shakespeare repeatedly conceives of strife "in terms of trees – the planting and grafting of saplings, the hewing and lopping of limbs." Pastoral images of tilling, planting, animal husbandry, and bee-keeping, so dear to Virgil, give way to contrasting images of despoiling (Bulman 1985b).

Rhetoric can be seen as another shaping and unifying force in *1 Henry VI*. Robert Turner finds in this play patterns of dialogue akin to those used in another early play, *The Comedy of Errors*. In the stychomythia of the Temple garden scene the antagonists devote themselves to insult and retort rather than reasoned discourse, with the actual cause of disagreement remaining unspecified; it is as though Shakespeare wishes to show that the impending civil conflict has "no basis in idea or value." In both ceremonious and witty dialogue in this play, the sounds of words are as important as their meanings; copious statements and highly schematic give-and-take supplant true dialectic. These characteristics, in Turner's view, "are the result of Shakespeare's train-ing in rhetoric and his early assumptions about the nature of drama." They argue for a single authorship and a coherent design of the arts of language. Shakespeare's char-acters in this early play reveal little about their inner feelings, "not because they lack a mastery of metaphor, but because Shakespeare's standards of relevance direct their choice of associations elsewhere." He wants us to understand the oral significance of historical events more than the play of emotions. His training at this early stage of his career is distinctly rhetorical, as we can see in his love for scenes of persuasion: Joan Pucelle persuading Charles to let her lead the French army, Joan vamping the Duke of Burgundy, Suffolk courting Margaret, Suffolk persuading Henry VI to marry her instead of the Earl of Armagnac's daughter. Our responses to the characters are directed by moral equations, inviting sympathy for the good and disapproval for the bad. The good speak their minds; the bad are secretive. Here, in Turner's view, are to be found the unifying identifications of Shakespeare's authorship as a young play-wright (Turner 1974: 15–50, 67–9, 122–6). Oaths perform a similar rhetorical func-tion, as shown by Faye Kelly: they offer a "principle of Shakespearean dramatic construction" (Kelly 1973).

Finally, staging of *1 Henry VI*, both as called for in the script and as realized in some recent productions, can be made to argue for a kind of theatrical coherence. Charles Edelman undertakes to confute the common impression of the play as "that drum-and-trumpet thing" (Edelman 1992: 60, citing Maurice Morgann) by showing how visible combat is used to depict "the heroic, but doomed, quality of the English expeditionary forces." The high incidence of military action is appropriate to the history being dramatized. Nashe saw the play as Talbot's play, and indeed Talbot is onstage extensively in scenes of combat. The prolonged sword-fighting invokes a lost medieval world of Malory, with Talbot as its chivalric hero doomed by the onrush of a more modern disillusioning world of political intrigue. Edelman sides with Michael Goldman, in whose view "the sweep of athletic bodies across the stage is used in *1 Henry VI* not only to provide an exciting spectacle but to focus and clarify, to render dramatic, the entire unwieldy chronicle" (Edelman 1992: 51–68; Goldman 1972: 161). Michael Hattaway shows how Shakespeare, in *1 Henry VI*, is not simply writing for an unadorned and unworthy scaffold, expecting the audience to conjure up what is to be imagined by verbal imagery alone; repeatedly, the stage becomes Orleans at dawn, or Bordeaux, with elaborate musical effects in the battle sequences (Hattaway 1982: 34, 61). Bevington (1984) reveals how the theatre space is repeatedly invoked in this play to represent conflict before walls under siege, complete with scaling ladders and hasty exists *"o'er the walls"* as the French are driven out of Orleans (pp. 102–3). Walter Hodges's illustrations for the New Cambridge Shakespeare do a fine job of suggesting how such an assault might have been managed in a London play-house (Hattaway 1990: 10, 19).

Recent productions, as at Stratford-upon-Avon in 1963 and again in 1977, have shown how well *1 Henry VI* can work onstage and also how eviscerated it can be when deprived of key scenes that are too quickly deemed extraneous. Too often the play has been cut to become part of a two-part version of all three Henry VI plays, and seldom if ever is *1 Henry VI* seen by itself. Lois Potter quotes John Barton and Peter Hall, directors of the 1963 two-part version, as saying that they found the original to be little more than "a mess of angry and undifferentiated barons, thrashing about in a mass of diffuse narrative" (Potter 1990). Barbara Hodgdon argues the importance of the pictorial, noting how the most comprehensive effects of the play "derive from spatial change"; hence the importance of letting *1 Henry VI* appear in full costume, as written. Its "syntax of stage pictures" (a phrase borrowed from Arthur Gerstner-Hirzel) is vital to an understanding of the play as a single and whole dramatic entertainment (Hodgdon 1980; Gerstner-Hirzel 1957). Students of staging thus join forces with more verbally-oriented critics in perceiving a unity in the play.

What we see, then, in an overview of critical studies of *1 Henry VI* in recent decades, is that critics have shown a consistent desire to find coherence and design in the play, even if that coherence is perceived as one of calculated disorder. Close analyses of imagery, of staging, of thematic focus all embrace the idea of a kind of authorial integrity. That general perception is, to be sure, a natural and even predictable one. Shakespeare is such a fabulous writer that one wants to see design even in his earliest work. Gary Taylor has mounted a real challenge by reviving and strengthening arguments for multiple authorship and for order of composition out of the chronological pattern. The jury is still out, and may remain deadlocked; no one wants to see Shakespeare executed for a crime he may not even have committed. Until something as reliable as DNA testing comes to the rescue, it remains unlikely that readers of *1 Henry VI* will come to a uniform verdict about its quality and its authorship. Certainly the debate adds materially to our interest in the play.

References and Further Reading

Alexander, P. (1929). *Shakespeare's "Henry VI" and "Richard III."* Cambridge: Cambridge University Press.

Bassnett, S. (1988). Sexuality and Power in the Three Parts of *King Henry VI*. *Shakespeare Jahrbuch*, 124, 183–90.

Belsey, C. (1985). *The Subject of Tragedy: Identity and Difference in Renaissance Drama*. London: Methuen.

Berman, R. S. (1962). Fathers and Sons in the Henry VI Plays. *Shakespeare Quarterly*, 13, 487–97.

Berry, E. I. (1975). *Patterns of Decay: Shakespeare's Early Histories*. Charlottesville: University Press of Virginia.

Bevington, D. (1966). The Domineering Female in *1 Henry VI*. *Shakespeare Studies*, 2, 51–8.

——(1984). *Action is Eloquence: Shakespeare's Language of Gesture*. Cambridge, MA: Harvard University Press.

Billings, W. L. (1972). Ironic Lapses: Plotting in *Henry VI*. *Studies in the Literary Imagination*, 5, 27–49.

Blanpied, J. W. (1975). "Art and baleful sorcery": The Counterconsciousness of *Henry VI, Part I*. *Studies in English Literature*, 15, 213–27.

——(1983). *Time and the Artist in Shakespeare's English Histories*. Newark: University of Delaware Press; London: Associated University Presses.

Boris, E. Z. (1978). *Shakespeare's English Kings, the People, and the Law: A Study in the Relationship between the Tudor Constitution and the English History Plays*. Rutherford, NJ: Fairleigh Dickinson University Press; London: Associated University Presses.

Born, H. (1974). The Date of *2, 3 Henry VI*. *Shakespeare Quarterly*, 1974, 323–34.

Brockbank, J. P. (1961). The Frame of Disorder – *Henry VI*. In J. R. Brown and B. Harris (eds.) *Early Shakespeare*. Stratford-upon-Avon Studies 3. London: Edward Arnold.

Bullough, G. (ed.) (1966). *Narrative and Dramatic Sources of Shakespeare*, vol 3. London: Routledge and Kegan Paul; New York: Columbia University Press.

Bulman, J. C. (1985a). *The Heroic Idiom of Shakespearean Tragedy*. Newark: University of Delaware Press.

——(1985b). Shakespeare's Georgic Histories. *Shakespeare Survey*, 38, 37–47.

Burckhardt, S. (1968). *Shakespearean Meanings*. Princeton, NJ: Princeton University Press.

Burns, E. (ed.) (2000). *King Henry VI Part I*. The Arden Shakespeare, 3. London: Thomson Learning.

Cairncross, A. (ed.) (1962). *The First Part of King Henry VI*. Arden Shakespeare 2. London: Methuen.

Campbell, L. B. (1968). *Shakespeare's "Histories": Mirrors of Elizabethan Policy*. San Marino, CA: Huntington Library.

Carroll, D. A. (1985). Greene's "Vpstart Crow" Passage: A Survey of Commentary. *Research Opportunities in Renaissance Drama*, 28, 111–27.

Chambers, E. K. (1923). *The Elizabethan Stage*, 2 vols. Oxford: Clarendon Press.

——(1930). *William Shakespeare: A Study of Facts and Problems*, 4 vols. Oxford: Clarendon Press.

Champion, L. S. (1980). *Perspectives in Shakespeare's English Histories*. Athens, OH: University of Georgia Press.

——(1990). *"The Noise of Threatening Drum": Dramatic Strategy and Political Ideology in Shakespeare and the English Chronicle Plays*. Newark: University of Delaware Press; London: Associated University Presses.

Cox, J. D. (1989). *Shakespeare and the Dramaturgy of Power*. Princeton, NJ: Princeton University Press.

——(2000). *The Devil and the Sacred in English Drama, 1350–1642*. Cambridge: Cambridge University Press.

Dean, P. (1982). Shakespeare's *Henry VI* Trilogy and Elizabethan "Romance" Histories: The Origins of a Genre. *Shakespeare Quarterly*, 33, 35–48.

Edelman, C. (1992). *Brawl Ridiculous: Swordfighting in Shakespeare's Plays*. Manchester: Manchester University Press.

French, A. L. (1968). Joan of Arc and *Henry VI*. *English Studies*, 49, 425–9.

——(1974). The Mills of God and Shakespeare's Early History Plays. *English Studies*, 55, 313–24.

French, M. (1981). *Shakespeare's Division of Experience*. New York: Summit Books.

Frey, D. L. (1976). *The First Tetralogy: Shakespeare's Scrutiny of the Tudor Myth*. The Hague: Mouton.

Gerstner-Hirzel, A. (1957). *The Economy of Action and Word in Shakespeare's Plays*. Bern: Peter Lang.

Goddard, H. C. (1951). *The Meaning of Shakespeare*, 2 vols. Chicago, IL: University of Chicago Press.

Goldman, M. (1972). *Shakespeare and the Energies of Drama*. Princeton, NJ: Princeton University Press.

Greenblatt, S. (1988). *Invisible Bullets: "Shakespearean Negotiations."* Berkeley: University of California Press.

Hammond, A. (ed.) (1981). *Richard the Third*. Cambridge: Cambridge University Press.

Hardin, R. F. (1990). Chronicles and Mythmaking in Shakespeare's Joan of Arc. *Shakespeare Survey*, 42, 25–35.

Hattaway, M. (1982). *Elizabethan Popular Theatre: Plays in Performance*. London: Routledge and Kegan Paul.

——(ed.) (1990). *The First Part of King Henry VI*. Cambridge: Cambridge University Press.

Hawley, W. M. (1992). *Critical Hermeneutics and Shakespeare's History Plays*. Bern: Peter Lang.

Helgerson, R. (1992). *Forms of Nationhood: The Elizabethan Writing of England*. Chicago, IL: University of Chicago Press.

Hodgdon, B. (1980). Shakespeare's Directorial Eye: A Look at the Early History Plays. In S. Homan (ed.) *Shakespeare's "More Than Words Can Witness": Essays on Visual and Nonverbal Enactment in the Plays*. Lewisburg, PA: Bucknell University Press.

Holderness, G. (2000). *Shakespeare: The Histories*. New York: St. Martin's Press.

Honigmann, E. A. J. (1985). *Shakespeare: The "Lost Years"*. Totowa, NJ: Barnes and Noble.

Howard, J. E. and Rackin, P. (eds.) (1997). *Engendering a Nation: A Feminist Account of Shakespeare's English Histories*. London: Routledge.

Jackson, G. B. (1988). Topical Ideology: Witches, Amazons, and Shakespeare's Joan of Arc. *English Literary Renaissance*, 18, 40–65.

Jones, R. C. (1991). *These Valiant Dead: Renewing the Past in Shakespeare's Histories*. Iowa City: University of Iowa Press.

Kahn, C. (1981). *Man's Estate: Masculine Identity in Shakespeare*. Berkeley: University of California Press.

Kastan, D. S. (1982). *Shakespeare and the Shapes of Time*. Hanover, NH: University Press of New England.

——(1986). Proud Majesty Made a Subject: Shakespeare and the Spectacle of Rule. *Shakespeare Quarterly*, 37, 459–75.

Kay, C. M. (1972). Traps, Slaughter, and Chaos: A Study of Shakespeare's *Henry VI* Plays. *Studies in the Literary Imagination*, 5, 1–26.

Kelly, F. L. (1973). Oaths in Shakespeare's *Henry VI* Plays. *Shakespeare Quarterly*, 24, 359–71.

Kelly, H. A. (1970). *Divine Providence in the England of Shakespeare's Histories*. Cambridge, MA: Harvard University Press.

Kirschbaum, L. (1952). The Authorship of *1 Henry VI*. *Publications of the Modern Languages Association*, 67, 809–22.

Levine, N. S. (1998). *Women's Matters: Politics, Gender, and Nation in Shakespeare's Early History Plays*. Newark: University of Delaware Press; London: Associated University Presses.

McCoy, R. C. (1989). *The Rites of Knighthood: The Literature and Politics of Elizabethan Chivalry*. Berkeley: University of California Press.

Mallin, E. S. (1990). Emulous Factions and the Collapse of Chivalry: *Troilus and Cressida. Representations*, 29.

Manheim, M. (1973). *The Weak King Dilemma in the Shakespearean History Play*. Syracuse, NY: Syracuse University Press.

Marcus, L. S. (1988). *Puzzling Shakespeare: Local Reading and Its Discontents*. Berkeley: University of California Press.

Mincoff, M. (1965). The Composition of *Henry VI, Part I*. *Shakespeare Quarterly*, 16, 279–87.

Norwich, J. J. (1999). *Shakespeare's Kings: The Great Plays and the History of England in the Middle Ages (1337–1485)*. New York: Scribner.

Orgel, S. (1985). Making Greatness Familiar. In D. Bergeron (ed.) *Pageantry in the Shakespearean Theater*. Athens, GA: University of Georgia Press.

——(2002). *The Spectacle of State: The Authentic Shakespeare*. New York: Routledge.

Ornstein, R. (1988). *A Kingdom for a Stage: The Achievement of Shakespeare's History Plays*. Cleveland, OH: Arden Press.

Pierce, R. B. (1971). *Shakespeare's History Plays: The Family and the State*. Columbus: Ohio State University Press.

Potter, L. (1990). Recycling the Early Histories: "The Wars of the Roses" and "The Plantagenets." *Shakespeare Studies*, 43, 171–81.

Price, H. T. (1951). *Construction in Shakespeare*. Ann Arbor: University of Michigan Press.

Prior, M. E. (1973). *The Drama of Power: Studies in Shakespeare's History Plays*. Evanston, IL: Northwestern University Press.

Rackin, P. (1990). *Stages of History: Shakespeare's English Chronicles*. Ithaca, NY: Cornell University Press.

Reese, M. M. (1961). *The Cease of Majesty: A Study of Shakespeare's History Plays*. London: Edward Arnold.

Ribner, I. (1965). *The English History Play in the Age of Shakespeare*, revd. edn. London: Methuen.

Richmond, H. M. (1967). *Shakespeare's Political Plays*. New York: Random House.

Riddell, J. A. (1977). Talbot and the Countess of Auvergne. *Shakespeare Quarterly*, 28, 51–7.

Riggs, D. (1971). *Shakespeare's Heroical Histories: "Henry VI" and its Literary Tradition*. Cambridge, MA: Harvard University Press.

Saccio, P. (1977). *Shakespeare's English Kings: History, Chronicle, and Drama*. New York: Oxford University Press.

Sanders, N. (ed.) (1981). *The First Part of King Henry the Sixth*. Harmondsworth: Penguin Books.

Sen Gupta, S. C. (1964). *Shakespeare's Historical Plays*. Oxford: Oxford University Press.

Siegel, P. N. (1986). *Shakespeare's English and Roman History Plays: A Marxist Approach*. Rutherford, NJ: Fairleigh Dickinson University Press.

Spurgeon, C. F. E. (1935). *Shakespeare's Imagery and What It Tells Us*. Cambridge: Cambridge University Press.

Taylor, G. (1995). Shakespeare and Others: The Authorship of *Henry the Sixth, Part One*. *Medieval and Renaissance Studies in English*, 7, 145–205.

Taylor, G. and Jowett, J. (1993). *Shakespeare Reshaped, 1606–1623*. Oxford: Clarendon Press.

Tillyard, E. M. W. (1964). *Shakespeare's History Plays*. London: Chatto and Windus.

Turner, R. Y. (1974). *Shakespeare's Apprenticeship*. Chicago, IL: University of Chicago Press.

Von Rosador, K. T. (1990). The Power of Magic: From *Endymion* to *The Tempest*. *Shakespeare Survey*, 43.

Warren, R. (1984). "Contraries Agree": An Aspect of Dramatic Technique in *Henry VI*. *Shakespeare Survey*, 37, 75–83.

Watson, D. G. (1990). *Shakespeare's Early History Plays: Politics at Play on the Elizabethan Stage*. London: Macmillan.

Wells, S. and Taylor, G., with J. Jowett and W. Montgomery (1987). *William Shakespeare: A Textual Companion*. Oxford: Clarendon Press.

Wilders, J. (1978). *The Lost Garden: A View of Shakespeare's English and Roman History Plays*. London: Macmillan.

Williams, G. (1974). Suffolk and Margaret: A Study of Some Sections of Shakespeare's *Henry VI*. *Shakespeare Quarterly*, 25, 310–22.

Willis, D. (1994). Shakespeare and the English Witch-Hunts: Enclosing the Maternal Body. In R. Burt and J. M. Archer (eds.) *Enclosure Acts: Sexuality, Property, and Culture in Early Modern England*. Ithaca, NY: Cornell University Press, 95–120.

Wilson, F. P. (1953). *Marlowe and the Early Shakespeare*. Oxford: Clarendon Press.

Wilson, J. D. (ed.) (1952). *The First Part of King Henry VI*. Cambridge: Cambridge University Press.

Wright, C. T. (1946). The Elizabethan Female Worthies. *Studies in Philology*, 43, 628–43.

15

Suffolk and the Pirates: Disordered Relations in Shakespeare's *2 Henry VI*

Thomas Cartelli

This essay builds on arguments advanced in my earlier essay (Cartelli 1994), but moves beyond them to a broader consideration of how disorder is discursively and dramatically constructed in this play. Whereas scholars like Richard Wilson had detected nothing but "animus" in the Jack Cade episodes of *2 Henry VI* that Wilson characterized as "one long orgy of scatological clowning, arson and homicide fuelled by an infantile hatred of literacy and law" (Wilson 1993: 27–8), I detected, instead, "a politically astute reckoning with a long list of social grievances whose inarticulate and violent expression does not invalidate their demand for resolution" (Cartelli 1994: 58). And I attributed "the astuteness of that reckoning to a playwright whose manifest literacy and identification with citizen values may actually have made possible his sympathetic appraisal of the people's claims" (ibid). At the same time, I identified the point of view of the play itself not with Shakespeare the private subject or individual, but with that of "the literate, industrious, law-abiding citizen class," which both in 1450 and 1590 could be held to remain "both stable and reliable in the face of wholesale social disorder," and whose interests Shakespeare could be held to be "representing, as well as promoting" (ibid). The constellation of values associated with this point of view may also help explain Shakespeare's provocative staging of an encounter that dramatically precedes Jack Cade's reckoning with Alexander Iden in the latter's garden, namely, the reckoning of the haughty Suffolk with the equally haughty "pirates" who capture him and in short order make him "shorter by the hedde" (Hall 1965: 207) in the first scene of what Wilson calls the play's "venomous fourth act" (Wilson 1993: 26).[1]

In his groundbreaking essay "Murdering Peasants," Stephen Greenblatt explores the social complications of representations of the great and powerful triumphing over those held to be lowly and contemptible, complications Shakespeare elides somewhat in the contention between Cade and Iden by making Cade so rich a prize for the aspiring squire and also by transforming "status relations . . . before our eyes into property relations" (Greenblatt 1990: 125).[2] In my own commentary on this scene, I acknowledged "the crucial role that property plays in this transaction," while contending that "Cade's braving of Iden with 'saucy terms' seems to arouse Iden more than does his mere transgression of freehold boundaries" and that "it is primarily Cade's obstreperousness . . . that motivates the violent turn in this encounter" (Cartelli 1994: 51), hence, that "status relations" remains a crucial pivot around which their contention turns. The otherwise very different encounter between Suffolk and the pirates reads rather similarly, dramatizing as it does the confident assault of two commoners on an aristocrat who (like Iden) takes every opportunity to remind his opponents of how radically unequal they are. Apart from Tamburlaine's assault on the astonished Persian king Cosroe in Marlowe's *Tamburlaine the Great*, there is little in the drama of the period to explain the presumption of Walter Whitmore in particular, Suffolk's self-styled scourge and executioner, even if we accept him at his word when he responds to Suffolk's assertion, "I am a gentleman," with "And so am I" (4.1.29, 31).[3] As Peter Laslett notes, "the word *gentleman* . . . [marked] a grade amongst other grades in a carefully graduated system of social status and had a critically important use," the term demarcating "the exact point at which the traditional social system divided up the population into two extremely unequal sections" (Laslett 1971: 27). Hence, it seems at first blush odd that a character acting the role of pirate or, at best, privateer, should so boldly claim this distinction. While lines like the following indicate that Shakespeare tried to underwrite Whitmore's presumption with a legitimate claim to an elevated social standing – "Never yet did base dishonour blur our name / But with our sword we wiped away the blot" (4.1.39–41) – they may also be aligned with Jack Cade's spurious claim to royal standing and with Cade's refusal to be intimidated by anyone of discernibly higher rank. In the world that obtains in *2 Henry VI* Whitmore's claim to gentlemanly status may be construed as yet another symptom – similar to Suffolk's aspiration to sovereign rule or to the Duchess of Gloucester's deluded machinations – of disordered social relations. This is, for obvious reasons, the opinion of Suffolk, who styles his unthinkably aggressive captors "paltry, servile, abject drudges" and "vile Bezonians." But whether it is also the "opinion" (if we can use such a word) of Shakespeare is quite another thing and one of the questions I will be pursuing in the body of this essay.

Historians have contended that "the circumstances of the duke of Suffolk's death . . . caused such alarm in Kent as to turn discontent into open action" (Harvey 1991: 73), basing their claim on the first article of complaints issued by the rebels which reads: "it is openlie noised that Kent should be destroyed with a roiall power, and made a wild forrest for the death of the duke of Suffolk, of which the commons of Kent thereof were neuer guiltie" (Holinshed 1807–8, III: 222). But Shakespeare appears to have preferred Holinshed's judgment that "those that fauored the duke of York and wished the crowne vpon his head procured [the] commotion in Kent" (p. 220) that became Cade's rebellion. I would like to take Shakespeare's cue and construe the execution of Suffolk as an event that has more pertinence to the sustained focus on aristocratic corruption and misrule of the first movement of his play than it does to what follows in its wake. In so doing, I would also like to redirect our attention from Jack Cade's effort to turn the world upside down in order to argue that the world of this play is upside down from the start, and that the disease of identity-distorting megalomania that afflicts Cade has not merely been transmitted by his tutor in disorder, Richard Duke of York, but has its root and source in a highly contagious aristocratic presumption that, quite literally, knows no bounds and affects virtually every character that steps onstage.

Much that is stiff, mannered, or rhetorically overblown in this play is chronically attributed to the earliness of its composition (the Shakespearean apprenticeship theory), the uncertainty of its authorship (the "other hands" theory), or factors related to the novelty of the chronicle genre itself, which had yet to evolve sufficiently to deliver characters and speeches of the conviction and quality we get in later plays like *Richard II* or *1 Henry IV*. Thus when we see characters like Warwick punning crudely on the loss of Maine (1.1.206–10) or witness them credulously accede to the opportunistic logic that informs York's tendentious assay at royal genealogy in 2.2, we understandably make allowances, and attribute the deficiency of the characters to a deficit in the art that creates them. Similarly, as we watch one character after another – from Queen Margaret and Suffolk on the one hand, to York and the Duchess Eleanor on the other – articulate their ambitions in the most self-deluding and blustering manner, and ride roughshod over the most obvious considerations of caution and restraint, it may seem that the world Shakespeare has summoned onstage in the first three acts is more residually Tamburlainean than it is proleptically "Shakespearean" (as the second tetralogy teaches us to understand that word). While I willingly admit all that is rough and residually imitative or emulative in Shakespeare's stagecrafting of *2 Henry VI*, I think we would do better to approach the parade of aristocratic presumption in the play's first three acts as something much more carefully and exactingly designed. As Brents Stirling long ago contended, "Elizabethan playwrights were very much concerned with disordered or 'sick' societies and built many of their plays around that concept to a degree not yet generally understood" (Stirling 1949: 12, n. 8). I take Stirling's point as the most promising point of access to Shakespeare's construction of aristocratic disorder in *2 Henry VI*, which may be said to dramatize a crisis of legitimacy that in turn "produces" not only Cade's rising and York's subsequent campaign of usurpation, but Suffolk's fatal encounter with his pirates.

Although this encounter is structurally and thematically tied to Cade's rebellion, which dramatically commences the moment Suffolk's body and head are removed from the stage, it is differently oriented in that it brings to a point of culmination or conclusion the play's sustained study of aristocratic corruption and in that, *as* a culmination or conclusion, the scene is end-directed, the pirates seeking neither reward nor recognition nor promise of advancement from the actions they undertake. In the structural economy of this play the pirates function in relation to the overweening aristocrat Suffolk in much the way that Iden functions in relation to Cade: as surrogate executors of the nation's will. Yet unlike Iden who, as I have elsewhere contended, seems more disingenuous than sincere when he claims he seeks "not to wax great by others' waning" (4.10.20) but then seeks immediate recognition for the killing of

Cade (see Cartelli 1994: 49–52), the pirates conspicuously *decline* the rewards of their piracy by choosing to kill Suffolk rather than to ransom him and by releasing without fee one of the two gentlemen they had planned to ransom. It is, in short, the patriotically motivated disinterestedness of the pirates I am seeking to isolate here, which operates as the polar opposite of the entirely self-interested motivation of virtually every aristocratic persona in the play, apart, that is, from Duke Humphrey, whose public-spirited absence the pirates effectively fill.

Who, then, are these men Suffolk (and no one else onstage) calls "pirates" and likens to the "vile Bezonians" that slew Tully, Caesar, and Pompey the Great? Who is the Lieutenant who opens 4.1 with such portentous, and obviously learned, language?

> The gaudy, blabbing and remorseful day
> Is crept into the bosom of the sea;
> And now loud-howling wolves arouse the jades
> That drag the melancholy night,
> Who with their drowsy, slow and flagging wings
> Clip dead men's graves and from their misty jaws
> Breathe foul contagious darkness in the air. (4.1.1–7)

And who is Walter Whitmore who, along with the Lieutenant, turns Suffolk's Tamburlainean vaunts back against him in the key of a self-styled junior Tamburlaine?

> *Suffolk.* Jove sometimes went disguised, and why not I?
> *Lieutenant.* But Jove was never slain as thou shalt be.
> *Suffolk.* Obscure and lowsy swain, King Henry's blood,
> The honourable blood of Lancaster,
> Must not be shed by such a jaded groom.
> Hast thou not kissed thy hand and held my stirrup?
> And bare-head plodded by my foot-cloth mule,
> And thought thee happy when I shook my head?
> How often hast thou waited at my cup,
> Fed from my trencher, kneeled down at the board
> When I have feasted with Queen Margaret?
> Remember it, and let it make thee crestfallen,
> Ay, and allay this thy abortive pride.
> And duly waited for my coming forth?
> This hand of mine hath writ in thy behalf
> And therefore shall it charm thy riotous tongue.
> *Whitmore.* Speak, Captain, shall I stab the forlorn swain?
> *Lieutenant.* First let my words stab him, as he hath me. (4.1.48–66)

Suffolk himself can be of some help to us in identifying the Lieutenant whom he confidently recognizes as a former servant who has even solicited and been rewarded at some point with Suffolk's written recommendation. Although the Lieutenant never responds specifically to Suffolk's claim of recognition, he is clearly provoked ("let my word stab him, as he hath me") by Suffolk's efforts to bring him back to a full consciousness of his inferiority ("Remember it, and let it make thee crestfallen"), which the Duke apparently believes will prove disabling. Of particular interest here is how Suffolk concludes his inventory of the Lieutenant's inferior parts with the claim that the same hand that "writ in thy behalf" shall "charm thy riotous tongue," giving a legalistic name to the radical social inversion the speech acts of a man who has "plodded by my foot-cloth mule" and "fed from my trencher" perform. That the Lieutenant responds to Suffolk's effort to "charm" him with the peremptory order to "Convey him hence, and on our longboat's side / Strike off his head" suggests a rather different understanding of established social protocols than Suffolk possesses. But even more striking is the 33-line speech Shakespeare next gives to this character who has no basis for this address in any of the sources we assume the playwright consulted, but whose words effectively reproduce the charges leveled against Suffolk by the formally assembled Commons in those very same sources.

Shakespeare's effort to establish Suffolk as the play's prevailing enemy of the people is telescoped by the unprofitable and self-advantaging marriage Suffolk negotiates for the King, which is dramatized in the play's first scene, but is given sustained dramatic treatment in the petitioners scene, 1.3. This scene seems directly modeled on the petitioners scene found at the beginning of Marlowe's *Edward II*, but works in very different ways. Whereas Marlowe's staging of the scene works against the grain of its formal structure as dramatic exemplum in a manner that privileges Gaveston's aestheticized opportunism at the expense of the three poor men who petition him for sponsorship (see Cartelli 1991: 123–30), Shakespeare uses his scene to paint a graphic picture of Margaret and Suffolk's predatory plans for the kingdom. Mistaking Suffolk for his ethical opposite, Humphrey Duke of Gloucester, the second petitioner, who holds in his hands a writ *Against the Duke of Suffolk, for enclosing the commons of Melford* and identifies himself as "but a poor petitioner of our whole township" (1.3.23–4), conveys in small space the larger crimes against the commonweal that Suffolk and his cohorts have been perpetrating. The speech that Margaret delivers after tearing the supplication and dismissing these "base cullions" is particularly revealing insofar as it negatively contrasts the English habit of allowing the commons to advance such petitions with the presumed French habit of sovereign indifference and contempt:

> My Lord of Suffolk, say, is this the guise,
> Is this the fashions in the court of England?
> Is this the government of Britain's isle,
> And this the royalty of Albion's king? (1.3.43–6)

The connection established here between Suffolk's contempt for the commons and Margaret's impatience with the structures of governance in England will later help underwrite and legitimate the simultaneously populist and patriotic cast of the Lieutenant's speech. At this point it helps to establish Suffolk, and his mutually opportunistic alliance with Margaret, as the most conspicuous source and symptom of the disordered relations that now obtain not only between ruler and ruled but within the King's court itself.

Although in Shakespeare's hands the story that Hall and Holinshed tell of the depredations visited on the kingdom by Suffolk and his associates is radically fore-shortened, it rises to the surface in the Lieutenant's speech, the first half of which reads:

> Now will I dam up this thy yawning mouth
> For swallowing the treasure of the realm.
> Thy lips that kissed the Queen shall sweep the ground;
> And thou that smiledst at good Duke Humphrey's death
> Against the senseless winds shall grin in vain
> Who in contempt shall hiss at thee again.
> And wedded be thou to the hags of hell
> For daring to affy a mighty lord
> Unto the daughter of a worthless king,
> Having neither subject, wealth nor diadem.
> By devilish policy art thou grown great
> And, like ambitious Sylla, overgorged
> With gobbets of thy mother's bleeding heart. (4.1.73–85)

As noted most recently by Ronald Knowles, "The catalogue of crimes and misde-meanours" iterated by the Lieutenant "can be documented from the chronicles, par-ticularly in the articles presented by the commons against Suffolk" (Knowles 1999: 369), and reiterate the claims against Suffolk summarized earlier in the play by Salisbury on the heels of Gloucester's murder (3.2.243–69). Indeed, some of the most potent phrases of the Lieutenant's indictment are direct borrowings from Hall's summary of the complaints formally lodged against Suffolk by the commons in par-liament, such that it may be said that he, as much as Salisbury, serves as their "ven-triloquist" or mouthpiece.[4] Motivated by their "disdain of lascivious souereignte which the Quene with her minions, and vnprofitable consailers daily toke and vsurped vpo[n] them," the "commonaltie," as Hall writes,

> began to make exclamacion against the Duke of Suffolke, affirming him, to be the onely cause of the deliuery of Angeow & Mayne, the chief procurer of the death of the good duke of Gloucester, the verie occasion of the losse of Normandy, *the most swallower vp and consumer of the kynges treasure*, . . . the expeller fro the kyng, of all good and verteous consailors, and the bringer in and auancer of vicious persones, common enemies and apparaunt aduersaries to the publique wealthe: So that the duke was called in euery mannes mouth, a traitor, a murderer, a robber of the kynges treasure, and worthy to bee put to moste cruell punishment. (Hall 1965: 217; my emphases)

In this respect among others, the Lieutenant's speech may be construed as the voice of the commonweal itself rising up in righteous indignation against what Hall elsewhere describes as the aristocratically induced "inward grudge, and intestine division, which to all Realmes is more pestiferous and noisome, then outward warre, dayly famine, or extreme pestilence" (ibid: 219). And it bears noting that the voice the Lieutenant ventriloquizes is not that of the many-headed mob but of what had become by 1450 a parliamentary membership comprised of "municipal officers and substantial citizens," such that it might be said that "There was nothing common about the incomes or social position of Commons" (Smith 1966: 49).

The indictments delivered by Salisbury and the pirate-Lieutenant, respectively, prompt responses from Suffolk that are stridently class (or status) conscious. In the face of Salisbury's recitation, for example, Suffolk brusquely remarks, "But all the honour Salisbury hath won / Is that he was lord ambassador / Sent from a sort of tinkers to the King" (3.2.275–7), his withering phrase carrying no hint of recognition of the well-ordered citizenry arrayed against him. His response to the Lieutenant's indictment is more elaborate:

> O, that I were a god to shoot forth thunder
> Upon these paltry, servile, abject drudges!
> Small things make base men proud: this villain here,
> Being captain of a pinnace, threatens more
> Than Bargulus, the strong Illyrian pirate.
> Drones suck not eagles' blood, but rob beehives.
> It is impossible that I should die
> By such a lowly vassal as thyself.
> Thy words move rage and no remorse in me. (4.1.104–12)

Suffolk's refusal to respond to the Lieutenant's indictment on any ground other than the Lieutenant's presumption not only seals his fate but leaves unanswered the charges leveled against him, while also vividly marking him as the play's (and the kingdom's) most insistent cultivator of social conflict and division. The direction those charges take in the words of the Lieutenant (I am thinking specifically of phrases like "swallowing the treasure of the realm," a clear borrowing from Hall) not only prove powerfully resonant but resonate powerfully with a long catalog of abuses Shakespeare chooses neither to stage nor refer to in any detail, but which Hall, among others, reproduces in painstaking detail (see Hall 1965: 217–18).

As a long list of authorities have noted, the historical Lord Suffolk played the role of ringleader of a group of powerfully placed individuals bent upon treating "the kynges treasure" as their private treasury, one of whom, Adam Moleyns, Bishop of Chichester, was attacked by "a mob of furious sailors and soldiers, said to number over 300 men, who on 9 January [1450] dragged him out of his lodgings to a field and killed him" (Harvey 1991: 63). This event occurred some five months before the capture and murder of Suffolk, but only about two weeks prior to an attempted uprising led by one Thomas Cheyne along the Channel coast in Kent. This failed uprising was notable on several accounts, first for its revival of "the notion, put into

effect in 1381 of addressing complaints to the king by raising the south-eastern counties into a mass demonstration converging on London"; second for the list the rebels
drew up of notables "they wanted to see beheaded" that "comprised William Ais-
cough, bishop of Salisbury, William, duke of Suffolk, [and] James, Lord Saye"; and
third for the carnivalesque cast of the proceedings, made manifest by the names chosen
by the leaders to hide their identities, which included "Blewbeard," "King of the
Fairies," "Queen of the Fairies," and "Robin Hood" (ibid: 64–5). While there is no
way to know what knowledge Shakespeare had of these events, he would know enough
from his reading of Holinshed that the king's earlier freeing of Suffolk from official
restraint "so much displeased the people" that "the commons in sundrie places of the
realme assembled together in great companies, and chose to them a capteine, whom
they called Blewbeard" and that the suppression of these assemblies coincided with
Suffolk's commitment to the Tower on January 29. And though he probably did not
know that "the more Suffolk came under attack [in official quarters] the better the
populace were liking it" and that "by late February or March the chanting in the
street seems to have become positively gleeful" (Harvey 1991: 680), he would have
read in Holinshed that the continuance and intensification of "the peoples furie" led
directly to Suffolk's banishment "as the abhorred tode and common noiance of the
whole realme" (Holinshed 1807–8, III: 220).

My aim in bringing this material to bear in the present context is to try to account
for the difference between the way Shakespeare stages the arraignment and execution
of Suffolk and the way he will later stage Jack Cade's arraignment and execution of
the Lord Say, who was closely linked to Suffolk in the collective mind of the commons
and whose murder in the process of the historical Cade's revolt was directly indebted
to that linkage. Why does Shakespeare make the Lieutenant a second, more eloquent
(than Salisbury) mouthpiece for the articles of complaint issued by the commons, one
who directly articulates a message that Salisbury only indirectly reports? How or why
does this conferral of righteousness and eloquence on the Lieutenant help legitimate
actions that would presumably abridge all established orders of legal and social authority? How can the Lieutenant and Whitworth take such a charge upon themselves
without being jointly linked to the Cade rising which Shakespeare begins to dramatize as soon as they leave the stage? Are we rather led to assume that the pirates are
executors of the will of the commons as expressed in the legally tendered complaint
against Suffolk earlier presented at court by Salisbury? And how, finally, do we assess
the passages of the Lieutenant's speech which reveal him to be an avowed partisan of
the Yorkist claim? Does this cast additional credit, or discredit, on the patriotic cast
of his speech and sentiments?

To help thicken my treatment of these questions, it may prove useful to return
to Holinshed and to other, less obvious sources of information to see just what
Shakespeare might have gleaned from the chronicles he consulted and from material
that might have come to his knowledge more circuitously. While Holinshed rather
plainly treats the particulars of Suffolk's capture and death – "[He] was incountered
with a ship of warre apperteining to the duke of Excester, constable of the Tower of

London, called the Nicholas of the Tower. The capteine of that bark with small fight entered into the dukes ship and perceiuing his person present, brought him to Douer road, and there, on the one side of a cock bote, caused his head to be striken off, and left his bodie with the head lieng there on the sands" (Holinshed 1807–8, III: 220) – his chronicle directly moralizes on Suffolk and the action taken against him. At the outset of its account of the duke's capture, for example, the chronicle remarks that "Gods iustice would not that so vngratious a person should so escape." And it concludes the account of Suffolk's execution in the following manner: "This end had William de la Pole duke of Suffolk, as men iudge by Gods prouidence, for that he had procured the death of that good duke Gloucester" (ibid).[5] In both passages we have providence to thank for the encounter between the "vngratious" Suffolk and the pirates, no mention being made of the possible anticipation of providence by the Duke of Exeter, or question raised regarding the qualifications of the ship's captain as a duly delegated executor of "Gods iustice." But what was this ship really doing in the area of Dover road? What relationship (if any) obtained between the Duke of Exeter and the ship's captain? Are such questions of any real interest to a project that was, in Annabel Patterson's words, "an expression of citizen consciousness" (Patterson 1994: xiii), and, hence, not prompted to dispute the actions of this peremptory agent of providence? Are they of any interest to Shakespeare?

A fuller account of Suffolk's capture and murder is found in a letter written on May 5, 1450 by William Lonmor to John Paston I which states that "the master of the *Nicholas* had knowledge of the Duke's coming" and that upon Suffolk's boarding of his ship this same master greeted him with the words "Welcome, traitor" (Davis 1963: 27). Lonmor says nothing more of this master but does say something about Suffolk's executioner that both departs from, and resonates in interesting ways with, Shakespeare's apparent invention of the tough-talking, self-styled gentleman, Walter Whitmore: "And in the sight of all his men, [Suffolk] was drawn out of the great ship, into the boat, and there was an axe and a stock; and one of the lewdest of the ship bade him lay down his head, and he should be fair ferd with, and die on a sword; and took a rusty sword, and smote off his head within half a dozen strokes, and took away his gown of russet and his doublet of velvet mailed, and laid his body on the sands of Dover" (ibid: 27–8). With little further ado, and no further notice paid to the rather shocking testimony of a great man's head being chopped at six times with a rusty sword by the "lewdest" of the ship, Lonmor moves on to remark a few pieces of news of the French wars before signing off. Apart from its graphic detailing of Suffolk's crude execution, the most notable aspects of this account are its apparent neutrality and the cues it leaves for the elaboration of the scene we find in Shakespeare, which fastens on the Lieutenant's treatment of Suffolk as a traitor and on Whitmore's irreverent approach to the body and persona of this most highly positioned aristocrat.[6]

It is worth noting here that neither Holinshed nor Lonmor ever uses the term "pirate" to identify Suffolk's captors, and that it is only the highly status-conscious Suffolk who does so, and only after first negatively comparing the threats of a mere "captain of a pinnace" to those of "Bargulus, the strong Illyrian pirate" (4.1.108). As Kingsford long ago noted, "The prevalence of piracy in the narrow seas was always a difficulty for the English government in the Middle Ages" (Kingsford 1925: 79), but it was even more difficult to generalize on the character and motivations of so-called pirates themselves, much less to identify seamen by this name. As Kingsford observes, when "we speak of these early seamen as pirates, it is necessary to bear in mind that the word had a wider meaning [in its day], and was applied alike to those who were at the worst unlicensed privateers and to those whose only object was plunder" (p. 78). Kingsford adds that two representative figures of the time, "the redoubtable privateer Harry Pay of Poole" and "the rich Dartmouth merchant John Hawley," played "the parts of patriot and pirate in turn, and in spite of occasional backslidings their careers were on the whole not unworthy" (pp. 78, 84).

While considerable collateral information regarding the ship's provenance and future associations is available, more reliable knowledge of the identities of its master and the "lewd" sailor who took Suffolk's life is nonetheless wanting. As Kingsford writes:

> The mystery of Suffolk's murder has never been solved. The *Nicholas of the Tower*, as the name shows, was a royal ship; but this would not have precluded its illicit employment by some person of influence . . . Later in the year the *Nicholas*, under the command of John Norton, was concerned in a piratical enterprise in the company of the notorious Clays Stephen. If this John Norton may be identified with the person of the same name who had been committed to prison for his share in the piracy of the *Edward* of Polruan, he was perhaps released as a fit agent for unlawful violence . . . The Duke of Exeter, who was Admiral and therefore in control of the *Nicholas*, was contracted to a daughter of Richard of York. It is conceivable, as some have suggested, that the murder was inspired by a political enemy. Or it may have been due to the same unpopularity which had been fatal to Moleyns. (Ibid: 172–3)

As we return to the scene of the crime, I would like to keep two of the possibilities outlined by Kingsford in play: that privateers could "play the part of patriot and pirate by turn" and that the assault on Suffolk was driven by, or on behalf of, York. If we add to this mix of motive and identity the material Shakespeare adds to his Lieutenant's characterization, we may conclude that the Lieutenant might well have been the pirate Suffolk claims he is, but such a pirate that Suffolk would not have previously been able to imagine: one who has risen from a former position of servility to some appreciable form of mastery; one considerably more capable than Suffolk of seeing himself as a patriotic subject of his nation, if not of his king, and capable as well of seeing himself as an armed extension of the legally assembled commons; one fueled by the same impatience and contempt for the corrupt nobility as the sailors and soldiers who murdered Suffolk's associate, Adam Moleyns; and one allied, if not officially, then surely sympathetically, with the emerging party and cause of Richard Duke of York. As the Lieutenant himself rather emotionally states towards the close of his peroration:

> And now the house of York, thrust from the crown
> By shameful murder of a guiltless king
> And lofty, proud, encroaching tyranny,
> Burns with revenging fire, whose hopeful colours
> Advance our half-faced sun, striving to shine,
> Under which is writ 'Invitis nubibus'.
> The commons here in Kent are up in arms;
> And, to conclude, reproach and beggary
> Is crept into the palace of our King,
> And all by thee. Away! Convey him hence. (4.1.94–103)

If all these qualities do not entirely license the action the Lieutenant bids Walter Whitmore to take against Suffolk, they add a conspicuously representative character to his motivations, and help to explain the confidence and fervor with which it is undertaken.

As opposed to Cade's riotously disposed murder of Lord Say – a character who "[pleads] so well for his life" (4.7.99–100) and whom Shakespeare chooses both to sentimentalize and misrepresent – the capture and execution of Suffolk is largely presented as something in the order of a high-mindedly motivated public service undertaken to advance the interests and concerns of the commons, its possible sponsorship by the soon-to-become-unruly York only residually apparent towards the scene's end. Arguably more provocative is the verbal sparring between the Lieutenant and Suffolk, on the one hand, and Whitmore and Suffolk, on the other, which deserves fuller treatment. Though the Lieutenant and Whitmore are identified as pirates and worse by Suffolk, both bitterly resent and resist their representation as mercenaries. Even before Suffolk has identified himself to his captors, Whitmore refuses to bargain with his captive, arguing that his claimed status as gentleman will not allow him to take money in place of revenge for an injury suffered:

> Never yet did base dishonour blur our name
> But with our sword we wiped away the blot.
> Therefore, when merchant-like I sell revenge,
> Broke be my sword, my arms torn and defaced
> And I proclaimed a coward through the world. (4.1.38–43)

In lines like these Whitmore oddly sounds more akin to the self-styled esquire of Kent, Alexander Iden, who encounters and kills Jack Cade in his garden, than he does to "the lewdest of the ship" who presumably slew Suffolk with six strokes of a rusty sword. Indeed, his rejection of the very idea that he might "merchant-like . . . sell revenge" presents him as an obvious alternative both to predatory aristocrats like Suffolk whose practice it is to plunder the "publique wealthe" and to self-regarding privateers who lack his sense of patriotism and honor. I would submit, on the basis of such evidence, that rather than overtly functioning as agents of the Duke of York or as anticipations of Jack Cade's riotous army, Whitmore and his Lieutenant are designed to operate both as extensions of the will of the commons and as idealized projections of the citizen consciousness that serves as something like the author-function of this play. That they may also be both more and less than this, products or symptoms of the disorder that reigns at the heart of the corrupt court and of the generalized misrule that will soon take full charge of the stage, is possibly signaled by the scene's last lines as uttered by the gentleman charged with delivering Suffolk's corpse to the Queen:

> O barbarous and bloody spectacle!
> His body will I bear unto the King.
> If he revenge it not, yet will his friends;
> So will the Queen, that living held him dear. (4.1.146–9)

But the oddly uncritical privileging of the Queen's disproportionate affection for Suffolk in these lines rather place this gentleman, along with his sentiments, in the party of those that still make their home in an unholy political dispensation instead of among those who can no longer suffer the prospect of an England bled dry by Suffolk and his followers. Indeed, what would this gentleman make of the "bloody spectacle" displayed in 4.4 of the sorrowing Queen holding the unrighteous Suffolk's head in her lap as the King looks on in dismay and their kingdom explodes in disarray around them?

In *Shakespeare's Heroical Histories* (1971), David Riggs makes the following point about this play's difference from influential predecessor plays like *Tamburlaine the Great*:

> From a loose rendition of heroic aspiration in an exotic setting, the emphasis has shifted towards a drama of ambition and disruption that anatomizes the ambivalent status of the Elizabethan peerage. In Lawrence Stone's analysis, a complex series of events was, by the 1590s, leading to a general failure of nerve among the aristocracy. Two familiar symptoms of that failure emerge directly from the social drama of *2 Henry VI*: Suffolk's fierce, reflexive pride in his noble blood and connections at court, and York's desperate impulse to restore his family's lost eminence by reckless military adventures. Just as these are indices of a more general failure to govern, the one tragic figure in the plan is a governor: Good Duke Humphrey. He can fill the administrative vacuum that results from the defection of Suffolk and York, but he is powerless to resist their determination to destroy and replace him. (Riggs 1971: 115)

As Riggs recounts, in scene after scene in the play's first three acts the "heroic" claims of York and Suffolk are found to be not only unequal, but inimical, to the needs of subjects and citizenry, "while Duke Humphrey suggests a new type of ideal ruler, the Ciceronian governor," who is willing to sacrifice even his own supremely erring wife for the good of the commonweal (p. 115). The weakness of this governor in the face of the machiavellian maneuvering of York, Suffolk, and the Cardinal, rather than reducing his dramatic status in the play, enhances it at the expense of characters whose actions seem opportunistically designed to throw the established social order into an "anarchic" state (p. 117). Scenes like those that focus on the intrigues hatched by Suffolk and the Cardinal to bring down the Lord Protector and his wife and on York's efforts to solicit support for his claim to the throne "serve to discount the value of ancestral name and martial fortitude, while laying stress on the importance of [virtues like] prudence [and] justice" which are clearly housed in Duke Humphrey, whose "judicial rectitude and expertise is established in a series of trial scenes" (p. 115). While the Duke himself is, of course, as much of an aristocrat as are his enemies, he is repeatedly represented in these scenes as the only remaining source of balance and fairness in the kingdom and as friend, if not always defender, of the common people. Indeed, the immediacy and fervor with which the commons bring their case against Suffolk on the heels of the discovery of Duke Humphrey's assassination in 3.2 – "Down with Suffolk! Down with Suffolk!" they are heard crying from offstage – demonstrates with unusual force the extent to which Shakespeare has them identify Duke Humphrey with their concerns.[7]

Riggs nonetheless claims that removal "from the scene [of] the one figure who embodies a thoroughgoing criticism of their personal aspirations" allows Suffolk and York to "enjoy a renewed vitality in the latter half of the play, as the social commentary, without Gloucester to interpret it, recedes into the background, and impinges less directly on the values of the two aristocrats" (p. 116). He adds that "the critique of Suffolk and York that is sustained by Gloucester never begins to generate a vision of the aristocratic life which convincingly supplants their own" (pp. 117–18). While York certainly does come to enjoy what Riggs terms "a renewed vitality" (however misdirected), Suffolk merely becomes more inexorably himself, stiffly insisting on his superannuated privileges and prerogatives to the end. Both, in any event, continue to model already discredited aristocratic values of pride and presumption while the "social commentary," which Riggs finds receding into the background, becomes instead translated into the domain of the protesting commons, achieving practical form in the exile of Suffolk and in his execution by the pirates before being retranslated into the carnivalesque idiom of collective misrule by Jack Cade and his "ragged multitude" (see Longstaffe 1998). Lacking any other qualified aristocratic aspirant, the space that Duke Humphrey once occupied becomes dramatically filled by the voice of the commons itself as reproduced by Salisbury, who functions as something like a bridge between the silenced Duke and the commons:

> Dread lord, the commons send you word by me,
> Unless Lord Suffolk straight be done to death,
> Or banished fair England's territories,
> They will by violence tear him from your palace
> And torture him with grievous lingering death.
> They say, by him the good Duke Humphrey died;
> They say, in him they fear your highness' death;
> And mere instinct of love and loyalty,

Free from a stubborn opposite intent,
As being thought to contradict your liking,
Make them thus forward in his banishment. (3.2.243–53)

In her provocative commentary on this moment Annabel Patterson sees Salisbury functioning here as "the temporary substitute" for Duke Humphrey and, consequently, as "the people's spokesman." Patterson adds that "The rhetorical 'They say' formula identifies Salisbury as ventriloquist, while the dramatic situation ensures his recognition as the people's sincere advocate," and concludes that "This protest is . . . both morally authoritative and, as petitioning from strength, effective" and, moreover, that it conveys Shakespeare's own "conditional approval of the role of popular protest in the play – conditional, that is, on rightful motives, a basic loyalty to the crown, and a proper spokesman" (Patterson 1989: 48).

These are large claims that it is not my purpose to examine or contest in great detail. Suffice it to say that I have as much trouble with Patterson's outright identification of Humphrey as "the people's spokesman" as I do with making Salisbury, through what Patterson calls his "formal act of ventriloquism" (p. 47), so complicit with the voice of the commons which he reproduces that he loses his highly differentiated place outside it. After all, what persuades the King to banish Suffolk is less Salisbury's ventriloquy than the far more direct threat from without that Suffolk will be taken by force if an "answer from the King" is not forthcoming (3.2.278). This is, of course, not to understate the powerful message sent by the commons through the medium of Salisbury. But what I prefer to take from Patterson are two other ideas, the first being that what might be called the Duke Humphrey alternative does not entirely dissolve with his death, leaving (as Riggs argues) either Suffolk or York in temporary command of what counts as noble or aristocratic; the second involving her notion of what conditions might inform the legitimation "of popular protest in the play," those conditions being "rightful motives, a basic loyalty to the crown, and a proper spokesman."

The fact is that until the emergence of Henry Tudor in the closing movement of *Richard III*, there are very few influential representatives of the aristocracy in this or the remaining plays of the first tetralogy who are free for very long of opportunistic motives that set them at odds with the common good. As in Marlowe's *Edward II*, the contentious barons are rather the source and symptoms of disorder than in any significant degree its potential solution or remedy, and the four plays that dramatize their misdeeds collectively "offer a searing indictment of aristocratic factionalism" (Hattaway 1988: 16). The only characters who can be said to escape the "sickness" of this society, and to see that sickness for what it is, namely, blind ambition, are those who have no real stake in the intra-aristocratic struggle for dominance or mastery. And these characters tend, for the most part, to belong to the citizen or "middling" class (see Leinwand 1993 on the "middling sort").

A better case for the legitimation "of popular protest in the play" can be made on behalf of the pirates who, in their arraignment and execution of Suffolk, not only see themselves acting in direct response to the murder of Duke Humphrey but also function, for Holinshed at least, as executors of "Gods iustice." Whether they also functioned in the same manner for Shakespeare remains an open question, but as Richard Strier has noted, it is not far-fetched to assume that Shakespeare was sufficiently responsive to a sixteenth-century discourse on civil disobedience to entertain the legitimacy of resistance to a corrupted authority. Strier largely isolates Shakespeare's responsiveness to the more provocative writings of John Ponet, Christopher Goodman, and George Buchanan to the period that begins with his composition of *Hamlet* and in particular application to *King Lear*, which he sees as "the culmination of a development in Shakespeare's political thinking from a focus on the problem of order to a focus on the problem of corrupt (and corruption-inducing) authority" (Strier 1995: 176). But in light of my own effort to connect Shakespeare's construction of *dis*order in *2 Henry VI* to the "problem of corrupt (and corruption-inducing) authority," and the focus of the play itself on popular protest, it is worth wondering to what extent Shakespeare was indebted to this discourse in shaping the assured and righteously indignant approach of his pirates to Suffolk.

Strier, for example, quotes Ponet to the effect that "he is a good citezin that dothe none evil," but "he is a better that letteth [prevents] others, that they shal not doe hurt nor uniustice" and quotes Goodman to the effect that "'comon and simple people' [who] think that they must be obedient 'because their doings are counted tumults and rebellion' wrongly 'suffer themselves like brute beastes rather than reasonable creatures, to be led and drawen where so ever their Princes commandments have called'" (Strier 1995: 173). And finally, and most suggestively, he speaks of Buchanan joining "what he sees as a scriptural injunction 'to cut off wickedness and wicked men, without any exception of a rank or degree' to a classical conception of tyrannicide: 'a Tyrant is a publick Enemy, with whom all good men have a perpetual warfare'" (p. 175).[8] Although Strier fails to demonstrate that Shakespeare had any direct knowledge of these writings, or that they impinged directly on his staging of Cornwall's servant's intervention in the blinding of Gloucester which Strier discusses in detail in *Resistant Structures* (1995), he makes a powerful case for the centrality of the servant's resistance to his master in this scene, and for the legitimacy of that servant's claim to be doing his master "better service" than he has ever done him before by intervening:

> Hold your hand, my lord!
> I have served you ever since I was a child;
> But better service have I never done you
> Than now to bid you hold.
> (*King Lear*, 3.7.75–8)

Strier grounds his reading of the servant's "treasonous" but licensed resistance on the "extrajudicial, purely private nature" of Cornwall's own actions for which "there is no legal or political point" and claims, further, that "the presentation of a world 'upside down' is made literal in the procedure Cornwall announces for the mutilation of Gloucester: 'Upon these eyes of thine, Ile set my foote' " (Strier 1995: 192). He goes on to contend that while the "better service" the servant attempts to supply is arguably equally "outrageous" and "unthinkable," Shakespeare "is presenting [this] most radical possible sociopolitical act in a way that can only be interpreted as calling for the audience's approval" (pp. 192–3):

> The servant is obviously not a "public person," and his action is one of militant inter-
> ference; it transcends and does not even involve nonobedience, since it is not clear that
> he has been directly commanded to do anything . . . The scene is that which Buchanan
> describes and endorses: "[when] from amongst the lowest of the people some very mean,
> and obscure" person is stirred up to revenge Tyrannical Pride. (Ibid: 193)

Although the capture and extrajudicial execution of Suffolk by pirates may seem to be a very different kind of act, and occurs in a play written at a stage in Shakespeare's career when his politics were allegedly more "conservative" (ibid: 192, n. 74), its status as an act of "militant interference" undertaken "to revenge Tyrannical Pride" not only makes it perfectly consistent with Strier's assessment of the higher legitimacy of the servant's revolt, but suggests also that Shakespeare's politics may have been at this time less conservative than Strier imagines.

Strier focuses his backward reference to (and judgment of) *2 Henry VI* on Green-blatt's (1990) discussion of "Shakespeare's depiction of the death of Jack Cade," a scene whose politics is (as I have elsewhere argued) considerably more complicated than Greenblatt allows, and not on Suffolk's fateful encounter with the pirates. Had he taken this scene into account, Strier might well have had to grapple, as I will in closing, with the difficulty of locating there the Shakespearean point of view. What, in my opinion, most differentiates the actions of the pirates from Cade's revolt, and links them so closely with Cornwall's servant's resistance to (and murder of) his master, is their own obvious "calling for" audience approval, and privileging of a point of view that both speaks to, and well of, the values of justice and fair play of "the lit-erate, industrious, [and otherwise] law-abiding citizen class."[9] Although neither Corn-wall's servant nor Suffolk's pirates are themselves members of this class, their actions operate in direct resistance to the kind of corrupt and corruption-inducing authority which, if allowed to flourish, would constitute a direct threat to the well-being of subject and citizen alike. For their part, Suffolk and Cornwall are both represented as dramatic embodiments of "Tyrannical Pride," inflexibly and unregenerately bent on satisfying their own ambitions and desires at the expense of the commonweal. Although their being brought to justice summons up the shock and indignation of their associates in crime – "O barbarous spectacle," says the first gentleman in *2 Henry VI*; "A peasant stand up thus?," exclaims Regan in *King Lear* – that shock is hardly meant to resonate as strongly in an audience presumably more shocked by the actions that have brought them to this pitch, the murder of the good Duke Humphrey, on the one hand, the blinding of Gloucester on the other.

Are these actions then as "radical" as Strier suggests? Only, I would imagine, to the class that suffers them, not to the one (or ones) whose survival and well-being are premised on their approval. What conceivably constitutes a more truly radical gesture, from both the citizen and Shakespearean point of view, would be something like Jack Cade's arraignment and execution of Lord Say, an act undertaken by a figure who, in Annabel Patterson's words, "fails every test for the proper popular spokesman" (Patterson 1989: 48), against a character who, as radically transmuted by Shakespeare, appears not only to be continuing to do the good work of the late Duke Humphrey, but also to have thrown his lot in with the citizens of London themselves, with whose cause he is dramatically associated and identified.[10] Yet given the disproportion between the isolated excesses of a short-lived popular rising and the horrors unleashed by a clash of aristocratic ambitions that would generate thirty-five years of civil war and wholesale disorder, what hard-working citizen or householder could fail to agree that "it was / never merry world in England since gentlemen came up" (4.2.7–8)?[11]

NOTES

1   I add this gloss on Suffolk's murder from Edward Hall's 1548 Chronicle to qualify Wilson's rather glib characterization of the Chronicle as a mere "glorification of the ruling dynasty" (Wilson 1993: 27). Indeed, in the passage from which the quote is drawn Hall shows a marked contempt for the presumptions of the ruling elite, suggesting that Suffolk might have kept his head on his shoulders "if he had remembred the consail of the popinjay, saying: when thou thynkest thy self in courte moste surest, then is it high tyme to get thee home to rest" (Hall 1965: 207).

2   I quote from the version of Greenblatt's essay published in *Learning to Curse* (1990). Cade's encounter with Iden is also discussed in detail by William Carroll (1994) in his essay on vagrancy, enclosure, and sedition.

3   I discuss the social implications of Tamburlaine's dramatic assault on Cosroe and the Tamburlainean orientation of Cade's rising and Suffolk's encounter with the pirates in *Marlowe, Shakespeare, and the Economy of Theatrical Experience* (1991: 77–80, 86–8). In those pages I claim that "*2 Henry VI* is virtually saturated in Tamburlainean statements of proud self-assertion" (p. 86), and that "at the time of *2 Henry VI*'s composition" Shakespeare "was too immersed in the Tamburlaine phenomenon to sustain a consistent critical detachment" (p. 88). As the rest of this essay should make clear, I now believe that Shakespeare *was* capable of sustaining "critical detachment" in his characterizations of figures like Suffolk and Richard Duke of York. All quotations from *2 Henry VI* are drawn from the Arden edition, third series, edited by Ronald Knowles.

4   See Patterson (1989: 48–9) on "Salisbury as ventriloquist" (and below).

5   I have been sufficiently tutored by Annabel Patterson's *Reading Holinshed's Chronicles* (1994) to recognize that the "Holinshed" I employ here to establish the point of view of the chronicler in question is not, strictly speaking, identifiable with the historical Raphael Holinshed but with "a giant interdisciplinary project" that was "a collaboration . . . between freelance antiquarians, lesser clergymen, members of Parliament with legal training, minor poets, publishers, and booksellers" (pp. vii–viii).

6   Norman Davis states that Lonmor was "a trusted agent of the Pastons," probably a blood relative, and also a soon-to-be-avowed Yorkist of some influence in that circle (Davis 1963: 26–7). Lonmor's "neutral" tone may convey his approval of the actions taken against Suffolk who had allegedly "imposed a reign of terror [in the Pastons's home county of Norfolk], using forcible methods to

extort money and gain possession of land, yet contriving to deny the victims the means of lawful redress" (Storey 1966: 54). Storey adds that "In 1448, Margaret Paston had written that it was being said in Norfolk that no man dared to do or say anything which might offend the duke and his clients, and that those who had been so foolhardy would 'sore repent them'" (ibid). In four letters written in 1448–9 Margaret Paston vividly describes these and other circumstances, including living in a state of siege in her own house in order to defend her family from the threats of Suffolk's close associate, Lord Moleyns (see Davis 1963: 10–21).

7   The fact that it actually took *three years* in historical time for the commons to bring their case against Suffolk indicates how invested Shakespeare was in making Suffolk appear the chief source and symptom of aristocratic disorder, and in linking "the good Duke Humphrey" to the cause and concerns of the commons.

8   The three texts in question are Ponet's *A Short Treatise of Politicke Power* (1556), Goodman's *How Superior Powers Ought to be Obeyed* (1558), and Buchanan's *De Jure Regni apud Scotos, or, a Dialogue, concerning the due Privilege of Government in the Kingdom of Scotland* ([1579] London, 1689).

9   For an informed discussion of the nature and extent of citizenship in early modern London, see Rapaport (1989: 23–60).

10   Shakespeare goes to great pains to place the historically predatory Say in direct dramatic linkage to the good Duke Humphrey by giving him lines like the following: "Tell me, wherein have I offended most? / Have I affected wealth or honour? Speak. / Are my chests filled up with extorted gold? / Is my apparel sumptuous to behold?" (4.7.90–3).

11   I am, of course, well aware that many London citizens (Shakespeare included) made it their life's ambition to achieve the honorific title of gentleman and that, as William Harrison long ago observed of his contemporaries, merchants "often change estate with gentlemen as gentlemen do with them, by mutual conversion of one into the other" (Harrison 1968: 271). What I seek to bring into focus here is less the disturbances produced by social mobility than the larger social and political disarray generated by the internecine conflicts of exclusively self-regarding aristocrats. In addition to Laslett's chapter on "social divisions and power relations" (Laslett 1971: 23–54), see Rapaport (1989: 285–376) on "patterns of mobility" in early modern England and, of course, Stone (1965) on "the crisis of the aristocracy."

References and Further Reading

Buchanan, G. (1689 [1579]). *De Jure Regni apud Scotos, or, A Dialogue, concerning the due Privilege of Government in the Kingdom of Scotland.* London.

Carroll, W. C. (1994). "The Nursery of Beggary": Enclosure, Vagrancy, and Sedition in the Tudor–Stuart Period. In R. Burt and J. M. Archer (eds.) *Enclosure Acts: Sexuality, Property, and Culture in Early Modern England.* Ithaca, NY: Cornell University Press, 34–47.

Cartelli, T. (1991). *Marlowe, Shakespeare, and the Economy of Theatrical Experience.* Philadelphia: University of Pennsylvania Press.

——(1994). Jack Cade in the Garden: Class Consciousness and Class Conflict in Shakespeare's *2 Henry VI.* In R. Burt and J. M. Archer (eds.) *Enclosure Acts: Sexuality, Property, and Culture in Early Modern England.* Ithaca, NY: Cornell University Press, 48–67.

Davis, N. (1963). *The Paston Letters: A Selection in Modern Spelling.* Oxford: Oxford University Press.

Goodman, C. (1972) [1558]. *How Superior Powers Ought to be Obeyed.* Geneva. Facsimile. *The English Experience*, no. 460. New York: Da Capo Press.

Greenblatt, S. J. (1990). Murdering Peasants: Status, Genre, and the Representation of Rebellion. In *Learning to Curse: Essays in Early Modern Culture.* New York: Routledge, 99–130.

Hall, E. (1965) [1548]. *The Union of the Two Noble and Illustre Families of Lancaster & Yorke.* London. New York: AMS Press.

Harrison, W. (1968) [1577]. *Description of England*, ed. G. Edelen. Ithaca, NY: Cornell University Press.

Harvey, I. M. W. (1991). *Jack Cade's Rebellion of 1450*. Oxford: Clarendon Press.

Hattaway, M. (1988). Rebellion, Class Consciousness, and Shakespeare's *2 Henry VI*. *Cahiers Elisabethans*, 33, 13–22.

Holinshed, R. (1807–8). *Holinshed's Chronicles*, 6 vols., ed. H. Ellis. London.

Jacob, E. F. (1961). *The Fifteenth Century: 1399–1485*. Oxford: Clarendon Press.

Kingsford, C. L. (1925). *Prejudice and Promise in XVth Century England*. Oxford: Clarendon Press.

Knowles, R. (ed.) (1999). *King Henry VI: Part II*. The Arden Shakespeare. Walton-on-Thames: Thomas Nelson.

Laslett, P. (1971). *The World We Have Lost*, 2nd edn. London: Methuen.

Leinwand, T. (1993). Shakespeare and the Middling Sort. *Shakespeare Quarterly*, 44, 3, 284–303.

Longstaffe, S. (1998). "A short report and not otherwise": Jack Cade in *2 Henry VI*. In R. Knowles (ed.) *Shakespeare and Carnival: After Bakhtin*. New York: St. Martin's Press, 13–35.

Patterson, A. (1989). *Shakespeare and the Popular Voice*. Oxford: Blackwell.

——(1994). *Reading Holinshed's Chronicles*. Chicago, IL: University of Chicago Press.

Ponet, J. (1972) [1556]. *A Short Treatise of Politicke Power*. Facsimile edn., *The English Experience*, no. 484. New York: Da Capo Press.

Rapaport, S. (1989). *Worlds within Worlds: Structures of Life in Sixteenth-Century London*. Cambridge: Cambridge University Press.

Riggs, D. (1971). *Shakespeare's Heroical Histories: Henry VI and Its Literary Tradition*. Cambridge, MA: Harvard University Press.

Shakespeare, W. (1999). *King Henry VI, Part II*, ed. R. Knowles. The Arden Shakespeare. Walton-on-Thames: Thomas Nelson.

Smith, L. B. (1966). *This Realm of England*. Boston, MA: Heath.

Stirling, B. (1949). *The Populace in Shakespeare*. New York: Columbia University Press.

Stone, L. (1965). *The Crisis of the Aristocracy, 1558–1641*. Oxford: Clarendon Press.

Storey, R. L. (1966). *The End of the House of Lancaster*. London: Barrie and Rockcliff.

Strier, R. (1995). *Resistant Structures: Particularity, Radicalism and Renaissance Texts*. Berkeley, University of California Press.

Wilson, R. (1993). A Mingled Yarn: Shakespeare and the Cloth Workers. In *Will Power: Essays on Shakespearean Authority*. Detroit, MI: Wayne State University Press, 23–46.

16

Vexed Relations: Family, State, and the Uses of Women in *3 Henry VI*

Kathryn Schwarz

It is clear then that a state is not a mere society, having a common place, established for the prevention of mutual crime and for the sake of exchange. These are conditions without which a state cannot exist; but all of them together do not constitute a state, which is a community of families and aggregations of families in well-being, for the sake of a perfect and self-sufficing life.

Aristotle, Politics, Book 3, Part 9

The family only represents one aspect, however important an aspect, of a human being's functions and activities. He cannot, she cannot, be divorced from the life of the social group, and a life is beautiful and ideal, or the reverse, only when we have taken into our consideration the social as well as the family relationship.

Havelock Ellis, "Children and Parents"

A King is a thing men have made for their own sakes, for quietness sake. Just as in a Family one Man is appointed to buy Meat.

John Selden, "King"

Henry VI, Part 3 has been many things to many readers: a history of kingship, a reformation of history, an exercise in source study, a study in bardic juvenilia, an apology for women, an apology for misogyny. It is also, structurally, a test case for the relationship between family and state. In two references to Priam and his sons the play condenses a host of questions about what it means when the family fully occupies the state, when statecraft and war are populated by men who share blood (2.5.120; 4.8.25). But where Priam, besieged by strangers, sends out his sons in a violent travesty of exogamy, *3 Henry VI* presents two families bound by an intimate and mutual knowledge. The title of Hall's history – *The Union of the two noble and Illustre famelies of Lancastre and Yorke* – stands behind this play as a proposition, a historical retrospective, and a bitter irony, the project of making state out of families at once inevitable and impossibly remote. We know that the union must take place, but the end seems at war with available means.

In this essay I want to interrogate the apparently natural parallel between family and state, and to pursue moments at which attempts to reason from one structure to another fail. Neither consolidation nor fragmentation is mimetic in *3 Henry VI*; family solidarity causes civil war, displaying the violence that irreducible relations do to more abstract systems of alliance. As it works through these causalities, the play posits a perhaps unexpected split in the roles played by women, distinguishing between the essentialism of generation and the transactions of marriage, between biological and contractual arrangements. Analyzing Levi-Strauss's description of kinship groups, Gayle Rubin writes, "As long as the relations specify that men exchange women, it is men who are the beneficiaries of the product of such exchanges – social organization" (Rubin 1975: 174). The exchange of women materializes relations among men who are not otherwise connected, broadening the scope of kinship. But the men of *3 Henry VI* illustrate this pattern only in its unraveling, defaulting instead to a more narrowly familial understanding of bonds. Family and state are not made or unmade in the same ways, or from or by the same things, and their incongruities sharply interrogate the relationship between descent and exchange. Patrilineality, the condition with which the play is largely preoccupied, connects men through maternal bodies, but such links do not accumulate to patriarchy in its larger social sense. As an anatomy of relations – relations of policy, relations of blood – the play invites us to scrutinize the relationship between patrilineal and patriarchal arguments, and to recognize that the disparate uses of women complicate the analogy between family and state.

Analogies linking family structures to those of the political state have strong currency in the early modern period; as Jonathan Goldberg writes, "The family/state analogy was embedded in the Renaissance habit of mind to think analogically and to explain events by understanding their origins; indeed, the analogy serves as an image of that ideational process."[1] Expressed as a relationship between microcosm and macrocosm, the analogy consolidates hierarchy, marking domestic insurrection, in the home or in the state, as treason. As Natalie Zemon Davis has argued, the apparent fact of sexual difference authorizes subordination, so that the command of subjects by sovereigns figuratively collapses into the control of women by men. "Sexual symbolism, of course, is always available to make statements about social experience and to reflect (or conceal) contradictions within it. At the end of the Middle Ages and in early modern Europe, the relation of the wife – of the potentially disorderly woman – to her husband was especially useful for expressing the relation of all subordinates to their superiors."[2] The analogy, despite its efficiency, occasionally finds women out of place; so in 1559 John Aylmer uses it to defend female sovereignty. "If then [women] may governe men in the house by saynt Paules commission, and an houshold is a lytle common welth, as Socrates in Xenophon saith: Then I can not see howe you can debarre them of all rule, or conclude that to be heads of men is against nature."[3] But for the most part the circle holds, linking men to kings and kings to men and excluding women from the places of power.

Formulated as a cliché, the analogy functions through assertions of self-evidence. Clearly (manifestly, but also transparently), men stand in a certain relationship to women; by extension (although that quality of extendedness is not stressed) certain men stand in the same relationship to the world at large. This after all is how ideology works, through extrapolation from what seems natural to what seems true. Althusser describes the phenomenon: "It is indeed a peculiarity of ideology that it imposes (without appearing to do so, since these are 'obviousnesses') obviousnesses as obviousnesses, which we cannot *fail to recognize* and before which we have the inevitable and natural reaction of crying out (aloud or in the 'still, small voice of conscience'): 'That's obvious! That's right! That's true!'" (Althusser 1971: 161). Obviousness has the power to approximate truth, or rather to project imposition backward into a condition of originality, leaving the subject unaware that any dislocation has occurred. That sense of grasping something always already true informs Edward Forset's *Comparative Discourse of the Bodies Natural and Politique*: "It is unfallable what I propound for my first principle, That in every particular person, there is both the seed and similitude of a State incorporat."

But Forset immediately qualifies his claim:

> Yet to imagine or seeke for in each severed or subdevided parts, such affinitie and fitnesse betwixt them, as may mutually illustrate each other; were not to tune but to crack the strings . . . Modestie and discretion bindeth us to a stint, beyond the which if we shall stretch or streine, we may justly be said to have borrowed of the wyer-drawers: we must not compell our applications there to shake hands and embrace, where discrepance of nature hath estranged and set apart. (Forset 1606: sig. A^v)

The warning against excessive interpretation, with its stretches, strains, and illicit embraces, might usefully hold us back from too quick a faith in the manifest identity of family and state. The logic that essentializes microcosm's correspondence to macrocosm begins not in the family, but in the individual body; it concludes not with the state, but with the world and God. "Moreover, as *Man* is called *Microcosmus*, a *little World*; so (to *fit* him to *it*;) his *head* is compared to the round *Heavens*; his *eyes* to the *Sunne* and *Moone*; his *haires* to the *trees* and *grasse*; his *flesh* to the *earth*; his *veines* to the *rivers*: but his more *solid bones* are compared to the precious *gemmes*, and hard *metals*, and *minerals*, which are the *riches* of the earth," William Austin writes (Austin 1637: 32). According to Helkiah Crooke, "This Little World therefore, which we call Man, is a great miracle . . . For, it is a farre easier thing to depaint our many things in a large and spacious Table, such as is the world; then to comprehend all things in one so little and narrow, as is the compasse of mans body" (Crooke 1615: 8). *The Problemes of Aristotle* argues that God created man as a "Microcosme, or little world, and in him printed his own image and similitude so lively, that no power whatsoever is able to blot it out" (sig. A2^v). Forset himself locates the state at a point intermediate between individual and cosmic bodies:

> The Commonweale with all her parts, orders, qualities, and requisites whatsoever, is (for better apprehension & illustration) set forth by sundry fit resemblances . . . but by none more properly than eyther by the universall masse of the whole world, (consisting of all the severall subsistances in that great frame by the high wisdome and might of God compact and united) or else by the body of man, being the lesser world, even the diminutive and modell of that wide extending universall (sig. ¶iij).

Where, we might wonder, is the family among all these relations?

Assumptions concerning the correspondence of family and state proliferate.[4] But in reading the family as a natural ground on which political abstractions work, we, like early modern political theorists, skip a step. The family is a socialized and secularized structure of connection, distanced through these processes from the immediacy that describes the body as a map of the world. I mention the obvious not to privilege embodiedness as an essential or originary condition, but to point out that even the fantasy of originality or essentialism recedes when the focus expands from individual to collective relations. To return to Davis's point, even if we accept that heterosexuality models the hierarchies of state control, we confront a set of discrete and potentially recalcitrant bodies whose relations might always shift. Nor is sexual superiority stable ground; for some early modern authors, the comparison of male to female bodies produces a different self-evidence. "[Woman] was not made of any uncleane, loathsome or base matter, as the body of man was: but even of his purity and most refined part, as may appear by her face, representing a very sweet and gracious complexion, without any ougly haires disfiguring" (*Other defence*: 63). Agrippa pursues a similar thought: having argued that "the essence of the Soul" reflects the creator's image equally in men and in women, he concludes, "In all other respects the *noble* and *delicate* Feminine Race, doth almost to infinity excell that *rough-hewn, boisterous* kind, the Male" (Agrippa 1670: 2). Misogyny and encomium may see the same thing without looking in the same way, so that patriarchal authority, as it rests on the clear meanings of sexed bodies, hardly seems grounded at all.

Considering the uses of analogy, George Puttenham writes, "This lovely conformitie, or proportion, or conveniencie betweene the sence and the sensible hath nature her selfe first most carefully observed in all her owne workes, then also by kinde graft it in the appetites of every creature working by intelligence to covet and desire" (Puttenham 1936: 262). But where the macrocosm is to a degree unknowable – the world, the universe, divine intention – the desire that pursues analogy must do so by way of synecdoche, a reliance on parts that at once condense and replicate the terms of the whole. Conviction that the available small object provides a reliable map requires a leap of faith, which proves not too difficult in the context of immanentist logics; belief in God or justice or a nice sense of proportion lends synecdoche its force. Kenneth Burke describes the privileged relation:

> The 'noblest synecdoche,' the perfect paradigm or prototype for all lesser usages, is found in metaphysical doctrines proclaiming the identity of 'microcosm' and 'macrocosm.' In

such doctrines, where the individual is treated as a replica of the universe, and vice versa,
we have the ideal synecdoche, since microcosm is related to macrocosm as part to whole,
and either the whole can represent the part or the part can represent the whole. (For
'represent' here we could substitute 'be identified with.') (Burke 1969: 508).

Synecdoche is the conceit of available knowledge; unlike metaphor, which keeps its
relations at least partly dark, or metonymy, which might always lead not inward but
away, synecdoche makes large truths accessible by inscribing them in small space.

Burke extrapolates this process into the social world, writing: "A similar synecdochic form is present in all theories of political representation, where some part of
the social body (either traditionally established, or elected, or coming into authority
by revolution) is held to be 'representative' of the society as a whole" (ibid). We might
be back again at the family, conceived as an element of the social body that mimics
that body's diseases, prophylactics, and cures. Yet families are structures, as political
states are structures, and the relation "as" may not imply the condition "like." As
Karen Newman writes, "Fathers were not sovereigns, nor even their representatives,
and many of these texts on marriage and the family betray their recognition of that
difference" (Newman 1991: 17). It is worth tracing fault lines in the processes of
analogy, if only to see how they lead from the premises that link familial to political
integrity to the conventions that define women simultaneously in terms of desire, use,
and trouble. The specific tensions between family and state, I suggest, reveal a great
deal about the ways in which women's roles are valued and understood.

Henry VI, Part 3 plays out a negotiation between family and state at once intimate
and adversarial. Leaving behind French challengers and vulgar dissidents, the play
creates a claustrophobic world opened up only intermittently and briefly by glimpses
of persons not named or claimed by blood.[5] This narrowness compresses familial and
political agendas, revealing a fracture in domesticity: the imperatives of blood are not
those of political coherence. *3 Henry VI* poses an analogic proposition through which
we see part and whole at the same time, and in which microcosm and macrocosm are
the same size. We do not scrutinize individuals to grasp an otherwise unimaginable
universe, or precipitate ourselves into orbit to parse the condition of personhood.
Instead, we see the structures of family and state overlap and interpenetrate, disjoin
and collide, and discover not an organic homology, or even a reciprocal tautology, but
a failure of extrapolation. "In a complex civilization any act of representation automatically implies a synecdochic relationship (insofar as the act is, or is held to be,
'truly representative')," Burke writes (Burke 1969: 508). In a civilization in which
two families battle for the right to *be* the state, synecdoche breaks down, and analogic
relations are contested at best.

Characters themselves invoke the family/state relation, as when Richard charges
Edward to fulfill filial duty through sovereignty: "For chair and dukedom, throne and
kingdom say, / Either that is thine, or else thou wert not his" (2.1.93–4). Warwick
accuses Edward of failings at home that breed crises abroad: "Alas, how should you
govern any kingdom, / That know not how to use embassadors, / Nor how to be

contented with one wife, / Nor how to use your brothers brotherly?" (4.3.35–40).
Edward himself reads familial and national harmony as mutual indices: "Now am I
seated as my soul delights, / Having my country's peace and brothers' loves"
(5.7.35–6). But from the vantage point of this last, misconceived complacency, already
deeply ironized by Richard's "I'll blast his harvest," we might regard those other analogies with a certain suspicion. The York family tells itself the story of the York state,
identifying patrilineality as the logic of kingship and placing faith in the force of
name (5.7.21). But when the correspondence of name to name, of head of family to
head of state, finds consummation, it does so in horrific, if also horribly comic, terms;
having killed the elder Richard, Margaret says, "Off with the traitor's head, and set
it on York gates, / So York may overlook the town of York" (1.4.179–80).

The convention that civil war tears families apart is at once recycled and traves-
tied as well. "[The family] functions almost entirely as a commentary on the causes
and consequences of political disorder," Robert Pierce writes of the *Henry VI* plays
(36), and the play's most famous setpiece embodies this effect in two men identified only by mistake, "*Enter a* SON *that hath kill'd his father, at one door*"; "*Enter a*
FATHER *that hath kill'd his son, at another door*" (2.5.54 s.d.; 2.5.78 s.d.). Father and
son cannot recognize kinship from opposite sides of battle: "Pardon me, God, I knew
not what I did! / And pardon, father, for I knew not thee!" says the son (2.5.69–70);
"But let me see: is this our foeman's face? / Ah, no, no, no, it is mine only son!"
(2.5.82–3), says the father. In the midst of this terrible misunderstanding both know
enough to blame their context, and the son's lament – "O heavy times, begetting such
events!" (2.5.63) – is parsed by the father's more elaborate denunciation. "O, pity,
God, this miserable age! / What stratagems! how fell! how butcherly! / Erroneous,
mutinous, and unnatural, / This deadly quarrel daily doth beget!" (2.5.88–91). In
that reiterated "beget" echoes the failure of another, more local begetting, as the chaos
of civil war unwrites the subjects and relations inscribed by domesticity. Lest we
should miss the point, Henry models audience response: "The red rose and the white
are on his face, / The fatal colors of our striving houses; / . . . / If you contend, a thousand lives must wither" (2.5.97–101). The story and its moral instruct us in the
processes that reason from homely to civil tragedies and back again. "How will my
mother for a father's death / Take on with me, and ne'er be satisfied!" says the son;
"How will my wife for slaughter of my son / Shed seas of tears, and ne'er be satisfied!" says the father; "How will the country for these woeful chances / Misthink the
King, and not be satisfied!" says the king (2.5.103–8).

And yet I would suggest that the instructional text misguides us. Families have a
kind of wild cohesion in *3 Henry VI*, coming together rather than falling apart in the
wake of civil violence. The play's early scenes compulsively repeat the modifiers of
familial place: "Father, tear the crown from the usurper's head," Richard demands
(1.1.114); "Sweet father, do so, set it on your head," adds Edward (1.1.115); "Good
brother, as thou lov'st and honorest arms, / Let's fight it out," Montague chimes in
(1.1.116–17); and York replies, "Sons, peace!" (1.1.119). "Why, how now, sons and
brother, at a strife?" York asks in the next scene (1.2.4); and, in greeting, "Sir John

and Sir Hugh Mortimer, mine uncles" (1.2.62). Chronicle plays are confusing, their characters requiring ingenious gloss, but surely this is more than information. The genealogies that link men to one another become irresistible, so that when Margaret taunts York to his death she recites a catalog that we and he know perfectly well.

> Where are your mess of sons to back you now,
> The wanton Edward, and the lusty George?
> And where's that valiant crook-back prodigy,
> Dicky, your boy, that with his grumbling voice
> Was wont to cheer his dad in mutinies?
> Or with the rest, where is your darling, Rutland? (1.4.73–8)

To the last, grim question she knows the answer. But the speech goes beyond prologue to a blood-soaked handkerchief, reminding us that the family does not end with York. "Richard, I bear thy name, I'll venge thy death, / Or die renowned by attempting it," Richard promises, and Edward adds, "His name that valiant duke hath left with thee; / His dukedom and his chair with me is left" (2.1.87–90). The iteration climaxes in the play's other famous setpiece, Edward's vision of three conjoined suns (2.1.34–8). And if the fraternal unity catalyzed by civil war is short-lived, it is nonetheless the play's most powerful fantasy, its closest approximation of harmonic ends.

The fantasy may seem narrow, conceived as it is among men from the same womb, but war is narrow in the same way. Variously completed, the accusation "you killed my" is its battle cry, a constant reminder of the intimacies of loss. "Earl of Northumberland, he slew thy father, / And thine, Lord Clifford, and you both have vow'd revenge / On him, his sons, his favorites, and his friends," Henry says. Clifford's proposal – "My gracious lord, here in the parliament / Let us assail the family of York" – identifies bloodshed as a logical effect of blood relation, as does Northumberland's response: "Well hast thou spoken, cousin, be it so" (1.1.64–6). Battle is joined in the name of lost fathers, identifying patrilineality as more potent than the bodies that inhabit it (1.1.89–100). Clifford's desire for revenge extends beyond the deaths of his enemies – "No, if I digg'd up thy forefathers' graves / And hung their rotten coffins up in chains, / It could not slake mine ire nor ease my heart" (1.3.27–9) – and that insatiable sense of implication shapes even his dying words. "Come, York and Richard, Warwick and the rest, / I stabb'd your fathers' bosoms, split my breast" (2.6.29–30). In his very extremity Clifford speaks for the play, and even Warwick, the consummate politician, knows this language. Explaining his change of allegiance, he reaches past the obvious reason – Edward has embarrassed him – to a more primal cause. "Did I forget that by the house of York / My father came untimely to his death?" he asks (3.3.186–7). It is a story more powerful than history, as *The Riverside Shakespeare's* footnote laconically informs us: "Actually, Warwick's father – the Earl of Salisbury of *2 Henry VI* – had been captured at the battle of Wakefield (1460) and executed by the victorious Lancastrians" (p. 691).

The statement that men fight in the name of family only reiterates the play's plot. But I want to take seriously the explicitness of that plot, with its obsessive insistence that family integrity causes civil war.[6] When Northumberland says of York, "Had he been slaughter-man to all my kin, / I should not for my life but weep with him," his gesture is extraordinary, at odds with the world in which he lives (1.4.169–70). "Think but upon the wrong he did us all, / And that will quickly dry thy melting tears," Margaret says; and Clifford, turning back to York, continues: "Here's for my oath, here's for my father's death! [*Stabbing him*]" (1.4.172–5). It seems as if the play cannot bear any logic, even the logic of survival or peace or human identity, that reaches across the boundaries of family, as if loss after loss only affirms the basic validity of these bonds. Warwick, learning of his brother's death, constructs a curious figure. "Why stand we like soft-hearted women here, / Wailing our losses, while the foe doth rage, / And look upon, as if the tragedy / Were play'd in jest by counterfeiting actors?" (2.3.25–8). A brother's death removes battle from abstraction – the stage, the genre play, the counterfeit – to lived experience, from a set of conventions acted out by rote to an urgent condition of necessity. The policy and statecraft that define Warwick's role become inadequate simulacra, irresponsibly distant from the real. In "Anti-Historians," Phyllis Rackin distinguishes between the theoretical agendas of men and the material insistence of women: "The whole issue of physical presence vs. historical record, dramatized in *1 Henry VI* as a conflict between English men and French women, is central, not only to this particular play, but to the history play genre itself."[7] *3 Henry VI* plays out this opposition, but deeply complicates it with the desire of men for imminent and knowable states of relation.

Men should not be women, nor their wars plays; such identities devalue heroic subjectivity, and in fantasizing his own feminized voyeurism Warwick signals something wrong.[8] But he hints as well at one of the play's great necessities, the consciousness of women as guarantors of relation. As it aggressively defines alliance in terms of kinship and kinship in terms of patrilineality, *3 Henry VI*, like other plays concerned with succession, places fierce pressure on sexual virtue. The play leaves no space for mothers to go astray; whether subjects or objects, onstage or off, they must create an absolute knowledge of uncontested legacy and uninterrupted line. "Conception is the male having an idea in the female body," in Thomas Laqueur's summary, but even in this most reductive of narratives the idea must be passed on.[9] The men of *3 Henry VI* recognize their shared inheritance from fathers because it has been ratified by mothers; blood as a patrilineal fantasy rests on the foundation of those more material blood products, menstruation and breast milk and female seed. Identity is secure as long as men trust their mothers, and *3 Henry VI* is unlike many of those other plays in defining male subjectivity through such trust.[10]

Men in this play locate familial relations beyond question, and brothers and fathers and sons and cousins die without dislodging that essential, essentialist, nuclear idea. Only by knowing who their fathers and cousins and brothers and sons *are* can they read loss as a sign of consolidation rather than a process of falling apart. Such faith in maternal virtue is odd enough for this story from this author in this time; perhaps more oddly, virtue works in contradictory ways. For the York family, maternity is an already-digested fact, a truth about the past that holds together the alliances of the present. York and his sons understand their connection to one another so thoroughly as to enable silence; the mother's absence demonstrates that nothing needs to be said. Mary Beth Rose writes:

> Since the mother would remove one from what is conceived as the world of action – the public, socialized world – the best mother is an absent or a dead mother. Thus . . . we can discern the outlines of what feminist and psychoanalytic criticism have identified as the oedipal plot: the essential separation from the mother (and consequent identification with the father) that proves the enabling condition for a full (i.e. both public and private) adult life. (Rose 1991: 301)

Male identity in the York family, aggressively both adult and public, proves the power of that invisible, private contract.

Margaret takes up power more directly. As many readers have observed, she erupts into this play, at once participating in and threatening to dismantle its masculinist, chauvinist, militarist presumptions.[11] Her martial role makes nonsense of Warwick's distinction between women and warriors; her sexual past violates the property rights of men and kings; her identity as a French woman threatens English maleness. I have argued elsewhere that, in the *Henry VI* trilogy, militant female agency detaches such qualities as masculinity, heroism, and sovereignty from any natural connection to men, and that Margaret represents an anxious domestication of that problem, forcing a reconceptualization of the roles of mother, mistress, queen, and wife.[12] She has so devastating an effect on policy that Edward of York blames her for the war: "For what hath broach'd this tumult but thy pride? / Hadst thou been meek, our title still had slept, / And we, in pity of the gentle king, / Had slipp'd our claim until another age" (2.2.159–62). This is the rhetoric of radical disaffection, of alienation catalyzed at a level of epic violence. And yet within the space of family politics Margaret reconnects her husband to his son.

> Hadst thou but lov'd him half so well as I,
> Or felt that pain which I did for him once,
> Or nourish'd him as I did with my blood,
> Thou wouldst have left thy dearest heart-blood there
> Rather than have made that savage duke thine heir,
> And disinherited thine only son. (1.1.220–5)

Even as she reproaches Henry, Margaret revalidates patrilineality, consolidating men who owe allegiance to a name.

In the families of Lancaster and York *3 Henry VI* turns radically different maternities to the same effect. Whether public or private, present or absent, mothers verify the patrilineality that provides the play's only constant argument. In both families the father is lost – York to death, Henry to the speech acts through which his wife and son abandon him – but the knowledge of patrilineal right remains. Margaret's responsibility for that knowledge troubles patriarchal agendas; when she parses the meaning of inheritance she occupies a decidedly odd place. Jean Howard and Phyllis Rackin write: "In separating herself from Henry's bed and table and taking on the job of championing her son's rights to the throne, Margaret is in a contradictory position within the patriarchal structures of family and state, but she is also a vehicle for exposing the ideological nature of many of patriarchy's claims" (85). In Margaret's doubled effect the split between patriarchy (the abstract conceiving of male privilege) and patrilineality (the concrete privileging of male conception) appears. Whatever damage she does to the theoretical naturalization of male homosocial power – and like many others, I believe that that damage is considerable – she does it in the course of a successful recuperation of her son's lineal claim. Militant maternity may have a shattering effect on political fictions, but it is one of the play's more provocative paradoxes that, within the fantasy of familial unity, Margaret quite simply does her job, enabling bonds to re-form in the father's name even when the father himself has abdicated the privileges and intentionalities that that name conveys.

In this chronicle of contested inheritance paternity is oddly secure. Genealogical faith, like Warwick's memory of his father's death, overwhelms historical evidence, so that Margaret's adultery in the second play of the tetralogy leaves little residue in the third. Richard, with his increasingly afamilial understanding of political advantage, reasons from her transgression – "Whoever got thee, there thy mother stands," he tells her son – but his initiative lacks momentum; the conventional insults of cuckoldry and bastardy, exchanged across patrilineal boundaries, do not dislodge the certainties within. Edward of Lancaster will lose his place if Edward of York has power to take it, an argument for armies of families rather than against inherited rights. Sovereignty can be detached and reassigned in a way that patrilineality cannot, and the play's large pattern of splitting the claims of blood from those of statecraft appears in this single act: Henry disinherits his heir without repudiating his son. "I'll leave my son my virtuous deeds behind, / And would my father had left me no more!" (2.2.45–50). Blood guarantees kinship but not kingship; as he disjoins bodily and ethical legacies from those imposed by social conventions, Henry disavows the analogic conceit.[13]

3 Henry VI does not limit female utility to the roles played by mothers, aspiring as well to the traffic in women that Rubin describes. But the project of homosocial exchange repeatedly falters, as when Edward of York describes Henry's marriage as an object lesson in misdirected exogamy.

> And had he match'd according to his state,
> He might have kept that glory to this day.
> But when he took a beggar to his bed,
> And grac'd thy poor sire with his bridal day,
> Even then that sunshine brew'd a show'r for him,
> That wash'd his father's fortunes forth of France,
> And heap'd sedition on his crown at home. (2.2.152–8)

Edward himself learns Henry's lesson in the mimetic rather than the aversive sense. "You'll think it strange if I should marry her;" he says of Elizabeth Grey, and Richard's reply — "That would be ten days' wonder at the least" — does not divert him (3.2.111–13). Edward wins his kingdom at the end of this play, and achieves his domestic desires as well. But rather than turning family solidarity to politic ends, this coincidence of sovereignty and uxoriousness confirms the narrowness of Edward's scope, frustrating the exogamy that might remake York through extended alliances. In Richard's words,

> And yet methinks your grace hath not done well
> To give the heir and daughter of Lord Scales
> Unto the brother of your loving bride.
> She better would have fitted me or Clarence;
> But in your bride you bury brotherhood. (4.1.51–5)

Through the act that alienates his brothers, Edward substitutes one patrilineal unit for another without questioning the priority itself.

Characters in *3 Henry VI* do not misunderstand the uses of exogamy; they are positively Rubinesque in the explicitness of their comprehension. "For how can tyrants safely govern home, / Unless abroad they purchase great alliance?" Margaret asks Lewis (3.3.65–70), and Henry, too, sees that Edward's availability for marriage gives him advantage in the contested French alliance (3.1.50–4). Montague rehearses the theory in response to Edward's choice: "Yet, to have join'd with France in such alliance / Would more have strength'ned this our commonwealth / 'Gainst foreign storms than any home-bred marriage" (4.1.36–8). But the play divorces knowledge from power. Describing the family/state relation through an analogy between good government and male sexual continence, Joyce Green MacDonald argues that in the *Henry VI* plays both break down. "When governors fail to discipline their sexual impulses toward pursuit of the greatest good for the state, chaos — both within families and in the commonwealth — inevitably follows" (MacDonald 1990: 211). *3 Henry VI* displays not only the triumph of lust, but the failure of strategy: Warwick marries one daughter to Clarence of York and the other to Edward of Lancaster, two well-conceived unions which produce betrayal in the first instance and futility in the second. Understanding contractual heterosexuality does not guarantee its effective consummation.

As a means to bonds among rather than within families, exogamy fails, leaving kinship narrowly and concretely rather than broadly and abstractly defined. Bodily links guaranteed by maternity, not social contracts formed through marriage, produce systems of connection. Coppélia Kahn has argued that, in history plays, "liaisons with women are invariably disastrous because they subvert or destroy more valued alliances between men" (Kahn 1981: 55). Howard and Rackin expand this point, describing the play as a catalog of male homosocial fractures — "*Henry VI, Part III* represents an extraordinary breakdown in the male bonds of filiation and loyalty, some biological and some not, that underwrote the feudal social order represented in this play" (84)

– and linking women to this effect. I want to sort out kinds of male bonds, and to argue that the play opposes familial to social relations. Women who prove connection by blood do different work than women who provide connection by marriage. Marriage, as Kahn argues, violates homosocial contracts, but this argument, like the play's own representations, makes a convention of what we should not expect. Invalidating the presumption that heterosexuality serves male homosocial interests, *3 Henry VI* identifies its marriages as failures of exogamy, privileging not social alliance but affective response. Edward and Henry choose wives based on the intimacy of desire, displacing statecraft for the more familiar spectacle of family. The nature of that choice – between abstract and material connection, between large and local worldviews – splits the imperatives of policy from those of blood, foreclosing kinship's expansion into a logic of state.

Clarence acts out the alternative, responding to Edward's marriage with his own calculated choice. "I will hence to Warwick's other daughter, / That though I want a kingdom, yet in marriage / I may not prove inferior to yourself. / You that love me and Warwick, follow me" (4.1.120–3). Reading marriage as instant male alliance, Clarence understands what Edward does not. But it is a partial and transient understanding, subject still to the desire for some primary unity; when Clarence commits his second betrayal, he does so in familiar terms. "Father of Warwick, know you what this means? / . . . / I will not ruinate my father's house, / Who gave this blood to lime the stones together" (5.1.81–4). Having crossed the gap between "father of Warwick," strategically acquired, and that other father's house and blood, Clarence crosses back. Richard and Warwick map out the no man's land between:

Richard. Welcome, good Clarence, this is brother-like.
Warwick. O passing traitor, perjur'd and unjust! (5.1.105–6)

If Richard, at this late moment, understands "brother-like" ironically, Clarence does not, and those simultaneous truths of loyalty and betrayal reflect a constant tension.

The play repeats Clarence's experiment on a larger scale, playing at pragmatic alliance but returning always to kinship narrowly defined. At the heart of the conflict, Henry attempts to invent an alternative version of inheritance: "Tell me, may not a king adopt an heir?" he asks, justifying his grandfather's usurpation of the throne, but anticipating as well his own compromise (1.1.135). Essex voices the play's resistance, "No; for he could not so resign his crown / But that the next heir should succeed and reign" (1.1.145–6). Only deviation from patrilineal inheritance can avert civil war, but the possibility appears deviant in that other, pejorative sense as well. "Richard Plantagenet, / Enjoy the kingdom after my decease," Henry resolves; and Clifford responds, "What wrong is this unto the Prince your son!" (1.1.174–6). When Henry tells York, "I here entail / The crown to thee and to thine heirs for ever," the statement has the form of a speech act but not its force, and York's response – "Now York and Lancaster are reconcil'd" (1.1.204) – is at once meaningful and empty. Its emptiness appears in its almost immediate negation; its meaning resides in the acknowledgment that only this can transfigure family into state. Only by expanding alliance beyond names and wombs, by attenuating the immediacy of shared bodily knowledge, can men join in policy rather than in war.

The terrible irony here is that the expansion is itself so narrow. York and Lancaster are linked by lineage as well as by ambition, descended together so closely that their arguments for kingship make equal if opposite sense. But even this added bit of interpretive room, this small relaxing of the conditions of bondage, implies an ideology too wide for the play's space. Henry, catalyzed by Margaret, abandons his compromise. Clifford echoes Margaret in explicitly resuturing the obligations of political place to those of fatherhood:

> He, but a duke, would have his son a king,
> And raise his issue like a loving sire;
> Thou, being a king, blest with a goodly son,
> Didst yield consent to disinherit him,
> Which argued thee a most unloving father. (2.2.21–5)

The play offers no effective defense against this argument, but requires us to recognize its costs. Men cannot agree arbitrarily on inheritance, even as the priority of blood tears apart the state by proscribing its consolidation through acts of will.

In a sense there are no effective acts of will in this play, but only presumptive statements of necessity. Men must know where they come from in order to know what to do; shared paternity, guaranteed by maternal bodies, displaces the lateral homosociality formed by marriage. Through marriage, men construct relationships to which women are useful; through maternity, men presume relationships to which women are essential. In a reasonably structured social universe, the first paradigm produces the second, which in turn reproduces the first, a neat tautology that seems endlessly self-perpetuating and smugly self-referential. But *3 Henry VI* does not take place in that universe. The bonds forged in heterosexual generation work against those formed by homosocial contract; the play is trapped in a rigid materiality, obsessed not with the advantages that women might provide but with the certainty they guarantee. Abstract power remains alien, the integrity of blood familiar, and two families pull the state to pieces. Puttenham writes of synecdoche, "Because it seemeth to ask a good, quick, and pregnant capacitie, and is not for an ordinarie or dull wit so to do, I chose to call him the figure not onely of conceit after the Greeke originall, but also of quick conceite" (Puttenham 1936: 185). The problem, for *3 Henry VI*, is that meanings are entirely too pregnant, too closely linked to the bodies that bear them. Conceit as an abstraction loosely linked to the thing it identifies gives way to that more intimate conceit, the arrogance of knowledge closely bound.

The men of *3 Henry VI* waver between local and general desires: Henry, with his contested legacy; Warwick, with his odd and inventive memory; Clarence, with his pique and its abeyance. Only Richard pursues a teleological course, from the man who says, "Methinks 'tis prize enough to be his son" to the would-be king for whom the blood of kinship signifies only in its spilling (2.1.20). And Richard carries no signs of his bearing. His attack on Prince Edward's paternity inspires Margaret's less conventional challenge: "But thou art neither like thy sire nor dam" (2.2.135). Richard's body does not bind him to his brothers, or to his father's memory, by referring him to his mother; in his own description, he is "Like to a chaos, or an unlick'd bearwhelp. / That carries no impression like the dam" (3.2.161–2). Dislocated from maternal essentialism and thus from family obligation, Richard represents the triumph of politic fictions, the embodied conviction that bonds can be bought and sold.

> I have no brother, I am like no brother;
> And this word "love," which greybeards call divine,
> Be resident in men like one another,
> And not in me: I am myself alone. (5.6.80–3)

Richard succeeds where his family and that other family of Lancaster have failed. In *Richard III* he falters only when he ceases to tend the alliances he has invented; and it is not, perhaps, an accident that he falls apart when he dreams of family.

Richard escapes from *3 Henry VI* into brief but effective kingship: however ill-meaning his desires, they distance him from the claustrophobic universe bounded by the bodies that produced him. The other men of *3 Henry VI* have what might be understood as a problem of knowledge. Knowing that familial bonds work through paternal certainty, and knowing as well that such bonds should model patriarchy, they aggressively produce the microcosmic artifact in all confidence that the macrocosm will follow. But unlike those early modern theorists of analogy, they cannot overleap the distance between material and abstract connections. The familial presumption of privileged indivisibility rests on maternity, on generative truth. Such truths are at once too much and too little to substantiate politic sociality: too much, as they put women at the center; too little, as they fail to encompass enough men. Patriarchy, as an argument about social organization, is not simply patrilineality writ large. Both systems rely on faith in the natural bonds among men, but where patrilineality embodies the natural in virtuous maternity, patriarchy claims more abstract ground, assuming a social condition of likeness rather than tracing the lines of blood. *3 Henry VI* demonstrates that bonds between men can convey relation without lending it a larger social significance. The play closes with the new king's rededication to familiar imperatives; claiming the son of his virtuous wife, he anticipates a sovereign future that we know he cannot encompass. "It is a wise father that knows his own child," says Launcelot Gobbo in *The Merchant of Venice* (2.2.76). *3 Henry VI* at once presumes that knowledge and questions its use.

Notes

1   Goldberg (1986: 9). Pierce, in *Shakespeare's History Plays*, traces the emergence of this analogy from classical and medieval drama. MacKenzie (1987) considers the familial and nationalistic myths

informing the tetralogy. MacDonald (1990) analyzes links between sovereignty and male sexuality. Lee (1986) characterizes Henry and Margaret in terms of role reversal, arguing that this reflects political chaos. For broader arguments concerning the relationship of political crisis to female dominance, see Bushnell (1992) and Davis (1975). For historical overviews of the family/state connection, see for example Schochet (1988) and Underdown (1985), especially chapter 2. Stone (1977) historicizes patriarchy as a familial structure; for readings that interrogate and complicate Stone's account of women's roles, see for example Ezell (1987), Newton (1990), and Amussen (1988).

2   Davis (1975: 127). See also Newman's (1991) discussion of the analogy's ordering function, especially pp. 16–18.

3   Aylmer (1559: sig. D1). In citing early modern texts, I have retained their spellings; however, I have modernized typography in several ways. Consonantal *u* and *i* have been revised to *v* and *j*, and vocalic *v* has been revised to *u*; long *s* has been revised to *s*; ligatures of æ and œ have been expanded; & and *y^e* have been altered to *and* and *the*; where a macron over a vowel indicates the suspension of *m* or *n*, I have supplied the letter.

4   For early modern theories of good government, with particular reference to the king's paternal relation to his subjects, see for example Beard (1648), Elyot (1544), Filmer (1680), Isocrates (1580), James I (1598 and 1603), and Nicole (1677).

5   For the tetralogy's treatment of women in relation to the investment in patrilineality, see for example Gutierrez (1990), Kahn (1981: ch. 3), and Rackin (1985).

6   Kahn (1981) argues that the investment in patrilineality, as it leads to vendetta, destroys the family, and links that effect to Henry's failure as king: "Because he has failed to be a strong father to his people, the paternal order has dissolved. Slaughter takes the place of succession . . . Both order and chaos are patriarchal" (p. 61).

7   Rackin (1985: 334). For an earlier version of this opposition of the material to the spiritual, see Bevington (1966: esp. 55).

8   Warwick invokes a specific site of cultural anxiety; for discussion of the implications of women watching plays, see Howard, "Women as Spectators."

9   Laqueur (1990: 35). There are of course more complicated, participatory or combative, ways of thinking about conception in the early modern period. For Laqueur's historicization of such ideas, see especially chapters 1 and 2. For a representative catalog of early modern theories, see *The Problemes of Aristotle*.

10 For discussion of Shakespearean maternity as a focus for concerns regarding paternal certainty and female sexual agency, see for example Adelman (1992), Kahn (1981), Rackin (1985), Roberts (1990), Rose (1991), Willis (1995), and Wilson (1994).

11 This disruptive effect has been described from a variety of perspectives. For consideration of Shakespeare's Margaret in relation to historical sources, see Lee (1986). For discussion of Margaret in relation to Elizabeth I, see Marcus (1988). Kahn (1981) analyzes Margaret's negative effect on male subjectivity; Howard and Rackin, in *Engendering a Nation*, and MacDonald (1990) describe her frustration of male homosocial bonds.

12 See Schwarz (1998).

13 For a contrasting reading, according to which broken political ties fracture biological bonds as well, see Howard and Rackin, *Engendering a Nation*, esp. 87.

REFERENCES AND FURTHER READING

Adelman, J. (1992). *Suffocating Mothers: Fantasies of Maternal Origin in Shakespeare's Plays, Hamlet to The Tempest*. New York: Routledge.

Agrippa, H. C. (1670). *Female Pre-eminence: or the Dignity and Excellency of that sex, above the Male*. Translated by H[enry] C[are]. London: Printed by T. R. and M. D. and sold by Henry Million.

Althusser, L. (1971). Ideology and Ideological State Apparatuses: Notes towards an Investigation. In *Lenin and Philosophy and Other Essays*, trans. B. Brewster. London: New Left Books, 121–73.

Amussen, S. D. (1988). *An Ordered Society: Gender and Class in Early Modern England.* Oxford: Blackwell.

Aristotle (1885). *The Politics*, trans. and ed. B. Jowett. Oxford: Clarendon Press.

Austin, W. (1637). *Haec Homo: Wherein the Excellency of the Creation of Woman is described, By way of an Essay.* London: Printed by Richard Olton for Ralph Mabb.

Aylmer, J. (1559). *An Harborowe for Faithfull and Trewe Subjectes, agaynst the late blowne Blaste, concerninge the Government of Wemen.* London: John Daye.

Beard, T. (1648). *The Theatre of Gods Judgements. The fourth edition, with additions.* London: Printed by S. I. and M. H.

Bevington, D. (1966). The Domineering Female in *1 Henry VI. Shakespeare Studies*, 2, 51–8.

Burke, K. (1969). Four Master Tropes. In *A Grammar of Motives*. Berkeley: University of California Press, 503–17.

Bushnell, R. (1992). Tyranny and Effeminacy in Early Modern England. In M. A. di Cesare (ed.) *Reconsidering the Renaissance*. Binghamton, NY: Medieval and Renaissance Texts and Studies, 339–54.

Crooke, H. (1615). *Microcosmographia. A Description of the body of man; together with the controversies thereto belonging.* London: W. Jaggard.

Davis, N. Z. (1975). Women on Top. In *Society and Culture in Early Modern France*. Stanford, CA: Stanford University Press, 124–51.

Ellis, H. (1957). Children and Parents. In *On Life and Sex*. New York: New American Library, 11–23.

Elyot, Sir Thomas (1544). *The boke named the governour.* London: In aedibus Thomae Bertheleti.

Ezell, M. J. M. (1987). *The Patriarch's Wife: Literary Evidence and the History of the Family.* Chapel Hill: University of North Carolina Press.

Filmer, Sir Robert (1680). *Patriarcha, or, The natural power of kings.* London: Printed by Walter Davis.

Forset, E. (1606). *A Comparative Discourse of the Bodies Natural and Politique. Wherein out of the principles of Nature, is set forth the true forme of a Commonweale, with the dutie of Subjects, and the right of the Soveraigne: together with many good points of Politicall learning, mentioned in a Briefe after the Preface.* London: Printed for John Bill.

Goldberg, J. (1986). Fatherly Authority: The Politics of Stuart Family Images. In M. W. Ferguson, M. Quilligan, and N. J. Vickers (eds.) *Rewriting the Renaissance: The Discourses of Sexual Difference in Early Modern Europe*. Chicago, IL: University of Chicago Press, 3–32.

Gutierrez, N. (1990). Gender and Value in *1 Henry VI*: The Role of Joan la Pucelle. *Theatre Journal*, 42, 183–93.

Herring, F. (1602). *The Anatomyes of the True Physition, and Counterfeit Mounte-banke, wherein both of them, are graphically described, and set out in their Right, and Orient Colours. Published in Latin by John Oberndorff, a Learned German: and Translated into English by F. H. Fellow of the Coll. of Physitions in London.* London: Printed for Arthur Johnson.

Howard, J. E. (1991). Women as Spectators, Spectacles and Paying Customers. In D. S. Kastan and P. Stallybrass (eds.) *Staging the Renaissance*. New York: Routledge, 68–74.

Howard, J. E. and Rackin, P. (1997). *Engendering a Nation: A Feminist Account of Shakespeare's English Histories.* London: Routledge.

Isocrates (1580). *A perfite looking glasse for all estates . . . nowe Englished to the behalfe of the reader, with sundrie examples and pithy sentences both of princes and philosophers gathered and collected out of divers writers.* London: Imprinted by Thomas Purfoote.

James, I. (1598). *The true lawe of free monarchies: or, The reciprock and mutuall duetie betwixt a free king and his naturall subiects.* Edinburgh: Printed by Robert Walde-grave, printer to the Kings Majestie.

——(1603). *Basilikon doron: or, His majesties instructions to his dearest sonne, Henry the prince.* London: Imprinted by Felix Kyngston, for John Norton, according to the copie printed at Edenburgh.

Kahn, C. (1981). *Man's Estate: Masculine Identity in Shakespeare.* Berkeley: University of California Press.

Laqueur, T. (1990). *Making Sex: Body and Gender from the Greeks to Freud.* Cambridge, MA: Harvard University Press.

Lee, P.-A. (1986). Reflections of Power: Margaret of Anjou and the Dark Side of Queenship. *Renaissance Quarterly*, 39, 183–217.

MacDonald, J. G. (1990). "Hay for the Daughters!": Gender and Patriarchy in *The Miseries of Civil War* and *Henry VI. Comparative Drama*, 24, 193–216.

MacKenzie, C. G. (1987). Myth and Anti-Myth in the First Tetralogy. *Orbis Litterarum*, 42, 1–26.

Marcus, L. (1988). *Puzzling Shakespeare: Local Reading and Its Discontents.* Berkeley: University of California Press.

Newman, K. (1991). *Fashioning Femininity and English Renaissance Drama.* Chicago, IL: University of Chicago Press.

Newton, J. (1990). Making – and Remaking – History: Another Look at "Patriarchy." In S. Benstock (ed.) *Feminist Issues in Literary Scholarship.* Bloomington: Indiana University Press, 124–40.

Nicole, P. (1677). *Moral essays, contain'd in several treatises on many important duties. First volume . . . faithfully rendred into English by a person of quality.* London: Printed for J. Magnes and R. Bentley.

Other defence of womens vertues, written by an Honorable personage, of great reckoning in Fraunce, and therefore thought meete to be joyned with the former discourse, An (1599). Bound with *A Womans Woorth*, translated by Anthony Gibson. London: Imprinted by John Wolfe.

The Problems of Aristotle, With other Philosophers and Physicians. Wherein are contained divers Questions, with their Answers, touching the estate of mans Bodie (1647). London: Printed by R. R. for R. W.

Pierce, R. (1971). *Shakespeare's History Plays: The Family and the State.* Columbus: Ohio State University Press.

Puttenham, G. (1936) [1589]. *The Arte of English Poesie*, ed. G. D. Willcock and A. Walker. Cambridge: Cambridge University Press.

Rackin, P. (1985). Anti-Historians: Women's Roles in Shakespeare's Histories. *Theatre Journal*, 37, 329–44.

Roberts, J. A. (1990). Birth Traumas in Shakespeare. *Renaissance Papers*, 55–66.

Rose, M. B. (1991). Where are the Mothers in Shakespeare?: Options for Gender Representation in the English Renaissance. *Shakespeare Quarterly*, 42, 3, 291–314.

Rubin, G. (1975). The Traffic in Women: Notes on the "Political Economy" of Sex. In R. R. Reiter (ed.) *Toward an Anthropology of Women.* New York: Monthly Review Press, 157–210.

Schochet, G. (1988). *The Authoritarian Family and Political Attitudes in 17th-century England: Patriarchalism in Political Thought.* New Brunswick, NJ: Transaction Books.

Schwarz, K. (1998). Fearful Simile: Stealing the Breech in Shakespeare's Chronicle Plays. *Shakespeare Quarterly*, 49, 2, 140–67.

Selden, J. (1689). King. In *Table-Talk: Being the Discourses of John Selden Esq.; Or His Sence Of Various Matters Of Weight and High Consequence, Relating especially to Religion and State.* London: Printed for E. Smith.

Shakespeare, W. (1974). *The Third Part of Henry the Sixth.* In G. B. Evans (ed.) *The Riverside Shakespeare.* Boston, MA: Houghton Mifflin.

Stone, L. (1977). *The Family, Sex and Marriage in England, 1500–1800.* New York: Harper and Row.

Underdown, D. E. (1985). *Revel, Riot, and Rebellion: Popular Politics and Culture in England, 1603–1660.* Oxford: Clarendon Press.

Willis, D. (1995). *Malevolent Nurture: Witch-Hunting and Maternal Power in Early Modern England.* Ithaca, NY: Cornell University Press.

Wilson, R. (1994). Observations on English Bodies: Licensing Maternity in Shakespeare's Late Plays. In R. Burt and J. M. Archer (eds.) *Enclosure Acts: Sexuality, Property, and Culture in Early Modern England.* Ithaca, NY: Cornell University Press, 121–50.

17

"The power of hope?" An Early Modern Reader of *Richard III*

James Siemon

Nothing could be more misleading in an attempt to recapture the experience of reading in the past than the assumption that people have always read the way we do today.

Darnton (1984: 215)

Despite considerable scholarly interest in early modern audiences, early readers of drama and their reading practices remain elusive objects of consideration. Recent work has made us aware of material and social circumstances affecting the production and reception of written materials such as pamphlets, ballads, and broadsides, and illuminating work has been done on individual readers of plays, such as Ben Jonson and Gabriel Harvey, even Shakespeare (see Evans 1995; Jardine and Grafton 1990; Miola 2000). Yet we know little about other readers who purchased plays, and who may have, as Joseph Hall and John Marston suggest, marked up their copies (Hall 1949: 15) or "made a common-place booke" out of them in order that they might speak "in print" from a "stock / Of well penn'd playes" (Marston 1598: H4r). This essay will consider one reader who, around 1630, recorded responses to Shakespeare's plays in a copy of the First Folio (Yamada 1998).

The focus will be annotations to *Richard III*. Other plays in the Folio are also copiously annotated, but the form and subject of *Richard III* make it a particularly interesting object of inquiry. Tillyard's unified Elizabethan world picture may no longer command assent or even rebuttal, but if ever a play approximated an identifiably early modern, even "Tudor," consciousness, *Richard III*, as scholars have repeatedly claimed, would seem to be it. One could contest aspects of Bernard Spivack's construction of the protagonist as a Vice figure (Spivack 1958: 386–407) or Paul Budra's claim that the play's outline is largely determined by *de casibus* tragedy (Budra 2000: 82), but such factors do arguably constitute the play, in Emrys Jones's phrase, as a "culmination and climax of 'Tudor' literature" (Jones 1977: 193). To what degree did the mid-seventeenth century reader find the play familiar or alien?

Recent scholarship has defined early modern reading communities that differed substantially in ideology and practice (Grafton 1997; Sherman and Jardine 1994; Ginzburg 1980; Stevenson 1984; Teague 1996; Watt 1991; Hackel 1999). Absent further evidence, there can be no grand claim that this particular reader's reactions and practices are typical of a well-defined community; however, at the very least, the annotations deserve consideration as pieces in an empirical puzzle that remains far from solution. The following account tracks a reader who was old enough, independent enough, literate enough, wealthy enough, and interested enough to mark up around 1630 the most expensive playbook that had ever been offered to the English public (Blayney 1996: xxviii), and who was somehow motivated to spend hours annotating plays without giving any sign of having seen them performed.[1] An overview of the marginalia will conclude by considering a speech by the Earl of Richmond that one of the play's most recent scholarly editors has defined as posing a special challenge to prevailing assumptions about the religious and social values of the early modern period.

Near the end of the play Richmond urges his "Fellowes in Armes" to throw off the "yoake of Tyranny" and take vengeance on King Richard, "The wretched, bloody, and vsurping Boare," by marching "In Gods name, cheerely on" (TLN 3406–20; 5.2.1–12),[2] and he concludes with lines concerning hope and aspiration that shock the editor of the new Oxford edition:

> All for our vantage, then in Gods name march,
> True Hope is swift, and flyes with Swallowes wings,
> Kings it makes Gods, and meaner creatures Kings. (TLN 3427–9; 5.2.22–4)

John Jowett reacts to this speech in appropriately early modern terms, calling the idiom of self-assertion here "perhaps . . . hubristic," and noting (rightly) that the use of "hope" to mean aspiration rather than patience renders this speech "disconsonant with hope as a Christian virtue." He might also have noted that Richmond echoes, as Richard himself does elsewhere, the aspiring language of familiar stage characters, sounding like Tamburlaine, who would be king and God or, more generally, like the Machiavells and malcontents who would be kings.[3] However, the seventeenth-century annotator, despite evident sensitivity to pious orthodoxies concerning God, monarchy, degree, and order, responds to Richmond's speech without disapproval, recording simply, "power of hope" (Yamada 1998: 160). Determining how this could be a possible response may help to remind one how little we know about early modern readers.

This is not to say that many elements of the annotations fail to conform to expectations as defined by modern scholarship. There is no mistaking a clear responsiveness to the Tudor political–dynastic interpretation of history. Even before the reader begins *Richard III*, the final remarks on *3 Henry VI* treat Richard of Gloucester as what Paul Budra calls "the great bugaboo of Tudor history" (Budra 2000: 82), characterizing his affront to social stability as "endlesse ambition" (Yamada 1998: 152). Similarly, the closing note to *Richard III* appears to sum up Tudor accomplishment: "Richmonds victorie and vowe to unite the white and red rose by his marieing of elizabeth and hopes therby to quench the fire of bypast miseries of warre and to establish peace and prosperitie" (ibid: 160). I will return to the form in which this response is articulated.

Paralleling their vilification of Richard for insatiable ambition, the annotations repeatedly register the value of a stable social order. For example, Queen Margaret's attack upon the newly prominent Woodevilles (TLN 726–31; 1.3.254–9) is termed her "reproach of the blind pride of new made noblemen" (Yamada 1998: 155), a formula that accepts her view and, for good measure, adds the term "blind" to characterize the proud demeanor of the nobles. Given the long-standing criticism of the Stuarts for advancing commoners to titles, this negative assessment is perhaps especially relevant to the reader, since George Villiers, Duke of Buckingham, had exacerbated political contentions during the middle 1620s by raising landless clients to titles and offices (Sharpe 1992: 131). The phrasing of the note also helps locate the annotator socially, since its intensified disapproval of upstarts expresses a prejudice against a group with which the annotator clearly does not identify. This evident social conservatism corresponds with the reader's equally clear responsiveness to representations of cosmic order. The notes assiduously record the play's omens and anticipations as "fearefull presagings" or "presages of mischance," and they second Buckingham's final observation about the implacability of divine justice: "falsified oath and Imprecation Iustlie remembred / and punished by god" (Yamada 1998: 157, 158, 160). The annotator also displays an appreciation of *de casibus* elements and ironies. Thus, Hastings's downfall bears witness to mortal over-confidence: "hastings securest confidence . . . of constant successe when he wes going to put his head in his ennemies hand to be cut off" (ibid: 157). In general, as one might expect from recent accounts of early modern commonplace books and the habits of mind that produced them (Crane 1993; Moss 1996), the annotator summarizes action or sentiments with generalizations about religion, state, and morality. Representative examples include: "how men sould gouerne in a change of things by the kings death"; "falshood of men couered with faire faces and words"; "precepts of deepe dissimulation And to say no and take it" (Yamada 1998: 156, 157, 158).

The remarks accompanying Clarence's death scene provide a sample of what one finds throughout:

Clarence his   dreame before   his death that he wes drowned

Clarence dreame   of his deserued torments in hell
princes happie in titles and miserable in effect

Torments on sea
Riches   in the sea bottome

powerfull operations of the conscience   of man
vexation of princes minds   Conscience derided

Conference betweene clarence and his murtherars
(Ibid: 155–6; TLN 851–1044; 1.4.1–210)

Plot summary and commonplaces alternate, without extended or explicit evaluation or overt interpretation. Still, the reportorial mode betrays signs of relative
weight and interest in the choice of elements to record and in the form of their
reportage.

This scene certainly offers a lot more that might have been glossed. The notes
might have responded to the stabbing of Clarence, the only dramatized physical
violence before Richard's death (TLN 1103; 1.4.268). They might have registered
the heavily ironic commentary on Richard's display of affection for Clarence (TLN
1060–81; 1.4.229–50). They do observe the murderers' treatment of conscience, but
they register none of its comic qualities nor its telling ironies in relation to
other characters; instead, the notes sternly pronounce, "conscience derided." Most
remarkably, they fail to mention the protracted debate concerning the loyalties of
subjects to king or God (TLN 1010–88; 1.4.195–204; 254–5), a highly charged
topic clearly related to Clarence's earlier lament about having served his brother-king
at cost to his own condition and spiritual well-being (TLN 902–4; 1.4.66–8). Seen
in the context of the bitter controversies in the mid-1620s about the limits of the
subject's duty to the sovereign (Cook and Wroughton 1980: 122), this omission is
historically striking, especially in light of what the annotator does seize upon
elsewhere in the scene. The annotations do react to the treatment of "conscience"
and related mental agonies, but only as they are felt by "princes." While we know
nothing specific about the annotator's religious orientation or rank outside of the
likelihood of substantial disposable fortune and the unlikelihood of belonging to
the newly ennobled, the potential implications of these selections and emphases are
suggestive.

Of course, the general importance of conscience is widely stressed in religious
discourses of all sorts during the early modern period. So it is not surprising that the
notes employ universalizing terms to refer to the "conscience of man," as elsewhere
they employ similarly undifferentiated plurals to record that "we affect the more the
grace of men" than that of God or to agree that "we" should react with patience to
the loss of a loved one (Yamada 1998: 158, 156). The two responses in 1.4 to the
dilemma of princes display, however, a more specific interest. The notes – "princes
happie in titles and miserable in effect" and "vexation of princes minds" – suggest a
high degree of responsiveness to Brakenbury's choric meditations on the vanity and
uneasiness that accompany royalty (TLN 913–20; 1.4.76–83). Since it is statistically
unlikely that the annotator is royal, this responsiveness at least potentially addresses
questions about the relation of some members of the early modern audience to what
Richard Helgerson has characterized as the regiocentric focus of Shakespeare's history
plays (Helgerson 1992: 195–245). Although the annotating discourse does not rise
beyond summary, the repetitions and the sympathetic evaluations implied in the
phrasing make the annotations appear literally to second Brakenbury's sympathies
for his superiors. They also lend support to the presumption of common empathy
in Clarence's demand, "A begging Prince, what begger pitties not" (TLN 1101;
1.4.267).

The typically reportorial mode of the annotations makes any strong statements especially noteworthy. Sometimes it is easy to discern what arouses pronounced responses because some notes affirm specific values. The note accompanying Richard's attempted manipulation of public opinion by appearing reluctant to leave his religious meditations and attendant bishops simply announces "damnable hypocrisie" (Yamada 1998: 158; TLN 2272–333; 3.7.57–115). A more complex example accompanies 3.1. Although the annotations offer no evaluation of Buckingham's egregiously sophistical arguments concerning sanctuary (TLN 1623–35; 3.1.44–56), they respond emphatically to values evident in other aspects of the scene:

> priuiledge of sanctuarie   Caesars high praise
> young king eduards royall courage
>
> meruellous sparkes of spirit and wit In
> the young duke of york
> (Yamada 1998: 157)

The passage that arouses the annotator's first enthusiastically positive response is that which expresses young Prince Edward's imaginary designs on France:

> An if I liue to be a man,
> Ile win our ancient Right in France againe,
> Or dye a Souldier, as I liu'd a King. (TLN 1670–2; 3.1.91–3)

These lines evoke the annotator's endorsement of martial values, awakening a sympathy that appears elsewhere in surprising circumstances. For example, when Richard proclaims his resolution to resist the forces of Ely, Richmond, and Buckingham, Richard's speech might be taken to sound desperate:

> Ely with Richmond troubles me more neere,
> Then Buckingham and his rash leuied Strength.
> Come, I haue learn'd, that fearfull commenting
> Is leaden seruitor to dull delay.
> Delay leads impotent and Snaile-pac'd Beggery:
> Then fierie expedition be my wing,
> Ioues Mercury, and Herald for a King:
> Go muster men: My counsaile is my Sheeld,
> We must be breefe, when Traitors braue the Field. (TLN 2759–67; 4.3.49–57)

But instead of registering the panic, haste, and impetuosity that this speech might suggest, the annotator sums it up in positive terms, remarking Richard's "resolution and diligence in warre" (Yamada 1998: 159).

Furthermore, in the Prince's enthusiastic dedication to the lost cause of English rights in France, the reader sees a courage that is specifically "royal." This assimilation of "royal" qualities to martial aims directed against France constitutes a notable, although somewhat ambiguous, sociopolitical alignment for the 1620s. Whatever such French dreams might have meant at the time of the play's composition in the early 1590s, in the years since King James's own failed attempt at continental intervention in 1624 with an expedition to aid his son-in-law, Frederick, the Elector Palatine, the reign of Charles I had seen military disasters on the Continent. Charles conducted a maritime war with Spain that eventuated in an utterly failed expedition against Cadiz in 1625. Subsequently, hostilities precipitated by a shipping dispute in 1626 led successively to the Duke of Buckingham's ill-fated 1627 expedition on behalf of the Huguenots against the Isle of Rhé, to additional failed expeditions to relieve La Rochelle in 1628, and finally to peace with France in 1629 and with Spain in 1630 (Cook and Wroughton 1980: 155). In the context of these developments, approval of Edward's martial ambition as individually courageous and specifically "royal" rather than half-baked, childish, futile, or, say, Protestant, implies a good deal about the persistent appeal of the personalized values of honor culture, even long after the administration of those values and their rewards had been claimed by the Tudors and their Stuart successors as a state monopoly (James 1986).

Equally suggestive in a social sense is the enthusiastic note concerning little York's exchanges with Richard. Ignoring Richard's own wit and sinister insinuations, the annotator focuses on the Prince's baiting of his uncle, characterizing it as "marvellous." Again, as in the notes to Brakenbury's meditations, the reader follows textual prompting; remarkably this susceptibility to prompting appears to be indifferent to the fact that the characters offering the prompts are sometimes compromised, or even thoroughly villainous. It is Buckingham who characterizes York's "sharpe prouided wit" (TLN 1716; 3.1.132), and Richard himself casts this wittiness as roughly synonymous with contemporary definitions of "spirit" when he calls the "perillous" boy "Bold, quicke, ingenious, forward, capable" (TLN 1741; 3.1.155). Such compliance with onstage evaluators may seem appropriate enough here, especially since Buckingham's positive evaluation of little York appears to be a personal opinion and seems to oppose his negative, rhetorical characterization of the boy to Richard as merely "prating" (TLN 1717; 3.1.151). The reader's tendency to chime in with onstage commentary is not uniform; there are moments when the glosses resist the text, although it is very difficult to predict where such objections will appear, as notes to 2.2 reveal.

Some glosses on this scene are hardly surprising. Queen Elizabeth's laments for King Edward's death prompt a garbled reaction that proves, when examined, unexceptionable in terms of contemporary theology (cf. Pigman 1985: 3). The reader's marginal note – "the Queenes extreame sorow for the kings death" – is followed by a further, more explicit evaluation: "reason why we sould sorrow Impatientlie for friends death." Despite its confusing articulation, this statement apparently follows the general tendency to accept textual prompting, for, taken in its context, the comment intends the opposite of what it literally says. A negative appears to have been omitted. It should read, "reason why we s[h]ould *not* sorrow impatientlie" since the annotated page exhibits utterly orthodox speeches by Dorset concerning God's displeasure at the Queen's objection to repaying "the Royall debt" lent her in the person of King Edward (TLN 1362–8; 2.2.89–100). Richard himself also contributes his equally orthodox (although utterly self-serving) support by observing "none can helpe our harmes by wayling them" (TLN 1378; 2.2.103). Again, the moral retains its recognition value independently of the motivation of the speaker. After all, the same character that opens the play eagerly anticipating the King's death here tells the royal widow to get over her grief. However, just after this positive response to Richard's hypocritical commonplace, the marginal remarks suddenly abandon their restrained tone to denounce "Richards vnspeakable malice & flatterie" (Yamada 1998: 156).

Richard has only three brief speeches that may have awakened this strong disapproval. "Flatterie" appears clearly in his fawning over Buckingham as "My other selfe, my Counsailes Consistory, / My Oracle, My Prophet, my deere Cousin" (TLN 1427–8; 2.2.151–2). His "vnspeakable malice" is less easily located. One might expect this uncharacteristically strong reaction to have been prompted by the first suggestions of plotting against Prince Edward. But the annotations to the contrivance against "the Innocent princes" (Yamada 1998: 159) assume a surprising, and perhaps culturally revealing, form.

Buckingham advises the various noble factions to bring Prince Edward from Ludlow to London with a "little Traine" (TLN 1395; 2.2.120). When charged to justify this potentially sinister proposal, Buckingham replies with smooth generalities about factional conflict:

> *Rivers.* Why with some little Traine,
> My Lord of Buckingham?
> *Buckingham.* Marrie, my Lord, least by a multitude
> The new-heal'd wound of Malice should breake out,
> Which would be so much the more dangerous,
> By how much the estate is greene, and yet vngouern'd.
> (TLN 1398–1403; 2.2.123–7)

Although this speech signals the first steps toward the imprisonment and murder of the princes, the annotation expresses neither shock nor disapproval. On the contrary, it echoes Buckingham's own language and logic: "It is dangerous after a greene reconciliation / of great quarrels to bring great parties / together with nombers and armies' (Yamada 1998: 157). The reader attends to extractable content, seconding a principle of state and ignoring its villainous application; in the process the marginalia display a tendency reminiscent of the ability of humanist readers like Gabriel Harvey to extract maxims from and record positive responses even to otherwise problematic authors like Machiavelli (Jardine and Grafton 1990: 161; cf. Stern 1979).

So, if appreciation of an abstract principle of statecraft can overrule moral qualms about its immediate employment, the question remains what there might be in surrounding passages to prompt anger at "Richards vnspeakable malice." On the relevant page Richard does have lines that are "vnspeakable" in that they are "inca-pable of being spoken or uttered" when he delivers a speech that most modern editors take to be an aside:

> *Richard.* . . . .
> Madam, my Mother, I do cry you mercie,
> I did not see your Grace. Humbly on my knee,
> I craue your Blessing.
> *Duchess.* God blesse thee, and put meeknes in thy breast;
> Loue Charity; Obedience; and true Dutie.
> *Richard.* Amen, and make me die a good old man,
> That is the butt-end of a Mothers blessing;
> I maruell that her Grace did leaue it out. (TLN 1379–86; 2.2.104–11)

Although unmarked as to delivery in Quartos and Folio, his last three lines appear to be unheard by the other characters (cf. TLN 791–2 (1.3.317), where Richard "*Speaks to himselfe*"). But is there a context in which these lines, frequently staged as comical (Colley 1992: 47), might offend the seventeenth-century annotator? Surely the phrase "vnspeakable malice" makes it likely that "vnspeakable" means "indescribable" and that the annotator reacts to promptings that are no longer self-evident.

One early modern context that might have rendered these lines repugnant could be that constituted by familiar period clichés about order and degree. Given the anno-tator's evident appreciation of hierarchy, perhaps he or she reacts to Richard's mockery of the content of his mother's speech. The Duchess prays that Richard might come to exhibit the cardinal Christian virtues officially demanded of the deferential subject by the Tudor–Stuart social order: "meeknes . . . / Loue Charity, Obedience, and true Dutie." That the reader ignores anything comical in Richard's famously funny lines would be in keeping with other instances in which the reaction is primarily or exclu-sively to the extractable burden of a passage rather than to its form or occasion.

However, there remains another potentially relevant set of contemporary contexts. The notes register a very high degree of responsiveness to family relationships. Despite the play's intense interest in the ambitions and downfalls of individuals, the reader frequently recurs to familial terms to designate the characters. Clarence is often the "brether" or "brother" of Richard and Edward, doing Edward "more then brotherlie duties" (Yamada 1998: 153, 156); the Queen's faction are repeatedly called her "kinred" (pp. 153, 154, 156, 157); Anne is Warwick's "daughter," "prince edwards widow," "the deceased princes widow," and Richard "her husband" (pp. 153, 154, 158); the princes are "king edwards children" (p. 158). Not surprisingly, the formu-lations that most strongly register such relationships occur in response to Richard's incestuous attempts to wed Princess Elizabeth. The notes record that Richard "plots to murther his nevewes and his owne wife and marrie his niece" and that "Richards mother vses bitter Imprecations agains him / he makes sute to haue his brothers daughter to wife" (pp. 158, 159).

This insistent familial focus makes it especially interesting that the reader's reaction to Richard's malice appears in proximity to a staged travesty of a family ritual. Recent accounts of parental blessings (Young 1992) and curses (Thomas 1971: 505–6) emphasize the prominence of the blessing ritual and the seriousness with which both blessings and curses were taken in early modern England. The widespread practice of parental blessing is recorded both by contemporary observations and by literature. Among other witnesses, an Italian account from the early seventeenth century claims that English children knelt to be blessed "in the public streets and in the most frequented and conspicuous places of the city, no matter what their age" (Young 1992: 188). No fewer than eighteen references to the practice appear in Shakespeare's plays (ibid: 179–81). Within *Richard III* itself, Richard's mockery of the ritual is contrasted with Clarence's credulous faith that brothers "blessed" by a father's "victorious Arme" must stick together (TLN 1069–71; 1.4.235–8). Yet despite evidence attesting to the frequency and importance of this ritual, an historically situated reconstruction of a reaction to its dramatic treatment demands theatrical as well as discursive complication.

First of all, mockery of parental blessing, even of parental blessing *in extremis*, seems to have been a standard feature of Tarletonian comedy. Not many years after the time of the Folio annotations, Henry Peacham recalls a stage routine of Tarleton's that he witnessed in his youth. As Peacham recounts this episode, two elder sons kneel at their father's deathbed to be blessed, the first with family lands, the second with means to maintain himself as a scholar. Each responds dutifully to his father with a tearful wish: "live to enjoy it yourselfe." Tarleton, playing the third son, travesties this patterned exchange:

> To the third, which was *Tarlton*, (who came like a rogue, in a foule shirt without a band, and in a blew coat with one sleeve, his stockings out at the heeles, and his head full of straw and feathers) as for you sirrah, quoth he, you know how often I have fetched you out of *Newgate* and *Bridewell*, you have beene an ungracious villaine, I have nothing to bequeath to you but the gallowes and a rope: *Tarlton* weeping and sobbing upon his knees (as his brothers) said, O Father, I doe not desire it, I trust in God you shall live to enjoy it your selfe. (Peacham 1638: 102–5)

Peacham ruefully concludes that "There are many such sons of honest and carefull parents in *England* at this day" (p. 105), a response that may be less vehement than the annotator's but that is consistent with its moralized interpretation. Yet the comic genre to which these mid-seventeenth century reactions respond so negatively appears to have been appreciated by Shakespeare.

Shakespeare prominently parodies the blessing ritual not only in *Richard III*, but also in *Two Gentlemen of Verona* and *Merchant of Venice*. In the former play, Lance enacts a pantomime in which his shoe stands in for his weeping "father" from whom he begs, "Father, your blessing" (2.3.23–4). In the latter, Launcelot Gobbo parodies both the contemporary ritual blessing and its biblical prototype, Isaac's blessing of Jacob, while offering a blasphemous echo of the *Gloria* from the Book of Common Prayer ("I am Launcelot, your boy that was, your son that is, your child that shall be"). Kneeling before his blind father, Lancelot replays a comic version of Jacob kneeling before Isaac, as old Gobbo feels the back of his head, mistaking his hair for a beard (2.2.81–98).

This parody of the archetypal biblical blessing *manqué* opens an interesting perspective onto the potential for diversity and competition among early modern values. The same social order that fostered the parental blessing not only witnessed its parody on the commercial stage but derived earnest counter-imperatives from its discursive prototype. Stable degree, order, and succession were indeed held to be divinely instituted, but it was also argued on the basis of the story of Jacob and Esau that there was another principle to be found in the biblical account. For example, Richard Lewes proclaims in a late sixteenth-century sermon the familiar, nearly ubiquitous principle of interlinked social hierarchies: if the "sonne bee obedient to his father, the subiect to his Prince, affection to reason" so that they keep "their proper place & office without vsurping," then all will be "quiet and orderly" in family, kingdom, and individual (Lewes 1594: B6r–B6v). And he also awards opponents of this principle their usual early modern designation as "Machiauelists" (ibid: C5v). Nevertheless, Lewes finds a strong message in the story of Jacob and Esau not so much for the "multitude" to submit to the demands of order as for "Magistrates" to "take heede" to "helpe poore Iacob to his right" (ibid: B7r). In fact, he interprets Jacob's successful deception of his father in order to steal the blessing from its rightful lineal inheritor as implicating the mystery of divine "election" or "prouidence" (ibid: C4v–C5r); namely, "They which the Lorde will aduance, shall be aduanced" (ibid: A6r). Here, as elsewhere, social advancement appears to acquire legitimacy and even a providential nature.

A similar doubleness of message – reverence for established order coupled with an appreciation of successful advancement – may be found in early modern civic discourse. For example, the Recorder of London's speech presenting the Lord Mayor, Sir John Spencer, to the Lord Chief Baron and his Brethren of the Exchequer in 1594 predictably proclaims submission to authority, asking rhetorically, "what order or government can there be where there is not one to commaund, others to obey, one to rule, and others that submit themselves?" (Nichols 1823, III: 255). The same speech also invokes different values in describing the mayoral election and office:

> this Chief Magistrate is not to be emposed upon us, or set over us without our consent and choise, but to be elected by ourselves, to be chosen not from amongest forrayners or strangers, but *de nobis ipsis*, a member of our body, a brother of our brotherhood, a Fellow Cittizen of the same society, whereof himself shall be the chiefest. What grant can be more grateful, or what princely gift more bounteous unto subjects, then for the inferiour to chuse his superior; the members their owne head; the Cittizens their own Magistrate? (Ibid)

The conclusion flies in the face of expectation. To ask what body could choose its own head should admit no possible positive answer; yet here, amid deference to "princely gift" and "bounty," an opening appears for self-assertion. The status and right of the "brotherhood" of "Fellow Cittizen[s]" are asserted in the act of choosing their own leaders rather than having superiors "emposed" upon them. As the speech continues an even more telling relationship to the theme of social advancement emerges from a consideration of mayoral election:

> To the well-disposed Cittizens; to stirr them up to ascend the same degrees that hath advanced others to that honourable dignity, when they see the self-same way for them as it was for others to attayne to the same, which is from vertue to vertue, from service to service, from one office to another, until they come to the highest office, which is the chiefest honour the Cittizens do bestowe, not upon him that will desire it, but by his vertues that deserve it. Honour is the reward of vertue. (Ibid: 256)

Simultaneously praising and disavowing ascent from degree to degree, the speaker proclaims that higher offices exist to be aspired to while demanding they should not be aspired to. "Vertue" should merit reward, but "desire" (read "ambition") should be eschewed; nevertheless, the ceremony of investiture and this very speech itself are said to be intended to stir the citizens to want to be "advanced" to the distinction of mayoral office.

Such doubleness of discourse, theological, civic, and social, may direct attention back to the lines from *Richard III* concerning hope, for a similar doubleness invests Richmond's declarations, and indeed to some extent the entire play, with a particular tension. In early modern usage "hope" manifests distinctly heteroglot tendencies that make it difficult to arrive at a single assessment of a speech by an invader who affirms hope in pursuing "vantage" and likens the prompting of his mission to the emotion that inspires kings to want to be gods and creatures to be kings: "then in Gods name march, / True Hope is swift, and flyes with Swallowes wings, / Kings it makes Gods, and meaner creatures Kings" (TLN 3427–9; 5.2.22–4).

The widely recognized negative connotations of "hope" inspire careful treading among contemporaries. The relevant concerns are evident in the history of the Percy family motto "esperaunce." As Mervyn James describes them, verses painted by the fifth Earl of Northumberland on his walls in Leconfield exemplify an aristocratic revision of sentiments in response to the large-scale recasting of values demanded by Tudor attempts to monopolize power and ideology through a "system of social controls and moral sanctions" (James 1986: 309). In place of the traditional family motto, *esperaunce ma conforte*, which implies a form of "hope" that could be taken as hope for advancement, the walls are repainted with a motto, *esperaunce in dieu*, rendering hope as a religious consolation and opposing it to honorable and worldly aspirations:

> Esperaunce in dyeu.
> Trust hym he is moste trewe.
> En dieu esperaunce.
> In hym put thyne affiaunce.

> Esperaunce in the worlde nay.
> The worlde variethe every day.
> Esperaunce in riches nay not so.
> Riches slidethe and sone will go.
> Esperaunce in exaltation of honoure.
> Nay it widderethe away lyke a floure.
> Esperaunce en dieu in him is all.
> Which is above fortunes fall. (James 1986: 89–90)

James notes the continuities of sympathy that connect these fifteenth-century pronouncements on religious detachment from honor, ambition, and the desire for wealth
with the later, more philosophical detachment of the earl's great-grandson, the ninth
earl, who wrote from his imprisonment in the Tower advising his son to "esteem
nothing of the world at an over-value" (p. 90). But such a carefully limited sense of
hope was by no means universally shared.

At its most conservative, contemporary usage could be positive about hope as the
consolation of the suffering and downtrodden, but this form of hope could hardly be
imagined, as it appears in Richmond's lines, exhibiting the speed of a swallow's flight.
Calvin's *Institutes* treat hope as endurance, rather than a spur to action. "The sufferãce
of hope" exercises a restraining function: "for hope, while it in silence loketh for y^e
lord, restraineth faith that it fal not hedlong with to much haste." Furthermore, Calvin
equates hope not with desire but with its suppression on behalf of God's will: "Paule
to the Philippians out of faith deriueth expectation, bicause in pacient hoping, we
holde oure desires in suspense, till Gods conuenient oportunitie be opened" (Calvin
1561: fol. 126r).

More negatively, hope frequently appears in the early modern period as a synonym
for carnal desires or presumption. William Cornwallis puts the proximity of hope to
ambition succinctly:

> What we call licorousnesse in children, greedinesse in Clownes, misery in couetous
> persons, the same is ambition in a higher fortune: the head of this humor is one, but in
> the disposing takes seuerall passages. To aspire is Ambition, which is hope attempting,
> heere hope is abused which is giuen to man not to clime with, but to keepe him from
> falling. It hurts not for all this, if we would allay the vigor, and prepare it as we do
> Quick siluer, which killing, cures. (Cornwallis 1600: F8v–G1r)

Within *Richard III* a similar contrast between the positive sense of generalized hope
as patient expectation of Christian redemption and the suspect sense of hope as worldly
desire appears in the erotic struggles between Richard and Anne:

> *Richard.* But shall I liue in hope.
> *Anne.* All men I hope liue so. (TLN 394–5; 1.2.199–200)

The joke depends upon the different meanings of the word in sonneting and salvific
usage, where hope means respectively the lover's desire and the Christian's redemp-
tive relationship with God. Similar plays of significance emerge in Clarence's lecture

to the murderers about their "hope for any goodnesse" from their king or God (TLN 1021; 1.4.89) and in Hastings's meditations on the false "hope" that trusts the "grace" of courtly politics rather than the "grace of God" (TLN 2069–71; 3.4.96–9). The suggestion of human futility conveyed in Hastings's invocation of the "momentarie grace of mortall men" also suggests the play's strong sense of hope as mortal presumption.

Richard III could be read as an extended ironic commentary on the falsity of worldly hopes for security and stability amid courtly contentions, a commentary that begins with the final line of *Henry VI, Part Three* as King Edward looks at his infant son and proclaims, in the presence of the child's future killer, "heere I hope begins our lasting ioy" (TLN 3217; 5.7.46; cf. Budra 2000: 81). The reader annotates this passage, remarking its immediate proximity to lines that convey "Richards endlesse ambition" (Yamada 1998: 152) and employing a favorite early modern buzzword – "secure" – to characterize Edward's hope as delusional: "king edward glories in the ouerthrow of his ennemies an promises to him self and his posteritie the secure possession of the crown" (pp. 151–2). Such usage acknowledges Hecate's claim that "security / Is mortals' chiefest enemy" (*Macbeth*, 3.5.32–3), a truism echoed in Hastings's laments about having trusted his political position to be "secure" (TLN 2064; 3.4.91).

Hastings's deluded faith in worldly security replays, of course, the foundational error of the princes whose falls make up the *de casibus* tradition of tragedies and *Mirrors*, reminding one that mortality cannot exceed itself; that, contrary to Richmond's claim, a king cannot be a god. Still, the proximity, even identity, of kings and gods appears widely asserted in early modern discourse. Such an assumption motivates the rhetoric of Shakespearean characters in *Richard II* like John of Gaunt, who affirms the sacred status of "God's deputy" (1.2.38), or like the Duchess of York, who proclaims King Henry "A god on earth" (5.3.136).[4] This phrasing draws on a biblical discursive tradition that was developed by figures like Calvin (1561: fol. 161r) and repeated by the *Homily against Disobedience* and *The Mirror for Magistrates*, in which Baldwin's 1559 dedication speaks of "God . . . honoring & calling all Kinges, & all officers vnder them by his owne name, Gods. Ye be all Gods, as many as have in your charge any ministracion of Iustice" (Baldwin 1938: 65). Henry Smith follows Calvin in quoting Psalm 82 to promulgate this idea in a widely reprinted sermon of the early 1590s addressing "Kings and Gouernours": "I haue sayed, yea are Gods, and ye all are the children of the most highest" (Smith 1594: 366). But despite the emphasis during the period on Christian subjection to rulers, there is not unanimity. Smith provides a relevant instance of complexity.

While Erasmus's *Adages* provide evidence that it was possible to resist the identification of kings with gods (Erasmus 1974: 115), Smith sides with mainline Elizabethan tradition to defend the equation. However, Smith suggests the complexity of the equation by emphasizing the duties of office:

> Princes and rulers haue many names of honor, but this is the honorablest name in their Titles, that they are called *Gods*: other names haue bin giuen them of men for reuerence

or flattery, but no man could giue them this name but God himselfe. Therefore their name is a glasse wherein they may see their duety, how God doth honour them, & how they should honor him. (Smith 1594: 371)

In keeping with this emphasis on the "duety" and responsibility for right thinking and responsive action that attend upon those who bear God's name, Smith points out the failure of many a "King, or Iudge, or Magistrate" to live up to the demands embodied in that name (p. 370). Smith also warns about a danger that inheres in the appellation itself insofar as it might encourage both tyrants and, surprisingly, another, and seemingly opposed category of political agents, ambitious rebels. Smith conjoins the two evil categories as he argues that "vngodly Rulers and gracelesse striuers against lawfull rule, in their owne heartes calling themselues *Gods*, not being so called of God, are cause of all disorder in euery Common weale" (ibid).

Although both may call themselves "Gods," tyrants and machiavellian "striuers" alike lack a true calling from God. Smith employs the period characterization of civil disorder as symptomatic of ambition, but in his invocation of "calling" Smith, like the also much-published William Perkins, opens a window onto some surprising individual and institutional dimensions of the concept. Although neither Smith nor Perkins is an extreme figure, their widely read texts suggest a remarkable early modern variety of thinking about government and subjection. True, Smith claims, with perfect orthodoxy, that the only rightful rulers are not those who rise to office prompted by their own "graceless" aspirations, but he also registers a positive role for subjects themselves in the calling of rulers and kings: "this name enformes vs what kind of Rulers & Magistrates we should choose: those which excell al othe[r] men like Gods amongst men" (p. 367). Tudor–Stuart kingship was hardly elective, but the continuity implied here between biblical kingship, early modern civic office, and monarchy presumes an element of acceptance and volition in the subject that bears on the calling of the true prince.

Such potentially opposing passive and active tendencies appear insistently in a work that brings the office of kingship into a detailed relation with the ordinary person's vocation, and the terms of William Perkins's *Treatise of Callings* are relevant to the problematic lines from *Richard III* concerning hope. As in the cases of Lewes's sermon and the City Recorder's speech, Perkins's *Treatise* eloquently invokes the ideal stability of an established order in which everyone is "placed" in a vocation by God and sticks to it. He, too, wastes no sympathies on "Machiauel his pollicies," which he denounces for exacerbating envy and resentment between different callings or social degrees (Perkins 1603: 932). However, Perkins also proclaims that "it is not vnlawfull to desire" offices, places, or callings (p. 918), and he even argues that one may want to change callings for all the wrong reasons, pursue the new vocation by evil means, and still end up ultimately and mysteriously having done the right thing, "for the after-approbation and acceptance (though it doth not iustifie the bad entrance) yet doth it make a supply thereof" (ibid; cf. Marshall 1996: 42). To illustrate this remarkable claim Perkins instances historical invasion and conquest:

A Prince as W. Conquerour, enters into a land or kingdome, & by warre and blood-shedde seekes to subdue the people, and to make them subiect vnto him: now by this bad entrance he is no lawfull king: for euery lawfull king is placed by God, and by men that are appointed vnder god to set vp princes ouer them, according to the lawes and customes of seuerall kingdomes. Yet if the people doe willingly submitte themselues to this vsurper, and be content to yeild subiection, & the king likewise to rule them by good & wholesome lawes, hee is nowe become a lawfull Prince, though his entrance was but tyrannical. (Perkins 1603: 918)

While it remains unclear just what this example should have to do with the ordinary commoner's entry into a vocation, it seems to me to come perilously close to suggesting that success in getting the position that one wants is its own justification – if, that is, one's new eminence is recognized by others.[5]

And this emphasis returns us to the end of *Richard III*. Tillyard claims that the end of the play provides Shakespeare's "full declaration of the principle of order, thus giving final and unmistakable shape to what, though largely implicit, had been all along the animating principle of the tetralogy. His instrument, obviously and inevitably, is Richmond" (Tillyard 1946: 201). But Andrew Gurr has rightly pointed out the play's emphasis on the participatory role of the whole realm in Richmond's accession (Gurr 1974). Richmond's final plea to the audience for acclamation appears designed to make up for the coercion of the London commoners by Richard in 3.7. The close of the play does present a final unity, to be sure, since even the ghosts cast votes against Richard and on behalf of the new order, but the new order is not a simple manifestation of a stable principle. Rather it appears to be founded upon desire and to need a favorable acquittal. Thus, Richmond's last speech in which, as the reader says, he "hopes . . . to quench the fire of bypast miseries of warre and to establish peace and prosperitie," constitutes, in effect, a sort of retroactive campaign address (cf. Campbell 1947: 333–4) that invites audience members – and readers – to add their "Amen" or else prove themselves to be "Traitor[s]." Thereby, the new ruler, however suspect his "hope" to attain office might otherwise have been, appears to seek, from the theatre audience and from readers, a measure of what Perkins calls "after-approval." Our reader adds no personal "Amen" to the margins, apparently content to characterize the play's concluding promises of peace and justice as Richmond's "hopes." Perhaps it says enough that he or she found the lines concerning "the power of hope" clearly unobjectionable. How typical or atypical were such reactions? If only we knew. How much more might other readers' assertions and reticence have to say to us?

NOTES

1 The Folio volume and its provenance are fully considered by Yamada, who finds calligraphic features of the notes consistent with a dating of "the 1620s or around 1630"; Yamada also argues on the basis of vocabulary that the author of the notes was a Scot (Yamada 1998: xix). The earliest known owner

is William Johnstoune, who apparently owned the volume ca. 1650 and who may have been a relative of Ben Jonson (Yamada 1998: xv–xx). I am grateful to Peter Stallybrass, Rachel Trubowitz, and
Jason Rosenblatt for valuable assistance with the research for this essay.

2   Quotations from *Richard III* will be included parenthetically from *The Norton Facsimile of the First
Folio of Shakespeare* with Through Line Numbers (TLN) followed by line numbers from *The Riverside
Shakespeare*. All other Shakespeare plays are quoted from the Riverside edition, unless otherwise noted.

3   Tamburlaine's classic speech of aspiration to the "sweet fruition of an earthly crown" occurs in *1
Tamburlaine* (2.7.12–29); Marlowe's Barabas is introduced in the Prologue to *Jew of Malta* by the
figure of "Machevill" as one who "favours" (i.e., resembles) him in villainy. For Richard's echoes of
Tamburlaine's aspiration to "golden crowns" and of the "murderous Machiavel" see *3H6* 3.2.128–95
and 5.6.68–93.

4   Cf. *Sir Thomas More* (Shakespeare 1997: 1786).

5   On the relation of Perkins's casuistic "prudence" to machiavellian "policy" see Mosse (1968: 48–67);
Mosse also considers the fact that Perkins, like Smith, terms kings "Gods upon earth" (p. 63).

REFERENCES AND FURTHER READING

Baldwin, W. (1938). *The Mirror for Magistrates*, ed. L. B. Campbell. Cambridge: Cambridge University
Press.

Blayney, P. (1996). Introduction. In *The Norton Facsimile of the First Folio of Shakespeare*, 2nd edn. New
York: Norton.

Budra, P. (2000). *A Mirror for Magistrates* and the *de casibus* Tradition. Toronto: University of Toronto
Press.

Calvin, J. (1561). *The Institution of Christian Religion*, trans. T. Norton. London: STC 4415.

Campbell, L. B. (1947). *Shakespeare's Histories: Mirrors of Elizabethan Policy*. San Marino, CA:
Huntington Library.

Colley, S. (1992). *Richard's Himself Again: A Stage History of Richard III*. New York: Greenwood Press.

Cook, C. and Wroughton, J. (1980). *English Historical Facts 1603–1688*. Totowa, NJ: Rowman and
Littlefield.

Cornwallis, W. (1600). *Essayes*. London: STC 5775.

Crane, M. T. (1993). *Framing Authority: Sayings, Self, and Society in Sixteenth Century England*. Princeton,
NJ: Princeton University Press.

Darnton, R. (1984). *The Great Cat Massacre and Other Episodes in French Cultural History*. New York: Basic
Books.

Erasmus, D. (1974–). *Collected Works of Erasmus*, vol. 31, trans. M. M. Phillips. Toronto: University of
Toronto Press.

Evans, R. C. (1995). *Habits of Mind: Evidence and Effects of Ben Jonson's Reading*. Lewisburg: Bucknell
University Press.

Ginzburg, C. (1980). *The Cheese and the Worms: The Cosmos of a Sixteenth-Century Miller*. Baltimore, MD:
Johns Hopkins University Press.

Grafton, A. (1997). *Commerce with the Classics: Ancient Books and Renaissance Readers*. Ann Arbor:
University of Michigan Press.

Gurr, A. (1974). *Richard III* and the Democratic Process. *Essays in Criticism*, 24, 39–47.

Hackel, H. B. (1999). The "Great Variety" of Readers and Early Modern Reading Practices. In
D. S. Kastan (ed.) *A Companion to Shakespeare*. Oxford: Blackwell, 139–57.

Hall, J. (1949). *Virgidemiarum*. In A. Davenport (ed.) *The Collected Works of Joseph Hall*. Liverpool:
Liverpool University Press.

Helgerson, R. (1992). *Forms of Nationhood: The Elizabethan Writing of England*. Chicago, IL: University
of Chicago Press.

James, M. (1986). *Society, Politics and Culture: Studies in Early Modern England.* Cambridge: Cambridge University Press.

Jardine, L. and Grafton, A. (1990). "Studied for Action": How Gabriel Harvey Read his Livy. *Past and Present,* 129, 30–78.

Jones, E. (1977). *The Origins of Shakespeare.* Oxford: Clarendon Press.

Jowett, J. (ed.) (2001). *Richard III.* Oxford: Oxford University Press.

Kintgen, E. R. (1990). Reconstructing Elizabethan Reading. *Studies in English Literature,* 30, 2–18.

Lewes, R. (1594). *A Sermon preached at Paules Crosse.* Oxford: STC 15556.

Marlowe, C. (1969). *Christopher Marlowe: The Complete Plays,* ed. J. B. Steane. Harmondsworth: Penguin Books.

Marshall, P. A. (1996). *A Kind of Life Imposed on Man: Vocation and Social Order from Tyndale to Locke.* Toronto: University of Toronto Press.

Marston, J. (1598). *The Scourge of Villanie.* London: STC 17485.

Miola, R. S. (2000). *Shakespeare's Reading.* Oxford: Oxford University Press.

Moss, A. (1996). *Printed Commonplace-Books and the Structuring of Renaissance Thought.* Oxford: Clarendon Press.

Mosse, G. L. (1968). *The Holy Pretence: A Study in Christianity and Reason of State from William Perkins to John Winthrop,* 2nd edn. New York: Howard Fertig.

Nichols, J. (1823). *The Progresses and Public Processions of Queen Elizabeth.* Rpt. New York: AMS Press, n.d.

Peacham, H. (1638). *The Truth of Our Times.* London: STC 19517.

Perkins, W. (1603). *Works.* Cambridge: STC 19647.

Pigman, G. W. (1985). *Grief and English Renaissance Elegy.* Cambridge: Cambridge University Press.

Shakespeare, W. (1996). *The Norton Facsimile of the First Folio of Shakespeare,* 2nd edn. New York: Norton.

——(1997). *The Riverside Shakespeare,* 2nd edn., ed. G. B. Evans and J. J. M. Tobin. Boston, MA: Houghton Mifflin.

Sharpe, K. (1992). *The Personal Rule of Charles I.* New Haven, CT: Yale University Press.

——(2000). *Reading Revolutions: The Politics of Reading in Early Modern England.* New Haven, CT: Yale University Press.

Sherman, W. H. (1995). *John Dee: The Politics of Reading and Writing in the English Renaissance.* Amherst: University of Massachusetts Press.

Sherman, W. H. and Jardine, L. (1994). Pragmatic Readers: Knowledge Transactions and Scholarly Services in Late Elizabethan England. In A. Fletcher and P. Roberts (eds.) *Religion, Culture, and Society in Early Modern Britain: Essays in Honour of Patrick Collinson.* Cambridge: Cambridge University Press, 102–24.

Slights, W. W. E. (1989). The Edifying Margins of Renaissance English Books. *Ren Quarterly,* 42, 682–716.

Smith, H. (1594). *The Sermons of Maister Henrie Smith.* London: STC 22720.

Spivack, B. (1958). *Shakespeare and the Allegory of Evil: The History of a Metaphor in Relation to his Major Villains.* New York: Columbia University Press.

Stern, V. F. (1979). *Gabriel Harvey: His Life, Marginalia, and Library.* Oxford: Clarendon Press.

Stevenson, L. C. (1984). *Praise and Paradox: Merchants and Craftsmen in Elizabethan Popular Literature.* Cambridge: Cambridge University Press.

Teague, F. (1996). Judith Shakespeare Reading. *Shakespeare Quarterly,* 47, 361–73.

Thomas, K. (1971). *Religion and the Decline of Magic.* London: Weidenfeld and Nicolson.

Thompson, A. and Roberts, S. (1997). *Women Reading Shakespeare, 1660–1900: An Anthology of Criticism.* Manchester: Manchester University Press.

Tillyard, E. M. W. (1946). *Shakespeare's History Plays.* New York: Macmillan.

Tribble, E. (1993). *Margins and Marginality: The Printed Page in Early Modern England.* Charlottesville: University Press of Virginia.

Wallace, J. M. (1974). "Examples Are Best Precepts": Readers and Meanings in Seventeenth-Century Poetry. *Critical Inquiry*, 1, 273–90.

Watt, T. (1991). *Cheap Print and Popular Piety, 1550–1640*. Cambridge: Cambridge University Press.

Yamada, A. (ed.) (1998). *The First Folio of Shakespeare: A Transcript of Contemporary Marginalia in a Copy of the Kodama Memorial Library of Meisei University*. Tokyo: Yushodo Press.

Young, B. (1992). Parental Blessing in Shakespeare's Plays. *Studies in Philology*, 89, 179–210.

18

King John

Virginia Mason Vaughan

Imagine this political scenario: two powerful leaders lay claim to the nation's highest executive office. Each offers elaborate rhetorical and legal arguments as to why he should be given authority. Each side offers a modicum of truth, but neither is totally convincing. The people are divided. The stalemate lingers until a third party enters the scene and for motives of its own declares one of the rivals to be the winner. To whom will the people give consent? And will the declared winner be able to assume the office's authority? The dispute over legitimacy is never completely resolved, but becomes moot when another nation attacks and the people unite behind the *de facto* leader.

In the United States after the election of 2000 this scenario ended peacefully with the majority of the electorate assenting to what many regarded as a legal fiction that George W. Bush had "won" the election, but in Shakespeare's *King John* this chain of events destabilizes England and subjects it to invasion by a foreign army. Indeed, instability is the defining characteristic of Shakespeare's version of John's troublesome reign, inherent in his shadowy claim to possess the throne through the "will" of Richard I despite Prince Arthur's superior pedigree, and in his inability to "order the present time." Set in medieval England, *King John* refracts political debates circulating in Shakespeare's early modern world (Lane 1995), even as its seeming inconclusiveness speaks to the twenty-first-century reader. Like the eclectic costuming in recent theatrical productions,[1] the text's multiple layers resist attempts to link it to a particular historical period or to arrive at a single, fixed meaning. Fractured and fragmented – radical at times – *King John* is Shakespeare's postmodern history play.

The troubles with *King John* begin with unusual textual instability. For over a century critics have debated the relationship between the First Folio's "The life and death of King John" and the anonymous two-part play text printed in 1591, *The Troublesome Raigne of King John.* These texts share only a couple of lines, but they follow, for the most part, the same structuring of chronicle material and order of plot. In his 1954 Arden edition E. A. J. Honigmann argued that *The Troublesome Raigne* has the textual features of a "bad quarto" and must have derived from Shakespeare's original, even though this meant dating *King John* as early as 1590. Few editors and critics have accepted Honigmann's thesis; most consider *The Troublesome Raigne* to be Shakespeare's source and argue that the dramatist exploited the earlier play's design and characters but rewrote the language with greater proficiency and different emphases.[2] The question remains vexed. As late as 1995 Brian Boyd contended that Shakespeare must have written first because only he would choose to organize the historical material around the death of Arthur, a fact of John's reign that ran counter to *The Troublesome Raigne*'s polemical purposes (Boyd 1995: 52–3). In the early twenty-first century we still know too little to decide this issue one way or the other. I wrote in 1974 that "There is no sure way of determining the exact relationship of the *TR* and Shakespeare's *KJ* until we have more external evidence. The plays may be related, but we cannot use internal evidence to decide exactly how they are related" (Carr 1974: 19). In the decades since, no new evidence alters that view.

Whichever text has priority, an intertextual relationship exists between *The Troublesome Raigne* and *King John* which makes it difficult to discuss one text without making comparisons to the other. The difference in emphasis is striking. In contrast to *The Troublesome Raigne* – which does everything it can to pin down its jingoistic and Protestant moralizing – *King John* is open, replete with gaps, ambiguities, and loose ends. In his production for the Royal Shakespeare Company (1974), John Barton inserted lines from *The Troublesome Raigne* to clarify motivations and events that Shakespeare left obscure.[3] But for readers, Shakespeare's elliptical text, like the language of politics that permeates our own culture, invites interpretation and analysis – "spin" if you will – and a multiplicity of responses. *King John*'s instability, this essay will argue, is not the result of the dramatist's ineptness (as E. M. W. Tillyard charged in 1944), but a deliberate interrogation of contemporary political assumptions.

Shakespeare's play discards the standard sixteenth-century image of John as a proto-Protestant martyr, who defied the pope's authority to assert English hegemony over matters temporal and clerical. This image of John circulated during the early days of the English Reformation in the writings of William Tyndale, John Bale, and John Foxe, resurfaced later in Elizabeth's 1571 *Homilie Against Disobedience and Wylfull Rebellion*, and dominates *The Troublesome Raigne of King John* (see Carr 1974: 21–41). Although his effort to free England from the yoke of papal tyranny was unsuccessful, John's defiance – or so these texts imply – was a proleptic promise of the success that would later fall to Henry VIII. John was a flawed hero, but in these texts his legitimacy is not in question, merely his judgment.

Not so with Shakespeare. The issue of legitimate succession opens the play, remains open to question through the middle scenes, and is resolved at the ending only by the accession of a new monarch. The final scene shows young Henry III as the indisputable heir, whether his predecessor be John or Arthur. Until that moment the ruler's authority is ambiguous. In the play's fourth line, Chatillon, the French Ambassador, describes John's majesty as "borrowed," and demands that he turn the throne over to his nephew Arthur, the "right royal sovereign" (1.1.15).[4] John defiantly maintains his right to the throne, threatening France with "blood for blood," calling on "Our strong possession and our right for us" (1.1.19–39), but his confident assertion is undercut by Queen Eleanor's aside, "Your strong possession much more than your right, / Or else it must go wrong with you and me" (1.1.40–1). Holding office, it would seem, is the only legitimacy John needs.

Possession is the key. By the strict rules of patrilineal inheritance, Arthur, son to John's older brother Geoffrey, should inherit the throne. But he is a mere boy, raised as a Frenchman, and precedent precluded foreign princes from inheriting the English throne (Lane 1995: 468–72). John's right is indeed a legal fiction, but in the monarchy's long history such fictions are commonplace. As the declared "bastard" daughter of Henry VIII, Elizabeth knew that bastardy and legitimacy were constructed categories. What mattered was the people's assent to the desired fiction. Authority, as Paola Pugliatti observes, is the real issue: "The main question, then, is not simply John's acquiring or affirming a right by vanquishing his opponents; it is, rather, his authority which is repeatedly contested, and without which neither right nor possession can be assured" (Pugliatti 1996: 83). The Folio's stage directions indicate that the Earls of Pembroke, Essex, and Salisbury accompany John in this scene, lending their silent consent to his authority. In the course of the play, John's real (or presumed) actions in killing Arthur take away that consent, making John's possession shaky, his right even more in doubt.

In a brilliant counterpoint, Shakespeare immediately interrupts the political action of 1.1 with an interrogation of legitimate inheritance on the private level. However he derived the Faulconbridge material, Shakespeare uses it to open "a space in the historical record – as Tudor audiences and politicians conceived that record – where he may dramatize issues of legitimacy and rule with less risk than any historian bound to use publicly endorsed names and chronology" (Braunmuller 1988: 314). At the death of his father Lord Faulconbridge, the younger brother Robert believes himself to be the rightful heir to his father's lands because his older brother Philip is really a bastard son of Richard Coeur-de-Lion. He claims his father made a will on his deathbed leaving the family lands to him. Both John and his mother read a "trick" of Coeur-de-Lion in the Bastard's face, a more empirical way of determining pedigree. Even so, John rules that the law accepts the legal fiction that children born to adulterous wives are legitimate. Whether or not Philip is a bastard, law requires that he inherit his father's lands. John thereby "exposes the weakness of any judgment based solely on bloodlines" and undermines his own claim to the English crown (Levine 1998: 135).

The issue of lawful inheritance is finessed in this instance when Eleanor invites the Bastard to forsake his fortune and follow her. He chooses the scambling world of court politics over the feudal ideal of inherited position. Like the Democratic presidential candidate in 2000, the Bastard is continually "reinventing" himself, deciding, as Peter Womack contends, "*who to be*," a radical move, because "if a man can decide which paternally given identity he wants, then clearly neither identity really determines the being of the chooser" (Womack 1992: 112); the Bastard iterates this himself when he claims, "I am I, howe'er I was begot" (1.1.175). He reconstructs himself as an early modern careerist and self-fashioner, a "'mounting spirit,' willing and eager to trade financial security and stability for a sixteenth-century version of upward mobility" (Gieskes 1998: 787).

Even though the issue seems settled, 1.1 concludes with an interview between the Bastard and his mother, Lady Faulconbridge. In a private conversation he asks his mother to tell the truth, and she confesses that Richard I seduced her, interposing his royal presence in her husband's bed. Phyllis Rackin argues that by her infidelity, Lady Faulconbridge has subverted the system of patrilineal inheritance that is so important to this play and "created the nightmare situation that haunts the patriarchal imagination, a son, not of her husband's getting destined to inherit her husband's lands and title" (Rackin 1990: 188). If Lady Faulconbridge had remained silent, the truth would remain "unwritten and unknowable" (ibid: 190), and as Nina Levine adds, even Lady Faulconbridge's confession of infidelity "does not affect the outcome of legal or political disputes within the play" because the law works to suppress women's subversive power (Levine 1998: 135).

Bastards are subversive too. The renaming of Philip Faulconbridge as Richard Plantagenet suggests his equivocal nature. Born outside the strict lines of patrilineal inheritance, he is in the nobility but outside of it at the same time, a "provocative mixture of centrality and alienation" (Womack 1992: 115), occupying a liminal space that enables him both to participate in and comment about what goes on. His propensity to play with categories that are generally assumed to be fixed is clear from his first entrance when he admits the uncertainty of his own parentage (pp. 60–3). Act 1 concludes with his demonstration to Lady Faulconbridge of such slippery categories as "legitimate," "illegitimate," "sin," and "virtue" when he asserts that only her refusal of King Richard would have been sin (1.1.275–6), transforming her infidelity into a virtue.

King John's opening scene thus suggests that legitimacy is a constructed category, that it depends on the consent of various political constituencies, and that it is subject to shifts as political circumstances change. From the start, *King John* exposes fissures in the system of patrilineal inheritance upon which the competing claims of both John and Arthur depend. Moreover, in 1.1, as in later scenes before the gates of Angers, Shakespeare's decision to make room in the historical narrative for the voices of women and a bastard suggests a more inclusive view of the body politic than is found in other history plays. As Richard Helgerson observes, the more inclusive a discursive form is and "the greater the place it gives women and commoners, the less concerned it will be to assert the prerogatives of monarchic rule" (Helgerson 1992: 298). Unlike Shakespeare's tetralogies which conclude with the imposition of a single, elite male authority and the establishment of a state (as opposed to Helgerson's notion of a nation), *King John* is preoccupied with the formation of a national consensus.

The play's middle scenes show King John and Arthur's supporters in an impasse; each side exploits language and military force to impose its vision of reality onto a skeptical audience. Like the Citizen atop the gates of Angers – and perhaps like US voters in 2000 – the audience is caught in a stalemate. Throughout, Shakespeare demonstrates the emptiness of political claims based on legal fictions.

All frames of reference are shown in the Angers scenes to be inherently unstable. Time itself, for example, loses its referential meaning. By anachronistically having King Philip and King John call for cannons[5] to topple Angers' intransigent walls, Shakespeare conflates medieval and early modern time frames. Deliberate anachronisms "that disrupt the historical context to create direct confrontations between past and present", as Rackin (1990: 94) contends, create radical dislocation. The mention of cannons in 1.1.26, 2.1.37, 210, 251, 382, 462, and 463 jolts the audience from the world of medieval kings to the world of sixteenth-century warfare.

Similarly, Chatillon describes the English army in terms more suitable to Elizabethan swashbucklers than medieval knights:

> all th' unsettled humours of the land –
> Rash, inconsiderate, fiery voluntaries
> With ladies' faces and fierce dragons' spleens –
> Have sold their fortunes at their native homes,
> Bearing their birthrights proudly on their backs,
> To make a hazard of new fortunes here. (2.1.66–71)

Among these voluntaries, as he reminds us, is the Bastard, who identifies himself "with the most individualistic elements in the play's audience: the young men – gallants, apprentices, students at the Inns of Court, discharged soldiers, masterless men – who are the least tightly attached to the framework of inheritance, patriarchy and service which ensures social cohesion" (Womack 1992: 113). The Bastard's voice, which frequently interrupts the flow of political rhetoric in these scenes, resonates with Shakespeare's world, suggesting that the issues of legitimacy and authority interrogated on stage are more germane to contemporary England than the medieval past.

When there is broad consensus in a society, there is less need for propaganda espousing that consensus. When, however, a society is divided, the decibel level of conflicting political interpretations becomes louder. Shakespeare shows such divisions in the seemingly endless debates before Angers. John and Arthur, contenders for patriarchal legitimacy, appear in these scenes accompanied by strong maternal figures whose strident interruptions undermine masculine authority. As early as 2.1.44 Constance tells Philip what to do when she bids him wait for the messenger from England before attacking Angers. Eleanor arrives with the English forces, presumably dressed as a "soldier" (1.1.150), and before John and Philip get very far with their claims to authority she begins a shouting match with Constance. Each woman charges the other with infidelity. Rackin describes the scene: "Speaking with strong irreverent voices, these mothers claim a place in the historical narrative and challenge the myths of patriarchal authority that the men invoke to justify their actions" (Rackin 1990: 178). With both Arthur's and John's legitimacy open to question, Eleanor closes her harangue by offering to produce a will that bars Geoffrey's title,[6] a tactic that directly contradicts John's previous action in disallowing the will of Sir Robert Faulconbridge. But this inconsistency escapes the notice of its stage auditors, and Philip calls for the citizens of Angers to announce "Whose title they admit, Arthur's or John's" (2.1.200).

Using elaborate and heroic rhetoric, John and Philip proceed to make their respective cases to the citizens on the city walls (and to the audience). These overblown speeches do not mask the basic assumption under which they speak, namely that the citizens of Angers have both the right and the competence to decide who is the rightful prince. Although I would not go so far as Robert Lane, who concludes that, "In this scene the consent of the public becomes the foundation for legitimate rule" (Lane 1995: 478), surely the resort to the people's judgment when patriarchy breaks down (or the true pedigree cannot be determined) is a radical notion in Elizabeth's England. The Citizen of Angers, however, doesn't accept this democratic ideal. He responds that it is up to the kings to decide "whose right is worthiest" (282), and until they do, Angers' walls will remain fortified against both claimants.

The formal stalemate continues when both armies exit. The Bastard calls for "blows, blood, and death!" (360), but the stage excursions result in another impasse with both sides claiming victory. Medieval trials by combat were intended to decide whose side God was on, but the ensuing stalemate suggests that God had better things to do that day. While John and Philip rant at each other, the Bastard sarcastically opines, "Ha, majesty! How high thy glory towers / When the rich blood of kings is set on fire" (2.1.350–1). John and Philip ask Angers once again, "who's your king?" (in what begins to seem like a political farce), only to hear that the city will acknowledge the king of England when it is decided who the king of England is. The Bastard compares these wayward citizens to theatre audiences that "gape and point / At your industrious scenes and acts of death" (375–6); he cajoles John and Philip to unite their forces and turn their artillery against Angers' "saucy walls" (404). This farcical solution to the conundrum would only delay the moment of decision, but as the Bastard gleefully notes, it smacks "something of the policy" (396).

The Bastard's interruptive asides, the references to anachronistic cannons, and repeated demands to *know* the unknowable – just who is the rightful king of England – break the fictional frame, casting the audience in the role of participants (Lane 1995: 464). The reversals before Angers reveal that the political world has no absolute value (Wormersley 1989: 501). Like the citizens of Angers, Shakespeare's spectators are subject to a world of political activity "where identity is not fixed but fluid, not immanent but assumed" (Kastan 1983: 9). Despite the claims of lineal right on either side, kingship increasingly seems more of a role than an essence.

The Citizen of Angers distracts John and Philip from their intended assault on the city by proposing a common diplomatic solution to a dynastic impasse; the marriage of John's niece, Lady Blanche, to Philip's son, Louis the Dauphin, settles the dispute, but only because Philip forgets the oath he had made to Constance to pursue Arthur's right. Angers' Citizen couches his proposal for the union of Louis and Blanche in the Neoplatonic terms of courtly love:

> He is the half part of a blessed man,
> Left to be finished by such as she,
> And she a fair divided excellence,
> Whose fullness of perfection lies in him. (2.1.438–41)

Although the discourse of courtly love is often relegated to the private sphere, the relationships it describes are invariably contested; Sidney's *Astrophil and Stella*, for example, depicts an ongoing struggle over who will control the relationship. Elizabeth I, who fashioned herself as the desired object of countless love poems, knew that the unobtainable lady could, in effect, be in charge. The Bastard sees Louis's play for power underneath the courtly language. When Louis professes to see his own shadow "Drawn in the flattering table of her eye," the Bastard undercuts the superficial rhetoric with an aside on drawing, hanging, and quartering, where Louis "doth espy / Himself love's traitor" (506–10). This play on words harks back to earlier scenes of face reading. Eleanor and John both claimed in 1.1 to be able to read the Bastard's true parentage in his face (85–90). Philip claimed Arthur's paternity is written on his face (2.1.99–103), but at the prospect of enhancing his son's territories with the extravagant dowry John offers, he forgets the original script. Louis's obvious exploitation of the face-reading trope, so easily satirized by the Bastard's barbed wit, suggests that however much one might want to read another's soul in his face, even this text is unstable, subject to distortion by the self-interested viewer.

As the Bastard realizes, the tension in this courtship is between the kings who negotiate the financial terms of marriage, not between man and woman. Blanche's response to Louis's courtship seems peculiarly tentative, even docile. She accepts her uncle's will as her own; if he points her in Louis's direction, she will "see" all that is "worthy love" in his face (2.1.518). Compliant with the wishes of the men around her, Blanche serves, as many princesses did, as a medium of exchange between men, "an instrument of kinship arrangements, political alliance, and patriarchal succession" (Rackin 1990: 180). The bargain is neatly and cleanly wrapped up with John's promise to make Arthur the Duke of Brittany and Earl of Richmond. It seems as if the contretemps before Angers has finally ended.

But at what price? The Bastard's soliloquy that ends act 2 spells out the hypocrisy in John's and Philip's arrangement: "John, to stop Arthur's title in the whole, / Hath willingly departed with a part," and France, "whose armour conscience buckled on," has been led by Commodity to make "a most base and vile-concluded peace" (563–87). "Tickling Commodity," not honor, underlies this agreement. And, as Christopher Z. Hobson perceptively notes, the Bastard's language mirrors his message:

> Syntax and rhetorical figures are used to express vehemence and to give concrete verbal form to the notions of shifting meaning and the inconstancy of moral order in the world of politics. The Bastard speaks of the power of commodity to "sway" the world, to act as a "byas" diverting it from its proper course, and he does so in language which itself continually turns aside from its own course. (Hobson 1991: 100)

The soliloquy concludes with the Bastard's avowal to conform to the patterns he has seen enacted before him: "Since kings break faith upon commodity, / Gain, be my lord, for I will worship thee!" (598–9). After serving as the outsider who provides satiric commentary on the action, the Bastard moves inside the frame, his analytic reasoning repeating "the less self-conscious hypocrisy of those around him" (Hobson 1991: 106). The Bastard reinvents himself once again.

Despite the United States' constitutional separation of church and state, organized religion plays a crucial role in national politics, often with different religious groups adopting conflicting positions. *King John* is timely here, too, for in this play the spokesperson for organized religion embodies another element that has the potential to destabilize the body politic. In addition, Pandulph suggests how external and diplomatic pressures from the rest of Europe could complicate England's internal politics.

Pandulph's confrontation with King John was the key episode in Protestant appropriations of his reign, and although Shakespeare shares some common language with *The Troublesome Raigne of King John* in this scene, his approach is less specific to Henry VIII, and as Donna Hamilton points out, directed more generally at episcopacy of any variety (Hamilton 1992: 46–9). Shakespeare omits the most virulent anti-Catholic aspects of *The Troublesome Raigne*: the abbey looting scene, a monk's plan to assassinate John for his crimes against the church, and John's dying prophecy forecasting England's split with Rome. The problem in Shakespeare's text is not so much with the specific authority of the Catholic church, but with institutionalized authority in general. John's resolution to disobey the church embodies early modern individualism: "I alone, alone do me oppose / Against the Pope, and count his friends my foes" (3.1.170–1). Pandulph, in response, insists on the church's universal authority and its unquestioned warrant for excommunicating and cursing deviant members.

Constance, not surprisingly, argues for individual rights as opposed to legal and clerical authority. Law, she claims, can neither give nor take away the right to curse; if John holds the kingdom, he holds the law: "Therefore since law itself is perfect wrong, / How can the law forbid my tongue to curse?" (189–90). Her verbal excesses in this scene underscore the equivocal nature of language and offer a site of resistance to masculine authority.

Pandulph places King Philip in an impossible political position. If he complies with the Cardinal's command and breaks with John, he will violate an oath newly sworn "With all religious strength of sacred vows" (229). If he disobeys Pandulph, the Cardinal threatens "A mother's curse, on her revolting son" (257). Constance and Louis urge him to break with John; Blanche earnestly begs him to keep the peace. The words "faith" and "curse" are bandied like tennis-balls. In a triumph of verbal legerdemain, Pandulph offers Philip a way out of his conundrum through equivocation:

> For that which thou hast sworn to do amiss,
> Is not amiss when it is truly done,
> And being not done, where doing tends to ill,

> The truth is then most done not doing it.
> The better act of purposes mistook
> Is to mistake again; though indirect,
> Yet indirection thereby grows direct,
> And falsehood falsehood cures, as fire cools fire. (270–7)

A second broken vow fires the first one out, transforming a double falsehood into truth. Shakespeare's Pandulph is, in other words, an early modern expert at political spin, who can manipulate events and language to his own advantage. Pandulph's language exemplifies the way political speech operates in these scenes – "not to bring men together into civil society, but to break down what little community exists into lonely fragments" (Donaworth 1984: 168).

As the cacophony rises, King Philip hesitates. Louis calls his father to arms, while Blanche falls to her knees and importunes him, "go not to arms / Against mine uncle" (308–9). When he finally drops King John's hand and breaks the peace, Constance's and Eleanor's interpretations seem equally valid, the action is both the "fair return of banished majesty" and the "foul revolt of French inconstancy" (321–2). Fair is foul and foul is fair, language itself has lost its stability.

But when words give way to actions, they have consequences. As the men rush to arms, Blanche speaks for an England soon to be torn apart by war: "each army hath a hand, / And in their rage, I having hold of both, / They whirl asunder and dismember me" (328–30). After excursions, the Bastard enters with Austria's head, Eleanor is assailed and rescued, and Arthur is captured by the English forces. The drama's shift from what seemed to be endless talk to short bursts of action indicates the inefficacy of language to contain, let alone solve, the political impasse.

As Shakespeare was to show in *Macbeth*, when language becomes equivocal the resort to violence is easy, perhaps inevitable. John cannot convey his dark and secret desires directly to Hubert. Instead, he uses hints that suggest *Macbeth*, he invokes the "midnight bell," whose "brazen mouth" sounds "into the drowsy race of night." He wishes to speak

> Without a tongue, using conceit alone,
> Without eyes, ears, and harmful sounds of words –
> Then, in despite of broad-eyed watchful day,
> I would into thy bosom pour my thoughts. (3.3.50–3)

Hubert finally comprehends John's meaning in the cryptic interchange:

John. Death.
Hubert.　　　My lord.
John.　　　　　　A grave.
Hubert. He shall not live.
John.　　　　　　　Enough. (3.3.66–7)

This sharp contrast to the lengthy speeches of earlier scenes strips John bare of any royal pretense. Here we see the tyrant's raw power naked and exposed, unadorned with stately rationalizations. The effect is chilling.

Act 3, scene 3 demonstrates the perfidy of kingly power. Act 3, scene 4 turns to the French camp to show the perfidy of church authority. As John had seduced Hubert, Pandulph seduces Louis, holding before him a vision of the English crown, his in right of his wife Blanche should Arthur die. That he will die, Pandulph predicts, is inevitable, and the scene is set for a French invasion of England.

Arthur and his mother Constance are the pawns in this elaborate chess game. The last we see of Constance — or any female in this play — is an image of a woman distraught, her unruly hair streaming around her face. Despite Philip's repeated request that she "Bind up those tresses," she refuses to "keep this form" upon her head. Her unbound locks visually emphasize not only her despair at the loss of her son, but also her struggle against patriarchal restraints, her refusal to confine her emotions within the yoke of policy.

Many critics have noted a shift in act 4 of *King John*; the action moves from France back to England where it remains, and as Womack contends, the movement embodies a shift in historical models, from a "dynastic model" — where the polity is organized by lord and servant relationships, and kings claim to possess territories without regard to culture, language, or natural boundaries — toward an early modern sense of England as a national community with commonalities in values and aspirations (136–8). Time is synchronic, the medieval era depicted on stage and the moment of production (late in the reign of Elizabeth I) are conflated. Acts 4 and 5 of *King John* show that body politic torn apart by a war for which both king and barons share the blame. King John's reign, after all, was the last period in which a foreign power had invaded England. The presence of Louis's French forces on English soil surely resonated with Elizabethan audiences, recalling their fears of a Spanish invasion, not completely quelled by the defeat of the 1588 Armada.

The play's finale also captures anxieties about the succession that were rampant in the last years of Elizabeth's reign. After undercutting John's legitimacy in the opening act, Shakespeare offers two other candidates to consider as possible successors: Arthur, whose title is unblemished but whose youth and tender nature make him unsuitable for political and military leadership, and the Bastard, who is illegitimate but demonstrates the leadership skills requisite in a king. After the relentless exposure of political hypocrisy dramatized before Angers, the last half of *King John* shows that none of the three candidates can assume the authority to govern.

The first to be eliminated is Arthur. Shakespeare's 4.1, the "blinding scene," is drastically different from its counterpart in *The Troublesome Raigne*, where Arthur is presented as a much older youth, who participates as a soldier in the battle scenes and adamantly insists on his right to the throne. Thus for the author of *The Troublesome Raigne*, the blinding scene is an opportunity to expound the doctrine of non-resistance. Arthur legalistically argues his way out of the blinding by convincing Hubert that it is unlawful to obey a king's immoral command. At first Hubert reiterates the key assumption of Tudor homilies: "a subject dwelling in the land / Is tyed to execute the Kings commaund" (1391–2), but, after being convinced by Arthur's counter-arguments, he concludes: "My King commaunds, that warrant sets me free: / But God forbids, and he commaundeth Kings" (1435–6).[7] Hubert then chooses the path of passive resistance, not defying the king but simply refusing to obey his order.

Shakespeare's version of the blinding scene is quite different from that of *The Troublesome Raigne*. Arthur, who is addressed as the "little prince," wishes he were a shepherd rather than a contender for the throne, or that he were Hubert's son "so you would love me" (4.1.24). When Hubert shows the boy his warrant from John to burn out his eyes, Arthur appeals to the man's emotions, not his reason. He reminds Hubert of his affection for him, and cries "O save me, Hubert, save me!" (72). Hubert yields out of pity and affection for the "pretty child" who pleads so pathetically for mercy, not out of legal principle. For Shakespeare, individual human feelings matter more than ideology; "Hubert's resistance," notes Pugliatti, "is a case of pure disobedience" to the king (Pugliatti 1996: 91–2) and a triumph of the individual human conscience.

The right of resistance is underscored in the following scene instead, when Pembroke, Salisbury, Bigot, and the other nobles protest John's decision to have a second coronation. Pembroke and Salisbury argue that John's repetition of the ritual that initially made him king casts doubt on its validity and "Makes sound opinion sick and truth suspected" (4.2.26). By re-crowning himself, John protests too much, the act displays John's "own lack of belief in what should be his ceremonious second body" and implies that he was never a legitimate monarch to begin with (Traister, in Curren-Aquino 1989: 93). The nobles, whose silent presence propped up John's claim to the throne in 1.1, are silent no longer and no longer give assent to his rule. When John announces that Arthur is dead, they question the monarch's actions and integrity, and rush off to spark rebellion, rebellion that under the circumstances seems warranted. The king's recognition that "There is no sure foundation set on blood" comes too late, and it is clear in Shakespeare's text that John's actions are the direct cause of England's internal disarray.

John's world crumbles around him. A messenger brings word of Louis's preparations for an invasion of England and news of Eleanor's and Constance's deaths. John panics at losing his mother's influence in France, but even worse, the Bastard brings news of turmoil in England: "I find the people strangely fantasied, / Possessed with rumours, full of idle dreams, / Not knowing what they fear, but full of fear" (4.2.144–6). John voices his fear that he has lost the consent of those he governs, sentiments that echo what must have been Elizabeth's fears during the Armada period: "O, let me have no subject enemies / When adverse foreigners afright my towns / With dreadful pomp of stout invasion" (171–3).

Shakespeare also makes it seem as if John is indirectly responsible for Arthur's death. After he leaps fearfully from the castle walls, Arthur finds his "uncle's spirit" in the stones beneath; hard and cruel, they break his body while heaven takes his soul. When Salisbury, Pembroke, and Bigot find Arthur's broken body, they assume his death can only be the murderous result of John's tyranny. The Bastard admits that "it is a damned and a bloody work" (4.3.57), but withholds judgment as to whether the death is the result of murder or an accident and defends Hubert from the nobles' wrath. When Hubert takes up Arthur's body, the Bastard describes it as "this morsel of dead royalty, / The life, the right, and truth of all this realm / Is fled to heaven" (4.3.142–5). These lines suggest that despite the loyalty he has previously shown John, the Bastard now thinks of Arthur as the legitimate heir to Richard I.

The Bastard's words here – "I am amaz'd, methinks, and lose my way / Among the thorns and dangers of this world" (140–1) – indicate a shift in his perspective and a further reinvention of his persona. The possibility of Arthur's kingship is ended by death. With John's authority undermined and the barons in revolt, this would be the opportune time for the Bastard to publish his own descent from Richard I, gloss over the fact of his illegitimacy, and seize the "bare-picked bone of majesty" for himself. But despite his earlier commitment to "tickling Commodity," the possibility hardly enters his mind. He sees the crisis both "for the individual and for the larger society of which he is a part" and realizes the "awfulness of living in a world without absolute values – a world stripped of life, right and truth" (Wormersley 1989: 509). The Bastard could not "figure as a patriot in the first half of the play because there was, effectively, no *patria* to which such a role could refer, only the patently empty formalism of a monarchical rhetoric." After the "delegitimation of the monarch through his personal failures," the Bastard embraces a new concept of national community (ibid: 125). No longer an outsider but a citizen of England, he works from inside the action to ensure the continuity of that community.

At the news of Louis's invasion, the Bastard charges John to

> Grow great by your example and put on
> The dauntless spirit of resolution.
> Away, and glisten like the god of war
> When he intendeth to become the field;
> Show boldness and aspiring confidence. (5.1.52–6)

By this time, however, John is incapable of acting like a king, and he turns the "ordering of the present time" over to the Bastard. The next time we hear of John, he is on his deathbed while the Bastard leads the English army. Although he now has the necessary military force and, as is suggested by his request to heaven that it "tempt us not to bear above our power!" (5.6.38), an inclination to assume power, the Bastard chooses to remain loyal to King John and, after his death, to John's successor.

King John's rushed conclusion repeats on a smaller scale the contretemps of the earlier scenes before Angers. As Barbara Hodgdon observes, act 5's short scenes each depict "a specific shift in allegiance or concern the results of those shifts" (Hodgdon 1991: 29). Act 5, scene 2 opens with the English lords Salisbury, Pembroke, and Bigot pledging to fight for Louis and his holy oath to reward them in return for their loyalty. But as soon as these vows of amity are proclaimed, Cardinal Pandulph enters (as he had in act 3) and asks that the vows be broken. This time, however, he is unsuccessful. Louis refuses to give up his quest for the English throne just because John has reconciled with the church, and in words resounding with the same individualism John had used in act 3, he insists on his own authority: "Is't not I / That undergo this charge? Who else but I, / And such as to my claim are liable" (5.2.99–101). Louis refuses to listen to either Pandulph, the church's spokesman, or the Bastard, who speaks for King John, opposing his will against the authority of both church and state.

When the Bastard learns of Louis's intransigence, he counters with a rhetorical fantasy of a warlike English king: "The King doth smile at, and is well prepared / To whip this dwarfish war, this pygmy arms / From out the circle of his territories" (134–6). But he does not chastise the barons for disloyalty to this king, their feudal lord, rather, it is their "dear mother England" they have betrayed, ripping up her womb. With Constance and Eleanor dead, England itself has become the mother figure and it is to England that the lords owe loyalty.

The Bastard describes a powerful king in whose forehead "sits / A bare-ribbed Death, whose office is this day / To feast upon whole thousands of the French" (176–8), but 5.3 belies this word painting by portraying John too sick with fever to rejoice at the news that Louis's supplies have been wrecked on Goodwin Sands. Then the action rapidly shifts to a part of the battlefield where Salisbury, Pembroke, and Bigot find the French Count Melun mortally wounded; the dying Frenchman reveals that Louis has no intention of keeping his sacred oath to reward them and has privately sworn another oath to execute them once the battle is over. As in the earlier Angers scenes, oaths are mere will-o'-the-wisps. Melun's motives for this deathbed confession are his love to Hubert and affection for a grandsire who was an Englishman; personal loyalties, not affairs of state and claims of legitimacy, elicit the truth. Perhaps Salisbury too retreats from dynastic politics to the level of personal commitment when he speaks for the rest of the nobles and promises that from now on they will "run on in obedience / Even to our ocean, to our great King John" (5.4.56–7).

One common resolution to a history play is a battle scene that clearly marks the winner, such as Shakespeare provided for Henry Tudor at Bosworth Field or for Henry V at Agincourt. But *King John* disappoints such generic expectations, ending not with a bang but with a proverbial whimper. The final scene introduces us to Prince Henry, John's lineal descendant, but presents him as young and untried (the boy actor who portrayed Arthur earlier in this play probably doubled this role).[8] Henry's paternity seems to solve the issue of legitimate inheritance, but he is not a heroic warrior king, just a boy who will need guidance and support (Levine 1998: 125). This time that guidance will not come from a mother with the power to confirm or deny biological legitimacy, but from the nobles who offer legitimacy derived from their assent to his royal claim.

Shakespeare hastily ties up the loose ends of his plot. John dies without paying much attention to the Bastard's announcement that he has lost much of his army in the Lincoln Washes. Salisbury reports that the threat from Louis has ended, because Cardinal Pandulph has finally persuaded him to abandon his military adventure and make peace. The offhand nature of this announcement, however, along with

Pandulph's absence from the final scene, minimizes the church's role in the play's final construction of England's commonwealth.

None of these incidents is fully explained; rather, "Shakespeare undermines rational explanation to such a degree as to call into question our ordinary faith in narrative exposition and our trust that events are knowable" (Hamel, in Curren-Aquino 1989: 53). Indeed, as these scenes progress, "natural forces (ill winds, John's fever, a slowly setting sun, tides) and human intervention (Melun's wounding, John's poisoning by the monks of Swinstead Abbey) combine in a cause–effect pattern of chance and coincidence to generate the impression that what *King John* does not show may have at least as much, if not more, import than what it dramatizes" (Hodgdon 1991: 29–30).

What the ending does show is consistent with the previous five acts; expectations are repeatedly disappointed and conventions undercut. Instead of seeing a climactic battle that resolves conflict by establishing one man's superiority, we learn that Louis's army is disbanding offstage and will slowly fade away, making combat unnecessary. There is no dynastic marriage to protect the future peace, as there is in Shakespeare's two tetralogies. When dynastic marriage was attempted in act 3, it led to war, and by the end of the play Louis subsumes Blanche's character and her title into himself. Not least, the play's final words are not spoken by the newly authorized ruling figure (Hodgdon 1991: 23) – such as Richmond, Henry V, Fortinbras, or Malcolm – but by the king's illegitimate cousin who speaks on behalf of the assembled king and nobles.

The play's final moments move out of the medieval world of John's reign to the 1590s, when "the need for security in the matter of the succession breeds a unity called 'England unto itself'" (Hodgdon 1991: 32). The barons who have rebelled return and voluntarily subject themselves to the new prince, as does the Bastard. We have a "settlement," a social compact between king and people. They will accept the king's legitimacy and subscribe to his "just and lineal descent," and he will build a functioning government on their acceptance of his claim. The ending is not a victory or a defeat but a compromise. The truism spoken by the Bastard, "Naught shall make us rue, / If England to itself do rest but true" (5.7.117–18), calls for loyalty to England, to the body politic, not to the person of a particular Plantagenet or Tudor. The play's final moments, like the debate before Angers and the actions that follow, indicate that loyalty rises from personal commitments and beliefs, not as a result of political pronouncements.

King Henry III's inability to speak (in contrast to the figures who take charge in Shakespeare's tetralogies) leaves the last words to the Bastard. It also accords with the subversive tendencies that occur elsewhere in *King John* because this last moment conveys a mutual dependency between king and subject, one feminized by weeping, the other a spokesman for masculine authority. Even in its patriotic conclusion, *King John* eschews absolutist rhetoric, calls for "limited monarchy and rule by law," and emphasizes "the king's obligations and indebtedness to a local, temporal and human realm" (Hamilton 1992: 49).

Shakespeare's *King John* presents two Englands: a medieval world which takes its identity from its hereditary rulers, and a community whose authority is ultimately derived from the people. Shakespeare's playing company, which was composed of players wearing the livery of a particular lord, but which performed for an unstructured and freely assembled audience, had similar tensions. Just as the play offers its audience a space where the two Englands could collide, negotiate, and transform one another, the space of the stage offered a place where the audience could imagine – and for a brief moment become – a shared community (Womack 1992: 137–8). If this is indeed the vision of England extolled by the Bastard in the text's final couplet, *King John*'s resolution is not the reimposition of Tudor doctrine (as I once thought),[9] but a radical call for limitations on absolute power in both church and state and mutual dependency between king and subject. In the final analysis, as Shakespeare shows, legitimacy is conferred by the people's assent – a willingness to see themselves as part of a body politic and to be ruled by its leader that is derived more from individual values and emotional needs than ideology – a lesson that kings and presidents would do well to remember.

Notes

I am grateful to Deborah Curren-Aquino, Richard Dutton, and Alden Vaughan for helpful suggestions on earlier drafts of this essay.

1   Deborah Warner's 1988–9 production of *King John* for the Royal Shakespeare Company at the Other Place is a good example. Cousin describes the costuming as "timeless modern" (Cousin 1994: 101).
2   For an overview of the textual dispute, see Carr (1974: 1–20) and Guy Hamel in Curren-Aquino (1989: 41–61).
3   Michael Kahn followed suit in his production for the Shakespeare Theatre of Washington, yet Deborah Warner saw no need to deviate from Shakespeare's original in her widely acclaimed RSC production.
4   Quotations from *King John* are cited from the Oxford Shakespeare, ed. A. R. Braunmuller (Oxford: Clarendon Press, 1989).
5   Cannons were a Renaissance invention. *OED* cites the first use of "cannon" to designate ordnance in 1525.
6   On his deathbed, Richard I did will the throne to his brother John.
7   Quotations from *The Troublesome Raigne of King John* are cited by line number from Geoffrey Bullough's *Narrative and Dramatic Sources of Shakespeare*, vol. 4 (London: Routledge and Kegan Paul, 1962).
8   Arthur and Henry were doubled, for example, in the 2000 production by Theatre for a New Audience at the American Place Theatre in New York.
9   See my "*King John*: A Study in Subversion and Containment," in Curren-Aquino (1989: 62–75).

References and Further Reading

Boyd, B. (1995). *King John* and *The Troublesome Raigne*: Sources, Structure, Sequence. *Philological Quarterly*, 74, 37–56.

Braunmuller, A. B. (1988). *King John* and Historiography. *English Literary History*, 55, 309–32.

Burckhardt, S. (1968). *Shakespearean Meanings*. Princeton, NJ: Princeton University Press.

Candido, J. (1996). *King John.* Atlantic Highlands, NJ: Athlone Press.

Carr [Vaughan], V. M. (1974). *The Drama as Propaganda: A Study of The Troublesome Raigne of King John.* Salzburg: Institut fur Englische Sprache und Literatur.

Cousin, G. (1994). *King John: Shakespeare in Performance.* Manchester: Manchester University Press.

Curren-Aquino, D. T. (ed.) (1989). *King John: New Perspectives.* Newark: University of Delaware Press.

——(1994). *King John: An Annotated Bibliography.* New York: Garland.

Donaworth, J. (1984). *Shakespeare and the Sixteenth-Century Study of Language.* Urbana: University of Illinois Press.

Dusinberre, J. (1989). *King John* and Embarrassing Women. *Shakespeare Survey*, 42, 37–52.

Gieskes, E. (1998). "He is but a bastard to the time": Status and Service in *The Troublesome Raigne of John* and *King John. English Literary History*, 65, 779–98.

Grennan, E. (1978). Shakespeare's Satirical History: A Reading of *King John. Shakespeare Studies*, 11, 21–37.

Hamilton, D. (1992). *Shakespeare and the Politics of Protestant England.* Lexington: University Press of Kentucky, 30–58.

Helgerson, R. (1992). *Forms of Nationhood: The Elizabethan Writing of England.* Chicago, IL: University of Chicago Press.

Hobson, C. Z. (1991). Bastard Speech: The Rhetoric of "Commodity" in *King John. Shakespeare Yearbook*, 2, 95–114.

Hodgdon, B. (1991). *The End Crowns All: Closure and Contradiction in Shakespeare's History.* Princeton, NJ: Princeton University Press, 22–43.

Howard, J. E. and Rackin, P. (1997). *Engendering a Nation: A Feminist Account of Shakespeare's English Histories.* London: Routledge, 119–33.

Kastan, D. S. (1983). "To set a form upon that indigest": Shakespeare's Fictions of History. *Comparative Drama*, 17, 1–16.

Lane, R. (1995). "The sequence of posterity": Shakespeare's *King John* and the Succession Controversy. *Studies in Philology*, 92, 460–81.

Levine, N. S. (1998). *Women's Matters: Politics, Gender, and Nation in Shakespeare's Early History Plays.* Newark: University of Delaware Press, 123–45.

Pugliatti, P. (1996). *Shakespeare the Historian.* New York: St. Martin's Press, 77–101.

Rackin, P. (1990). *Stages of History: Shakespeare's English Chronicles.* Ithaca, NY: Cornell University Press.

Shirley, F. A. (ed.) (1988). *King John and Henry VIII: Critical Essays.* New York: Garland.

Vaughan, V. M. (1984). Between Tetralogies: *King John* as Transition. *Shakespeare Quarterly*, 29, 407–20.

Womack, P. (1992). Imagining Communities: Theatres and the English Nation in the Sixteenth Century. In D. Aers (ed.) *Culture and History, 1350–1600.* Detroit, MI: Wayne State University Press.

Wormersley, D. (1989). The Politics of Shakespeare's *King John. Review of English Studies*, 40, 497–515.

19

The King's Melting Body: *Richard II*

Lisa Hopkins

When Steven Poliakoff recently directed Samuel West in a highly acclaimed RSC production of *Richard II*, Benedict Nightingale, on its transfer to London, complained that though the lead actor gave a tremendous performance, the production as a whole lacked period detail:

> Add a growing wisdom, and a genuinely thoughtful, moving prison-monologue, and you've a picture of a man better equipped to be a 21st-century Windsor or post-Windsor than a 14th-century Plantagenet. But wouldn't that point be more evident in a revival that clanked and banged with noxious late-medieval earls and barons? I think so. (Nightingale 2000: 14)

This demand for period accuracy, so rarely encountered in professional criticism of Shakespearean productions (and indeed an element much criticized when Barry Kyle did mount a conscientiously medievalizing production of *Richard II* for the RSC in 1986: see Shewring 1996: 59), may perhaps have something to do with the fact that in many respects *Richard II* does indeed seem to depict a world more remote from us than that of other Shakespearean history plays. As the first play of the second tetralogy, it is set longest ago of the well-known plays; the only ones to depict an earlier period are *King John* and (if it is indeed by Shakespeare) *Edward III*. The insistence in *Richard II* on chivalric rites such as the trial by combat and the throwing of the gages confirms the sense that we are paying a visit to a world we have well and truly lost.

Our sense of the play's medieval setting may be further bolstered by the fact that Richard II is one of the few kings in Shakespeare's histories of whom a strong, pre-Shakespearean visual image might perhaps come to mind. Rather than the contemporary representation offered by a Branagh, a McKellen, or an Olivier, as in the case of Richard III or Henry V, at the name "Richard II" we are perhaps at least as likely to think of the *Wilton Diptych*, the splendid double-panelled painting which shows the king praying to the Virgin Mary and is now in the National Gallery, or perhaps the splendid 7-feet-tall coronation portrait of the king in Westminster Abbey, rather than any particular Shakespearean production. Moreover, both these paintings, with the flat, iconic style of the first and the obviously pre-Reformation piety of the other, are clearly products of an age very different from our own, but also from Shakespeare's (indeed the king looks so ethereal in both that he seems to belong not just to another time but almost to another world). Yet I am going to argue that *Richard II*, far from being the play most remote from the concerns of an Elizabethan audience, was in fact the most closely connected to them of all Shakespeare's history plays. And the key to these vitally contemporary concerns can be found in those remote, iconic portraits of a medieval king.

It may seem strange to begin a discussion of a play by reference to paintings, but Shakespeare himself may well have seen at least one of them, and perhaps both. Caroline Barron observes of *Richard II* and the *Wilton Diptych* that

> Several passages in the play are suggestive of the painting. John of Gaunt's description of England as "this little world, / This precious stone set in the silver sea" recalls the tiny map of a green island set in a sea of silver leaf recently discovered on the orb at the top of a banner in the right-hand panel of the diptych. Moreover, the eleven angels who all clearly display their support for Richard by wearing the king's badge of the white hart, may have been in Shakespeare's mind when he wrote: "God for his Richard hath in heavenly pay / A glorious angel." (Barron 1993: 13)

We cannot guess *where* Shakespeare might have seen the *Wilton Diptych*; though his putative connection with the third Earl of Pembroke might seem to be suggestive, the painting did not in fact arrive at the Pembrokes' great house of Wilton until the eighteenth century, and its whereabouts before that are unknown. The Westminster Abbey painting, however, was certainly already in the abbey by 1611, and since it has clear iconographic links with *freschi* there, it seems reasonable to assume that, as Frederick Hepburn argues, the abbey was probably always its home (Hepburn 1986: 20, 16, 22). Moreover, Shakespeare could also be expected to have seen the magnificent portrait effigy of the king on his tomb in the abbey. Indeed, it is possible that Shakespeare's creation of a poetic persona for his Richard might be seen as in some way correlating to the splendor of the visual imagery more normally associated with him: John Halverson comments that "Richard's astonishing eloquence seems to have been Shakespeare's invention – none of his sources credits the king with a reputation for fine speech, although they do regularly mention his handsome features and dress" (Halverson 1994: 360), and in *Historia Vitae et Regni Ricardi II*, attributed to a monk of Evesham, the king is specifically said to have been a stammerer (Hepburn 1986: 18). By making Richard poetic, then, Shakespeare may perhaps have been attempting to endow him with a different kind of magnetism to compensate for one which it was no longer possible to reproduce, but of which he perhaps expected his audience to be aware.

More centrally, Shakespeare may have found the portraiture of the historical Richard, and indeed visual modes of representation in general, of particular interest

and relevance for his play. Many of Shakespeare's history plays are clearly centrally concerned not only with what happens in England but also with how those events are represented, and indeed with how England itself is represented. Balancing Hall against
Holinshed, choosing what to include and what to omit, taking details now from one
source and now from another, Shakespeare shows himself keenly aware of the political
pressures on the writing of England's history and the extent to which that history is
written by the winners; but as a dramatist, he also inevitably goes beyond this to the
question of how one person, or one incident, can be used to represent a crucial truth
of the history of the many. Indeed, *Richard II* offers a miniature disquisition on just
such issues in the gardener scene, which not only explicitly compares the microcosm
with the macrocosm but explores how far metaphors drawn from the one can be legitimately and helpfully used to figure the other. *Richard II* is all about who owns England,
but it is also interested in what England is and how it can be figured.

In particular, *Richard II*, like *King Lear* and *Henry IV, Part One*, is about ways in
which England can be represented in one of the most economically and politically
charged modes of representation available to early modern society, the map. For the
painter of the *Wilton Diptych*, this had been simple: a small green island, with no specific geographical features, is enough to do duty. Shakespeare, however, could expect
his audience to have a more sophisticated understanding of the problematics of
mapping. When the gardeners describe the garden, they are commenting only on
what they can see, and what it is their own peculiar business to touch and tend; but
when the whole realm of England is translated onto a map, that immediacy and tac-
tility must inevitably be lost, and the protocols and codes of visual representation
must be understood to be at work. When Bolingbroke refers to "here, or elsewhere
to the furthest verge / That ever was survey'd by English eye" (1.1.93–4) he actually
evokes one of the primary mechanisms both for deciding who owned land and for producing representations of the land – surveying, the cornerstone of mapping. Garrett
Sullivan argues that "while no map appears directly in *Richard II*, the play echoes
and builds upon *Woodstock*'s investigation of the nature and social function of maps"
(Sullivan 1998: 59). The visual protocols associated with surveying and mapping were,
however, different from those governing other forms of visual representation such as
that of the portraiture with which Richard was so closely associated, and could often
be in tension with them. Philip Armstrong argues that

> from the fifteenth to the seventeenth centuries, a powerful cartographic paradigm
> emerges alongside the early modern developments in linear perspective, mathematics
> and optics . . . In the cartographic transactions of Shakespeare's time . . . it is possible to
> glimpse, inextricably caught up in the development of this visual and representational
> economy, one ancestor of that "modern" subjectivity typified by and reliant upon its
> occupation of a single, fixed and centralized viewpoint. (Armstrong 2000: 135)

A comparison can readily be made with the distance perceived, on the one hand,
between mapping techniques as opposed to medieval images, and, on the other, the

analogous gap between the complex and multivalent viewpoint encouraged by Shakespeare's plays as opposed to the flattened ethos and didactically monolithic nature of the medieval dramatic tradition. Indeed, Armstrong quotes Richard II and Julius Caesar aligning themselves with the sun and the Pole Star before their respective defeats to argue that "whenever it appears in Shakespearean drama, this guaranteed stability granted by the privileged central viewing position in the scopic economy will prove to be both illusory and liable to dissolution" (Armstrong 2000: 135). Certainly a central viewing position is hard to achieve or maintain in *Richard II*: is the king hero or villain, is the play history or tragedy? And this is obviously, to some extent, a problem anchored in the play's foregrounding of different modes of representation: it can be argued that in one way Richard's predilection for poetry virtually hijacks Shakespeare's own status as dramatist, structurally forcing competing viewpoints to proliferate as the king, marginalized in the political arena which has so far appeared to be the play's main area of interest, unexpectedly fights back to establish himself as having at least some of the credentials of the hero of the rather different genre of tragedy. To think of the differences between the shifting perspective of the itinerant surveyor and the single, fixed centrality of Richard II's coronation portrait, then, may well be to achieve some purchase on how this play both evokes the world of the past and forces us, by adopting a modern perspective, to perceive it as such.

The paintings of the historical Richard II, as well as serving as potent reminders of the wide variety of protocols of visual representation, also serve as emblems of the ways in which this play, more perhaps than any of Shakespeare's other histories, depends on knowledge of things outside itself for full comprehension, which is of course one of the reasons why it is so hard to maintain a coherent perspective. As a play, *Richard II* seems more reluctant than perhaps any other Shakespearean history to seem to present a full and freestanding account of events. Not only is a sophisticated ability to recognize and respond to generic conventions required to negotiate its affective and narratological terrain, but also a knowledge both of the historical period and of previous historiography of it proves essential to grasping much of what happens. In particular, it is almost impossible to follow the course of events and various characters' reactions to them without some knowledge of Richard's alleged role in the murder of his uncle, Thomas of Woodstock, Duke of Gloucester, the younger brother of both his own father and the play's Duke of York and John of Gaunt. Halverson observes that "The omission of so much 'prehistory' of the drama has the effect of trivializing Richard's motives" (Halverson 1994: 363), and indeed the treatment of events is so allusive that the play is often felt to have a missing Part I, sometimes identified with the anonymous play *Woodstock* (and indeed as part of its 1999 season the Royal Shakespeare Company offered a matinee reading of *Woodstock* as an aid for people attending the *Richard II* in the evening, while Manchester University Press is currently preparing the launch of a new edition of the play provocatively entitled *Thomas of Woodstock, or King Richard the Second, Part One*). Phyllis Rackin argues that "Richard II cannot allow the fight between Mowbray and Bullingbrook to proceed because . . . Richard really does believe in trial by combat, and he knows that Bullingbrook's charges are true" (Rackin 1990: 52); but it is only the application of independent external knowledge that can possibly wrest this reading from the play. Another striking lacuna is the circumspect treatment of the king's possible homosexuality, which is confined to some structural parallels with Marlowe's *Edward II* and one brief remark that Bushy and Greene have "Broke the possession of a royal bed" (3.1.13), although Ordelle G. Hill and Gardiner Stillwell argue that the historical Richard II was so clearly labeled as a homosexual that Chaucer's *Parliament of Fowles* was meant to warn the young king against this tendency, and point out that "Richard himself is implicated by two of the chroniclers for unnatural relationships," including an alleged one with Thomas Mowbray, the Norfolk of the play (Hill and Stillwell 1994: 321, 322). The sexuality of the monarch is, indeed, something that this play seems careful to avoid, just as the fact that Richard has no child, and hence no heir, is left implicit rather than ever explicitly mentioned. At the same time, though, enough hints are dropped to suggest to the audience that what they are seeing is only part of the picture.

What the omission of these background details may primarily suggest is that the play is not consciously medievalizing and concerned with actual reconstruction of the past, but is in fact fundamentally concerned with the present: in the last years of the unmarried Elizabeth, the problem of a childless monarch was not one to be discussed too loudly, and this may be part of the reason for the play's reticence. This idea is reinforced by the ways in which spectral presences of Elizabeth and her troublesome favorite the Earl of Essex haunt it, in ways which could not be made explicit but which were nevertheless abundantly clear to Shakespeare's original audience, as the commissioning of a special performance of the play by Essex's steward on the eve of his rebellion attests. Indeed, this could perhaps be at least part of the reason for the omission of any clear indication of Richard's guilt in the murder of his uncle: the murder of close relations was a subject a bit too close to the bone for the Tudors, since Henry VIII had ordered the execution of his aged aunt, the Countess of Salisbury, and Elizabeth that of her cousin Mary, Queen of Scots and of Sir John Perrot, who was rumored to be a bastard son of Henry VIII, and thus her own half-brother. There is perhaps a suggestive contrast here with *Richard III* and *King John*: Shakespeare could be lavish and graphic in his depiction of nephew-murdering, because this was one charge of which the small-familied Tudors could never have been guilty.

And indeed, as these potential Tudor resonances suggest, the play itself is, despite its various chivalric trappings and its occasionally archaic feel, *not* medieval. Certainly some features are – Edgar Schell (1990), for instance, compares the treatment of time in the play to medieval drama, and Paul Budra (1994) remarks on the use of the medieval *de casibus* tradition in the play. But *Richard II* is also strongly rooted in its own, distinctively Elizabethan, historical moment. Comparisons were often made between Richard and Elizabeth, but, as Alzada J. Tipton has recently shown, they were even more pertinent than usual at the particular point in Elizabeth's reign at which *Richard II* was written:

The play's interest in the events which can lead up to a prince's deposition is not merely an academic political exploration. The comparison between Elizabeth and Richard always underlay Elizabethan accounts of Richard's reign in a provocative way. This was especially true in the 1590s, which saw an increase in social and political problems and a relative explosion of works treating the reign of Richard II. (Tipton 1996: 48)

Elizabeth herself was of course acutely aware of this, and indeed her own response to a portrait of the king – we do not know which, and it was probably not the Westminster Abbey one, though it may well have been one based on it – was to identify with it, and indeed to say "I am Richard II, know ye not that?" (Hepburn 1986: 21–2). And Phyllis Rackin points out that a

tiny anachronism, not likely to attract attention in a modern theater, occurs . . . when one of the fourteenth-century conspirators against King Richard charges that the king has used benevolences to extort money from his subjects . . . the authorities in Elizabeth's England certainly knew that Richard II never used benevolences because this very anachronism, present not only in Shakespeare's play but also in a seditious *Life of Henry III* by John Hayward, was cited at the trial of Essex as evidence that "the times of Elizabeth rather than those of Richard II were in question." (Rackin 1990: 93)[1]

It is also, I think, appropriate that we do not know *which* picture of Richard II Elizabeth was looking at when she made her famous remark comparing herself to him, and that there should be more than one portrait of the king of which we might think, because the play itself, in keeping with its insistence that there is always more to the story and another possible point of view, insists on creating figures of duality and mirroring. The idea of the king's two bodies is often important in Shakespeare, but rarely is it so centrally exploited as in this play, which stages not one but two kings of England in competition with each other. Richard himself obviously represents the body politic, initially at least, while Janet M. Spencer points out that "Henry IV . . . was associated not merely with succession debates and the distinctions drawn between the king's two bodies but also and more particularly with the king's natural body" (Spencer 1990: 70). The distinction is not so simple as that, however, as we see in the following exchange:

North. Well, lords, the Duke of Lancaster is dead.
Ross. And living too, for now his son is Duke. (2.1.224–5)

Here Bolingbroke is clearly associated with the ceremonial body even before his accession. The fact that it is impossible to pin down the moment when one of these two men ceases to be king and the other becomes so underlines this blurring of the differences between them, as does the fact that Bolingbroke's anxiety to receive the crown from Richard in person works to underline Richard's importance as well as his own: indeed, a famous production had Ian Richardson and Richard Pasco alternating between the two roles (Shewring 1996: 122–37). This is consonant with a motif of constitutive duality in the play, seen first when Bolingbroke declares

> O thou, the earthly author of my blood,
> Whose youthful spirit in me regenerate
> Doth with a twofold vigour lift me up (1.3.69–72)

This confusion of identity proves the prelude to a more general blurring of selves, as Northumberland says "The king is not himself" (2.1.241) and Ross declares "We three are but thyself" (2.1.275). Twinning also continues with the Duchess's "Ah, my sour husband, my hard-hearted lord, / That sets the word itself against the word!" (5.3.119–20) and her "Twice saying 'pardon' doth not pardon twain" (5.3.132), the only use in Shakespeare of twain as a verb. Indeed, perhaps the only person who is *not* twinned or paralleled is Aumerle, which is, of course, the source of his value to his mother as her unique and irreplaceable only son – and even he has a dual identity when his name changes. Just as the play itself seems to offer a hidden anamorphic parallel between Ricardian rule and Elizabethan rule, then, so each character seems to have a shadowy alternative identity.

Identity in this play is habitually fluid, partly because, as with paintings, it is viewed so much from the outside. Frank Kermode argues that

> All the Shakespeare kings (except on occasion Henry VI) profess assurance in their king-ship, and some emphasize its sacredness; they are also inclined to dwell on the intoler-able responsibilities and insecurities of their state. But Richard II alone has a habit of studying himself from the outside, as it were, a habit emblematized in the scene where he sends for a looking glass . . . In a sense he is always calling for a mirror, finding in his reflection a king stripped of all his belonging (3.3.142ff.), seeing himself as an ana-logue of Christ, betrayed by Judases and condemned by Pilates (4.1.239–40), develop-ing . . . the figure of the two buckets (4.1.184ff.). (Kermode 2000: 43)

The use of the mirror in this play encodes a positively modern understanding of mir-roring effects which in many ways seems to be Lacanian *avant la lettre*: Jonathan Gold-berg argues that "when Richard looks in the glass, the text refuses to confirm what he would see there. It deposes him, too, beguiling him with a false image; it refuses to deliver the present or to offer an outer image that would correspond to what Richard supposes he will see" (Goldberg 1988: 9). When Richard says "As brittle as the glory is the face" (4.1.287), the spectacular, foregrounded change of one single syllable to change the meaning enables us to hear almost a textbook explication of the difference that produces *différance*.

The constitutive duality of *Richard II* is more far-reaching than this, though, and has eschatological as well as psychological overtones, since so many of its uses in the play touch on the distinction between soul and body. Here, too, both the gap and the similarities between the medieval and early modern worlds would be strongly

relevant: the Richard of the *Wilton Diptych* is praying to the Virgin Mary and is accompanied by his patron saints, testifying to a unitary theology lost forever at the
Reformation. Very early in the play Bolingbroke declares to Norfolk,

> what I speak
> My body shall make good upon this earth,
> Or my divine soul answer it in heaven. (1.1.36–8)

Similarly, he later says,

> Bushy and Greene, I will not vex your souls,
> Since presently your souls must part your bodies. (3.1.2–3)

In drama the inevitable mediation of thought through speech means that we do not
have direct access to souls, and in *Richard II* we are unusually aware of that because
of the play's self-conscious theatricality. As Sharon Cadman Seelig argues, this is felt
with particular acuteness in the beggar and the king scene, where "in its labeling of
this material as a scene, an artificial construction, Bullingbrook's distancing remark
provides the kind of explicit reference to the fictional quality of the dramatic illusion
that we are accustomed to find in Shakespeare's comedies" (Seelig 1995: 347). Moreover, the generic indeterminacy that Seelig hints at here has in itself both political
and theological resonances. In her very interesting article on *Richard II*, Janet M.
Spencer points out that "when staged in the public playhouses outside London . . .
the tragicomic proceedings of the royal pardon scene often received disruptively and
self-consciously *comic* treatments capable of questioning royal power, or at least of
revealing the layers of conflict which limit it", and therefore contends that the beggar
and the king scene "takes on a tone of mock-seriousness in which generic questions
become political ones" (Spencer 1990: 57, 65); indeed, the lines "my dangerous
cousin" (5.3.80), spoken by an English monarch to a traitor, would have had an elec-
trifying subtext in the years after the execution for treason of Mary, Queen of Scots
by her cousin Elizabeth. However, since pardon scenes occurred in the specific context
of determining and forgiving guilt, the political overtones also have inherently spiritual consequences: the process of trial, particularly for treason, attempted, however
crudely, to uncover the truth of the soul, and the offering of pardon, whether deserved
or not (and in Aumerle's case it is clearly not), in itself eerily mimicked and doubled
the Calvinist concept of grace which descended on the elect regardless of their personal behavior. The fact that Henry IV can pardon while Richard II could not or
would not ironically marks the decisiveness of the shift in power which has taken
place both between Ricardian and Henrician terms on the intradiegetic level and,
extradiegetically, between Ricardian and Elizabethan ones.

Particularly interesting from the point of view of genre, politics, and the soul is
the way in which, within all the other doublings of the play, Richard himself seems
further split into two entities, a masculine one and a feminine one, with the feminine

explicitly identified as the soul: "My brain I'll prove the female to my soul" (5.5.6). From one angle, this emphasis should be unsurprising in a theatrically self-conscious play because it is a staple condition of early modern drama that the gender of the person acting need not match the gender of the person represented. Maurice Hunt also argues that self-conversion is integral to Richard's character, but is, too, what ultimately destroys him, and does so largely because of the generic sophistication of the audience:

> Richard eventually finds that the rich inner life made possible by the conversion of selves becomes disorienting, debilitating, and finally a paradoxical existence based on "nothing." The protagonist's self-flattering "original" scheme of tragedy, by which he avoided the humiliation of a prince's conventional fall, itself proves surprisingly conventional when Richard sadly concludes that his nihilistic inner life is Everyman's. His final struggle proudly to construct a tragic death for himself requires a heroic deconstruction and arrest of the perpetual inner conversion of opposites. This process, for educated playgoers at least, resembles that of a conventional Aristotelian catastrophe. Richard's tragedy, in the final analysis, is that his compelling, singular attempts to define his ruin never break free of the conventional – a just punishment, perhaps, for this vain monarch. (Hunt 1999: 1)

Richard, then, seems paradoxically almost to be defined by change and alteration. But conversion to femininity seems the most marked of his alterations, as when he declares

> As a long-parted mother with her child
> Plays fondly with her tears and smiles in meeting,
> So weeping, smiling, greet I thee, my earth. (3.2.8–10)

or asks

> Was this face the face
> That every day under his household roof
> Did keep ten thousand men? (4.1.281–3)

which clearly works to compare him with Helen of Troy.

Nor is gender uncertainty confined to Richard: Bolingbroke refers to his son Hal as a "young wanton, and effeminate boy" (5.3.10). This also reminds the audience at the same time that, firstly, the historical Henry V was devoted to the memory of Richard II (James 1990: 138), even, as he reminds us on the night before Agincourt, reburying him (*Henry V*, 4.1.289–302), and, secondly, that *Richard II* is not only a freestanding drama but also the first play of the second tetralogy, and that at least part of its function is thus to introduce us to the story of Hal, so that, especially in view of Hal's later friendship with the famously feminized Falstaff (Hawkes 1998: 128), it is of considerable interest for our later sense of Hal that our first introduction to him should be in connection with an accusation of effeminacy. It is little wonder that for all that Mowbray declares "'Tis not the trial of a woman's war" (1.1.48), many critics have found gender representation one of the most interesting facets of the play. R. A. Martin suggests that "women are thoroughly assimilated to the existing values and hierarchies of a monolithic patriarchal state even when they might appear to be criticizing them" because "While the impartial mirror had been smashed by Richard earlier because it had shown him something he did not like, Isabel makes sure she always reflects back to him the face he wants to see, for her primary concern is to preserve the dominant values of paternal authority as vested in her husband and her king" (Martin 1989: 256, 257). Here, Shakespeare seems to anticipate not only Lacan but also the recent feminist theory which has focused on how women "mirror" men.

Isabel was also a resonant name in terms of the succession to the English crown, since the Infanta Isabella of Spain was one of those regularly proposed as a possible successor to Elizabeth, and perhaps this concern with gender arises because the play is always aware of being shadowed by Elizabeth, the hidden double of its nominal hero. Indeed, gender issues might well suggest national ones in the Elizabethan context, especially in view of the ways in which ideas of femininity and of mirroring also map onto another issue which the play is reluctant to discuss: colonialism. Despite the importance of Ireland in the play, *Richard II* is set in England/Wales, and therefore may initially seem to be entirely removed from the concerns of colonialism and conquest; it certainly seems ironic that Essex should have found this play more fitting to have staged on the eve of his rebellion than *Henry V* (Montrose 1996: 52–3), which actually refers admiringly to him. Perhaps, however, this is because Essex was in fact attentive to a subtext which we would do well to investigate. No history play of Shakespeare's is hermetically sealed from the discourses of colonialism, in that all are concerned with the relationship between England and other countries, and countries, to the Renaissance mind, are always liable metaphorically to morph into "cuntries," conceived, moreover, within a sexualized model of international relations which assumes that what is masculine is always stronger and must therefore conquer what is feminine. Armstrong, for instance, argues that Shakespeare's "delineation of the geographical relationship between England and France" is habitually "reliant . . . on a correlation between the land and a 'girdled' female body, protected by inviolable boundaries" (Armstrong 2000: 164). But what if, as was the case with the young and military-minded Essex confronting the aged Elizabeth, the holder of power is gendered female?

It is in the light of that political situation that it is of particular interest that boundaries in this play are pointedly not inviolable, and are also figured as both personified and indeed as inherently analogous to individual identities. Mowbray, told that he is to be exiled, says:

> The language I have learnt these forty years,
> My native English, now I must forgo,
> And now my tongue's use is to me no more

> Than an unstringed viol or a harp,
> Or like a cunning instrument cas'd up —
> Or being open, put into his hands
> That knows no touch to tune the harmony.
> Within my mouth you have engaol'd my tongue,
> Doubly portcullis'd with my teeth and lips (1.3.159–67)

Mowbray's figuring of geographical exile in terms of the human face draws our attention to the extent to which human and physical borders may be analogous, just as when Bolingbroke speaks of "the furthest verge / That ever was survey'd by English eye," he is, Garrett Sullivan argues, working to a conception of "an English identity constituted here in terms of a history of English travel" rather than of one bounded by the geographical limits of England itself (Sullivan 1998: 114).

Mowbray's metaphor also directs our attention upwards to the face, and perhaps especially the face of Richard II himself, whose stammering may be recalled here, and it thus specifically reminds us that the question "Was this face the face?" does double damage to the image of the king. Not only does it feminize Richard by comparing him with Helen of Troy, but also both terms of the equation are operative: it aligns him with Troy, and with the Celtic parts of the British Isles which emblematized the supposed British descent from Trojan Brutus, but which also represented that which was not English and was indeed, in the case of Ireland, in rebellion against the Queen of England. The question "Was this face the face?," in short, trails with it thoughts not only of Helen of Troy but of the *translatio imperii* of which her abduction was the nominal cause, reminding us that the whole philosophy of imperialism, as inherited by the English "heirs of Troy," was predicated on a myth of origins which inscribed male as conqueror and female as to-be-conquered. Not only the feminized Richard but also, behind him, the far more conflicted figure of Elizabeth are thus indicted.

In many early modern texts the discourses of sexuality and gender are significantly inflected by the experiences of colonization; as Elaine Showalter wittily remarks, "discovered by an anatomist appropriately named Columbus in the sixteenth century, the Renaissance clitoris was the brave new world" (Showalter 1991: 130). In almost all Elizabethan and Jacobean writing on Ireland, images of monstrous femininity figured very prominently. Ireland itself was often represented as a woman, as in the often-quoted description by Luke Gernon:

> This Nymph of Ireland is at all poynts like a yong wenche that hath the greene sicknes
> for want of occupying. She is very fayre of visage, and hath a smooth skinn of tender
> grasse . . . Her breasts are round hillockes of milk-yeelding grasse, and that so fertile,
> that they contend with the vallyes. And betwixt her leggs (for Ireland is full of havens),
> she hath an open harbor, but not much frequented . . . It is nowe since she was drawne
> out of the wombe of rebellion about sixteen yeares, by'rlady nineteen, and yet she wants
> a husband, she is not embraced, she is not hedged and ditched, there is noo quicksett
> putt into her. (Hadfield and Maley 1993: 4)

Gernon's envisaging of Ireland as a nubile virgin desperate for sex draws on a common Renaissance trope which analogizes land to be conquered to women to be married; the English were fond of labeling Spanish colonial activity as rape while simultaneously glorifying their own as "husbandry," and in the imagined "Shee-landt" of the second book of John Healey's *The Discovery of a New World* (1609) the dominance of women harms the land, since "the soile thereof is very fruitfull, but badly husbanded" (Healey 1609: 1). As Lynda Boose comments,

> although the equation between land and the female body which makes rape and imperialism homologous is a metaphor of masculine ownership that is neither peculiarly English nor new to England's enclosure period, the collocation of the two discursive fields clearly acquired new energy at precisely this historical moment of heightened land anxieties. (Boose 1994: 203)

One of the principal reasons for these heightened anxieties undoubtedly lay in the gender of England's own ruler for much of the relevant period. The imagery of conquest as husbandry fitted a nation ruled by a queen far less well than one ruled by a king, and indeed was dangerously open to inversion. As a result, considerable ideological and emotional energy was poured into figuring Elizabeth's virginity as a strength rather than a weakness, and into making political capital of this. As Jeffrey Knapp points out, as a virgin "Elizabeth could seem . . . the providential consummation of England's efforts to realize itself *as* an island. William Paten (1575) lists 'Ad Insulam' or 'To the Isle' . . . as one derivation of the queen's name" (Knapp 1992: 67).

Nevertheless, even the emphasis on Elizabeth's virginity was not enough to ward off the fear of contamination associated with female rule and its imagined vulnerability to conquest and colonization. Marlowe's tragic but ineffectual Dido dies praying,

> from mine ashes let a conqueror rise,
> That may revenge this treason to a queen
> By ploughing up his countries with the sword! (5.1.306–8)

Dido can imagine a virile, all-powerful conqueror who can phallically plough up countries/cuntries (and a Renaissance audience would be well aware that her wish would eventually be fulfilled in the person of Hannibal), but the fact of her gender means that she can never be it. The always latent pun on country/cuntry is made even clearer when "writing in his *Admonition to the Nobility and People of England* (1588), Cardinal Allen . . . impugns the queen's chastity and with it the 'cuntry' itself: . . . '[S]hamefully she hath defiled her person and cuntry'" (Levine 1998: 110). And perhaps it ought to be Hamlet's pun on "country matters" which invites us to be alert to unease about the succession in the play, even more than "crowner" jokes, the possible echoes of the Essex Rebellion and the parallels between the Claudius/Gertrude story and that of Henry VIII and Katherine of Aragon.

Richard II, a play which was probably written not long before *Hamlet* and which some have seen as linked to it by the Essex story, is haunted by shadowy questions about national identity, and they are doubly mediated through discourses of Ireland and discourses of gender. At an early stage of the play, John of Gaunt refers to

> England, bound in with the triumphant sea,
> Whose rocky shore beats back the envious siege
> Of wat'ry Neptune. (2.1.61–3)

This has become perhaps the most famous speech of the play, but its celebrity should not blind us to its basic lack of truth: England is surrounded not only by sea, but by the Celtic fringe of Wales, Scotland, and, with only a narrow intervening channel, Ireland. War in Ireland proves a structuring event of the play, as of Richard's reign – indeed the *Wilton Diptych* may have been originally designed as a battle icon intended for use in Ireland (Gordon 1993: 62). Ireland does not, however, operate in entirely predictable ways within the play. One might expect it to be aligned entirely with ideas of enmity, rebellion, and the Other. Initially, this does seem to be the case. Greene says of Bolingbroke,

> Well, he is gone; and with him go these thoughts.
> Now for the rebels which stand out in Ireland. (1.4.37–8)

Here, the Irish seem to function almost as a narratological replacement for Bolingbroke. But it soon becomes apparent that they are not only opposed to the official English establishment, but also uneasily echo and displace it. One of the gardeners demands,

> Why should we, in the compass of a pale,
> Keep law and form and due proportion,
> Showing, as in a model, our firm estate,
> When our sea-walled garden, the whole land,
> Is full of weeds, her fairest flowers chok'd up,
> Her fruit-trees all unprun'd, her hedges ruin'd,
> Her knots disordered, and her wholesome herbs
> Swarming with caterpillars? (3.4.40–7)

The gardener here directly echoes John of Gaunt's idea of the safe enclosure of England in his phrase "sea-walled," but his use of "pale" equally firmly reminds us of the existence of Ireland, and of the attempts to maintain the authority of the English pale around Dublin.

Patterns of alignment rather than difference are equally clear in the play's second reference to the wars in Ireland, which is uttered by the king himself:

> Now for our Irish wars;
> We must supplant those rough rug-headed kerns,
> Which live like venom where no venom else,
> But only they, have privilege to live. (2.1.155–8)

The pattern of displacement and reversal inaugurated by the chiasmus of "live . . .
venom . . . venom . . . live" leaches into Richard's curious choice of the verb "supplant," which is more usually an action applied *to* a king than *by* one, and thus works
to drain off the iconography of royalty from the king himself and transfer it, aston-
ishingly, to the Irish.

The idea of venom also introduces the traditional motif of the uncanniness of the
Irish. Again, though, this is not unique to them, but is also seen to characterize other
members of the Celtic fringe, notably the Welsh – the nation which most clearly
encapsulated the Trojan heritage and from which Elizabeth herself, with her Tudor
blood, was descended. Indeed, it is the superstition for which the Welsh were notorious in Elizabethan literature which leads directly to the king's undoing, as we see
when the Welsh captain says:

> 'Tis thought the king is dead; we will not stay.
> The bay-trees in our country are all wither'd,
> And meteors fright the fixed stars of heaven,
> The pale-fac'd moon looks bloody on the earth,
> And lean-look'd prophets whisper fearful change,
> Rich men look sad, and ruffians dance and leap –
> The one in fear to lose what they enjoy,
> The other to enjoy by rage and war.
> These signs forerun the death or fall of kings.
> Farewell: our countrymen are gone and fled,
> As well assured Richard their king is dead. (2.4.7–17)

Nor are the Welsh alone in seeming on the edges of the natural. In a vivid demonstration of the extent to which England is *not* in fact isolated by the sea, Bagot accuses
Aumerle,

> I heard you say "Is not my arm of length,
> That reacheth from the restful English court
> As far as Callice, to mine uncle's head?" (4.1.11–13)

The Irish then are not alone in being uncanny, and cannot be so easily demonized for
it. Most strikingly, Richard himself repeatedly associates himself with supernatural
powers. He calls on chthonic forces:

> Feed not thy sovereign's foe, my gentle earth,
> Nor with thy sweets comfort his ravenous sense,

But let thy spiders that suck up thy venom
And heavy-gaited toads lie in their way,
Doing annoyance to the treacherous feet,
Which with usurping steps do trample thee;
Yield stinging nettles to mine enemies;
And when they from thy bosom pluck a flower,
Guard it, I pray thee, with a lurking adder,
Whose double tongue may with a mortal touch
Throw death upon thy sovereign's enemies. (3.2.12–22)

He descends still further into the realms of the underground when he avers:

within the hollow crown
That rounds the mortal temples of a king
Keeps Death his court. (3.2.160–2)

And he both evokes duality and aligns himself with the non-human when he says:

O that I were a mockery king of snow,
Standing before the sun of Bolingbroke,
To melt myself away in water-drops! (4.1.260–2)

Most importantly, his own Celtic ancestry is stressed when he is twice associated with Trojan ancestry, when the Queen, having first referred to him coming from "Julius Caesar's ill-erected tower" (5.1.2), calls him "the model where old Troy did stand!" (5.1.11). Especially given the marked feminization of the king, this reference to Trojan/Welsh ancestry aligns him even more unmistakably than ever with Elizabeth, and reminds us that despite all the splendor of Ricardian visual imagery, the face we should really see when we look at this play is Elizabeth's, and that, as so often with Shakespeare's history plays, what we are being offered is as much politics as history.

We are also, however, being offered a sustained meditation on the ways in which the representation of history is always already political. Richard II may be a poet and a visionary, but poetry has never been the dominant discourse of historiography, and indeed, since Shakespeare's very representation of Richard as eloquent and poetic is contrary to any of his sources, it serves in itself to underline the ways in which representations of the historical past may differ and diverge from each other. Bolingbroke, by contrast, is a man of many voices: though it is Richard who wished he could melt, it is Bolingbroke who actually displays fluidity and flexibility in his rapid adjustment to the shifting tones of the pardon scene, even himself rising to ruefully doggerelly verse in his "Our scene is altered from a serious thing, / And now changed to 'The Beggar and the King'" (5.3.78–9). In the self-conscious metatheatricality of this speech, Shakespeare reminds us not only that all the world's a stage, but that history plays can never deal only with history; like all drama, they only come truly alive when they can touch the widest possible emotional range and deploy the maximum number of resonances. Foraying into both comedy and tragedy, activating contemporary political concerns while dealing in unusual detail with the political intrigues of the past, *Richard II* offers a complex vision of not just a section of English history, but also of the processes that shape both the unfolding of historical events and our own subsequent representation and understanding of them.

NOTE

1 It is part of Rackin's argument that *Richard II* presents the medieval world as irretrievably lost. Christopher Highley similarly comments that the play's imaging of the financing of the Irish wars makes it "a cautionary example, a veiled warning, to the rulers of Elizabethan England of embroilment in Ireland" (Highley 1997: 64).

REFERENCES AND FURTHER READING

Armstrong, P. (2000). *Shakespeare's Visual Regime: Tragedy, Psychoanalysis and the Gaze*. Basingstoke: Palgrave.

Barron, C. (1993). Richard II: Image and Reality. In D. Gordon (ed.) *Making and Meaning: The Wilton Diptych*. London: National Gallery Publications.

Boose, L. E. (1994). *The Taming of the Shrew*, Good Husbandry, and Enclosure. In R. McDonald (ed.) *Shakespeare Reread: The Texts in New Contexts*. Ithaca, NY: Cornell University Press, 193–225.

Budra, P. (1994). Writing the Tragic Self: *Richard II*'s Sad Stories. *Renaissance and Reformation*, 18, 4, 5–15.

Goldberg, J. (1988). Rebel Letters: Postal Effects from *Richard II* to *Henry IV*. *Renaissance Drama*, 19, 3–28.

Gordon, D. (ed.) (1993). *Making and Meaning: The Wilton Diptych*. London: National Gallery Publications.

Hadfield, A. and Maley, W. (1993). Introduction: Irish Representations and English Alternatives. In B. Bradshaw, A. Hadfield, and W. Maley (eds.) *Representing Ireland: Literature and the Origins of Conflict, 1534–1660*. Cambridge: Cambridge University Press, 1–23.

Halverson, J. (1994). The Lamentable Comedy of Richard II. *English Literary Renaissance*, 24, 343–69.

Hawkes, T. (1998). Bryn Glas. In A. Loomba and M. Orkin (eds.) *Post-Colonial Shakespeares*. London: Routledge, 117–40.

Healey, J. (1609). The description of *Shee-landt*, or *Woman deçoia*. In *The Discovery of a New World*. London.

Hepburn, F. (1986). *Portraits of the Later Plantagenets*. Woodbridge: Boydell Press.

Highley, C. (1997). *Shakespeare, Spenser, and the Crisis in Ireland*. Cambridge: Cambridge University Press.

Hill, O. G. and Stillwell, G. (1994). A Conduct Book for Richard II. *Philological Quarterly*, 73, 3, 317–28.

Hunt, M. (1999). The Conversion of Opposites and Tragedy in Shakespeare's *Richard II*. *Explorations in Renaissance Culture*, 25, 1–18.

James, T. B. (1990). *The Palaces of Medieval England*. Oxford: Alden Press.

Kermode, F. (2000). *Shakespeare's Language*. London: Allen Lane.

Knapp, J. (1992). *An Empire Nowhere: England, America, and Literature from Utopia to The Tempest*. Berkeley: University of California Press.

Levine, N. S. (1998). *Women's Matters: Politics, Gender, and Nation in Shakespeare's Early History Plays*. Newark: University of Delaware Press.

Marlowe, C. (1999). *Dido, Queen of Carthage*. In M. T. Burnett (ed.) *Christopher Marlowe: The Complete Plays*. London: Dent.

Martin, R. A. (1989). Metatheater, Gender, and Subjectivity in *Richard II* and *Henry IV*, Part I. *Comparative Drama*, 23, 3, 255–64.

Montrose, L. (1996). Shakespeare, the Stage, and the State. *SubStance*, 25, 2, 46–67.

Nightingale, B. (2000). Clever-clever Dick. *The Times*, Arts supplement, December 27.

Rackin, P. (1990). *Stages of History: Shakespeare's English Chronicles*. Ithaca, NY: Cornell University Press.

Schell, E. (1990). *Richard II* and Some Forms of Theatrical Time. *Comparative Drama*, 24, 3, 255–69.

Seelig, S. C. (1995). Loyal Fathers and Treacherous Sons: Familial Politics in *Richard II*. *Journal of English and Germanic Philology*, 94, 3, 347–64.

Shakespeare, W. (1956). *Richard II*, ed. P. Ure. London: Methuen.

——(1980). *Hamlet*, ed. H. Jenkins. London: Methuen.

——(1995). *King Henry V*, ed. T. W. Craik. London: Routledge.

Shewring, M. (1996). *King Richard II*. Manchester: Manchester University Press.

Showalter, E. (1991). *Sexual Anarchy: Gender and Culture at the Fin de Siècle*. London: Bloomsbury.

Spencer, J. M. (1990). Staging Pardon Scenes: Variations of Tragicomedy. *Renaissance Drama*, 21, 55–89.

Sullivan, G. A., Jr. (1998). *The Drama of Landscape: Land, Property, and Social Relations on the Early Modern Stage*. Stanford, CA: Stanford University Press.

Tipton, A. J. (1996). *Richard II* and Theories of the Subaltern Magistrate. *The Upstart Crow*, 16, 48–69.

20

1 Henry IV

James Knowles

Since 1597 *The History of Henrie the Fovrth* has occupied an especially resonant place in the Shakespeare canon. Judging from contemporary allusions, the numbers of copies apparently printed, and the continued performances of the play right through the Caroline and Carolean periods, the play achieved popular success. It penetrated both aristocratic culture (such as the household performances mounted by Sir Edward Dering in the 1620s) and popular culture (instanced by the "droll" or short play that dates from the Interregnum). The Caroline period renamed the play "Falstaff" in a manner that provides a clue to the enduring popularity of the play: Falstaff – rather than Henry IV or his son, Prince Henry – emerged as the dominant figure of the play. Indeed, Falstaff and the Cheapside scenes inspired many of the appropriations of the text in the centuries that followed, from Morgann's "Essay on Dramatic Character" (1777), to the Verdian opera (based on *The Merry Wives of Windsor*), to Elgar's symphonic movement (*Falstaff*, Op. 68, 1913), and films by Welles (*Chimes at Midnight*) and Gus Van Sant (*My Own Private Idaho*). More recently, the play has prompted Stephen Greenblatt's highly influential "Invisible Bullets," the signature essay of new historicism.

The popularity of Falstaff has often meant that *The History of Henrie the Fovrth* as a play in its own right has often been overshadowed. Even though the title page of the first edition highlighted three elements to appeal to contemporary readers (the history of the king, the battle of Shrewsbury and, only finally, "the humorous conceits" of Falstaff) the importance of the political narrative has often been neglected. The situation is further complicated by the uncertain relationship of the earlier play to *Henry IV, Part 2* (1598), which has often led to the play being treated as the first part of a pair or "two-part" play. Many critical essays, although purportedly about the "Henry plays," largely focus on the rejection of Falstaff (usually in the *Part 2* version) sometimes at the expense of the different qualities of *The History of Henrie the Fovrth*. The purpose of this essay is to return to the play in 1597, before the impact of the Falstaff effect, and consider why the title page balances the three elements and how that should shape our interpretation of the play.[1]

Whereas *Part Two* is marked by a mixture of decay and an elegiac quality, with a Falstaff much reduced from the flamboyant and confident figure found in *The History of Henrie the Fovrth*, the first play is characterized by its sense of a poised moment with events and emotions on the cusp, and the "Falstaff comedy" (Weis, in Shakespeare 1993: 3) is matched, if not outdone by, a complex political narrative. From its opening with King Henry's desire to turn from civil war to a crusade and in his description of Hotspur as "Fortune's minion" (1.1.82) the play continuously twists and turns, nowhere more so than in the fortunes of the rebels (4.1). This mutability and the issue of its motives and origins is reinforced as many of the characters raise the possibility of redemption or restoration (1.3.180–2). In a play marked by rapid shifts in fortune another important dynamic lies in the narrative of Hal's more calculated "reformation" (1.2.201). Yet although the play alludes to the possibility of a moral pattern, especially in the repeated pattern of fathers, sons, and surrogate fathers redolent of the prodigal son plays of the Elizabethan tradition, the pattern is only ever filled in an ambiguous fashion.

Indeed, *The History of Henrie the Fovrth* has affinities with the later traditions of city comedy, where biblical patterns of moral order are juxtaposed with classical New Comedy and its vision of a world of witty sons outfoxing their elders. In *The History of Henrie the Fovrth* the repeated instances of "redeem" and "redeeming" (1.3.180, 1.3.206, 3.2.132, 5.4.48; 1.2.205) may suggest a moral possibility; the various uses in the play slip disconcertingly between moral, legal, and economic meanings. Thus in 5.4 when Hal rescues the king, his father's cool response emphasizes the ambiguity of moral reform:

> Thou hast redeemed thy lost opinion,
> And showed thou mak'st some tender of my life
> In this fair rescue . . . (5.4.47–9)

Although a "fair rescue" the ethical ideals implicit in "redeemed" are undermined by the more commercial senses of "tender" (an offer of money that discharges a debt) and even "fair" suggests that the action is possibly a rational exchange based on calculation rather than idealism.

The History of Henrie the Fovrth assumes a darker tone, perhaps partly because Falstaff appears a less sympathetic figure than in *2 Henry IV*, becoming a braggart soldier who is hardly funny in his deliberate destruction of his enlisted troops, and partly because the play ends not with the coronation of Henry V and the movement into national myth, but with a far less comfortable continuance of the civil wars. Indeed, the dark and uneasy ending of *The History of Henrie the Fovrth* echoes contemporary events, as in 1597 England was mired in crisis. Although historians debate precisely how deep and widespread the economic crisis of the 1590s may have been, both the queen and her regime were under great strain (Guy 1995: 10). Elizabeth, despite the fixity of her iconography, was clearly ageing. The French ambassador, de Maisse, may have commented favorably on her breasts (displayed to him as she "open[ed] the front of [her] robe with her hands as if she was too hot"), but he also mercilessly described her large red wig and how "her face . . . is and appears to be very aged. It is long and thin and her teeth are yellow . . . Many of them are missing" (cited in Somerset 1991: 556–7). Moreover, the almost continual state of war in the 1590s had stretched Elizabethan finances and, more crucially, the patronage system. Naunton described her court as divided between "militi" and "togati" and the last decade of the reign saw stagnant promotion prospects amongst the military figures and an intensified struggle for patronage and political dominance between the Cecil and Essex factions. The Earl of Essex, in particular, strained the court system with his preeminence and demands for precedence and he was widely regarded as a popular military hero – and even a possible successor to the queen (McCoy 1989: 79–102). In 1600 a picture of Essex on horseback, with his conquest arrayed in the background and verses describing him as "Gods elected," was printed and rapidly suppressed by the Privy Council as it was thought "not meete such publique setting forth of anie pictures but of her most excellent Majesty" should occur (ibid: 97–8).

The History of Henrie the Fovrth was, then, published in a climate marked by a sense of *fin de siècle* where political sclerosis combined with pressures for change, accusations of cultural degeneracy and a marked shift towards a harsher attitude towards criticism and a government which was moving towards a more absolutist view of royal prerogative. If the early Elizabethan period had been characterized by a "monarchical republic," the period after 1585 saw a decline in attention to the role of the monarch in parliament and rather an adumbration of royal supremacy. The political model most pursued in this period was one of "imperial sovereignty." It is precisely this climate that is represented in Shakespeare's play and, as many contemporaries noted, the political problems of the reign of Henry IV seemed to provide an important image of current events. In *The History of Henrie the Fovrth* many of these issues around the conflict of rights, the place of honor and militarism in society, and even the definition of manliness are explored and the analysis offered is unremittingly pessimistic.

"The History of Henrie the Fovrth"

Henry IV is a strangely marginalized figure in the play that bears his name (he only appears in six scenes), yet the play was obviously presented to its first audiences as a "history" of his reign. The dominant critical focus upon Hal and Falstaff has, perhaps, obscured the political significance of Henry IV's reign to contemporary commentators. Yet the play represents a working out of the politically charged narratives of Richard II and his dispossession and many of the same issues that fueled discussions of the Riccardian regime recur under Henry IV. Despite this, as Lorna Hutson has noted, many current interpretations, while conceding that *Richard II* "permits a sceptical view of absolutist claims" and promotes a "discernible civic consciousness," suggest this critical stance has dissipated into a concern with the legitimizing of "illegitimate power" in *The History of Henrie the Fovrth* (Hutson 2001: 178–9). This, indeed, is the common New Historicist view of the play that regards Hal's tavern sojourns as parallel to the activities of colonial governors, recording native voice as a means to extend his power through knowledge.

The concentration on Henry's manipulation of power, the aristocratic intrigues of his regime, and Hal's growth into kingship (whether regarded as a positive growth into authority or more as machiavellian ploy), raises acutely the issues of royal prerogative and power seen in Richard's reign and, rather than simply concerning itself with the legitimization, *The History of Henrie the Fovrth* provides a troubling critique of precisely the ancient feudal rights and chivalric culture that were seen as the basis of aristocratic republicanism. Indeed, *The History of Henrie the Fovrth* was written at a point when early modern political thought and historiography had started to articulate a shrewd and skeptical political analysis rooted in Machiavelli and Tacitus. This efflorescence included translations of Lipsius, Savile, and Greneway's translations of Tacitus (1591, 1592, and 1597), and Hayward's *Historie of the Life and Raigne of Henrie IIII* (1599).[2] As Malcolm Smuts has argued, Tacitus acted as "a surrogate for Machiavelli since he did not advocate the amoral behaviour he described" (Smuts 1994: 30, 25). Nonetheless, translations of Machiavelli also circulated quite widely and it is possible that another key subversive text, Marlowe's translation of Lucan's republican and anti-tyrannical *Pharsalia*, was also disseminated by this means, although it remained unpublished until 1600.

Daniel's *First Fowre Bookes of the Ciuile Wars* (1595) – a source that Shakespeare used for *The History of Henrie the Fovrth* – provides a parallel interpretation of the events depicted in the play. Although Daniel apparently frames his narrative within a paean to the stability of the current regime ("blisse of thee Eliza"), the providential pattern that traces the happy arrival of the Tudors from the fall of Richard II, along with the Virgilian echoes at the outset (Book 1, stanza 2) are rapidly undermined by the narrative of a "flexible" (weak) king (Book 1, stanza 37). Daniel depicts ambitious and self-serving nobles, the subornation of established law by both king and aristocracy, actions often undertaken under the cloak of "publique good" (Book 1, stanza 42), a monarch reduced to a beast (an "vnbridled" lion crazed with blood-lust), and a kingdom transformed into a wilderness. Daniel's narrative establishes its skepticism in two remarkable passages. In the first, the populace watching Bolingbroke depart to exile lament:

> Are we lockt vp poore soules, here t' abide
> Within the watery prison of thy waues,
> As in a fold, where subiect to the pride
> And lust of rulers we remaine as slaues. (Book 1, stanza 69)

The passage with its compelling images of the common people imprisoned on their island (the absolute opposite of Gaunt's fortress England in *Richard II*) "subject to the pride / And lust of rulers we remaine as slaues" could almost come from Blake's *Visions of the Daughters of Albion*. The "lust of rulers" is not the sole cause, however, and in a second radical moment Daniel notes how "ambitious unckles," "th' indiscreet young king," his minions and "the greedy counsell" "all were in the fault" and "all togither did this tempest bring" (Book 1, stanza 38). Later, even Bolingbroke's justifications for ascending the throne are questioned: "How iust 'tis done and on how sure a ground" (Book 3, stanza 18).

Although Daniel's poem does not use the language of civic humanism or appeal to the aristocratic republicanism that some critics have seen as a critique of the Elizabethan regime, Daniel was deeply interested in Lucan and his text manifests a concern for law, right, and parliament against the "exactions" of war tax and even warns of the failure of royal terror: "in vaine with terrour is he fortified / that is not guarded with firme lawe beside" (Book 1, stanza 58). Importantly, Daniel invokes the Norman yoke and – implicitly at least – the ideals of ancient English feudal liberties. His tone, however, is more pessimistic and there appears to be no way to "redeem this wrong-detained honor" (Book 1, stanza 20). Yet, instead of simply sliding into a providential relief at the arrival of the Tudor peace, the text strongly suggests that chance was more in action and that without parliamentary agreement and proper law there can be no legitimacy.

In comparison to Hayward's *Historie* with its sophisticated invocation of Cicero and Tacitus and its allusion to the royal prerogative and clashes with the "auncient libertie," Daniel's text may seem rather naive, but like the Hayward *Historie*, simply retelling this story could have radical implications (Hayward 1599: sig. C3r). Elizabeth I herself commented that the history of this period was "a seditious prelude to put into the peoples heades boldnesse and faction" and so although the text may not have invoked the possibility of a plural political agency and consciousness directly, Elizabeth I clearly saw that it could be inferred from the story (Manning 1991: 2). Although the main source for much of the narrative in *The History of Henrie the Fovrth* was researched through Holinshed and the chronicles tradition, Shakespeare's text adopts some of Daniel's details and also the questioning framework, implicitly echoing Daniel's question, "How iust 'tis done and on how sure a ground?" In so doing Shakespeare's play articulates a bleak critique of aristocratic culture and the possibilities of political action where militarism and terror outstrip debate and law.

The clash between royal authority and aristocratic culture is seen most clearly in 1.3, where Hotspur refuses to hand over his prisoners to Henry. The key issue of the scene – Henry's demand for the prisoners – embodies a clash familiar to the Elizabethans between the customary rites of knighthood, justified by honor, and the duty of obedience to the monarch. Henry was entitled to the noble prisoners, while Hotspur only offers him the Earl of Fife (automatically a royal prisoner due to his own royal blood) and oversteps the bounds by detaining the other four captive Scottish earls (1.1.72–3). Equally, Henry's demand for all the prisoners without exception (1.3.120) and without the payment of the traditional royal gratuity compromises Hotspur's honor.

The failure to find a compromise between royal and aristocratic rights is exacerbated by the problematic legitimacy of Henry's kingship. Although Henry insists

"I will from henceforth rather be myself, / Mighty and to be feared" (1.3.5–6) his position is more tenuous, as Worcester reminds that although he is "sovereign liege" his family advanced Henry to that "greatness" that he now uses against them (1.3.10–13) and later he interprets the king's unwillingness to ransom Mortimer as fear of his claim to the throne as Richard II's heir presumptive (1.3.145–6). The shifting terms of address in the scene encapsulates this tension as Henry moves from "I" to the royal "we" as he addresses Worcester (1.3.15–21), an effect that is replayed as he describes Mortimer's treachery (1.3.84–92) and reiterated when he gives Northumberland "license" to leave the court (1.3.123–4). Indeed, he asserts his royal superiority even further when he addresses Hotspur as "sirrah" (1.3.118).

The changing pronouns of the scene encapsulate the translation in Henry's own status and the awkward relationship between his past identity as "Bolingbroke" and his current position as king – and, indeed, Hotspur's use of the former name marks his revolt from royal authority (1.3.137). But the question of address also highlights the internecine nature of this feud. Almost everyone in the play is, in Elizabethan terms at least, "cousin" to everyone else and they are addressed as such. Westmoreland is "gentle cousin" and "coz" (1.1.31 and 90) and Worcester constantly addresses Hotspur as "Good cousin" or "cousin" (1.3.187, 211, 226, 290). The importance of these relationships is marked in Hotspur's description of Bolingbroke's arrival at Ravenspurgh (dramatized in *Richard II*, 2.3.1–50), where rather than "sirrah" he termed Hotspur "gentle" and "kind cousin" (1.3.252). Hotspur's anger and his punning "the devil take such cozeners" (1.3.253) illustrates how much this represented a struggle between family members and the perilously nuanced distinctions of rank and position that actually separate them. As Hotspur comments, it is no wonder that Mortimer's "cousin king" (1.3.158), knowing of his proclamation as Richard's heir presumptive, would be willing to see "him on barren mountains starve" (1.3.159–60).

The significance of this kinship lies in the honorable conduct that Hotspur expects and which shapes his interpretation of events. Thus rather than straightforward dealing according to the honor code, Henry is regarded as "subtle" (1.3.169) and "a vile politician" (1.3.240) who deploys "a candy deal of courtesy" (1.3.249) rather than the codes of honor. Indeed, Hotspur even interprets the death of Richard and their implication in it within the honor code, suggesting that their "nobility and power" have been shamed as they "Did gage them both in an unjust behalf" (1.3.173). The image of the "gage" echoes the interrupted combat at the start of *Richard II* (one of the key accusations against Richard was his interference in the judicial trial by combat) and depicts aristocratic resistance to royal authority as a matter of honor:

> Yet time serves wherein you may redeem
> Your banished honours, and restore yourselves
> Into the good thoughts of the world again;
> Revenge the jeering and disdained contempt
> Of this proud king . . . (1.3.179–84)

Hotspur also harps upon their "shame" and "these shames ye underwent" (1.3.177 and 179, but also 170) in supplanting Richard and supporting Bolingbroke's "murderous subornation" (1.3.163), again stressing the chivalric issues of honor and dishonor, placing the aristocratic code above royal powers.

The dominant sense of the political machinations in *The History of Henrie the Fovrth*, then, is of an aristocratic order in conflict with royal power and of the interconnections between the extended kinship network of the aristocracy destroying the country in its pursuit of power. Shakespeare's view of Henry's reign seems closer to Daniel's shared blame than Hayward's greater emphasis upon the extension of royal prerogative, but it also concurs with the skepticism of both of those texts towards power and the modes of behavior of the powerful. Unlike other early modern historical texts that depict the evils of rebellion, the analysis presented here is closer to Henry Savile's extension of Tacitean readings which sees misrule and underlying structural weakness as the cause of civil wars:

> As in a body corrupt, and full of ill humours, the first pain that appeareth, be it never so slender, draws on the rest, discloseth old aches and strains, actuateth what else is unsound in the body: so in a state universally disliked, the first disorder disolveth the whole. (Smuts 1994: 26)

But the play also depicts the venality of the political class, so that Savile's "universally disliked" regime is simply disliked by those who erected it. In this sense Shakespeare's play is more radical in presenting a critique of the very aristocratic culture that many saw as required to hold royal prerogative in check.

The skepticism about aristocratic chivalric culture permeates the play. Hotspur's rashness and ultimate brutality brings out the violence implicit in this culture, while figures like Glendower with his reliance on portents (3.1.12–41), prophecies, and magic are used to associate chivalric values with a comic archaism. This process continues in the use of romance motifs throughout the text, so that the aristocratic use of these ideas (Worcester describes the rebellion as "the unsteadfast footing of a spear": 1.3.193) is undermined by the broader resonances of chivalric culture in the text. In 1.2, "the wandering knight so fair" becomes Falstaff's bombastic synonym for the sun (perhaps an allusion to the romance hero, the Knight of the Sun: see 1.2.14), while the "squires" cease to be noble servants and instead are thieves (1.2.23). Even the chivalric titles adumbrated by Glendower (and which exasperate Hotspur) are burlesqued in Falstaff's description of Bardolph as the "knight of the burning lamp" (3.3.25). Indeed, it is Falstaff as a knight who presents the most formidable critique of the chivalric ideal.

Falstaff is often discussed as if he somehow is outside the aristocratic world and he is frequently described within the play as a "base" companion. Yet, crucially, he is *Sir* John Falstaff, and he belongs to the elite chivalric class. The symbolic importance of this role is glossed by Daniel's description of Richard II's murder by Sir Piers of Exton when he comments:

This knight, but o why should we call him knight
To giue impiety this reuerent stile,
Title of honour, worth and vertue's right . . .
(Daniel, Book 3, stanza 58: sig. P3r)

Falstaff certainly belies the notion that this is a "reuerent stile" and his activities as thief and coward undermine the image of the knight. In this the play echoes the critique of knighthood in plays such as *Every Man In His Humour* (1598), where the braggart Bobadilla claims his sword exceeds "Morglay, Excalibur, Durindana" (3.1.134–5), or even *Eastward Ho* (1605), where Gertrude and Sindefy, exemplifications of the dire effects of romance-reading upon fertile minds, concede that their knights fail to live up to the Palemerins, Tristrams, and Lancelots: "They were still pressed to engage their honour, ours still ready to pawn their clothes. They would gallop on at the sight of a monster, ours run away at the sight of a sergeant" (*Eastward Ho*, 5.1.25–37).

Although the critique of knighthood was accelerated by the Jacobean period's promiscuous creations, *The History of Henrie the Fovrth* also suggests how the cult of the Fairy Queen served by a court of knights in imitation of the Arthurian round table had become threadbare as the queen aged and as the "knights" struggled for power as much as honor or the cause of courtesy. Indeed, in the 1590s knighthood became a vexed issue between the queen and the Earl of Essex who regarded the conferring of knighthoods as part of his rights as a commander (and would-be commander-in-chief) and as a fit reward for his soldiers. Elizabeth, on the other hand, was concerned to preserve the social distinction of the rank and once when Essex created twenty-four knights in one batch commented that "my lord would have done well to have built his alms-house before he made his knights" (Hammer 1999: 223). The figure of the poor or decayed knight was easily recognizable to the audience of 1597.

Interestingly, Falstaff's description of thieving deploys chivalric and courtly terms, even almost echoing the terms that had saluted Elizabeth herself. The description of his band of footpads as "squires of the night's body" and "gentlemen of the shade, minions of the moon" and the image of the "noble and chaste mistress" affirm Falstaff's link with aristocratic culture. For him, courtiership is clearly about theft, and his later interest in the court as a route to reward suggests that the connection is deliberate. Indeed, the tavern world of East Cheap is often depicted as the antithesis of the court (and some resonances are clearly developed from morality plays where the tavern is depicted as the devil's kitchen), but given the manner in which Falstaff's band parodies court structures, the tavern starts to look like an inversion of the court rather than its opposite, especially as it is here that Falstaff and Hal play at ruling. The sense of an upside-down court accentuates the awareness of the origins of disorderly conduct within the aristocratic culture rather than from beyond.

If earlier criticism tended to regard Falstaff's antics as a light relief from the civil war narrative of the main text, more recent approaches have stressed the political implications of the education of Hal (almost transforming the play into the education of a Christian prince). This politicizing trend now concentrates on how Falstaff represents either the forces of disorder that monarchy needs to learn to control or – more positively – the "refusal of monarchic order," a symbol of political agency that can contest royal will. More recently, Lorna Hutson has argued that the motif of the prodigal prince's involvement with Falstaff "offers the disturbing spectre of the repetition of Richard II's tyranny" (Hutson 2001: 180). Many of the accounts of Riccardian misrule highlight the king's assumption that he embodied the law, asserting "laws are in the King's mouth, or sometimes in his brest," and Hayward certainly attributes to Richard the destruction of parliamentary liberty, especially freedom of speech (ibid; Hayward 1599: sig. C3r). Hutson argues that this tyrannical behavior can be seen in the well-known anecdote of Prince Henry's attempt to subvert the course of the law, his boxing of the Lord Chief Justice's ears and his imprisonment for contempt that leads Henry IV to concede the righteousness of the law (Hutson 2001: 181). This famous incident is dramatized in *The Famous Victories* but only obliquely alluded to in *The History of Henrie the Fovrth* (less so in *2 Henry IV*) when Falstaff asks Hal "shall there be gallows standing in England when thou art king?" (1.2.56–7). Although Falstaff disguises this as preventing "resolution" (courage) being cheated by the law his description of "old Father Antic the law" (1.2.58) reveals his underlying contempt. Falstaff's appeal may appear to be one of mercy ("Do not thou, when thou art king, hang a thief") it in fact presages a disregard for law and this impression is confirmed as Hal apparently offers the "old Father Antic" Falstaff a legal role which Falstaff takes to be membership of the bench but is, in fact, the hangman's office. Although the exchange is brief and jokey, the implications are serious, as the law is not only to be traduced by Falstaff's planned peculation (he'll gain from the sale of the dead victims' suits) but how Hal, once king, might ignore the proper bounds of law.

In *2 Henry IV* the threat is more serious, as Falstaff will become chief justice and his words law ("the laws of England are at my commandment") (Hutson 2001: 182), whereas in *The History of Henrie the Fovrth* the offense is simply aiding Falstaff's avoidance of the sheriff (2.4.488–503) as against a full-scale assault by the prince in *The Famous Victories*. Nonetheless, the episode raises the question of what kind of king Hal will make and this is illuminated by the famous scene where Falstaff initially plays Hal's father interrogating his son over the Falstaff association and when the knight fails to match Hal's idea of kingly speech, Hal assumes the role. The scene has been the subject of much commentary, not least the extent to which Hal provokes Falstaff's playing the king, seen by New Historicist critics as a demonstration of the way that authority provokes disorder in order to justify its own oppression of that subversive force. This pattern has been challenged by other critics who see the theatricality of the situation and Falstaff's charisma as effectively undermining the authoritarian desire to contain and control.

While it is possible that both these patterns are present – authority producing the very disorder that justifies its own existence, and a theatrical energy that makes the audience aware of precisely that process in operation – the scene also contains a more direct (and in the context of a discussion of the king's word as law operating without parliamentary sanction) more threatening moment of royal authority. As the sheriff hammers at the door and Falstaff pleads to continue the play so that he can argue against his banishment, Hal closes all argument with his stark phrase: "I do, I will" (2.4.463). Although this "will" may defer the actions into the future, it is also promissory and reminds the listener forcefully of the central issue of the politics of Richard II's deposition, the royal will. Hal's words have a chilling effect on the scene and are a harsh reminder that he will exercise his power and that the populace depends on his will to operate within the law – a law which he clearly disregards as and when it suits him.

The History of Henrie the Fovrth centers upon aristocratic politics. When the king raises his son's "vile participation" and his popularity, the appeal is to Hal to involve himself with the political nation – the aristocracy and the court. Indeed, the play is notably skeptical, too, about the role of London and its citizens in political events. In plays as diverse as Heywood's *Edward IV* (1599), *The Famous Victories* (1586), and even Dekker's *Shoemaker's Holiday* (1600), London is depicted as loyal, its citizens engaged in political actions (see Heinemann 1990). Yet in *The History of Henrie the Fovrth* Hal rapidly learns the language of the drawers and the comic confusion of Francis in 2.4.84 almost stands as an emblem of the situation of the populace, divided between two forces. Even if the term "commonwealth" (2.1.77–80) has become debased in the play (it is the subject of a joke), the play still adopts a highly critical stance towards not only the claims of imperial sovereignty exercised by monarchs, but also the aristocratic republicanism that tempered royal excesses. Indeed, it is the critique of aristocratic values, especially the militarism inherent in chivalric culture, which powers the play's sharpest political commentary.

"With the battell at Shrewsburie"

When Jonson added a new Prologue to *Every Man in His Humour*, probably around 1613, he surveyed his theatrical competitors and the popularity of their plays and the audience appetite for "popular errors," among which he numbered the "three rusty swords" used to "Fight over York and Lancaster's long jars" (Prologue, lines 26, 9–11). Jonson's complaints are a forceful reminder that history plays retained a continued popularity even as theatrical and literary fashion shifted, and even as the number of new English history plays declined, their Elizabethan forebears remained widely read and performed. His attack on the "three rusty swords" of Elizabethan theatre suggests incredulity at the representations of battles on stage, yet these were a staple of the Elizabethan repertoire and, indeed, many companies advertised sword fighting displays to attract an audience, as in the playbill to *England's Glory* (1602), which offered "a great triumph . . . made with the fighting of twelue Gentlemen at Barriers" (see Braunmuller and Hattaway 1990: plate 5).

Although it is tempting to see these features as part of an outdated citizen fashion for chivalric narratives, in fact chivalric ideals remained powerful throughout the period, for both aristocratic and other social classes. Even though chivalric ideals were undergoing some transformations in this period, the knight remained a key figure in aristocratic culture, and jousts, tilting at the ring, and other martial exercises remained an important feature of court life and provided major arenas for public display. The chivalric offices, such as Earl Marshall, and the chivalric orders, such as the Order of the Garter, were still highly valued, not least in the case of the marshallship, for the prestige, preeminence, and real power they bestowed. Even as late as the 1640s, parliamentarian and royalist generals offered their opponents single combat as a means to avoid bloodshed (Adamson 1994: 183). Indeed, the leading parliamentary general, the third Earl of Essex, even quoted Hotspur in parliament (ibid: 185).

The significance of honor as a defining quality of manliness in early modern England suggests how apparently archaic ideas still retained their potency. Even though the sixteenth century also saw a shift towards the importance of humanism and learning in the definition of courtesy, manly, military exercises still played a crucial role and events such as the Accession Day tilts helped "contain the latent violence within acceptable limits" and tame the "competitiveness of honour" (James 1986: 313). The Accession Day tilts, in particular, were venues for spectacular public display of the aristocratic self and of the power of one's following, but they also belonged to a process whereby honor was centralized by the monarchy. From Henry VIII onwards, and especially under Elizabeth I who used it as a political strategy to balance the competing factions of aggressive male magnates, monarchs depicted themselves as the fount of all honor against the older notion of a self-validating honor community. Although honor was itself a personal quality, the implication of the honor system and its chivalric culture was that the great chivalric offices (especially the earl marshalcy and the constableship) meant that the officeholders accrued great political power and several contemporary theorists saw these positions as maintaining a check on royal power. Thomas Starkey's *Dialogue Between Reginald Pole and Thomas Lupset* (ca. 1529–32) is remarkable in this sense, mixing Venetian oligarchical Republicanism, appeals to the ancient constitution, and feudal offices to claim that "our old ancestors . . . considering well this same tyranny . . . ordained a Constable of England to counterpoise the authority of the prince and temper the same" (McCoy 1989: 93).

It is unsurprising that early modern monarchs like Elizabeth I (and later James VI and I) often preferred to keep these offices unfilled, but in 1596–7 Essex increasingly lobbied for the role, as it would establish him as commander-in-chief. This context, however, lends particular resonance to Hotspur's chivalric code and the way in which he constructs politics through the language of honor. When Hotspur describes his father and uncle as having been shamed by their support of Henry IV, it is in terms of chivalric contest; they have "gage[d]" their "nobility and power" "in an unjust behalf" (1.3.173). This translates the political action into a cause of honor and – as such – as members of the honor community provides them with the justification to act – to protect their own, self-defined honor. It is almost as if this is to be a trial by combat – a form that symbolized the independence of the aristocracy from royal interference and whose interruption by Richard II had been regarded as one of his main offenses.

Although for many of the characters in the play (not least Henry, who describes him as "the theme of honour's tongue": 1.1.80) Hotspur symbolizes the power of the honor culture and the importance of chivalric manliness, equally he also suggests the failures of such a culture, especially the indiscriminate aggression (seen in his exchanges with Glendower in 3.1) and its rashness and rejection of the possibility of persuasion and argument (some of this is, perhaps, suggested by Hotspur's rejection of poetry as "mincing"). Hotspur's own enthusiasm for martial combat produces an uneasy and unstable violence that increases as the play progresses. His description of the rebellion as "sport" (1.3.300) and his indiscriminate desire for war marks him out as less the perfect knight than a thug. In 4.1, where he is faced with the decline of his forces and the augmentation of his enemies, he insists:

> Let them come.
> They come like sacrifices in their trim,
> And to the fire-eyed maid of smoky war
> All hot and bleeding will we offer them.
> The mailèd Mars shall on his altars sit
> Up to the ears in blood. I am on fire
> To hear this rich reprisal is so nigh
> And yet not ours. (4.1.114–20)

Although the images of bloody Mars and Bellona are the commonplaces of chivalric and martial writing, the indiscriminate lust for blood undermines any sense of "sacrifice," while the "reprisal" is not only a "prize" but carries inferences of retaliatory force and the seizure of property. Beneath the language of chivalry lies violence and the seizure of property.

It is in the musters that the starkest critique of militarism occurs in *The History of Henrie the Fovrth*. Not only does Falstaff abuse the "press" to obtain profit by extorting money from those wishing to avoid military service and by promoting non-existent officers and pocketing their wages (4.2.10–24), but also his "scarecrows" are even mistaken for "dead bodies" (4.2.35–6). These "pitiful rascals" are not only unfit as soldiers but – worse – Falstaff merely regards them as "food for powder" (4.2.62); that is, they are suitable only to fill up the rolls of the dead from which Falstaff will profit again. In 5.3 he reveals that he has deliberately led his troops to "where they are peppered" (5.3.37), reducing his 150 men to three remaining cripples. Again, the callousness of Falstaff's actions and his pursuit of illicit profit not only satirizes contemporary abuses of the military system and suggests the degree of his own self-interest; it also highlights the reality of early modern knighthood. While Henry, Hal, Hotspur, and others imagine a world on "noble horsemanship," the more mundane world of the foot-soldier is brutal and brief. As Worcester says of Hotspur's chivalric mission to "pluck bright honour from the pale-faced moon" (1.3.202), it is "a world of figures" and "not the form." The figures of this world are casualty figures and not rhetorical tropes, its "form" the "shot" that kills but ultimately pays Falstaff's tavern "scoring" (5.3.30–2).

The violent militarism underlying chivalric rhetoric is emphasized in Falstaff's address to Blunt's body: "There's honour for you" (5.3.32). Here the dead body is a forceful reminder of the potential end of the chivalric honor code, taking Falstaff's witty conclusion that "Honour is a mere scutcheon" (5.1.139) to its logical end. Falstaff's ironic affirmation of the truth of his observation "Here's no vanity!" also suggests that this is, indeed, no *memento mori* (another meaning of "vanity"); this is the brutal reality of warfare. Indeed, throughout this scene – and especially the exchange with Hal – the skull beneath the skin is a constant presence: "I like not such grinning honour as Sir Walter hath" (5.3.57–8). The rictus of the dead knight contrasts with Falstaff's prayer "Give me life, which if I can save, so; if not honour comes unlooked for, and there's an end" (58–9), while the language often used in heroic drama (in the bungled comparison with the Turk (5.3.45) and the Marlovian "carbonado" (5.3.57) becomes frighteningly literal and plausible.

The overwhelming presence of death at the end of *The History of Henrie the Fovrth* brings out the savagery of the "furious close of civil butchery" (1.1.13). In particular, the almost ritualistic attitude towards death and honor expressed by Hal in his speech pledging the expunging of the "long-grown wounds of . . . intemperature" (3.2.156), and the expiation of his shame ("I will wear a garment all of blood"), is undermined by Percy's death. Although this too is depicted in the heroic terms of blood sacrifice and honor in a noble death, the reality is "the loss of brittle life" (5.4.77) and the "mangled face" (95) hidden beneath the ceremonial "favours." The gesture may be chivalric but it foregrounds again the ways in which aristocratic culture glosses violence and that the "Fair rites of tenderness" are only available to the dead. Indeed, Falstaff's later abuse of the corpse and the degradation of Hotspur (marked in a "sirrah" that cruelly echoes King Henry's own put-down in 1.3.118) as he becomes "noble luggage" (that is, inconveniently heavy baggage) with its comic implications undermines any sense of the heroic end. The "fair rites of tenderness" which dignify Hotspur's bloody end are, ultimately, only available after death when he is "food for – / For worms" (5.4.85–6).

This whole section of 5.4 yields a queasy humor. Falstaff – recently himself thought to be a dead "deer" ready for the "powder" and consumption – now treats the fallen hero as a piece of meat. Moreover, the thigh wound he administers receives an awkward echo in the images of sexual initiation used by Hal to Lancaster (as if brothel and battle haunting and hunting are parallel actions). But it is Hal's attitude – apparently a moment of graceful acquiescence to Falstaff – that actually throws the nature of chivalry into clearest relief: "If a lie may do thee grace, / I'll gild it with the happiest terms I have" (5.4.152–3). The willingness to lie – to return to the shame that chivalric deeds were supposed to have expunged – and to countenance Falstaff again not only undermines the chivalric code, it returns to the question of what kind of king will Hal make. King Henry's final line reminds the audience, forcefully, that the point of such chivalric endeavor lies in possession and ownership: "Let us not leave till all our own be won" (5.5.44).

Hayward's *Historie of the Life and Raigne* described the battle at Shrewsbury as a "mercilesss match" and Shakespeare's play prefigures that description. Although the play ends with a series of gestures towards chivalry and military courtesy, the final momentum is towards further battles and the problematic inheritance of a prince who will "lie" to spare Falstaff just as he is prepared to "falsify men's hopes" (1.2.199) in order to secure political advantage. Indeed, the final chivalric encounter of the play is also based on a lie. In 5.2 after Henry has parleyed with Worcester and Vernon and offered terms, the "liberal and kind offer" (5.2.2) is hushed up as Vernon concurs: "Deliver what you will; I'll say 'tis so" (5.2.26). Worcester's cynical summation of the political situation (he thinks Henry will blame him and Northumberland for corrupting Hotspur whilst excusing the younger man's actions as mere youthful rashness) prompts him to conceal the offer of terms and sacrifice his nephew by depicting Henry as "haughty" and determined to battle. The incident neatly inverts the prodigal play pattern to which Worcester even alludes (the older generation forgives the younger its follies) and, instead, the older generation betrays the younger. It is a stark instance of political manipulation that matches the brutality of the play's final confrontations. At the start of act 5 Henry summarizes the situation in terms of winning and losing, rejecting any glosses or mitigations (5.1.1–8), and the rest of the act confirms this realism. Indeed, at the end of the play, Hotspur and the chivalric culture he embodies are dead, Hal has only redeemed "some" (5.4.48) of his position, and events simply move on. The call to "business" (5.5.43) in the final lines imbues the play with a stark realism and the sense of pessimism as royal power grips ever more tightly.

"With the humorous conceits of Sir Iohn Falstaffe"

There is a devil haunts thee in the likeness of an old fat man; a tun of man is thy companion. Why dost thou converse with that trunk of humours, that bolting-hutch of beastliness, that swollen parcel of dropsies, that huge bombard of sack, that stuffed cloak-bag of guts, that roasted Manningtree ox with the pudding in his belly, that reverend Vice, that grey iniquity, that father Ruffian, that Vanity in years? (2.4.431–8)

The chivalric culture that pervades *The History of Henrie the Fovrth* was intimately concerned with the body, notably the training of the male body (from the handling of arms and horsemanship to matters of deportment and decorum in speech). But the play is overshadowed by another body: the physical bulk of Falstaff. Falstaff, despite his knightly title, literally embodies the opposite of the chivalric male body – gross, unfit, uncontrolled, and corrupt. The 1597 title page notices the importance of this body, as "humorous conceits" seems to associate the play less with laughter (though in the Stationer's Register entry the title is given as "humorous mirth") than to appeal to the new vogue for humor plays that was emerging in 1597. Falstaff has much in common with the humor-driven figures of Chapman and Jonson's early comedies, but the nuanced shift between "mirth" and "conceits" in the register and on the printed page may suggest some recognition that Falstaff's body was more than simply a joke. As a humorous body it symbolized the failure of bodily control – of all forms of appetite – that lay at the heart of the polities of *The History of Henrie the Fovrth*.

Although the most obvious connection between "that stuffed cloak-bag of guts" Falstaff's body and the politics of the play lies in the suggestions of a corrupt political state (compare, for instance, the passage cited from Smuts (1994: 26), above), the main connection lies in the more attenuated concerns with ideas of self-control and discipline of the appetites, ideas that were central to the early modern conception of masculinity. Indeed, the body – and the contrast between the fat Falstaff and the lean Hal – is used to explore another important idea in the play: political manliness. Hal represents precisely the kind of male charismatic body that was displayed at the tournament and tilt, designed to inspire the spectators with a manliness that demonstrated virtue (and, indeed, *virtù*), and the capacity for governance, while also providing an example for would-be followers to emulate. The target of this display and the subject of the gaze was other men, because men were the power brokers. The idea of dancing in elaborate costumes, jousting in barriers, posing for stylized pictures, especially those in elaborate armor or expensive robes or clothes, was to attract the gaze and thus the appreciation and approbation of other men.

The overarching aim of these displays, epitomized in the elaborate rituals of the Accession Day tilts of the Elizabethan court, was to display the control of self (and, indeed, the horse) that established manly honor and showed suitability for governance. Beyond the tilting field the aim was to govern the self much as a kingdom might be ruled, so that failure of self-control can be seen to epitomize personal and political weakness, as in 3.1 where Mortimer warns Hotspur, commending Glendower's "high respect" for Hotspur's "temper . . . And curbs himself even of his natural scope / When you come 'cross his humour" (3.1.165–7). Within the lines are not only an implicit reproof for Hotspur's high-handed treatment of Glendower, and the sense that he regards the Welsh prince's fascination with signs and portents as superfluous and even effeminate, but also the kernel of the idea that manliness is defined by the ability to "curb" the "natural scope."

Worcester's speech that follows links the personal and political qualities more explicitly, warning that his "too wilful-blame" (3.1.172) courts political failure:

> Though sometimes it show greatness, courage, blood –
> And that's the dearest grace it renders you –
> Yet often times it doth present harsh rage,
> Defect of manners, want of government,
> Pride, haughtiness, opinion, and disdain,

The least of which haunting a nobleman
Loseth men's hearts and leaves behind a stain
Upon the beauty of all parts besides,
Beguiling them of commendation. (3.1.176–84)

For Worcester, the central issue here is that "want of government" does not only debase Hotspur's blood, "It loseth men's hearts," crippling his ability to attract followers by his chivalric bearing. It is this homosocial, even homoerotic, charismatic manliness that is the basis of political success in welding together a following that will produce power.

This manliness – and its management – also figures centrally in Hal and his father's disagreement in 3.2, where Henry rails against the prince's loss of his offices and "princely privilege" through "vile participation" (3.2.86–7). Significantly, whilst the chroniclers and later historians emphasized Richard's loss of power due to his interference in aristocratic and parliamentary rights, King Henry argues Richard "enfeoffed himself to popularity" (69), perhaps developing the arguments about the king's base followers, such as the Duke of Ireland. Henry's warning speech becomes a textbook exemplification of how to manage public appearances: "being seldom seen . . . / . . . like a comet I was wondered at" (46–7). The manipulation of an appearance of humility, courtesy matched with occasional sumptuousness to stress rank, was designed to create an impression of an almost religiously virtuous character ("My presence, like a robe pontifical") and win "by rareness such solemnity." Each of these features is designed to "pluck allegiance from men's hearts" (51) and garner "admiring eyes" (80) and to be "wondered at" (57).

Of course, this is very much Hal's own plan, so that his "reformation, glitt'ring o'er my fault / Shall show more goodly and attract more eyes" (1.2.201–2), and indeed his language and reasoning even resemble those of his father (2.1.192–4 and 3.2.70–6) as he plans to exploit men's enchantment by his charisma. The sun imagery in both the father's and the son's speeches encapsulates the political aim, that all men will gaze upon and respect "sun-like majesty." As this makes clear, the disagreement is not about the tools of manipulation, the aims and ends, but the means. The king emphasizes that Hal must match proper appearance with chivalric deeds to counter Percy's "worthy interest to the state" against the mere arguments of "succession." Again, the codes of chivalric manliness insist that display must be matched by competence and ability – and, indeed, although the throne was supposed to descend by lineage, early modern political theorists stressed the importance of merit in occupying the throne. Hal's victory over Hotspur is a perfect demonstration of that merit.

The play also, however, resounds with the dangers of too much manly association – the concerns that homosociality provoked and the fears over the male body and male interaction, especially in a society in which the very bonds which structured society were also regarded as potentially sinful and subversive (Bray 1990). Writing in 1615, Francis Bacon commented that Sir Thomas Overbury, a close friend of the Earl of Somerset, the king's favorite, had erred in making his friend "his Idol," suggesting how the boundaries of acceptable and unacceptable kinds of male relationship were hard to define and even dangerously permeable. These questions around the uses of the male body and male friendship, especially in *The History of Henrie the Fovrth*, have become an important critical issue spurred on – in part – by Gus Van Sant's deployment of parts of 1.2 (spliced with other parts of the text and lines from *Part 2*) in *My Own Private Idaho* (1991), set in contemporary Portland and Seattle. In particular, the film has opened up discussion of the relationship between Falstaff and Hal, especially its sexual ambiguities in the context of Renaissance anxieties about sexuality and the role of the boy actor (Roman 1994).

Van Sant's film throws into stark relief the issue of who misleads who in the play. Falstaff's claims that Hal has "damnable iteration" and is "indeed able to corrupt a saint" has often been read as merely another example of Falstaff's self-serving blame-shifting (1.2.87–8). Yet Gus Van Sant's version of Scott's seductive charms (the Hal figure played by Keanu Reeves) presses the accuracy of these statements and the possibility that Falstaff's claim "Before I knew thee Hal, I knew nothing" (1.2.89–90) may contain some truth. Indeed, Hal's response "Where shall we take a purse tomorrow, Jack?" (1.2.91) seems significant in this connection, reflecting the prince's ability to deflect others from investigations of himself and his motives (reiterated in his avoidance of Falstaff's charge "Thou art essentially made without seeming so": 2.4.474–5) and the insistent and "endemic predation" (Goldberg 1992: 153) that characterizes the play. The potential role of Hal in the seduction of Falstaff into misdeeds presents another reversal of the prodigal paradigm that runs throughout the play but, more importantly, it reflects upon Hal's acts of political seduction as it undermines the whole premise of much criticism of the play that interprets Hal's time in Cheapside as forming an education for kingship. Indeed, Van Sant's film owes something to Greenblatt's version of Hal as neocolonialist accumulating the slang of his lower orders to attain better social control.

This exploration of the male body and the cultural anxieties surrounding it and male bonding draws attention to the very corporeality of the historical figures in the play: the ageing king, the "humorous" Falstaff and, most centrally, the heroic bodies of Hotspur (later merely "food" and "luggage") and Hal. Worcester's punctuation of Hotspur's "world of figures" with "the form of what he should attend" (1.3.209–10) and Falstaff's insistence to Hal that "Thou art essentially made" (2.4.474–5) further draw attention to the material world beneath the tropes of the chivalric body. Indeed, it is as if the play entirely demystifies the aristocratic body, making even the sun (as frequent symbol of royalty) nothing more than a transvestite ("a fair hot wench in flame-coloured taffeta": 1.2.9–10), while many of the bodies of the play's protagonists are ageing (Henry IV) and corrupt (Falstaff). These body metaphors were, of course, the foundation of political discourse in the period, from the image of the state as body to ideas of the royal and mystical body of the king. The depiction of an aged king, an ambivalent princely body, and the corrupt knightly body constantly foregrounds the material reality that underlies any mystical or figurative use of the body. Rather than a chivalric or ideal body we are offered a pragmatic political body, one that is open to change and decay as much as it is fashioned by education and discipline. This rational attitude, rather than the sacramental attitude that some have traced in early modern notions of kingship, accentuates the skepticism that pervades the play.[3]

The representations of political manliness in the play and Hal's manipulation of his charisma are demystifications of the royal image. By locating political manliness within the troubled and contested spaces of the actor's body, and the ambiguous pedagogic and pederastic relationships of the play, the implications of manly display are explored. These issues had become particularly acute in the 1590s, as the struggle over control of royal policy raged among the queen's favorites and counselors with, in the mid-1590s, the Earl of Essex looking likely to dominate. In some ways, even more so than with *Richard II* which may have been performed on the eve of the Essex revolt, this play is haunted by Essex, although unlike *Henry V* there is nothing that can be construed as a direct allusion. Yet much of the historical stance of the play and the materials it drew upon were of great interest to the Essex circle that cultivated Tacitean political analysis. Indeed, a contemporary notebook which also contains materials perhaps by Thomas Harriot (an associate of the ninth Earl of Northumberland) and which may derive from a member of Essex's circle, cites passages from *The History of Henrie the Fovrth* (including Henry's analysis of political manipulation in 3.2.29–91 and one extract in which the text is altered to refer to Elizabeth I).[4]

Whether or not the play was understood by contemporary readers as applying to Essex, it is clear that the political potential of the narrative of Henry IV's reign was widely recognized in the late 1590s and it is even possible that some of the furore over the naming of Falstaff (Oldcastle) originates in the political sensitivity of the play's subject matter. Whereas later ages have often extracted the "Falstaff comedy" and taken less from the political narrative, at least one contemporary, Francis Meres in *Palladis Tamia*, viewed the play as a "tragedy," perhaps in recognition of the dark tone and political seriousness of the play. The question left for the audience of *The History of Henrie the Fovrth* is exactly whose tragedy this might be. Given the dark tone, the pervasive violence, and uneasy image of chivalric culture and its would-be heroes, it is tempting to suggest that the tragedy lies in the victims of the play, the robbed merchants, the sacrificed soldiers and, even, the hapless, confused and duped drawers, such as Francis. It is as if the hopes embodied in *Richard II* for control of prerogative power through aristocratic republicanism and even parliamentary oversight have dissipated, to be replaced by militarism and a regime devoted to political control and its self-perpetuation.

Notes

1   In 1597 the play was not divided into acts, although I have retained these for ease of reference to modern editions (only the Oxford *Complete Works* prints the play with scenes). The effect of this arbitrary division is most noticeable in the current act 5, which segments the battle into many scenes, while in the Quarto (Q1) the action ebbs and flows seamlessly, giving a much greater sense of the mobility – and confusion – of the battle, which with its multiplication of kings stalking the stage

perhaps looks forward to the battle scenes of *Troilus and Cressida*. In addition, in 1597 the play did not contain the character named Falstaff; instead he was called Sir John Oldcastle (1.2.40–1). Again, I have retained the more familiar name to help reference to modern editions. For a good summary of the Oldcastle affair and the early playing history of the play, see Shakespeare (1993: 9–13).

2   In addition to the Lipsius translation (*Sixe Bookes of Politickes* (1594)), the most important Tacitean books were *The Ende of Nero and the beginning of Galba. Fower bookes of the Histories of Cornelius Tacitus*, trans. Henry Savile (Oxford, 1591), with a second edition in 1598, and *The Annales of Cornelius Tacitus*, trans. R. Greneway (1598).

3   The idea of the "king's two bodies" which argues for a sacramental and mystical attitude to kingship has come under sustained attack recently, and David Norbrook has ably demonstrated the relatively confined use of the idea in contemporary political discourse, as well as exploring the implications of the "doctrine" for the politics of Shakespeare criticism (see Norbrook 1996b). The key issue is that a mystical attitude to kingship removes monarchy from the arena of rational political debate, from the realms of civic consciousness, and denies the possibility of a language of state formation and political thought. Plays like *The History of Henrie the Fovrth* suggest a much wider political consciousness based on rationality and debate rather than simple adherence to mystical notions of sovereignty.

4   Such political applications were not unusual in the period, and plays like Marlowe's *Edward II* (another king whose reign was often paralleled with Richard II's as an exemplar of contemporary political issues) used the male favorites of a male king to reflect on Elizabeth's male courtiers (see Knowles 1998: 14).

REFERENCES AND FURTHER READING

Adamson, J. (1994). Chivalry and Political Culture in Caroline England. In K. Sharpe and P. Lake (eds.) *Culture and Politics in Early Stuart England.* Basingstoke: Macmillan, 161–98.

Allen, M. J. B. and Muir, K. (eds.) (1981). *Shakespeare's Plays in Quarto.* Berkeley: University of California Press.

Braunmuller, A. R. and Hattaway, M. (eds.) (1990). *The Cambridge Companion to Renaissance Drama.* Cambridge: Cambridge University Press.

Bray, A. (1990). Homosexuality and the Signs of Friendship in Elizabethan England. *History Workshop Journal*, 29, 1–19. Reprinted in *Queering the Renaissance*, ed. J. Goldberg (Durham, NC: Duke University Press, 1994), pp. 40–61.

Burgess, G. (1992). *The Politics of the Ancient Constitution: An Introduction to English Political Thought, 1603–1642.* Basingstoke: Macmillan.

Cohen, D. (1985). The Rites of Violence in *1 Henry IV. Shakespeare Survey*, 38.

Corbin, P. and Sedge, D. (eds.) (1991). *The Oldcastle Controversy.* Manchester: Manchester University Press.

Crewe, J. (1990). Reforming Prince Hal: The Sovereign Inheritor in *2 Henry IV. Renaissance Drama*, n.s. 21, 225–42.

Findlay, H. (1989). Renaissance Pederasty and Pedagogy: The "Case" of Shakespeare's Falstaff. *Yale Journal of Criticism*, 3, 229–38.

Goldberg, J. (1992). Desiring Hal. In *Sodometries: Renaissance Texts, Modern Sexualities*. Stanford, CA: Stanford University Press.

Greenblatt, S. (1985). Invisible Bullets: Renaissance Authority and its Subversion, *Henry IV* and *Henry V*. In J. Dollimore and A. Sinfield (eds.) *Political Shakespeare: New Essays in Cultural Materialism.* Manchester: Manchester University Press, 8–47.

Guy, J. (ed.) (1995). *The Reign of Elizabeth I: Court and Culture in the Last Decade.* Cambridge: Cambridge University Press.

Hamilton, D. (1983). The State of Law in *Richard II. Shakespeare Quarterly*, 34, 5–17.

Hammer, P. E. J. (1999). *The Polarisation of Elizabethan Politics: The Political Career of Robert Devereaux, 2nd Earl of Essex, 1585–1597*. Cambridge: Cambridge University Press.

Hayward, J. (1599). *The Life and Raigne of Henrie IIII*. London.

Heinemann, M. (1990). Political Drama. In A. R. Braunmuller and M. Hattaway (eds.) *The Cambridge Companion to Renaissance Drama*. Cambridge: Cambridge University Press, 161–205.

Hutson, L. (2001). Not the King's Two Bodies: Reading the "Body Politic" in Shakespeare's *Henry IV*, Parts 1 and 2. In L. Hutson and V. Kahn (eds.) *Rhetoric and Law in Early Modern Europe*. New Haven, CT: Yale University Press, 166–98.

James, M. (1986). *Society, Politics and Culture: Studies in Early Modern England*. Cambridge: Cambridge University Press. [This volume contains two important essays: "English Politics and the Concept of Order, 1485–1642" and "At a Crossroads of the Political Culture: The Essex Revolt, 1601."]

Kelliher, H. (1989). Contemporary Manuscript Extracts from Shakespeare's *Henry IV, Part 1*. *English Manuscript Studies*, 1, 144–81.

Knowles, J. (1998). Marlowe and the Aesthetics of the Closet. In G. McMullan (ed.) *Renaissance Configurations*. Basingstoke: Macmillan, 3–29.

——(ed.) (2001). *The Roaring Girl and Other Plays*, with notes by G. Giddens. Oxford: Oxford University Press.

McCoy, R. C. (1989). *The Rites of Knighthood: The Literature and Politics of Elizabethan Chivalry*. Berkeley: University of California Press.

Manning, J. J. (ed.) (1991). *The First and Second Part of John Hayward's "The Life and Raigne of Henrie IIII."* London: Royal Historical Society.

Norbrook, D. (1996a). "A Liberal Tongue": Language and Rebellion in *Richard II*. In J. M. Mucciolo (ed.) *Shakespeare's Universe: Renaissance Ideas and Conventions. Essays in Honour of W. R. Elton*. Aldershot: Scolar Press, 37–51.

——(1996b). The Emperor's New Body? *Richard II*, Ernst Kantorowicz, and the Politics of Shakespeare Criticism. *Textual Practice*, 10, 329–57.

Orgel, S. (1985). Making Greatness Familiar. In D. Bergeron (ed.) *Pageantry in the Shakespearean Theatre*. Athens, GA: University of Georgia Press, 19–25.

Patterson, A. (1994). *Reading Holinshed's "Chronicles."* Chicago, IL: University of Chicago Press.

Roman, D. (1994). Shakespeare Out in Portland: Gus Van Sant's *My Own Private Idaho*, Homoneurotics, and Boy Actors. *Genders*, 20, 311–33.

Shakespeare, W. (1974). *The History of King Henry the Fourth, as revised by Sir Edward Dering, Bart*, ed. G. W. Williams and G. B. Evans. Washington, DC: Folger Books.

——(1987). *Henry IV, Part 1*, ed. D. Bevington. Oxford: Oxford University Press

——(1993). *Henry IV, Part 2*, ed. R. Weis. Oxford: Oxford University Press.

Smuts, M. (1994). Court-centred Politics and the Uses of Roman Historians, c. 1590–1630. In K. Sharpe and P. Lake (eds.) *Culture and Politics in Early Stuart England*. Basingstoke: Macmillan, 21–44.

Somerset, A. (1991). *Elizabeth I*. London: Weidenfeld and Nicolson.

Tuck, R. (1983). *Philosophy and Government, 1572–1651*. Cambridge: Cambridge University Press.

Wommersley, D. (1996). Why is Falstaff Fat? *Review of English Studies*, n.s. 47, 1–22.

21
Henry IV, Part 2:
A Critical History
Jonathan Crewe

Introduction

The body of criticism dealing with *2 Henry IV* isn't as large or compelling as that dealing with *1 Henry IV* or *Henry V*. It is, however, a body of criticism in which the key issues aren't trivial. On the contrary, they are ones that implicate a surprisingly wide range of Shakespeare criticism and have a way of putting critics on the spot. Those are the features of the criticism I shall emphasize.

Much discussion of *2 Henry IV* is, of course, linked to discussion of *1 Henry IV* or of larger units like Shakespeare's second historical tetralogy, the so-called Henriad (Kernan 1970; Berger 1991), or Shakespeare's Tudor "epic" (Tillyard 1944).[1] Obviously, all views of *2 Henry IV* are conditioned by the existence of these larger units, as they are by discussions of *1 Henry IV*. In the pages that follow, however, I shall mainly consider criticism elicited by *2 Henry IV*'s distinctive features and challenges (see also Young 1968; Hunter 1970; Bevington 1986; Bloom 1987; Taylor 2001). Criticism of *1 Henry IV* as well as of the larger units is more extensively reviewed elsewhere in this volume.

Although it *is* an issue that arises in connection with *2 Henry IV*, I shall touch only in passing on the question of whether *1* and *2 Henry IV* should be treated as a unit or as two separate plays.[2] Upton (1750) set the ball rolling by concluding on Aristotelian grounds that each play had its own beginning, middle, and end (cited in Jenkins 1956: 155). Johnson (1765) responded that the plays are "two only because they are too long to be one" (Woudhuysen 1989: 201). Most modern critics who have taken up the issue have sided with Upton, among them, Shaaber (1948), Cain (1952), Hunter (1954) and, notably, Jenkins (1956). Readers can still do no better than consult Hawkins (1982) for a survey of the issue and its critical history.[3]

While Wilson (1943), Tillyard (1944), Calderwood (1979), and Berger (1991) are among those who argue for unity or continuity at some level between the two plays, their arguments encompass more than the two Henry IV plays. Other arguments concern the relation between the two plays alone, about which various proposals have been offered. Shaaber (1948), for instance, regards *2 Henry IV* as an unpremeditated addition. For Hunter (1954), the plays form a diptych; for Jenkins (1956), the plays are complementary and mutually exclusive; for Kerrigan (1990), they are parallel. Since Knights (1959), one broadly perceived difference between the two plays has been that between undiminished vitality in *1 Henry IV* and the passing of time, sickness, aging, melancholia, and death in *2 Henry IV*. Most critics have backed away from Shaaber's extreme position by treating the play as a vaguely anticipated sequel rather than just an afterthought. If arguments on this subject have run out of steam, that is mainly because the formal structures of Shakespeare's plays no longer engage a great deal of critical attention.

I shall also mention only in passing the view of René Weis, in his recent Oxford edition of *2 Henry IV* (1998), that "all roads in *2 Henry IV* including its textual and bibliographical history, lead to Falstaff and Oldcastle" (p. 7).[4] Weis is referring to the evidence, familiar even to non-specialists since the publication of the Oxford Shakespeare (1986), that Sir John Falstaff in *1* and *2 Henry IV* was named Sir John Oldcastle in pre-publication performances of *1 Henry IV*.[5] Evidence strongly suggests that Shakespeare changed the name Oldcastle to Falstaff under pressure from Oldcastle's powerful collateral descendants, Sir William Brooke, Lord Cobham, the then Lord Chamberlain, and his son Sir Henry Brooke, Lord Cobham.[6] Traces of this change remain in a few speech prefixes in *2 Henry IV* and in a disclaimer included in the play's Epilogue: "Falstaff shall die of a sweat, unless already a be killed with your hard opinions. For Oldcastle died martyr, and this is not the man" (Epilogue, 29–31).[7] In the 1986 Oxford edition, the name Oldcastle is "restored," thereby supposedly reversing a historical act of censorship and upholding Shakespeare's intention.[8]

Although important critical issues are at stake, among them the nature and claims of historical interpretation, and the legitimacy of editorial decisions based on evidence regarding the early performances of the plays (Taylor 1985), I shall not review the Falstaff/Oldcastle question at greater length here for two reasons. First, not all roads, or necessarily the most interesting ones, have always led to Oldcastle/Falstaff in criticism of *1* and *2 Henry IV*. Second, the Oldcastle/Falstaff issue doesn't arise primarily in connection with *2 Henry IV*.

The history of *2 Henry IV* criticism could be narrated in simple, chronological fashion or, especially in the twentieth century, through the succession of critical paradigms evident in this chronology: historical, anthropological, psychoanalytic (old and new),[9] deconstructive, New Historicist, feminist, queer, etc. I shall follow neither of these courses, however, but rather organize the narrative, chronologically for the most part, under what I consider to be the most salient topics of *2 Henry IV* criticism.

Few readers will be surprised to learn that the main preoccupation of *2 Henry IV* criticism has been the play's double ending, where Hal is first reconciled with his father and then rejects Falstaff following his coronation. Those episodes, especially the latter, produce so great an impact that they continue to prompt sometimes agonized rereading of what leads up to them in *1 Henry IV* and follows them in *Henry V*. Coming at the end of the third play in the second historical tetralogy, these episodes have also, when treated as conclusive, underpinned many teleological approaches to the history plays if not to History in general. Moreover, the rejection of Falstaff remains more than just the "nagging problem" Greenblatt (1994) called it. The episode inflicts a wound that will not heal, and not just on Falstaff. It is around that episode that what we might call sentimental and anti-sentimental approaches to the history plays have often organized themselves. (I use these terms *faute de mieux*, without pejorative intent.)

The Rejection of Falstaff

Bradley (1902) is rightly credited with summarizing nineteenth-century attitudes to Falstaff and making an issue of the rejection for his twentieth-century successors. He did not, however, launch the topic. Hazlitt (1817) wrote: "The truth is that we could never forgive the Prince's treatment of Falstaff . . . Falstaff is the better man of the two" (Bevington 1986: 63–4). Before Hazlitt, Morgann (1777) had already remarked that "we can scarcely forgive the ingratitude of the Prince in the new-born virtue of the King, and we curse the severity of the poetic justice which consigns our old, good-natured companion to the custody of the warden, and the dishonours of the Fleet" (Hunter 1970: 29). Bradley's argument thus has precedents. Since, moreover, his essay is heavily freighted with prior Shakespeare criticism, including Maurice Morgann's defense of Falstaff *in extenso*, let us begin with Bradley's predecessors.

Johnson (1765), in his notes on *1* and *2 Henry IV*, remarked in passing that Falstaff is a coward (Woudhuysen 1989: 205). It was in response to this remark, or perhaps to a more widely shared belief that Falstaff's cowardliness is part of what makes him funny, that Morgann wrote his celebrated "Essay on the Dramatic Character of Sir John Falstaff" (1777). It is that essay, according to Empson, that "started the whole snowball of modern Shakespeare criticism" (Hunter 1970: 135). To be more precise, Empson writes that "the question whether or not Falstaff is a coward . . . was the chief topic of Morgann's essay nearly two hundred years ago. It was the first time a psychological paradox was dug out of a Shakespeare text" (ibid: 136).

These are large claims. Even if Empson is right about Morgann's originality in eliciting a "psychological paradox," more explanation is needed for the fact that this essay started a snowball so enormous. We should not ignore Morgann's own claim to be undertaking the first-ever close reading of a Shakespeare play: "But general criticism is as uninstructive as it is easy: Shakespeare deserves to be considered in detail; – a task hitherto unattempted" (Hunter 1970: 31). Furthermore, Morgann is arguing for a notion of Shakespearean character – and of the Shakespearean text – as complex and contradictory. Finally, Bate (1989: 201) goes so far as to credit Morgann with initiating Shakespearean character study and psychological criticism as such. Wittingly or not, by characterizing Falstaff as a coward, Johnson had invoked the one-dimensional classical stereotype of the *miles gloriosus*, the stereotype Morgann explicitly rejected (p. 41). However responsive Johnson may have been to Falstaff's multiplicity, he was not free of preconceptions regarding essentialized character types. Morgann's essay represented an important departure from these preconceptions.

Previous discussions of Morgann have generally overlooked one additional feature of his essay that may have contributed to its long-term effect. Recently, as questions about the recruitment of Shakespeare in the cause of English imperialism have come to the fore, Dobson (1992) has highlighted a passage that was eagerly taken up by contemporary journals:

> when the very name of *Voltaire*, and even the memory of the language in which he has written, shall be no more, the *Apalachian* mountains, the banks of the *Ohio*, and the plains of *Scioto* shall resound with the accents of this Barbarian: In his native tongue he shall roll the genuine passions of nature. (Ibid: 228)

Such naturalizing assertions of preeminence became even more strident in English Shakespeare criticism written in the post-Revolutionary period of intense English rivalry with France, as noted by De Grazia (1991: 6–8). Without necessarily recognizing any descent from Morgann, critics like Wilson (1943) and Tillyard (1944) seemingly endorse continuing English *racial* assertion in Shakespeare's histories; both critics use that term.

Concerning *2 Henry IV*, it need only be said that Morgann's most telling evidence in Falstaff's defense comes from this play. While the prima facie evidence of Falstaff's cowardice occurs mainly in *1 Henry IV* – the Gadshill robbery and playing dead on the battlefield – Morgann's strongest evidence in rebuttal comes mainly from *2 Henry IV*. It includes testimonies from Mistress Quickly and Doll Tearsheet to Falstaff's bellicosity and the fact that Falstaff *led* his ragamuffins into battle, where they were peppered. Morgann further adduces Falstaff's jests on the battlefield and his fatalistic rather than terrified acceptance that he might die. It counts for a good deal with Morgann that Falstaff stands up to Prince John and that he is a respected participant in the play's council of war. Morgann does not, however, remark on the fact that most of his evidence in rebuttal is gleaned from *2 Henry IV*, thereby missing an opportunity to ask whether Falstaff really is a "Whole" (p. 55) character or one significantly revised in *2 Henry IV*, with the addition of "supplementary" biographical information about Falstaff's early life. The presumption of Unity is too powerful for Morgann to relinquish.

When Morgann broaches the topic that will be central to Bradley's essay, namely Falstaff's rejection, he does not, as we have seen, appear unduly distressed. For him, a question of fact – that of Falstaff's courage – always takes precedence over questions of affect. Not so Bradley, for whom the question of what we "feel" (Hunter 1970: 57), or are intended to feel, is paramount.

In elevating affect to a primary critical datum, Bradley elicits a traumatic potential in Falstaff's rejection that later critics have confirmed by repetition if nothing else. Like many after him, Bradley would like Falstaff let down lightly.[10] Since it is inconceivable to Bradley that Shakespeare would have wanted to end the play disagreeably ("no one who understands Shakespeare at all will consider that supposition for a moment credible": p. 66), it follows that Shakespeare failed to realize his intent. Falstaff simply got away from him, or, to put it differently, Shakespeare got carried away by his own creative, freedom-loving superabundance, leaving readers with an unintended residue of pain (p. 60).[11] For Bradley, the pain of the rejection is at once confirmed and articulated for Shakespeareans in the death of Falstaff in *Henry V*, a death reported, as Bradley insists, "by persons not very sentimental" (p. 60).

Bradley's allegiance to Falstaff is also an avowed allegiance to more expansive human possibilities than those represented by the politician prince. Since Bradley, critics have continued to work the antithesis between the human and the political: politics and their discontents remain a persistent topic in criticism of the history plays (see, for example, Hazlitt 1817; Hunter 1955; Barish 1965; Bloom 1999). This is not an antithesis I shall track in the criticism, since I accept the now prevailing view that an opposition between the political and the human is ill-conceived and anachronistic.[12] It is certainly ill-conceived insofar as it calls into play the "essentialist humanism" Dollimore, speaking for a generation, dismissed in 1984. It also preemptively depoliticizes popular allegiance to Falstaff in the seventeenth century, a popularity attested by numerous allusions to him (Hunter 1970: 16). Any assumption that Falstaff represents an extra-political humanity, or, for that matter, a utopian freedom belonging only to the genre of comedy, is always questionable. Recognizing a split between sentimental and anti-sentimental criticism allows more productive consideration of what is at issue than trying to locate a split between the political and the human in Shakespeare's text.

Coming back to the main point, then, Bradley's appeal to shared feeling as distinct from the "objective" properties of the text might be read, notwithstanding his disclaimer, as a manifestation of the sentimentality for which F. R. Leavis (1962) took his reading of *Othello* to task. In fact, Bradley has persistently been charged with sentimentality in the weak sense. Yet if we may distinguish between a "weak" and a "strong" sentimentality, it is to the latter that Bradley lays claim. For him, the denial or bracketing of what we feel amounts to an impairment of critical competence. So does feeling incorrectly: those who feel disgust or indignation at Falstaff, and therefore rejoice in his fall, reveal "that kind of inability to understand Shakespeare with which it is idle to argue" (Bradley, in Bevington 1986: 60).[13]

Bradley's "strong" sentimentality enables him to argue a case rather than just appeal to shared feeling. The reported death of Falstaff in *Henry V* does hark back to the rejection and confirm it as a mortal wound for Falstaff. That it is such a wound is by no means clear at the end of *2 Henry IV*, where it appears that Falstaff's resilience may carry him through. Rephrasing Bradley, it might now be possible to say that *Henry V* belatedly articulates the unvoiced trauma of the rejection – or reconstitutes the rejection as traumatic after the fact. It does so for Falstaff, but also, at a remove, for susceptible readers and theatregoers. There is no question that the effects of the rejection linger, not just in *Henry V* but in post-Bradley criticism of the play. The rejection also disturbs generic alignment of the two Henry IV plays with (festive) comedy by allowing a tragic potential, which Knights (1959) detected early on in the play, to erupt unexpectedly, even though Hal has put Falstaff (and the rest of us) on notice in *1 Henry IV*.

It would be too much to say that post-Bradley criticism that seeks to bypass or minimize the rejection constitutes a denial of the injury it inflicts. Post-Bradley, it does, however, require a significant devaluation or relocation of affect to neutralize this moment in the play. If an outright critique of sentimentality is not necessarily required, then what typically is required is a reading of the plays in which the stakes are higher and more public than those of personal interaction and injury.

The Politics of History

One way of depersonalizing the history plays and raising their stakes has been to take seriously their representations of English history or destiny, of which characters in the plays then become the bearers. That depersonalization was affected in Tillyard's enormously influential *Shakespeare's History Plays* (1944). Yet it is precisely the historical credentials of Tillyard's approach, or at least its claim to any historical disinterestedness or ideological neutrality, that has been most strenuously challenged by New Historicist and Cultural Materialist critics.[14] The phrase "Political Shakespeare," used as the title of a volume edited by Dollimore and Sinfield (1994), not only asserts the fundamentally political character of Shakespeare's writing in the history plays and elsewhere – for these editors, politics has no outside – but also implies the no less fundamentally political character of criticism, especially of the historicizing variety. The choice is not whether or not to be political but whether or not to be consciously and/or avowedly political.

My choice of "The Politics of History" as a subheading implies my general acceptance of this view, from which it follows that I shall not attempt to reclaim Tillyard or anyone else for Historical Criticism.[15] At the same time, I credit the precedent set by Tillyard and his successors in taking seriously Shakespeare's representations of English history or destiny. Repeated attacks on Tillyard from the political left constitute a form of backhanded recognition: Pugliatti (1996) observes that "no work has been so vehemently confuted, none has been more radically demolished; nevertheless, all readings of the history plays take us back to Tillyard as the necessary starting point" (p. 10).

As Hunter (1970) noted, Wilson (1943) set the stage for Tillyard and for later critics by refocusing *1* and *2 Henry IV* on Prince Hal (as their "technical centre": p. 17) and launching him on a trajectory that supposedly culminates in his metamorphosis into the ideal king in *Henry V* (p. 92). Instead of summoning up classical conventions and prototypes for the history plays, Wilson invokes those of the English Morality tradition. Characters in the plays, especially Hal and Falstaff, are thereby transformed for the most part into personified abstractions and the plays take on a distanced, allegorical cast. Capitalizing on Hal's self-consciousness regarding the dramatic prototypes he and Falstaff are enacting ("that reverend Vice, that grey Iniquity, that father Ruffian, that Vanity in years": 2.4.442), Wilson makes Falstaff an incarnation of Riot and/or Vice and/or Vanity leading astray the Prodigal prince. The invocation of Morality conventions also reroutes the plays back to classical prototypes. The figure of the Prodigal is one from Latin comedy, on which, as Wilson notes, Tudor dramatists had superimposed the biblical story of the Prodigal Son. Wilson even sees the *miles gloriosus* as an element in Falstaff's composition. In a sense, then, Wilson restores the *status quo ante* from which Morgann had departed.[16]

Furthermore, while conceding a certain perennial, low-life appeal to Falstaff – a class limit thus being imposed on Falstaff's power of attraction – Wilson's schematizing approach solicits a moralistic understanding, projected as that of the Elizabethan audience. Implicitly, we should be pleased when the Tempter is defeated and the Prodigal Son returns to the Father. Still in keeping with Morality conventions, Wilson perceives a degeneration of Falstaff in *2 Henry IV* that alienates whatever sympathies he has been able to muster in the earlier play. Wilson concludes by assimilating Falstaff to Milton's Satan and Hal to Milton's Christ. Falstaff's role, then, is only to magnify the importance of Hal's eventual reformation and emergence as ideal king. Wilson is not the only critic for whom Shakespeare's meaning is definitively "realized" in Milton.

Although preceded by the explicitly political Charlton (1929), who somewhat mysteriously made a point of Henry IV's competence as a ruler and of Hal's admirable, unpunished mediocrity, Tillyard pursued an approach centered on the nature of rule and the fortunes of England in the history plays. Both *1* and *2 Henry IV* iterate the Morality structure: "The Prince . . . has to choose between Sloth or Vanity, to which he is drawn by his bad companions, and Chivalry," and "again he is tested . . . he has to choose, Morality fashion, between disorder or misrule . . . and Order or Justice" (Tillyard 1944: 265). Reducing characters to types facilitated a recentering of the plays on Hal as the sole locus of moral–political transformation and the ideal bearer of the national (or racial) destiny. This reduction cuts Falstaff down to size and practically eliminates the shock of his rejection. Giving short shrift to Bradleyans, Tillyard writes: "Those who cannot stomach the rejection of Falstaff assume that in some ways the Prince acted dishonestly, that he made a friend of Falstaff, thus deceiving him, that he got all he could out of Falstaff and then repudiated the debt. They are wrong. The Prince is aloof and Olympian from the start, and never treats Falstaff any better than his dog" (pp. 271–2).

For Tillyard, it does not even suffice that Shakespeare wrote serial history plays. He recasts Shakespeare's second tetralogy as a single, unified Tudor epic, written in emulation of such contemporaries as Sidney, Spenser, and Daniel. The telos of the epic narrative is the ultimate triumph of English Order and Justice in the person of King Henry, about whose comprehensive nature Tillyard can hardly say enough: "he is Shakespeare's studied picture of the kingly type" (p. 269).[17] Although Tillyard (unexpectedly) finds Hotspur "adorable" (p. 280), he can cast him only as the boorish provincial foil to the internationally sophisticated Hal.

As discussion of Laurence Olivier's film of *Henry V* frequently reminds us, World War II, during which Tillyard's book appeared, created a market – or a Tory niche-market – for patriotic reprocessing and sanitization of the history plays (see Hodgdon 1991: 195–7). The critical idealization of absolute monarchy in the person of Shakespeare's Henry V clearly isn't just an attempt to understand the history plays in their own time. Indeed, as Hunter (1970) remarked, the English patriotic exploitation of the history plays at least from the nineteenth century onward "bears little relation to . . . *Henry IV* or *Henry VI*" (p. 13).[18] Hunter additionally notes that the mid-twentieth-century Shakespeare, whom we might now regard as a Cold War product, is generally a conformist, upholding Order, the Tudor state, and the official homilies with few questions asked (e.g., Campbell 1947; Danby 1949; Reese 1961).[19] An unsentimental rejection of Falstaff becomes a moral and logical necessity in all these schemas, and *2 Henry IV* the key text.

Although the work of Barber (1959) belongs to this period, and still centers *1* and *2 Henry IV* on Hal as "an inclusive, sovereign nature fitted for kingship" (p. 195), its invocation of precedents from saturnalian popular culture rather than from the Morality tradition brings the plays into the orbit of "festive comedy." Barber characterizes the plays as "masterpieces of the popular theater" (p. 195).[20] These precedents necessarily highlight Falstaff's brilliantly improvised, parodic performances as clown and Lord of Misrule; he is the plays' figure of "predominating imaginative significance" (p. 215). As parodic Lord of Misrule, he also exposes counterfeiting as the basis of kingship in the plays, a motif to which Empson (1950) had previously drawn attention, and which is now universally recognized.

While Barber (1959) settles for the conservative thesis regarding misrule – "misrule works . . . to consolidate rule" (p. 205)[21] – his argument makes far more generous allowance than those just discussed for animation, mobility, and Disorder in the plays. Indeed, Barber's argument that drama constitutes a departure from the fixity of ritual, hence from the names and meanings fixed *in* ritual, establishes drama as an indefinite "interlude" of slippage and free play no matter what form of closure is plotted in any given play. (In *2 Henry IV* "the holiday-everyday antithesis is [Hal's] resource for control, and he makes it stick": p. 196.)

As the above account will have suggested, it is the Falstaff of *1*, not *2*, *Henry IV* who principally interests Barber. For him, both Carnival and Falstaff are merely placed on trial in *2 Henry IV*. Duly convicted, Falstaff falls properly under Henry's judgment. Indeed, Barber explicitly counsels against attending to Falstaff's "personal" (p. 218) feeling for Hal, the feeling that allows Hal to "kill his heart" (*Henry V*, 2.1.92). For Barber, the personal should be subordinated to larger considerations: Falstaff becomes the sacrificial scapegoat carrying away the "bad luck" of the previous reigns and allowing Hal a "fresh start" (p. 227). In the end, Barber's anthropological reading practically displaces *2 Henry IV* and "drama" along with it, while sacrifice emerges as the other face of festivity. By merging Falstaff wholly into his function,

Barber, unlike Shakespeare, banishes the "unpleasantness," not just of the play's ending, but of sacrificial politics in general: the objects sacrificed are invariably human ones.[22] Shakespeare allows that to be seen – and felt.

It has become a commonplace that "political Shakespeare" as we now understand him is as much a post-Vietnam product as the conformist Shakespeare was a Cold War product. The widespread political disaffection and skepticism produced by Vietnam, coupled, not just coincidentally, with the advent of critical theory (chiefly Marxist, deconstructive, and Foucauldian at first) produced an account of the "political" more disillusioned, consciously sophisticated, tough-talking, and uncircumscribed than had typically been the case in earlier Shakespeare studies.[23] An avowed commitment to radical critique and a corresponding anti-sentimentalism featured in all this criticism, although the real implications of both the radicalism and the anti-sentimentalism have remained in contention ever since. To go directly to what applies to *2 Henry IV*, however, I shall turn to the essay that did so much to launch the New Historicism and change the terms for discussion of the history plays, namely Greenblatt's "Invisible Bullets" (1994).[24]

The startling, counter-intuitive, and brilliantly sophisticated proposition of "Invisible Bullets" was that powerful cultures and/or political societies – power being given in advance – propagate and expand their power by *subverting* their own most cherished ideals and values – only to impose and disseminate them all the more relentlessly. "Indeed . . . subversiveness is the very product of . . . power, and furthers its ends" (Greenblatt 1994: 24) and "actions that should have the effect of radically undermining authority turn out to be the props of that authority" (p. 40). Having rehearsed subversion, so to speak, these powerful societies (e.g., England in the new world) can radically subvert the beliefs and ideals of those they set out to conquer (e.g., Native Americans) in order to fill with their own content the vacated space. Proto-ethnographic data-collection by imperialist conquerors, especially regarding the beliefs and values of native peoples, is conducted entirely in the service of containing and evacuating the Other.

The plays from *1 Henry IV* through *Henry V* not only reveal subversion/containment as the very model of early modern power production, but track a process of internal conquest that progressively incorporates all Others into the unitary political nation-state. Hal alone seems to have something approaching a cognitive grasp of these mechanisms, enabling him to exploit them more successfully than anyone else. Such are the devices of his ideal kingship, the charismatic theatrical show of which constitutes its only sacred substance.[25] No real distinction exists between theatre and state: Renaissance England *is* the theatre-state.

The arguments pursued by Greenblatt and other New Historicists (e.g., Tennenhouse 1986, 1994; Mullaney 1988; Goldberg 1983), have been sharply distinguished from those of Old Historicists, not only on grounds of their dark vision of power but of vastly increased sophistication regarding the nature of textuality and so-called cultural poetics. They have been distinguished as well on grounds of their skeptical understanding of the manipulable constructedness rather than givenness of

History. It will nevertheless be apparent that Greenblatt's account of the history plays not only shares with those of his predecessors the crucial impulse to take Shakespeare's representations of English history or destiny seriously, but recapitulates in more saturnine fashion the conservative, imperialistic accounts of those predecessors. In the end, the point for him is still "to understand Shakespeare's whole conception of Hal, from rakehell to monarch." Such understanding will now entail the adumbration of "a poetics of Elizabethan power" (Greenblatt 1994: 44).

Greenblatt follows Bradley in finding "the mood at the close . . . an unpleasant one – the rejection of Falstaff has been one of the nagging 'problems' of Shakespearean criticism" (p. 41). For Greenblatt, the explanation of the unpleasantness is, however, that the rejection again instantiates the subversion/containment dynamic of the play. This is Greenblatt's version of politics and its discontents. It is in *2 Henry IV* that the mechanisms at work become more fully exposed than they are in *1 Henry IV*. More precisely, subversion/containment emerges clearly in this play as the general structure of power, and less as Hal's own manipulative strategy. Hal thus becomes less a compromised agent and more a passive cipher than in the previous play. His action in banishing Falstaff accordingly becomes less "personal."

In "Invisible Bullets," then, *2 Henry IV* is no mere continuation of *1 Henry IV*: "there is manifestly a single system now, based on predation and betrayal" (Greenblatt 1994: 34–5). By invoking system, Greenblatt unobtrusively capitalizes on the poststructuralist legacy of diminished personal agency and increased structural determination to capture the particularity of *2 Henry IV*. If Falstaff is injured and the spectator left "frustrated" (p. 41) – if, indeed, Falstaff is betrayed by Prince Hal, as Greenblatt strongly puts it (p. 40) – that merely instantiates the effects of the system.

For Greenblatt, in short, the political Shakespeare is one who exposes a power (contingently English and Renaissance power) in the operations of which he fully participates. The legitimacy (or legitimation) of that power seems wholly beside the point. Dispensing with the feel-good arguments for which Hunter (1970: 13–14) mocked earlier critics, Greenblatt conspicuously bypasses the legitimation process of the plays, including the reconciliation between Hal and his father.

Initially, the most consequential counter-views to Greenblatt's were embodied in some ambitious rereadings of the history plays by feminist critics. The way for decisive feminist entry into the field of the history plays had been prepared by feminist theorists of the caliber of Jacqueline Rose (1985) and Catherine Belsey (1985), and by Boose's (1987) polemic directed at male New Historicists.[26] One of the first to enter was Rackin (1990), pursuing a metahistorical approach with a strong feminist orientation. Despite footnoting Greenblatt, she reclaims a good subversion for the women who speak (one in Welsh) in *1 Henry IV*. It appears, however, that Shakespeare "contrives his action to subvert the subversive female voices and ratify the masculine vision of the past" (p. 149). Regarding *2 Henry IV*, Rackin argues that in the Epilogue "the players defer to the economic power of their female customers and the authority of their queen, the present realities of female power and authority that hovered at the margins of their historical stage. In the central scene of historical representation, women have no place" (pp. 146–7). Rackin projects fully polarized sexual difference between "male" and "female" actors on the stage of history.

As part of a larger critique of prevailing feminist approaches to early modern texts, Goldberg's "Desiring Hal" (1992b) took aim at Rackin. (Hodgdon (1991), to whom I will turn shortly, wasn't cited.) From Goldberg's point of view, Rackin, along with many others, subscribes to an unexamined gender binarism manifesting itself in the belief that the only sexuality – or the only sexuality that counts, politically or otherwise – is normalized heterosexuality. What typically accompanies that belief, both in and out of feminist criticism, is a naturalized scenario of masculine "maturation" that relegates homosexuality to adolescence or tolerated "immaturity," but denies it any further recognition. Indeed, such criticism joins in the broader culture's heavy breathing as soon as "perversity" presumes to leave its adolescent enclosure and resist inscription within a normative, heterosexual telos.

For Goldberg, not only do these hetero-normative approaches reinstantiate a major form of historical oppression, but they also radically undermine the credibility of any claimed *historicizing* account of the history plays. Not just the history of gender but of sexuality (Foucault 1978; Bray 1982) must crucially inform any attempt to think through history. Additionally invoking Sedgwick's (1985) critique of homosociality, Goldberg (1992b) writes that "the plays forever transgress even as they seem to be producing the boundaries between legitimate and illegitimate male–male relations" (p. 161).

Accounting for Hal's appeal to feminist and non-feminist critics alike, Goldberg writes that

> [The plays'] project is to produce Hal as the legitimate son of his father, but, bypassing biology as the means to do so, this legitimizing project is . . . wholly allied to the artifices of image-production, the simulations of paternity based on similitude; this is the economy of narcissistic image-production – the production of an ego ideal – but not simply of uninflected sameness. (Ibid: 161)

In the course of his critique, Goldberg relocates the "unpleasantness" that is so much a leitmotif of *2 Henry IV* criticism. Following Empson, Goldberg finds it, not in the rejection of Falstaff, but in Shakespeare's performance of abjection *through* Falstaff, for which the trade-off is his identification with the prince. The Young Man sonnets supply the model. It follows, then, that Falstaff's desire, on which that of the reader "floats" (Goldberg 1992b: 162), is the desire to take abuse. Perhaps rejection *is* the payoff Falstaff unconsciously sets off to claim from the moment he hears of the king's death.

If weak sentimentality includes taking the pain of characters or readers unreflectively, at face value, Goldberg's approach must surely count as the most astringent one to date. He refuses to separate Falstaff's pain or the critics' from their pleasure and desire, or locate that pain outside a compensatory economy. What gives Goldberg's reading its closural power, however, is not just its methodological rigor and consistency, but its partially displacing importation of the sonnet scenario. This tight reframing changes the picture.

In almost concurrent work, Hodgdon (1991) capitalized on the evolving discourses of theory, including deconstruction, to present a strongly anti-closural account of the history plays, emphasizing their fractures, doublings, substitutions, and often indeterminate or unstable constructions of gendered identity.[27] *2 Henry IV* strongly contributes to this indeterminacy since, as Hodgdon notes (citing Calderwood (1979) and Berger (1987)), Rumor begins the play by revoking the narrative of royal victory at Shrewsbury in *1 Henry IV*, thereby plunging us into the world of "misreport" (Hodgdon 1991: 166) that constitutes the medium of History. Noting that the boundaries of the plays, and of the Shakespearean text in general, are weak, she locates forms of attempted closure in criticism and performance rather than in the texts. She accordingly reviews a wide range of theatrical productions that seek to impose (or sometimes resist) closure in the service of varying political agendas. In keeping with a growing trend in Shakespeare criticism, the performance history of the plays becomes integral to her critical argument. In performance, the ending of *2 Henry IV* can "be re-formed to neutralize or repress Falstaff's presence and so to manage the anxieties he represents" (p. 168). That strategy was adopted in the 1951 Redgrave production of the *Henriad*, for example, designed to uphold "the mythos of England as a unified whole, still powerful and powerfully intact" (p. 169). In contrast to her predecessors, Hodgdon avows the purpose of keeping the plays open to an undetermined future rather than treating them as texts in which historical options are steadily being foreclosed.

In its gendered aspect, Hodgdon's argument also capitalizes on the critique of homosociality launched by Sedgwick (1985). Referring to *1 Henry IV*, Hodgdon writes:

> In this extremely limited gender economy, structured by a desire for the male other that takes the form of aggression, women are positioned at history's margins . . . Only the rebel leaders . . . have wives, whose presence functions primarily to separate public from private domains and, by proving their husbands' heterosexuality, deflects the homoerotic into the homosocial. (Hodgdon 1991: 155)

In Goldberg's argument, of course, this "deflection" is far from complete.

For Hodgdon, Falstaff figures above all a destabilizing "semi-androgyny" (p. 157) in the plays' fluid circulation of roles, bodies, and personae. Following Traub (1989), she observes that "although . . . Falstaff figures as Hal's surrogate father, he is coded in feminine, maternal terms" (Hodgdon 1991: 155). His feminized Misrule exposes yet ultimately facilitates (through his rejection) the counterfeiting of masculine identity and reinstatement of exclusive patriarchal legitimacy in the plays.

Finally, Hodgdon observes that in *2 Henry IV* "the potential threats Carnival represents [to the exclusively masculine domain of royal power being re-formed in the play] are displaced on to the play's women. Beadles arrest Mistress Quickly and Doll Tearsheet" (p. 172). In short, women are multiply positioned and perform multiple functions in the history plays, but the bottom line is still polarized exclusion.

In their gender-historicizing collaboration, Howard and Rackin (1997) incorporate and consolidate much of this earlier feminist work while elaborating it in two principal directions. The first is that of foregrounding public and domestic sexual violence, both threatened and actual, against women in the plays' nation-centered representations. Although referring primarily to *Henry V*, the following comment bears on all the plays: "In the struggle for power between men of two nations, the sexualized bodies of women become a crucial terrain where this battle is played out" (p. 5). The second is that of focusing on women in their socioeconomic roles both in Shakespeare's plays and the broader culture.

This elaboration of a hint in Rackin's earlier discussion of the Epilogue to *2 Henry IV* necessarily directs attention to Eastcheap: "Mistress Quickly's tavern in Eastcheap is a plebeian, comic, theatrical – and strikingly contemporary – place that mirrors the disorderly push and shove of the theater itself. The women in the tavern are theatergoers, entrepreneurs, and purveyors of commercial sex" (p. 164). It is "the only place where non-aristocratic women enter the Shakespearean history play . . . [but] they can do so only on sexualized and criminalized terms" (p.180). No wonder the "feminized," transgressive, histrionic Falstaff finds himself at home there. It follows that, in *2 Henry IV*, "Hal's final rejection of Falstaff . . . produces a theatrical power purged of its feminine pollution" (p. 166). Howard and Rackin nevertheless wish to reclaim the alternative, oppositional energies of the women and their economic milieu. Indeed, the fact that Eastcheap is "strikingly contemporary" optimistically implies that it *has* prevailed over the plays' forces of masculine absolutism, and even over Shakespeare's own purification agendas. Finally, Laurie Shannon (2001) shifts the interpretive frame by examining the Hal–Falstaff relationship in the context of *mignonnerie*, the opprobrious term for too-personal relations between early modern sovereigns and their social inferiors.

Gloucestershire

Relative lack of critical attention to the Gloucestershire scenes reinforces whatever impression exists that those scenes (3.2, 5.1, 5.2) are a backwater in the play. Insofar as the scenes are so perceived, it is because Hal is separated from Falstaff, Gloucestershire is separated from the main scenes of action, and Shallow and Silence inhabit their own domain of rustic self-absorption.[28] More conspicuously than any others, these diversionary scenes make *2 Henry IV* a "holding action" pending the death of Henry IV and the accession of Henry V (Calderwood 1979: 134). When the news arrives in 5.2 of the king's death, Falstaff and his cronies don't linger in Gloucestershire but gallop post-haste to Westminster, the scene of action. Yet Gloucestershire isn't necessarily or only represented as a backwater in the play.

Since Knights (1959), these scenes have certainly been connected to the play's dominant motifs of passing time, sickness, and aging. Complicating that connection, Hunter (1978) characterized the Gloucestershire episodes as "senility's saturnalia" (p. 357). He thereby captured something of the complex doubleness Kerrigan (1990) later uncovered in these scenes: they at once manifest and resist the decline of festivity in the plays. Kerrigan further suggests that the version of pastoral these scenes invoke, with Shallow's "bullock[s] at Stamford Fair" (3.2.36) and "sow[ing] the headland with wheat" (5.1.12), is the Georgic: these are among "the activities thought to reflect as well as belong to a flourishing commonwealth" (p. 28).[29] The Gloucestershire scenes are thus arguably more "political" than the scenes dealing with centralized royal power and rebellion. Moreover, even without Falstaff's intrusive recruiting mission, Gloucestershire is not necessarily marginal to the play's larger national scene.

Rackin (1990: 24–5) notes that the emergence of chorography as a field of early modern knowledge gave studies of regions and localities a new importance, and offered an alternative to centralizing national/dynastic histories. Kerrigan (1990) observes, on the other hand, that "Gloucestershire was no backwater, it remained from the fourteenth to the seventeenth centuries a crossroads between North and West, with thriving ports and an affluent hinterland . . . nor should the post-Restoration tendency to find rural life inane obscure the importance of Shallow's farm" (p. 27). Concerning Shallow and Silence, Kerrigan makes the point that "Early audiences would have seen the pair as more than rustic babblers. The government of Elizabethan England extended power far from the center" (ibid).[30] Justices of the Peace represented that centralized power even if their positions enabled them to create their own local fiefdoms. Finally, the Gloucestershire scenes participate in the spatial multiplicity of the Henry IV plays – in the disparate worlds and languages the plays seek to encompass. Pugliatti (1996: 119–36) not only draws attention to the multi-directional "invasion" of discrete spaces in the play, but also reads the spread of "corruption" under the usurper Henry IV into the Gloucestershire world of unscrupulous military impressment and judicial favors. In work forthcoming, Patricia Cahill connects Falstaff's recruiting to broad changes in the "norms of manhood" in early modern England. Suffice to say that, even if not a locus of major critical attention, the Gloucestershire scenes have been placed on the critical map.

NOTES

1   Whether or not Kernan (1970) coined the term, his "The Henriad: Shakespeare's Major History Plays" certainly gave currency to it.

2   I shall even more completely bypass pre-Johnsonian (1765) discussion of whether or not Shakespeare's plays conform to the Rules of Drama (Hunter 1970: 11). I will merely note that Elizabeth Montagu (1769) made an important argument for waiving the rules in the case of the histories.

3   A survey that includes extensive review of Hal's "double reformation" (Hawkins 1982: 288–94), a topic foundationally discussed by Schell (1970) and addressed in Crewe (1990). Schell makes a point

of Shakespeare's transformation of the "folkloric" materials regarding the wild prince into drama. Hawkins argues that the double reformation is set up in *The Famous Victories of Henry V*.

4 My citations from the text of the play will be to this edition.

5 Or possibly in an Ur-play that preceded the two printed plays (Melchiori 1989: 12–13), or some other play.

6 For textual editors, the Oldcastle/Falstaff issue is connected to differences between two versions of the 1600 Quarto edition of *2 Henry IV*, and between those and the 1623 Folio edition (Weis 1998: 78–9). Shakespeare's puzzling transformation of the upstanding proto-Protestant martyr Sir John Oldcastle (1378–1417) into the monumentally disreputable Falstaff has speculatively been attributed to Elizabethan anti-Puritan sentiment. As Goldberg (1992a) summarizes: "The part involves Protestant posturing, claims to vocation, [and] biblical allusions all apt for Oldcastle" (p. 77).

7 Cognate name changes are those of Russell and Harvey to Bardolph and Peto. The name Sir John Falstaff is a transliteration of Sir John Fastolf (1378–1459), a historical contemporary of Oldcastle. For an extensive discussion of names in the play, see Weis (1998: 27–40) and Goldberg (1992a).

8 For an argument against this alleged restoration of what Shakespeare allegedly intended, see Goldberg (1992a: 76–8), who takes issue with Taylor's attachment to historical referentiality in the plays – an attachment some have recently begun to call Historical Correctness.

9 Despite or because of its markedly oedipal narrative, *2 Henry IV* has not become a *locus classicus* for psychoanalytic decoding, most of which is now "post-oedipal" in any case (see Lupton and Reinhard 1993). After Kris's (1952b) pioneering essay, the principal follow-up was Traub's (1989) Lacanian-feminist revision, in which Falstaff figures the preoedipal maternal domain to Hal. Goldberg's (1992b) account of Hal's ability to excite desire includes an important psychoanalytic component. Crewe (1992) touches on the play's oedipal narrative as a homosocial one. That Falstaff is a father surrogate is now a critical commonplace.

10 The obvious question, then, is why Shakespeare didn't or couldn't let him down lightly. Instead of wishing the unpleasantness away, many critics have treated it as a basic datum of the play. Stewart (1949) and Kris (1952a) inaugurate the view that the harsh rejection is a displacement of Henry's parricidal impulse towards his father. Hal can both be reconciled with his father and "kill" him in the person of Falstaff. The contexts for these claims are anthropological and psychoanalytic respectively.

11 Falstaff's uncontainable exorbitance figures centrally in later accounts of *2 Henry IV* by Calderwood (1979) and Bloom (1999).

12 The unprecedented bestseller success of Bloom's (1999) book, devoted to Shakespeare's "invention of the human," does, however, constitute something of an embarrassment for contemporary antihumanist critics.

13 *Pace* Leavis, we might speculate that Bradley's attitude owes more to a subjectivization of criticism successively pursued by Walter Pater and Oscar Wilde against Matthew Arnold's object-centered criticism than it does to any generalized sentimentality. Bloom (1999) situates himself in the same lineage.

14 Tillyard's *The Elizabethan World Picture* (1943) has, of course, been the primary target for a generation of critics. See, for example, Sanders (1968), Kelly (1970), Dollimore (1984), Dollimore and Sinfield (1994), Rackin (1990), Taylor (2001).

15 Since, as Hunter (1970: 14) notes, Tillyard's work derives from that of Lovejoy (1936) and Craig (1936), it might more appropriately be classified under history-of-ideas than history.

16 There is no need to imagine how repellent this approach would have been to Empson (1953): his essay speaks for itself.

17 In addition to comprehending practically all the manly virtues, Tillyard's Henry is Castiglione's courtier personified. His low-life escapades (of which Castiglione would surely have disapproved) enable him to "practice the regal touch among his inferiors" (Tillyard 1944: 281). Where *sprezzatura* fails, the lower orders can by subjugated by more brutal means, as in the prince's treatment

of Francis: "The subhuman element in the population must have been considerable in Shakespeare's day; that it should be treated almost like beasts was taken for granted" (p. 277).

18 Hodgdon mentions the practice of playing the English national anthem at the end of *1 Henry IV* performances from the late nineteenth century down through the 1950s.

19 Ornstein (1972) seriously begins to question this postwar trend.

20 A historically important discussion of the mingling of high and low in *2 Henry IV* appears in Auerbach (1953). See also Empson (1950: 27–88).

21 Differing in this respect from Bakhtin (1968), for whom the "carnivalesque" works against any such consolidation.

22 For Calderwood (1979) it is not Falstaff but Henry IV who must be sacrificed, and who accepts the fact, so that Hal can "look to the future" (p. 126).

23 This is not the place to attempt a general history of this change or of succeeding phases of critique and infighting. Few current readers of this essay will be unfamiliar at least with the outlines of this history and most will have participated in one phase or another.

24 First published in *Glyph* 8 (1981: 40–61), the essay was revised and republished in Dollimore and Sinfield (1994: 18–47), Bloom (1987: 125–50), and in Greenblatt (1988b: 21–65). I have used the 1994 version.

25 These provocative theses resulted in widespread debate about subversion/containment that still flares occasionally. For many, the issue has now been talked to death, however, and investment in the politics of subversion (a police term more than a revolutionary one) is not what it once was.

26 Insofar as the history plays show men trying to construct and defend an all-male world of power, rivalry, and bonding, Boose saw the same pattern being repeated in the work of New Historicist men.

27 See also Kerrigan (1990) for a virtuoso reading of doubling, duplicity, and counterfeiting in *2 Henry IV*.

28 For many readers these self-enclosed scenes are, however, the highlight of *2 Henry IV*, and they were invested with an almost magical aura by Orson Welles's (1966) film *Chimes at Midnight*. Kerrigan (1990) believes that "there is a warmth and quirky affirmation here far more confident than anything in Westminster" (p. 27).

29 Responding to diffuse suggestions that these generically anomalous scenes show affinities with the emergent genre of City Comedy, Melchiori (1989: 21–2) proposes Country Comedy as a more plausible designation.

30 The legibility of these scenes in an Elizabethan context can also, of course, make them seem anachronistic in the play's represented historical world.

References and Further Reading

Auerbach, E. (1953). *Mimesis*. Princeton, NJ: Princeton University Press.

Bakhtin, M. (1968). *Rabelais and His World*. Cambridge, MA: MIT Press.

Barber, C. L. (1959). Rule and Misrule in *Henry IV*. In *Shakespeare's Festive Comedy: A Study of Dramatic Form and its Relation to Social Custom*. New York: Meridian.

Barish, J. (1965). The Turning Away of Prince Hal. In D. Bevington (ed.) *Henry the Fourth Parts I and II: Critical Essays*. New York: Garland, 277–88.

Bate, J. (1989). *Shakespearean Constitutions: Politics, Theatre, Criticism, 1730–1830*. Oxford: Clarendon Press.

Belsey, C. (1985). Disrupting Sexual Difference: Meaning and Gender in the Comedies. In J. Drakakis (ed.) *Alternative Shakespeares*. New York: Methuen, 166–80.

Berger, H., Jr. (1987). Sneak's Noise, or Rumor and Detextualization in *2 Henry IV*. In H. Bloom (ed.) *2 Henry IV: Modern Critical Interpretations*. New York: Chelsea House, 105–24.

————(1991). On the Continuity of the *Henriad*: A Critique of Some Literary and Theatrical Approaches. In I. Kamps (ed.) *Shakespeare Left and Right*. New York: Routledge, 225–40.

Bevington, D. (ed.) (1986). *Henry the Fourth Parts I and II: Critical Essays*. New York: Garland.

Bloom, H. (ed.) (1987). *2 Henry IV: Modern Critical Interpretations*. New York: Chelsea House.

————(1999). *Shakespeare: The Invention of the Human*. New York: Riverhead.

Boose, L. (1987). The Family in Shakespeare Studies; or – Studies in the Family of Shakespeareans; or – The Politics of Politics. *Renaissance Quarterly*, 40, 4, 707–42.

Bradley, A. C. (1902). The Rejection of Falstaff. In D. Bevington (ed.) *Henry the Fourth Parts I and II: Critical Essays*. New York: Garland, 77–99.

Bray, A. (1982). *Homosexuality in Renaissance England*. London: Gay Men's Press.

Cain, H. E. (1952). Further Light on the Relation of 1 and 2 *Henry IV*. *Shakespeare Quarterly*, 3, 21–38.

Calderwood, J. L. (1979). *Metadrama in Shakespeare's Henriad*. Berkeley: University of California Press.

Campbell, L. B. (1947). *Shakespeare's "Histories": Mirrors of Elizabethan Policy*. San Marino, CA: Huntington Library.

Charlton, H. B. (1929). *Shakespeare: Politics and Politicians*. Oxford: Oxford University Press.

Craig, H. (1936). *The Enchanted Glass: The Elizabethan Mind in Literature*. New York: Oxford University Press.

Crewe, J. (1990). Reforming Prince Hal: The Sovereign Inheritor in 2 *Henry IV*. *Renaissance Drama*, n.s. 21, 225–42.

————(ed.) (1992). *Reconfiguring the Renaissance: Essays in Critical Materialism*. Lewisburg, PA: Bucknell University Press.

Danby, J. F. (1949). *Shakespeare's Doctrine of Nature: A Study of King Lear*. London: Faber and Faber.

De Grazia, M. (1991). *Shakespeare Verbatim: The Reproduction of Authenticity and the 1790 Apparatus*. New York: Oxford University Press.

Dobson, M. (1992). *The Making of the National Poet: Shakespeare, Adaptation and Authorship, 1660–1769*. Oxford: Clarendon Press.

Dollimore, J. (1984). *Radical Tragedy: Religion, Ideology, and Power in the Drama of Shakespeare and his Contemporaries*. Chicago, IL: University of Chicago Press.

Dollimore, J. and Sinfield, A. (eds.) (1994). *Political Shakespeare: Essays in Cultural Materialism*. Ithaca, NY: Cornell University Press.

Drakakis, J. (ed.) (1985). *Alternative Shakespeares*. New York: Methuen.

Empson, W. (1950). Double Plots. In *Some Versions of Pastoral*. London: Chatto and Windus, 27–88.

————(1953). Falstaff and Mr. Dover Wilson. In G. K. Hunter (ed.) *Shakespeare: Henry IV Parts I and II. A Casebook*. London: Macmillan, 135–54.

Foucault, M. (1978). *The History of Sexuality*, vol. 1, trans. R. Hurley. New York: Pantheon Books.

Goldberg, J. (1983). *James I and the Politics of Literature: Jonson, Shakespeare, Donne, and their Contemporaries*. Baltimore, MD: Johns Hopkins University Press.

————(1992a). The Commodity of Names: "Falstaff" and "Oldcastle" in 1 *Henry IV*. In J. Crewe (ed.) *Reconfiguring the Renaissance: Essays in Critical Materialism*. Lewisburg, PA: Bucknell University Press, 76–88.

————(1992b). Desiring Hal. In *Sodometries: Renaissance Texts, Modern Sexualities*. Stanford, CA: Stanford University Press, 145–78.

Greenblatt, S. (ed.) (1988a). *Representing the English Renaissance*. Berkeley: University of California Press.

————(1988b). *Shakespearean Negotiations: The Circulation of Social Energy in Renaissance England*. Berkeley: University of California Press.

————(1994). Invisible Bullets: Renaissance Authority and Its Subversion in *Henry IV* and *Henry V*. In J. Dollimore and A. Sinfield (eds.) *Political Shakespeare: Essays in Cultural Materialism*. Ithaca, NY: Cornell University Press, 18–47.

Hawkins, S. (1982). *Henry IV*: The Structural Problem Revisited. *Shakespeare Quarterly*, 33, 3, 278–301.

Hazlitt, W. (1817). *Henry IV in Two Parts*. In D. Bevington (ed.) (1986) *Henry the Fourth Parts I and II: Critical Essays*. New York: Garland, 55–64.

Hodgdon, B. (1991). *The End Crowns All: Closure and Contradiction in Shakespeare's History Plays*. Princeton, NJ: Princeton University Press.

Howard, J. (ed.) (1997). *The Second Part of Henry the Fourth. The Norton Shakespeare: Histories*, ed. W. Cohen, J. Howard, and K. Eisaman Maus. New York: Norton.

Howard, J. and Rackin, P. (1997). *Engendering a Nation: A Feminist Account of Shakespeare's English Histories*. New York: Routledge.

Hunter, G. K. (1954). *Henry IV* and the Elizabethan Two-Part Play. *Review of English Studies*, n.s. 5, 236–48.

———(1955). Shakespeare's Politics and the Rejection of Falstaff. *Critical Quarterly*, 1, 1–15.

———(ed.) (1970). *Shakespeare: Henry IV Parts I and II. A Casebook*. London: Macmillan.

Hunter, R. G. (1978). Shakespeare's Comic Sense as it Strikes us Today: Falstaff and the Protestant Ethic. In D. Bevington (ed.) (1986) *Henry the Fourth Parts I and II: Critical Essays*. New York: Garland, 55–64.

Jenkins, H. (1956). The Structural Problem in Shakespeare's *Henry IV*. In G. K. Hunter (ed.) *Shakespeare: Henry IV Parts I and II. A Casebook*. London: Macmillan, 155–73.

Johnson, S. (1765). The First Part of *King Henry IV*, and The Second Part of *King Henry IV*. In H. R. Woudhuysen (1989) *Samuel Johnson on Shakespeare*. Harmondsworth: Penguin Books, 195–200.

Kamps, I. (1991). *Shakespeare Left and Right*. New York: Routledge.

Kelly, H. A. (1970). *Providence in the England of Shakespeare's Histories*. Cambridge, MA: Harvard University Press.

Kernan, A. (ed.) (1970). The Henriad: Shakespeare's Major History Plays. In *Modern Shakespearean Criticism: Essays on Style, Dramaturgy and the Major Plays*. New York: Harcourt, Brace and World, 245–78.

Kerrigan, J. (1990). *Henry IV* and the Death of Old Double. *Essays in Criticism*, 40, 1, 24–53.

Knights, L. C. (1959). Time's Subjects: The Sonnets and *King Henry IV, Part 2*. In *Some Shakespearean Themes*. London: Chatto and Windus, 45–64.

Kris, E. (1952a). Prince Hal's Conflict. In *Psychoanalytic Explorations in Art*. New York: International Universities Press, 273–90.

———(1952b). *Psychoanalytic Explorations in Art*. New York: International Universities Press.

Leavis, F. R. (1962). Diabolical Intellect and the Noble Hero. In *The Common Pursuit*. Harmondsworth: Penguin Books, 136–59.

Lovejoy, A. (1936). *The Great Chain of Being: A Study of the History of an Idea*. Cambridge, MA: Harvard University Press.

Lupton, J. and Reinhard, K. (1993). *After Oedipus: Shakespeare in Psychoanalysis*. Ithaca, NY: Cornell University Press.

Melchiori, G. (ed.) (1989). *The Second Part of King Henry IV*. Cambridge: Cambridge University Press.

Montagu, E. (1769). *Essay on the Writings and Genius of Shakespeare, Compared with the Greek*. In D. Bevington (ed.) (1986) *Henry the Fourth Parts I and II: Critical Essays*. New York: Garland, 9–14.

Morgann, M. (1777). An Essay on the Dramatic Character of Sir John Falstaff. In G. K. Hunter (ed.) (1970) *Shakespeare: Henry IV Parts I and II. A Casebook*. London: Macmillan, 24–55.

Mullaney, S. (1988). Strange Things, Gross Terms, Curious Customs: The Rehearsal of Cultures in the Late Renaissance. In S. Greenblatt (ed.) *Representing the English Renaissance*. Berkeley: University of California Press, 82–9.

Ornstein, R. (1972). *A Kingdom for a Stage: The Achievement of Shakespeare's History Plays*. Cambridge, MA: Harvard University Press.

Pugliatti, P. (1996). *Shakespeare the Historian*. New York: St. Martin's Press.

Rackin, P. (1990). *Stages of History: Shakespeare's English Chronicles*. Ithaca, NY: Cornell University Press.

Reese, M. M. (1961). *The Cease of Majesty: A Study of Shakespeare's History Plays*. New York: St Martin's Press.

Rose, J. (1985). Sexuality in the Reading of Shakespeare: *Hamlet* and *Measure for Measure*. In J. Drakakis (ed.) (1985) *Alternative Shakespeares*. New York: Methuen, 119–43.

Sanders, W. (1968). *The Dramatist and the Received Idea*. Cambridge: Cambridge University Press.

Schell, E. T. (1970). Prince Hal's Second Reformation. *Shakespeare Quarterly*, 21, 11–16.

Sedgwick, E. K. (1985). *Between Men: English Literature and Male Homosocial Desire*. New York: Columbia University Press.

Shaaber, M. (1948). The Unity of *Henry IV*. *Joseph Quincy Adams Memorial Lectures*. Washington, DC: Folger Library, 217–27.

Shannon, L. (2001). *Sovereign Amity*. Chicago, IL: University of Chicago Press.

Sinfield, A. and Dollimore, J. (eds.) (1994). *Political Shakespeare: Essays in Cultural Materialism*. New York: Cornell University Press.

Stewart, J. I. M. (1949). *Character and Motive in Shakespeare's Plays*. London: Longmans, Green.

——(1970). The Birth and Death of Falstaff. In G. K. Hunter (ed.) *Shakespeare: Henry IV Parts I and II. A Casebook*. London: Macmillan, 127–34.

Taylor, G. (1985). The Fortunes of Oldcastle. *Shakespeare Survey*, 38, 85–100.

Taylor, G., Wells, S., Jowett, J., and Montgomery, W. (eds.) (1986). *The Oxford Shakespeare: The Complete Works*. Oxford: Clarendon Press.

Taylor, M. (2001). *Shakespeare Criticism in the Twentieth Century*. Oxford: Clarendon Press.

Tennenhouse, L. (1986). *Power on Display: The Politics of Shakespeare's Genres*. New York: Methuen.

——(1994). Strategies of State and Political Plays: *A Midsummer Night's Dream, Henry IV, Henry V, Henry VIII*. In J. Dollimore and A. Sinfield (eds.) *Political Shakespeare: Essays in Cultural Materialism*. Ithaca, NY: Cornell University Press, 109–28.

Tillyard, E. M. W. (1943). *The Elizabethan World Picture: A Study of the Idea of Order in the Age of Shakespeare*. London: Chatto and Windus.

——(1944). *Shakespeare's History Plays*. New York: Macmillan.

Traub, V. (1989). Prince Hal's Falstaff: Positioning Psychoanalysis and the Female Reproductive Body. *Shakespeare Quarterly*, 40, 4, 456–74.

Upton, J. (1750). *Critical Observations on Shakespeare*. Cited in H. Jenkins (1956) "The Structural Problem in Shakespeare's *Henry IV*," p. 155.

Veeser, H. A. (ed.) (1989). *The New Historicism*. New York: Routledge.

Weis, R. (ed.) (1998). *Henry IV, Part 2*. Oxford: Clarendon Press.

Wilson, J. D. (1943). The Falstaff Myth. In *The Fortunes of Falstaff*. Cambridge: Cambridge University Press.

Woudhuysen, H. R. (1989). *Samuel Johnson on Shakespeare*. Harmondsworth: Penguin Books.

Young, D. P. (ed.) (1968). *Twentieth Century Interpretations of "Henry IV, Part II."* Englewood Cliffs, NJ: Prentice-Hall.

22

Henry V

Andrew Hadfield

In the chorus to *Every Man in His Humour* Jonson launched into a concerted attack on Shakespeare's histories, which, he claimed, could be classified as the work of a "poetaster," lacking serious moral purpose, designed to please the multitude rather than serve a serious, corrective moral purpose, and violating the rules of mimesis and classical decorum:

> Though need make many Poets, and some such
> As art, and nature have not bettered much;
> Yet ours, for want, hath not so much loved the stage,
> As he dare serve th'ill customs of the age:
> Or purchase your delight at such a rate,
> As, for it, he himself must justly hate.
> To make a child, now, swaddled to proceed
> Man, threescore years: or, with three rusty swords,
> And help of some few foot-and-half foot words,
> Fight over York, and Lancaster's long jars:
> And in the tiring-house bring wounds, to scars.
> He rather prays, you will be pleased to see
> One such, to-day, as other plays should be.
> Where neither Chorus wafts you o'er the seas;
> Nor creaking throne comes down, the boys to please. (Chorus, lines 1–16)

The Chorus that "wafts you o'er the seas" is a reference to the Chorus to act 5 of *Henry V*, in which Shakespeare urged his audience to follow the action of the play: "Now we bear the King / Toward Calais: grant him there; there seen, / Heave him away upon your winged thoughts / Athwart the sea" (lines 6–9), and imagine the assembled English ranks returning to their native land.[1]

It is hard to know how serious Jonson's strictures of Shakespeare were meant to be: after all, he praised Shakespeare fulsomely after his death. The attack on Shakespeare's histories – one he sustained in other works such as *The Devil is an Ass* (1616) (Kastan 2001: 173) – shows that Jonson thought they were inauthentic, designed to pander to the basest instincts of the theatre audience and could not even deliver what they promised (three rusty swords and bombastic speeches failing to capture the essence of the protracted Wars of the Roses). Given that the play was dedicated to William Camden, author of *Britannia* (1587), Jonson's former history teacher, who was regarded by many as the most serious historian to emerge in Elizabeth and James's reigns (Trevor-Roper 1971), the strength of the public insult aimed at Shakespeare can be gauged.[2]

Jonson's attack shows that Shakespeare's histories, and *Henry V* in particular, were controversial works from their very first performances and that they existed within a critical tradition of debate and argument centered on the staging of English history, its significance and meaning. *Henry V*, as is well known, has aroused serious debate, especially in the twentieth century. On the one hand, it has been cast as Shakespeare's contribution to English patriotism, a gung-ho drama enshrined in the famous Rank Organisation film version of 1944 starring Laurence Olivier (Davies 2000: 164–70).[3] On the other hand, it has often been read as a work which is sharply critical of the patriotic ambitions of its subject, and the methods he uses to secure his goal of conquering France.[4]

Recent productions, representations, and discussions of the play have been equally divided. In many ways Kenneth Branagh's 1989 film version inverts the values and attitudes of Olivier's, stressing the horror and cost of war, and replacing the heroic glory of the 1944 version of the Battle of Agincourt with "a grimy, decidedly unheroic mud-laden battle scene" (Crowl 2000: 228; Holderness 2001: ch. 4). However, the film does not challenge Henry's status in every way and leaves the viewer with the clear understanding that Henry is an ambiguous figure, part tyrant and part noble Christian king. It is an indication of the impact of *Henry V* as a modern popular phenomenon – Branagh's film, for example, has been credited with "spark[ing] a revival of the creative and commercial interest in Shakespeare as a source for films" (Crowl 2000: 222) – that John Sutherland and Cedric Watts should entitle their popular collection of pithy essays on Shakespearean conundrums, *Henry V, War Criminal? & Other Shakespeare Puzzles* (Sutherland and Watts 2000). It is equally pertinent that in the title essay, John Sutherland should come down on Henry's side, arguing that his orders to kill the French prisoners were either not fully obeyed because they were given in the heat of battle, or applied only to the lower-class prisoners, "And who cares about them? as well shed tears for the dead horses festering in Agincourt's fields" (ibid: 116). But in the following essay, "Henry V's claim to France: valid or invalid?," Cedric Watts argues that Henry did not have a legitimate claim to France, meaning that his triumphs would have been regarded ironically by the audience who know that "it all came to nothing" (p. 125).

One further example will indicate the complexity of recent responses to the play. While many academics seem to be consciously reacting to the nationalistic fervor productions of the play were designed to inspire when it was staged or filmed in the middle years of the last century, recent stage experiments indicate that theatre audiences read *Henry V* as a celebration of English patriotic triumphs.[5] When *Henry V* was staged at the New Globe Theatre in 1997, as an attempt to return to the original conditions under which Shakespeare's plays were performed, the audience responded to Henry's campaign as if they were part of his assembled army. The French soldiers were booed and hissed, while the English army were enthusiastically supported, especially at key moments in the play such as the "tennis ball scene":

> King Henry, seated on his throne in the authority position in front of the central opening, would encourage the audience to support him in his confrontation with the French ambassador with a slight movement of the head. When Henry stood up and dextrously juggled three of the balls in the air to turn the gesture of humiliation on its head the playgoers cheered. (Kiernan 1999: 54)

The audience's reading of *Henry V* is especially intriguing given that reconstructing the conditions of the theatre in Shakespeare's time made the stage darker than modern audiences are used to, and so placed more emphasis on what was said than on what was seen (ibid: 5). Equally, however, it might be argued that so strong is the patriotic interpretation of the play on the modern theatregoer's imagination that this was one ingrained belief that the experiments at the New Globe could do little to shift.

It is hard to solve the riddle of *Henry V* and I suspect that it will never be satisfactorily resolved whether Henry is meant to inspire our devotion or contempt. Of course, it is likely that he is supposed to do both, as Kenneth Branagh's film suggests. However, if Andrew Gurr is right that the First Quarto of the play (1600) is not a "bad quarto" based on the memorial reconstruction of an actor, but a record of the first run of performances, then perhaps we should concede that the New Globe audience are indeed recreating the first audience's probable responses to the play.[6] As Gurr points out:

> The underlying emphasis of the changes is . . . to intensify Henry's heroism and to play down the setbacks to his campaign. From the opening where the whole scene between the two bishops is cut, so that the exposition of the case for Henry's title to the French crown becomes less an expedient tactic on Canterbury's part than an open statement of a good legal case, through Henry's royal "we" and the later elimination of references to his rejection of Falstaff, the Q text affirms the depersonalised rightness of war. (Gurr 2000: 22)

It is possible that the choruses, which undoubtedly direct and qualify our conception of the play, were not heard on stage until the eighteenth century (ibid: ix; Pugliatti 1996: 148–53; Williams 1969). The evidence of the First Quarto suggests that Shakespeare's play, whatever the intentions of the author himself, resembled the stirringly patriotic *Famous Victories of Henry V* (published in 1598), rather than qualified or complicated that popular play's representation of the king's life, as the Folio text of Shakespeare's play undoubtedly does (Corbin and Sedge 1991).

Such issues raise the problem of texts and which one should be used and why. Should we try to recover what the author intended – insofar as we can reconstruct this aim; should we try and analyze the text as it was performed, a solution that many contemporary bibliographers and critics favor; or should we try and analyze the different forms of the texts that we have, accepting that each version plays a different role in the world of early modern literature?[7] My suggestion is that we can, as often as not, recover what Shakespeare's working text was and that we should not simply abandon our critical faculties and assert that every text is equally valuable as a material object. As Richard Dutton has argued it is likely that Shakespeare's texts did circulate as manuscripts among a coterie audience, and that they seem to bear the status of works produced by an important author. Many of the texts are obviously too long to be conveniently staged and so must have existed as texts to be read, eventually appearing in the 1623 Folio (*Hamlet* being the most obvious example of this process (Irace 1998)). Whether they were intended as reading texts or were simply failed dramatic texts is a further question to be considered. Shakespeare may not have actually published his texts himself as Ben Jonson did, probably because he was "a company man," but the fact that so many manuscripts found their way into circulation suggests that their release to a wider public was deliberate and that Shakespeare had a clear sense of himself as an author, an identity as a writer distinct from – albeit related to – his identity as a working dramatist (Dutton 1997).[8]

The point that needs to be made is that we have to use our judgment when deciding how to interpret a complex and alien tradition of textual production and circulation. Although determining the status of the authorship of dramatic – but not poetic – works is problematic and sometimes impossible, it does not follow that we should assume that authors did not exist as we know them.[9] Furthermore, we should be skeptical of any claim that employing the notion of "intention" signals a reactionary approach to the politics of literature, and denying its use as a heuristic tool signals a radical approach.[10] Getting rid of the author, as often as not, gets rid of the politics of the text, whatever the intentions of the critic. If I am right, then it is plausible that the authorial text of *Henry V* was a challenging or even a radical work, which was extremely skeptical about the rights and actions of kings, whereas the performance text, produced by the theatrical company, presumably after extended discussion, rehearsal, and cooperation, was more straightforward and politically safe.

In this essay I will provide a reading of the Folio (what I have assumed to be the authorial) text of *Henry V* in terms of its historical and political context. I shall concentrate on Shakespeare's exploration of the concept of legitimate sovereignty at the very end of Elizabeth's long reign, the last years of the Tudor dynasty.[11] I make no attempt to provide a comprehensive analysis of a complex work – I have included little on Henry's wooing of Katherine, for example, owing to pressures of space. Rather, my aim is to suggest one way of reading the play in the light of the successes and failures of a scholarly and critical tradition.

Shakespeare's representation of kings in all his history plays is governed by the understanding that it is what kings do rather than what they are or claim to be that is important. That genealogical arguments are given little weight in the histories can be seen at the start of *Henry V*, which, for the first time, represents a conspicuously successful king. The opening scene shows the Archbishop of Canterbury and the Bishop of Ely debating how to persuade Henry to abandon a bill passed in his father's reign that would seize all the temporal wealth of the church.[12] The bishops praise the king for his newly acquired religious devotion and wisdom, and convince themselves that he can be made to listen to reason and they will not have to face the awful prospect of losing half their revenue. The lines "Turn him to any cause of policy, / The Gordian knot of it will he unloose" (1.1.45–6) seem to disclose the central issues of Henry's approach to the monarchy. The Gordian knot, tied by Gordius, the father of Midas, was proverbial for being impossible to untie, and it was prophesied that whoever managed to unloose it would rule Asia. Alexander the Great simply cut the knot with his sword. Henry is here implicitly compared to Alexander, the greatest conqueror of the ancient world, a prophetic allusion to what Henry will achieve in France and his reputation as the most successful warrior king in English history, and an allusion repeated later in the play (3.1.19; 4.7.12–40) (Herman 1995: 219–20). But do the Archbishop's words indicate that Henry is able to go beyond Alexander and untie the most complex knots; or do they indicate that Henry, like Alexander, chooses to cut through them and use whatever information there is at his disposal to support the claims he would have made anyway? The comparison of Henry to Alexander – and by the head of the church – is double-edged. Alexander was admired for his military prowess, but notorious for his cruelty and the fact that he had apparently learnt very little from having been taught by Aristotle.[13] Henry has undergone a different but equally important education in *Henry IV, 1* and *2* through his dissolute life with the rogues in the Eastcheap Tavern. His behavior in France will show him to be a ruthless leader like Alexander or, even, the other famous conqueror of Asia, Tamburlaine, whose story had been one of the great dramatic successes of the 1590s.[14]

The conversation further heightens the importance – as well as the irony – of these lines. The Archbishop's calculation that the king will be inclined to their cause if they support his claims to France and his intention to "give a greater sum / Than ever at one time the clergy yet / Did to his predecessors part withall" (79–81) shows that he understands the world of political reality astutely, as his earlier use of the machiavellian term "policy" indicates (Raab 1965: ch. 3). The plan to give the money to Henry suggests that the decision to reveal "The severals and unhidden passages / Of his true titles to some certain dukedoms, / And generally to the crown and seat of France, / Derived from Edward, his great-grandfather" (86–9), is a cynical maneuver that mirrors Henry's designs for personal and national aggrandizement. The church and the king speak the same political language.

In scene 2 Henry asks the Archbishop to expound his right to France, warning him that he must convince the king that his cause is just given the high stakes of Henry's claim and the fearful consequences that will ensue:

> For never two such kingdoms did contend
> Without much fall of blood, whose guiltless drops
> Are every one a woe, a sore complaint
> 'Gainst him whose wrongs gives edge unto the swords
> That makes such waste in brief mortality. (1.2.24–8)

Henry is effectively transferring the guilt of the campaign on to the advisers, making it clear that if he succeeds he will accept the glory himself, but if he fails then others can take the blame, a characteristic strategy (Herman 1995). In a lengthy and intricate speech (62 lines) the Archbishop explains that the French have unjustly assumed that the Salic Law stipulating that "No woman shall succeed in Salic land" (39) applies to the whole realm of France, whereas the law really only applies to certain German principalities.[15] Hence Henry can claim his title through his descent from Edward III, who was the son of Isabella, the daughter of Philip IV of France. However, it is noticeable that the Archbishop does not state the actual claim itself and appeals instead to the "warlike spirit" of Henry's great-uncle, Edward the Black Prince, and his victories over the French at the Battle of Crécy (1346) (103–10). The subsequent rallying cries by nobles and churchmen reveals a series of interchangeable bellicose sentiments and arguments (115–35).

It is hard to take Henry's claim seriously, especially when read alongside the bogus claims to crowns made throughout the first tetralogy – significantly enough, staging the bloody course of English history after Henry's death – and given the motives of the prelates supporting the campaign. There is a bitterly comic element to Henry's claims to France on the grounds of their usurpation, given his dubious right to the English crown, acknowledged at key points in the play (Sutherland and Watts 2000: 117–25). The invocation of the Salic Law by the French and the pious English desire to negate its use cannot but seem ironic given the exclusion of Mary, Queen of Scots from her rightful succession, or the wealth of criticism against the female monarch on the grounds of her sex's natural unsuitability for government (McLaren 1999). Furthermore, as the play makes increasingly clear, Henry's success in uniting the four nationalities of Britain, explicitly signaled in the scenes containing Fluellen, Gower, Jamy, and Macmorris (3.2; 3.6) after the Siege of Harfleur and before the Battle of Agincourt, depends on a successful foreign war and is radically unstable (Edwards 1979: 74–86; Jardine 1996: 7–11). The Chorus's admission that the achievements of Henry came to nothing with the advent of his son – "Whose state so many had the managing / That they lost France and made his England bleed, / Which oft our stage hath shown" (Epilogue, 11–13) – is a sharp reminder of the insubstantial nature of Henry's success, and an anticlimax after the bellicosity of the prologues to each act, the fabulous victories against all odds, and the carefully negotiated marriage alliance and peace treaty (Herman 1995: 207, 219; Corbin and Sedge 1991: 21–8). Exactly like Alexander the Great's empire, in fact, which broke up when he died, prematurely (Henry was 34 when he died; Alexander, 32) (Mossman 1994).

One of the key images recurring throughout *Henry V*, as in many of the other history plays, is that of the king as player/actor. In *2 Henry IV* Hal/Henry had appropriated his father's crown, mistakenly thinking that the king was dead, and asserted: "My due from thee is this imperial crown, / Which, as immediate from thy place and blood, / Derives itself to me" (4.5.41–3). The obvious irony of these lines is spelt out when Henry wakes up and Henry IV makes his last speech to his son, pointing out what care and trouble the crown has caused him because "It seemed in me / But as an honour snatch'd with boist'rous hand" (190–1). Henry hopes for better things for Hal but comments that "all my reign hath been but as a scene / Acting that argument" (198–9), and he dies in the pretend landscape of the chamber called "Jerusalem" to complete his performance. Henry hopes that his son will be a real rather than a pretend king:

> To thee it shall descend with better quiet,
> Better opinion, better confirmation;
> For all the soil of the achievement goes
> With me into the earth. (188–91)

Henry's hopes of having dug and manured the ground ready for his son to rule properly refer back to the imagery of gardening prevalent throughout *Richard II* (Spurgeon 1965: 220–3). However, such natural imagery ceased to be relevant once Henry had deposed Richard and the image of the king as actor assumed center-stage throughout the tetralogy. Henry IV's hope that he has established a dynasty proves as delusive as his hope that he will lead a crusade (the real "crusade" turns out to be against the French). His need to justify his rule by ceaselessly playing the role of king is a performative burden he bequeathes to his heir. Monarchs who have no natural right to rule – i.e., no English monarchs after Richard – have to prove themselves worthy of the people's support, endlessly playing a part (Rackin 1990: 71–2, 78). Henry's reputation as a king, as the chronicles available to Shakespeare made clear, was not based on the truth or falsity of his claim, which Shakespeare's play appears to treat as bogus, but on the purpose and success of his war in France and establishment of a secure peace.

Henry V is replete with scenes that reflect on the problem of the nation and its political identity, from the opening comments of the Chorus and the machinations of the bishops to the final scene with its descriptions of France devastated by war, followed by the misunderstandings and broken macronic dialogue of Henry and Katherine (Neill 1994; McEachern 1996: ch. 3; Baker 1997: ch. 1; Jardine 1996: 10–12). A key exchange takes place when Henry, repeating the class transposition of his youth, disguises himself as a common soldier and mingles with three of his soldiers, John Bates, Alexander Court, and Michael Williams, at dawn before the Battle of Agincourt, a scene that has no precedent in any of the sources. Henry introduces the question of the identity of the king, having suggested that the English commanders think they are doomed to defeat in combat. Henry argues that

> The King is but a man, as I am: the violet smells to him as it doth to me; all his senses
> have but human conditions; his ceremonies laid by, in his nakedness he appears but a
> man; and though his affections are higher mounted than ours, yet when they stoop they
> stoop with the like wing. Therefore when he sees reason of fears as we do, his fears, out
> of doubt, be of the same relish as ours are. Yet, in reason, no man should possess him
> with any appearance of fear, lest he, by showing it, should dishearten his army.
> (4.1.101–12).

The sentiments are meant to appear democratic and egalitarian, but are actually
authoritarian. Henry's argument is: the king has to lead the army; the king is a man
like the men in his army; all these men feel fear; therefore, no one should show any
fear as it will prevent the king from leading the army. The implication is clearly that
no one ought to question the king, a point made clearly when the disguised Henry
asserts that he would willingly die for the king, "his cause being just and quarrel honourable" (127–8). Williams responds, "That's more than we know" (129) (but,
arguably, less than the audience does).

As the opening exchange in the play demonstrates, Henry's war with France is
based on questionable grounds and is in fact justified as a means of thwarting the
demands of parliament, the elected body designed to represent the people.[16] Henry
has to rely on Williams, Bates, and Court to fight his wars, but he is effectively invoking the social analysis of Sir Thomas Smith, one of the key political theorists of
Elizabethan England in his influential *De Republica Anglorum* (published 1583, but in
circulation from 1565). Smith divided society initially into two sorts of people: those
"that beare office, the other of them that beare none: the first are called magistrates,
the second private men" (Smith 1972: 30–1). He further divides English society into
a hierarchy of four classes: gentlemen (including the king and nobles), citizens,
yeoman artificers, and laborers (p. 31). Only the fourth sort or class, who include "day
labourers, poore husbandmen, yea marchantes or retailers which have no free lande,
copiholders, and all artificers, as Taylers, Shoomakers, Carpenters, Brickemakers,
Masons, &c," cannot become magistrates. Smith is somewhat ambivalent about their
political role: "These have no voice nor authoritie in our common wealth, and no
account is made of them but onelie to be ruled, not to rule other, and yet they be not
altogether neglected" (p. 46). Smith does not endorse this confused situation, merely
describes it (McLaren 1999: 210–11).

This scene in *Henry V* could have been written with Smith's words in mind.
Although it is not stated what Williams, Bates, and Court do when they are not
soldiers, they clearly belong to this fourth class, the class that Machiavelli argued
produced the best soldiers (Machiavelli 1560: 44). And it might also be argued
that Henry does what Smith suggests a ruler should do in refusing to neglect men
who otherwise do not feature in the political landscape by moving among them before
the battle. However, Henry is there to persuade them to fight loyally and to learn
how to be a successful military commander, as manuals on military science urged
(Machiavelli 1560: 80–1). We are always aware that we are not seeing an ideal of

England, but England organized for military success. Henry's attention to the arguments of the men he commands is only partial, and he evades key issues, trying to manipulate them to follow his line of reasoning. Bates and Williams point out that the cause of war must be honorable, or else the crimes of war will be the king's responsibility and weigh on his conscience. Williams comments:

> But if the cause be not good, the King himself hath a heavy reckoning to make when all those legs and arms and heads chopped off in a battle shall join together at the latter day and cry all: "we died at such a place", some swearing, some crying for a surgeon, some upon their wives left poor behind them, some upon the debts they owe, some upon their children . . . Now if these men do not die well it will be black matter for the King, that led them to it, who to disobey were against all proportion of subjection. (134–46)

Williams represents the king as responsible for the fate of his army on the Day of Judgment, a theological image that, once again, reflects no credit on the bishops who supported Henry's claims for their own ends, and stands in pointed contrast to Henry's attempts to remove the hierarchies between rulers and subjects. Henry's response to Williams misses the point. Henry argues that the king should not be held responsible for the afterlife of his subjects should they die sinfully for his cause (147–84). Henry is right, but his argument only serves to emphasize the cynical manner in which the common people have been used by the church and their leaders who are prepared to risk their deaths in a cause of dubious justice. As Williams notes in the last line cited above, subjects are not permitted to disobey and, for all the horizontal bonds formed here between men at war, the king still rules and leads his men into battle. The scene can be read as a carnivalesque interlude in the progress of war. As in another play which deals, albeit less explicitly, with Henry's French campaign, Thomas Dekker's *The Shoemaker's Holiday* (1599), the horrors of war can only briefly be suspended (Dekker 1990: xvii–xxv). When Williams and Henry exchange gloves as a sign that they will fight a duel if they survive the battle, Bates urges them to "Be friends, you English fools, be friends! We have French quarrels enough" (219–20), a reminder that war was a democratizing force only as long as everyone obeyed orders.

Henry's soliloquy is a meditation on the doctrine of the king's two bodies, whereby a monarch was deemed to have a private and a public persona (and so straddling the divide between private citizens and magistrates articulated by theorists such as Smith) (Kantorowicz 1957). Henry now feels the acute burden of office, and the personal responsibility for those he commands, something he had earlier passed on to his enemies, in his speech to the governor of Harfleur (3.3.1–43), and, through his ambassador, his uncle, the Duke of Exeter, to the King of France, who is warned that unless he resigns his crown, on his head will be "the widows' tears, the orphans' cries, / The dead men's blood, the pining maidens' groans, / For husbands, fathers and betrothed lovers / That shall be swallowed in this controversy" (2.4.106–9). It is only after his conversation with Bates and Williams that Henry acknowledges that all responsibility lies with him, suggesting that his education as a ruler is only now nearing completion, and indicating that kings have to learn to govern through an understanding of the lower orders (those who Smith claims are not really to participate in the process of government):

> Upon the King! "Let us our lives, our soul,
> Our debts, our careful wives,
> Our children and our sins lay on the King!"
> We must bear all. O hard condition,
> Twin-born with greatness, subject to the breath
> Of every fool whose sense no more can feel
> But his own wringing! What infinite heart's ease
> Must kings neglect that private men enjoy!
> And what have kings that privates have not too,
> Save ceremony, save general ceremony?
> And what art thou, thou idol ceremony? (227–37)

Several points can be made here because this is Shakespeare's most sophisticated reflection on the problem of kingship in the English history plays and concludes his historical sequence written in the 1590s. There is no historical precedent for this scene or this speech in the chronicle sources or earlier plays. Henry finally starts to understand the power and responsibility of kingship – although even at this point he dismisses those who risk their lives for his cause as fools. His educational journey neatly reflects and inverts that taken by Richard II, who also realizes the burdens and duties of the king, but only when he has surrendered his crown. Henry, in contrast, is about to become the only successful king in Shakespeare's history plays, an achievement, significantly enough, founded on the pursuit of an aggressive foreign war.

The soliloquy also draws our attention to what actually makes a king or gives him the right to rule, a question that has been considered at key points throughout the sequence of the history plays. Henry is concentrating on the burdens he must support and justify as ruler, effectively answering the questions that Bates and Williams raised in their exchange – but only after they have departed, a detail that enables the mystery of kingship to be preserved for the characters within the play, while the audience is granted a more penetrating insight. Henry admits that only ceremony separates the king from his subjects, which, given his precarious claim to the throne, is a startlingly accurate assessment (and a revelation he is wise not to spread further afield). The remainder of the speech consists of Henry's reflections on this thin line between subjects and rulers, and shows him to be self-absorbed and not to realize the full significance of his insight. Henry dismisses ceremony as a "proud dream" (254) and lists the forms and manifestations that are used to justify and express the aura of majesty:

> I am a king that find thee [i.e., ceremony], and I know,
> 'Tis not the balm, the sceptre and the ball,
> The sword, the mace, the crown imperial,
> The intertissued robe of gold and pearl,

The farced title running 'fore the king,
The throne he sits on, nor the tide of pomp
That beats upon the high shore of this world,
No, not all these, thrice-gorgeous ceremony,
Not all these, laid in bed majestical,
Can sleep so soundly as the wretched slave. (256–65)

The list is a comprehensive survey of what transforms the private body of the king into his public body and singles him out as a sacred ruler. The lines would seem to reflect directly on the ways in which Elizabeth sought to preserve her mystery as ruler of state and anointed queen, ceremonies, pageants, and costumes which, in the late 1590s, had come to attract severe criticism as means of disguising the dying body of a very old queen (Hackett 1995: ch. 6). As is well known, *Henry V* was written at the height of the Nine Years War in Ireland, directly alluding to the war in the chorus to act 5 with an optimistic prediction of the outcome of the Earl of Essex's campaign, and indirectly through a "Freudian slip" in act 5 of the folio text when Queen Isabel of France opens her speech with "So happy be the issue, brother Ireland" (5.2.12), instead of "brother England" (Maley 1997: 98). Henry's French wars have to be read in terms of Elizabeth's Irish wars, and, implicitly, his reflections on kingship reflect also on her role as queen.

The result of Henry's analysis of his duties as king before Agincourt is that he envies the lowest of his subjects ("the wretched slave"), because he, unlike the king, can sleep soundly. This seems a perverse conclusion to his thoughts, which can easily be read in a different way, The king's soldiers are, after all, drawn from the lower classes of society and if they sleep soundly, they are also likely to be killed in battle the next day. As Graham Holderness has pointed out, the list of the English dead read out after the battle (4.8.81–113) concentrates on all those with titles from duke to esquire, but omits those of lower social status, "None else of name" (106), effectively deleting them from the historical record. However, the list "might have contained, among those nameless common soldiers, Henry's companions of the previous night, John Bates and Alexander Court, whose names he never sought to know" (Holderness 2000: 155). What really affects Henry's peace of mind, as he acknowledges later in the scene, is not the fate of the army he leads in pursuit of glory and success, but his guilty conscience at the fate of Richard (289–302). Henry's reflections on the signs and images that single him out as king demonstrate the flimsy justification of his kingship, suggesting that he could easily be replaced by someone else, just as his father replaced Richard. The "anointed balm" has been transferred into a series of symbols and shows that must be reproduced and performed time and again to remind his subjects that they are in the presence of a king. By the same token, when Henry does not act like a king, he ceases to be one.

Henry V can be read as a republican play; or, perhaps, more accurately, a work that does not discount the possibility that England could be ruled better by a strong leader than a hereditary monarch, someone who had no claim to govern apart from his intrinsic merit. The logic of Henry V's meditations on the question of his kingship is that a king should rule because he – or she – is the best suited for the role. The play flirts dangerously with this reading in the notorious chorus to act 5, describing the triumphant return of Henry to London:

> But now behold,
> In the quick forge and working-house of thought,
> How London doth pour out her citizens.
> The Mayor and all his brethren in best sort,
> Like to the senators of th'antique Rome
> With the plebians swarming at their heels,
> Go forth and fetch their conquering Caesar in;
> As, by a lower but as loving likelihood,
> Were now the General of our gracious Empress,
> As in good time he may, from Ireland coming,
> Bringing rebellion broached on his sword,
> How many would the peaceful city quit
> To welcome him! (22–34)

Henry, albeit in carefully qualified terms, is compared to Robert Devereux, second Earl of Essex, imagined returning in triumph from his Irish campaign, a clear, if unsustained, suggestion that he might be a suitable king, as he and many of his supporters undoubtedly thought (Heinemann 1991). Elizabeth, in her often cited comments to William Lambarde, almost exactly six months after Essex's rebellion, acknowledged that she was represented as Richard II on stage. Equally important is her recognition that the staging of that play before the uprising was not the only example of this identification. When Lambarde sought to comfort his queen by isolating the comparison, "Such a wicked imagination was determined and attempted by a most unkind Gent. The most adorned creature that ever your Majesty made," she responded with a more gloomy assessment of the situation: "He that will forget God, will also forget his benefactors: this tragedy was played 40[tie] times in open streets and houses" (Ure 1961: lix). Elizabeth recognized that there was more general and aggressive disaffection with her rule, pointing to the proliferation of plays targeted at her at the turn of the century. If *Richard II* was used to represent Elizabeth as the feeble, corrupt, and doomed king who lost his crown, *Henry V* cast her most ambitious courtier as England's most successful and popular monarch.

Equally important, Henry is imagined here as Julius Caesar, entering Rome after his victory over Pompey's sons, with the mayor and citizens envisaged as the senators of Rome. This image invites comparison with the opening scene of Shakespeare's next play, *Julius Caesar*, produced later in the same year (1599). Here the tribunes, annually elected intermediaries between the plebians and the senate, are shown disparaging Caesar's triumph and praising the dead Pompey, and urging the people to return to their houses. Shakespeare would undoubtedly have been familiar with Caesar's career from having read Sir Thomas North's translation of Plutarch's *Lives* (1579), before he wrote the play. On the one hand, Caesar was famous for having reached his eminent position and achieved his successes through merit rather than birth and having seized power in Rome. On the other hand, he not only ended the Roman republic and inaugurated the Empire, but in his extensive military experience in Europe (58–49 BC) he conquered Britain. Just as Caesar was ruthless in his pursuit of personal glory, Henry was prepared to destroy besieged cities (3.3), slaughter prisoners (4.7), and lay waste vast areas of rural France (5.2.23–67) in order to further his ambitions. If *Henry V* recognizes the merits of Essex, it also hints at the dangers of his ambitious rise to power.

Shakespeare's representation of the British army at war also suggests that the play may have a more radical political agenda than is usually assumed. Henry's rousing patriotic speech on the feast of St. Crispian appeals to a common experience among the soldiers, arguing that when the survivors show their wounds, these will become signs of a glorious moment in English history, one that will help define the nation. Their names will become synonymous with an ideal representation of England and

> We in it [the day] shall be remembered,
> We few, we happy few, we band of brothers,
> For he today that sheds his blood with me,
> Shall be my brother, be he ne'er so vile,
> This day shall gentle his condition.
> And gentlemen in England now abed
> Shall think themselves accursed they were not here. (4.3.59–65)

Of course, the speech is propaganda and is undercut by the fact that the army is patently British rather than English, a point Shakespeare is at pains to make, and the promise that all men are in this moment equal does not prevent the lack of equality demonstrated when the lists of the dead are read out. Nevertheless, the play explores the idea, so familiar in machiavellian republicanism, that the most actively virtuous state is one that is constantly at war, because only then can the worthiness of the citizens be put to the test. Put another way, the same logic decreed that a state constantly at war would be able to enfranchise more of its citizens than one that remained constantly at peace. As J. G. A. Pocock comments on the arguments of *The Arte of Warre* and *The Discourses*:

> Military *virtù* necessitates political virtue because both can be presented in terms of the same end. The republic is the common good; the citizen, directing all his actions toward that good, may be said to dedicate his life to the republic; the patriot warrior dedicates his death, and the two are alike in perfecting human nature by sacrificing particular goods to a universal end. If this be virtue, then the warrior displays it as fully as the citizen, and it may be through military discipline that one learns to be a citizen and to display virtue. (Pocock 1975: 201)

Such arguments could have been gleaned from the translation of *The Arte of Warre* published in 1560, as well as consulting the Latin or Italian editions of *The Discourses* (Machiavelli 1560: 80–1; 1970: 274–81).

However, if war enfranchises and makes citizens or gentlemen of the army, it is a limited and unstable moment, a carnivalesque utopian hope that cannot survive the transition back to ordinary life. The universal brotherhood of military conflict could only preserve liberty for a relatively short space of time. Military values would eventually lead to "a tyranny, which may well be exercised by a Pompey or Caesar, once a citizen but now so far perverted as to use the sword as an instrument of political power" (Pocock 1975: 201). Machiavelli was acutely aware of this problem, and, as the startling juxtapositions in *Henry V* demonstrate, so was Shakespeare (Skinner 1981: 73–7). All men can be brothers in war, but not when the war draws to a close. Moreover, war, as often as not, starts off by encouraging virtuous citizens and ends in tyranny.

Henry V, far from being a crudely patriotic play, or even an exposé of conduct in war, is Shakespeare's most sophisticated analysis of kingship, and forces the audience/ reader to reconsider the career of England's most celebrated ruler, one who had been represented on the stage a few years previously in an uncritical light. In the end, we have to judge the king on his merits. Shakespeare's other history plays show unhappy kings behaving more or less badly and failing to gather the popular support they require to enable them to function as rulers. The relationship between the play as Shakespeare wrote it and as it was performed on the public stage will remain a matter for conjecture unless further evidence emerges. Nevertheless, the textual evidence would suggest that the version of *Henry V* that the Elizabethan audience saw was much more in line with the representation of the king in *The Famous Victories of Henry V* and Thomas Dekker's *The Shoemaker's Holiday* than the unsettling authorial version which appeared in the Folio in 1623.

NOTES

1 All references to *Henry V* are to the edition edited by T. W. Craik (1998), unless otherwise stated. All other references are to the Arden editions, third series, when available, otherwise second series.

2 As is well known, Shakespeare's major source of historical material was Raphael Holinshed's *Chronicles of England, Scotland and Ireland* (1577, 1587). It is likely that Jonson was suggesting that his association with a "proper" historian such as Camden elevated him above the status of Shakespeare, who relied on a mere chronicler.

3 It is a rather splendid irony that not only were the magnificent battle scenes shot in county Wicklow, Ireland, but that they helped to bankrupt the producers, London Films, resulting in the takeover by the J. Arthur Rank Corporation (Gurr 1992: 52).

4 For a recent view see Holderness (2000 ch. 6); for an older one, see Gould (1969).

5 Academics are no doubt reacting against such interpretations of *Henry V* as part of the widespread rejection of once ubiquitous works such as Tillyard (1943), which saw the Renaissance as a time of fervent patriotism.

6 The alternative possibility is that a fuller version of the text was performed in 1599, but later cut, either through casting difficulties or because the association with the disgraced Earl of Essex was obviously undesirable after his failed coup (Patterson 1989: 76–7).

7 For a convenient overview of the state of Shakespeare bibliographical questions, see Mowat (2001).

8   For a more extended discussion, see Brooks (2000: ch. 1).

9   On the authorship of poetry and its growing significance in the sixteenth and seventeenth centuries, see Helgerson (1983).

10   For discussion, see Patterson (1984).

11   For an incisive discussion of Shakespeare's analysis of the problem of the succession in his history plays, which perhaps underestimates the radical charge of some of the works, see Erskine-Hill (1996: pt. 1).

12   As related in Holinshed, 1587, III, p. 545–6. Holinshed does not show the machinations of the bishops which is Shakespeare's invention.

13   The most likely source for information on Alexander was Plutarch. See Plutarch (1998: 385–465).

14   On Henry's education, see Greenblatt (1988: 40–56). For a comparison between the two plays, see Battenhouse (1974).

15   Based on Holinshed (1587, III: 545–6).

16   On the status and role of later Tudor parliaments, see Jones (1995).

References and Further Reading

Baker, D. J. (1997). *Between Nations: Shakespeare, Spenser, Marvell and the Question of Britain*. Stanford, CA: Stanford University Press.

Battenhouse, R. W. (1974). The Relation of *Henry V* to *Tamburlaine*. *Shakespeare Quarterly*, 27, 71–9.

Brooks D. A. (2000). *From Playhouse to Printing House: Drama and Authorship in Early Modern England*. Cambridge: Cambridge University Press.

Corbin, P. and Sedge, D. (eds.) (1991). *The Oldcastle Controversy: Sir John Oldcastle, Part 1 and The Famous Victories of Henry V.* Manchester: Manchester University Press.

Craik, T. W. (ed.) (1998). *Henry V*. London: Nelson.

Crowl, S. (2000). Flamboyant Realist: Kenneth Branagh. In R. Jackson (ed.) *The Cambridge Companion to Shakespeare on Film*. Cambridge: Cambridge University Press, 222–38.

Davies, M. (2000). The Shakespeare Films of Laurence Olivier. In R. Jackson (ed.) *The Cambridge Companion to Shakespeare on Film*. Cambridge: Cambridge University Press, 163–82.

De Grazia, M. and Wells, S. (eds.) (2001). *The Cambridge Companion to Shakespeare*. Cambridge: Cambridge University Press.

Dekker, T. (1990). *The Shoemaker's Holiday*, ed. A. Parr. London: Norton.

Dutton, R. (1997). The Birth of the Author. In C. C. Brown and A. F. Marotti (eds.) *Texts and Cultural Change in Early Modern England*. Basingstoke: Macmillan, 153–78.

Edwards, P. (1979). *Threshold of a Nation: A Study in English and Irish Drama*. Cambridge: Cambridge University Press.

Erskine-Hill, H. (1996). *Shakespeare and the Realm of Politics: Shakespeare to Dryden*. Oxford: Clarendon Press.

Gould, G. (1969). Irony and Satire in *Henry V*. In M. Quinn (ed.) *Henry V: A Selection of Critical Essays*. London: Macmillan, 81–94.

Greenblatt, S. (1988). Invisible Bullets. In *Shakespearean Negotiations: The Circulation of Social Energy in Renaissance England*. Oxford: Oxford University Press, 21–65.

Gurr, A. (ed.) (1992). *Henry V*. Cambridge: Cambridge University Press.

——(ed.) (2000). *The First Quarto of King Henry V*. Cambridge: Cambridge University Press.

Hackett, H. (1995). *Virgin Mother, Maiden Queen: Elizabeth I and the Cult of the Virgin Mary*. Basingstoke: Macmillan.

Heinemann, M. (1991). Rebel Lords, Popular Playwrights, and Political Culture: Notes on the Jacobean Patronage of the Earl of Southampton. In *The Yearbook of English Studies*, 21, 63–86.

Helgerson, R. (1983). *Self-Crowned Laureates: Spenser, Jonson, Milton and the Literary System*. Berkeley: University of California Press.

Herman, P. C. (1995). "O, 'tis a gallant king": Shakespeare's *Henry V* and the Crisis of the 1590s. In D. Hoak (ed.) *Tudor Political Culture*. Cambridge: Cambridge University Press, 204–25.

Hoak, D. (ed.) (1995). *Tudor Political Culture*. Cambridge: Cambridge University Press.

Holderness, G. (2000). *Shakespeare: The Histories*. Basingstoke: Macmillan.

——(2001). *Cultural Shakespeare: Essays in the Shakespeare Myth*. Hatfield: University of Hertfordshire Press.

Holinshed, R. (1587). *Chronicles of England, Scotland and Ireland*, 2nd edn.

Irace, K. O. (ed.) (1998). *The First Quarto of Hamlet*. Cambridge: Cambridge University Press.

Jackson, R. (2000). *The Cambridge Companion to Shakespeare on Film*. Cambridge: Cambridge University Press.

Jardine, L. (1996). *Reading Shakespeare Historically*. London: Routledge.

Jones, N. (1995). Parliament and the Political Society of Elizabethan England. In D. Hoak (ed.) *Tudor Political Culture*. Cambridge: Cambridge University Press, 226–42.

Jonson, B. (1966) [1616]. *Every Man in His Humour*, ed. M. Seymour-Smith. London: Ernest Benn.

Kantorowicz, E. H. (1957). *The King's Two Bodies: A Study in Medieval Political Theology*. Princeton, NJ: Princeton University Press.

Kastan, D. S. (2001). Shakespeare and English History. In M. De Grazia and S. Wells (eds.) *The Cambridge Companion to Shakespeare*. Cambridge: Cambridge University Press, 167–82.

Kiernan, P. (1999). *Staging Shakespeare at the New Globe*. Basingstoke: Macmillan.

McEachern, C. (1996). *The Poetics of English Nationhood, 1590–1612*. Cambridge: Cambridge University Press.

Machiavelli, N. (1905) [1560]. *The Arte of Warre*, trans. P. Whitehorne. The Tudor Translations 39. London: Nutt.

——(1970). *The Discourses*, ed. B. Crick. Harmondsworth: Penguin Books.

McLaren, A. N. (1999). *Political Culture in the Reign of Elizabeth I: Queen and Commonwealth, 1558–1585*. Cambridge: Cambridge University Press.

Maley, W. (1997). "This sceptred isle": Shakespeare and the British Problem. In J. J. Joughin (ed.) *Shakespeare and National Culture*. Manchester: Manchester University Press, 83–108.

Mossman, J. (1994). *Henry V* and Plutarch's *Alexander*. *Shakespeare Quarterly*, 45, 57–73.

Mowat, B. A. (2001). *The Reproduction of Shakespeare's Texts*. In M. De Grazia and S. Wells (eds.) *The Cambridge Companion to Shakespeare*. Cambridge: Cambridge University Press, 13–29.

Neill, M. (1994). Broken English and Broken Irish: Nation, Language and the Optic of Power in Shakespeare's Histories. *Shakespeare Quarterly*, 45, 18–22.

Patterson, A. (1984). *Censorship and Interpretation: The Conditions of Writing and Reading in Early Modern England*. Madison: University of Wisconsin Press.

——(1989). *Shakespeare and the Popular Voice*. Oxford: Blackwell.

Plutarch (1998). *Selected Lives of the Noble Grecians and Romans*, ed. J. Mossman. Ware: Wordsworth Editions.

Pocock, J. G. A. (1975). *The Machiavellian Moment: Florentine Political Thought and the Atlantic Republican Tradition*. Princeton, NJ: Princeton University Press.

Pugliatti, P. (1996). *Shakespeare the Historian*. Basingstoke: Macmillan.

Quinn, M. (ed.) (1969). *Henry V: A Selection of Critical Essays*. London: Macmillan.

Raab, F. (1965). *The English Face of Machiavelli: A Changing Interpretation, 1500–1700*. London: Routledge and Kegan Paul.

Rackin, P. (1990). *Stages of History: Shakespeare's English Chronicles*. Ithaca, NY: Cornell University Press.

Skinner, Q. (1981). *Machiavelli*. Oxford: Oxford University Press.

Smith, T. (1972). *De Republica Anglorum: A Discourse of the Commonwealth of England*, ed. L. Alston. Shannon: Irish University Press.

Spurgeon, C. (1965). *Shakespeare's Imagery and What It Tells Us*. Cambridge: Cambridge University Press.

Sutherland, J. and Watts, C. (2000). *Henry V, War Criminal? & Other Shakespeare Puzzles*. Oxford: Oxford University Press.

Tillyard, E. M. W. (1943). *The Elizabethan World Picture*. London: Chatto and Windus.

Trevor-Roper, H. (1971) *Queen Elizabeth's First Historian: William Camden and the Beginnings of English "Civil History."* London: Cape.

Ure, P. (ed.) (1961). *King Richard II*. London: Methuen.

Williams, C. (1969). The Honour of King Henry V. In M. Quinn (ed.) *Henry V: A Selection of Critical Essays*. London: Macmillan, 108–15.

Index